Get up and running right away with this exclusive hands-on book

Learn the basics — in under one hour!

Master hot new features quickly and easily

Microsoft®

Office 2000

Bible
Quick Start

Edward Willett

What's New in Microsoft Office 2000?

✦ **Improved Web-centered document creation:** Office 2000 lets you save your documents as Web pages and turn them back into Office documents without losing most of your special formatting, which in turn makes it easier than ever to share documents with others, no matter what system or software they use.

✦ **Easier to use:** Office 2000 is smarter than its predecessors. It remembers your usage patterns and customizes itself to adapt to them.

✦ **Better support for international users:** Office 2000 makes it possible to work in multiple languages and exchange files with other Office 2000 users around the world.

✦ **Real-time collaboration:** Office 2000 makes it easier for Office users to collaborate over a network.

✦ **Better support for Internet standards:** Outlook 2000 ensures that your message gets through to just about anyone, no matter what kind of system they're using.

✦ **Improved e-mail and information management:** Outlook 2000's e-mail, calendar, and contact management programs have all been made easier to use, and work together more closely than ever before. In addition, in cooperation with Outlook 2000, Word 2000 can be used to create and edit all e-mail. Formatting and inserted special elements such as tables and pictures are preserved when the e-mail is sent (provided that the recipients are using a program that permits them to view HTML e-mail).

✦ **Improved remote usage functionality:** Outlook 2000 makes it easier for people to access their information even when they're away from the office where it's stored.

Microsoft® Office 2000 Bible Quick Start

Edward Willett

Hungry Minds™

HUNGRY MINDS, INC.

New York, NY ◆ Cleveland, OH ◆ Indianapolis, IN

Microsoft® Office 2000 Bible Quick Start

Published by
Hungry Minds, Inc.
909 Third Avenue
New York, NY 10022
www.hungryminds.com

Part Number: D471

Printed in the United States of America

10 9 8 7 6

1B/RT/QT/QS/FC

Distributed in the United States by Hungry Minds, Inc.

Distributed by CDG Books Canada Inc. for Canada; by Transworld Publishers Limited in the United Kingdom; by IDG Norge Books for Norway; by IDG Sweden Books for Sweden; by IDG Books Australia Publishing Corporation Pty. Ltd. for Australia and New Zealand; by TransQuest Publishers Pte Ltd. for Singapore, Malaysia, Thailand, Indonesia, and Hong Kong; by Gotop Information Inc. for Taiwan; by ICG Muse, Inc. for Japan; by Intersoft for South Africa; by Eyrolles for France; by International Thomson Publishing for Germany, Austria and Switzerland; by Distribuidora Cuspide for Argentina; by LR International for Brazil; by Galileo Libros for Chile; by Ediciones ZETA S.C.R. Ltda. for Peru; by WS Computer Publishing Corporation, Inc., for the Philippines; by Contemporanea de Ediciones for Venezuela; by Express Computer Distributors for the Caribbean and West Indies; by Micronesia Media Distributor, Inc. for Micronesia; by Chips Computadoras S.A. de C.V. for Mexico; by Editorial Norma de Panama S.A. for Panama; by American Bookshops for Finland.

For general information on Hungry Minds' products and services please contact our Customer Care Department within the U.S. at 800-762-2974, outside the U.S. at 317-572-3993 or fax 317-572-4002.

For sales inquiries and reseller information, including discounts, premium and bulk quantity sales, and foreign-language translations, please contact our Customer Care Department at 800-434-3422, fax 317-572-4002, or write to Hungry Minds, Inc., Attn: Customer Care Department, 10475 Crosspoint Boulevard, Indianapolis, IN 46256.

For information on licensing foreign or domestic rights, please contact our Sub-Rights Customer Care Department at 650-653-7098.

For authorization to photocopy items for corporate, personal, or educational use, please contact Copyright Clearance Center, 222 Rosewood Drive, Danvers, MA 01923, or fax 978-750-4470.

For information on using Hungry Minds' products and services in the classroom or for ordering examination copies, please contact our Educational Sales Department at 800-434-2086 or fax 317-572-4005.

Please contact our Public Relations Department at 212-884-5163 for press review copies or 212-884-5000 for author interviews and other publicity information or fax 212-884-5400.

Hungry Minds™ is a trademark of Hungry Minds, Inc.

Contents

Welcome to the *Microsoft Office 2000 Bible Quick Start*

This *Microsoft Office 2000 Bible Quick Start* is designed to give you a quick introduction to Office 2000, the latest version of the world's most popular office productivity software. This convenient booklet is a pullout section of the *Microsoft Office 2000 Bible* published by IDG Books Worldwide, which covers the full gamut of the Office 2000 suite of applications in exceptional detail. Here's what you'll find:

✦ **What's New:** On the inside front cover of this booklet, you'll find a brief overview of the new features of Office 2000. For full coverage, see Appendix A: What's New in Office 2000, at the end of the *Microsoft Office 2000 Bible*.

✦ **Word:** In this section you'll find the basic information you need to create a document in Microsoft Word. Microsoft Word is a word processor: a tool for writing, editing, and formatting words. It can't actually write your document for you, but it can help you enhance your document with interesting fonts, tables, and pictures; and lay it all out on the page any way you wish. It can even check your spelling and grammar for you — in more than one language.

✦ **Excel:** You can find a ton of detailed information about Excel in the *Microsoft Office 2000 Bible* (check out the entire part dedicated to Excel), but if you're brand-new to Excel, or if you're just in a hurry to find out what's new in Excel 2000, then this is the place to start. This section tells you just what you need to start making use of Excel's capabilities — fast.

✦ **PowerPoint:** People using PowerPoint are driven by deadlines: they don't have time to waste. This section will have you creating your own eye-catching PowerPoint presentation in no time.

✦ **Top Office Time-savers:** In this final section, you'll find many useful tips designed to help you use Office 2000 more efficiently and enjoyably.

✦ **Keyboard Shortcuts:** On the inside back cover of this booklet you'll find a listing of the most important Office 2000 keyboard shortcuts. It's designed so you can fold the page open, keeping the list next to your computer until these shortcuts are committed to memory.

In a few short pages, the unique format of this *Quick Start* booklet gives you all the basic information you need to begin using Word, Excel, and PowerPoint 2000 productively — in just hours.

How Does This Booklet Work with the *Microsoft Office 2000 Bible?*

No matter how you got hold of this booklet — by pulling it from the inside of your own copy of the *Microsoft Office 2000 Bible* or acquiring it from a friend or coworker — you're probably wondering how it works with the comprehensive *Bible* it originally came packaged with. Here are a few pointers:

✦ The *Office 2000 Quick Start* is designed with flexibility in mind. It provides quick tutorials and an overview of basic features and shortcuts. You can take the Quick Start with you anywhere, as an instant source of information and aid to updating your Office 2000 skills, even if you're an experienced user of previous versions of Microsoft Office.

✦ The *Microsoft Office 2000 Bible* provides a comprehensive view of Office 2000 — everything you need to know to master the program. Expert authors Edward Willett, David and Rhonda Crowder, David Karlins, and Jackie Leech cover every feature and capability of Office 2000 and show you how to make them work for you. The book is loaded with advice, tips, tutorials, cross-references, and sources of other information; and also features a CD-ROM loaded with clip art, utilities, and useful shareware ranging from a business-plan generator to a label-printing program. If you want or need to become an Office 2000 power user, the *Office 2000 Bible* is for you.

For More Information

If you've found this *Quick Start* useful and want to increase your skill to encompass the full power of Office 2000, you would be wise to follow the instructions at the back of this booklet. They tell you how to order the full-length *Microsoft Office 2000 Bible* — the single most comprehensive source of information on the topic.

IDG Books Worldwide also has other books you can order via this Quick Start, which may better suit your style. Check out *Teach Yourself Microsoft Office 2000,* which provides a visual, hands-on approach to learning, and our *Microsoft Office 2000 One Step at a Time,* which includes unique interactive training software on a companion CD-ROM. Although these books may take another route to learning, they meet the same impeccable standards of clarity and accuracy you can expect from any IDG publication.

Contact Us!

At IDG, we're always striving you make our books more useful to you — our readers. We welcome your input! Please feel free to contact us in any of the following ways:

✦ Through our Web site: www.hungryminds.com

✦ Send mail to us: Hungry Minds, Inc. ATTN: Customer Care, 10475 Crosspoint Blvd., Indianapolis, IN 46256

✦ Call us: 800-762-2974

Creating a Document with Word

Figure 1-1 shows you exactly what you see when you first start Word 2000. By default, Word 2000 opens in Print Layout view, which shows you almost exactly what you'll see on the printed page when you're done.

The *document area* is where you'll create your document. Within it, you can place your *insertion point* wherever you like, using your mouse. This is where text will appear when you start typing. Use the *rulers* to position your text and other elements exactly where you want them and to set margins, tabs, and indents.

Use the horizontal and vertical *scrollbars* to move sideways or up and down through your document. The horizontal scroll-bar includes buttons that let you switch among Normal, Outline, Web Layout and Print Layout views; the vertical scrollbar includes buttons to take you to the previous page or the next page, or to browse through your document for par-ticular sorts of objects: tables, for instance, or pictures.

The *status bar* tells you where the cursor is, how many pages your document has, which page you're on, and more. Double-clicking on some items lets you change their status: for exam-ple, double-clicking on the page number opens a dialog box that lets you go to a particular page.

The *menu bar* contains menus of commands that are common to almost all Windows programs — File, Edit, View, Window, Help — plus some that are specific to Word, such as Format and Table. *Toolbars* contain buttons that activate a variety of features. The Standard and Formatting toolbars, which con-tain the most-used features, appear by default. Other toolbars appear automatically as you carry out certain tasks. You can also choose to display whichever toolbars you want by choosing View ➪ Toolbars.

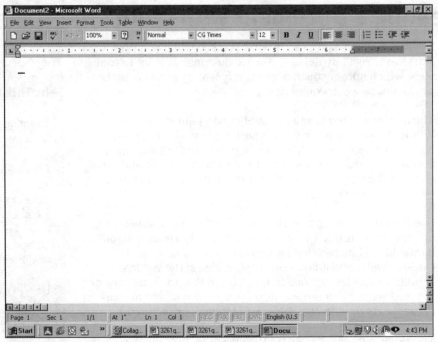

Figure 1-1: When you first start Word 2000, this is what you see.

Entering, editing, and formatting text

The moment Word opens, the insertion point is already located in the document area, so Word is ready to receive text. Just type as though you were working on a typewriter; the only difference is that instead of pressing Enter at the end of each line, you only have to press Enter at the end of each paragraph.

Editing text

Once you have some text to work with, you can begin whipping it into shape. To make changes and corrections, move your insertion point to the place where you want to make changes by placing the mouse pointer there and clicking once. To add a word or phrase, just type it in. The existing text will move to the right to make way for it. To replace a word or phrase, select the text you want to replace by placing the insertion point at the beginning or end of the text, and then clicking and dragging the mouse pointer over it. This highlights the text. Then type in the new text. It automatically replaces the highlighted text.

To delete a word or phrase, highlight it and press Delete. To delete just a few characters, place the insertion point immediately to the left of the string of characters you want to remove, and then press Delete once to delete a single character or press and hold Delete to delete characters repeatedly. Alternately, you can place the insertion point immediately to the right of the character you want to delete and press Backspace to delete to the left.

Selecting text

In addition to clicking and dragging, you can select text by holding down the Shift key while moving through the text with the arrow keys. Holding down the Ctrl key at the same time lets you select a word at a time with the left and right arrow keys, or a paragraph at a time with the up and down arrow keys.

You can select an entire word by double-clicking anywhere inside it, or select an entire paragraph by triple-clicking anywhere inside it. You can select an entire line by moving the mouse pointer to the left edge of the document until it changes to a right-pointing arrow, and then pointing at the line you want to select and clicking; and you can select the entire document by choosing Edit ⇨ Select All or pressing Ctrl+A.

Formatting text

The most common tools for formatting text are all available on the Formatting tool-bar. Additional buttons become visible when you click the More Buttons button at the extreme right end. To use the formatting tools, highlight the text you want to format, and then click the button of your choice on the toolbar.

Choose the font (typeface) you want from the Font pull-down list of all the fonts installed on your system. Each font name appears in that font, so you can see what it looks like. Click the name of the font you want and the highlighted text will change. Then you can choose the font size from the drop-down list right next to it. Sizes are given in points (approximately 1/72 of an inch) and refer to the height of the capital letters. Make text bold or italic or underline it just by clicking on the appropriate buttons, and choose Align Left to align it against the left indent stop or Center to center it between the left and right indent stops.

Click Numbering or Bullets to create a numbered or bulleted list. If you click either before you start typing, every time you press Enter, a number or bullet appears in front of the next item in the list. To stop it, press Backspace to delete the last number or bullet, and then resume typing. Click either button after you've highlighted a section of text to turn it into a numbered or bulleted list, adding a new number or bullet to begin each paragraph. The Decrease Indent and Increase Indent buttons adjust the left indentation for selected text to the left or the right by a set amount.

Choose a preset format, such as Heading 1 or Envelope Return, from the Style list box. The name of each style appears in that particular style. To apply a style, high-light the text you want to apply it to and select the name of the style from this list-box; or, for a paragraph style, just place the insertion point anywhere within the paragraph. Align Right lines up the right edge of the selected text with the right indent stop, while Justify adds space between words to line up both the left and right edges of the text with the indent stops.

Click Border to draw a border around a selected word or paragraph. Click the little downward pointing arrow to see a selection of other borders. Clicking Highlight places a transparent color over selected text, similar to drawing over text on paper with a highlighting pen. Click the downward-pointing arrow to select the color.

Click the Highlight button before you select text, and you can use your cursor exactly like a highlighting pen, painting a color over any text in your document. Click Font Color to change the color of text; again, click the downward-pointing arrow to choose the color you want. The Single Spacing and Double Spacing buttons adjust the amount of space between lines of text.

Note   All of these formatting options can be combined with one another, and many other formatting options are available through the dialog boxes you can access from the Format menu.

Moving around and viewing your document

To move around in Word, you can use the mouse, the scrollbars, the keyboard, the Go To command, or the Navigation tool. Using the mouse, you can place the pointer wherever you want to start typing and click once. Using the scrollbars, you can click the single arrows at the top or bottom of the vertical scrollbar to move up or down one line at a time, or click the light-colored area above or below the box-shaped slider to move up or down one screen at a time. Dragging the slider moves you smoothly through the document. Use the horizontal scrollbar in a similar fashion to move left or right through documents that are too large to fit on the screen.

The cursor keys on the keyboard move your insertion point up or down one line at a time, or left or right one character at a time. By holding down the Ctrl key, you can also use them to move left or right one word at a time, or up and down one paragraph at a time. Home moves you to the beginning of a line, and End to the end. Ctrl+Home takes you to the top of the document, Ctrl+End to the end, and Page Up one screen up and Page Down one screen down. Press Ctrl+G to open the Go To dialog box. Enter the page number you want to go to, or a plus or minus sign and the number of pages you want to go forward or back, and then click Go To.

Finally, the three buttons at the bottom of the vertical scrollbar let you browse through your document the way that suits you best. Click the button in the middle, and then choose the item you want to browse for: for example, tables. The arrow buttons will then take you to either the previous occurrence of that item or the next.

Word also offers you several ways to view your document. The three you'll use most often are available in the View menu. They are Normal view, Page Layout view and Web Layout view. Normal view (see Figure 1-2) hides page boundaries and special items such as headers and footers. It's most useful if your document is mostly text. Print Layout view (see Figure 1-3) shows you exactly how text, graphics, and other elements will appear when you print your document; it's useful if you're using lots of pictures, tables, etc. Finally, Web Layout view (see Figure 1-4) shows you what your page will look like when viewed with a Web browser, and is most useful if you're creating a Web page.

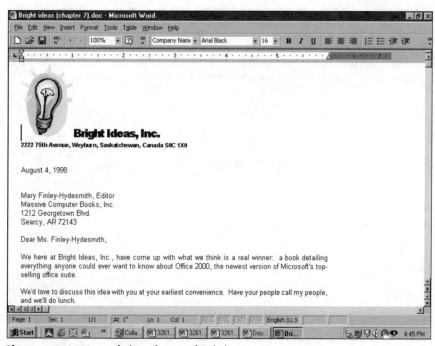

Figure 1-2: In Normal view the emphasis is on text.

Figure 1-3: Print Layout view gives you a better idea of what your document will look like when printed.

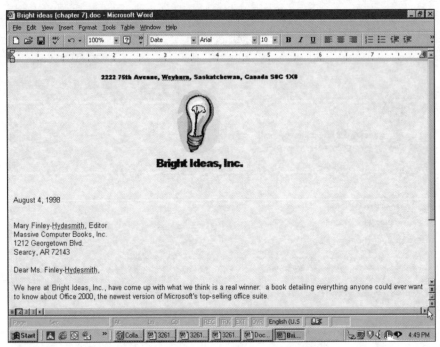

Figure 1-4: Use Web Layout view if you're creating a Web page.

Saving, opening, and closing documents

Once you've created your document, you'll want to save it so you can call it up again in the future for further revision or reference. To save a document, click the Save button on the Standard toolbar, or choose File ⇨ Save. This opens the Save As dialog box. Browse until you find the file folder you want to save your new document in, and then double-click on the folder to open it. Type a name for your document in the File Name box; then, in the Save As Type box, select the format in which you want to save the document. Normally you'll save it as a Word document, but you can also choose to save it as an HTML (Web) document, as plain text, or in a format readable by earlier versions of Word or other word processors. Finally, click Save.

Tip   To save a copy of a document, or save it in a different format, without losing the original document, choose File ⇨ Save As. You can save the copy in a different place, under a different name, or in a different file format, as you wish.

To open a saved document, click the Open button on the Standard toolbar, or choose File ⇨ Open. Using the Open dialog box, browse for the document you want to open. When you find it, double-click on it, or click on it once and then click Open. When you're done working with a document and want to close it, choose File ⇨ Close, or simply click the Close Window button at the far right end of the menu bar.

Caution If you click Save after making changes to a previously saved document, the changed version of the document replaces the original version. To preserve the original version, use Save As.

Page properties, previewing, and printing

Once you're happy with the content and formatting of your document, you're just about ready to print it. Before you do, though, you need to make a few final decisions.

Setting page properties

Choose File ⇨ Page Setup to open the Page Setup dialog box shown in Figure 1-5.

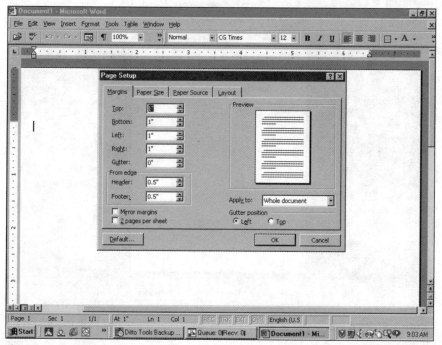

Figure 1-5: Make decisions about the appearance of your document here.

For most documents, you'll only need to worry about three of the tabs in this dialog box: Margins, Paper Size, and Paper Source. Set top, bottom, right, and left margins by entering measurements into the various boxes or by clicking on the arrows to increase or decrease the default measurements. If your printer supports it, you can also add a gutter on the left or top side, if you want to leave extra white space for a binding.

The Paper Size tab lets you choose from a variety of standard paper sizes—letter, legal, AR, etc.—or enter the dimensions of a custom size. You can also choose whether to have your document print across the narrower dimension of the page (portrait style) or across the longer dimension (landscape style). Finally, the Paper Source tab lets you choose which source of paper available to your printer you want to use: upper tray, lower tray, manual feed, etc.

Previewing your document

To see exactly what your document will look like once it's printed, choose File ⇨ Print Preview. You'll see what looks a bit like a photograph of the first page of your document (see Figure 1-6).

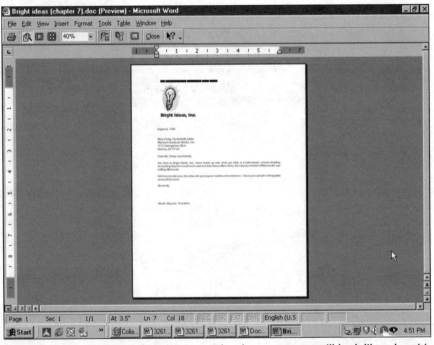

Figure 1-6: Print Preview shows you exactly what your page will look like when it's printed.

Click the Magnifier button to zoom in for a closer look, or change the size of the preview using the Zoom drop-down list. To see more than one page at a time, click the Multiple Pages button, and then drag your mouse through the box that opens to choose how many pages you want to display at once and in what configuration. Navigate through the pages exactly as you would in Normal view, using the scrollbars, the keyboard, the Navigation tool, Go To, etc.

You can edit in Print Preview just as though you were in Normal or Print Layout view. (Although the Formatting toolbar isn't visible, you can call it up by choosing View ➪ Toolbars ➪ Formatting.) Or, if you prefer, you can return to Normal or Print Layout view by opening the View menu.

Printing

When you're finally 100 percent satisfied with your document, you're ready to commit it to paper. Click the Print button on the Standard toolbar to begin printing immediately or choose File ➪ Print to open the Print dialog box, where you can choose a printer from those installed on your system, set specific properties of that printer, and choose how much of your document to print and the number of copies. You can even choose to print more than one page per sheet of paper or scale your document to fit on a different size of paper than you designed it for: for example, legal-size instead of letter-sized. When you're satisfied with your choices, click OK, and your document will print.

Creating a Spreadsheet with Excel

Microsoft Excel is a spreadsheet application. Spreadsheets are the modern-day equivalent of the ledgers and adding machines of half a century ago. They let you enter, edit, track, analyze, and perform calculations on data. With Excel, you can display data in a wide variety of formats. For example, you can display numeric values with or without decimals, or as currency amounts or exponential values. You can also enter text, and display dates and times. Finally, you can carry out calculations on all this data using Excel's functions, which include mathematical, statistical, financial, logical, date and time, text, and special-purpose operations. In other words, Excel 2000 puts the power of an entire computer department on your desktop, at your fingertips.

Introducing the Excel interface

The first thing to understand about Excel is the difference between a workbook and a worksheet. A *worksheet* is a single spreadsheet, while a *workbook* is a collection of worksheets. When you start Excel 2000, it automatically opens a new workbook, called Book1, which contains three worksheets, and by default displays Sheet1 (see Figure 1-7).

An Excel worksheet has 256 columns, labeled across the top with the letters of the alphabet. When it gets to Z, it starts over with AA, AB, AC, AD, etc.; then BA, BB, BC, and so on, all the way up to IV. Going the other way, a worksheet has 65,536 rows. The place where each column and row meets is called a *cell*. (We'll save you the trouble of doing the math: An Excel worksheet contains 16,777,216 cells. You're welcome.) You store your data in these cells. Each cell is identified by its column and row number. For example, the cell in the upper left corner of the worksheet is referenced as A1, while the cell in the bottom right corner would be IV65536. You have to be able to identify cells in order to create formulas that make use of your worksheet data.

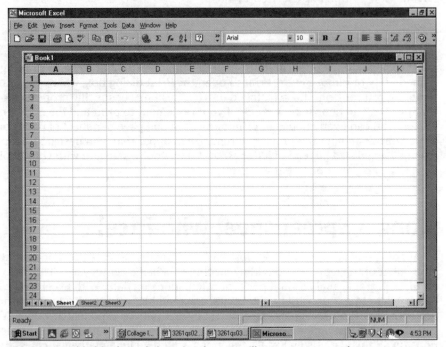

Figure 1-7: This blank worksheet is where you'll enter your own data.

Besides worksheets, cells, rows, and columns, other major parts of the Excel 2000 interface include the vertical and horizontal *scrollbars,* which you use to move up and down or sideways through your worksheet, and the *worksheet navigation controls,* which take you from worksheet to worksheet within your current workbook. (Click the leftmost arrow to go to the first worksheet in the workbook, the middle two arrows to move one worksheet backward or forward through the workbook, and the rightmost arrow to go to the last worksheet in the workbook. You can also go directly to any workbook by clicking the appropriate tab.) The *Name box* displays the name of the currently active cell or, as you're highlighting multiple cells, the dimensions of that range of cells. The *formula bar* is where you enter data and create and apply formulas.

The *menu bar* contains menus of commands that are common to almost all Windows programs — File, Edit, View, Window, Help — plus some that are specific to Excel, such as Data and Chart, while the *toolbars* contain buttons that activate a variety of features. The Standard and Formatting toolbars appear by default, because they contain the most-used features, but other toolbars appear automatically as you carry out certain tasks, and you can choose to display whichever toolbars you want by choosing View ➪ Toolbars.

Entering, editing, and formatting data

The simplest way to enter data in Excel is to type it in: Click the cell into which you want to enter data and type away. You can also move from cell to cell with the Tab or Enter keys. Excel is most commonly used to manage numerical data. (You *can* use it to create lists and databases as well, but for most text-based information, you might be better off using Microsoft Access, Office's database program. (For basic information about using Access, see the chapters on Access in Part V of the Office 2000 Bible.) By default, Excel displays a maximum of eleven digits in a cell (ten if the number includes a decimal point).

You can also enter dates and times as numbers. For dates, use slashes or hyphens to separate the elements. For instance, 12-30 or 12/30 would be interpreted as December 30. If you don't add a year, it assumes that it's the current year; if you do want to enter a year, add it with another slash or hyphen. (With the year 2000 coming up, it's a good idea to add the year as a full four-digit number.) For times, use colons: 3:00 is interpreted as 3 A.M. To tell Excel you want the date to be P.M., type a space and a **p** or **pm** following the time.

Whatever you enter in the formula bar appears in the cell and vice versa (assuming you're in edit mode; if you're not, formulas are displayed in the formula bar, and formula results in the cell.) Either one acts like the window of a little word processor: You can use the arrow keys to move around, jump to the beginning or end of the data by pressing Home or End, use Delete or Backspace to take out characters, or select data and cut, copy, or paste it.

Copying the information from one cell to another is useful when you have a lot of repeating data, or when you need to reorganize your worksheet. To copy a cell to another location, click on the cell you want to copy, and then click the Copy button on the Standard toolbar. (The border around the cell will change from a solid line to a moving dotted line.)

Next, click on the cell you want to copy the data to; its border becomes a solid line. Click the Paste button on the Standard toolbar, and the data from the first cell appears in the new cell, complete with formatting. You can paste the same information to as many new cells as you want by clicking on additional cells and clicking Paste. You can also copy and paste to and from a range of cells instead of just one. To move a cell, click anywhere on the border of the active cell (except the fill handle in the bottom right corner), and then hold down the mouse button and drag the cell to a new location.

Adding and deleting cells, rows, and columns

To insert a single cell, row or column, right-click on the cell located where you want the new cell to appear, and select Insert from the pop-up menu. In the Insert dialog box, decide whether you want to shift the existing cells right or down to make room for the new one. You can also choose to insert an entire row or column instead of a single cell. Then click OK.

To delete a cell, follow the same procedure, but choose Delete instead of Insert. In the Delete dialog box, choose whether to shift the remaining cells left or up to fill in the space vacated by the cells you've deleted. To insert an entire row or column, select a cell anywhere in the row or column currently located where you want the new row or column to appear, and then choose Insert ⇨ Rows or Insert ⇨ Columns.

Changing column widths and row heights

Rows change their height automatically to fit your data, but columns don't. To change the width of a column to fit your data, place your mouse pointer on the boundary between its header and the next one to the right, and double-click. You can also simply drag the header boundaries left or right (or up and down, in the case of rows).

Formatting data

The easiest way to format your worksheet attractively is to use AutoFormat, which applies a preset design to whatever range of cells you select. To use AutoFormat, select the range of cells you want to format, select Format ⇨ AutoFormat from the menu, and then choose the format you like from the AutoFormat dialog box. To make adjustments or apply only certain elements of the AutoFormat, click Options. When you're satisfied, click OK. The AutoFormat formatting is automatically applied to your selection (see Figure 1-8).

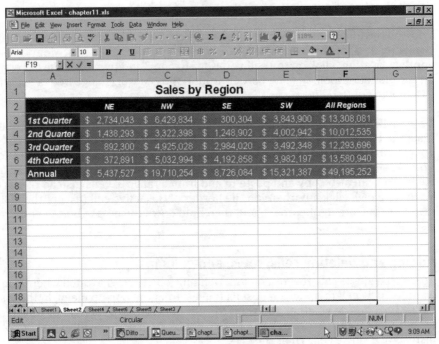

Figure 1-8: Here's what the worksheet looks like with AutoFormat applied.

If you change your mind about AutoFormatting, select the AutoFormatted cells, choose Format ⇨ AutoFormat and, in the AutoFormat dialog box, choose the design labeled None. Click OK to remove all formatting. Note that any formatting you applied before applying AutoFormat will not reappear.

Using Excel functions and formulas

The easiest way to perform analysis and calculations on data in Excel is with the Function wizard. To use it, select the cell where you want the results of the function to appear, and then click the Paste Function button on the Standard toolbar to open the Paste Function dialog box (see Figure 1-9).

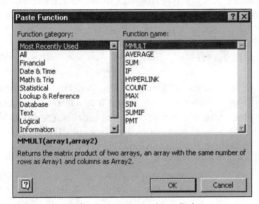

Figure 1-9: The Paste Function dialog box lets you choose from the functions Excel supports.

Click on the category of function you want on the left-hand side of the dialog box (e.g., statistical, database, math & trig, and so on). You can also choose from Most Recently Used (which keeps track of the functions you've used lately), and All (which lists every available function). Then choose the function you want from the list at the right. A description of what it does and how it works appears at the bottom of the dialog box to help you choose.

Click OK to open the second screen of the Function wizard. Excel automatically guesses what range of cells you intend to apply the function to, but you can adjust the range if it guesses wrong. The result of the formula if applied to the current range is shown at the bottom of the dialog box. Adjust the range as required, using your mouse on the worksheet; then, when you are satisfied, click OK. The function result will appear in the active cell.

The most commonly used Excel function, Sum, has been given its own button on the Standard toolbar. To use Sum, highlight the cells you want to add together, and click the Sum button. The values in those cells will be added and the answer displayed either at the bottom of a column or at the end of a row, depending on the shape of the range you selected.

Saving, opening, and closing workbooks

To save a workbook, click the Save button on the Standard toolbar, or choose File ⇨ Save. In the Save As dialog box, look for the folder you want to save your workbook in. Double-click on the folder to open it. Change the default name Excel has assigned your workbook (for example, Book1), if you wish; then in the Save As Type box, select what format you want to save the document in. Normally you'll save it as a .xls document, the default, but you can also choose to save it as an Excel template (so you can use its formatting and functions on a regular basis) or in a variety of other formats, ranging from database formats to formats for earlier versions of Excel to HTML. Finally, click Save.

To save a copy of your workbook or save it in a different format without losing the original version, choose File ⇨ Save As instead of Save; once a workbook has been saved, simply clicking Save will replace the old version of the workbook with the new, changed version. To open a saved workbook, click the Open button on the Standard toolbar, or choose File ⇨ Open. Using the Open dialog box, browse for the workbook you want to open. When you find it, double-click on it, or click on it once, and then click Open. When you're done working with a workbook and want to close it, choose File ⇨ Close, or simply click the Close Window button at the far right end of the menu bar.

Setting page properties, previewing, and printing

Before you print, you should set your page properties. Choose File ⇨ Page Setup to open the Page Setup dialog box. The Page Setup dialog box offers you four tabs. Under Page, you can choose between portrait and landscape orientation, select a paper size and print quality, and scale your pages (shrinking or expanding them) to fit your paper. Under Margins, you can set top, bottom, left, and right margins; and the distances from the top and bottom that headers and footers should appear. Under Header/Footer, enter the text for headers and footers, and under Sheet, select other printing options, such as the range of cells you want to print.

When you're happy with your choices, click Print to open the Print dialog box, described in a moment; or Print Preview to make sure everything is the way you want it (see Figure 1-10). You can also access Print Preview by choosing File ⇨ Print Preview.

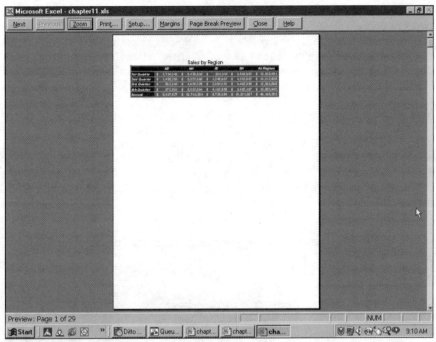

Figure 1-10: Print Preview gives you a sneak peek at your finished document.

Creating a Presentation with PowerPoint

Presentation software like PowerPoint helps you communicate your ideas to an audience, whether it's an audience of one in your own office or an audience of millions on the World Wide Web. When you first start PowerPoint, it offers you three ways to proceed: AutoContent Wizard, Design Template, or Blank Presentation.

Using the AutoContent Wizard

The easiest way to create a presentation is with AutoContent Wizard, which lets you choose a look that appeals to you and even suggests content for several common types of presentations. To use AutoContent Wizard, either select its radio button from the start-up screen, or choose File ⇨ New, click the General tab in the New Presentation dialog box, and then double-click AutoContent Wizard. From the initial screen of the wizard, click Next.

From the second screen, choose a presentation type. Click All to see all of the types of presentations AutoContent Wizard can help you create, or click General, Corporate, Projects, Sales/Marketing or Carnegie Coach to see just the presentations filed under those subject headings. (Carnegie Coach presentations are designed to help you hone your presentation and public speaking abilities.) Highlight the presentation type you want, and then click Next.

Next, choose the method you will use to make your presentation (e.g., on a computer, on the Web, as 35mm slides, etc); then, in the final screen, enter a title for your presentation and any text you'd like to use as a footer on each slide, and select other presentation options. Finally, click Finish. AutoContent Wizard creates a presentation based on your guidelines (see Figure 1-11). You'll have to enter your own text and graphics to complete the presentation, but your basic design is in place.

Figure 1-11: With AutoContent Wizard's help, you're already well on your way to a finished proposal.

Introducing the PowerPoint Interface

The easiest way to move through your presentation in PowerPoint is to use the Outline pane. Click anywhere on a slide title or within its text to open that slide in the Slide View pane. You can also use Slide Sorter view, which shows you thumbnail versions of all your slides. Choose View ⇨ Slide Sorter (see Figure 1-12), and then click on the slide you want to edit. Slide Sorter view also allows you to easily move slides around and change their properties.

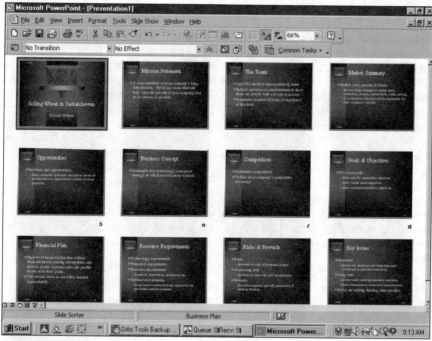

Figure 1-12: Slide Sorter view is useful for moving around in your presentation and for editing and formatting it.

Editing and formatting slides

Now you have an AutoContent Wizard-generated presentation that you want to make your own. Here's how.

Replacing and adding text

To replace existing text on a slide, find the slide you want to edit and click once inside the text you want to replace. This selects the text box that contains the text. Highlight the text you want to change, and then type in the new text to replace it. Finally, click anywhere outside the selected text box to deselect it. If you prefer, you can highlight text you want to change in the Outline pane and type over it there. You can insert text by simply placing your cursor where you want changes to be made, and then typing in the new text (the existing text moves aside to make room for it). To delete text, highlight it and press Delete.

Formatting text

To format text, click to select the appropriate text box, and then highlight the text you want to format. Finally, click the appropriate button on the Formatting or Drawing toolbars. Choose the typeface you want to apply from the Font list box, and the size from the Font Size list box. Make text bold or italic. Underline or shadow it to make it stand out. Align it within its text box with *Align Left, Center,* or *Align Right*. To create a numbered or bulleted list within a text box or change an existing list to a numbered list, click *Numbering* or *Bullets*. (To stop the numbering/bulleting, press Backspace to delete the last number or bullet.) Click *Increase Font Size* to boost the size of selected text to the next-highest size in the Font Size list box, or click *Decrease Font Size* to shrink it to the next-lowest size.

Demote moves an item in a list one step lower in the hierarchy of the outline (which generally means it becomes smaller and gets indented further to the right.) *Promote* moves it up in the hierarchy, which makes it larger and moves it back toward the left margin. Click *Animation Effects* to apply one of several preset animation effects to text.

Additional formatting commands can be accessed by clicking the *More Buttons* button on the Formatting toolbar and then clicking the Add or Remove buttons, or by choosing Format from the menu bar. Also, the Drawing toolbar includes one particularly useful formatting command, Font Color, which applies the color currently shown on it to the selected text. To choose a different color, click the down arrow beside the Font Color button.

Changing your presentation design

You may not like the default design provided by AutoContent Wizard. To change it, you apply a design template. (You can also start your presentation with a design template; it's one of the options in PowerPoint's start-up box. Like AutoContent Wizard, a design template takes care of the design work for you; unlike AutoContent Wizard, it doesn't provide suggested content.)

To apply a design template to your current presentation, choose Format ➪ Apply Design Template, and then choose the design template you want from the list provided. (A preview is provided.) The new template is applied to your current presentation, without changing any of the content (see Figure 1-13).

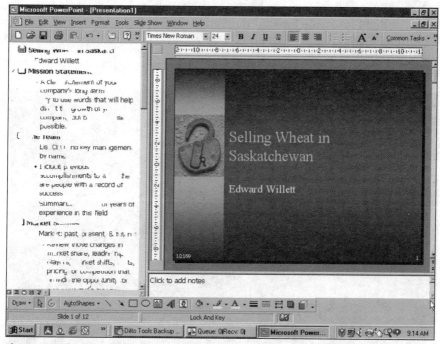

Figure 1-13: With a different design template applied, the presentation looks quite different — even though none of the content has changed.

Saving, opening, and closing presentations

To save your presentation, choose File ➪ Save or click the Save button on the Standard toolbar. In the Save As dialog box, find and open the folder where you want to save the presentation, enter a name for your presentation, and then choose the format in which you want to save it: the standard PowerPoint presentation format, HTML, an earlier PowerPoint format, or even a series of graphics. You can also save it as a template, which allows you to apply the same design to future presentations. Finally, click Save.

To save a copy without losing the original version, choose File ➪ Save As and use a new file name and/or format type. To open a presentation, choose File ➪ Open, locate the presentation you want to open in the Open dialog box, and then double-click on it. To close your presentation, choose File ➪ Close. If you've made changes since the last time the presentation was saved, you'll be prompted to save it before it closes.

Previewing and showing your presentation

Before you show your presentation, it's important to preview it. To do so, choose Slide Show ➪ View Show, or press F5. You'll see a full-screen view of your first slide (see Figure 1-14). Navigate through the slide show using the keyboard (Page Down, Down, or Right takes you forward through the show; Page Up, Up, or Left takes you back). You automatically return to PowerPoint at the end of the show; you can also end the show at any time by pressing Esc.

Figure 1-14: Here's the way the first slide will look during the actual presentation.

If you're happy with your presentation, choose Slide Show ⇨ Set Up Show, and select the options you want from the Set Up Show dialog box. You can preview the show again to see how it will play. Once you're completely satisfied, save your presentation again, and it's ready to go.

Printing your presentation

PowerPoint presentations aren't often printed, just viewed on the screen, but sometimes you'll want a paper copy to hand out to your audience or for your own reference. In addition, you may want to print your outline or notes. To print a presentation, you first need to set up your pages. Choose File ⇨ Page Setup. In the dialog box, choose the size of paper on which you'll print. (PowerPoint automatically resizes the slides to fit, but if you prefer, you can size them yourself.) Choose the orientation of the slides and the notes, handouts, and outline, and the starting number for numbering the slides, and then click OK.

To print, choose File ➪ Print. In the dialog box, choose a printer, which slides to print, the number of copies to print, and whether or not to collate them. You can also choose which aspect of the presentation to print: slides, notes, handouts, or the outline. (If you choose handouts, you'll be asked to choose the number of slides to print on each page and how to arrange them.) Finally, choose Grayscale (good for photographs and shaded graphics) or Pure Black and White (good for text and line art), whether to frame slides, and whether to scale them to fit the paper. When you've made all your decisions and are happy with them, click OK to print.

Top Office Time-savers

We've looked long and hard for tips that can help you use Office 2000 as efficiently as possible. Here are ten we think you'll find useful.

Copying an object's format to several others

The Format Painter tool appears on the Standard toolbar of every Office application. It's a highly useful tool for copying formatting from one item to another. Select the object (text, graphic, etc.) whose formatting you want to copy and click the Format Painter tool. The mouse pointer will change to look like a paintbrush. Click on the object you want to apply the formatting to.

To copy the formatting to several objects at once, select the object whose format you want to copy, double-click the Format Painter tool, and then click on each object you want to copy the formatting to in turn. When you have finished, click the Format Painter tool again to deactivate it.

Automatically addressing envelopes in Word

When you write a letter in Word that includes the address of the recipient, you can automatically create an envelope with that address on it. Just highlight the address within the letter and then choose Tools ➪ Envelopes and Labels. In the resulting dialog box, the address will automatically appear in the Delivery Address box. Enter your return address in the Return Address box. (Note that the Return Address box may already contain your return address, if you entered it during the initial setup of Office or by choosing Tools ➪ Options and clicking the User Information Tab.)

Using Word master documents

A master document is a document that contains a set of related documents: for example, a corporate annual report could be stored as a master document with reports from each department as related subdocuments. Many people can work on the subdocuments, and their changes are automatically incorporated into the master document.

To create a master document and subdocuments, you must first create an outline of your master document. Use the same heading style for each section you want to turn into a subdocument. Select the portion of the outline for which you want to create subdocuments, and then click the Create Subdocument button on the Outline toolbar. Word creates a new subdocument everywhere in the selection where the heading style that begins the selection appears. Once you save the outline, it becomes the master document.

Using Excel's Go To command

Excel's Go To command is very useful for quickly finding ranges or cells in a large spreadsheet. If you have so many named ranges that they've gone missing in your worksheet, choose Edit ⇨ Go To. In the Go To dialog box, all the named ranges are listed. Select the one you want to go to and click the OK button (or just double-click on the name of the range).

To compare values among the cells in a range and automatically locate and select those that are different from a particular set of values, first make sure the values you want to use as the basis for your comparison are entered in either a single row across the top of the range you want to conduct the comparison in, or in a single column to the left. Next, select the range, including the comparison row or column, making sure they form either the top or left edge of the range. Then select Edit ⇨ Go To from the menu. In the Go To dialog box, click the Special button. In the Go To Special dialog box, pick either the Row Differences radio button (if your base values are in a row) or the Column Differences radio button (if your base values are in a column). Click OK. All cells in the range that do not match the base values will be selected.

Changing the design of PowerPoint presentations

PowerPoint's master slides contain the basic formatting information for all the slides in your presentation. Any changes made to the master slides affect all the slides based on them. There are masters for Title slides, regular slides, Notes, and Handouts.

To change the appearance of slides, choose View ⇨ Master ⇨ Slide Master (or Title Master), and make the changes you want to fonts, font sizes, backgrounds, colors, and graphics. When you're satisfied, click Close on the Master toolbar. The changes will appear throughout your presentation, and by default any new slide you insert will also reflect the new formatting.

Automatically creating PowerPoint summary slides

In PowerPoint, you can automatically create a single slide that summarizes your presentation by listing the titles of selected slides. Go to Slide Sorter view, hold down Ctrl and click on each slide you want to include in the summary; then click the Summary Slide tool on the Slide Sorter toolbar. The summary slide is inserted before the first selected slide. The title of each selected slide appears as an element in a bulleted list.

Saving chart designs for future use

You can save the design of any chart you create with Microsoft Graph to use over and over again. To save the design, first create your chart and then choose Chart ⇨ Chart Type. Click the Custom Types tab and select the User-Defined radio button. Click the Add button and name your design and type in a description. The design is added to the list of user-defined chart types.

When you want to use your design for another chart, choose Chart ⇨ Chart Type. Select the Custom Types tab and the User-defined radio button. You should see your design on the list. Select it, click OK, and it will be applied to your graph.

Speeding up queries in Access

One of the easiest ways to speed up queries is to create thorough indexes. When a field is indexed, Access doesn't have to search through it; instead it goes straight to the index, just as you use the index of a book to find exactly what you want. It's best to put indexes on fields you're likely to use in a query.

To see if a field is indexed, put the table into Design view, select the field, and look at the General tab. Next to the word Indexed are three possible values: No, Yes (Duplicates OK), and Yes (No Duplicates). If the value is No, click on it and select one of the other options from the drop-down list that appears.

Announcing something new on your FrontPage Web

With FrontPage, you can automatically place the date the page was last changed anywhere on any Web page. Click in a Web page (in Page view) to place your insertion point where you want the date to appear, and then select Insert ⇨ Date and Time.

The first radio button in the Date and Time Properties dialog box will update the timestamp whenever the page is edited. The second option updates the page whenever it is changed automatically (this applies if you have placed a component on the page that automatically updates; such as a counter, for example). Finally, select a date format from the Date Format drop-down list and a time format (or None) from the Time Format drop-down list, and click OK to place the date on your page.

✦   ✦   ✦

For every level, for every learning style...
Hungry Minds has you covered!

SERIES	USER LEVEL	MAIN FEATURES OF SERIES	TOPICS	PAGE COUNT*
...FOR DUMMIES®	Beginning to intermediate	**...For Dummies Series** • Practical, fun, and easy-to-use books that cover topics with humor and entertainment • Filled with simple explanations, helpful icons, and clear, on-the-mark cartoons	Hundreds of computer-related books and over 100 other how-to books, covering topics from business to fitness to self-help	384–504
...FOR DUMMIES® QUICK REFERENCE	Beginning to advanced	**...For Dummies Quick Reference Series** • Pocket-size guide that offers easy-to-follow advice and easy-to-use steps for executing a program • Lay-flat, comb binding and small trim size for easy "in and out" access to software or technology features	Windows, Mac, Internet, word-processing, databases, spread-sheets, HTML, programming	220
MORE ...FOR DUMMIES®	Beginning to intermediate	**MORE ...For Dummies Series** • Starting where ...For Dummies books leave off, with more depth and breadth of topic coverage • Filled with simple explanations, helpful icons, and clear, on-the-mark cartoons	Windows, Internet, wordpro-cessing, databases, spread-sheets, suites, programming	420
DUMMIES 101®	Beginning to intermediate	**Dummies 101 Series** • Easy-to-follow tutorial with step-by-step lessons that take readers to a level of basic competency • Interactive CD-ROM with ready-to-use templates	Windows, Internet, HTML, word-processing, spreadsheets, data-bases, suites, programming	288
SMALL BUSINESS ...FOR DUMMIES®	Beginning to experienced small business technology implementers	**Small Business ...For Dummies Series** • Shows small business owners/employees how to apply technology to everyday small business situations • Filled with helpful icons and "what it means to your business" explanations • CD-ROMs with tools and applications for small businesses	Windows, networking, suites, Internet	325–400
CERTIFICATION FOR DUMMIES®	Intermediate to advanced software professionals	**Certification For Dummies Series** • Fast, focused, fun and easy reference guides that help candi-dates hone in on exam objectives and maximize study time • Written and reviewed by certified industry experts • CD-ROMs with exclusive QuickLearn™ game and Dummies test engine	Microsoft MCSE, A+ Certification	500
ONE STEP AT A TIME™	Beginning to intermediate	**One Step at a Time Series** • Book/CD-ROM combo with step-by-step, self-paced lessons • On-screen lessons with three levels of interactivity • Landscape 9" x 8" trim size and lay-flat binding • Interactive, sound-enhanced software	Office applications, Windows, Internet Explorer, graphics	350+
...SIMPLIFIED™	Beginning	**...Simplified Series** • Exclusive award-winning 3-D Visual™ learning system • Full-color illustrations and screenshots • Friendly, animated disk characters who explain terms and topics simply	Office applications, Windows, Internet, HTML, hardware, America Online	200–350
TEACH YOURSELF VISUALLY™	Beginning to intermediate	**Teach Yourself VISUALLY Series** • Exclusive award-winning 3-D Visual® learning system • Full-color graphics on every page • Step-by-step, clear, concise instructions	Windows, Internet, hardware, Access, Office, Netscape Navigator, Networking, Word	350

Microsoft®
Office 2000 Bible

Microsoft®
Office 2000 Bible

**Edward Willett, David Crowder, Rhonda Crowder,
David Karlins, and Jackie Leech**

Hungry Minds™

HUNGRY MINDS, INC.

New York, NY ◆ Cleveland, OH ◆ Indianapolis, IN

Microsoft® Office 2000 Bible

Published by
Hungry Minds, Inc.
909 Third Avenue
New York, NY 10022
www.hungryminds.com

Screen shots reprinted with permission from Microsoft Corporation.

Library of Congress Catalog Card Number: 98-75378

ISBN: 0-7645-3261-8

Printed in the United States of America

10 9 8 7 6

1B/RT/QT/QR/FC

Distributed in the United States by Hungry Minds, Inc.

Distributed by CDG Books Canada Inc. for Canada; by Transworld Publishers Limited in the United Kingdom; by IDG Norge Books for Norway; by IDG Sweden Books for Sweden; by IDG Books Australia Publishing Corporation Pty. Ltd. for Australia and New Zealand; by TransQuest Publishers Pte Ltd. for Singapore, Malaysia, Thailand, Indonesia, and Hong Kong; by Gotop Information Inc. for Taiwan; by ICG Muse, Inc. for Japan; by Intersoft for South Africa; by Eyrolles for France; by International Thomson Publishing for Germany, Austria and Switzerland; by Distribuidora Cuspide for Argentina; by LR International for Brazil; by Galileo Libros for Chile; by Ediciones ZETA S.C.R. Ltda. for Peru; by WS Computer Publishing Corporation, Inc., for the Philippines; by Contemporanea de Ediciones for Venezuela; by Express Computer Distributors for the Caribbean and West Indies; by Micronesia Media Distributor, Inc. for Micronesia; by Chips Computadoras S.A. de C.V. for Mexico; by Editorial Norma de Panama S.A. for Panama; by American Bookshops for Finland.

For general information on Hungry Minds' products and services please contact our Customer Care Department within the U.S. at 800-762-2974, outside the U.S. at 317-572-3993 or fax 317-572-4002.

For sales inquiries and reseller information, including discounts, premium and bulk quantity sales, and foreign-language translations, please contact our Customer Care Department at 800-434-3422, fax 317-572-4002, or write to Hungry Minds, Inc., Attn: Customer Care Department, 10475 Crosspoint Boulevard, Indianapolis, IN 46256.

For information on licensing foreign or domestic rights, please contact our Sub-Rights Customer Care Department at 650-653-7098.

For authorization to photocopy items for corporate, personal, or educational use, please contact Copyright Clearance Center, 222 Rosewood Drive, Danvers, MA 01923, or fax 978-750-4470.

For information on using Hungry Minds' products and services in the classroom or for ordering examination copies, please contact our Educational Sales Department at 800-434-2086 or fax 317-572-4005.

Please contact our Public Relations Department at 212-884-5163 for press review copies or 212-884-5000 for author interviews and other publicity information or fax 212-884-5400.

Hungry Minds™ is a trademark of Hungry Minds, Inc.

Credits

Acquisitions Editor
Andy Cummings

Development Editors
Alex Miloradovich
Kenyon Brown

Technical Editor
Rob SanFilippo

Copy Editors
Luann Rouff
Amanda Kaufmann
Anne Friedman

Production
Foster City Production Department

Proofreading and Indexing
York Production Services

Cover Design
Murder By Design

About the Authors

Edward Willett is a freelance writer in Regina, Saskatchewan, Canada. He's the author of several previous computer books, most recently *America Online's Creating Cool Web Pages,* also published by IDG Books Worldwide. In addition, he writes a science column for radio and television, and children's science books. He is the author of three young adult fantasy novels, *Soulworm* and *The Dark Unicorn,* published by Royal Fireworks Press, and *Andy Nebula: Interstellar Rock Star*, published by Roussan Press, and is also a professional actor and singer.

David Crowder and Rhonda Crowder have been involved in the online community for over a decade, and they run Far Horizons Software, a Website design firm. The Crowders' other book credits among many include *Setting Up an Internet Site For Dummies, Microsoft, Teach Yourself the Internet,* and *Teach Yourself FrontPage 2000* published by IDG Books Worldwide.

David Karlins teaches web design with FrontPage. Visit David any time at www.ppinet.com.

Jackie Leech has been working with PCs for 15 years, initially evaluating software. For the last 10 years she ran her own computer training business in Cape Town, South Africa, and has written many training courses. She currently lives on a yacht traveling around the world.

Preface

Welcome to *Microsoft Office 2000 Bible!* This is your guide to the latest and greatest version of Microsoft's immensely popular suite of office applications. Within these pages you'll find everything you need to know to make immediate, effective use of Microsoft Word, Microsoft Excel, Microsoft PowerPoint, Microsoft Outlook, Microsoft Access, Microsoft FrontPage, and Microsoft Publisher. You'll learn how to use each program separately. You'll also learn how to use them together to create integrated documents that draw on the strengths of all these programs to help you do your work better.

Is This Book for You?

If you use, or will soon be using, Microsoft Office 2000, then this book is for you. Beginners should start with the special Quick Start pullout section; experienced users can move straight on to the sections devoted to each of the applications, or plunge immediately into the chapters in Part VIII: Cutting-Edge Office or Appendix A: What's New in Office 2000, which explore some of the exciting new capabilities of Office 2000 in detail. Throughout this book you'll find useful tips and step-by-step guides to carrying out the most common Office tasks. The excellent index and thorough table of contents can both help you find the topics that interest you.

How This Book Is Organized

In addition to the special Quick Start pullout section, the main body of the Office 2000 Bible is divided into eight parts and three appendixes, which are described in the following overviews.

Special Quick Start Pullout Section

This booklet tells you just what you need — no more, no less — to start using Word, Excel, and PowerPoint immediately for their primary purpose: creating a document, a spreadsheet, and a presentation. A final section covers the ten best tips we could find to help you use Office 2000 as efficiently as possible. The inside front and back covers of this booklet also provide quick overviews of what's new in Office 2000 and a brief look at some of the most commonly used keyboard shortcuts. Even if you're already an experienced Office user, you'll want to turn here first!

Part I: Word

The heart of any office suite is the word processor, and with Word, Microsoft Office 2000 has the most popular and powerful word processor in the world. Chapters 1-9 show you how to put Word's power to work for you.

Part II: Excel

Excel is Office's spreadsheet application, and, like Word, it's pretty much the standard in its field. Chapters 10-19 show you how to get the most from your worksheets.

Part III: PowerPoint

PowerPoint is Office's presentation software. Chapters 20-27 demonstrate how to make great presentations that communicate your message clearly and effectively.

Part IV: Outlook

Outlook is Office's application for managing messages, such as faxes and e-mail, and your time. Chapters 28-34 help you get the most from Outlook's powerful features.

Part V: Access

Just as Outlook lets you manage messages and your time, so Access lets you manage data—and use it in other Office applications. Chapters 35-41 explain how.

Part VI: Web and Desktop Publishing Tools

Chapters 42-50 introduce FrontPage, Publisher, and PhotoDraw, the newest additions to the Office suite of applications. FrontPage helps you create professional-looking Web pages and manage them effectively. Publisher is a full-featured desktop-publishing program, perfect for creating everything from newsletters to annual reports. PhotoDraw complements FrontPage and Publisher in particular, and every Office application in general, by providing powerful graphic creation and editing tools.

Part VII: Integrating and Automating Office Applications

Office's most powerful attribute is the way all of its applications work closely together to accomplish things none of them could on their own. Chapters 51-56 explore Office's cooperative capabilities.

Part VIII: Cutting-Edge Office

Office 2000 has capabilities no version of Office has ever had before. Chapters 57-59 illustrate ways to put Microsoft's latest innovations to work for you.

Appendixes

Appendixes A-C include additional valuable information. Appendix A, What's New in Office 2000, contains handy tables laying out the most important new features that Microsoft has packed into the latest version of each Office application. If you've used previous versions of Office and just want to know what's different about Office 2000, this resources should prove invaluable. Appendix B, Sources of Office Info on the Web, points you to Web sites where you'll find more information and lots of useful tips, tricks, templates, and more, for use with Office 2000. Appendix C explains what you'll find on the CD-ROM that accompanies this book, and why you'll find it useful.

Conventions This Book Uses

We've made finding your way through this massive tome easier by including a variety of signposts that point you to useful information. Look for these icons in the left margin:

Notes highlight something of particular interest about the current topic, or expand on the subject at hand.

These icons clue you in to hot tips, or show you faster, better ways of doing things.

If a process holds some risk of losing data or irrevocably altering a document, this icon will warn you of it.

This icon points you to another section of the book where additional information on the current topic can be found.

What You'll Find in Sidebars

Sidebars provide related information, examples, or additional detail about a topic. Generally the information in sidebars, while interesting, isn't critical to understanding how to use an application, so you can skip them if you like. (Although we'd prefer you didn't — after all, we put a lot of work into writing them!) The following points are (in fact) helpful in using this book:

✦ When we tell you to use a particular command from a menu, we'll write it like this: choose File ➪ New. That tells you to pull down the File menu and click on the New command. If there's another level of menu beyond that, it'll look like this: choose View ➪ Toolbars ➪ Formatting.

✦ Keyboard commands are written like this: press Ctrl+A. That means to press the Ctrl key and continue to hold it down while you press the A key.

Where Should I Start?

With a such a complete and thoughtfully designed resource (a book as comprehensive as its subject), it may difficult to decide where to begin. Here are a few helpful hints:

✦ **If you're entirely new to Office** — start with the special Quickstart pullout section. It will have you using Office's applications in minutes.

✦ **To learn what's new in Office 2000** — start with Appendix A, where all that information is conveniently gathered in one spot.

✦ **To work with a specific application** — with Word, Excel, PowerPoint, Outlook, Access, or FrontPage, or if you're interested in creating integrated documents and automating Office applications, or learning how to put Office 2000's new features to work for you in brand-new ways, refer to the pertinent parts and chapters in the book.

✦ **To work with a specific topic** — let the table of contents or the complete index at the back of the book be your guide.

✦ **To find additional sources of information or what's on the CD** — refer to Appendixes B and C.

✦ **If all else fails** — simply turn the page and begin. We're sure you'll find reading this book as enjoyable a process as using Microsoft Office 2000.

Acknowledgments

Many thanks to the fine team at IDG Books Worldwide, especially our long (and we really mean long!) suffering editors — Andy Cummings, Ken Brown, Alex Miloradovich, Rob Sanfilippo, and Luann Rouff — without whom, you wouldn't be reading this today.

A very special thanks to my even more long-suffering wife, Margaret Anne, for understanding why I sometimes spend more time with my keyboard than I do with her.
—*Edward Willettt*

We'd also like to thank David Fugate, our agent, who's always there when you need him.
—*David and Rhonda Crowder*

And thanks to Denise Snaer-Gauder for the photo used in the FrontPage section of this book.
—*David Karlins*

I would like to acknowledge the invaluable support I received from Cyril Wallis, John Ingram from Carriacou, and Bertrand Bhikarry from Tobago.
—*Jackie Leech*

Contents at a Glance

Contents

Part II: Excel   219

Chapter 10: Worksheets and Workbooks 221

Chapter 11: Entering and Formatting Information 245

Part III: PowerPoint   437

Part VI: Web and Desktop Publishing Tools   827

Word

Creating and Managing Documents

"**A** journey of a thousand miles," an old proverb says, "begins with a single step." In Word, a manuscript of a thousand pages begins with the creation of a new document. Word makes beginning and carrying out a new project easy, providing you with a variety of tools, many of them customizable, that can even help you with the look and content of your document.

Creating New Documents

Creating a new document in Word is so easy you don't have to do anything at all: Word automatically opens a blank document the moment you start the program (see Figure 1-1).

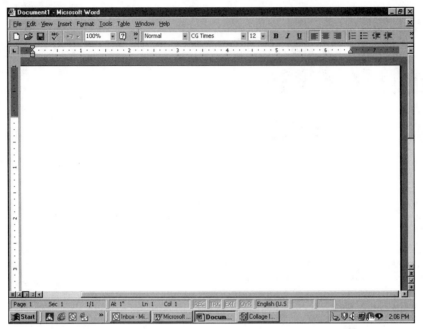

Figure 1-1: When you open Word, a blank document automatically appears.

To start a new document, just start Word. That doesn't mean you have to restart Word every time you want to create a new document, however. You can also create a new document at any time by choosing File ➪ New. This opens the New dialog box (see Figure 1-2).

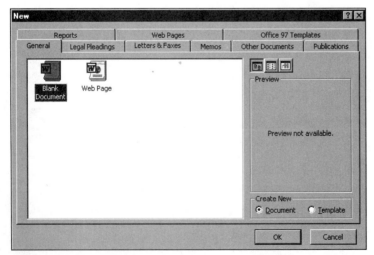

Figure 1-2: You can start a new document from within Word by bringing up the New dialog box.

We'll look at a number of tabs in this dialog box in detail later in this chapter, but by default, the General tab is selected, which offers you two options:

✦ **Blank Document.** If you're creating an ordinary paper document, choose this option. This will begin a new document just as Word normally does when you start it.

✦ **Web Page.** If you're using Word to create a page intended for display on the World Wide Web or an intranet, double-click this icon. The only difference between the display for a new Web page and that for a blank document is that the New button in the Standard toolbar changes slightly to indicate that clicking it will start a new Web Page, not a regular document.

For detailed instructions on entering text into new Word documents, see Chapter 2, "Working with Text."

Navigating in Word

There are several ways to move around your Word document. However, before you set out on a journey, it's important to know where you're starting from. Your current position — the place where text will be entered if you start typing — is called the *insertion point*. It's represented by a flashing vertical bar. Once you know where you are, you can move around your document in many different ways:

✦ **Use the mouse.** Inside a document, your mouse pointer appears as a vertical bar with smaller crossbars at the top and bottom, like a capital letter I. Place this wherever you want the insertion point to appear and click once.

✦ **Use the scrollbars.** You can only move the insertion point within the portion of the document currently displayed. If the document extends beyond the top, bottom, left, or right sides of the screen, you can use the scrollbars to see the rest of it.

- *To move up or down one line at a time*, click the single arrows at the top or bottom of the vertical scrollbar.

- *To move up or down one screen at a time*, click in the light-colored area above or below the box-shaped slider.

- *To scroll smoothly through the document*, click and hold the single arrows or drag the slider up and down. The advantage of using the slider is that as you scroll through your document, pop-up windows will appear that show you what page you're on and, if your document is divided into sections, what section you're in (see Figure 1-3). You can navigate left or right through an extra-wide document in similar fashion, using the horizontal scrollbar.

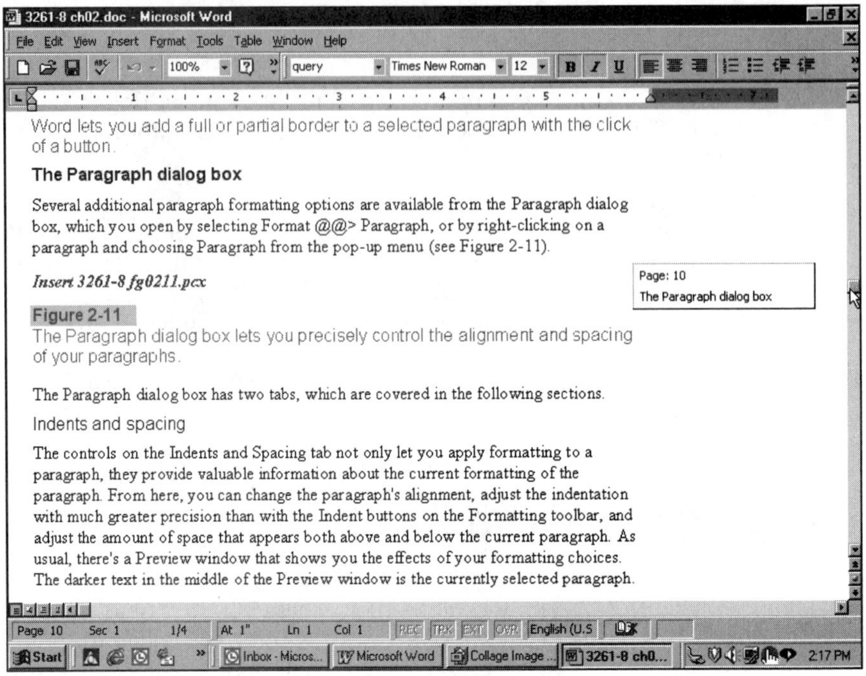
3261-8 ch02.doc - Microsoft Word
File Edit View Insert Format Tools Table Window Help
100%
query
Times New Roman
12
Word lets you add a full or partial border to a selected paragraph with the click of a button.
The Paragraph dialog box
Several additional paragraph formatting options are available from the Paragraph dialog box, which you open by selecting Format @@> Paragraph, or by right-clicking on a paragraph and choosing Paragraph from the pop-up menu (see Figure 2-11).
Insert 3261-8 fg0211.pcx
Page: 10
The Paragraph dialog box
Figure 2-11
The Paragraph dialog box lets you precisely control the alignment and spacing of your paragraphs.
The Paragraph dialog box has two tabs, which are covered in the following sections.
Indents and spacing
The controls on the Indents and Spacing tab not only let you apply formatting to a paragraph, they provide valuable information about the current formatting of the paragraph. From here, you can change the paragraph's alignment, adjust the indentation with much greater precision than with the Indent buttons on the Formatting toolbar, and adjust the amount of space that appears both above and below the current paragraph. As usual, there's a Preview window that shows you the effects of your formatting choices. The darker text in the middle of the Preview window is the currently selected paragraph.
Page 10 Sec 1 1/4 At 1" Ln 1 Col 1 REC TRK EXT OVR English (U.S
Start
Inbox - Micros...
Microsoft Word
Collage Image...
3261-8 ch0...
2:17 PM

Figure 1-3: The slider in the vertical scrollbar tells you what part of your document you've moved to.

✦ **Use the keyboard.** You can also move easily through your document using your keyboard. The cursor keys move your insertion point up or down one line at a time, or left or right one character at a time.

- You can move through your document faster by holding down the Ctrl key at the same time: In that case, the left and right cursor keys move you through your document one word at a time, while the up and down keys move you one paragraph at a time.
- Four other keys are also particularly useful for navigation. *Home* moves you to the beginning of the line that contains your insertion point; *End* moves you to the end of the line. *Ctrl+Home* takes you to the top of the document; *Ctrl+End* takes you to the end. *Page Up* moves you one screen up in the document; *Page Down* moves you one screen down.

✦ **Use Find and Replace.** Finally, you can navigate through a Word document by using the Find and Replace dialog box, which you access by choosing Edit ➪ Find ➪ Replace or Go To (each one takes you to a different tab). You can also press Ctrl+F for Find, Ctrl+H for Replace, or Ctrl+G for Go To.

Using Find and Replace

Use Find to locate and move to specific bits of text in the document. Type the text you want to find in the Find What box, and then click Find Next (see Figure 1-4). The next instance of the word after the current location of the insertion point is highlighted. (The Find and Replace dialog box automatically repositions itself so as not to hide the highlighted word.) To move to the next instance of the word, click Find Next again.

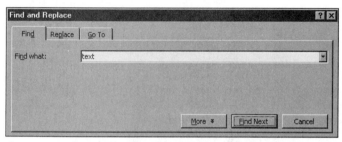

Figure 1-4: The Find and Replace dialog box can take you to the exact point in your document you want to reach, even when you don't know where it is.

The Replace tab works similarly, except it not only finds the word or words you're looking for, it lets you replace them with something else. This is particularly useful if, for example, you've spelled Mr. Remple's name as Mr. Ripple throughout a long document (something I actually did once!).

As before, type the text you want to find in the Find What box, and then type the text you want to replace it with in the Replace With box (see Figure 1-5). Click Find Next to find the next instance of the chosen word. If you want to replace it with your new text, click Replace; that will replace it, and then automatically find and highlight the next instance of the word. This gives you the opportunity to either replace it or click Find Next to leave it as it is and move on to the next instance. If you're sure you want to replace all instances of the selected text, click Replace All.

Figure 1-5: Replace lets you act on second thoughts about some of the words you've used in your document.

Find and Replace can be used to search for and change more than just text. You can also use Find to look for formatting elements such as specific font and paragraph styles, as well as special characters such as tab stops, line breaks and em dashes; and use Replace to replace those special elements and characters with other special elements and characters. For example, you could use Replace to find all the instances of bold text in your document and replace it with underlined text — or to italicize every instance of the title of a book you referred to frequently.

To access these additional capabilities, click More in the Find and Replace dialog box. This increases the size of the box and adds several more controls (see Figure 1-6).

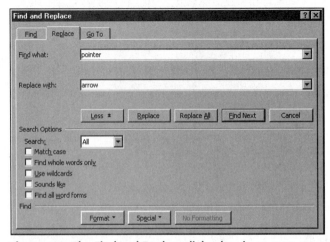

Figure 1-6: The Find and Replace dialog box is an even more powerful navigation and editing tool when you take advantage of its additional capabilities by clicking More.

At the top of this expanded section is the Search Options area, which offers a pull-down menu that lets you choose All, Down, or Up. If you choose All, Find and Replace will go through the whole document. If you choose Down, Find and Replace will search down from the insertion point, and ask you if you want to search the rest of the document once it gets to the end. If you choose Up, Find and Replace will search up from the insertion point, and ask you if you want to search the rest of the document once it gets to the top.

The following check boxes offer more search options:

✦ **Match case.** Checking this box ensures that Word only finds instances of text whose letters match the case of those you entered. For example, it would distinguish between the word "cart," and the acronym CART (Championship Auto Racing Teams).

✦ **Find whole words only.** This treats the search text as a whole word, which is important if the search text can also be found as part of other words. If you're searching for every instance of the word "dog," you don't want to locate every instance of the words "boondoggle," "dogwood," and "doggerel" too.

✦ **Use wildcards.** This lets you search for words or phrases that begin or end with specific words or phrases by inserting an asterisk to represent what comes before or after the selected text. The search term "the*end," for instance, would find everything from "the living end" to "the flexible teacher taught the whole class how to bend." On the other hand, it wouldn't find "The End" because Use Wildcards only finds text that exactly matches the case of the search term.

✦ **Sounds like.** This lets you search for words that sound vaguely like the search text. For example, a search for "cat" with this option selected turned up "quite," "good," "got," and "cut" in one of the chapters of this book.

✦ **Find all word forms.** Used smart, smarter, and smartest when you meant to use dumb, dumber, and dumbest? Choose this option and enter "smart" as your search text and "dumb" as your replace text. Word will find all forms of the word and change them.

✦ **No formatting.** When you click this button, Word ignores the format of the text it's searching for, which means it will find the word whether it's in 72-point Helvetica Bold or six-point Times New Roman Italic.

✦ **Format.** If you want to take format into account, click the Format button and choose which formatting options you want to search for (if your insertion point is in the Find What box), or apply (if your insertion point is in the Replace With box).

✦ **Special.** Click this button to search for or insert special characters and other document elements such as tabs, footnote marks, and even graphics. The options in the Special list vary depending on whether your insertion point is in the Find What box or the Replace With box.

Using Go To

Go To, the remaining tab in the Find and Replace dialog box (see Figure 1-7), takes you to a specific area of your document without regard for content.

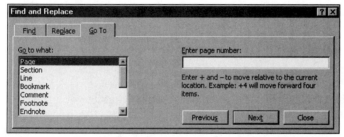

Figure 1-7: The Go To tab of the Find and Replace dialog box can take you to specific areas of your document.

Here you have a whole new series of search criteria:

✦ **Page.** This lets you move to a specific page of your document, by entering the page number and clicking Next, or by entering a certain number of pages forward or backward from your current location. Enter +n or -n, where n is the number of pages you want to move.

✦ **Section.** If you've used section breaks (see Chapter 2, "Working with Text") in your document, you can move among those sections just as you moved among pages, by entering a specific section to go to or the number of sections you want to move forward or backward.

✦ **Line.** Again, you can enter a specific line to move to, or a certain number of lines to move forward or backward.

✦ **Bookmark.** You can insert a bookmark, and give it a name, by choosing Insert ⇨ Bookmark. Then you can use Go To to move to a specific bookmark by selecting the bookmark's name from the pull-down menu.

✦ **Comment.** This lets you jump to comments entered by any reviewer or by a specific person.

✦ **Footnote.** Use this option to find a specific footnote (by number) or jump a certain number of footnotes forward or backward.

✦ **Endnote.** Use this option to find a specific endnote or jump a certain number of endnotes forward or backward.

✦ **Field.** Jump to a specific field by selecting the field type from the drop-down list.

✦ **Table.** Jump to a specific table or a certain number of tables forward or backward.

✦ **Graphic.** Jump to a specific graphic (by number) or a certain number of graphics forward or backward.

✦ **Equation.** Jump to a specific equation (by number) or a certain number of equations forward or backward.

✦ **Object.** Jump to a specific type of ActiveX object, chosen from the pull-down menu. These can include such things as embedded sounds and video clips, Excel spreadsheets, and more.

✦ **Heading.** Jump to a specific heading (by number) or a certain number of headings forward or backward.

The navigation tools

At the bottom of the vertical scrollbar are three controls that let you browse through your document in the way that suits you best. To use these tools, first click the Select Browse Object button. This opens the small menu shown in Figure 1-8.

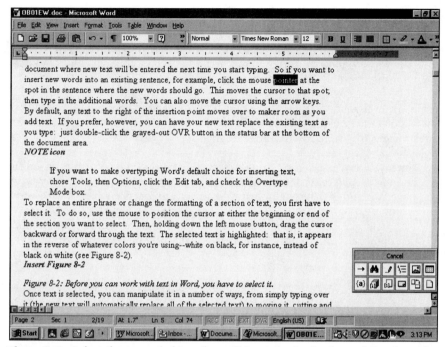

Figure 1-8: Select the type of object that will form the basis of your browsing using the Select Browse Object menu.

From this menu, select the type of element you want to use as the basis of your browsing; then use the Previous and Next buttons to move through your document. The twelve choices in the Select Browse Object menu are Go To, Find, Edits, Heading, Graphic, Table, Field, Endnote, Footnote, Comment, Section, and Page.

Go To and Find open their respective tabs in the Find and Replace dialog box; once you've entered search text or selected search options in those tabs, the Previous and Next buttons will move you to each occurrence of your selected criteria (enabling you to close the dialog box while continuing to search through the document). With the other options, Previous and Next simply move you from instance to instance of the selected browse object — up to the previous location at which you edited text, for instance; or down to the next occurring graphic.

With so many ways to navigate through your Word document, there's no reason to ever get lost!

Word's Views

Just as Word offers you many ways to move around within a document, so it offers you many ways to view your document. In fact, it offers you six: print layout, Web layout, normal, outline, Web page preview, and print preview.

Normal, print layout, Web layout, and outline views are accessed by opening the View menu and choosing the view you want from the list; Web page preview and print preview are available from the File menu.

✦ **Normal view,** as its name suggests, is the standard view for typing, editing, and formatting text. Because its focus is on text, it simplifies the layout of the page, and hides page boundaries, headers and footers, objects with text wrapping, floating graphics, and backgrounds (see Figure 1-9). You can vary this view with the Zoom control box on the Standard toolbar, which lets you specify what percentage of full size you want the page displayed.

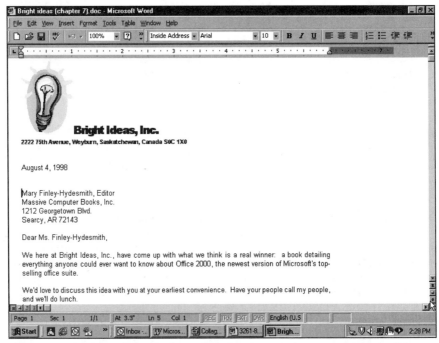

Figure 1-9: The normal view is the easiest view to use when entering and editing text.

✦ **Print layout view** shows you exactly how text, graphics, and other elements will appear in the final printed document. Print layout makes it easier to work with elements in addition to regular text, such as headers and footers, columns, and drawings (see Figure 1-10).

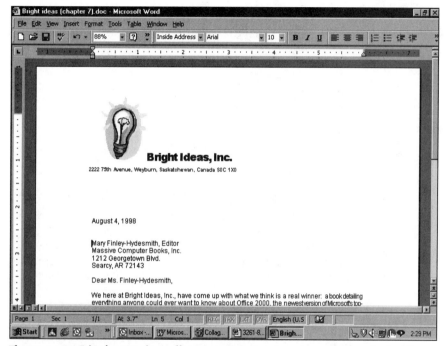

Figure 1-10: Print layout view offers a more accurate representation of what the finished document will look like.

✦ **Web layout view** is used when you're creating a Web page or any other document that's going to be viewed on a monitor. In Web layout view you can see backgrounds, text is wrapped, and graphics are placed the same way they are in a Web browser (see Figure 1-11).

✦ **Outline view** lets you see the structure of a document and reorganize text simply by dragging headings (see Figure 1-12). If you wish, you can collapse documents to see only the main headings.

Cross-Reference

For more detailed information on working with outlines, see Chapter 5, "Outlines, Tables of Contents, and Indexes."

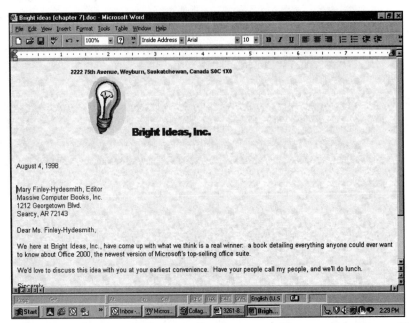

Figure 1-11: If you're creating an online document, it's a good idea to use Web layout view while you work; otherwise, you may find that things don't appear quite where you expect them to. Notice where the return address shows up now that we've switched from normal or print layout view to Web layout view.

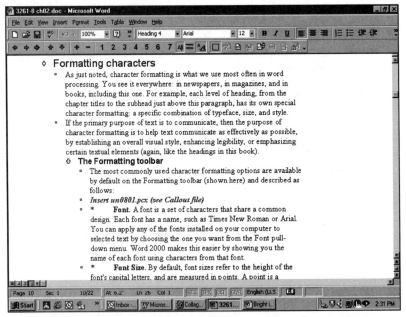

Figure 1-12: Outline view makes it easier to organize and reorganize your document.

✦ **Web page preview** shows you how your document will appear when viewed online using a Web browser by displaying it with Internet Explorer. You can't edit in this view; it's just a way of checking the final appearance of your work (see Figure 1-13). (Clicking the Edit button in Internet Explorer 5 won't work because, since the file is already open in Word, it can't be opened again. To edit, return to Word and use one of the other views.)

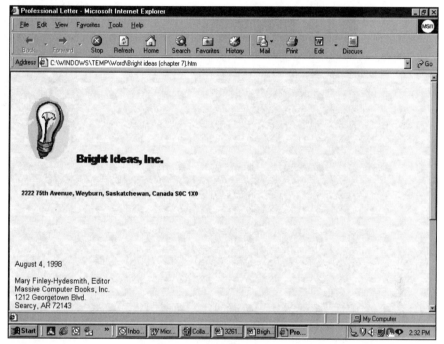

Figure 1-13: Check the final appearance of your online document using Web page preview.

✦ **Print preview,** similarly, shows you how your document will appear when printed (see Figure 1-14). By default this view shows you the whole page, but notice in the figure that the mouse pointer has taken on the shape of a magnifying glass. By pointing at the document and clicking, you can toggle back and forth between a view of the whole page and a larger view that makes it easier to read the text.

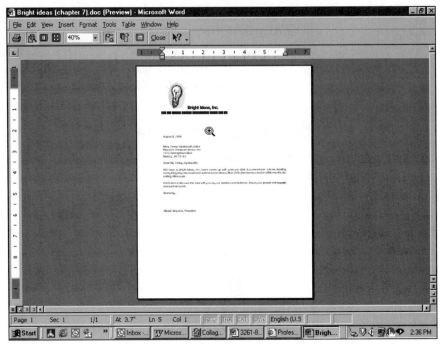

Figure 1-14: Print preview shows you exactly how your printed document will look.

You also have several other controls on a new toolbar, which are shown in Figure 1-14. From left to right, these controls let you:

- ✦ Print the document

- ✦ Toggle the magnifying glass pointer on and off (when it's off, you can edit the page as you would in normal view)

- ✦ Display one page or, in a larger document, several pages at once (as many as six or more at a time depending on the size of the Word desktop windows and your screen resolution)

- ✦ Display the page at a specific percentage of full size

- ✦ Toggle the ruler on and off

- ✦ Shrink the document by one page so that a small portion doesn't spill onto another page

- ✦ Toggle Full Screen display (which hides everything except the print preview toolbar and the page you're previewing)

- ✦ Close the print preview

- ✦ Get context-sensitive help (that is, help that's related to the task you're trying to perform).

Word's Wizards

Sometimes when you're creating a document you want to do it from scratch. Other times you wouldn't mind a little help. As you've seen, Word makes it easy to open a blank document, but it's also standing by with a selection of wizards to guide you in your document creation.

To access the wizards, choose File ➪ New. From the New dialog box, choose the tab that matches the type of document you want to create. For example, if you choose Other Documents, you'll see the selection shown in Figure 1-15. Some of these are templates, another excellent tool Word provides to help you design effective, eye-catching documents. However, among them you'll also find several wizards, such as the Resume Wizard.

Cross-Reference
Templates are dealt with in detail in Chapter 6, "Styles and Templates."

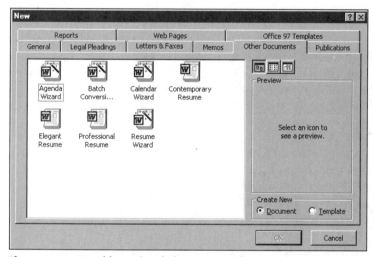

Figure 1-15: Word has wizards for many of the most common types of documents.

To use a wizard, simply double-click its icon. You'll be presented with a screen something like the one in Figure 1-16 (obviously the details will vary depending on what kind of wizard you're using).

Click Next to proceed through the wizard. You'll be asked to choose from a series of options. For example, with the Resume wizard, the first thing you have to do is choose from one of three styles of resume: professional, contemporary, or elegant (see Figure 1-17). A thumbnail sketch of each gives you a good idea of what they'll look like.

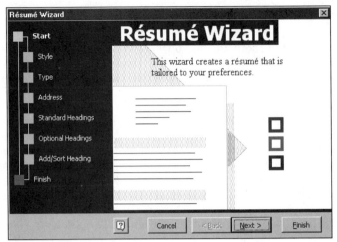

Figure 1-16: Whenever you select a wizard, the first thing you'll see is something like this.

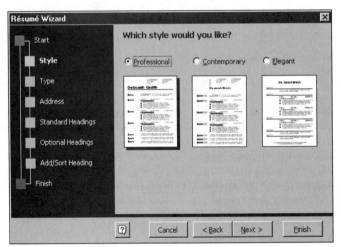

Figure 1-17: In many wizards, you're first asked what overall design style you'd like to apply to your document.

As the wizard progresses, you're asked to make other choices (such as how you want to organize the information) and enter such basic information as your name and address.

When you've completed going through the wizard, click Finish. Voilà! Your document is complete — well, except for the small detail of adding your own words and graphics to it (see Figure 1-18).

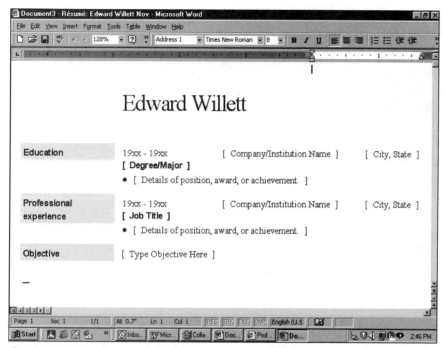

Figure 1-18: Word's wizards will design documents for you, but they leave the actual words and images to you.

Other wizards provided by Word can help you design envelopes, faxes, letters, mailing labels, memos, agendas, calendars, legal pleadings, and Web pages.

Tip   One of the most useful Word 2000 wizards is one that converts whole batches of files from another format into Word files—or vice versa. This Batch Conversion wizard, located on the Other Documents tab in the New dialog box, lets you choose what format of file you want to convert to or from, and then specify the files you want to convert. It's a great time-saver, especially if you've switched to Word from some other word-processing system.

Word's Automatic Functions

As you'll see in the next chapter, "Working with Text," Word makes it easy for you to correct and format text once you've entered it. If you want or need it, however, Word also offers help automatically as you enter text.

To access Word's automatic functions, choose Tools ➪ AutoCorrect. This opens the dialog box shown in Figure 1-19, which has four tabs: AutoCorrect, AutoFormat As You Type, AutoText, and AutoFormat.

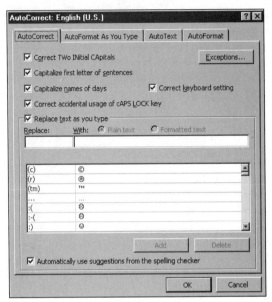

Figure 1-19: Word offers a number of automatic functions that can help you create documents more quickly and efficiently.

AutoCorrect

AutoCorrect watches for common typing errors and corrects them as you make them — sometimes before you're even aware you have made them. Choose which errors you would like automatically corrected from the list. If you want it to, Word will automatically correct words or sentences with two initial capitals (a common mistake for fast typists with sluggish keyboards), capitalize the names of days and the first word of sentences (which it assumes to be any word following a period or other typical sentence-ending punctuation mark), and correct accidental usage of the Caps Lock key.

If you select Replace As You Type, Word will watch for the spelling errors contained in the list at the bottom of the tab and automatically correct them. For example, if you type "accomodate," Word will automatically change it to "accommodate" as soon as you hit the space bar to move on to the next word. You can teach Word to correct your own most common misspellings by entering the wrong spelling in the Replace box and the correct spelling in the With box, and then clicking Add. If you want to remove an existing entry in the AutoCorrect list, highlight it and click Delete. If you'd like Word to automatically replace words it doesn't recognize with suggestions from the spelling checker, click the check box at the bottom of the tab.

Sometimes AutoCorrect can be a nuisance. The famous poet e.e. cummings, for example, would have hated it, because he never used capital letters to start his sentences. To tell Word to ignore certain specific usages that look like mistakes but really aren't, click Exceptions. You can teach Word not to capitalize after abbreviations ending in a period (a list of common ones is provided), to ignore certain words that are supposed to have two initial capital letters (like CSi, the official abbreviation for CompuServe), and to not correct other words you can add to a list.

AutoFormat As You Type

Word can do more than correct mistakes automatically; it can even automatically apply formatting, which can save you a lot of mouse clicking and dragging. To fine-tune this capability, open the AutoFormat As You Type tab of the AutoCorrect dialog box (see Figure 1-20).

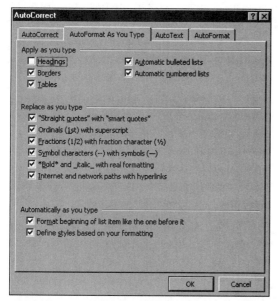

Figure 1-20: The AutoFormat As You Type options apply formatting automatically, which can save you a lot of mouse dragging and clicking!

There are three sections to this tab: Apply As You type, Replace As You Type, and Automatically As You Type.

Apply As You Type

These five commands format text as you enter it, so you don't have to go back and do it later:

✦ **Headings.** If this is selected, Word automatically applies Heading styles 1 through 9 to the headings and subheadings in your document (Word assumes a paragraph is a heading if it doesn't end in a punctuation mark and you hit Enter twice after it).

Cross-Reference

For more information on styles, see Chapter 6, "Styles and Templates."

✦ **Borders.** Select this, and Word will automatically apply a border to your current paragraph if you enter three or more hyphens (for a thin border), underscore marks (for a thick border), or equal signs (for a double-line border).

✦ **Tables.** If this is selected, Word will draw a table if you enter a series of plus signs and hyphens, such as +— —+— —+. Word will create a column between adjacent plus signs.

✦ **Automatic bulleted lists.** Select this, and Word will assume you're creating a bulleted list whenever you type a -, >, or asterisk at the beginning of a paragraph and follow it by a space or tab mark, or type an O (uppercase letter O) and follow it with a tab mark. The current paragraph will be tabbed as a list item (much like this list item), and subsequent paragraphs will also be tabbed and bulleted as list items until you press Enter twice or press Backspace to delete the last bullet in the list.

✦ **Automatic numbered lists.** This works exactly the same way as automatic bulleted lists, except it looks for a number or letter, followed by a period, followed by a tab or space, at the beginning of a paragraph.

Replace As You Type

Replace As You Type will automatically replace certain items that can be readily entered via the keyboard with others that can't but might look or work better: For example, you can ask Word to replace the straight quotation marks on the keyboard with the curly ones that are usually used in books and magazines. These options are self-explanatory: just click their check boxes to activate them.

Automatically As You Type

There are two options in this section:

✦ **Format beginning of list item like the one before it.** This can save you time in creating lists. If, for example, you want the first word of each list item to be italicized, click this; and once you've formatted the first list item, each subsequent list item will have its first word italicized automatically.

✦ **Define styles based on your formatting.** Select this, and Word automatically creates new styles based on the manual formatting you apply to paragraphs in your document. If you want to format subsequent paragraphs in the same way, all you have to do is apply the style instead of manually formatting again.

See Chapter 6, "Styles and Templates," for more information about applying styles.

AutoText

AutoText, the third tab in the AutoCorrect dialog box (see Figure 1-21), tries to figure out what word or phrase you're typing, based on the first four letters, and offers to complete that word or phrase for you. It draws on information entered into the current template. If you're using the Normal template (which you use by default), for example, and you type the first four letters of any month of the year, a little pop-up tip will show you the complete name of the month. Press Enter or F3, and Word inserts the complete word for you. If you want to ignore the AutoText suggestion, just keep typing.

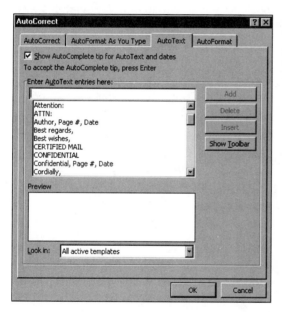

Figure 1-21: AutoText tries to save you keystrokes by guessing what word or phrase you're typing and offering to insert it automatically.

You can make your own additions to AutoText. To do so:

1. Type a word or phrase you often use and want AutoText to help you with.

2. Highlight it.

3. Choose Tools ➪ AutoCorrect.

4. Click the AutoText tab.

5. Type a name for the entry in the Enter AutoText Entries Here box, and click Add. The next time you type the first four letters of that word or phrase, Word will offer to complete it for you.

AutoText entries can include formatting and even objects such as graphics. To delete AutoText entries, highlight them and click Delete. Click Insert to insert a highlighted AutoText entry into the current document.

AutoFormat

AutoFormat, the final tab in the AutoCorrect dialog box, has most of the same options as AutoFormat As You Type. The difference is that AutoFormat is applied to the whole document at once, and takes effect only when you choose Format ⇨ AutoFormat. By default, AutoFormat preserves styles you've added to the current document, which is probably what you want, though you can turn that option off if you wish.

AutoSummarize

AutoSummarize, activated by choosing Tools ⇨ AutoSummarize, analyzes your document to determine the key sentences, and then automatically creates a summary (see Figure 1-22). You can choose how long you want the summary to be (anywhere from 10 sentences to 75 percent of the length of the original), and choose how to present it: as highlighted sentences in the original document, as a separate document, as an executive summary or abstract at the top of the original document, or by hiding everything except the summary (in that case, a toolbar pops up that lets you show or hide more of the original document as you see fit).

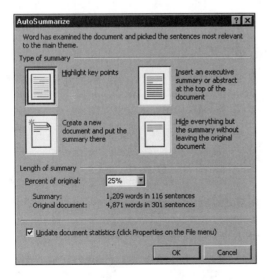

Figure 1-22: AutoSummarize analyzes your document and does its best to boil it down to a few key sentences.

AutoSummarize is just a starting point toward an effective summary — you'll undoubtedly have to edit the result considerably to get what you want — but it can save you a lot of time and effort.

Using Simple Macros

Macros are instructions to Word to perform an action or series of actions. Every command built into Word is a macro; by creating your own, you can automate common tasks that may currently require you several steps and several minutes.

You can create a simple macro at any time by recording it: You perform the action you want to turn into a macro, and Word remembers how to do it. The next time you want that action performed, you issue a single command, and Word carries it out much faster than you could.

To record a macro:

1. Choose Tools ➪ Macro ➪ Record New Macro. (You can also choose View ➪ Toolbars ➪ Visual Basic to call up the Visual Basic toolbar, and then click Record Macro.) This opens the Record Macro dialog box (see Figure 1-23).

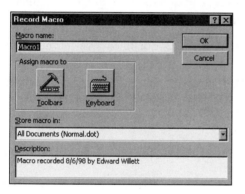

Figure 1-23: Assign a name and a command to your macro in the Record Macro dialog box.

2. Give your macro a name.

3. Assign your macro a command. You can create a new toolbar button for your macro by clicking Toolbars, and/or assign your macro a keyboard shortcut by clicking Keyboard.

4. Decide whether to store your macro in the current template, which means it will be available whenever you create documents using that template, or to store it in the specific document you're creating, which means it will only be available when you're working on that document.

5. Type a description of the macro in the box at the bottom. This can help you remember what that macro does, especially if you label it with a cryptic name like Macro1.

6. Click OK. The Record Macro dialog box disappears, replaced by a much smaller dialog box with two buttons, Stop Recording and Pause Recording; and the image of a cassette appears next to your mouse pointer to indicate you're recording.

7. Carry out the task you want recorded. If you need to do something you don't want recorded, click Pause Recording. To resume recording, click Resume Recording (the same button as the Pause Recording tool).

8. When you're finished, click Stop Recording.

To run the macro, click the toolbar button you've assigned or press the keyboard shortcut. You can also choose Tools ➪ Macro ➪ Macros, pick your macro from the list, and click Run. You can also edit macros from this dialog box.

Cross-Reference   For detailed information on creating and editing macros, see Chapter 55, "Creating Macros."

Summary

In this chapter, you learned about some of the tools Word offers to help you create documents, and how to move around and find things in documents once they're created. Major points of this chapter included the following:

✦ Word automatically creates a new, blank document every time you start the program.

✦ You can move around in Word using the mouse, the keyboard, or the scrollbars. Also, Find and Go To can help you locate specific places within your document, and Replace can help you replace words or formatting throughout your document.

✦ Word's navigation tool is a powerful method of browsing for specific elements within a long document.

✦ Word offers many different ways to view your document, including views that show you exactly how the completed document will look on paper or when viewed with a Web browser on the World Wide Web or a corporate intranet.

✦ Word's wizards can help you create a professional-looking, eye-catching document by doing most of the design work for you. You just have to add your own text and pictures.

✦ Word's automatic functions can correct typing errors as you type, as well as apply popular formatting touches. AutoText can save you keystrokes by automatically inserting commonly used words and phrases, and AutoSummarize can even help you create an executive summary.

✦ You can save yourself even more time by recording macros—complex tasks you carry out regularly. Once you've turned a task into a macro, a single mouse click can accomplish what might otherwise take several minutes.

✦   ✦   ✦

Working with Text

Word has a lot of advanced capabilities that allow you to create documents containing graphics, tables, bulleted lists, and more (we'll be looking at those in the next few chapters). But above all else, Word is a word processor — a piece of software designed to manipulate text, to make it easy to alter, rearrange, and reformat your words until they deliver your message in the most effective way possible. In this chapter, we'll walk through Word's basic tools for working with text, from entering it to formatting it to adding headers, footers, page numbers, and footnotes.

Entering Text

Before you can process words, you have to enter them. Generally, whenever you start Word (which automatically opens a blank Word document) or create a new Word document from within Word, you can start entering words immediately: the cursor is already ready and waiting for you in the document area. Just start typing, and your text appears (see Figure 2-1).

Later in this chapter we'll look at the various formatting options for text. Formatting can be applied either before you begin entering text, by setting options before you start typing, or to text you've already entered — in which case you need to select the text to which you want the formatting to apply.

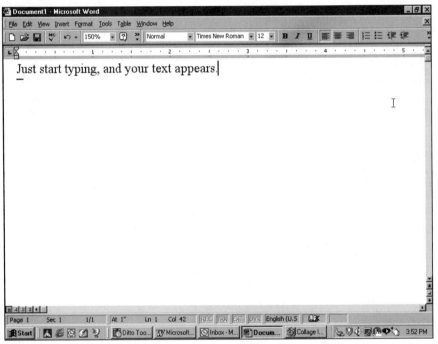

Figure 2-1: On start-up, Word automatically opens a blank document into which you can immediately enter text.

Selecting and Editing Text

To edit text, you first have to move the cursor to the place in the document where you want to make changes. Recall that inside the document area, your mouse pointer is a vertical bar with two smaller horizontal bars on either end, like a capital I. This special pointer allows you to precisely position the cursor within the document. Simply move the mouse pointer to the desired location and click once. The cursor, a solid, flashing vertical line, will appear where you click.

The position of the cursor also marks the position of the *insertion point*, the point in the document where new text will be entered the next time you start typing. So if you want to insert new words into an existing sentence, for example, click the mouse pointer at the spot in the sentence where the new words should go. This moves the cursor to that spot; then type in the additional words. You can also move the cursor using the arrow keys.

By default, any text to the right of the insertion point moves over to make room as you add text. If you prefer, however, you can have your new text replace the existing text to the right as you type: just double-click the grayed-out OVR button in the status bar at the bottom of the document area.

Note If you want to make overtyping Word's default choice for inserting text, choose Tools ⇨ Options, click the Edit tab, and check the Overtype Mode box.

To replace an entire phrase or change the formatting of a section of text, you first have to select it. To do so, use the mouse to position the cursor at either the beginning or end of the section you want to select. Then, holding down the left mouse button, drag the cursor backward or forward through the text. The selected text is highlighted: that is, it appears in the reverse of whatever colors you're using—white on black, for instance, instead of black on white (see Figure 2-2).

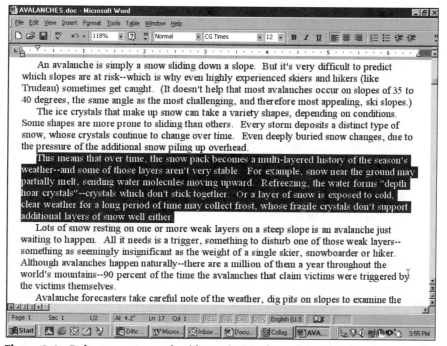

Figure 2-2: Before you can work with text in Word, you have to select it.

Once text is selected, you can manipulate it in a number of ways, from simply typing over it (the new text will automatically replace all of the selected text) to moving it, cutting and pasting it, and changing its formatting.

Although clicking and dragging is the most common way to select text, there are alternate methods as well:

✦ Position the insertion point, and then hold down the Shift key and select text using the arrow keys. If you hold down the Ctrl key, too, you can select larger chunks of text at once: one word at a time, if you're using the right or left arrow keys; or one paragraph at a time, if you're using the up or down arrow keys.

✦ You can select an entire word by double-clicking anywhere inside it; you can select an entire paragraph by triple-clicking it.

✦ You can select an entire line by moving the mouse to the left edge of the document until the usual I-beam cursor changes to an arrow. Use the arrow to point at the line you want to select, and then click once.

Formatting

Word supports four different levels of formatting, applying to successively larger sections of text:

✦ **Character formatting** applies to all selected characters, or all the characters you type after you've established the formatting. When you make a single word or sentence bold or italic, you're using character formatting.

✦ **Paragraph formatting** applies to all the text between two paragraph marks, which are entered whenever you press the Enter key. You can apply many of the same formatting options as you can to characters — e.g., bold or italics — but you also have additional options with regard to spacing, alignment, and indents.

✦ **Page formatting** affects the formatting of every page in the document, and includes settings such as page size, tabs, and margins.

✦ **Section formatting** is useful if you want to have several different types of formats within the same document. You can divide it up into several sections, and then format each section individually, with different indents and margins, or even different numbers of columns.

These various kinds of formatting overlap quite a bit: You can make a paragraph bold by using paragraph formatting, for example, but you can also make it bold by selecting all the text in it and using character formatting. Generally, because character formatting is what we use most often, we tend to make it our first choice, but if you're working with a large section of text, it's important to remember there are other formatting methods available that may be more efficient.

Formatting characters

As just noted, character formatting is what we use most often in word processing. You see it everywhere: in newspapers, in magazines, and in books, including this one. For example, each level of heading, from the chapter titles to the subhead just above this paragraph, has its own special character formatting: a specific combination of typeface, size, and style.

If the primary purpose of text is to communicate, then the purpose of character formatting is to help text communicate as effectively as possible, by establishing an overall visual style, enhancing legibility, or emphasizing certain textual elements (again, like the headings in this book).

The Formatting toolbar

The most commonly used character formatting options are available by default on the Formatting toolbar (shown here) and described as follows:

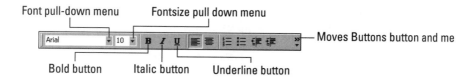

Font pull-down menu   Fontsize pull down menu

— Moves Buttons button and me

Bold button   Italic button   Underline button

✦ **Font.** A font is a set of characters that share a common design. Each font has a name, such as Times New Roman or Arial. You can apply any of the fonts installed on your computer to selected text by choosing the one you want from the Font pull-down menu. Word 2000 makes this easier by showing you the name of each font using characters from that font.

✦ **Font Size.** By default, font sizes refer to the height of the font's capital letters, and are measured in points. A point is a printer's measure equivalent to 1/72 of an inch, so 72-point characters may be up to an inch high when printed (depending on design; capital letters in some designs don't take up all the height available), 36-point characters are half an inch high, 18-point characters are a quarter of an inch high, and so on. Remember that characters get proportionally wider as they get taller. You apply a font size to selected text just as you apply a font: choose the size you want from the Font Size pull-down menu.

✦ **Bold.** Click this button to make the selected text thicker and darker than usual.

✦ **Italic.** Click this button to make the selected text slant to the right.

✦ **Underline.** Click this button to underline the selected text.

Note   Note that as you use commands from the More Buttons box, they're added to the visible toolbar, which grows longer to accommodate them — which can cause the Standard toolbar to get shorter as a result, dropping some of its commands into the More Buttons box.

✦ **Highlight.** Highlighting selected text in Word is just like highlighting it with a highlighting pen. Click the downward-pointing arrow next to the Highlight button to call up a small menu of possible highlight colors. Choose the one you want, and a strip of that color will overlie the selected text. It's a great way to make important text stand out visually on your monitor.

Note   If you click the Highlight button before you select any text, you'll get a special cursor that you can use exactly like a highlight pen: click and drag it over text to apply your selected Highlight color wherever you like.

✦ **Font Color.** Whereas highlighting text lays a strip of color over it; the Font Color button changes the color of the text itself. Again, click the downward-pointing arrow next to the button to see a menu of possible colors. Choose the one you want, and the selected text changes color.

The Font dialog box

Several additional character formatting options are available that aren't included on the Formatting toolbar. Instead, you have to open the Font dialog box, shown in Figure 2-3, by selecting Format ➪ Font, or by right-clicking and choosing Font from the pop-up menu.

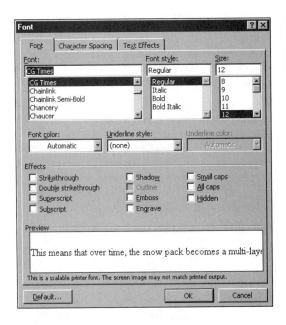

Figure 2-3: The Font dialog box lets you take advantage of all of Word's character formatting options.

The Font dialog box has three tabs, each of which controls a different aspect of character formatting:

Font

Under the Font tab, you can access most of the character-formatting options available on the formatting toolbar, sometimes with enhancements. For example, not only can you choose to underline selected text, you can choose what type of underlining you want to use (including Single, Words Only, Double, or Dotted). You can also choose to use a different color for underlining than you do for text.

You also have entirely new formatting options, called Effects, which include strikethrough, double strikethrough, superscript, subscript, shadow, outline, emboss, engrave, small caps, all caps, and hidden. These effects are illustrated in Figure 2-4; you can also see them as you apply them in the Preview window at the bottom of the Font dialog box.

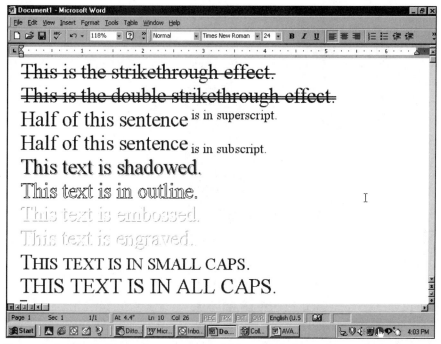

Figure 2-4: Word offers numerous eye-catching effects for you to apply to your text.

Character spacing

The Character Spacing tab offers a new set of controls (see Figure 2-5).

✦ **Scaling** adjusts the width of the selected text without affecting its point size. If you adjust this upward, the letters look fat and squat; if you adjust it downward, the letters look tall and skinny. The Preview window at the bottom of the dialog box shows you what your text will look like.

✦ **Spacing** adjusts the amount of space between letters. You select whether you want the text spacing Normal, Expanded, or Condensed; and then you specify the amount of space (in points) you want to add to or subtract from between letters. Again, use the Preview window to get just the effect you want.

✦ **Position** adjusts the location of the selected text relative to the normal baseline for text. As with spacing, you select whether you want the text Normal, Raised, or Lowered; and then you specify how many points you want to raise or lower the text above or below the baseline.

✦ **Kerning** adjusts the spacing between certain letters to make text as legible and attractive as possible. If you select the Kerning check box, Word will automatically adjust kerning in TrueType or other scalable fonts whenever they're equal to or larger than the size you specify.

Figure 2-6 demonstrates some of these formatting options.

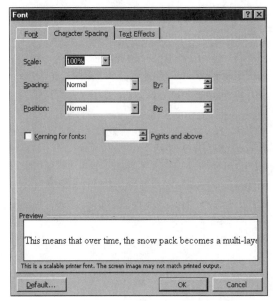

Figure 2-5: Fine-tune your characters with these controls.

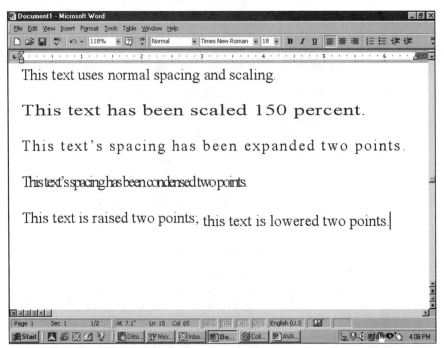

Figure 2-6: Character spacing can be used to achieve a number of interesting effects.

Text effects

The third tab in the Font dialog box, Text Effects (see Figure 2-7), won't do you much good if you're preparing a document for printing, but if your document is going to be read on other computers, you might find that making characters blink, shimmer or sparkle really makes them stand out!

To apply any of the text effects, just select the text you want to animate, open the Font dialog box, and then choose the effect you want to apply and click OK. You can preview each effect in the Preview window to be sure you've chosen the one you want.

Setting default text

You can also use the Font dialog box to change your default text; for example, from the usual 10-point Times New Roman to 24-point shimmering, bold, italic, blue Arial. Or anything else. Just apply the formatting you'd like to be the new default, and click the Default button at the bottom of the dialog box. Word will ask you if you're sure; if you are, click Yes. From then on, whenever you start a new document in Word, text will automatically have the new formatting.

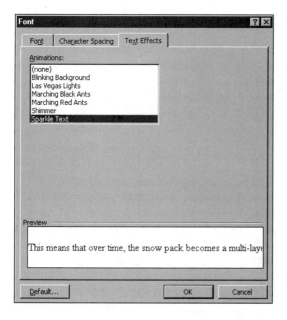

Figure 2-7: If your readers will be using computers to peruse your document, you can spice it up with one of these snazzy animation effects!

Keyboard shortcuts

You have one other way to apply formatting to selected text: use the shortcut keys, which some people find quicker to use when typing than reaching for a mouse. The keyboard shortcuts for formatting are shown in Table 2-1.

One of the most useful of these shortcuts is Ctrl+Spacebar, which cancels all character formatting, returning text to the default.

Table 2-1
Keyboard Shortcuts for Character Formatting

Format	Shortcut
Bold	Ctrl+B
Italic	Ctrl+I
Underline	Ctrl+U
Word underline	Ctrl+Shift+W
Double underline	Ctrl+Shift+D
Subscript	Ctrl+EQUAL SIGN
Superscript	Ctrl+Shift+PLUS SIGN
Small caps	Ctrl+Shift+K
All caps	Ctrl+Shift+A
Change case	Shift+F3
Hide text	Ctrl+Shift+H
Remove formats	Ctrl+SPACEBAR
Font	Ctrl+Shift+F
Symbol font	Ctrl+Shift+Q
Point size	Ctrl+Shift+P
Next larger size	Ctrl+Shift+>
Next smaller size	Ctrl+Shift+<
Up one point	Ctrl+]
Down one point	Ctrl+[

Formatting paragraphs

In addition to formatting characters, Word provides tools to let you apply formatting to whole paragraphs at a time. Word considers a paragraph to be any section of text that falls between two paragraph marks, which are inserted whenever you press Enter. (The only exception to that rule is the first paragraph of a document, which Word recognizes as being the text from the top of the document to the first paragraph mark.)

To see where the paragraph marks are in your document, click the Show/Hide ¶ button in the standard toolbar (if you can't see it, you can find it by clicking the More Buttons button). This will make all the paragraph marks visible (see Figure 2-8).

Paragraph formatting affects the spacing and alignment of all the lines in a paragraph. As with character formatting, you have more than one way to format a paragraph, but all of them begin with you placing your cursor somewhere inside the paragraph you want to format (it doesn't matter where, as long as it's between the two paragraph marks that define the paragraph).

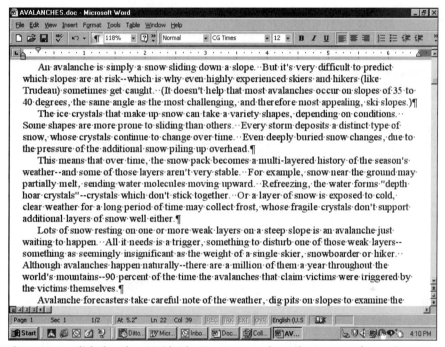

Figure 2-8: Click the Show/Hide¶ button to see where the paragraphs are in your document.

The Formatting toolbar

The most commonly used paragraph formatting options, as with character formatting, are available on the Formatting toolbar (shown here), beginning with four buttons that determine the paragraph's alignment.

- ✦ **Align left.** This aligns all the lines in the selected paragraph with the left margin.

- ✦ **Center.** This centers all the lines in the selected paragraph on the page.

- ✦ **Align right.** This aligns all the lines in the selected paragraph with the right margin.

- ✦ **Justify.** This adds space between words so that all the lines in the paragraph (except the final one) appear to be the same length and are aligned with both the left and right margins.

The effects of these buttons are illustrated in Figure 2-9.

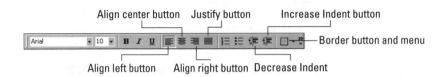

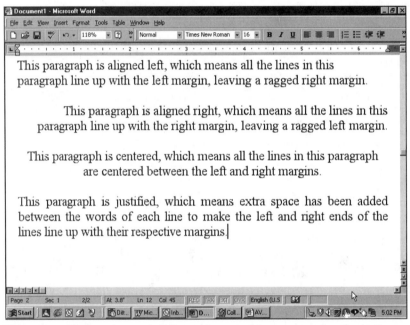

Figure 2-9: Paragraphs can be aligned in one of four ways using the buttons on the Formatting toolbar.

There are three other buttons on the Formatting toolbar that apply to paragraphs:

✦ **Increase Indent.** Each time you click this button, the selected paragraph is indented an additional one-half inch.

✦ **Decrease Indent.** Each time you click this button, any existing indent on the selected paragraph is reduced by one-half inch. If the paragraph isn't currently indented, this button has no effect (it doesn't move the paragraph to the left of the current document margin).

✦ **Border.** Click on the downward-pointing arrow next to this button to see a menu of the possible borders you can add to the selected paragraph. You can enclose the entire paragraph in a border, or simply apply a partial border, with lines along only one, two, or three sides. Note that some of these options show an inside border; those apply primarily to tables and can't be used as paragraph formatting. You can also use the Border menu to insert a horizontal line. Figure 2-10 illustrates some of the border possibilities.

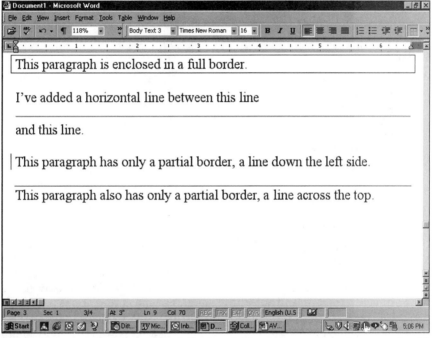

Figure 2-10: Word lets you add a full or partial border to a selected paragraph with the click of a button.

The Paragraph dialog box

Several additional paragraph formatting options are available from the Paragraph dialog box, which you open by selecting Format ➪ Paragraph, or by right-clicking on a paragraph and choosing Paragraph from the pop-up menu (see Figure 2-11).

The Paragraph dialog box has two tabs, which are covered in the following sections.

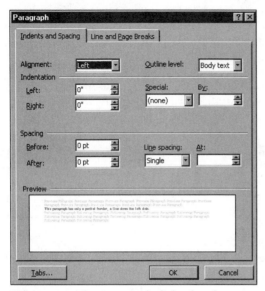

Figure 2-11: The Paragraph dialog box lets you precisely control the alignment and spacing of your paragraphs.

Indents and spacing

The controls on the Indents and Spacing tab not only let you apply formatting to a paragraph, they provide valuable information about the current formatting of the paragraph. From here, you can change the paragraph's alignment, adjust the indentation with much greater precision than with the Indent buttons on the Formatting toolbar, and adjust the amount of space that appears both above and below the current paragraph. As usual, there's a Preview window that shows you the effects of your formatting choices. The darker text in the middle of the Preview window is the currently selected paragraph.

The Paragraph dialog box also gives you control over line spacing, the amount of space between lines. You have six options:

✦ **Single.** This leaves a minimum amount of space between lines, just enough that their characters don't overlap.

✦ **1.5.** This leaves one and a half times as much space between lines as Single does.

✦ **Double.** This leaves the equivalent of a blank line between lines.

✦ **At Least.** When you choose this, Word will automatically adjust line spacing in the paragraph to allow for smaller or larger font sizes or graphics, but it will never leave less space between lines than the point size you specify.

First-Line and Hanging Indents

One of the indentation controls gives you the option to apply First Line or Hanging indents. Both align the first line of a paragraph differently from the following lines.

A *first-line indent,* like the one that starts this paragraph, begins the paragraph's first line to the right of the rest of the lines. This is the kind of indent usually used to set off the first line of a paragraph in many books, magazines, and newspapers.

A *hanging indent,* like the one that starts this paragraph, begins the paragraph's first line to the left of the rest of the lines. It's often used to start off a list of items.

✦ **Exactly.** When you choose this and enter a value in points, Word will use that line spacing regardless of font size or graphics.

✦ **Multiple.** This lets you enter line spacing as a multiple of single spacing: 1.6, for example, or 2.4.

Line and page breaks

The Line and Page Breaks tab (see Figure 2-12) lets you control the flow of text within a paragraph. It offers several options:

✦ **Widow/Orphan control.** This prevents widows (the first line of a paragraph that appears all by itself at the bottom of a page) and orphans (the last line of a paragraph that appears all by itself at the top of a page).

✦ **Keep lines together.** This prevents any page break at all in the middle of a paragraph, even if it doesn't result in a widow or orphan.

✦ **Keep with next.** This prevents a page break from occurring between the selected paragraph and the one that follows.

✦ **Page break before.** This inserts a page break before the selected paragraph.

✦ **Suppress line numbers.** If you've got line numbering turned on within a document, this option keeps those line numbers from being displayed for the currently selected paragraph.

✦ **Don't hyphenate.** This prevents the selected paragraph from being automatically hyphenated if Hyphenation is enabled.

Tabs

In addition to the preceding tabs, the Paragraph dialog box includes a button, Tabs, that brings up the Tabs dialog box shown in Figure 2-13. (You can also access this dialog box by choosing Format ⇨ Tabs.)

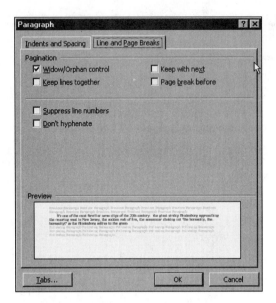

Figure 2-12: Controlling the flow of text with these controls can make your document look cleaner and more professional.

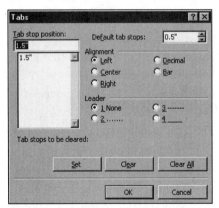

Figure 2-13: Set tabs and their leaders using the Tabs dialog box.

Enter the tabs you want in the box at left, and then set their alignment at right. You have several options:

✦ **Left.** If you press Tab, the cursor will go to this spot, and any subsequent text you type will appear to the right of the Tab stop.

✦ **Right.** Press Tab, and again, the cursor will go to this spot, but any subsequent text will appear to the left of the Tab stop.

✦ **Center.** Press Tab to send the cursor to this spot, and any subsequent text will be centered on the Tab stop.

✦ **Decimal.** This is most commonly used when you're creating a column of monetary figures. Set the Tab stop where you want the decimal to appear. Press Tab, and then type in the number. The numerals to the left of the decimal will appear to the left of the Tab stop, but once you enter a decimal, subsequent numerals appear to the right of the Tab stop.

✦ **Bar.** This draws a vertical bar at the spot where you insert the Tab stop. It has no effect when you press the Tab key.

In addition to setting Tab stop alignments, you can assign each Tab stop a leader — characters that will be inserted in the tabbed line before the stop. You can use dots, dashes, or underline marks.

Keyboard shortcuts
Shortcut keys are also provided for paragraph formatting. They're shown in Table 2-2.

Table 2-2 Keyboard Shortcuts for Paragraph Formatting	
Format	**Shortcut**
Left-align text	Ctrl+L
Center text	Ctrl+E
Right-align text	Ctrl+R
Justify text	Ctrl+J
Indent from left	Ctrl+M
Remove indent from left	Ctrl+Shift+M
Increase hanging indent	Ctrl+T
Decrease hanging indent	Ctrl+Shift+T
Single-space lines	Ctrl+1
Use 1.5-line spacing	Ctrl+5
Double-space lines	Ctrl+2
Add or remove 12 points of space before a paragraph	Ctrl+0 (zero)
Remove paragraph formats not applied by a style	Ctrl+Q
Restore default formatting (reapply the Normal style)	Ctrl+Shift+N
Display or hide formatting marks and nonprinting characters	Ctrl+*

Using the ruler

You can also set indents and tabs using the ruler (shown here) as follows:

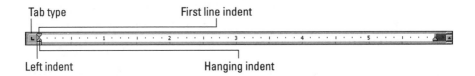

+ **Left indent.** Go to the left end of the ruler and click and drag the little square below the two diamond-shaped arrows pointing at each other. Place the arrows however far from the left margin you want the indent to be set, and release the square.

+ **First-line indent.** Drag the top diamond to the right of the bottom arrow by the amount you want the first-line indent to be.

+ **Hanging indent.** First set a left indent as above, and then drag the top arrow to the left of the bottom arrow by the amount you want the hanging indent to be.

+ **Right indent.** To change the right margin of a paragraph, drag the arrow at the right end of the ruler to the left.

To set tabs:

1. Click the button at the far left of the ruler to cycle through the various types of Tab stops. Pick the one you want.

2. Click on the ruler at the point you want the Tab stop to be set.

3. Adjust the Tab stop as necessary by dragging it left or right along the ruler.

4. If you make a mistake, delete the Tab stop by dragging it off the ruler.

Formatting pages

Page formatting controls the appearance of all the pages in the document — page size, orientation, margins, and so on.

To set page formatting, choose File ⇨ Page Setup. This opens the Page Setup dialog box, which has four tabs: Margins, Paper Size, Paper Source and Layout. We'll look at the first three tabs in this section, and then look at the Layout tab in detail in "Formatting Sections."

Margins

The Margins tab (see Figure 2-14) lets you set margins — the distance between the edge of the page and the start of text — all around the page.

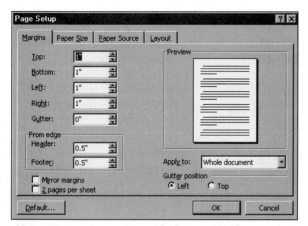

Figure 2-14: Set margins with these controls.

Enter the width you want each margin to be in the Top, Bottom, Left, and Right boxes. You can also use the little arrow buttons to the right of each box to adjust the number displayed up or down, one-tenth at a time.

Check the Mirror Margins box if you're creating a document that will have two facing pages, like a book or magazine. This changes the Left and Right options to Inside and Outside, inside being the margin closest to the center of the two-page spread, and outside being the margin on the outside edges. If you're printing two pages per sheet of paper (if you will be folding the paper, for example), click the 2 pages per sheet box.

If your document is going to be bound on the left-hand side, click the Left radio button under Gutter Position. This adds the amount of extra space you specify in the Gutter box to the left margin (if you haven't selected Mirror Margins) or the inside margin (if you have). If your document is going to be bound at the top, click the Top button, which adds the space you specify in the Gutter box to the top of each page to make room for the binding.

You can also set the distance from the top and bottom that you want any headers or footers to appear (we'll look at headers and footers in more detail later in this chapter). Note that you will normally set this amount to be less than the amount entered for the top and bottom margins!

Tip   If a header or footer is too big to fit in the margin, Word will automatically adjust the margins of the page so they fit. To avoid that, enter a hyphen before the Top or Bottom margin setting. Word will then keep the margins of the page constant no matter how big the header or footer gets. (Of course, if either one is too big, it may overwrite part of the main text.)

Finally, using the Apply To list box, you can choose whether to apply your page formatting to the whole document, only to those pages that come after the current insertion point, or to the section of text you currently have selected.

Paper size

The Paper Size tab (see Figure 2-15) lets you specify what paper size you'll be printing your document on. You can choose one of the commonly used sizes (e.g., Letter, Legal, A4, depending on what your printer supports) from the Paper Size list box, or specify a size of paper using the Width and Height controls. You can also decide how you want the paper to be oriented: Portrait style (in which the longest dimension is the height) or Landscape (in which the longest dimension is the width). And, again, you can choose whether to apply this formatting to the whole document, just to those pages that come after the insertion point, or just to whatever text you currently have selected — which means you can print half your document on letter-sized paper and half on legal-sized, if you wish!

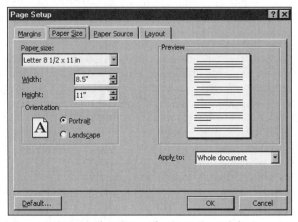

Figure 2-15: Set the size and orientation of the paper you'll be printing to here.

Paper source

The Paper Source tab (see Figure 2-16) lets you specify which bin of paper available on your printer you want to use, or if you want to feed the paper in manually. The list of available sources varies from printer to printer.

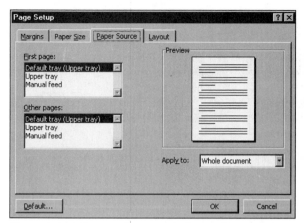

Figure 2-16: Choose the source of your document's paper here.

You can also choose to have the first page drawn from a different bin than subsequent pages — an option you might want to use if one bin is loaded with color paper, which you want for the front of your document, and another with white paper, which you want for your document's interior. And, again, you can apply these choices to the whole document, just to the pages that come after the current insertion point, or to selected text.

Formatting sections

Word's section-formatting capability lets you apply different formats to different parts of the same document, something you've seen already in each of the Page Setup tabs, which let you decide how much of the document you want to apply the page formatting to.

A typical use of this capability is to mix text set in columns with text that isn't, or to use different page numbering (Roman numerals, for instance) in one part of a document.

When you use Page Setup to format part of your document differently from another part, Word creates a new section. To control how Word deals with those sections, open the Page Setup dialog box again by choosing File ➪ Page Setup, and click the Layout tab (see Figure 2-17).

Word offers you five ways to start each new section:

✦ **Continuous.** The section will immediately follow the preceding text, without a page break.

✦ **New Column.** The section will start at the top of the next column.

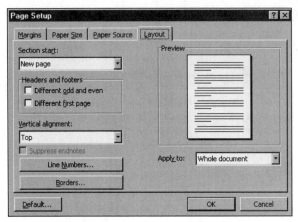

Figure 2-17: The Layout tab of the Page Setup dialog box lets you control the flow of sections within your document, among other things.

✦ **New Page.** The section will start at the top of the next page. In other words, this option adds a page break between the preceding text and the text you've just selected to make a new section.

✦ **Even Page.** This starts the section at the top of the next even-numbered page.

✦ **Odd Page.** This starts the section at the top of the next odd-numbered page.

You can tell where one section begins and another ends, because Word inserts a line in the document space labeled "Section Break" (see Figure 2-18).

The Layout tab also contains several other commands:

✦ **Vertical alignment.** Use this drop-down list to control the spacing of the text in your document between the top and bottom of the page. You can align it with the top (the default), align it with the bottom, vertically center it, or vertically justify it (which adds spaces between the lines of full pages to ensure they extend completely to the bottom margin).

✦ **Line Numbers.** Click this button to open the Line Numbers dialog box shown in Figure 2-19. Check the Add Line Numbering box to add a number to selected lines. In the Start At box, enter the starting number for line numbering; in the From Text box, enter how far to the left of the text you want the numbers to appear; and in the Count By box, enter the increment you want to count by (one, five, ten, etc.). Click the appropriate radio button under Numbering to restart numbering on each page, in each new section, or to make numbering continuous throughout the document.

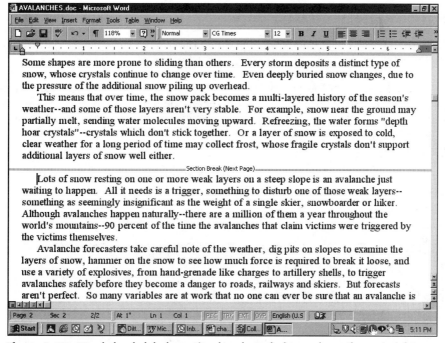

Figure 2-18: Word clearly labels section breaks to help you keep them straight.

✦ **Borders.** Click this button to apply borders and shading to your pages using the Borders and Shading dialog box.

For details on using Borders and Shading, see Chapter 7, "Adding Graphics and Fancy Formatting."

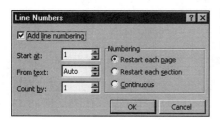

Figure 2-19: Line numbering, controlled from this dialog box, is often used in contracts and other legal documents.

You can apply any of these layout options to the whole document, to only those pages that come after the current insertion point, or to selected text.

Headers and Footers

A header is text or a graphic that appears at the top of every page in a document; a footer is text or a graphic that appears at the bottom of every page.

To create a header or footer, select View ➪ Header and Footer. Word automatically switches to Print Layout view. The main text in the document is grayed out; at the top and bottom of the page, you'll find boxes into which you can enter text or graphics for your headers and footers. You'll also see the Header and Footer toolbar, shown in Figure 2-20.

Type text into the header and footer boxes just the way you would into the main document. All of the formatting options available for regular text are also available for headers and footers.

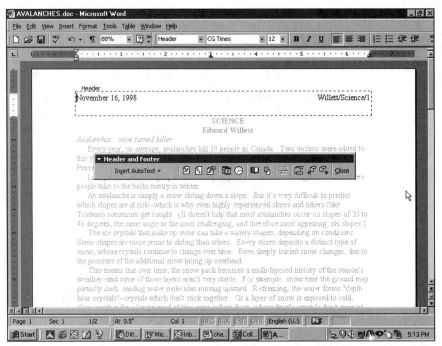

Figure 2-20: The Header and Footer toolbar lets you control the placement and content of your headers and footers.

In addition, you can use the Header and Footer toolbar to automatically add certain features to your headers and footers, including the following:

✦ **AutoText.** Click Insert AutoText to pull down a menu of AutoText items you might want to add to your headers or footers, including the date it was last printed, the date on which it was created, who created it and the filename, and so on. Just select the AutoText item you want to use, and Word automatically adds it to the header or footer you're currently creating.

✦ **Insert Page Number, Insert Number of Pages, and Format Page Number.** We'll look at all three of these in more detail in the next section.

✦ **Insert Date.** Click this button to insert the current date into your header or footer. The date is inserted as a field, so it will always display the current date when you view the document.

✦ **Insert Time.** Click this button to insert the current time as a field.

For detailed information on using fields in Word, see Chapter 4, "Forms, Fields, and Merging."

The Header and Footer toolbar also includes several other useful buttons:

✦ **Page Setup.** This opens the Page Setup dialog box we looked at earlier in this chapter. Under the Layout tab of that dialog box, you can choose to have different headers and footers on odd and even pages, and a unique header and footer for the first page. If you choose those options, place your insertion point on an even page before opening the Header and Footer toolbar in order to create the header and footer for even pages, and then do the same for odd pages and/or the first page.

✦ **Show/Hide Document Text.** Clicking this button hides even the grayed-out version of the document's main text, so you can work on your header or footer without distraction.

✦ **Same as Previous.** This button is only active if you have more than one section in your document. If you do, it makes your header or footer for the current section the same as the header or footer for the previous section.

✦ **Switch Between Header and Footer.** You can get from the header box to the footer box (or vice versa) by scrolling down (or up) the page — or you can simply click this button to instantly switch back and forth between them.

✦ **Show Previous, Show Next.** If your headers and footers are different on odd and even pages, or on the first page, or across sections, you can move from one to the other using these buttons.

Page Numbering

One of the most common uses of headers and footers is to add page numbers. All you have to do to add a page number to either a header or footer is click the Insert Page Number button on the Header and Footer toolbar. There are also several AutoText options that include the page number.

If you want to automatically include the total number of pages in the document, click the Insert Number of Pages button on the Header and Footer toolbar.

Of course, you have more than one way to indicate page numbers. For instance, sometimes you want Roman numerals, sometimes you want Arabic. That's where the Format Page Number button on the Header and Footer toolbar comes in. Click it to bring up the Page Number Format dialog box shown in Figure 2-21.

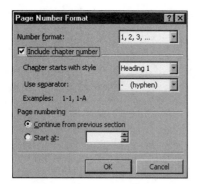

Figure 2-21: Use this dialog box to tell Word how you want your page numbers to appear.

Here you can choose a format for your page numbers: regular numerals, Roman numerals (both uppercase and lowercase) or letters (again, both uppercase and lowercase). If you like, you can ask Word to add a chapter number in front of the page number, and specify the character that will separate the two numbers (e.g., 1-2 or 2:A). You can also specify how Word will recognize the beginning of a chapter, by telling it which style of text is used to start one. Finally, you can have page numbering be continuous from section to section, or start anew at the beginning of each new section — and specify which number page numbers in a new section should start with.

Cross-Reference   For more on styles, see Chapter 6, "Styles and Templates."

If all you want in your header or footer is the page number, you don't have to use the Header and Footer toolbar at all. Simply choose Insert ➪ Page Numbers. This opens the Page Numbers dialog box, shown in Figure 2-22.

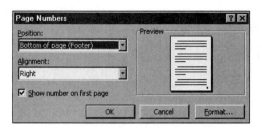

Figure 2-22: Adding page numbers to your document is a breeze, thanks to the Page Numbers dialog box.

Choose a position for your page numbers (top or bottom of the page — as a header or footer, in other words) and an alignment (right, left, center, inside or outside — the latter two only apply if you're creating a document that will be bound and have mirrored margins). You can also choose whether or not to show a page number on the first page.

Creating Footnotes

Word makes creating footnotes easy, and offers you the option of placing them directly beneath the text where they appear, at the bottom of the page, at the end of a section, or at the end of the document (in which case they're called *endnotes*).

To insert a footnote, place the insertion point where the footnote reference (usually a superscripted number) will appear, and then choose Insert ⇨ Footnote to open the Footnote and Endnote dialog box, shown in Figure 2-23.

Figure 2-23: When you insert a footnote, this dialog box is the first thing you see.

Here you're asked to decide if you want to insert a footnote (at the bottom of the page) or an endnote (at the end of the document). Then you have the option of having Word automatically number footnotes sequentially. If you'd prefer to use a symbol of your own choosing, click the Custom Mark button instead, and type what you want to use (e.g., an asterisk) in the space provided. If you're looking for a symbol more exotic than anything that's on the keyboard, click the Symbol button to bring up the Symbol dialog box, shown in Figure 2-24, from which you can select any character from various fonts installed on your computer.

To fine-tune the look of your footnotes even more, click the Options button. This opens the Note Options dialog box, which has two tabs, one for All Footnotes and one for All Endnotes. The options for each are basically the same: You can choose where to place the notes (beneath text or bottom of page for footnotes; end of document or end of section for endnotes), a number format (numbers, letters, or symbols), a starting number, and whether you want the numbering to be continuous throughout the document or to restart in each section. (For footnotes, you can also choose to restart numbering on each page.)

Once you're happy with your footnote or endnote setup, click OK in the Footnote and Endnote dialog box. This opens a footnote pane in the bottom portion of the screen (see Figure 2-25). Type your footnote into this pane. You can change its size by dragging the split bar (at its top) up or down. Once you're done entering footnotes, you can close the pane by clicking the Close button; or you can simply return your insertion point to the main document area and keep typing with the footnote pane open.

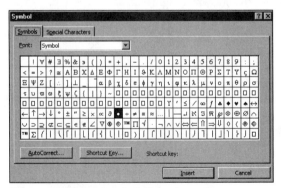

Figure 2-24: The Symbol dialog box gives you access to any character in various fonts.

Footnotes are only visible when the footnote pane is open or in Print Layout view.

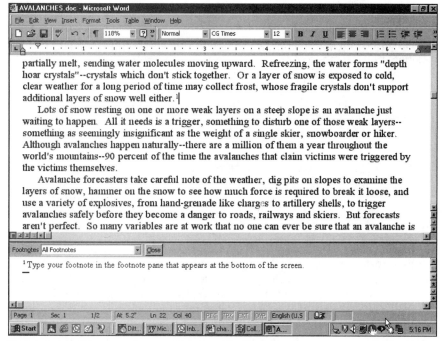

Figure 2-25: When you insert a footnote, the footnote pane opens at the bottom of your screen; type the text for your footnote into it.

As you continue to add footnotes throughout the document, they'll all appear in the footnote pane, where you can easily move through them and edit them as necessary. To move a footnote, all you have to do is move its reference mark in the text: just select the reference mark, cut it, and paste it in its new location. Similarly, you can delete a footnote simply by selecting and deleting its reference mark. If Word is auto-numbering footnotes for you, it will automatically adjust the numbering of all footnotes as needed.

You can change footnotes to endnotes or vice-versa by selecting the footnotes you want to convert in the footnote pane, and then right-clicking and choosing Convert to Endnote or Convert to Footnote from the pop-up menu.

Summary

In this chapter, you learned the basics of entering and editing text, and learned how to format at all the different levels Word allows: character, paragraph, page and section. Some of the major points covered included the following:

✦ To format characters (select their font, size, style and other attributes), first select them, and then choose the formatting commands you want by using the Formatting toolbar; by using the keyboard shortcuts; or by choosing Format ➪ Font.

✦ To format all the lines in an entire paragraph (select their alignment, indentation, spacing, tabs, and other characteristics), place your insertion point anywhere within the paragraph, and then choose the formatting commands you want by using the Formatting toolbar; by using the keyboard shortcuts; or by choosing Format ➪ Paragraph. You can also use the ruler to set indents, margins, and tabs.

✦ Page formatting affects all the pages in a section, and because by default Word documents are created with a single section, it generally affects all the pages in the document. You access page formatting by choosing File ➪ Page Setup, which also gives you access to formatting commands for sections — pieces of the document with their own unique page formatting.

✦ Headers and footers can be easily added by choosing View ➪ Header and Footer. The Header and Footer toolbar includes buttons for adding many often-used elements, including the date, time, and page numbers. Page numbers can also be added by choosing Insert ➪ Page Numbers.

✦ Footnotes and endnotes are inserted by choosing Insert ➪ Footnote. Word makes it easy to place them where you want them and edit, move, and delete them. It even renumbers them for you after a change has been made.

✦   ✦   ✦

Tables

T ables are among Word's most useful ways of organizing information to the benefit of both the creator and the reader. Readers benefit from a clearer understanding of the relationships among the various items inserted into the table. Creators benefit from Word's ability to sort, sum, and otherwise manipulate information entered into tables. Recognizing their importance, Word 2000 makes tables easy to set up and use.

Creating Tables

You have more than one way to create a table in Word. In fact, there are three: a tool on the Standard toolbar and two different menu commands.

The Table tool

The quickest way to create a table is to click the Insert Table tool on the Standard Toolbar. Clicking this tool brings up the small grid shown in Figure 3-1, which represents the rows and columns of a table. You can select how many rows and columns you want simply by running your mouse pointer over the grid; the grid squares you've selected turn dark. In Figure 3-1, I've elected to create a table three rows high and four columns wide.

Once you've chosen the number of rows and columns, click the bottom right cell of the grid on the tool. Your table is automatically created.

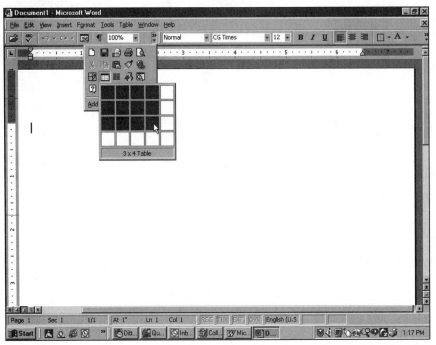

Figure 3-1: Run your mouse pointer over this grid to choose the number of rows and columns you want in your table.

Draw Table

The second way to create a table is to choose Table ➪ Draw Table. When you choose this command, your mouse pointer changes to an image of a pencil, which you can use to draw the rows and columns of your table just as you might draw a table on a piece of paper with a regular pencil and a ruler. You can make the table as large as you want, and add as many vertical and horizontal lines as you want (see Figure 3-2).

Draw Table is a very powerful command for creating nonstandard tables: tables that have different numbers of columns in different rows, for instance; or tables in which columns and rows are of varying widths and heights. Notice that when you choose Draw Table, you also automatically open the Tables and Borders toolbar. This toolbar provides handy access to tools for applying borders and shading.

Cross-Reference   See Chapter 7, "Adding Graphics and Fancy Formatting" as well as many of the formatting tools for tables discussed in detail later in this chapter.

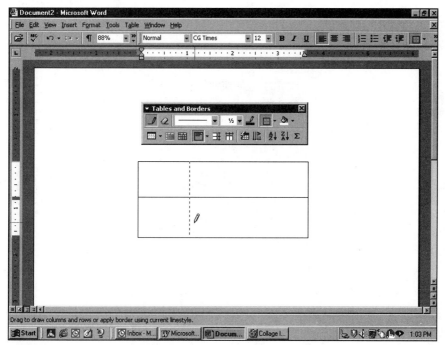

Figure 3-2: Here are two rows of the table; adding vertical lines will create columns.

Insert Table

The third way to create a table is to choose Table ➪ Insert ➪ Table. This opens the Insert Table dialog box shown in Figure 3-3.

In the top section, enter the number of rows and columns you want your table to have. In the second section, choose how columns will act when you enter information in them. With a fixed column width (which can be set automatically by Word or which you can specify), columns never get wider, only deeper, when data too wide for the current width is entered in them. If you choose AutoFit to Window, the table's width changes to keep it within the margins you have set for the page. If you choose AutoFit to Contents, columns get wider to accommodate whatever you put into them (for more details on AutoFit see the section "AutoFit" later in the chapter).

If the size of table you're creating is one you're going to want to use again and again, check the Set as Default for New Tables box at the bottom of the dialog box before clicking OK.

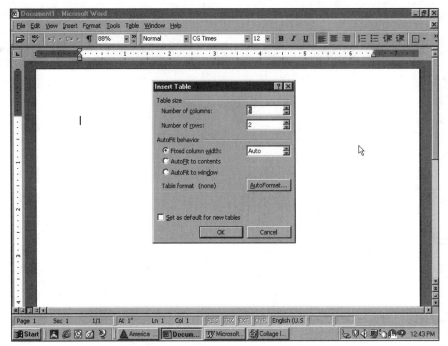

Figure 3-3: Specify the size of the table you want to create in this dialog box.

The other button in this dialog box, AutoFormat, we'll look at in the section on formatting tables a little later in this chapter.

Adding data

The simplest method of adding data to a table is to type it in. In a sense, each cell of the table is a separate little word-processing window; just place your insertion point in the cell you want to enter information into and type away.

You can also add data by copying it from elsewhere into the Clipboard, and then pasting it into your table cells. If you have a lot of data already in tabular form in another Office application, such as Excel or PowerPoint, you don't have to rely on cut-and-paste or retype it. You can import that table directly into Word as a linked or embedded object.

Cross-Reference   For more information on linked and embedded objects and sharing data among Office 2000's various components, see Chapter 52, "Building Integrated Documents."

Editing and Formatting Tables

Once you have created your table and entered data in it, you may want to make changes. Editing text in a table is the same as editing text anywhere else in Word. You can copy text from place to place, highlight it and type over it or delete it, etc.

Cross-Reference For more details on editing text in Word, see Chapter 2, "Working with Text."

You can also format text the same way you do in the main body of a document, with one major difference: You can set individual margins, indents, and even tab stops for each cell in a table.

Whenever you click inside a cell, you'll see the same controls that appear in the main document area ruler appear inside a smaller ruler that corresponds to the size of the cell. You can use these controls just as you do in your main document, moving the upper triangular slider at the left to set an indent, clicking on the ruler to create a tab stop, and moving the left bottom and far right triangular sliders to set margins (see Figure 3-4).

Note To use a tab stop within a table cell, press Ctrl+Tab instead of just pressing Tab. The latter will move you to the next table cell instead of to the tab stop.

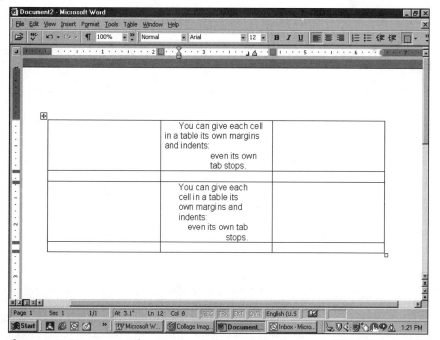

Figure 3-4: You can set the margins, indents, and tab stops individually for each cell in a Word table.

Similarly, you can change fonts and their sizes and styles within each cell just as you do anywhere else in your Word document, using the usual text formatting commands.

In addition to formatting the text within a table, however, you'll probably want to format the table as a whole, to give it a unified look or simply to make the information you've entered into it more easily accessible to your audience.

Word provides many tools for fine-tuning the appearance of a table — most of them, as you might expect, listed under the Table menu.

The Table menu

Choose Table, and you'll find many commands to help you make your table look just the way you want to. The first three commands, covered in the following sections, let you add or delete cells, rows, columns, or whole tables.

Insert

Choose Table ➪ Insert, and you're presented with a new menu featuring several options:

✦ **Table.** This inserts a new table into your document, as described in the earlier section of this chapter on creating tables.

✦ **Columns to the left.** This inserts a new column into the table to the left of the column where your cursor is currently located.

✦ **Columns to the right.** This inserts a new column to the right of the column where your cursor is located.

✦ **Rows above.** This inserts a new row above the row where your cursor is currently located.

✦ **Rows below.** This inserts a new row below the row where your cursor is located.

✦ **Cells.** This brings up yet another menu (see Figure 3-5) that asks you if you want to shift cells down or shift cells right when you insert your new cell. If you choose to shift cells down, the new cell will force all the cells below it in its column down one to make room for it. If you choose to shift cells right, all the cells in the new cell's row will shift to the right to make room for it. You can also choose to insert a whole column or a whole row using this menu.

Delete

Choose Table ➪ Delete, and you're presented with commands that are essentially the opposite of the Insert commands. You can delete the entire table, or just the row or column where your cursor is currently located. If you choose Table ➪ Delete ➪ Cells, you'll see a Delete Cells dialog box just like the Insert Cells dialog box in Figure 3-5, except instead of being asked if you want to shift the other cells in the column or row down or right, you're asked if you want to shift them up or left.

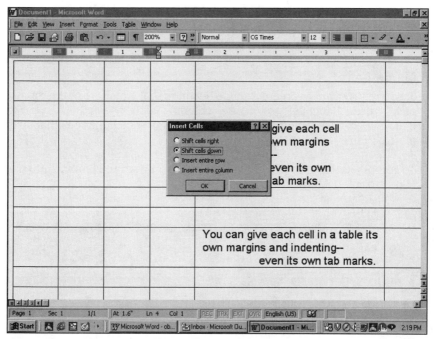

Figure 3-5: Specify how you want your new cell to affect the rest of your table in the Insert Cells dialog box.

Note

Insert Cells and Delete Cells work a little differently if you use them with multiple cells selected (see the next section of this chapter to learn how to select more than one cell). If you choose to shift cells to the right in the Insert Cells dialog box, Word inserts the same number of cells as you've selected, and shifts the rows in which they appear to the right. If you choose to shift cells down, however, Word doesn't just insert the number of cells you've selected; it inserts a number of rows equal to the number of rows of cells in your selection. In the Delete Cells dialog box, you can choose only to shift cells left; if you choose to shift cells up, Delete Cells has no effect at all.

Select

Table ⇨ Select offers you the same options. Click Table to highlight the whole Table for formatting, Column to select the entire column where your cursor is located, Row to select the entire row, or Cell to select the cell where you've placed your cursor.

Note

You can also select parts of a table with your mouse. To select a cell, triple-click anywhere inside it. To select an entire row, move your mouse pointer to the left edge of the table. Just outside the table boundaries, the pointer will turn into a white arrow pointing back at the row. Click once to select the row. Similarly, to select a column, move your pointer to just outside the table's top edge. Your pointer will turn into a black arrow pointing down at the column. Click once to select the column.

You can also select a specific range of cells by clicking and dragging from one cell to another. The next section of the Table menu lets you merge and split cells, or even split the entire table.

Merge Cells

Suppose you want to create a single headline that runs across the top of your table, or subheads that cover two or three columns further down inside your table. To do that, you need to combine two or more cells into one larger cell that spans one or more columns or rows.

To combine cells, simply highlight the cells you want to combine into one, and then choose Table ⇨ Merge Cells (see Figure 3-6).

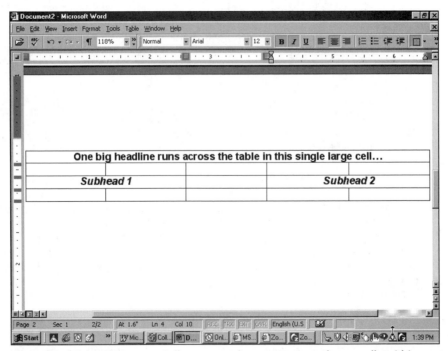

Figure 3-6: Using the Merge Cells command, you can create larger cells within your table's regular grid.

Split Cells

Sometimes, of course, you want to do just the opposite: you want to subdivide an existing cell into two or more smaller cells. To do that, select the cells you want to subdivide, and then choose Table ⇨ Split Cells. You'll see the dialog box shown in Figure 3-7.

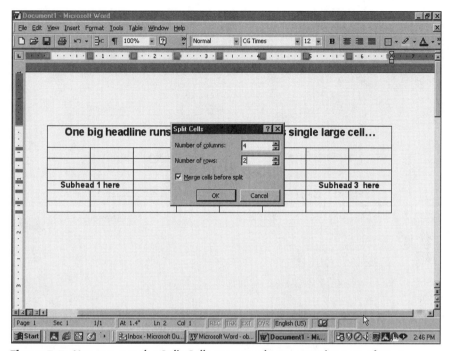

Figure 3-7: You can use the Split Cells command to reorganize part of your table, or even to completely reconfigure it.

Choose how many rows and how many columns you want to subdivide the selected cell or cells into. You can choose to split each cell you've selected individually into that many rows or columns, or, by checking Merge Cells Before Split, combine all the selected cells into one large cell that is then subdivided into the number of rows and columns you've specified.

Note

You can use the Split Cells command to quickly change the number of rows and columns in your whole table. Choose Table ➪ Select ➪ Table to highlight every cell in your table, and then choose Table ➪ Split Cells. Enter the new number of rows and columns you want in your table, making sure Merge Cells Before Split is checked, and then click OK. Your table will instantly change from whatever it was before to the number of rows and columns you've specified.

Split Table

You can turn a single table into two separate tables with the Split Table command. Just place your cursor in the row that you want to be the first row of the bottom table and choose Table ➪ Split Table. The table will split apart above the row you've selected (see Figure 3-8).

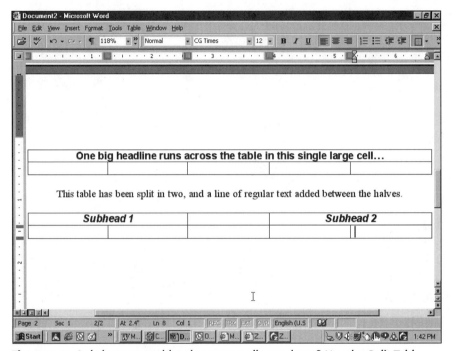

Figure 3-8: Only have one table when you really need two? Use the Split Table command to remedy the situation.

Tip

The cursor, after the Split Table command, is between the two tables. This allows you to enter text before the second table (see Figure 3-8 again). If you've created a table as the first thing in a new document, place your cursor in the top row of the table and use this command to make room for text above the table, if you need it.

Using automatic formatting with tables

Also within the Table menu are several options to apply automatic formatting to Tables. Automatic formatting can save you time and effort and ensure a consistent, professional look to your tables.

AutoFormat

AutoFormat automatically applies shading, borders, colors, and other interesting formatting elements to your table. You can apply AutoFormat to a table either when you first create it (by clicking AutoFormat on the Insert Table dialog box) or at any time by placing your cursor anywhere within the table and choosing Table ➪ Table AutoFormat (see Figure 3-9).

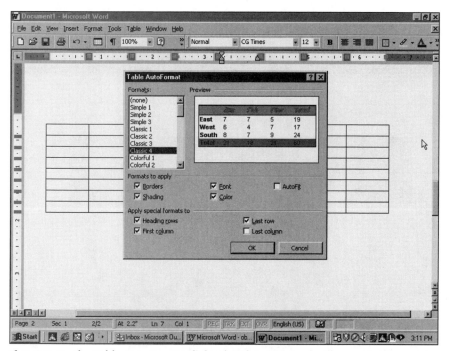

Figure 3-9: The Table AutoFormat dialog box lets you apply all or parts of several pre-designed formats to your table.

Choose the format you want from the Formats scroll-down list; the Preview box will show you exactly what it will look like. You don't have to apply the entire format. Instead, you can choose to apply only those parts that you like by checking boxes in the Formats to Apply area. You could choose, for example, to apply only borders, shading, fonts, or color, or you could choose to apply any combination of them. You can also choose whether or not to accept any special formatting that might be included in the design for the heading (top) row, first column, last column, or last row.

Applying an AutoFormat won't change the size of your table unless you check AutoFit; if you do, then your table's columns and rows may change to fit snugly around the text they contain.

Cross-Reference   See the next section of this chapter for more details on how AutoFit works.

Once you're happy with your choices, click OK to see your new table (see Figure 3-10).

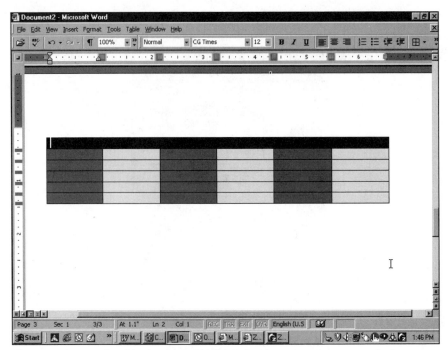

Figure 3-10: Here's a blank table with the Columns 4 AutoFormat applied.

AutoFit

AutoFit, the next option in the Table menu, determines how rows and columns change to accommodate the text you enter into cells. AutoFit offers five options:

- ✦ **AutoFit to Contents.** If you choose this option, your table will automatically adjust itself to wrap snugly around the text entered in cells.

- ✦ **AutoFit to Window.** If you choose this option, your table will adjust its width to fit within the margins you have set for the page.

- ✦ **Fixed Column Widths.** If you choose this option, your column widths will remain the same, and text will automatically wrap when it comes to the end of the column, instead of making the column expand.

- ✦ **Distribute Rows Evenly.** This makes all rows in your table the same height — the same height as the tallest row in your table, which means your table may suddenly get much taller.

- ✦ **Distribute Columns Evenly.** This makes all columns the same width, by subdividing the width of the column evenly. In other words, while Distribute Rows Evenly makes your table higher, Distribute Columns Evenly keeps the column the same width and makes some rows wider and some narrower.

Heading Rows Repeat

This command is useful if your table is going to span more than a single page. To use it, select the top row or rows of your table, and then choose Table ➪ Heading Rows Repeat. If your table jumps to another page, the top rows you selected will be displayed again as heading rows.

Other Table menu commands

The remaining commands on the Table Menu are Convert, Sort, Formula, Hide Gridlines, and Table Properties. We'll look at Table Properties, Sort, and Formula in detail in a moment.

Convert

Convert allows you to turn a table into text, or text into a table.

Table to text

To convert a table to text:

1. Select the portion of the table that you want to convert to text.

2. Choose Table ➪ Convert ➪ Table to Text.

3. From the dialog box, choose what you want to use to separate the items from the table once it's converted into text (see Figure 3-11): paragraph marks, tabs, commas, or any other character you specify.

4. If any of the cells in the table you're converting contains a nested table, check Convert Nested Tables; if you'd like to keep the nested table as a table, don't check it.

5. Click OK.

Text to table

Convert also allows you to turn text into a table. To do so:

1. Highlight the text you want to convert.

2. Choose Table ➪ Convert ➪ Text to Table.

3. A dialog box almost identical to the usual Insert Table dialog box appears (see Figure 3-12), with one difference: At the bottom, you have to tell Word what character it should look for to figure out how to break the text into table entries. Also, note that while you can choose the number of columns, you can't choose the number of rows — it's set automatically. That's because the total number of cells created has to match the number of entries that Word will form from the converted text.

4. Click OK.

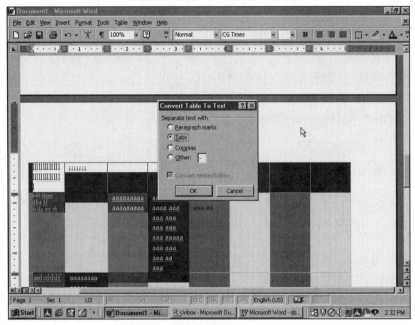

Figure 3-11: Word lets you specify what character you want to use to separate entries from a table when it's converted into text.

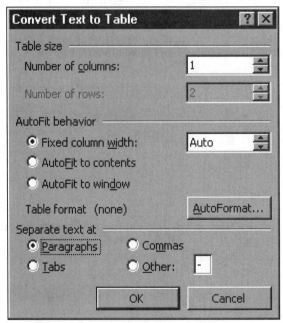

Figure 3-12: You can instantly place text into a table by using the Convert Text to Table command.

Hide Gridlines

This command does just what it says: Click on it to hide the gridlines that Word otherwise provides to outline your table's cells. Click Show Gridlines to bring the gridlines back.

Note These gridlines are not the same as the borders you can apply to tables (outline borders are used by default on new tables — unless you change these borders, this command will appear to have no effect). Also note that this command applies to all tables in the document.

Table Properties

Table Properties, at the bottom of the Table menu, is one of the most powerful commands the menu has to offer. It opens a dialog box that lets you handily specify most of your table's characteristics. The Table Properties dialog box has four tabs:

Table

Here you can specify three major properties of your table as a whole (see Figure 3-13):

✦ **Size.** Set the preferred width of your table, in inches or a percent of the page width. Note that this width may change later as you add or edit entries to the table, depending on your AutoFit choices.

✦ **Alignment.** Set your table against the left margin, centered on the page, or against the right margin, or enter a specific amount for it to be indented. (Note that the Indent from Left command is available only if you choose left alignment.)

✦ **Text wrapping.** Choose None if you want text to appear only above or below your table; choose Around if you'd like text to wrap around the table on the page. Around can sometimes improve the look of your page, particularly if your table is small. If you choose Around, click Positioning to detail exactly how you want text to relate to your table; options including horizontal and vertical positioning relative to margins, columns, paragraphs, or the page as a whole, and how much white space you want to add around the table. You can also choose whether to let the table move with the text or allow text to overlap it.

Row

Use the Row tab (see Figure 3-14) to specify the height of a range of rows (if you've highlighted several of them) or individual rows (if you haven't). Here's how the options work:

✦ **Size.** Word tells you which row or range of rows you're working with. Specify the height you want the row or rows to be and whether you want the row(s) to be exactly that height, or if that's a minimum measurement.

✦ **Options.** You can choose to allow or disallow the row to break across pages. If you're working with the first row, you can choose to make it a header row that will repeat on each page the table takes up.

◆ **Previous Row or Next Row.** Click here to adjust the next row above or below the currently selected row or rows.

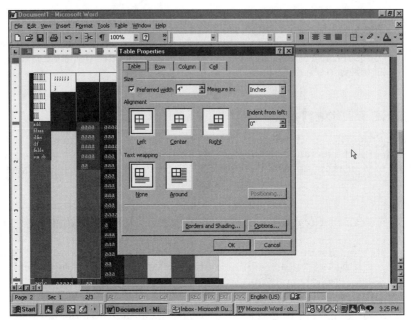

Figure 3-13: The Table tab of the Table Properties dialog box lets you position your table just where you want it on the page.

Column

The Column tab looks very much like the Row tab, and behaves exactly the same way, except you specify width, not height. There are no options for breaking across pages, and you can specify width not only in inches but as a percentage of the total table width.

Cell

The Cell tab (see Figure 3-15) lets you specify the preferred width for a selected cell or cells. Again, you can specify width in inches or as a percentage of the total table width. Below that, you can choose how to align text within the cell: flush against the top, centered vertically, or flush against the bottom.

Finally, clicking Options brings up a small dialog box in which you can set the cell's margins (or choose to leave them the same as for the rest of the table), and whether to wrap text when it gets too long or to squeeze or widen it to make it fit the width of the cell.

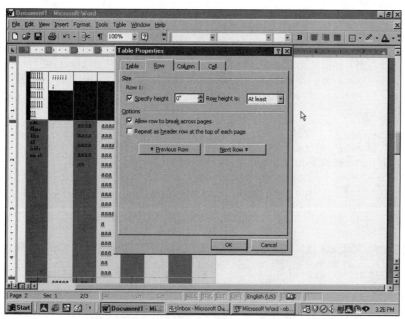

Figure 3-14: Specify row height, and other options, from the Row tab of the Table Properties dialog box.

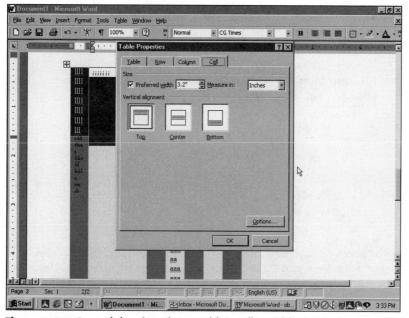

Figure 3-15: Control the size of your table's cells, and how text fits within them, with these controls.

Using Sort and Formulas

If you're planning to sort, sum, or otherwise manipulate a lot of data, chances are you're better off doing it in Excel than you are in Word. But if all you need is some simple calculations or you want to create an alphabetically sorted list of names, then Word's tables can probably do it for you.

Using Sort

To use Sort, make sure your cursor is inside the table you want to sort, and then choose Table ⇨ Sort. Word automatically selects the entire table. The table in Figure 3-16 is unsorted. After choosing Table ⇨ Sort, the Sort dialog box appears, looking like the one shown in Figure 3-17.

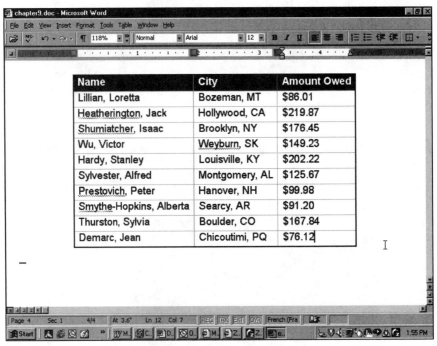

Figure 3-16: Here's a table in dire need of sorting.

Word lets you sort your table in three ways: by text, by number, or by date (depending on what type of data is entered). In the Sort By area, you choose which column you primarily want to sort, whether to sort by text, number, or date, and whether to sort in ascending order or descending order. In the two Then By areas, you enter the criteria you want to apply to settle any ties, where the initial criteria are identical for two or more entries. You should choose to use the data in one of your remaining columns to decide which of the tied entries comes first. Then choose whether to sort the tied entries in ascending or descending order.

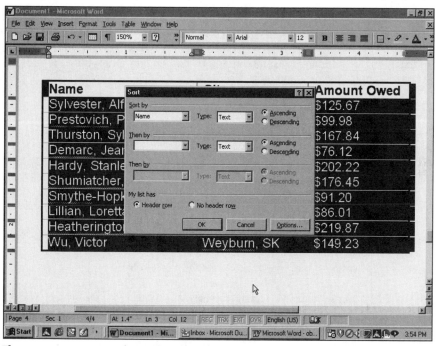

Figure 3-17: Here are the options Word provides for sorting tables.

At the bottom, indicate if your table has a header row or not. If you indicate that it does, the entries in the top row will not be sorted with the others. Also, columns will be indicated by the entries associated with them in the header row, instead of just being listed as Column 1, Column 2, etc., as they otherwise are.

When you've made the selections you want, click OK. The table from Figure 3-16, sorted in descending order by amount owed, is shown in Figure 3-18.

Click Options to fine-tune the sorting command. For example, you can specify what language Word should use to sort with and whether the sorting order should be case-sensitive.

Sorting Tips and Tricks

To sort a single column without affecting the columns on either side of it, first highlight the column, and then choose Table ➪ Sort and click Options. Check the box marked Sort Column Only, and then return to the main Sort dialog box and choose your criteria as usual. Click OK. Only the selected column will be sorted.

You can also sort a text list that isn't in a table with the Table ➪ Sort command, provided each item in the list ends with a paragraph mark. Highlight the list, and then choose Table ➪ Sort. A dialog box will open; choose ascending or descending order and whether you're sorting text, numbers, or dates, and then click OK.

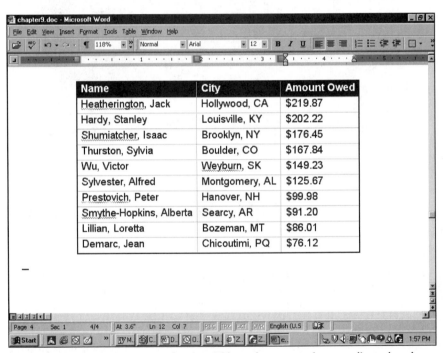

Figure 3-18: The Sort command can quickly make sense of a complicated and convoluted list.

Using formulas

Formulas let you perform calculations on the entries in your table's cells. The calculations aren't limited to the cell in which you place the formula; they can reference other cells in the table or any data in the document (provided you've marked it with a bookmark).

Word keeps track of the cells in a table with a simple reference system that combines the column and the row with a colon. B:3, for instance, would be the third cell down in the second column from the left. You can also reference an entire row or column by using the column letter or row number twice, separated by a colon; B:B would reference the entire second column, while 3:3 would reference the entire third row.

Quite complex formulas can be devised in Word tables that let you, for example, add together all the values of a row in one table, which you've bookmarked Expenses, and then subtract that from the sum of all the values of a column in another table, bookmarked Income. The formula might look like this:

```
{=(SUM(Income C:C)) - (SUM(Expenses 4:4))}
```

Cross-Reference Formulas are a form of field code. For more detailed information on field codes, see Chapter 4, "Forms, Fields, and Merging."

You can enter a formula by typing it directly into a cell, but an easier method is to click in the cell where you want the formula to appear, choose Table ⇨ Formula, and use the resulting dialog box (see Figure 3-19) to enter the formula. You can type it directly into the Formula blank; the Paste function list box at the bottom of the dialog box provides you with a complete list of all the formula functions available to you. Just click on the one you want to have it automatically entered into your formula.

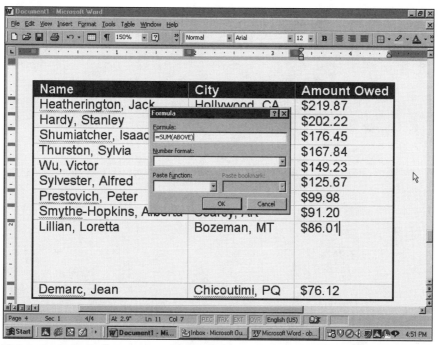

Figure 3-19: Formulas are powerful tools for automatically generating new data from data you've already entered into tables.

Choose the format in which you wish to display the results of your calculation from the Number Format drop-down list (e.g., do you want it to appear as a percentage, or in dollars and cents?). If you want to reference a bookmarked table, you'll find all of the ones available in your document listed under Paste Bookmark. Again, just click on the one you want to enter it into your formula.

Once your formula is complete, click OK.

The Tables and Borders Toolbar

One last thing before we leave this chapter: another, and sometimes easier, way to access the table formatting tools previously discussed.

As mentioned early on, when you use the Draw Table tool, you also automatically open the Tables and Borders toolbar (see Figure 3-20). You can also bring up this toolbar by choosing View ➪ Toolbars ➪ Tables and Borders. Most of the tools on the bottom half of this toolbar relate to tables, and most of them we've already looked at. From left to right, they are Insert Table, Merge Cells, Split Cells, Alignment, Distribute Rows Evenly, Distribute Columns Evenly, Table AutoFormat, Text Direction, Sort Ascending, Sort Descending, and AutoSum.

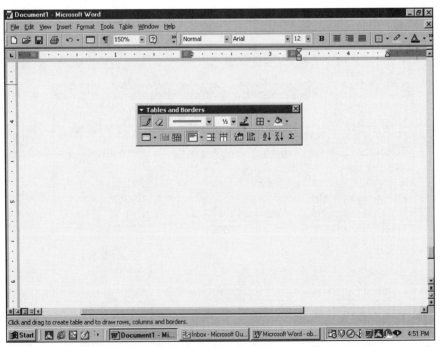

Figure 3-20: The Tables and Borders toolbar provides one-click access to many of the most useful table-formatting tools.

Cross-Reference The tools in the top half of this toolbar are discussed in detail in Chapter 7, "Adding Graphics and Fancy Formatting."

The Text Direction command

One of the commands we haven't yet looked at is the Text Direction command, which is also available by right-clicking on a table. Text Direction lets you run text vertically on the page instead of horizontally. To use it, highlight the text you want to apply it to, or simply place your cursor inside the cell where you want it to apply, and click the Text Direction button. The text will move from horizontal to vertical, with what was at the left margin now at the top. Click the button again and the text will remain vertical, but what was at the left margin when the text was horizontal is now at the bottom. Click the button a third time and the text returns to its original horizontal position.

If you choose this command from the right-click pop-up menu instead, you'll get a dialog box that shows you the three positions and illustrates what each looks like to help you make your choice.

Using AutoSum

Another useful command on this toolbar is AutoSum. This calculates and displays the sum of the values in the cells above or to the left of the cell containing the insertion point.

Summary

In this chapter, you learned several ways to create and format tables in Word. Major points included the following:

✦ Word gives you three methods to create tables. For a small table, you can click the Insert Table button; for a larger table, you can choose Table ➪ Insert ➪ Table, and to create a complex, custom table, choose Table ➪ Draw Table.

✦ Use the Table menu to add, delete, and format rows, columns. and individual cells.

✦ Why recreate the wheel? Let AutoFormat give your table a sharp, professionally designed look at the click of a button.

✦ Use the Table Properties dialog box to adjust the size of rows, columns, cells, and the table as a whole as you see fit. Specify exactly how you want other text to fit around your table.

◆ Convert text to tables and tables to text by choosing Table ⇨ Convert.

◆ Choose Table ⇨ Sort to organize your table in the way you think works best. You can also choose to sort a single column.

◆ Formulas are powerful tools that you can use to generate new data from information you've already entered into tables. You can add entries together, average them, and more.

◆ The Tables and Borders toolbar provides one-click access to the most common table formatting commands.

◆   ◆   ◆

Forms, Fields, and Merging

◆ ◆ ◆ ◆

In This Chapter

Using field codes

Creating and
using forms

Protecting forms
and fields

Performing a
mail merge

◆ ◆ ◆ ◆

Entering information in Word is most often done by typing, but that's not always the best way. Sometimes the information you need isn't at your fingertips, and has to be fetched from some other document. Sometimes there's a lot of repetition in the information, so typing it over and over again is terribly inefficient. Sometimes numerical information has to be calculated from other information elsewhere in the document. And sometimes the information has to be obtained from the person reading the document. Word has powerful tools that can help you in all of these situations and many more: field codes, forms, and merging capabilities.

Using Field Codes

Field codes are Word's way of letting you insert dynamic data—information that changes over time—into your document. The date is a good example of dynamic data. So is the amount of time you've spent working on a particular document. With field codes, you can automatically insert either of these values into a header or footer, or anywhere else in the document. They're used extensively in Word's templates to automatically insert information. The automatic page numbering feature available in headers and footers is another good example of a field code at work, as are Word's tools for automatically creating an index or table of contents.

Cross-Reference
Fore more information on this topic, see Chapter 5, "Outlines, Tables of Contents, and Indexes."

What can field codes do?

Word has more than 70 field codes available for your use, grouped by general purpose. The names of these groups are a pretty good indication of some of the uses field codes are put to:

Note What follows here is only a brief introduction to the topic of field codes: a complete exploration of all of the field codes Word offers (more than 70) and their options would make a pretty good-sized book all on its own. However, once you know the basics of using field codes, you can experiment with them on your own. How you use them depends on what you need them for, and is really limited only by your imagination.

✦ **Date and Time.** Using these field codes, you can automatically insert temporal information such as the current date and time; when the document was created, last printed, or last saved; and how much time has gone into editing it.

✦ **Document Automation.** These field codes allow you to perform tasks such as moving the insertion point, running macros, sending commands to a printer, inserting variables, comparing values, and carrying out conditional branching.

✦ **Document Information.** These field codes insert information about the document itself, such as who created it, its size and name, how many pages it contains, and the comments included in its Summary Info.

✦ **Equations and Formulas.** Carry out calculations on numerical data using these field codes. Others in this group also let you offset the text that follows the field to the left, right, up, or down to make way for the calculated data.

✦ **Index and Tables.** These field codes help you automatically construct tables of contents, indexes, and tables of authorities.

Cross-Reference See Chapter 5, "Outlines, Tables of Contents, and Indexes," for a detailed look at these processes.

✦ **Links and References.** Insert AutoText items, graphics, links, and other objects with these codes.

✦ **Mail Merge.** Most commonly used to create form letters, these codes let you combine saved data with a template to create individualized documents. (We'll look at merging documents in detail later in this chapter.)

✦ **Numbering.** Anything to do with numbering can be inserted with these codes, including page numbers, the number of times the document has been saved, the current section number, list elements and more.

✦ **User Information.** Tools ➪ Options ➪ User Information lets you enter your name, initials, and mailing address. These codes automatically insert that information into your document.

Viewing field codes

Most of the time, field codes are invisible, because what's important is the information they insert into the document, not the codes themselves. However, sometimes you may want to check which field codes are at work, or edit them (many codes have options that you can change which affect, for example, how the displayed information is formatted).

To see field codes in a document, you have to turn them on by pressing Alt+F9. This turns on all the codes in the document. Pressing Alt+F9 again turns them off.

To display a single field code, place your insertion point inside it and press Shift+F9. You can also use Shift+F9 to display a selected group of field codes (see Figure 4-1).

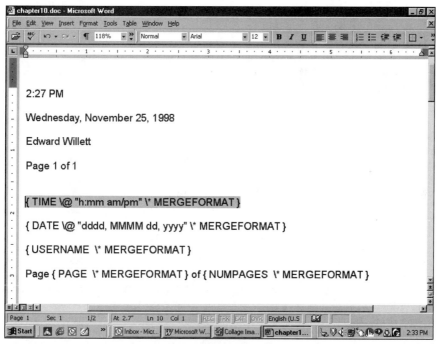

Figure 4-1: At the top, this document displays the information automatically inserted by the same field codes that are displayed below. Note that the currently selected field is highlighted with gray.

Inserting field codes

Inserting a field code is very much like inserting anything else in Word. To insert a field code:

1. Choose Insert ➪ Field. This opens the Field dialog box (see Figure 4-2).

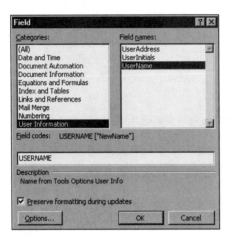

Figure 4-2: The Field dialog box includes a complete menu of all the field options available in Word.

2. Choose the category of field you're interested in. To insert my name as I did in Figure 4-1, for example, I chose User Information.

3. From the Field Names list, choose the field you want to insert — in this case, UserName (the other options are UserInitials and UserAddress). The actual code that will be used appears in the Field Codes area of the dialog box, as does a brief description of what that code does.

4. Choose Options to specify attributes unique to the chosen field code, such as how it will display the information it obtains. This opens a new dialog box, something like the one shown in Figure 4-3. For UserName, the choices are simple, and related to what case will be used for the letters. Other field codes have many more options, usually listed under two tabs, General Switches and Field-Specific Switches. Again, the Description area at the bottom of the dialog box provides a brief explanation of the effects of the various options.

5. When you're happy with your selection, click Add to Field. If you abruptly change your mind after doing so, there's no need to panic: just click Undo Add.

6. Click OK to return to the Field dialog box.

7. Some field codes allow you to enter optional information. This is indicated by square brackets to the right of the field code, just below the Categories menu. You can enter this additional information in the Field Codes blank. For

example, I can change the name the UserName field code inserts by typing in a new name (see Figure 4-4). Note that you don't type in the square brackets; they're just displayed to show you that that information is optional.

8. Once you're satisfied with your field code, click OK. The new field is automatically entered in the document wherever your insertion point is.

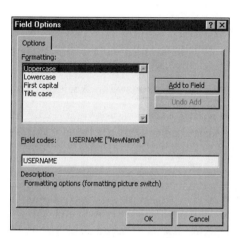

Figure 4-3: Each field code has its own unique formatting and other options that you can set.

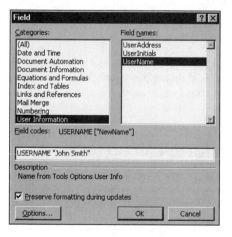

Figure 4-4: Some field codes let you enter optional information that changes what the field would otherwise display.

Tip   Word uses a backslash (\ ) in field codes to indicate that what follows is a switch of some kind. This can be a problem if you're adding optional information, such a file location, that also uses the backslash character. To make a backslash character appear without messing up the field code syntax, use it twice: for example, "C:\\Webpages\\FP Web\\index.htm."

Updating field codes

When you first insert a field code, the information displayed in it is current as of that moment. However, the whole point of field codes is that they can display dynamic information, which means that by the time you print your document, the information displayed in the various fields may be out of date. To ensure that it isn't, you have to update your fields:

✦ To update a single field, click on it and press F9.

✦ To update several fields at once, highlight the area of the document that contains the fields you want to update and then press F9.

✦ To update all the fields in the document, choose Edit ➪ Select All, and then press F9.

This causes all the selected fields to calculate or fetch the latest version of the data they display—for example, the current time.

Formatting field codes

As noted earlier, you can preset some of the formatting of field codes from the Field Options dialog box—determining whether the date will be displayed as "Wednesday, August 12, 1998" or as "08/12/98," for example. You can also format field codes just as you do any other text, by highlighting them and using the formatting options discussed in detail in Chapter 2, "Working with Text."

Tip   If you want any formatting applied to a field to remain in place even after the contents of the field changes due to updating, make sure that the Preserve Formatting During Updates check box in the Field dialog box is checked when you insert the field into your document. Checking this box includes the * MERGEFORMAT switch in the field code.

Using field codes to perform calculations

As explained in Chapter 3, "Tables," field codes can be used to perform calculations on the contents of the cells of a table. They can also be used to perform calculations involving any other numerical data in your document, provided that data can either be returned by another field code or has been bookmarked.

For example, suppose you've written a report that contains total annual sales figures from two different stores in two different locations in the document. Now you want to calculate the average monthly sales for the operation as a whole and include that figure in your closing paragraph. To do that, you would first have to bookmark the two stores' sales figures as, say, North and South. Then you could create a field code that will add the two together and divide them by 12, as follows:

1. Choose Insert ➪ Field.

2. Select (All) from the list of categories, and = (Formula) from the list of Field names (it appears right at the top).

3. In the blank at the bottom, after the =, enter the formula (North + South) / 12.

4. Click OK. The results of your calculation are displayed (see Figure 4-5).

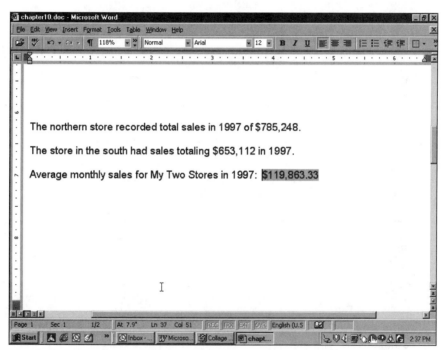

Figure 4-5: The formula entered in the field in the last paragraph adds the figures from the previous two paragraphs and divides the total by 12.

What makes formulas so powerful, in this and other instances, is that if you have to revise the information referenced in the formula, you don't have to recalculate the final result yourself; just update your fields, and the formula field recalculates and displays the new result.

Creating and Using Forms

Forms allow you to create documents into which you or someone else can easily enter data. A good example of the use of forms is the fax cover letter shown in Figure 4-6, one of the templates that comes with Word. In this case, the fields allow you to enter your own information in several places, and even to check off checkboxes. Another field automatically enters the date.

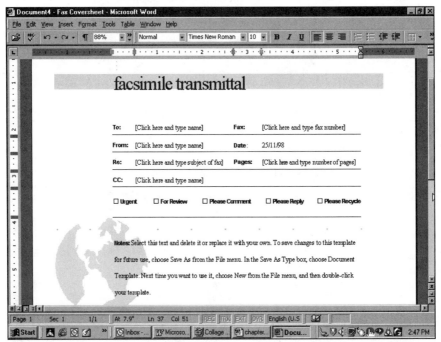

Figure 4-6: Word's forms capabilities can help you create professional-looking documents like this one.

Most forms are set up as templates. This makes it easier to, for example, send out invoices that share the same look, while still individualizing the portions that need to be individualized—such as who's being billed, what for, and how much.

Cross-Reference   For more information on templates, see Chapter 6, "Styles and Templates."

To create a form template, first create the information that won't change very often, if at all: the name of the form, the name and address of the company, logos or other graphics, etc. Then, when you're ready to begin entering form fields, choose View ⇨

Toolbars ⇨ Forms, to call up the Forms toolbar (see Figure 4-7). Enter and edit the forms as you see fit, and then save the document as a document template (*.dot) file.

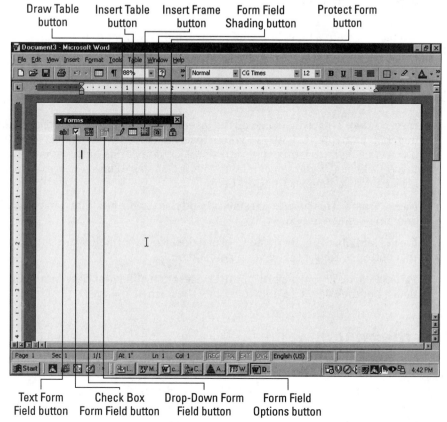

Figure 4-7: The Forms toolbar puts all the tools you need to create your own forms at your fingertips.

The Forms toolbar

The Forms toolbar (refer to Figure 4-7) contains the controls you will most often need in creating forms of any type:

✦ **Text Form Field.** One of the most common elements of a form is a place for the user to enter text. Click this button to create such a field.

✦ **Check Box Form Field.** Check boxes are also common elements in forms. Click this button to place a check box in your document. If the form is being filled out onscreen, a user can check or uncheck this box by clicking it.

✦ **Drop-Down Form Field.** This form field is only useful in an onscreen form. It creates a drop-down list from which the user can make a selection.

✦ **Form Field Options.** This lets you set various options (which we'll look at in detail a little later) for any of the form fields.

✦ **Draw Table.** This opens the Tables and Borders toolbar. You can use this toolbar to create a table into which you can then enter static text or form fields.

Cross-Reference

See Chapter 3, "Tables," for details on how to use this toolbar to create tables.

✦ **Insert Table.** This is the same as the Insert Table command, also discussed in detail in Chapter 3. It allows you to insert a table of whatever size you like. If you click on an existing table and select a column, this button changes to Insert Columns; if you select a table row, it changes to Insert Rows; if you select a cell, it changes to Insert Cells.

✦ **Insert Frame.** This inserts a frame, a handy, resizable box that can be used to contain graphics or text.

✦ **Form Field Shading.** By default, form fields, like other fields, are shaded. Click this button to toggle that shading off and on.

✦ **Protect Form.** If you click this button, users can still enter data into your form fields, but they won't be able to modify the form field codes.

Inserting a form field

To insert a text, check box, or drop-down form field, place your insertion point wherever in your document you want the field to appear, and then click the appropriate button on the Forms toolbar. Text and drop-down form fields appear as shaded rectangles; check-box form fields appear as shaded, black-bordered boxes (shading appears only if the Form Field Shading tool is turned on).

Once you've inserted the field, you can fine-tune it by clicking on it and then clicking the Form Field Options button on the Forms toolbar, or simply by double-clicking it.

Note

The Form Field Options dialog box offers different options for each type of form field.

Text form fields

When you insert a text form field, the Form Field Options dialog box looks like the one shown in Figure 4-8.

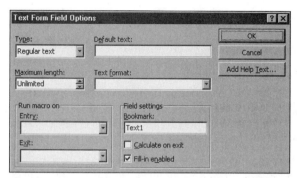

Figure 4-8: Use the Text Form Field Options dialog box to set the size and other specific properties of your text form field.

You have several options here to help you fine-tune your text form field:

✦ **Type.** From this drop-down list, choose what type of text you want entered in this field: regular text, a number, a date, the current time, the current date, or a calculated value.

✦ **Default Text.** Type in whatever you want to appear in the field by default. Note that if you indicate that you want a number or date in the field, this box changes to Default Number or Default Date. If you choose to enter the current time or current date in the field, this box isn't available. If you've associated the field with a calculated value, then this is where you enter the formula that produces that value (see the section on formula field codes earlier in this chapter).

✦ **Maximum Length.** Specify the maximum length the text field can expand to, in characters, if you're worried about it messing up your form's overall layout, or leave it at the default Unlimited if you're not.

✦ **Text Format.** Use this drop-down list to specify the format for text entered in the text field. What's on the list changes depending on what type of text you've chosen. For regular text, the options are limited to uppercase, lowercase, first capital, and title case; but for numbers and dates you have many more options to choose from.

✦ **Entry.** You can create macros for your form that will run when a user clicks on certain fields. If you want to associate a macro with this field, choose it from the list here.

Cross-Reference

To learn more about creating macros, see Chapter 55, "Creating Macros."

✦ **Exit.** Like entry, except the macro you choose here runs when the user exits a field by pressing Tab or clicking outside it.

✦ **Bookmark.** This assigns a bookmark name to the field.

✦ **Calculate on Exit.** Check this if you want Word to recalculate the contents of the field once the user leaves it.

✦ **Fill-In Enabled.** Check this box if you want the user to be able to fill in the field onscreen. If you just want it to display a predetermined value and don't want users messing with it, uncheck this box.

✦ **Add Help Text.** Click here to create your own help messages, which will appear in Word's status bar and/or in a small message box when the user selects the field and presses F1.

Check Box form fields

When you insert a check box form field and double-click on it or click the Form Properties button, you get slightly different options in the dialog box (see Figure 4-9).

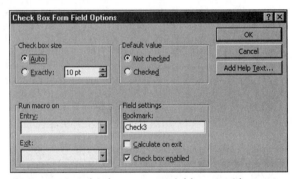

Figure 4-9: A Check Box Form Field, as you'd expect, has slightly different properties you can specify.

Some of the options are exactly the same as in the Text Form Field Options dialog box: Entry and Exit, Bookmark, Calculate on Exit, Check Box Enabled, and Add Help Text. However, there are a few differences:

✦ **Check box size.** In this area, you can choose Auto, which automatically adjusts the size of the check box to correspond to the size of the text around it, or Exactly, which lets you specify a size for the box in points.

✦ **Default value.** There are two options: Not Checked or Checked.

Drop-Down form fields

Drop-down form fields let you create the same kind of drop-down lists Windows software is always presenting you with. To create and edit such a list:

1. Place your insertion point where you want the drop-down list to appear and click the Drop-Down Form Field button on the Forms toolbar. The drop-down list initially looks like a text form field.

2. Double-click the form field to call up the Drop-Down Form Field Options dialog box (see Figure 4-10).

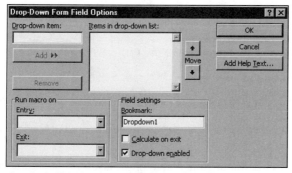

Figure 4-10: The Drop-Down Form Field Options dialog box lets you add whatever options you like to a drop-down list.

3. Type the first option you want in the list in the Drop-Down Item text box and click Add. Repeat this procedure until you've added all the options you want to the list.

4. To move an item up or down within the list, highlight it by clicking on it, and then click the up or down arrows labeled Move. To remove an item, click on it, and then click Remove.

5. As with text form fields and check box form fields, you can assign a macro to run when the user either clicks on the drop-down list or leaves it by choosing the macros you want from the Entry and Exit lists; you can also assign a bookmark to the list, set it to perform a calculation when the user exits it, enable or disable it, and assign help text to it.

6. When you're satisfied with your drop-down list, click OK.

Note

You'll notice as soon as you click OK that your drop-down list doesn't actually look like a drop-down list, and your check box doesn't behave like a check box (because you can't check it). That's because your form is still in an editable format, so you can make changes to it. Drop-down lists and check boxes don't begin acting the way they're supposed to until you *protect* the document—as described in the next section.

Protecting your form and fields

At the moment, your form is rather useless, because anyone using it online is not only free to type in information, but is also free to change what goes into text form fields, fiddle with check box form fields, and alter the list of items in drop-down list form fields. Generally, to make an online form work, you have to protect your forms: Tell Word that only authorized people such as yourself are to be allowed to alter their properties.

Note   You can protect your document in other ways, as well, to ensure that unauthorized people can't make changes to it. You can even stop unauthorized people from opening the file in the first place, by attaching a password to it.

Protecting forms

To protect the forms in your document, click the Protect Form button on the Forms toolbar.

Cross-Reference   For more information on protecting your documents, see Chapter 54, "Collaborating on a Network."

Locking fields

You can't protect the other fields in your document the same way you protect forms. Anyone who can change any other part of the document can change the field codes. You can, however, lock individual fields so that they aren't updated when the rest of the fields in the document are. To lock an individual field, click on it and press Ctrl+F11. Click on the locked field and press Shift+Ctrl+F11 to unlock it.

Using Mail Merge

"Mail merge" is a misleading term. Although it is probably most commonly used to create individualized form letters, address labels, and the like, it can in fact be used to merge any kind of data with any kind of document to create a single Word file containing a whole series of individualized documents. No matter what kind of document and data you're merging, the basic process is the same:

1. *Create the main document.* This is the "boilerplate," the part of the document that doesn't change no matter what data is merged with it. If you're creating a form letter, for instance, this will probably include most of the letter's main body.

2. *Create the data that will be merged with the document.* This is the information that will be used to personalize each document: typically, names, addresses, and other data about the individuals the document is intended for. You can create this mail-merge data source directly in Word, or take it from an existing Access or Outlook database.

3. *Define the merge fields in the main document.* These fields tell Word where to put the data from the data source: the first name after "Dear" in the salutation line, for instance.

4. *Merge the data and the main document.* Word follows your instructions to create a series of individualized documents based on the main document, each containing one set of data from the data source.

5. *Print.* You can print all the documents or a range of them, because they're all part of a single Word document file.

It's helpful to know the process, but Word doesn't even require you to remember these steps on your own: it has provided a handy Mail Merge Helper that leads you through them one at a time.

The Mail Merge helper

To begin a mail merge, choose Tools ⇨ Mail Merge to call up the checklist shown in Figure 4-11.

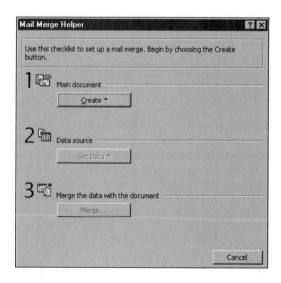

Figure 4-11: Word takes you through the mail merge process step by step.

Under Main Document, click Create. Mail Merge Helper lists four types of documents it can help you create:

✦ **Form Letters.** These are letters where the address, salutation and any other information you want are personalized based on the information in your data source. When the mail merge is finished, you have a single Word file containing all the personalized letters. Because each one is its own section, it's easy to print a single letter, a range of them, or the entire set.

✦ **Mailing Labels.** You specify the size of label you want to use, and then Word creates a main document for you that consists of a single page of appropriately sized labels. Each label contains the fields you specify. After the merge, you have a single document file consisting of many pages of labels. Unlike the form letters, all the labels are in one section.

✦ **Envelopes.** As with labels, Word lets you specify the size of envelope you're using, and then add the fields you want to it. The resulting merged file contains all the envelopes, each in an individual section.

✦ **Catalogs.** Whereas a form letter mail merge creates one document per record in the database, a catalog creates one large document containing all the data, forming a list — descriptions and prices of various items for sale in your store, for instance.

Click Create and then choose the type of document you want to create from the list. From that point on, the options for each type of mail merge vary somewhat. We'll look first at creating a form letter, because that's probably the most common type of document created using mail merge. After that, we'll look at the ways in which creating other sorts of mail-merge documents differ (not as much as you might think — many of the steps are identical).

Creating a form letter

When you choose Form Letters from the Mail Merge Helper Create list, you're first asked if you want to create the form letter in the current document window (if one is active) or create a new document window.

That decided, the Mail Merge Helper returns with a new button, Edit, alongside the Create button. You can change your main document to a different type of mail-merge main document, work on more than one main document of different types, or work on more than one main document of the same type, by clicking Create again and choosing another option from the list. You'll be asked if you want to change the document to the type you've selected (if you've selected a different type) or open a new main document.

You can also choose to stop the whole process by clicking Restore to Normal Word Document. This won't change any text you've entered in your main document; it just stops the Mail Merge Helper process.

Creating your main document

Click Edit to bring up a list of any mail-merge main documents you're currently working on. Choose the one you want to edit. Mail Merge Helper disappears. For your form letter, enter any text that won't change in the main document and edit and format using the usual text editing and formatting tools.

When you're done editing, choose Tools ➪ Mail Merge again to call up the Mail Merge Helper once more.

Creating or locating your data source

Next, you need to specify the data that will be inserted into your form letter. Click Get Data. Mail Merge Helper provides you with four options:

✦ **Create data source.** Choose this option to create a new data source by entering data directly into Word.

✦ **Open data source.** Choose this to bring up the Open Data Source dialog box, which is very similar to Office's standard Open dialog box. Word lets you use Microsoft Query, Excel, and Access databases, as well as several non-Microsoft database programs, as sources of data for mail merges. Locate the database you want to use, click on it, and click OK.

✦ **Use address book.** Access and Outlook address books and Schedule+ contact lists can also be used as data sources for mail merge.

✦ **Header options.** Whatever source you use for your data, mail merge considers the first row of data to be a header. The entries in that row are interpreted as the names of the data columns and will be used to name the merge fields that you'll be inserting into your main document. By clicking Header options, however, you can choose to import headers and data from two different sources. Click Create or Open here to create or choose the source of your header names, and then choose one of the preceding options as your data source.

If you choose Create data source, you'll see the dialog box shown in Figure 4-12.

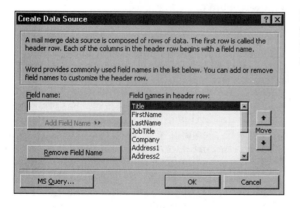

Figure 4-12: Create or select the fields of data you need in the Create Data Source dialog box.

To create a new data source using Word:

1. Choose your field names. As the dialog box explains, mail merge looks for data organized into rows and columns. The top row is the header row; its entries are the field names for the data in each column. Word provides a list of common field names. Delete any that you don't want by clicking on them, and then clicking Remove Field Name; add additional ones by entering their names in the Field Name box and then clicking Add Field Name. You can change their position by clicking on them, and then clicking the Move buttons to move them up or down.

2. Once you're happy with your field names, click OK. Word prompts you to save your new data source document. The first time you save it, Word warns you that the data source is empty, and lets you edit it or the main document.

3. Return to the Mail Merge Helper. There is now an Edit button in the Data Source area. Click it. Choose the name you just gave your data source from the list that appears; this brings up the Data Form dialog box (see Figure 4-13).

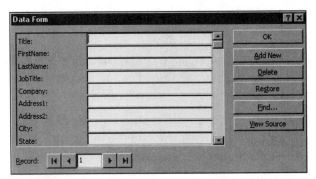

Figure 4-13: Enter the data for your form letter in the Data Form dialog box.

4. This dialog box contains a blank for each field name you chose, and represents the information that will be inserted into a single letter after merging. Enter the information for the first letter into the blanks.

5. To enter the information for the second letter, click Add New to create a new record. Enter the information. Continue this process until you've entered information for all the letters you're planning to create. You can move from record to record to make changes or corrections by using the Record controls at the bottom of the dialog box: Click the inner controls to move one record at a time forward or backward; click the outer controls to jump to the beginning or end of the records. You can also find specific text within your data records by clicking Find and entering the text you're looking for. To erase an entry, click Delete; to undo a change, click Restore.

6. When you've entered all the necessary data, click OK.

What you're really creating with this dialog box is another Word document: specifically, a table, which has the field names in the top row and the information from each record in each subsequent row. You can edit this document directly by clicking View Source. This can be an easier way to check for mistakes and make corrections, because it allows you to see many records at once and use tools such as Find and Replace.

When you view your data source document (see Figure 4-14), you'll also discover a new toolbar has opened. This database toolbar includes several useful buttons (from left to right):

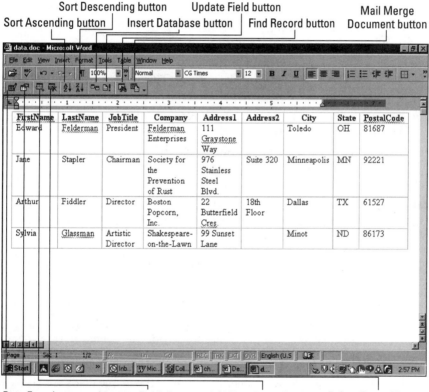

Figure 4-14: Sometimes it's easier to edit the data source you're creating by going straight to the source — the Word document itself.

✦ **Data Form.** This opens the Data Form dialog box (refer to Figure 4-13).

✦ **Manage Fields.** This opens a version of the Create Data Source dialog box in which you can add, delete, or rename the existing fields.

✦ **Add New Record.** This adds a blank row to the table in which your data is stored, into which you can add the information for a new record.

✦ **Delete Record.** To remove a record from the database, place your insertion point anywhere in that record's row, and then click this button.

✦ **Sort Ascending; Sort Descending.** Place your insertion point anywhere within the column of the field by which you wish to sort your data, and then click one of these two buttons. If it's a text field, all the records will be sorted alphabetically (or reverse-alphabetically), based on the information within that field; if it's a numerical field, all the records will be sorted numerically (or reverse-numerically), based on the information within that field.

✦ **Insert Database.** You can insert data from another database as a table in your document by clicking this button.

✦ **Update Field.** Select the field or fields you want to update and click this button to insert the latest data into them. (This applies to fields that call for the current time or other dynamic data.)

✦ **Find Record.** This calls up a dialog box that allows you to search any field for a specific word or phrase.

✦ **Mail Merge Main Document.** Click this button to view the mail-merge main document associated with the data source.

Inserting merge fields

Now you have to indicate in the main document where the information from the data source should go. To do so:

1. Return to your main document. Notice, if you haven't already, that there's a new toolbar open above your document.

2. Place the insertion point where you want to insert a merge field.

3. Click Insert Merge Field on the Mail Merge toolbar. This drops down a list of all the merge fields in the specified data source for this document (see Figure 4-15).

4. Choose the field you want. Word inserts it into your main document.

5. Continue editing the main document until all the merge fields are inserted. The finished document will look something like the one shown in Figure 4-16.

6. Save your main document.

Note

The Insert Word Field button beside the Insert Merge Field button allows you to insert various other field codes that you can use to customize your mail-merge main document. For details on using field codes, refer back to the beginning of this chapter.

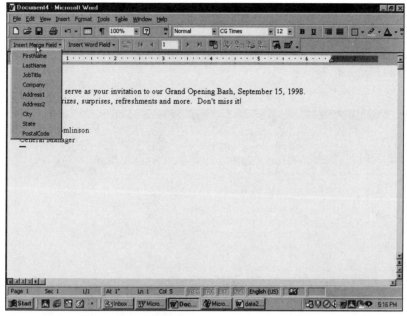

Figure 4-15: Choose the merge field you want to insert into your main document from this handy menu.

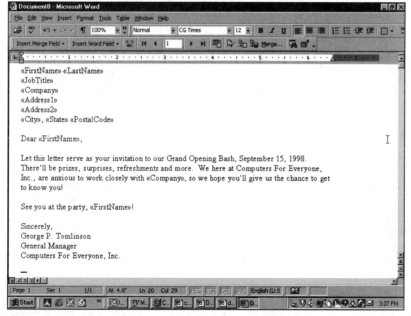

Figure 4-16: Here's what your final document will look like with all the merge fields inserted.

Previewing your document

Once you've inserted merge fields and have chosen or created a data source, all the tools in the Mail Merge toolbar are active, including several that allow you to preview your merged document and even check it for errors before committing it to disk or printer (see Figure 4-17):

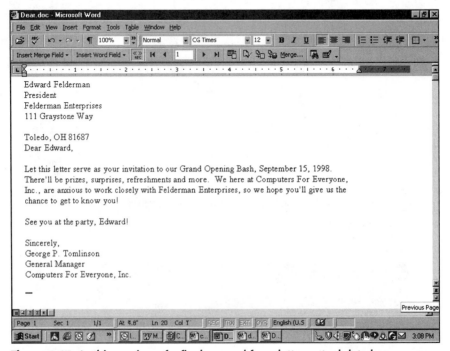

Figure 4-17: In this preview of a final merged form letter, actual data has replaced the merge fields.

✦ **View Merged Data.** This button conducts a trial run of the mail merge and lets you see what your letter will look like with the data included.

✦ **First Record, Previous Record, Go to Record, Next Record, Last Record.** These buttons form a mini control panel rather like the controls of a CD player. Use them to see a preview of the letter using any record in the database. You can click the arrows to move directly to the first and last records or one at a time backward or forward through the records, or enter a specific record's number in the Go to Record blank.

✦ **Check for Errors.** Click this button to check your merged document for errors before you print it. You're given three options: You can simulate the merge and get an error report in a new document, proceed with the merge and see each error as it occurs, or simply proceed with the merge and get a report of all the errors that occurred when it's over.

Merging document and data

Once you've previewed and corrected to your heart's content, you're ready to actually carry out the mail merge and create your individualized form letters. To do so, click the Mail Merge button on the Mail Merge toolbar. (If you'd like to return to the Mail Merge Helper, do that, and then click the Merge button.) This opens the Merge dialog box (see Figure 4-18), which is used as follows:

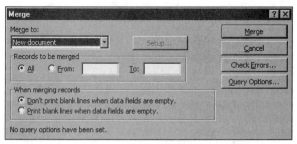

Figure 4-18: Fine-tune your mail merge before you carry it out with the tools included in the Merge dialog box.

✦ First, choose whether you want the finished product to become a new document, to go straight to the printer, or to go out by e-mail or fax. (If you choose one of the latter two, click Setup to indicate the data field that contains the e-mail address or fax number, insert a subject line, and choose whether to send the file directly or as an attachment.)

✦ Next, select whether you want to merge all the records or just some of them; if the latter, you must enter a range.

✦ Then, decide if you want to print blank lines to represent empty records. (In our example, the Address 2 field is sometimes empty. Because leaving a blank line, as I did in Figure 4-17, can make the address at the top of the letter look odd, my choice would be to not have empty records leave blank lines.)

Note This dialog box also contains a button to check errors, as described in the section on previewing documents.

Using Query Options

There's one more button, which also appears in the Mail Merge Helper: Query Options, which opens a dialog box with two tabs, Filter Records and Sort Records.

By using Filter Records (see Figure 4-19), you can exert detailed control over which records are used in the mail merge. Choose the field you want to filter in the first column, and then choose the type of comparison you want to make (equal, not equal, greater than, less than, greater than or equal, less than or equal, blank or not blank), and finally enter what you want to compare the field to.

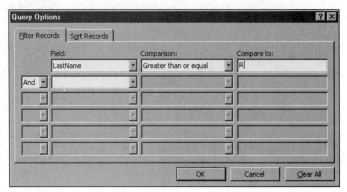

Figure 4-19: Use these controls to choose which records should be merged and which shouldn't.

In Figure 4-19, I've filtered the records so that only those in which the last name begins with the letter R or above will be merged.

Tip   You can create extremely fine filters, up to six layers deep, by using all the blanks in the Filter Records tab. The small list boxes at the left let you choose AND or OR to apply additional filters.

The other tab, Sort Records (see Figure 4-20), lets you sort your records by up to three fields. Enter the first field you want to sort the records by in the first blank, and whether you want to sort in ascending or descending order; then, in the remaining blanks, enter the fields you'd like to use to settle any ties among records sorted by the first field.

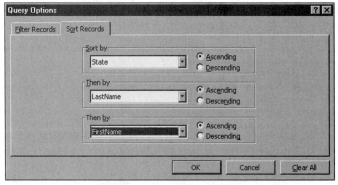

Figure 4-20: Sort your records just the way you want them with the Sort Records tab of the Query Options dialog box.

Completing the merge

Once you've set the Query Options you want, click OK to return to the Merge
dialog box, and click Merge to (finally!) create your individualized form letters
(see Figure 4-21).

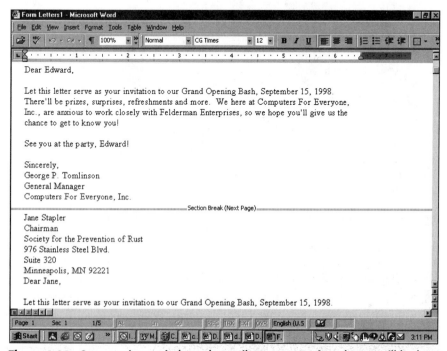

Figure 4-21: Once you've carried out the mail merge, your form letters will look
like this: individual sections in a single document file.

Creating mailing labels

Creating mailing labels is generally the same as creating form letters. The
differences are that you have to choose the size of mailing label you want to
create, and instead of creating individual sections from each record, Word
creates pages of labels, each containing many records. To create mailing labels:

1. Choose Tools ⇨ Mail Merge to open the Mail Merge Helper.

2. Choose Create ⇨ Mailing Labels from the Mail Merge Helper. As with all
   mail merge documents, Word asks you to choose between using the current
   document and creating a new one.

3. Choose Get Data, and create or obtain a data source as with Form Letters.

4. Word will prompt you to set up the main document. Clicking the Setup button will open the Label Options dialog box (see Figure 4-22).

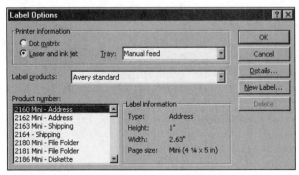

Figure 4-22: Whatever type of mailing label you use, chances are good it's included in the Label Options dialog box.

5. Enter the appropriate printer information and then choose the type of label you'll be using from the lists. The Label Products drop-down list lists major label manufacturers, while the Product Number list lists some of their most popular products. If your particular label doesn't appear, go through the available options and check the Label Information area for something that corresponds.

6. If you need to modify an existing label to suit your needs, click Details; if you want to create an entirely new type of label, click New Label. Both options bring up a version of the dialog box shown in Figure 4-23.

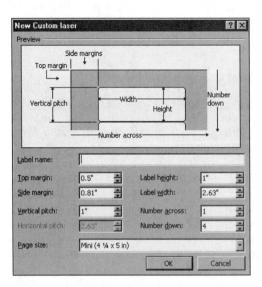

Figure 4-23: You can customize the size of labels you want to create using this dialog box.

7. Once you've set the required parameters, click OK, and then click OK again in the Label Options dialog box. Now Word opens the Create Labels dialog box (see Figure 4-24).

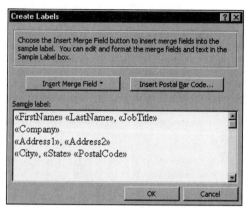

Figure 4-24: Instead of creating a main document as you did in creating form letters, you use this dialog box to insert merge fields for mailing labels.

8. Click Insert Merge Field to see a list of available fields. Select the field you want. Continue inserting fields until they're all in place.

9. If you want to insert a postal bar code, click Insert Postal Bar Code. You'll be asked to specify the merge field that includes the zip code and the field that includes the street address. Click OK to return to the Create Labels dialog box.

10. Click OK in the Create Labels dialog box to return to the Mail Merge Helper, and click Edit in the Main Document area to see what your page of labels looks like with field codes added (see Figure 4-25).

11. Make any formatting changes you'd like, and then continue with the merge just as with form letters: you can preview it, set Query Options, etc., just as before.

12. Once everything's set, click Merge. The final result will be a set of individualized mailing labels (or name tags, or something else similar) ready to be peeled off and used.

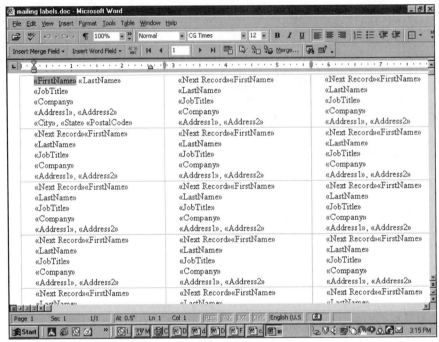

Figure 4-25: Word creates a page of mailing labels ready to be merged with your data. (Note that I chose Table ⇨ Show Gridlines so I could more clearly see where one label ends and the next begins.)

Creating envelopes

Creating envelopes is very similar to creating mailing labels, except you specify the type of envelope to use instead of the type of label — and, of course, you choose Envelopes when you click Create in the Main Document section of the Mail Merge Helper.

Creating a catalog

Creating a catalog is the same as creating a form letter, except the final result is a single document with a single section, instead of a single document with multiple sections. That's because a catalog is typically used to create a single document containing a list of product names, descriptions, and prices.

A catalog also often contains pictures of products, ordering and company information, and more. You'll probably find it easier to make the final document look aesthetically pleasing if you set up your merge fields and data first, go ahead with the merge, and then enter text and graphics around the results.

Summary

In this chapter, you learned ways to use dynamic, changeable data in Word documents, how to create forms, and how to carry out a mail merge. Major points included the following:

✦ Field codes are Word's way of letting you insert dynamic data—information that changes from time to time—into your document.

✦ To insert a field code, choose Insert ➪ Field, and then choose the type of field code you want from the list.

✦ Field codes displaying ever-changing data have to be updated from time to time. Use F9 to update a single field code or range of codes.

✦ Field codes can be used to carry out complex calculations that draw on information contained elsewhere in your document.

✦ Use the Forms toolbar to create professional-looking forms that include text fields, check boxes, and even drop-down lists (the latter for online forms only, obviously!).

✦ For online forms to work properly, they have to be protected by choosing Tools ➪ Protect Document ➪ Forms.

✦ The Mail Merge Helper (Tools ➪ Mail Merge) takes you step-by-step through the process of creating individualized form letters, mailing labels, catalogs, or envelopes, beginning with the creation of a main document.

✦ You can create the data for a mail merge yourself in Word or use other databases, including those from Access and Excel—and even draw information from Outlook address books.

✦ You can preview your mail merge before actually carrying it out, to make sure the result matches your needs.

✦ Query options provide powerful filtering tools to help you merge only the records you want.

✦   ✦   ✦

Outlines, Tables of Contents, and Indexes

Good organization is crucial to the success of any document. If the information presented isn't in some sort of logical order, it's much harder for the reader to understand it. That not only undermines communication (the primary purpose of creating a document in the first place), it undermines your credibility. Fortunately, Word provides several organizational tools that can help you present your thoughts in crystal-clear fashion, and make it easier for your audience to find the information they're looking for within your documents.

What Is an Outline?

An outline is simply a hierarchical listing of the headings within a document. This book, like most nonfiction books, began life as an outline, and that outline can still be traced in the various levels of headings that appear in each chapter. Major headings, like "What Is an Outline?" above, use the largest type; each subsequent level of heading uses slightly smaller type. Sub-subheadings all relate in some way to the subheadings they're grouped under, which in turn relate in some way to the major heading under which they are grouped.

Word includes, as part of its normal template, several levels of heading styles. By using these styles for your headings (Heading 1 for main headings, Heading 2 for subheadings, Heading 3 for sub-subheadings, etc.) as you build your outline, you can create an organizational structure that's easy to modify and easy to move around in within Word.

Using Outline View

Word offers a special view, Outline View, to help you work with outlines. A typical outline in Outline View looks something like the one shown in Figure 5-1, which is part of the outline for this book. You can turn on Outline View by choosing View ➪ Outline.

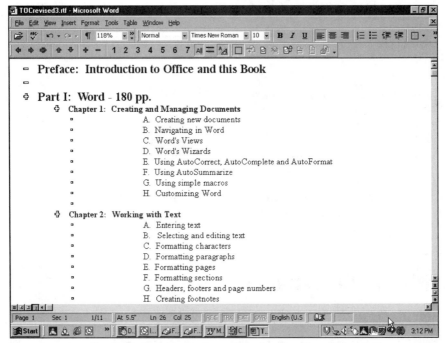

Figure 5-1: Outline View shows you the various levels of headings within your document.

In Outline View, Word automatically indents headings to show their relative importance to one another. In addition, it allows you to view only the level of headings that you want by using the Outlining toolbar, which you can see in Figure 5-1 just above the document window. This offers you several useful tools:

✦ **Click 1** to view only your most important headings. This hides everything except headings that use the Heading 1 style (see Figure 5-2).

✦ **Click 2** to see only the headings that use Heading 1 and Heading 2 style, 3 to see the headings in the top three levels, and so on.

✦ **Click All** to see the entire document, including paragraphs that don't use a heading style.

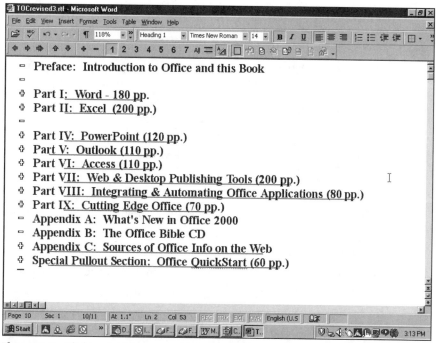

Figure 5-2: Clicking 1 hides everything except the top-level headings in your outline.

✦ **Click Show First Line Only** to see only the first line of all the paragraphs in your document (of all the styles you're viewing).

✦ **Click Show/Hide Formatting** to toggle formatting on and off. In general, though it varies from template to template, every heading style has its own character formatting, which can be distracting when all you want to do is organize your document.

We'll look at the other buttons on the Outlining toolbar in the next section.

Creating and Modifying Outlines

All you have to do to create an outline is assign each level of the outline the appropriate heading style: Heading 1 for top-level heads, Heading 2 for subheads, and so on. You can write your outline first, and then assign heading styles as appropriate, or you can assign heading styles as you go along. It doesn't matter.

Rearranging your outline

Rearranging the order of your outline is also easy. If you're not already in Outline View, choose View ➪ Outline to get there. The first five buttons on the left end of the Outlining toolbar are controls for quickly and easily reorganizing your outline — and your thoughts. Place your cursor anywhere inside the outline element you want to rearrange, and then press the appropriate button. From left to right, the buttons are as follows:

✦ **Promote.** This moves the selected item one notch higher in the hierarchy by assigning it the next-highest outline level.

✦ **Demote.** This moves the selected item one notch lower in the hierarchy, assigning it the next-lowest outline level.

✦ **Demote to Body Text.** This assigns the normal style to the selected item.

✦ **Move Up.** This moves the selected item above the item above it. The outline level doesn't change.

✦ **Move Down.** This moves the selected item below the item below it. Again, the outline level doesn't change.

Using outline paragraph levels

Although the Heading 1, 2, 3, etc., styles are assigned outline levels 1, 2, 3, and can't be changed, you can apply the same outline levels to other paragraph styles. You could choose to make Normal style correspond to outline level 1 just like Heading 1 style, if you wished. This gives you enormous flexibility in designing your outline.

There are nine outline levels in all. You can't change the outline levels assigned to various paragraph styles directly from Outline View, oddly enough; instead, you have to return to Normal or Print Layout View. Once you've done that, click on the paragraph you want to apply an outline level to, and then either choose Format ➪ Paragraph, or right-click and choose Paragraph from the pop-up menu. Either method will open the Paragraph dialog box shown in Figure 5-3.

Choose an outline level from the Outline Level drop-down list. To remove an existing outline level, choose Body Text.

The effects can't be seen in Normal or Print Layout View (see Figure 5-4), which is the strength of using outline paragraph levels: unlike heading styles, they allow you to "invisibly" outline a document. You could, for example, use levels simply as way to remind yourself which paragraphs are most important, in the event you have to later shorten the document, without someone reading a printed copy ever being able to tell.

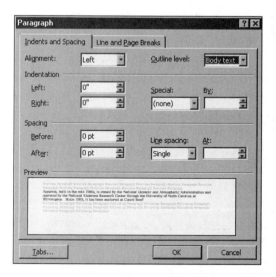

Figure 5-3: The Paragraph dialog box allows you to apply one of nine outline levels to your paragraph styles.

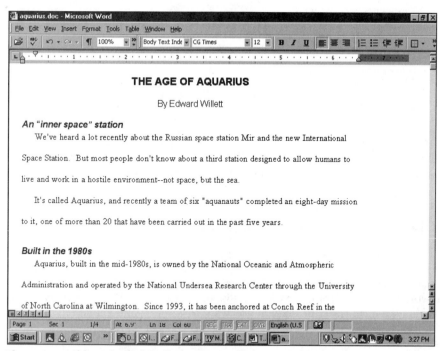

Figure 5-4: Although the heading styles applied are readily apparent in Normal view, you can't tell by looking here, or on the printed page, which outline levels were applied to the individual paragraphs.

To view the results of your outline paragraph levels, switch to Outline View (see Figure 5-5). Level 1 paragraphs are flush with the left margin, Level 2 paragraphs are indented, Level 3 paragraphs are indented still further. Body text paragraphs are always indented one level further than the heading level they are within. Note that the paragraph outline levels are independent of the heading levels.

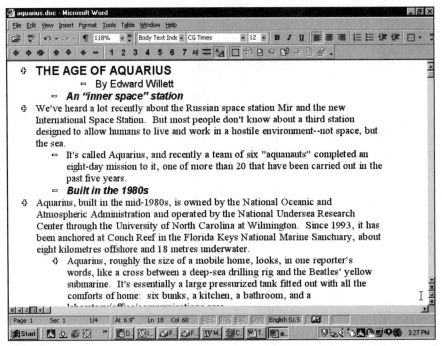

Figure 5-5: In Outline View, the outline levels applied to the paragraphs become clear.

Using the outline to navigate

An outline not only keeps you organized, it also makes it easier to move around in a lengthy document. By going to Outline View and collapsing a lengthy document to first-level heads alone, you can effectively shrink the document to a size much easier to work with — it might fit on one page instead of a hundred. Then you can simply click on the heading of the section you want to work on and expand it, make your changes, and then collapse that section again. This can save you a lot of scrolling.

Printing an outline

You can print an outline just like you would any other document. Go to Outline View, collapse or expand sections as you see fit, and then choose File ⇨ Print or click the Print button on the Standard toolbar.

Building a Table of Contents

A table of contents (TOC) is very similar to an outline, in that it displays the information contained within a document in the form of a series of headings, usually arranged in a hierarchical format. In Word, however, the big difference between an outline and a table of contents is that the table of contents also lists the page in the document on which the information can be found.

Creating and formatting a TOC

You could create a table of contents by printing an outline, printing the whole document, and then figuring out which page the various headings fall on. Fortunately, you don't have to. Word will automatically build a table of contents for you, and let you format it as you see fit. To create a table of contents:

1. Apply a consistent series of paragraph styles to your document. The simplest ones to use are the same ones you use to create an outline: Heading 1, Heading 2, Heading 3, and so on. If you haven't used heading styles, however, you can still build a TOC, as long as you use a different style in your document for each level you want to show in the TOC: chapter heads, section heads, etc.

2. Place your insertion point where you want the TOC to be inserted into your document, then choose Insert ➪ Index and Tables, and click on the Table of Contents tab (see Figure 5-6).

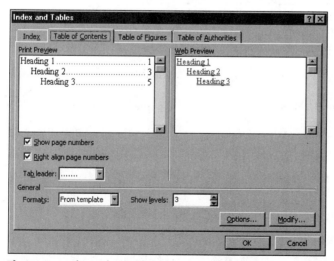

Figure 5-6: The Index and Tables dialog box includes controls for designing and formatting a table of contents for your document.

3. The window at the left shows you what your TOC will look like in a printed document; the window at the right shows you what your TOC will look like in an HTML document. In Print Preview, by default, page numbers are displayed and right-aligned, and a tab leader is already assigned. You can remove the page numbers and the right-alignment, and remove or change the tab leader, as you see fit. (In the HTML version, your TOC entries are direct links to the appropriate pages.)

4. By default, your TOC is formatted in the way your current template calls for, which is pretty basic if you're using the Normal template. Word offers you a list of other formats to choose from in a drop-down list. Select each to see it previewed, and then choose the one you want. Also, choose how many levels you want in your TOC.

5. Click Options to open the Table of Contents Options dialog box (see Figure 5-7).

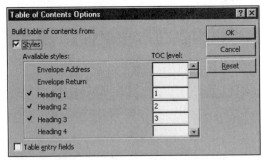

Figure 5-7: Set the styles Word should look for when selecting items for the TOC using the Table of Contents Options dialog box.

6. This dialog box lists all the currently available styles and shows you which ones Word is currently looking for to include in the TOC. By default, TOC level 1 is assigned to paragraphs with Header 1 style, TOC level 2 to those with Header 2, etc. If you outlined your document in the usual way, these default options should work well for your table of contents. If you didn't, however, you can scroll through the list of styles to find the ones that you did apply to your headings and indicate which level of the TOC you'd like items bearing those styles to appear as. Type the TOC level you'd like to assign to it in the space next to each style's name.

7. Click OK to return to the Index and Tables dialog box.

8. Click OK to insert the TOC into your document (see Figure 5-8).

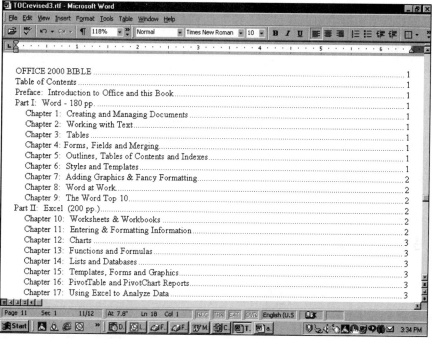

Figure 5-8: A newly inserted table of contents looks like this.

Keeping your TOC current

The entries in the Table of Contents are built using field codes. This is helpful, because as headings and page numbers change due to editing of the document, you can keep the TOC current simply by updating the field codes. To do so, right-click on any entry in the TOC and choose Update Field. This opens the little dialog box shown in Figure 5-9.

Choose whether you want to update the page numbers alone or the page numbers and the TOC entries' names, and then click OK.

Cross-Reference For more information on editing, formatting, and updating field codes, see Chapter 4, "Forms, Fields, and Merging."

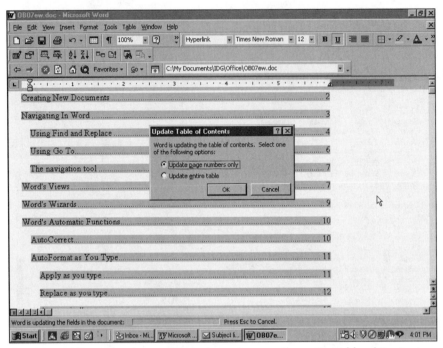

Figure 5-9: You can update page numbers alone, or the entire Table of Contents, automatically.

Building a Table of Figures

A table of figures is a list of all the figures, equations, or illustrations in a document. Building one is very similar to a building a table of contents: Word looks for a set of elements that all have the same style (the Bullet style, for instance; another common choice is the style applied to captions, as each figure is probably accompanied by one) and places them in a table linked to the pages they appear on. To create a table of figures (TOF):

1. Consistently apply styles to your figures or their captions.

2. Place your insertion point where you want the TOF to appear, and then choose Insert ➪ Index and Tables, and click on the Table of Figures tab (see Figure 5-10).

3. Word shows you what your TOF will look like in print and in an HTML document. For the print version, you can choose whether or not to display page numbers and if you want them right-aligned with a tab leader, whether to include a label and number (e.g., Figure 3, Figure 4), and which items you want to include in the table: Captions (the default), Equations, Figures, or Tables. (By repeating this process and changing this option, you can create separate tables listing each type of item.)

4. Choose which format to apply to your table of figures.

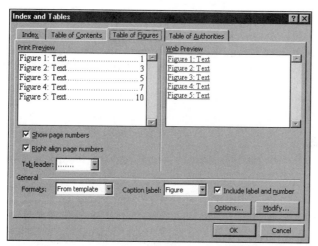

Figure 5-10: The Table of Figures tab in the Index and Tables dialog box includes all the controls you need for creating and formatting a table of figures.

5. Click Options to open the Table of Figures Options dialog box (see Figure 5-11). Choose the style you want Word to look for when selecting the items to be included in your TOF.

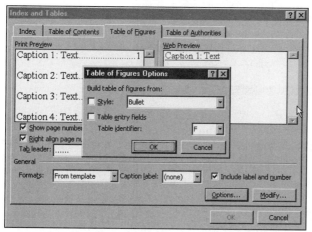

Figure 5-11: Use this dialog box to specify the style Word should look for when finding the items you want included in your table of figures.

6. Click OK to return to the Index and Tables dialog box.

7. Click OK to insert the TOF into your document.

Building a Table of Authorities

A table of authorities is used primarily in legal documents: it's a list of references made to other legal documents. Although the process is essentially the same as building a table of contents or a table of figures, marking the citations you want to add to the table is a little more complicated than simply assigning each the same style.

Marking citations

To mark citations:

1. Select the first full citation.

2. Choose Insert ⇨ Index and Tables; select the Table of Authorities tab.

3. Click Mark Citation. This opens the Mark Citation dialog box shown in Figure 5-12.

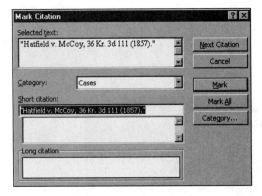

Figure 5-12: Mark your citations using this dialog box before creating your table of authorities.

4. In the Selected Text box, edit the long citation until it looks the way you want it to appear in the table of authorities. (You can also format it using keyboard shortcuts such as Ctrl+B to bold it, Ctrl+I to italicize it, etc.)

5. Select the category that applies to the citation from the Category drop-down list.

6. In the Short Citation box, enter any short versions of the citation that appear in the document, so Word can search for them.

7. To mark a single citation, click Mark; to mark all the citations that match both the long and short versions you've just entered, click Mark All.

8. To move on to the next marked citation in the document, click Next Citation. To mark another citation, return to the document, highlight it, and then repeat the steps above.

9. Once you've marked all your citations, Click Close.

Inserting your TOA

You can insert a table of authorities (TOA) just as you would a table of contents or a table of figures. Place your insertion point where you want the TOA to appear; then, as before, open the Index and Tables dialog box. From the Table of Authorities tab:

1. Click the category of citation you want to include in your TOA, or click All to include them all.

2. Choose the format you want to use from the Formats list box.

3. If you want to replace any instance of five or more page references to the same citation with the text "passim," make sure the Use Passim check box is checked.

4. If you want to keep long citations' original formatting in the TOA, make sure Keep Original Formatting is checked.

5. Click OK.

Creating an Index

Personally, I can think of few things more annoying than a lengthy reference article or book without an index—especially these days, when more and more people are accustomed to the search function built into so many Web sites. A good index isn't as handy as that, but it's as close as you can get to it in a print document.

Creating an index by hand is a tedious and difficult task. Fortunately, Word can simplify the procedure for you somewhat (although it can't take it out of your hands altogether). Just as with building the various sorts of tables discussed earlier, Word does require you to first mark the words or phrases that are to be included in the index. You can either do this one word or phrase at a time, or you can use a concordance file to semi-automate the process.

By marking words and phrases

To create an index by marking individual words and phrases:

1. Start at the very beginning (a very good place to start). Locate the first word or phrase you want to include in the index.

2. Highlight it, and then choose Insert ➪ Index and Tables.

3. Click the Index tab; choose Mark Entry. This opens the Mark Index Entry dialog box (see Figure 5-13). The word or phrase you highlighted appears in the Main Entry box.

4. If you want to add another word or phrase as a subentry under the main entry, type it into the Subentry box.

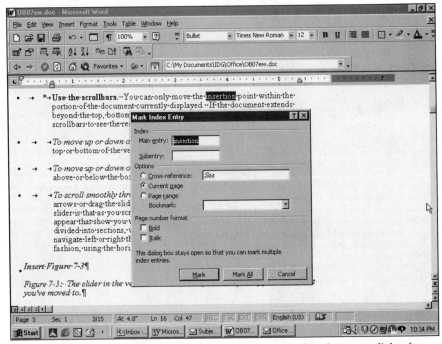

Figure 5-13: Build an index word by word using the Mark Index Entry dialog box.

5. Sometimes, instead of giving a page number, you want to point readers to a different entry in the index. If that's the case, click the Cross-reference radio button and enter the appropriate text in the Cross-reference box.

6. By default, Word inserts the page number of the highlighted word or phrase into the index. This is what the Current Page option does.

7. If you'd prefer to have Word insert a range of pages instead of a single page number, click Page Range. (You can only do this if you've already bookmarked the range; you select the range by choosing the correct bookmark from the drop-down list.)

8. If you'd like page numbers to be in bold or italic, click the appropriate Page Number Format check boxes.

9. Once you're satisfied with your choices, click Mark to mark the current selection as you've indicated, or click Mark All to mark every instance of the highlighted text within the document.

10. Repeat this procedure with every word or phrase you want to add to the index.

Using a concordance file

The other method of creating an index, with the use of a concordance file, is particularly useful if many of the documents you create contain the same key words or phrases. If you're already looking for a tool on any of the Word toolbars to help you create a concordance file, you can stop looking: it doesn't exist. A concordance file is simply a separate Word file, set up as a two-column table.

 Cross-Reference See Chapter 3, "Tables," for detailed information on how to create a table in Word.

Creating a concordance file

To create a concordance file:

1. Create a two-column table.

2. In the left column, enter the text you want Word to search for and mark as an index entry.

3. In the right column, enter what you want to appear in the index for that entry. You can create a subentry by typing the main entry followed by a colon, and then the text for the subentry.

4. Do the same for every other word or phrase you want Word to search for and create an index entry for.

5. When you're done, save the concordance file. (You can use any name you want.)

Marking index entries

Once you have a concordance file, you can use it to quickly mark index entries in any document. To do so:

1. Open the document you want to index.

2. Choose Insert ⇨ Index and Tables; click the Index tab (see Figure 5-14).

3. Choose AutoMark.

4. Word shows you the standard Open File dialog box; find the concordance file, and then click Open. Word searches for the words and phrases you entered in the left-hand column and marks them as you indicated in the right-hand column.

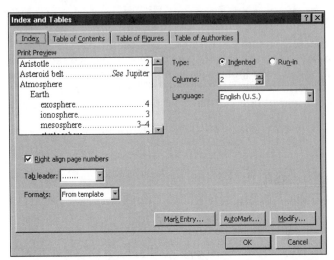

Figure 5-14: The Index tab of the Index and Tables dialog box controls the appearance of your index.

Building your index

Once you've marked all the entries for your index, either one at a time or by using a concordance file, you're ready to create your index:

1. Place your insertion point wherever you want the index to appear (typically at the end of the document, but it doesn't have to be).

2. Choose Insert ➪ Index and Tables. This again opens the dialog box shown in Figure 5-14.

3. Select a format for your index from the Format drop-down list. You can see what each format looks like in the Print Preview box.

4. Fine-tune the formatting with the other controls: you can right-align the page numbers and add a tab leader, change the number of columns used to display the index, and choose to indent subentries or simply run them straight on after the main entry.

5. Once you're satisfied with your formatting choices, click OK. Your index will be automatically inserted into your document in a new section of its own.

Updating your index

As with the three types of tables (table of contents, table of figures, and table of authorities), what you really end up with is a series of field codes, which you can update at any time to reflect the changing page numbers of the words and phrases you've marked as index entries. Just place the insertion point anywhere in the index and press F9, or right-click and choose Update Field from the pop-up menu.

Summary

In this chapter, you learned about some of organizational tools Word provides to help you and your readers find your mutual ways around your documents more easily. Some important points included the following:

✦ An outline is a hierarchical listing of the main points of a document.

✦ By using Word's built-in headings styles (Heading 1 for main headings, Heading 2 for subheads, etc.), you can easily create an outline that will aid you both in organizing your document and in moving around in it.

✦ Outline View makes the organization of your document very clear by automatically indenting each level of heading further than the one above it.

✦ With the tools on the Outlining toolbar, which shows up automatically in Outline View, you can easily rearrange your outline, promote and demote items within it, and collapse and expand sections of it.

✦ You can apply any outline level to any style of paragraph, giving you greater flexibility in the organization of your outline. One possible use is to create an invisible outline that lets you organize your document without affecting its final appearance.

✦ Word can easily create a table of contents, a table of figures, or a table of authorities for you, which you can insert wherever you wish in your document and format as you like.

✦ Word can also help you build an index; you can either choose the words and phrases you want to add to your index one by one, or create a concordance file that contains words and phrases that occur in your document, and have Word add them to the index automatically.

✦ All tables and indexes really consists of a series of field codes, which means the page numbers they display can be automatically updated by clicking anywhere within any of the tables or the index and pressing F9.

✦   ✦   ✦

Styles and Templates

In this chapter you learn how useful styles and templates can be—and how easy they are to use. When getting a new word processor up and running, one of the first things to do is set up templates for letterheads and faxes. When typing letters using the template, your address and logo are automatically put in their proper places.

Styles can be part of a template. I use templates mainly when typing longer documents to save time and avoid repetition when formatting headings, subheadings, lists, and so on. Using styles and templates ensure that your documents have a consistent look—the headings, subheadings, lists, etc., are all formatted in the same way.

What Are Styles?

A style is a set of text formats (which can include the size, the font, the indent, and the border) that is given a name. You can apply a style to a paragraph of text, or to a few words, and all the formatting is done at once. For example, in this book, all the major headings are one style, called "Heading 1," and all the second-level headings are another style, called "Heading 2."

Cross-Reference

Styles are also used to format automatic tables of contents and outlines. See Chapter 5, "Outlines, Tables of Contents, and Indexes," for more information.

One of the major advantages of using styles is that when you make a change to a style (for example, you decide to change the font of your headings) all the paragraphs using that style are also changed, throughout your document. This saves you searching through your document and changing each paragraph individually.

Paragraph and character styles

There are two types of styles: paragraph and character.

✦ **Paragraph styles.** These styles, as the name implies, format a whole paragraph. Paragraph styles can include not just font type and size, but any formatting that can be applied to paragraphs, including alignment, indents, and justification. The style called "Normal" is the default paragraph style. This means that if you do not choose another style, all text is formatted with the Normal style.

Caution   Be aware that there is both a Normal style and a Normal template (covered later in this chapter) — it's easy to confuse the two.

✦ **Character styles.** These styles are used to format words and phrases instead of whole paragraphs. Unlike paragraph styles, they do not include alignment, indents, spacing, etc. You could use a character style if you regularly need to highlight words in your document by making them bold, underlined, or italic. The character style called "Default Paragraph Font" contains the same character formatting information as the Normal paragraph style. (You can use a paragraph style as a character style — it just ignores all the alignment and indent information.) Character styles can only include the formatting options that are available when you choose Format ➪ Font, Format ➪ Borders and Shading, or Tools ➪ Language.

Tip   One of the advantages of using a character style is that you can use it to change the look of text without changing the size. For example, you may want to use blue, bold Arial text whenever you refer to one of your company's products. You can select the product name and apply the character style; the text size, whatever it is, remains the same.

Saving style information

When you save any document, both the character and paragraph styles used within it are also automatically saved, so they're automatically available the next time you edit that document. However, if you want to use those styles in another document, you'll have to copy them from the first document to the second. If you find you need to use the same styles over and over again in a multitude of documents, it's time to create a template.

What Are Templates?

A template is a special Word document with the filename extension .DOT that is used to maintain a consistent look from document to document. Word comes with templates for many common types of documents, including letters and faxes, memos, reports, newsletters, and Web pages.

In a template, all the unchanging items — the company logo and company name and address, for example, in the case of a letterhead — are inserted automatically. As a result, when you create a document using a template, all the fixed text and pictures are already in place, and you only need to enter your additional text.

How templates relate to styles

Templates also contain styles, as well as macros and any changes that have been made to Word's default menus, keyboard shortcuts, and toolbar settings. Using the styles included with the template ensures that all documents created using that template will use the same fonts, sizes, alignment, etc. For example, in the Professional Letter template (see Figure 6-1) styles are provided for the company name, address lines, salutation, body text, and closing.

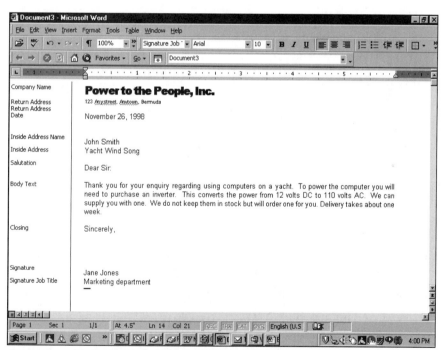

Figure 6-1: This letter was typed using a template. Different styles (shown in the column down the left side) are used to format the various sections of the letter.

The default Normal template

Actually, all documents are based on templates — even the blank document Word opens automatically when you start the program. The default template is called Normal.dot; if you haven't chosen another template, that's the one you're working with.

The Template That Wrote This Book

Templates are very useful for long documents. This book is a good example: It was written using a special template created by IDG Books Worldwide for all the books in its *Bible* series.

The page formats and the styles for the headings, bullets, lists, and so on, which all stay the same from book to book, are all stored in the template. This ensures that all the *Bible* books have the same "look," and also makes the formatting of each book a quick and simple task.

In addition to the many templates you can use as is or modify, Word provides several wizards, mini-programs that can help you automatically create faxes, letters, and other documents.

Cross-Reference For more information on wizards, see Chapter 1, "Creating and Managing Documents."

Applying Styles

The Normal template includes several built-in styles. You can use them as they are, or change them to suit yourself. Later in this chapter you'll learn how to create your own styles and modify them, but in this section you'll simply apply them.

Applying a style with the toolbar

The two easiest ways of applying a style are to use the Formatting toolbar or a keyboard shortcut. Here's how to use the toolbar:

1. If the Formatting toolbar is not visible, choose View ⇨ Toolbars, and then select the Formatting toolbar to switch it on.

2. Select the text to be formatted as follows:

   • If you want to apply a style to a whole paragraph, place the insertion point anywhere in the paragraph.

   • If you want to apply a style to several consecutive paragraphs, highlight the paragraphs to be changed.

   • If you want to apply a style to selected text only, highlight the text to be changed.

3. Click on the arrow at the right of the Style drop-down list on the Formatting toolbar to open a list of available styles (see Figure 6-2).

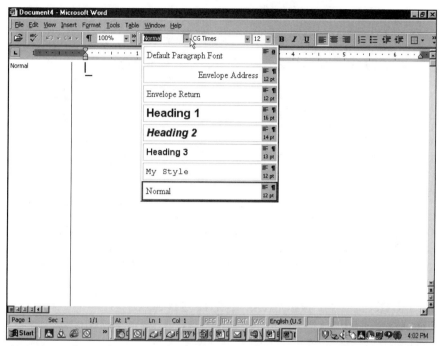

Figure 6-2: The Style drop-down list shows all the styles currently available for you to apply.

Note

In Figure 6-2, note that all of the styles except Default Paragraph Font have a paragraph symbol in the gray box at the right end. It has an underlined "a." That tells you it's a character style.

4. Click on the style you want to apply. If you simply placed your insertion point somewhere in a paragraph, that paragraph changes to the new style; if you highlighted several paragraphs, all of them will change to the new style. If you just highlighted a few words, the formatting is only applied to those words.

Tip

If the list of styles becomes long, you may find yourself wasting time scrolling up and down to find the style you want. Try this trick: Click on the Style drop-down arrow and then type the first letter of the style you are looking for. For example, press H if you are looking for Heading 1. The first style starting with H moves into view in the list, where you can select it with a click.

Applying a style with a keyboard shortcut

You can also apply styles with keyboard shortcuts; just select the paragraph(s) or text you want to apply the style to as outlined above, and then press the appropriate key combination. Table 6-1 lists the keyboard shortcuts assigned by default to the Normal template.

Table 6-1 Built-In Styles		
Style Name	**Main Features**	**Shortcut Key**
Heading 1	Arial, 16 pt, bold	Ctrl+Alt+1
Heading 2	Arial, 14 pt, bold, italic	Ctrl+Alt+2
Heading 3	Arial, 13 pt, bold	Ctrl+Alt+3
Normal	Times New Roman, 10 pt	Ctrl+Shift+N

Note If you apply a style containing certain character formatting options such as bold or italic to text that already has that formatting, the existing formatting is canceled out. For example, if you bold some text and then apply a style that includes bold text, the existing bold text will no longer be bold. To avoid this, select the text and remove the formatting by pressing Ctrl+SPACE before applying the new style.

Alternative ways to apply styles

Word provides many way to apply styles to your documents. The following sections explore these other methods.

Using AutoCorrect

Word can automatically apply some styles as you type. For example, you can set Word to apply the style Heading 1 to the text you've just typed whenever you press Enter twice. These options are controlled by choosing Tools ➪ AutoCorrect, and then opening the AutoFormat As You Type tab.

Cross-Reference For detailed information about using AutoCorrect, see Chapter 1, "Creating and Managing Documents."

Using Repeat

Another method is to use Repeat:

1. Apply the style to the first paragraph you want to format.

2. Move your insertion point to the next paragraph you want to format.

3. Choose Edit ➪ Repeat Style, or press Ctrl+Y.

4. Move to the next paragraph you want to format and repeat Step 3.

5. Continue until you've applied the style to all the paragraphs you want.

Using the Format Painter

When applying styles to a document you have already typed, you often want to format all the headings the same way. One method is to use the Format Painter:

1. Apply the style you want to the first heading in your document.

2. Highlight the heading or place the insertion point anywhere inside it.

3. Click the Format Painter tool on the Standard toolbar to switch it on.

4. Click on the next heading you want to apply the style of the first heading to. It will change, and the Format Painter will automatically switch off.

5. Repeat Steps 3 and 4 until you reach the end of your document.

You've probably already recognized the problem with the Format Painter: It requires you to change headings one at a time, and if you decide to change the heading style later, you'll have to go back and change each heading individually again. Styles give you much more power.

Removing a style from text

If you apply a style to a paragraph by mistake, you can re-apply the default Normal style by selecting the paragraph and pressing Ctrl+Shift+N.

Similarly, if you have applied a character style and want to remove it, select the text and change it back to Default Paragraph Font by pressing Ctrl+SPACE.

Seeing which styles have been applied

You can see which style has been applied to a paragraph by clicking on it and looking at the Style box on the Formatting toolbar.

If you're in Outline or Normal view, you can also have Word display style names down the left side of the screen (see Figure 6-3). If you use styles a lot, this can be very helpful.

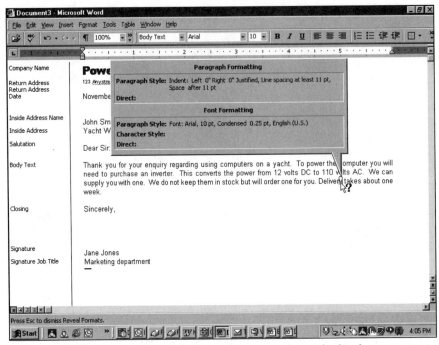

Figure 6-3: You can make Word display style names alongside the document text.

Displaying style names

To make Word display style names:

1. Make sure you are in Normal or Outline view.

2. Choose Tools ⇨ Options, and go to the View tab.

3. In the Style Area Width box in the Outline and Normal Options section at the bottom of the View tab, enter how wide you would like the area used to display style names to be.(One inch is a convenient width.)

4. Click OK. The style names are now displayed down the left side of the document. You can adjust the width of the style names display area by dragging the onscreen divider left or right.

Using the Show/Hide Paragraph tool

If you switch on the Show/Hide Paragraph tool on the Formatting toolbar, you'll also see a small black spot to the left of each paragraph that has had a style other than Normal applied to it.

Tip

You can find out more information about how a paragraph has been formatted by choosing Help ⇨ What's This? A question mark will appear beside your mouse pointer. Click on the text you want to know about: A box will appear telling you what paragraph and character formatting has been applied (see Figure 6-3). Note that this box does not show you the style name.

Creating Styles

You have two ways to create a style:

✦ Name a style and use dialog boxes to select the formatting features you require. This is the most complete method, as it gives you access to some features that are not easy to see (such as rules for page endings and special line spacing).

✦ Create the style using some existing text, which you have already formatted the way you want. In effect, you are giving Word an example of what the style should look like.

Creating a style using dialog boxes

To begin, choose Format ⇨ Style. This opens the Style dialog box (see Figure 6-4). To continue:

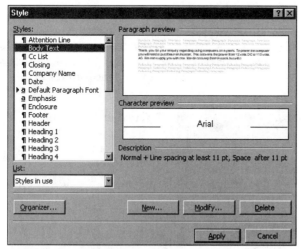

Figure 6-4: The Style dialog box lists the existing styles and describes their characteristics.

1. Click the New button. This opens the New Style dialog box (see Figure 6-5).

Figure 6-5: The New Style dialog box lets you set the attributes for a brand-new style.

2. Type a name in the Name box. Note that the style name is case-sensitive. This means that you could create a style named Heading and another one called heading. The style name can be up to 253 characters. You cannot use the backslash(\), curly braces ({ }), or the semicolon (;), but you can use spaces.

Tip   Names appear in alphabetical order, so it's a good idea to name related styles in a similar way. For example: Head 1, Head 2, Head 3, rather than Major head, Subhead and Sub-subhead. This makes styles easier to find because they end up grouped together in the Style list box.

3. Click on the Format button to display its menu (see Figure 6-6). This gives you access to the formatting dialog boxes, which are normally accessed by choosing Format from the menu bar. The Preview box shows a thumbnail view of what your paragraph looks like, and the Description box lists the features of this style.

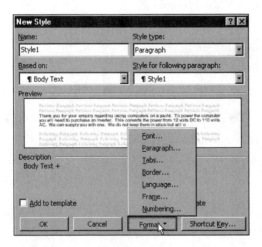

Figure 6-6: The Format pop-up menu of the New Style dialog box lets you fine-tune the formatting of your new style.

4. Other options in this dialog box include the following:

- **Style type.** You can choose character or paragraph. See the section earlier in this chapter describing the difference between paragraph and character styles.

- **Based on.** If you base your new style on an existing style, all the formatting of the existing style is used; you need only make the changes in format where the two styles differ. For example, if your base style is Arial 12-point normal, your new style will also be Arial 12-point normal. If you want your new style to be bold and italicized, you only need to add those two formatting instructions. Also, if the base style changes — say, the font is changed to Times New Roman instead of Arial — then all the styles based on it change, too. This is particularly useful for keeping documents looking consistent. Suppose you want all headings in a document to use the same font. Create the major heading and use it as the base style, and then base the rest of the headings on this style. But be careful — you might find yourself changing a base style without realizing that all the dependent styles are going to change!

- **Style for following paragraph.** This feature sets which style will be used in the paragraph following any paragraph that uses the style you're currently defining. For example, suppose you're defining your Heading 1 style. If you know that every time you use the Heading 1 style, the next paragraph in the document should be in Normal style, then choose Normal here.

- **Shortcut Key.** This opens the Customize Keyboard dialog box (see Figure 6-7), with the insertion point flashing in the Press New Shortcut Key box. Type in the shortcut you would like to use; for example, Ctrl+Alt+H. If it has already been assigned to another function, Word informs you in the area labeled Currently Assigned to. You can choose to assign the style to this shortcut anyway, or try to find one that is unassigned by pressing Backspace and entering another shortcut. When you're happy with your shortcut, click Assign, and then Close.

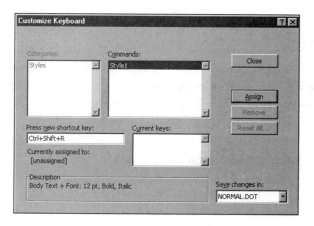

Figure 6-7: The Customize Keyboard dialog box lets you change currently assigned keyboard shortcuts and create new ones.

- **Add to template.** New and modified styles are automatically saved with the document, but not the current template. If you want to save the new style information so that it is available for all new documents created with this template, you need to check this option.

- **Automatically update.** This has no effect when using the Normal template. If you are using any other template and change the format of a paragraph, the style gets redefined and all the paragraphs using the same style are automatically changed. This can surprise you if you are not expecting it! We'll look at how to modify styles in the next section of this chapter.

Tip   Word has several ready-made styles for you to use besides the ones you see in the Normal template. To access them, choose Format ⇨ Style and click the drop-down arrow on the List box. Choose All Styles and you'll see a long list. Click on any style to see a preview and description. Click Apply to add it to the list of styles available in the document you're currently working on. Why waste time creating styles that already exist?

Creating a style by using an example

To create a style by using an example:

1. Format a paragraph the way you would like your style to look. Use any of the Word formatting tools, such as font, borders, indents, and so on.

2. Click anywhere in the paragraph. You should see the insertion point flashing.

3. Click on a style name (not on the drop-down arrow) in the Style box on the Formatting toolbar. The style name becomes highlighted. (It doesn't matter which style name it is.)

4. Type the new style name and press Enter. The new style name is added to the list and assigned to your paragraph.

Modifying Styles

Just as there are two ways of creating styles, there are two ways of modifying them. You can use dialog boxes or use an example. If you are not using the Normal template, then you can also choose to have some styles updated automatically. This feature is discussed in the section "Creating a style using dialog boxes."

Modifying a style using dialog boxes

To modify a style using dialog boxes:

1. Choose Format ⇨ Style.

2. Select the style you wish to modify from the Styles list and click Modify.

3. The Modify Style dialog box appears. You can now change any of the settings; click on the Format button or click the Shortcut key button. These features are described in the section "Creating a style using dialog boxes."

4. When you have finished, you'll find that all text formatted with the same style has changed.

Modifying a style by using an example

This is a quick and easy way to modify a style.

1. Select any paragraph using the style you wish to change by clicking anywhere in the paragraph or by highlighting some text.

2. Make whatever changes to the paragraph you want to make a part of the modified style.

3. Click on the name of the paragraph's original style in the Style drop-down list on the Formatting toolbar. The Modify Style prompt appears (see Figure 6-8), asking if you want to change the style or revert to the previous formatting for the style.

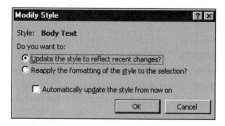

Figure 6-8: The Modify Style prompt gives you the option of changing a style or reverting to the previous formatting.

4. Click OK or press Enter to modify the style.

5. You should find that all paragraphs using the same style have changed.

Changing the Normal style

You cannot change the Normal style using this last method (modifying by example). You can use the dialog box method, but there is an easier way if you just want to change the default font. Choose Format ➪ Font, make your changes, and then click Default. You are asked whether you want to change the default font, as it will affect all new documents based on the current template. If you reply Yes, then the Normal style changes.

Copying, deleting, and renaming a style

You can copy a style from one document or template to another using the Organizer. To access the Organizer, choose Format ➪ Style and then click Organizer (see Figure 6-9).

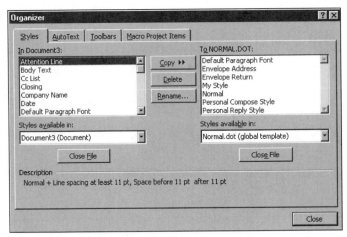

Figure 6-9: The Organizer dialog box lets you copy styles from one document or template to another.

This dialog box has two sides: In (on the left) and To (on the right). You can open and close the files of your choice on either side. If one of them shows the incorrect document or template, click Close File under the incorrect one first, and then click Open File to bring up the Open dialog box. Make sure you have the correct setting in the Files of Type box. To open a document choose Word Documents and to open a template choose Document Templates.

✦ **To copy a style** using the Organizer, make sure the source file is on one side and the destination file is on the other. Highlight the style you want to copy by clicking on it, and then click Copy. You should see the selected style appear in the destination file's style list.

✦ **To delete a style** click on the style name and then click Delete. However, you cannot delete the two built-in styles from the Normal template.

✦ **To rename a style** click on the style name on either side of the dialog box and then click Rename. Type a new name for the style, click OK, and then click Close.

Using the Style Gallery

The Style Gallery is a tool to help you find styles, no matter which template they are in. It shows you an example of the style and tells you in which template it is saved. To use the Style Gallery:

1. Choose Format ⇨ Theme. Click Style Gallery to open the Style Gallery dialog box (see Figure 6-10).

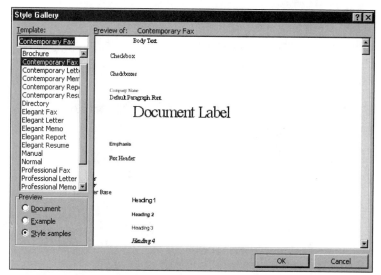

Figure 6-10: The Style Gallery dialog box can help you find the style you want from all those Word has to offer.

2. Select the template you want to look at.

3. Click the Document radio button to see what your document would look like formatted with the styles in the selected template. Click Example to see a sample document formatted with the template. Click Style samples to see a document showing a sample of each style in the template.

Once you have found a style you wish to use, you can copy it into your template using the Organizer.

Applying a Template

As noted earlier, when you create a new document by clicking the New button on the Standard toolbar, you are creating a document based on the Normal (default) template.

However, if you create a new document using the menu instead of the toolbar, you can choose from a variety of other templates. Choose File ➪ New to open the New dialog box (see Figure 6-11). The templates available are grouped by type under various tabs. Word has several built-in templates and you can add your own later. You can also use the wizards supplied with Word to create your own documents

Cross-Reference   See Chapter 1, "Creating and Managing Documents," for more details on using wizards.

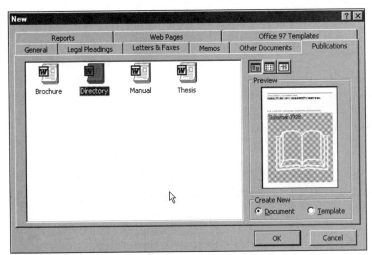

Figure 6-11: The New dialog box offers a multitude of templates for you to choose from.

Creating a new document with a template

To use a template, select the tab you require and then the template. When you create a document using a template other than Normal, it has no filename; you can treat it just as you would a document created using the Normal template and name it whatever you wish.

Applying a template to an existing document

To apply a template to a document you have already created, choose Tools ➪ Templates and Add-Ins. The dialog box shows the current template in use. Click Attach to select another template to use with the document. The styles from the attached template are added to the current document. Any fixed text or pictures stored in the template are not added.

You can choose whether to automatically update the document with the styles in the saved template each time you open the document.

To also add fixed text or pictures from a template to an existing document:

1. Choose File ➪ New, and select the appropriate template. All the fixed material in the template will appear.

2. Click where you want to insert the text that has already been typed.

3. Choose Insert ➪ File and locate the document you typed.

4. Save the document under a new name.

Creating a Template

You can create a new template in two ways:

✦ From scratch

✦ From an existing document

Creating a template from scratch

To create a template from scratch:

1. Choose File ➪ New to open the New dialog box.

2. Click on the Template radio button in the Create New section of the dialog box and then click OK. The document name at the top of the window will be Template1 instead of Document1.

3. Create a document containing all the elements you would like to be part of your new template: text, pictures, styles, fields, forms, etc. You can also include macros, special toolbars or menus, AutoText, and shortcut key entries.

4. Save the document as usual. It will be automatically saved with the filename extension .DOT in the Templates folder.

Tip   To add a new tab to those on the New dialog box, add a new folder under the Templates folder and add one or more templates to that folder. A new tab by that name, containing the templates you've stored in that folder, will automatically appear the next time you open the New dialog box. Note that the tab will not appear if your new folder doesn't contain any templates.

Creating a template from an existing document

If you have an existing document that you would like to use as a template—maybe you've created a document you've been using as your letterhead but you've only just learned about the template feature—follow these instructions:

1. Open the document you want to use as a template.

2. Choose File ➪ Save As. The Save As dialog box appears.

3. Type a name for your template, and then select Document Template in the Save as Type box. Word automatically switches you to your Templates folder.

4. Click Save.

Adding an automatic date field

In a template for a letterhead, memo, or fax, it's handy to include an automatic date field. The current date is automatically inserted in this field whenever you call up the template. To add an automatic date field, choose Insert ➪ Date and Time, and then choose the date format you prefer.

Cross-Reference   For more detailed information on using fields, see Chapter 4, "Forms, Fields, and Merging."

Modifying Templates

You can modify a template in much the same way you modify any other document. The difference is in the way you open it.

1. Choose File ➪ Open, to bring up the Open dialog box.

2. Choose Document Templates from the Files of Type box. Locate the folder in which the template is located.

3. Open your template.

4. Make the changes you require.

5. Save the template as usual.

Note You cannot save changes to a template when it is in use. If you created your current document by choosing File ➪ New and then selecting the template, you cannot save it as a template using the same name. You have to give it a different name, or cancel the procedure and use the File ➪ Open method described in the previous section.

Modifying the Normal Template

For certain features, you need not use the method described in the previous section to modify the Normal template. If you wish to change the default font, choose Format ➪ Font, select the font you wish to use, and click the Default button. You are prompted to verify that you really want to change the Normal template.

The same Default button appears in the Page Setup and Language dialog boxes. Choose File ➪ Page Setup to set the default paper size, printer bin, margins, and many other options. Choose Tools ➪ Language ➪ Set Language to select the default language for spell checking, the thesaurus, and grammar checking. (Some language dictionaries have to be purchased separately.)

To change any of the styles other than the Normal style in the Normal template, you need to open the template as instructed in the previous section.

Note You may have difficulty locating the file Normal.dot. (On my system it is in c:\Windows\Application Data\Microsoft Office\Templates.) You may need to do a search to find it on your system. Click Tools on the toolbar of the Open dialog box to search for document templates on your disk.

Summary

Styles and templates are special features used to make your documents look consistent in style and to save you repetitive work. This chapter covered the following points:

✦ A style is a set of formats that has been given a name.

✦ Word has several built-in styles in the Normal template, which are ready for you to use.

✦ Styles can be created using dialog boxes or by defining them by example.

✦ Styles can be modified; when they are, all text using that style in a document is changed automatically.

✦ Word can show you which styles have been assigned to each paragraph.

✦ The Style Gallery helps you find styles in various templates. The Organizer lets you copy styles from one template to another, and rename and delete styles.

✦ A template is a predesigned document that not only includes styles, but also text, pictures, menus, shortcut keys, and macros.

✦   ✦   ✦

Adding Graphics and Fancy Formatting

Word is more than just a glorified typewriter. You can also use it to add pictures, drawings, graphs, and other graphics to your document or add special formatting touches such as bulleted lists, columns, and borders. While Word isn't a full-featured desktop publishing program like Microsoft Publisher, it can still create a sharp, professional-looking, eye-catching design for just about any type of document.

Creating Bulleted and Numbered Lists

One of the most common types of "fancy formatting" is a bulleted or numbered list. You can create such a list with a combination of indents, tabs, and typing, or you can enlist Word's help to eliminate most of these concerns, so all you have to do is enter the information for each item. An example of each type of list is shown in Figure 7-1.

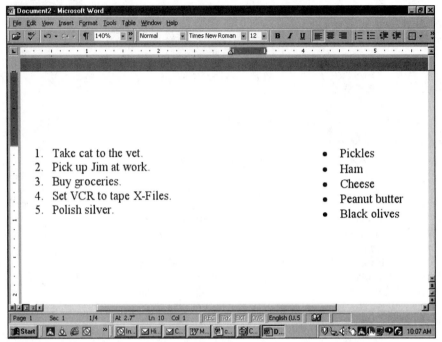

Figure 7-1: Word makes it easy to create numbered and bulleted lists like these.

Using the Formatting toolbar

The tools to create a bulleted or numbered list are right on the Formatting toolbar. To create a numbered list, click the Numbering button; to create a bulleted list, click the Bullets button.

When you click either button, Word inserts either a number or a bullet. Whenever you press Return at the end of a line, the next number or another bullet is inserted. When you've finished typing the list, press Return, and then press the Backspace key to delete the bullet or number for that row. After that you can continue typing normally.

Formatting your lists

The lists in Figure 7-1 show the default formatting for numbers and bullets. You're not limited to the defaults, however. You can format your numbered and bulleted lists any way you like. To do so, Choose Format ⇨ Bullets and Numbering. This opens the Bullets and Numbering dialog box (see Figure 7-2).

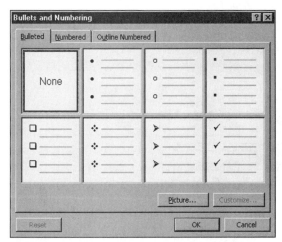

Figure 7-2: Choose the types of symbols and numerals you want to use in your bulleted and numbered lists in this dialog box.

Using the standard settings

The Bullets and Numbering dialog box has three tabs: Bulleted, Numbered, and Outline Numbered (which applies numbering to the various headings and subheadings of an outline). Choose the style of list you like from the options provided and click OK.

Note   The Bulleted tab has a button labeled Picture. This feature is brand-new in Office 2000: it lets you use any picture you like as a bullet. Clicking the Picture button opens the Clip Gallery. Choose the image you want to use as a bullet and click OK.

If you don't like any of the options Word provides, you can custom-design your bullet or numbering scheme by clicking Customize on whichever property sheet you've opened. Each of the resulting dialog boxes is similar, with slight differences.

Customizing bulleted lists

The Customize Bulleted List dialog box (see Figure 7-3) lets you choose any symbol you want to use as a bullet. You can choose from the six bullets shown at the top, or click Font to change the font from which those symbols are taken and apply other formatting options.

Cross-Reference   See Chapter 2, "Working with Text," for more detailed information on the Font dialog box.

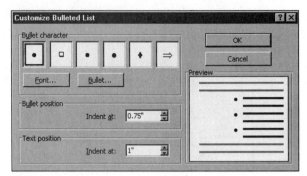

Figure 7-3: Word lets you choose any symbol you want to use as a bullet.

To use different symbols entirely, click Bullet. This opens the Symbol dialog box, from which you can choose any character from any symbol font installed on your computer.

Use the Bullet position and Text position controls to adjust the indentation of bullets and text from the left margin. By changing these you can get various effects, which are illustrated in the Preview box.

Customizing numbered lists

The Customize Numbered List dialog box is very similar to the Customize Bulleted List dialog box — it lets you set indents and choose and format a special font for your numbers. You can also choose a number style (1, 2, 3 or i, ii, iii, or even A, B, C, which aren't exactly numbers, but never mind) and choose whether to start the list at 1 or some other number.

The Customize Outline Numbered List dialog box is basically the same as the Customize Numbered List dialog box, except it lets you customize each of the nine possible levels of an outline. In addition, by clicking More you can change which styles are associated with which outline numbers and what character appears between the number and the start of the outline text, among other things.

Note   You can set the options for bulleted and numbered lists before you begin creating them; you can also change the formatting of a list after it's finished. Just place your insertion point anywhere inside the list, choose Format ➪ Bullets and Numbering, and customize it as described above. When you click OK, the new design is automatically applied to your list.

Using Columns

Arranging text in columns is a good way to break up an otherwise gray mass of print with a little white space. You can set columns before you begin entering text into a document, or you can apply columns to a document that's already underway.

To set columns:

1. Choose Format ⇨ Columns. This opens the Columns dialog box (see Figure 7-4).

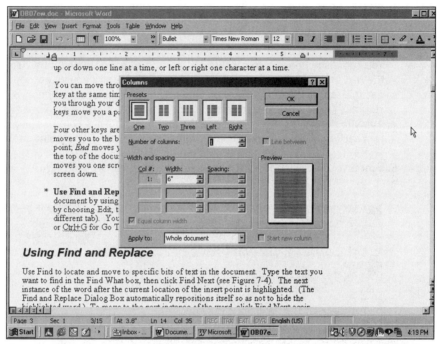

Figure 7-4: Setting your text in columns, using these controls, can make it more visually appealing.

2. Decide how many columns you want. Word offers you five preset column designs: One, Two, Three, Left, or Right. The latter two create pages with two columns of unequal width: If you choose Left, the left column is narrower than the right; if you choose Right, it's the other way around. If you want more columns, enter the number you want in the Number of Columns box.

3. By default, the check box marked Equal Column Width is checked. To specify different widths for different columns, uncheck it; then enter the width of each column in the Width boxes above it, followed by the amount of space you want between that column and the next one to the right in the Spacing boxes. The Preview box will show you roughly what your document will look like with those settings.

4. If you would like to draw a dividing line between columns, check the Line Between box.

5. Finally, use the Apply To drop-down list to choose whether to put the whole document into columns, or just use columns from the current location of your insertion point onward. If you choose the latter, you also have the option to have the columns start immediately, even if they're in the middle of a page, or check the Start New Column box to jump to a new page to start the columns. If you're already using columns, checking this box forces your current column to end, and any text after the insertion point will go into the next column on the same page.

Note   You can also choose to set a selected portion of text into columns. Just highlight the text you want in columns before beginning the procedures above; when you get to Step 5, the Apply To drop-down list will include the option of applying columns just to the selected text. If your document has more than one section, the Apply To drop-down list will include the option of applying columns just to the current section, the whole document, or just from your insertion point onward.

6. When you're satisfied with your selections, click OK (see Figure 7-5).

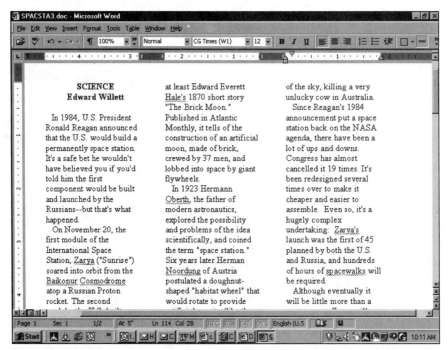

Figure 7-5: Text set in columns can be easier to read, and more pleasant to look at, than text that runs across the page. Note that you can only see what the columns will look like by using Print Layout view; Normal view shows only a single column.

Inserting Pictures and Graphics

Word's very name makes it clear that its primary function is processing text, but that doesn't mean it can't handle pictures. In fact, it handles them quite well. You have three ways to insert pictures into a Word document:

✦ You can insert a picture file from your own computer, a floppy, a CD, or some other data storage device.

✦ You can insert a picture from the Clip Gallery.

✦ You can input an image from a scanner or digital camera.

In addition, you can insert other specialized graphical elements such as AutoShapes, WordArt, a new drawing, or a chart.

Inserting a picture file

To insert a picture file:

1. Place your insertion point where you want the picture to appear.

2. Choose Insert ➪ Picture ➪ From File. This brings up the standard Open File dialog box.

3. Locate the picture file you want to insert. Double-click it or click Insert.

4. Word inserts the picture into your document (see Figure 7-6).

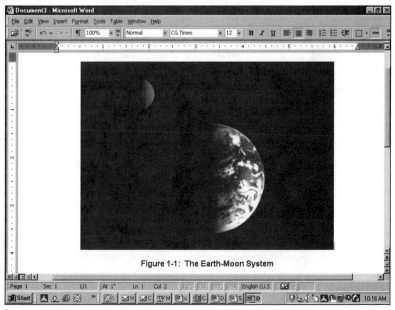

Figure 1-1: The Earth-Moon System

Figure 7-6: Word makes it easy to insert picture files into your documents.

Inserting a Clip Gallery clip

Although the Open File dialog box lets you easily identify files that are in a picture format supported by Word, finding the precise file you want can be difficult, especially if the files aren't clearly labeled. That's where Clip Gallery comes in.

Clip Gallery is a separate piece of software that catalogs images into categories and makes it easy to browse through those categories to find the file you want. You can also search Clip Gallery's collection of pictures by keyword.

Cross-Reference   For more details on using the Clip Gallery, see Chapter 53, "Universal Drawing and Graphics Features."

To insert a picture from the Clip Gallery:

1. Place your insertion point where you want to insert the picture.

2. Choose Insert ➪ Picture ➪ Clip Art. This opens the Clip Gallery.

3. In the Search for Clips box, type a keyword (or words) that describes the subject matter you want an illustration for. For example, in Figure 7-7 shows what results from entering the word "oil."

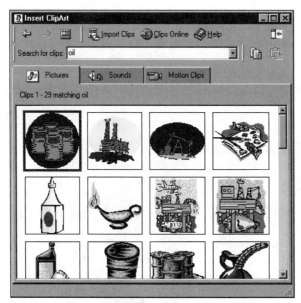

Figure 7-7: The Clip Gallery puts a well-organized collection of clip art at your fingertips. Here's a selection of clips related to oil.

4. Choose the artwork you want from those displayed. (If there are more than 60 clips that match your keyword, you'll find a "More clips" hyperlink once you've scrolled to the bottom.) Click on the clip you want to bring up the pop-up menu shown in Figure 7-8.

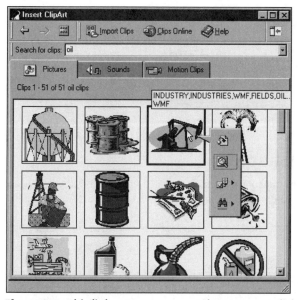

Figure 7-8: This little menu pops up whenever you click on a picture in the Clip Gallery.

5. This menu offers you four options. In this chapter, we're just concerned with the top two: Insert Picture and Preview Picture. Click Preview Picture to see a larger version of the selected clip; click Insert Picture to place it in your document.

6. Close Clip Gallery. The clip art you selected is now in your document.

Inserting an image from a scanner or camera

To insert an image from a scanner or camera, choose Insert ⇨ Picture ⇨ From scanner or camera. Windows presents you with a list of all the scanners or cameras connected to your computer; choose the one you want to use and decide whether you want the picture's resolution to be Web-quality or print-quality. (Print-quality is of higher resolution than Web-quality.) Then click Insert. To adjust the device's settings, click Custom Insert.

Advanced Picture Editing Tools

Word's picture-editing tools are fairly rudimentary. To get the most out of a scanned or digital-camera image, it's a good idea to first import it into a dedicated graphics or photo-editing program. All versions of Office come with Microsoft Photo Editor, which allows you to improve a photo's appearance, crop it, rotate it, and even apply a number of special effects. You can access it by clicking Start, then Programs ⇨ Office Tools ⇨ Microsoft Photo Editor.

In addition, some versions of Office include a powerful graphics and photo-editing application called Microsoft PhotoDraw. For detailed information on using PhotoDraw, see Chapter 50, "Using PhotoDraw." For additional information on Photo Editor, see Chapter 53, "Universal Drawing and Graphics Features."

Inserting AutoShapes

AutoShapes are shapes that Word can draw automatically. They include everything from boxes and ovals to arrows and starbursts. To insert an AutoShape:

1. Choose Insert ⇨ Picture ⇨ AutoShapes. This displays the AutoShapes toolbar (see Figure 7-9).

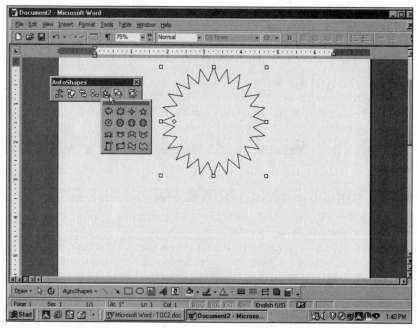

Figure 7-9: Here you can see the AutoShapes toolbar, one of its menus, and a 24-point starburst created by clicking on that menu. Note the diamond inside the shape; by clicking and dragging it, you can alter the starburst's appearance significantly.

2. Each button on the AutoShapes toolbar displays a different menu of shapes. Find the shape you want and click on it.

3. Your cursor changes to a crosshairs. Center the crosshairs where you want the center of the AutoShape to be and click. The AutoShape appears.

4. Most AutoShapes can be adjusted. Those that can display one or more yellow diamonds. Click and drag these diamonds to adjust the AutoShape.

5. When you're satisfied with your shape, click anywhere outside it to return to normal text editing mode.

Inserting WordArt

WordArt is a separate program that you can use in any of Office's applications to insert fancily formatted text. To insert WordArt in Word:

1. Choose Insert ➪ Picture ➪ WordArt. This opens the WordArt Gallery (see Figure 7-10).

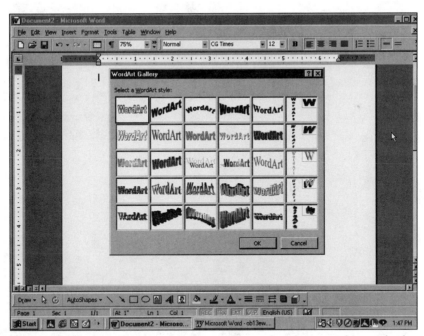

Figure 7-10: You can insert text in any of these colorful, eye-catching styles by using WordArt.

2. Choose the style of WordArt you want and double-click on it.

3. In the resulting dialog box, enter your text where it says Your text here; choose the font, size, and style (bold or italic) and click OK.

4. Your text, in the WordArt style you selected, will appear on the current page of your document. Drag it to where you want it, and edit it using the WordArt toolbar that appears at the same time.

5. When you're done, click anywhere outside the WordArt to deselect it and return to normal text editing mode.

Cross-Reference   For more detailed information on using WordArt, see Chapter 53, "Universal Drawing and Graphics Features."

Inserting a drawing

In addition to AutoShapes, Word has other powerful drawing tools. To access all of them, choose Insert ➪ Picture ➪ New Drawing. Word draws a frame (at the location of your insertion point) to contain the drawing, and opens the Drawing Toolbar (see Figure 7-11). (You can also open the Drawing Toolbar by choosing View ➪ Toolbars ➪ Drawing.)

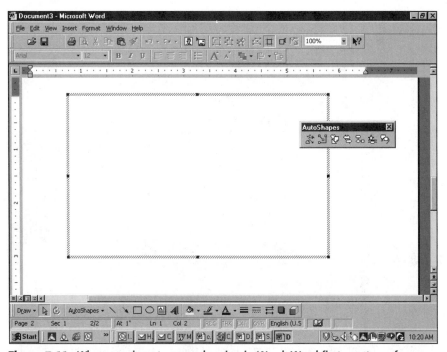

Figure 7-11: When you insert a new drawing in Word, Word first creates a frame, and then provides you with drawing tools just below the document area to help you create a drawing.

Use the tools in the Drawing toolbar to create the image you want within the frame, and then click anywhere outside the frame to return to normal editing mode.

Editing Pictures

No matter how you insert a picture, most of the ways you can edit it are the same. The most common change you'll want to make to pictures is to their size. Most will either be too large or too small when you first insert them.

Resizing a picture

To resize a picture, click on it. A set of eight handles will appear around it, forming a rectangle that closely frames the picture. To adjust the overall size of the picture without affecting the proportions of the image, click and drag any of the corner handles. To squash or elongate the picture horizontally or vertically, click and drag one of the handles on the sides (see Figure 7-12).

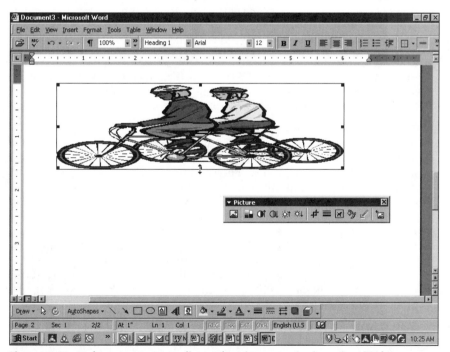

Figure 7-12: Unless you want to distort the picture you're inserting, it's better to use the corner handles to resize it instead of those along the sides. In this case, the bottom handle has been moved up.

Using the Picture tools

Also notice in Figure 7-12 that a new toolbar has appeared. The Picture toolbar contains other useful tools for editing your picture. From left to right, they are described as follows:

✦ **Insert Picture.** Clicking this button is equivalent to choosing Insert ➪ Picture ➪ From File.

✦ **Image Control.** You can use this to turn color pictures into black-and-white or into a watermark, a faded image often used to build backgrounds on Web pages (because they're faded, they don't interfere with text). Choose how you want the image displayed from the pull-down menu.

✦ **More Contrast; Less Contrast.** Click the one on the left to increase contrast; click the one on the right to decrease it.

✦ **More Brightness; Less Brightness.** Ditto the above, only this time the controls affect brightness instead of contrast.

✦ **Crop.** Click this and your pointer changes to a cropping tool. Click and drag the cropping tool on the handles to hide portions of your picture so they don't show up on the screen or when you print. (Don't worry, the hidden areas are still there — you can uncover them by choosing Crop again and dragging the handles out to their full extent.)

✦ **Line Style.** This lets you choose the weight of line you'd like AutoShapes and other drawings to be made of. You can also choose dotted, dashed, and other specially formatted lines. (Note that line style is disabled for pictures; you can't use it to create a border around a picture.)

✦ **Text wrapping.** This is a particularly important option when you're inserting a picture in Word, because the odds are good there's some text around it somewhere. From this drop-down menu, choose how you want the picture to interact with text. Five of the six possibilities are illustrated in Figure 7-13; the remaining one, Top and Bottom, places the graphic by itself, with text appearing only above and below it, not to its right or left.

✦ **Format picture.** This opens the Format Picture dialog box. It contains several property sheets that let you change the colors and lines making up graphics; adjust the size; change text wrapping options and horizontal alignment; crop the picture and alter its contrast and brightness; and even assign alternative text that will be displayed if the picture is posted to the Web and called up by a text-only browser.

✦ **Set transparent color.** Sometimes you'd like to get rid of the background behind an image, or let text show through part of a picture, but not other parts. Office lets you make one color in most pictures and some clip art transparent. In the printed document, the transparent area will be the same color as the paper underneath; on the Web, the page background will show through. To make a color transparent, click this button, and then click the resulting pointer inside the picture on the color you want to make transparent.

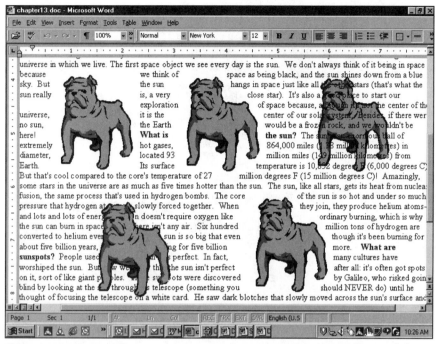

Figure 7-13: Here are five ways you can wrap text around a picture. Top row, left to right: Square, Tight, Behind Text. Bottom row, left to right: In Front of Text and Through.

✦ **Reset picture.** If you change your mind about the alterations you've made to a picture, just click this button to restore it to its original appearance.

Inserting and Editing Charts

Like WordArt, Microsoft Graph is a separate program that works with all the applications of Office to help you create what Microsoft calls charts and most of us call graphs (although Microsoft calls the program that creates them Microsoft Graph. Go figure).

To insert a chart into your Word document:

1. Place your insertion point where you want the chart to appear.

2. Choose Insert ➪ Picture ➪ Chart. This creates a sample chart and a datasheet (see Figure 7-14).

3. To simply edit the sample chart, type the names you want to give the columns of your chart in the top row of the datasheet, under the A, B, C, D, etc., and type the names you want to give the data you're displaying in the first column, next to the 1, 2, 3, etc. Enter your data in the corresponding cells of the datasheet. The chart will change appearance to match your data as you change each cell.

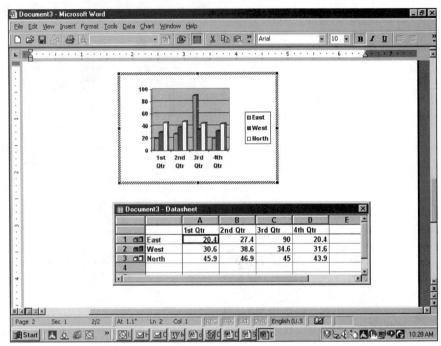

Figure 7-14: Whenever you create a chart, this is what you'll see first. You can then replace the data in the datasheet with your own and format the chart to your liking.

4. To create a different type of chart than the default bar chart, choose Chart ➪ Chart Type. This opens the Chart Type dialog box (see Figure 7-15). Choose the type of chart you want to create, and then choose the appropriate chart type from the Chart sub-type menu at right. Click and hold the bar below the Chart sub-type menu to see a preview of that chart. A brief description below that bar explains how each type of chart is created.

5. Click OK to create a chart of the type you've chosen and return to the datasheet. Enter your data.

6. When you're finished entering data, close the datasheet. You can then resize your chart just as you would any other picture.

Tip You can create additional rows and columns for your chart at any time by simply labeling and filling in more rows and columns in the datasheet. Microsoft Graph automatically adjusts the chart accordingly, even choosing new colors as necessary to display the new data.

To fine-tune your chart's appearance, choose Chart ➪ Chart Options. The Chart Options dialog box lets you change or eliminate gridlines, alter labels, move the legend around, and more.

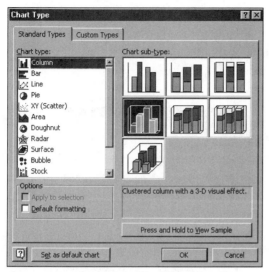

Figure 7-15: The Chart Type dialog box offers dozens of chart types and sub-types to choose from, making it easy to find one that perfectly displays your data.

You can also format the various parts of your chart as you wish, changing color, for example, applying patterns and even pictures to the chart's background or to individual data series, and altering the size and font of labels. To format any part of the chart, first double-click on the chart as a whole, and then single-click on the part you want to format.

When you're finished formatting your chart, click anywhere outside it to return to normal editing mode.

Adding Borders and Shading

You can add borders not only to pictures, but also to selected bits of text, from a single character to an entire document.

Adding a simple border

To add a simple border to text:

1. Highlight the text you want to add the border around (unless it's a single paragraph, in which case you only have to click somewhere within the paragraph).

2. Click the Border button on the Formatting toolbar. By default, this draws a simple rectangular box around the selected text (see Figure 7-16). If you want something a little different, click the down arrow next to the Border button and select the kind of border you want from the menu. You can choose to draw a line only along one side, for example.

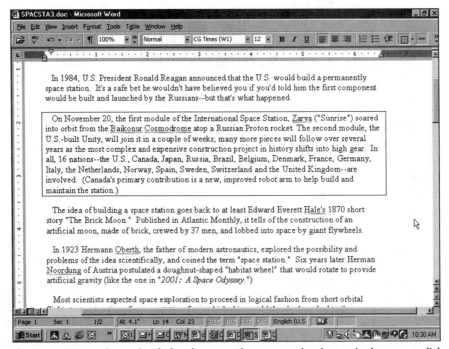

Figure 7-16: Drawing a simple border around a paragraph takes a single mouse-click.

Adding borders to tables

Note that some of the Border options involve drawing inside borders on a grid. These borders are intended for use with tables. To add a border to a table, simply draw the table as usual, and then click the Border button and choose the kind of border you want. A typical choice would be All Borders, which outlines every cell and can make it easier for readers to see where rows and columns come together.

Fine-tuning your borders

For more complex borders, Word provides a dialog box, which you access by choosing Format ➪ Borders and Shading (see Figure 7-17).

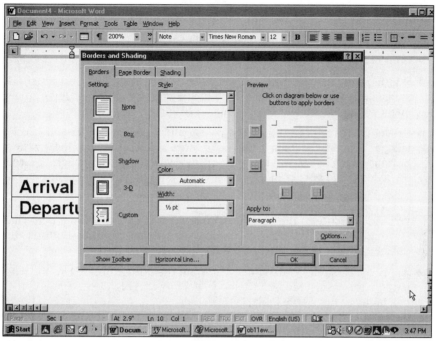

Figure 7-17: When you want a more sophisticated border than you can get with the Border button, bring up the Borders and Shading dialog box.

The first two property sheets, under the Borders and Page Border tabs, are virtually identical. (However, the Borders property sheet changes somewhat when you're applying borders to a table instead of text.) Use the Borders property sheet to apply a border to a selected section of text or a table; use the Page Border property sheet to apply borders to entire pages. The controls the two property sheets share include the following:

✦ **Setting.** This determines the type of border you're going to use. None, of course, means just what it says; so does Box. Shadow applies a drop shadow to the box; 3-D applies a preset effect that gives some borders the appearance of a picture frame. Custom applies to borders where you've removed one or more sides (more on that in a minute) or otherwise altered the preset options. If you're applying a border to a table, All and Grid replace Shadow and 3-D; All applies the same border to all the cells in the table, while Grid applies your chosen border just to the outside of the table, and outlines the cells with simple lines (which you can then format as you see fit).

✦ **Style.** From the scroll box, choose the kind of line you want to use to draw the border, from a simple straight line to dashed lines, dotted lines, combinations of thick and thin lines, and even wavy lines.

✦ **Color.** Pick a color, any color, for the lines of your border.

✦ **Width.** Select the width of line you want to use. How many and which widths are available depends on what kind of line you choose. Some lines come in many widths; some, like the double wavy line, come in only one.

✦ **Preview.** This not only shows you what your selected border will look like, it lets you remove the lines from one or more sides, either by clicking the buttons to the left of and below the Preview window, or by clicking directly on the sides of the border in the preview. In addition, you can change any line by choosing a different style, color, or width, and then clicking one of the buttons or on one of the lines. If you're working with a table, you have more controls; you can adjust both the outside edge of the table and the inner lines that surround the cells. You can even add diagonal lines with the buttons at the bottom left and right corners of the preview.

✦ **Apply to.** This tells Word where you want the border applied: to the whole paragraph, to selected text (if you've got any text highlighted); or, in the case of a table, to the whole table, to selected cells, or to the paragraph the table appears in. Click the options button to set how much space you want to leave between the text and the border (this button is only active if you're working with a paragraph border).

Note   One difference between the Page Border property sheet and the Borders property sheet is in the Apply to options. You can choose to apply page borders to the entire document, to just the current section, to just the first page of the current section, or to every page in the current section except the first page. (If the whole document is a single section, the latter two options can be used to apply borders to everything except the first page of the document or to the first page only.)

The Page Border property sheet adds the following option to the mix:

✦ **Art.** This allows you to add a decorative border to your pages. Just choose the design you want from the drop-down list (see Figure 7-18). Word automatically assigns a width to the border art, but you can increase or decrease it as you wish.

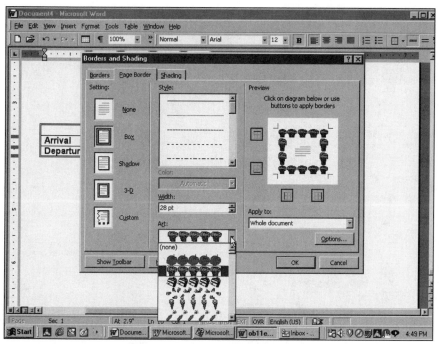

Figure 7-18: Add a decorative border to your pages. Muffin, anyone?

Adding shading

In addition to, or instead of, using a border to set off a paragraph, table, section of text, or whole pages, you can use shading. Click on the Shading tab in the Borders and Shading dialog box to bring up the Shading property sheet (see Figure 7-19). Here's how it works:

✦ Choose the color you want to use to shade the selected text or paragraph from the Fill palette, or click More Colors to access all the colors your computer and monitor are capable of displaying.

✦ In the Patterns area, use the Style drop-down list to choose from various shades (given in percentages of the solid color) or a variety of patterns.

✦ The Color drop-down list lets you choose a second color to use to draw the selected pattern over the Fill color.

✦ The Preview area shows you what the fill looks like, and Apply To lets you apply the fill to just selected text or to an entire paragraph.

Tip

There's no provision to apply shading to an entire page, but you could do so by selecting all the text on the page before applying shading. If you have a table selected, you can apply shading to the whole table or just to the selected cell.

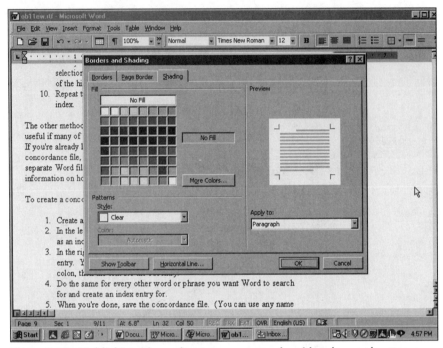

Figure 7-19: Highlight sections of text, or a paragraph, with colors and patterns.

Using Word for Desktop Publishing

Although Word isn't specifically designed for desktop publishing, you can tell from the impressive capabilities it has displayed in this chapter that it can certainly be used to create documents using graphics as well as text to communicate effectively.

Word's wizards and templates reflect this, offering many well-designed documents that include both graphics and text. Word provides wizards for faxes, memos, agendas, calendars, resumes, and newsletters; and templates for all of those plus brochures, invoices, purchase orders, time sheets, manuals, directories, and reports, all of which require some graphical elements, even if it's just simple boxes in some cases.

Cross-Reference See Chapter 1, "Creating and Managing Documents," and Chapter 6, "Styles and Templates," for more information on wizards and templates.

By combining Word's world-leading word processing capabilities with the impressive graphical capabilities you've seen in this chapter, you can create just about any sort of document you can think of without necessarily turning to a full-fledged desktop publishing program. You're really only limited by your imagination.

Summary

In this chapter, you've learned several ways to make your documents more graphically interesting. In the next chapter, "Word at Work," we'll walk through the process of using Word to create some of the documents just mentioned, and get you started creating the specialized documents that meet your specific needs. Some important points in this chapter included the following:

✦ Bulleted and numbered lists are excellent ways to organize information — and by choosing Format ⇨ Bullets and Numbering, you can customize them to suit your needs.

✦ Choose Format ⇨ Columns to set selected text or your whole document into columns. You can create columns of equal width, or make each column a different width. You can also add lines between columns.

✦ Word lets you insert several different types of pictures and other graphics. Choose Insert ⇨ Picture, and then the type of picture you want from the list provided. Among others, you can insert any picture file you have stored on your computer or get a picture from a scanner or digital camera.

✦ Clip Gallery organizes your available clip art into a virtual catalog that you can search by keyword.

✦ WordArt adds extra oomph to text with colors, shadows, bending and twisting, and other special effects.

✦ The Drawing toolbar gives you access to another powerful set of tools that you can use to create special shapes.

✦ Microsoft Graph is a powerful utility shared by all Office applications that you can use to automatically create and insert into your document dozens of different types of graphs to illustrate your data.

✦ Choose Format ⇨ Borders and Shading to add borders to selected text, whole paragraphs, tables, or even whole pages. You can set the width and style of the border lines; page borders even include decorative art.

✦ Shading can be used with or instead of borders to highlight paragraphs or selected text. You can use a variety of patterns and set colors as you see fit.

✦ ✦ ✦

Word at Work

In previous chapters you learned the basics of using Word, but it's all been pretty general. In this chapter you'll learn how you can customize Word to better suit your needs, and then you'll examine, step by step, how to use Word to perform some common business tasks, from creating a newsletter to creating a Web page.

Customizing Word

You can customize just about every aspect of Word, from how it displays text to how it lets you edit it. You're not even stuck with the toolbars Microsoft has created: You can create your own toolbars, and, with macros, even your own customized tools to go on them. Two dialog boxes give you control over all of this: the Customize dialog box, and the Options dialog box.

Cross-Reference For more information on macros, see Chapter 55, "Creating Macros."

Customizing toolbars

To open the Customize dialog box (see Figure 8-1), choose Tools ➪ Customize, or View ➪ Toolbars ➪ Customize. Three property sheets, which are covered in the following sections, let you customize your toolbars as you see fit

The Toolbars property sheet

This essentially works the same as the View ➪ Toolbars commands: checking a toolbar makes it appear. You can use this property sheet to specify which toolbars you want to have open all the time. You can also use this property sheet to create a custom toolbar. Click New; you'll be prompted to name your new toolbar and choose whether to associate it just with the current document or with the current template (in which case it will be available to every document created with that template in the future). When it's first created, the new toolbar is just a small, empty gray box. To add commands to it, go to the next property sheet.

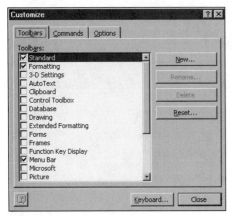

Figure 8-1: You can customize your toolbars using the Customize dialog box.

The Commands property sheet

This lists all of Word's available commands (see Figure 8-2). You can pick a category from the Categories list to see just the commands in that category, or choose the Category called All Commands to see them all. The commands and their associated icons (if any) are displayed in the Commands scroll-box. To add a command to your new toolbar, or any existing toolbar, just click and drag it from the Customize dialog box to the toolbar. To see a description of the command as in the figure, click Description.

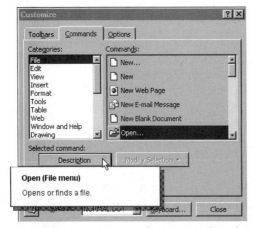

Figure 8-2: The Commands property sheet lets you add any of Word's commands to any toolbar.

Note Note that one of the categories of commands is Macros. Every macro you create becomes a command you can insert into a toolbar, just like the commands Word supplies by default.

Modifying a toolbar button

Once a command has been added to a toolbar, you can change its appearance. With the Customize dialog box open, click the button you wish to modify on a toolbar that's visible, and then click Modify Selection. This opens a new menu. Commands on this menu let you copy the button (so you can assign the button image to a different command, if you like, or insert it into a document as a picture), paste in a button image you've already copied to the Clipboard, reset the button to its original image, edit the button image using the Button Editor (see Figure 8-3), or choose a new button image from a pop-up menu. You can also choose whether to display the command as text only or both text and image.

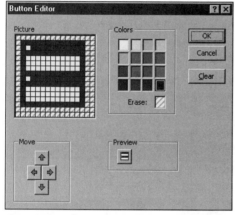

Figure 8-3: The Button Editor lets you redesign Word's buttons pixel by pixel, or draw your own buttons for new commands.

Assigning hyperlinks and shortcut keys

Finally, you can change the button's function entirely by assigning it a hyperlink to an existing file (either a document or picture) or Web page. This could be useful, for example, if you insert the same picture — say, a company logo — into many different documents. By clicking the Keyboard button in the Customize dialog box, you can change shortcut keys for any command and/or assign shortcut keys to your macros.

The Options property sheet

The final property sheet in the Customize dialog box, Options, lets you modify the way Word displays commands. By default, Word 2000 places the Standard and Formatting toolbars on the same row; you can change that here. You can also turn off the function whereby Word moves the commands you most recently used to the top of menus, and shows you full menus after a short delay if you keep pointing at them. Other default options you can turn off here include the Font list-box's ability to show you font names in their font and show ScreenTips on toolbars (ScreenTips are the little pop-up boxes that give you the name of a command when you point at a button). Options you can turn on that are off by default include large icons (useful for people who have difficulty reading the screen), showing shortcut keys in ScreenTips, and menu animations (which changes the way menus appear on the screen—instead of just popping into existence, they can appear to unfold or slide open).

Other options

Word also lets you set many, many other options by choosing Tools ➪ Options. This opens the Options dialog box (see Figure 8-4), which has ten tabs, each of which offers numerous options.

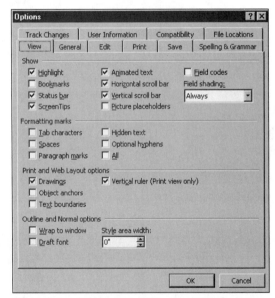

Figure 8-4: The Options dialog box gives you access to dozens of customizable features in Word.

There are too many options here to explore in detail, but in brief, here's what you can find under each tab:

✦ **View.** This property sheet lets you customize the way Word displays your document while you're working on it. For example, if you don't want field codes to appear shaded, you can turn off that option here; you can even remove the vertical and horizontal scrollbars if you wish. Among other options, you can also choose to display formatting marks such as tab characters and paragraph marks, or turn on and off the Wrap to Window function, which makes lines of text automatically restart on a new line in your display when they reach the right edge.

✦ **General.** This property sheet contains options that didn't fit into any of the other categories. For example, here you can change your display from black characters on a white background to white characters on a blue background (sure to make WordPerfect 5.1 users feel more at home). Special help and navigation keys for WordPerfect users can also be activated here. Other options include the ability to change the number of files in the recently opened list on the File menu (by default, four are listed) and to change the measurement system from inches to centimeters, millimeters, points, or picas.

✦ **Edit.** These options affect the way you insert, alter, and move text. For example, you might find drag-and-drop text editing and Word's propensity to automatically select an entire word when you select text annoying; you can turn these off here. This property sheet lets you set several other editing options, as well, including which program you want to use to edit pictures (by default, Microsoft Draw, but you might have another graphics program you prefer).

✦ **Print.** This property sheet lets you set a number of printing options, including the option to automatically resize documents intended for letter-sized paper to fit on A4 paper, and the option to automatically update fields and links before printing. You can also tell Word to automatically include comments, field codes, drawing objects, document properties, and hidden text when you print, and even specify which tray of your printer should be used by default to print Word documents.

✦ **Save.** These options determine how Word saves documents. You can tell it, for example, to always save a backup copy as well as the main copy, to prompt you to specify document properties when you save (normally you have to open File ⇨ Properties manually to fill out the various property sheets of the Properties dialog box), and to embed TrueType fonts (which ensures, if you send the file to someone else, that he and she will have the necessary fonts to see it the way you want it to look). This is also where you can set the default format for Word to save files in: regular Word format or HTML. (One of the most powerful new abilities of Office 2000 is that it can save documents in HTML format and open them again with almost no loss of formatting or other features of the original document.) You can also set document-sharing properties here, including assigning the passwords others must know in order to read or modify your documents. Another option is to make them read-only recommended, which suggests, but does not require, that the user open the document read-only.

✦ **Spelling & Grammar.** Are you spelling-challenged? Then make sure you use this property sheet to tell Word to check spelling as you type. You can also ask it to check grammar as you type, as well as to always suggest spellings when you run spell-checking and to ignore words in uppercase, words that include numbers, and Internet and file addresses. Choosing a Writing style from the drop-down list tells Word how aggressively to check grammar, and you can customize the grammar-checking further by clicking Settings.

✦ **Track Changes.** When I write a computer book, I know my first draft is going to pass through the hands of several editors before returning to me for author review. By that time, my original clean, black-and-white Word file is full of multicolored revisions and comments. Text that's been deleted or changed is still visible, but has changed color and has a strike-out line through it. All of this is activated by choosing Tools ⇨ Track Changes, and it's modified here. This property sheet lets you set how revisions will appear when you track changes, from how the revisions are marked to what color is used to show them.

✦ **User Information.** Some documents insert information about their creator automatically. That information (name, initials, and mailing address) can be edited here.

✦ **Compatibility.** To make it easier for people using earlier versions of Word, Macintosh versions of Word, or even some versions of WordPerfect to read your document, Word lets you set a number of options here, involving everything from how tab spaces are handled to how margins are measured.

✦ **File Locations.** Use this property sheet to set the default locations Word should go to to find various types of files. For instance, Word looks in the My Documents folder by default when you choose File ⇨ Open; if most of your documents are in a different folder, you can use this property sheet to tell Word to go to that folder first when you choose File ⇨ Open. You can also specify the locations for templates, AutoRecover files, clip art, user options, tools, and startup files.

Creating a Resume

Once you've got Word set up just the way you want it, you're ready to start using it for your own projects. In the remainder of this chapter, we'll look at how to put Word through some of its most popular paces, step by step — starting with a resume. To create a resume:

1. Choose File ⇨ New.

2. From the New dialog box, choose the Other Documents tab (see Figure 8-5).

3. Double-click Resume Wizard. This opens the initial window shown in Figure 8-6.

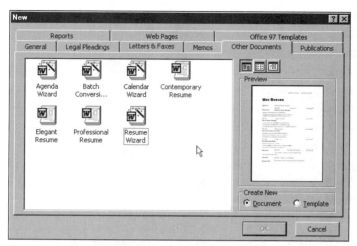

Figure 8-5: The Publications tab contains templates and wizards for a number of different types of documents, including a resume.

Figure 8-6: The first step to creating a resume: open Resume Wizard.

4. Click Next, and choose a style for your resume: Professional, Contemporary, or Elegant (see Figure 8-7). (You can get some idea of what each style looks like from the preview pictures provided.)

5. Click Next, and in the next window, choose which type of resume you'd like to create: entry-level, chronological, functional, or professional (see Figure 8-8).

6. Click Next again, and enter your name, mailing address, phone and fax numbers,. and e-mail address.

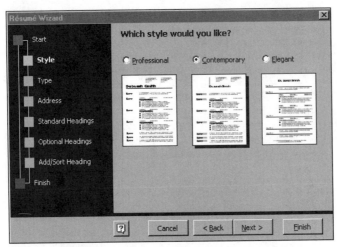

Figure 8-7: Choose a style, any style, for your resume.

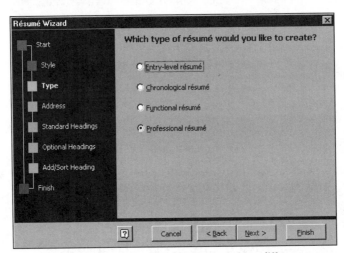

Figure 8-8: The Resume Wizard can create four different types of resumes for you.

7. Click Next again, and you'll see a list of headings that are typically included in the kind of resume you're creating. Check the boxes of the headings you want to keep. Click Next once more, and make additional selections from a list of optional headings. Finally, click Next one more time and add any additional headings you'd like to create, then use the list of headings provided and the Move Up and Move Down buttons to arrange the headings in the order you'd like them to appear in.

8. If you want to go back and change any of the choices you've made, click Back or use the navigation bar at the left of the window; if you're happy with the choices you've made, click Finish. (Clicking Next from this window just takes you to a message window that tells you to click Finish, so you might as well click Finish now and save yourself a step!) Word opens a resume template (see Figure 8-9).

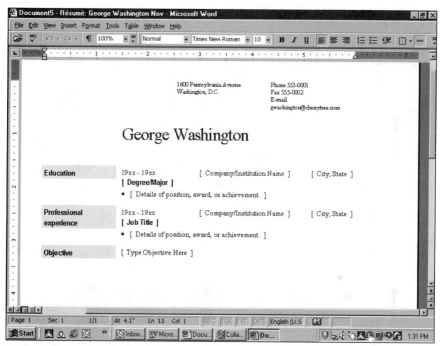

Figure 8-9: The resume, in the style you requested and containing the information you provided, is now ready for you to enter your own text.

9. The resume template includes a number of fields where you can enter the information appropriate for that section of the resume. Edit and format the text as you would for any other document. You can add any of the elements we've discussed in this section, including graphics, tables, and charts. You can apply your own styles to headings, captions, and text. The template isn't a straitjacket for your creativity: it's just a springboard. However, if you're not confident of your eye for design, don't change the template too much. That way you can be sure of ending up with a professional-looking publication.

Tip Many templates include text that provides helpful information about the template and how to use it. Choose File ➪ Print and print the template before you replace any of the text in it with your own so you can refer to those instructions as necessary.

10. When you're finished editing the template, save it under any name you want. If you made any changes to the styles included with the template, you might want to consider saving your finished resume as a template as well as a regular document. That way you can use your own template, instead of the generic one, to create future resumes and cut down on the amount of editing you have to do.

11. Print your resume or, if you've saved it in HTML format, post it on your local network or the Internet.

Creating a Web Page

Because you can choose to save any Word document in HTML format, you're really creating a potential Web page even if you're just writing a letter. However, it probably wouldn't be a very interesting Web page. Because of their reliance on hyperlinks and added touches like background images, Web pages are usually designed a little differently than an ordinary document. If you know your document is going to end up on the Web, it's a good idea to keep that in mind from the very beginning of the design process. To that end, Word provides you with a Web-page wizard. To create a Web page:

1. Choose File ➪ New.

2. From the New dialog box, choose the Web Pages tab (see Figure 8-10).

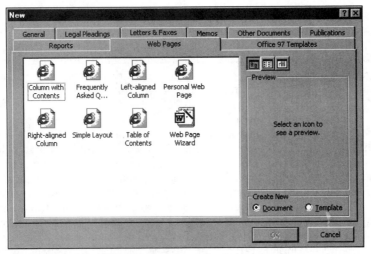

Figure 8-10: The Web Pages tab contains templates for some common types of Web pages, plus a Web Page wizard.

3. Double-click Web Page Wizard.

4. Despite its title, Web Page Wizard actually is a Web Site Wizard, letting you create a multi-page site complete with navigation tools and a professionally designed theme (as the initial window informs you). Click Next, and in the next window, give your Web site a name and choose a location on your computer to save it to.

5. Click Next, and choose a navigation scheme (see Figure 8-11). The options are Vertical Frame, in which links to the other pages in the site appear in a separate vertical frame to the left of the main frame; Horizontal Frame, in which the links appear in a separate horizontal frame above the main frame; and Separate Page, which doesn't use frames, but instead creates a list of links to all the pages in the site on a separate page and includes links on every page to all the other pages.

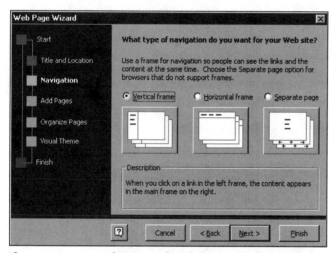

Figure 8-11: A good system of navigation is vital to a good Web site. Web Site Wizard offers you three types to choose from.

6. Click Next again and add all the pages you want to your site (see Figure 8-12). You can add blank pages, pages based on Word's existing templates (refer back to Figure 8-10), or pages you've already created. All the pages added here will be included in the navigation scheme you picked in Step 5.

7. Click Next, and in the next window, which is almost identical to the Add Pages window, organize your pages by highlighting them and clicking Move Up or Move Down to rearrange their relative positions. Changes here are reflected in the order in which pages appear in the navigation links. You can also rename pages here by highlighting them, and then clicking Rename.

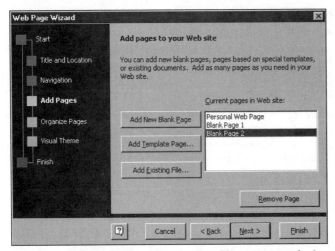

Figure 8-12: Add as many pages as you like to your Web site with these handy controls.

8. Click Next one last time, and choose a visual theme for your page — if you want to use one. (If you don't, all your pages will have a plain white background to start with. However, you can always add a background of your own choosing later.) To preview the available themes, click Browse Themes. This opens the Theme dialog box shown in Figure 8-13.

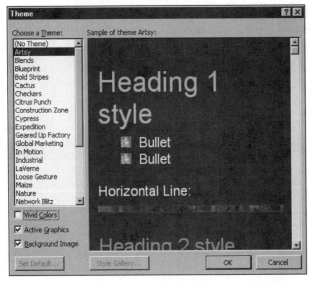

Figure 8-13: Word offers many different visual themes, each with its own special buttons, lines, and colors, for your Web pages.

9. When you've picked a theme you're happy with, click OK. This returns you to the Wizard.

10. Click Finish. Word builds your Web site, and automatically switches to Web Layout View to show it to you (see Figure 8-14).

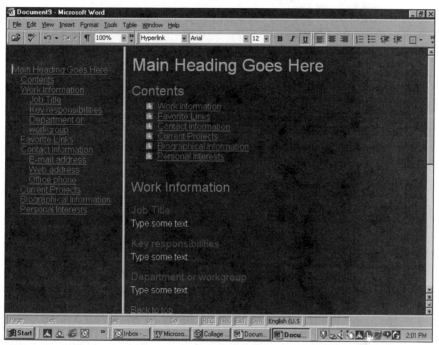

Figure 8-14: Web Layout View shows you your Web site approximately as it will look in a browser.

11. Edit your Web page. You can edit text just as you would in any Word document, changing fonts, styles, etc. You can insert pictures and other graphics as well. You can also edit hyperlinks. To assign a hyperlink to a picture or bit of text, or to change an existing hyperlink, select it and press Ctrl+K. This opens the Edit Hyperlink dialog box shown in Figure 8-15.

12. In the first blank at the top of the dialog box, you can change the text you want the hyperlink to display — or leave it just the way it is. If you want to enter specific text for a pop-up ScreenTip (supported by Internet Explorer 4.0 and later), click ScreenTip and enter the text in the dialog box that appears. (If you don't enter anything here, Word uses the assigned address for the hyperlink as its ScreenTip.)

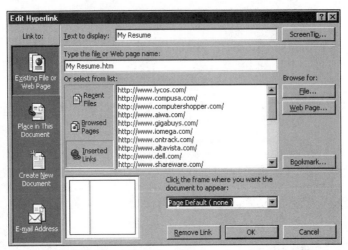

Figure 8-15: Assign and edit hyperlinks using this dialog box.

13. To the left, in the Link To area, choose the type of hyperlink you want to attach to the selected item:

- **Existing File or Web Page** gives you the options you see in Figure 8-15. You can type in the path to a file or the URL of a Web page, or choose one from one of three lists: Recent Files, which displays a list of Office files you've recently worked on; Browsed Pages, which displays pages stored in your browser's cache; and Inserted Links, which displays links you've manually typed into your browser. You can use the Browse buttons to browse for a file on your computer or on the Web: clicking Web Page opens your browser. Find the page you want, and then return here to create a hyperlink to it. You can also make a link to a specific part of any pages or files that contain bookmarks; click the Bookmark button to do so.

- **Place in This Document** lets you choose a location within your Web site to link to. Clicking this opens an Explorer-like list of pages within the site, which can be expanded to include a list of headings. You can link to the top of a page or to any particular heading.

- **Create New Document** lets you create a brand-new document to link to. You don't have to edit the document right away, although you can: You can also choose to simply create it and link to it, and then edit it later. Click the radio button that matches your selection.

- **E-mail Address** lets you create a link that, when clicked, will automatically bring up a form in which your Web site visitors can enter e-mail that will be sent to the address you specify. You can also pre-enter a subject for the e-mail. Type in an e-mail address or choose from a list of recently used addresses.

14. Finally, if you're using a page with frames, you need to enter where you want the linked document to appear: in the left frame, in the main frame, as a whole page without any frames, in the same frame as the hyperlink, or in a new window.

15. When you're finished editing a hyperlink, click OK to return to the main document (see the sidebar "Creating Hyperlinks to Other Office Documents.)"

16. Choose File ⇨ Save As Web Page to save your page. Word automatically saves any associated graphics files into special folders and converts your document into HTML.

17. To see what your page looks like in a Web browser, choose File ⇨ Web Page Preview. Word automatically opens your browser and displays your Web page with it (see Figure 8-16).

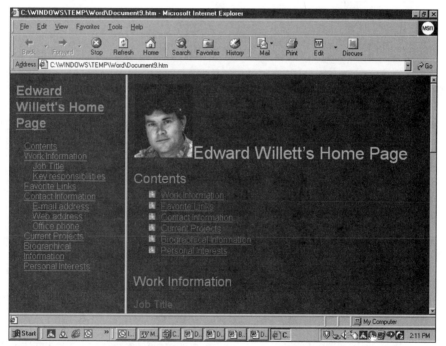

Figure 8-16: Web Page Preview shows you your new Web page using your Web browser.

18. Publish your new Web pages to the Web or your local intranet via your usual method.

Creating Hyperlinks to Other Office Documents

You can also create a hyperlink to other Office documents by copying and pasting into your Web site selected text or graphics from a Word document or PowerPoint slide, a selected range in Microsoft Excel, or a selected database object in Microsoft Access. Word automatically recognizes the location of the information. To do so, display both files on the screen (you can do that with two Word files by opening both of them, and then choosing Window ⇨ Arrange All), and then select the material you want the hyperlink to point to. Copy it to the Clipboard, return to your Web page, place your insertion point where you want the hyperlink to appear, and then choose Edit ⇨ Paste as Hyperlink.

You can then edit the new hyperlink as described in Steps 12 to 15 in the section "Creating a Web Page." (If you have drag-and-drop text editing enabled in the Tools ⇨ Options ⇨ Edit property sheet, you can do the same thing by clicking on the selected text with the right mouse button, dragging it to where you want the hyperlink to appear on your Web page, and then clicking Create Hyperlink Here from the pop-up menu that automatically appears.)

Writing a Business Letter

Writing a business letter is one of the most basic of business tasks. Often, business letters are written on preprinted stationery, and you can certainly use Word to do that. However, Word can go one better: It can create electronic stationery that you can easily change or redesign as necessary. To write a business letter:

1. Choose File ⇨ New.

2. Choose the Letters and Faxes tab from the New dialog box.

3. Word offers three templates and a wizard for creating business letters. This time we'll use a template instead of the wizard. The three options are contemporary, elegant, and professional; Figure 8-17 shows the "Professional Letter" template.

4. Replace the text "Company Name Here" in the text frame with your own company's name, and then click on the field that says "Click here and type return address," and do just that in the resulting text frame.

5. The next field down contains the current date; you can change this if necessary by highlighting it and typing over it. Then type the recipient's address into the field below that.

6. The "Dear Sir or Madam" field and the "Sincerely" field can both be changed to other common forms of greetings and closures by right-clicking and choosing from the resulting pop-up menu (see Figure 8-18). Click once on the phrase you want to automatically insert it.

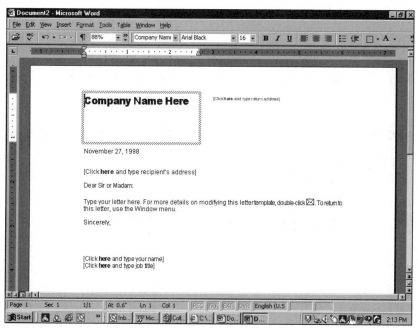

Figure 8-17: All the letter templates are similar, but the "Professional" template is appropriate for a business letter.

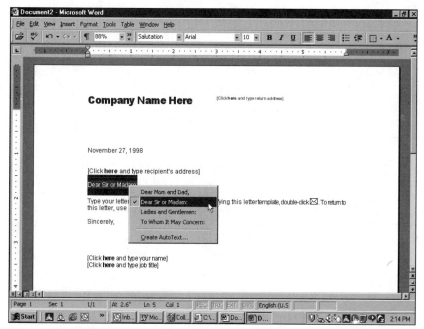

Figure 8-18: Common salutations are just a mouse-click away when you create a business letter using one of Word's templates.

7. Type the text of your letter over the body of the template letter; finally, type your name, title, etc., in the two fields at the bottom of the letter.

8. Now go back and format the letter however you wish. For example, you may want to change the typeface, or even insert a picture — the company logo, for instance. By doing so, you can create attractive stationery right on your own computer (see Figure 8-19).

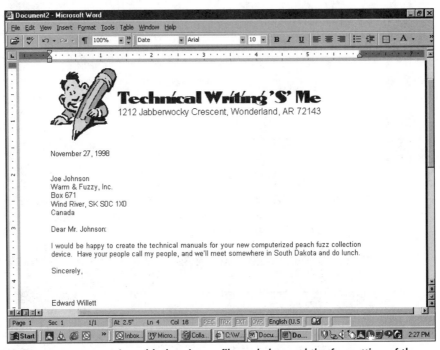

Figure 8-19: Here we've added a picture file and changed the formatting of the company name to create sharp-looking stationery for our fictitious technical writing company.

9. Save the letter. If you plan to use your new virtual stationery for other letters, it's a good idea to save it as a template, not just as a document. To do so, choose File ⇨ Save As, then choose Document Template in the Save As Type box. To protect Word's original template, change the name. The next time you start a new document, the template you just created will appear with the other templates in the New dialog box (see Figure 8-20).

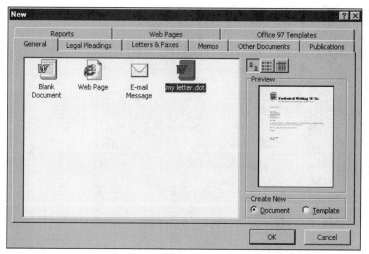

Figure 8-20: Your new business letter template is now available for use every time you start a new document.

Writing a Memo

Another common business use for Word is writing memos. Recognizing this, Word again offers several templates and a Wizard for memo creation. To create a memo using the Memo Wizard:

1. Choose File ➪ New.

2. From the New dialog box, choose the Memos tab.

3. Double-click Memo Wizard.

4. In the initial window of the wizard, click Next.

5. Choose a memo style: professional, contemporary, or elegant (note that these correspond to the letter styles we just looked at). Click Next.

6. If you want to title your memo, do so in this window. If you're going to use a preprinted memo form, you probably won't want to do this. Click Next.

7. In the next window (see Figure 8-21) you're given the option of adding several useful fields, including the date, who the memo is from, and the subject. You can also include a priority label from this window. Click Next.

8. Next, enter a list of recipients for the memo (see Figure 8-22). You can type these in or insert them from your Address Book. You can also create a list of people to send copies of the memo to. Finally, you can choose to create your distribution list on a page separate from the memo, if you don't want it to appear right on the memo. When you're done, click Next.

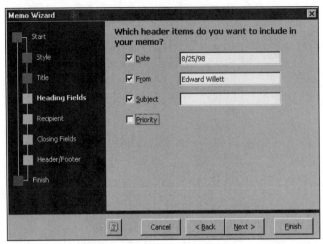

Figure 8-21: Word can automatically add several useful fields, both to the front of the memo and (from another step later on in the wizard) to the end.

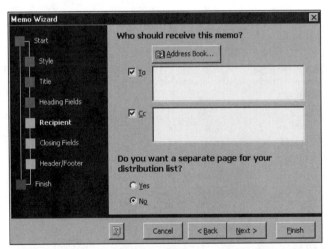

Figure 8-22: Enter a list of recipients, and a list of people to CC the memo to, in this window of the wizard.

9. In the next window, you can add several more useful fields that will appear at the bottom of the memo: author's initials, typist's initials, an enclosures field in which you can enter a number or text, and a note that there are attachments. When you've made your selections, click Next.

10. In the final window, you choose from still more fields, three for header pages after the initial page (you can choose from date, topic — which you can enter — and page number); and three for footers, which will appear on all pages (choose from date, a "confidential" label, and the page number).

11. If you want to go back and change anything you've entered in the wizard, do so by clicking Back or clicking on the name of the part of the wizard you want to return to in the navigation bar at the left. When you're satisfied, click Finish. Word opens a memo template that reflects the selections you made (see Figure 8-23).

12. Enter your memo text in the field that says "click here and type your memo text." You can also edit the memo in all the usual ways—changing fonts, styles, sizes, etc. When you're done, save and print.

13. If all your memos will follow the same basic style, choose File ⇨ Save As, and choose Document Template in the Save As Type box. Name the template whatever you like. Now, the next time you create a new document, you can use your new memo template instead of the memo wizard.

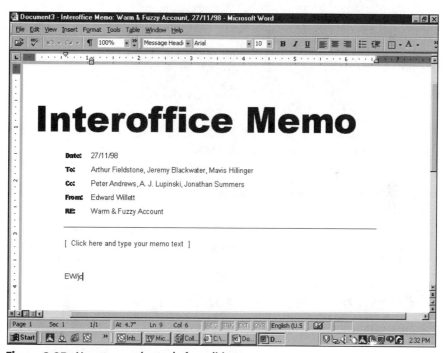

Figure 8-23: Your memo is ready for editing.

Using Word As Your E-mail Editor

To use Word as your e-mail editor, you first have to tell Outlook that you want to use Word for that purpose. (You have to do this in Outlook; you can't do it in Word.) To do so:

1. Open Outlook and choose Tools ⇨ Options.

2. From the Options dialog box, click the Mail Format tab, and check the Use Microsoft Word to Edit E-mail Messages check box (see Figure 8-24).

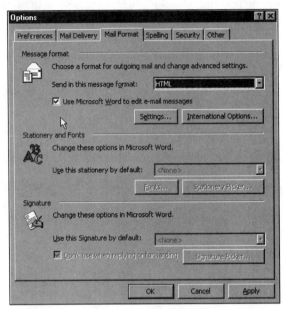

Figure 8-24: This dialog box in Outlook is where you have to go to set Word as your e-mail editor.

3. From the Send in This Message Format list box, select HTML format.

4. Click OK.

Now you can use Word to create or edit e-mail just as you can use it to create or edit other documents.

Creating a new message in Word

To create a new e-mail message in Word:

1. Choose File ➪ New.

2. From the General tab in the New dialog box, select E-mail message.

3. Word opens a new document window that looks a bit different than the others we've seen (see Figure 8-25).

4. Enter the e-mail addresses of the recipients you're sending this e-mail to in the blank marked To. Click the little address book icon to open your Outlook Address Book, if you want to use addresses that you've already got on file.

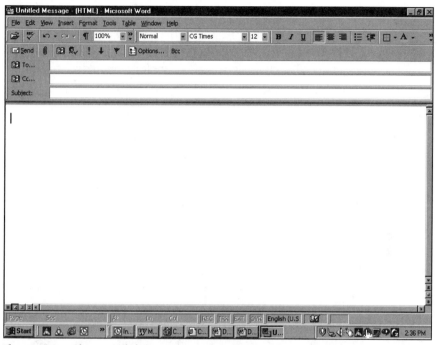

Figure 8-25: The e-mail document window in Word has a slightly different look than you might be used to.

5. Enter the e-mail addresses of anyone you want to send copies of the e-mail to in the blank marked CC. Again, you can use addresses from your Address Book just by clicking the icon. If you want to blind-copy people on this message (recipients that receive the message don't see the blind copy list, but they do see the To and CC lists), click the Bcc button in the E-mail toolbar and enter the addresses of people on that list as well.

6. Enter the subject of the e-mail in the Subject blank.

7. Enter the text of your message in the document window. You can edit and format it as you would any other Word document; just remember that you're really creating an HTML document, so it's a good idea to preview your message by choosing File ➪ Web Page Preview to see how well your formatting translates to HTML.

8. To add an attachment to your e-mail, click the button with the paperclip on it to open the Insert File dialog box, and then locate the file on your computer and click OK.

Note

You can send any Word document via e-mail just by opening the document, and then clicking the E-mail button on the Standard toolbar. The same kind of header you see on a regular e-mail appears; enter the recipient information and subject and click Send, and the document is on its way.

9. Mark the e-mail message as you see fit. You can click the red exclamation mark to mark it high priority, the blue downward arrow to mark it low priority, or the red flag to flag it for follow-up. If you flag it, a dialog box opens that lets you flag it in a number of different ways (e.g., For Follow Up or No Response Necessary) and even lets you pick a date for a reminder.

10. When you're happy with your message, click Send.

Themes, stationeries, and signatures

Word offers a number of additional user-defined options regarding how your message looks. For example, because you're essentially creating a Web page when you create a mail message in Word, you can also draw on all of the Web page themes that we looked at in the section on designing a Web page, as well as stationeries (which are like themes but intended specifically for e-mail).

Applying a theme or stationery

To apply a theme or stationery to your e-mail, choose Format ➪ Theme, and then select the one you want from the resulting dialog box. The e-mail message in Figure 8-26, for instance, uses the Kids theme.

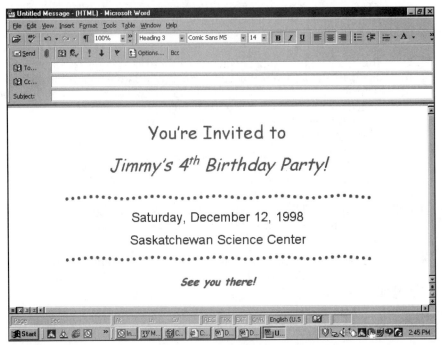

Figure 8-26: This is just one of the colorful stationeries Word offers you for e-mail messages.

Note You can edit e-mail created with stationery just as you would a Web page: insert pictures, change the font and size of the text, etc.

Creating a signature

Another option Word gives you as your e-mail editor is the ability to create a signature that will be automatically appended to every e-mail you create. To create a signature:

1. Choose Tools ➪ Options.

2. From the Options dialog box, choose the General tab, and then click E-mail Options.

3. This dialog box (see Figure 8-27) has two tabs. The second, Personal Stationery, lets you set a default stationery to be used automatically whenever you create a new e-mail. You can also set default fonts and colors. The first, E-mail Signature, lets you create your signature file using a miniature Word document window, complete with the ability to use different fonts and styles and add pictures and hyperlinks. First type a title for your signature, and then create the signature. Click Add.

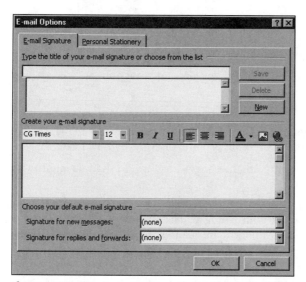

Figure 8-27: Create a signature that will automatically be added to your e-mail messages.

4. The new signature will appear in the list boxes at the bottom of the dialog box. If you have more than one signature, you can choose different ones to be appended to new messages and to replies and forwards. When you've chosen the signatures you want to use, click OK.

Setting delivery options

Finally, you can set delivery options for each message. To access them, click the Options button on the E-mail toolbar. This opens the Message Options dialog box shown in Figure 8-28. If you are using Outlook as your e-mail client, there are four areas to this dialog box (if you're using a different client, there may be variations):

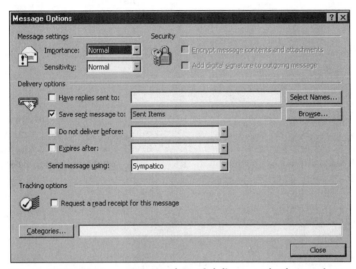

Figure 8-28: You can set a number of delivery and other options for e-mail from here.

+ **Message settings.** Set the importance (low, normal, or high) and the sensitivity (normal, personal, private, or confidential) here.

+ **Security.** Encrypt outgoing messages and/or add digital signatures to them here.

+ **Delivery options.** Here you can decide where replies should be sent (it doesn't have to be your e-mail address); choose where to save sent messages; set a date when the message should be delivered and another for when it expires; and choose the network you want to use to send the message.

+ **Tracking options.** Click the check box to request a read receipt for the message, and, if you wish, file it away in a specific category—which could help you find it again later.

Summary

In this chapter, you learned ways to put Word to work: ways to customize it to fit your needs, and then how to use it to perform some common (and highly useful) tasks. Major points of this chapter included the following:

✦ You can create your own toolbars by choosing Tools ⇨ Customize, and add any commands Word has to offer to them — in addition to commands you create yourself as macros.

✦ You can change the appearance of any tool using the Button Editor that's included on the Customize dialog box under the Commands tab.

✦ Just about every aspect of Word's editing functions are customizable by choosing Tools ⇨ Options, from how editing functions work to how the final document is printed.

✦ Word's Newsletter Wizard takes you step by step through the process of creating a newsletter, and the text in the template used by the wizard is full of helpful information about how to make the best use of it.

✦ You can not only create a single Web page, but an entire Web site in Word (as you can in all the other Office applications). Apply themes to instantly give your pages a professional appearance. Add new pages or already existing pages to your Web site with ease.

✦ Word's business letter templates let you create you own virtual stationery, which you can then save as a template and have available whenever you need to write another letter. You can add a logo or other graphics or anything else that you want to appear on all your letters.

✦ Memo Wizard lets you put all the recipients on the memo sheet itself, or on a separate page, if you don't necessarily want everyone who receives the memo to know who else received it.

✦ To set Word as your e-mail editor, go to Outlook and choose Tools ⇨ Options ⇨ Mail Format and check the appropriate check box. After that, any time you create a new mail message, you'll have the features of Word available to you.

✦ You can create e-mail directly in Word in HTML format. You can then format it just as you do a Web page, complete with background colors, pictures, hyperlinks, and more.

✦ You can send any Word document as e-mail just by clicking the E-mail button on the Standard toolbar and filling in the list of recipients.

✦ Choose Tools ⇨ Options, and then choose the General tab and click E-mail Options to create a signature (which can also include graphics and hyperlinks) to be automatically appended to all your new e-mail messages in the future.

✦   ✦   ✦

Word Top 10

Questions, questions, questions. Everyone has questions. In this chapter we'll look at answers to ten commonly asked questions about Word in general and Word 2000 in particular. If your question isn't answered in this chapter (or elsewhere in this book), you might try one of the lists of common questions, and their answers, maintained by Microsoft on the World Wide Web at http://support.microsoft.com.

How Do I Convert Word-Processing Formats with Word 2000?

Word comes with converters for most popular word-processing formats. As long as the correct converter is installed, you don't have to do anything special to convert a document in another format into a Word 2000 document: just open it as you would any other document.

You can find out which converters you have installed by choosing File ➪ Save As, and then looking in the Save as Type list box in the Save As dialog box (see Figure 9-1). All of the installed converters appear in this list. As you might guess from that, you can also convert your Word documents into any of these formats simply by choosing File ➪ Save As and choosing the format in which you want to save it from this same list.

If the file format you're looking for doesn't appear in this list, that doesn't necessarily mean you don't have it; it could have been supplied with Word but not installed, in which case you can install it simply by rerunning the installer program.

Note
You'll notice that there's not a Word 97 converter. That's because Word 97 files are already fully compatible with Word 2000; Word 2000 doesn't need a converter to read them, and Word 97 doesn't need a converter to read Word 2000 files.

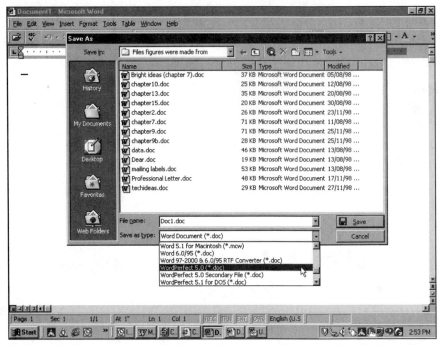

Figure 9-1: The Save as Type list box in the Save As dialog box lists all of the file format converters currently installed in Word.

File Format Converters Included in Word

The following file format converters are included with Word 2000:

✦ **WordPerfect for MS-DOS, versions 5.x and 6.x.** Note that this converter will only open version 6.0 documents, it won't let you save your Word documents in WordPerfect 6.x format.

✦ **WordPerfect for Windows, versions 5.x and 6.x.** Again, you can only open version 6.0 documents; you can't save your Word documents in that format.

✦ **Microsoft Excel, versions 2.x to 97.** This converter, too, only opens documents; it won't let you save a Word document in Excel format.

✦ **Microsoft Word 2.x for Windows.** This converter exists only to let you save Word 2000 documents in the earlier format. Word will open all earlier versions of itself without any converter.

✦ **Word 6.0/95**

✦ **Word 97 & 6.0/95-RTF**

✦ **Word (Asian versions) 6.0/95**

✦ **Microsoft Word.** Word doesn't use this converter itself; instead, Word 6.0, Word 95, PowerPoint, Works, and Publisher use this converter to open Word documents.

✦ **Microsoft Word for the Macintosh, versions 4.x and 5.x.** Word can also open these file formats without a converter, but the converter enables you to save your documents in these formats as well.

✦ **Microsoft Works 3.0 for Windows**

✦ **Microsoft Works 4.0 for Windows**

✦ **Lotus 1-2-3, releases 2.x, 3.x and 4.0.** This converter only opens documents; it won't let you save in these formats.

✦ **Lotus Notes.** This converter is used by Lotus Notes to import Word documents, not by Word itself.

Tip   To find additional converters, visit Microsoft Support on the World Wide Web at http://www.microsoft.com/support. Converters for various other file formats are available free for download from that site.

Text-only Formats Supported by Word

There are also five text-only formats into which you can save documents. Even programs for which no converter exists are generally able to open text-only documents. Word 2000's five text-only formats are

✦ **Text only.** This uses the ANSI character set, and removes all formatting, converting section breaks, page breaks, and new line characters to paragraph marks.

✦ **MS-DOS text.** This works the same way, but it uses the extended ASCII character set. This is the best format for sharing information with non-Windows-based programs.

✦ **Text only with line breaks, MS-DOS text with line breaks.** As above, except these convert line breaks as well as section breaks and page breaks to paragraph marks. This can be useful with some e-mail systems; it means the converted text will still fit within a single window and the reader won't have to do a lot of side-scrolling.

✦ **Text with layout, MS-DOS text with layout.** These preserve line breaks and insert spaces to approximate indents, tables, line spacing, paragraph spacing, and tab stops.

✦ **Rich Text Format (RTF).** This is a text-only format that preserves all formatting by converting it into instructions that other programs can read.

Converting Several Documents at Once

If you have a lot of documents in another file format that you would like to convert to Word format, or from Word format to another, you can use the Batch Conversion Wizard. To do so:

1. Place the files you want to convert in a single folder.
2. Choose File ⇨ New.
3. In the New dialog box, click the Other Documents tab.
4. Double-click the Batch Conversion Wizard to start the wizard.
5. In the first window of the wizard, click Next. This opens the window shown in Figure 9-2.

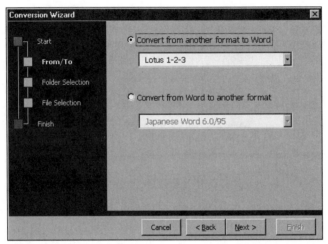

Figure 9-2: Choose which format you want to convert files from or to from this window of the Batch Conversion Wizard.

6. Here you have two choices: convert from another format to Word, or convert from Word to another format. Whichever way you're going, choose the other format from the list boxes provided. Click Next.
7. Locate the file folder containing the files you want to convert and choose a file folder into which you want to place the converted files. Click Next.
8. In the next window (see Figure 9-3), the wizard shows you all the files in your selected format that are in the chosen folder. Double-click the files you want to convert (this moves them from the Available list to the To Convert list), or click Select All to add all of the available files to the list of those to be converted. Click Finish.

9. Word converts your selected files into your chosen alternate format, and places the new files in the destination folder you selected in Step 7.

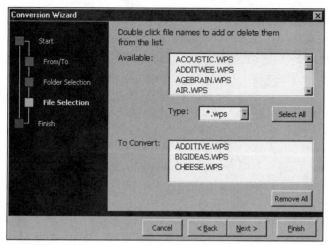

Figure 9-3: Pick the files you want to convert from the list of those available.

How Do I Send a Fax from Word?

First, your computer must support faxing—which means you have to either have a fax modem or be connected to a network that allows you to send faxes, and you must have fax software. With most fax software, sending a fax is as easy as printing. In fact, it's exactly the same procedure:

1. Open the document you want to fax.

2. Choose File ⇨ Print.

3. Look in the list of printers in the Print dialog box for your fax software, which should be listed there, and select it (see Figure 9-4).

4. Change any of the options you wish to adjust, and follow the instructions your fax software presents you with to send a fax.

Word can also help you create a professional-looking fax with the Fax Wizard. To use the Fax Wizard:

1. Choose File ⇨ New.

2. In the New dialog box, click on the Letters and Faxes tab.

3. Double-click the Fax Wizard icon. This opens the wizard's introductory screen; click Next to begin creating your fax.

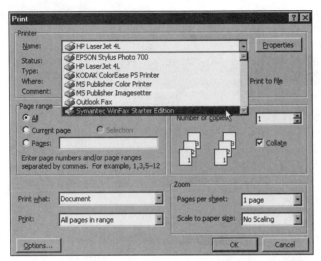

Figure 9-4: Fax software usually appears as an option in the Printer list in the Print dialog box.

4. In the first window (see Figure 9-5), you're asked to choose a document to fax, and whether you want to send it with or without a cover sheet. You can also choose to simply create a cover sheet and write a note directly on it. Once you've made your selections, click Next.

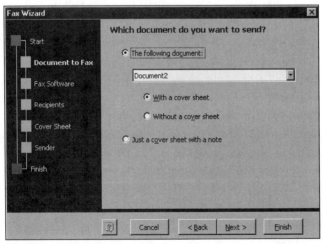

Figure 9-5: The Fax Wizard lets you choose a document to fax and how you want to fax it.

5. In the next window, you're asked to choose a fax program; either Microsoft Fax (the default) or another one you may have installed on your system. You can also choose to simply print out the fax for faxing from a regular fax machine. Make your selections and click Next.

6. The next window lets you enter names and fax numbers of the recipients of the fax, or select them from your Outlook Address Book. Once you've entered all the recipients, click Next.

7. Now choose a style for your cover sheet: Professional, Contemporary, or Elegant (see Figure 9-6). Click Next.

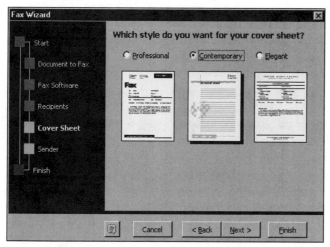

Figure 9-6: Choose from one of three pre-designed styles for your cover sheet.

8. Finally, enter information about yourself, or whomever you're sending the fax for; then click Finish. (Information entered in the User Information tab of the Tools ⇨ Options dialog box is defaulted in this step.)

9. Word creates a cover sheet that you can edit as you see fit and opens a small toolbar with only one command: Send Fax Now (see Figure 9-7). When you're ready to send the fax, click that command, and Word will fax your cover sheet and attached document (if any).

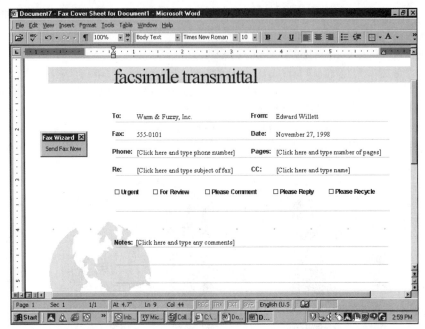

Figure 9-7: The Fax Wizard creates a snazzy cover sheet for you and provides you with a handy one-click toolbar for sending your fax.

How Can I Address an Envelope with Word?

Word provides a special tool for addressing envelopes that makes the process easy — particularly if you're writing a letter in which you've already included the address of the recipient. To address an envelope:

1. Choose Tools ⇨ Envelopes and Labels. This opens the Envelopes and Labels dialog box shown in Figure 9-8.

2. Enter the delivery address in the Delivery Address box, and the return address in the Return Address box. Note that the Return Address box may already contain your return address, if you entered it during the initial setup of Office.

Tip

If you're writing a business letter, you can avoid typing the delivery address twice by opening the letter, highlighting the address you've already typed into it, and then opening the Envelopes and Labels dialog box. The delivery address will automatically be inserted. That's how the address in Figure 9-8 was entered.

3. You can specify the envelope size and the placement of the delivery and return addresses by clicking the Preview area. This opens another dialog box that lets you select an envelope type from a list and enter the distances from the top and bottom edges of the envelope you want the addresses to appear.

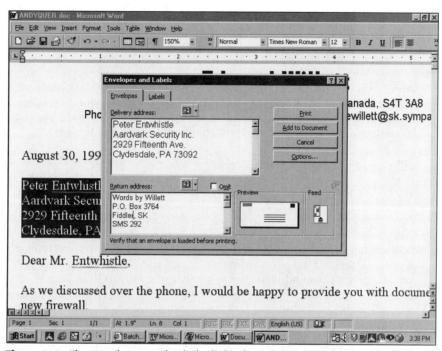

Figure 9-8: The Envelopes and Labels dialog box makes it easy for you to address envelopes.

4. To specify printing options, click the Feed image in the bottom right-hand corner. This opens a third dialog box, in which you can change the direction you feed the envelope into the printer, whether it goes in face up or face down, and which tray the printer should look for the envelope in. Note that only certain settings may work with your printer, so make sure you know what those are before you change things here!

5. If you'd like to add the envelope to the currently open document, click Add to Document. This places the envelope at the top of the document as page (and section) 1, so you can print it first, followed by the document. This can be very handy for printing letters.

6. To print the envelope, click Print.

Why Aren't All Toolbar Buttons Visible All the Time?

If you've used previous versions of Word, or, for that matter, most other Windows-based programs, you probably noticed immediately that there seem to be fewer toolbars at the top of your Word 2000 document than you might expect.

A closer inspection reveals that the usual Standard and Formatting toolbars are both still there, but they're now on the same level instead of a different level. In addition, they don't display all their buttons all the time, as you've probably come to expect. And not only that, but the buttons they do display seem to change.

Word 2000 does this not only to reduce clutter, but also as a way of automatically customizing itself to better fit your specific needs. When you first open Word, only the most commonly used commands are visible on the toolbars. As you work with Word, it adds other commands you commonly use to the toolbars.

The first time you click on a command, it's automatically made visible on the short toolbar, replacing a button that hasn't been used for a while. In this way, you eventually end up with toolbars that display the commands you use most often. The menus in the menu bar work the same way.

You can access all the available commands of any toolbar by clicking the More Buttons button at the toolbar's right end — it's the one with two sideways pointing arrows on top and a downward-pointing arrow at the bottom (see Figure 9-9). To see all the items available in any menu, just continue to hold your mouse pointer over the menu name for a few extra seconds or click on the double down arrow at the bottom of the menu.

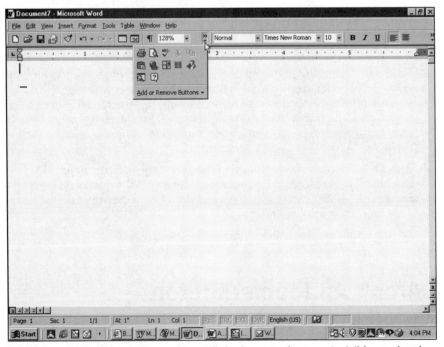

Figure 9-9: Click More Buttons to see all the buttons that aren't visible on the short toolbars.

If you'd prefer to have the Standard and Formatting toolbars appear the same way they do in earlier versions of Word, choose View ⇨ Toolbars ⇨ Customize, go to the Options tab, and then check the check box labeled "Standard and Formatting toolbars share one row."

How Can I Delete Word Documents in Word?

It's easy, but a bit counterintuitive, to say the least: to delete a Word document, don't look for a Delete command. Instead:

1. Choose File ⇨ Open to bring up the standard Open dialog box.

2. Locate the file you want to delete and highlight it.

3. Press the Delete key or click the Delete tool.

4. Windows will ask you if you're sure you want to send the selected file to the Recycle Bin. Click Yes.

5. To permanently delete the file, go to your Windows desktop, right-click on the Recycle Bin, and select Empty Recycle Bin from the shortcut menu.

How Can I Set a Different Default Font?

If Word begins all new documents using Times New Roman, and you'd rather be using Arial, you may want to change the default font in the Normal.dot template. To do so:

1. Choose Format ⇨ Font.

2. In the Font dialog box, select the font, font style, and size you want to make the default.

3. Click Default (see Figure 9-10).

4. Word asks you if you're sure; click OK.

The next time you start a new document, your new font, style, and size will be applied automatically.

How Do I Use AutoRecover to Prevent Data Loss?

It's important not to rely too much on AutoRecover, because it doesn't guarantee that parts of your document won't disappear into the ether in the event of a power failure or system crash. While AutoRecover does automatically save a copy of your document, it does so at specified intervals. If a crash happens near the end of one of those intervals, you may have made several changes that didn't make it into the AutoRecover file.

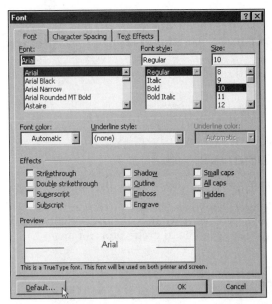

Figure 9-10: Click the Default button in the lower-left corner of the Font dialog box to make the font you've just set the default font for future Word documents.

It's also important to remember that AutoRecover files are temporary. They're erased when you save a file yourself and they are deleted completely when you close a file. That means that if you simply turn off Word without saving your file, you won't be able to get it back later from the AutoRecover file.

To change the amount of time that passes between AutoRecover saves:

1. Choose Tools ➪ Options, and click on the Save tab.

2. Make sure the Save AutoRecover Info Every check box is selected.

3. Enter the interval you want to elapse between AutoRecover saves in the box just to the right of that (see Figure 9-11). The default is 10 minutes.

4. Click OK.

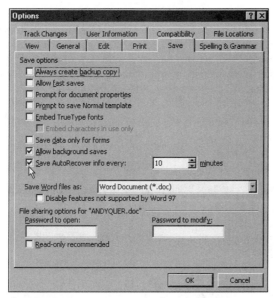

Figure 9-11: You can set the interval between AutoRecover saves in the Options dialog box.

How Can I Recover Damaged Documents?

Word includes a special converter called Recover Text from Any File that lets you extract text from any file, including non-Word files. Special formatting and anything that isn't text — such as pictures and tables — cannot be recovered, but text elements such as headers, footers, footnotes, and endnotes can.

To use the converter on a Word file, simply choose File ➪ Open, find and select the damaged file, select "Recover Text from Any File" in the Files of Type box in the Open dialog box, and click Open. To use the converter on a non-Word file:

1. Choose Tools ➪ Options.

2. Select the General tab and check the "Confirm Conversion at Open" check box.

3. Click OK.

4. Choose File ➪ Open.

5. Locate and select the file you want to recover and click Open.

6. Select the Recover Text From Any File converter (see Figure 9-12), and click OK.

Word will convert the damaged document and recover any text from the document.

Caution

Sometimes, after Word quits unexpectedly, the AutoRecover file may be damaged. In that case, the next time you open Word you'll get a message that says Word encountered file corruption, and you'll be asked if you want to attempt recovery. If you click No, the document will be permanently lost; if you click Yes, Word will automatically attempt to recover the document using the Recover Text from Any File converter. If it's successful, the recovered document will be opened in normal Word format.

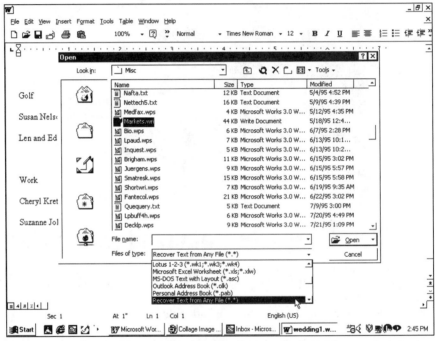

Figure 9-12: Choose this converter from the list to recover text from a damaged or non-Word file.

How Do I Work with Master Documents?

A master document is a document that contains a set of related documents. For example, if you were writing a book, you could create a master document (the book as a whole) made up of, say, 25 subdocuments (the chapters of the book). In a network environment, master documents can be even more useful. A corporate annual report could be stored as a master document while the subdocuments that made it up — reports from various departments, etc. — could be worked on by different individuals. In that way the master document itself would always be as up-to-date as possible and could be referred to by all the people working on its various components.

Creating Master and Subdocuments

To create a master document and subdocuments:

1. Create an outline of your master document. For each section you want to turn into a subdocument, be sure to use the same heading style.

2. Select the part of the document you want to break into subdocuments. Make sure it begins with the heading style you've selected.

3. On the Outline toolbar, click the Create Subdocument button. Word creates a new subdocument everywhere in the selection where the heading style that begins the selection appears. For example, if the selected area begins with Heading 2, a new subdocument will be inserted everywhere you used the Heading 2 style (see Figure 9-13)

4. Save the outline. It becomes the master document; each subdocument is saved with a name based on the text you used in its heading.

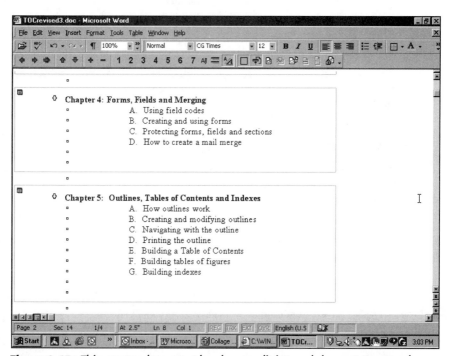

Figure 9-13: This master document has been split into subdocuments at each chapter heading.

Tip   You can also convert an existing document to a master document and then divide it into subdocuments simply by going to Outline View and following the same procedure.

Converting Documents to Subdocuments

You can also turn an existing document into a subdocument of a master document. To do so, open the master document, place the insertion point where you want to insert the new subdocument, click the Insert Subdocument button on the Outlining toolbar, and locate and select the file you want to insert.

Rearranging and Editing Subdocuments

You can quickly change the structure of a master document by adding, removing, combining, splitting, renaming, or rearranging its subdocuments. By default, the subdocuments are hidden when you open a master document, but you can use the Expand and Collapse Subdocuments buttons on the Outlining toolbar to see them in detail. When they're collapsed, each subdocument's name appears as a hyperlink; clicking on the link opens that subdocument.

You can edit each subdocument just as you would a regular Word document. The master document's template applies to all the subdocuments, which ensures a consistent design, and you can print all of the subdocuments at once simply by printing the master document.

Master and Subdocument Security

Within a workgroup, if someone is working on a subdocument, that document is "locked" to everyone else. Users can view it, but they can't modify it until the subdocument is closed. Also, master documents and subdocuments can both be assigned passwords to limit access.

Cross-Reference   For more information on protecting documents, see Chapter 54, "Collaborating on a Network."

How Can I Prevent Unwanted Page Breaks?

Word provides you with a number of ways to control where your pages break. The most straightforward way to ensure that page breaks occur only where you want them is to insert them yourself. To insert a page break, go to Print Layout View, place your insertion point where you want the break to occur, and press Ctrl+Enter.

Automatic Page Break Controls

Automatic methods of controlling page breaks can be found by choosing Format ⇨ Paragraph, and then selecting the Line and Page Breaks tab (see Figure 9-14). Four options here can help you:

✦ **Widow/Orphan control.** Despite its ominous-sounding name, this is simply an automatic method of keeping your text looking good. It prevents Word from printing the last line of a paragraph all by itself at the top of a page (a widow) or the first line of a paragraph all by itself at the bottom of a page (an orphan).

✦ **Keep with next.** This prevents a page break from being inserted between the selected paragraph and the one that follows it.

✦ **Keep lines together.** This prevents a page break anywhere within the selected paragraph.

✦ **Page break before.** This inserts a page break in front of the selected paragraph.

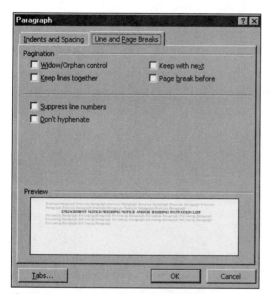

Figure 9-14: Word offers several methods of controlling page breaks in paragraphs.

Note

You can also control page breaks by altering your margins and viewing the results in Print Layout View. However, altering margins can sometimes have unintended consequences in other parts of your document, so be sure to examine the entire document carefully before printing.

Controlling Page Breaks in Tables

Sometimes page breaks fall in the middle of tables, sometimes even splitting a row. To keep the entire table on the same page, put a page break just above it. To simply prevent rows from splitting:

1. Place your insertion point in the row that is being split.

2. Choose Table ➪ Table Properties.

3. Click on the Row tab.

4. Clear the Allow Row to Break Across Pages check box.

5. Repeat Step 4 for each row you want to prevent from breaking. You can change rows without closing the Table Properties dialog box by using the Previous Row and Next Row buttons. When you're done, click OK.

Excel

P A R T

In This Part

Chapter 10
Worksheets and
Workbooks

Chapter 11
Entering and
Formatting
Information

Chapter 12
Charts

Chapter 13
Functions and
Formulas

Chapter 14
Lists and Databases

Chapter 15
Templates, Forms,
and Graphics

Chapter 16
PivotTable and
PivotChart Reports

Chapter 17
Using Excel to
Analyze Data

Chapter 18
Excel at Work

Chapter 19
Excel Top 10

Worksheets and Workbooks

Workbooks, not worksheets, are the basic file in
Excel — even if you're only using a single worksheet,
it's still contained in a workbook. Workbooks, in essence, are
the containers for worksheets. Think of workbooks as the
ledger books that contain the pages on which you enter
information. Worksheets are grids of cells arranged in rows
and columns. When you first start Excel, or any time you
create a new workbook, you'll notice that you have three
different worksheets in your workbook. Each worksheet is
independent of the others.

Understanding Workbooks

Excel starts with a blank workbook titled "Book1" (see Figure
10-1). If you are just starting a new project, simply use the
blank default workbook and save it under a new name. (See
the section on saving workbooks later in this chapter.)

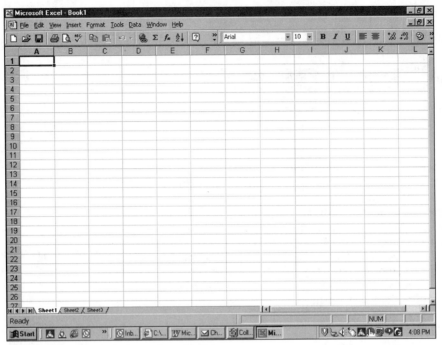

Figure 10-1: The default Excel workbook.

Opening new workbooks

There are times when you might want more than one workbook open at the same time. To open another new workbook, select File ➪ New from the menu. This brings up the New dialog box (see Figure 10-2).

Select the General tab, click Workbook, and then click the OK button to create a new workbook.

Tip   The other tab in the New dialog box is labeled Spreadsheet Solutions, and contains templates for pre-designed projects like invoices and expense reports. If one of the templates fits your needs, you can select it for your new workbook and have a head start on completing your work.

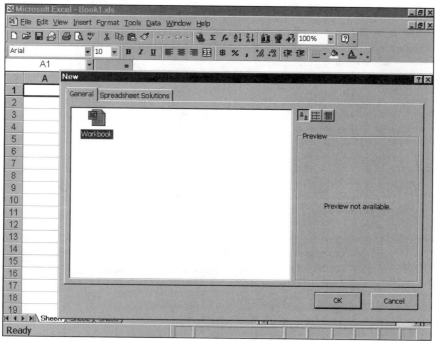

Figure 10-2: The New dialog box.

Opening existing workbooks

If the workbook you want to open is one you've recently had open, it'll be listed in your File menu. Select File from the menu, and then look at the bottom of the drop-down menu options. Your most recently used files will be listed just above the Exit option. Click on the name of the file you want to open.

Otherwise, you'll have to use the standard Open method. Either click on the Open tool or select File ➪ Open from the menu. The Office 2000 Open dialog box has a new look to it, and you can choose from History, My Documents, Desktop, Favorites, or Web Folders (see Figure 10-3). The initial file listing is from the default file folder. This is C:\ My Documents (assuming you've done a standard installation on drive C).

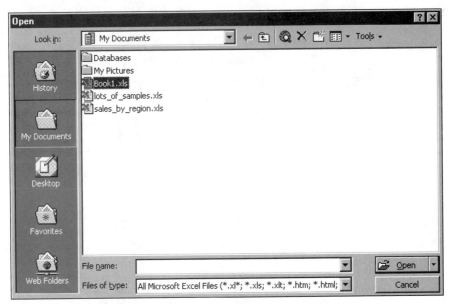

Figure 10-3: The Open dialog box.

Select the file you want, and then click the Open button (or just double-click on the desired file). If the file you want isn't in the default folder, use the folder navigation buttons to find the correct folder or use the file finding methods detailed later in this chapter.

Adding More Files to the List

The recently used files list has only four files in it by default, but you can set it to display up to nine files. To do this, follow these steps:

1. Select Tools ➪ Options from the menu.

2. Click on the General tab.

3. Make sure that the Recently Used File List check box has a checkmark in it.

4. Under entries, enter the number of files you want listed. You can either use the arrows to scroll through the numbers or type the number in directly.

5. Click the OK button and the number of files retained will be reset.

Working with Worksheets

When you first start Excel, or any time you create a new workbook, you'll notice that you have three different worksheets in your workbook. Each worksheet is independent of the others, and they're accessed by clicking on the tabs labeled "Sheet1," "Sheet2," and "Sheet3" at the bottom of the screen (see Figure 10-4) on the same level as your horizontal scrollbar. The tabs are called, appropriately enough, *sheet tabs*. You don't have to use all of the worksheets. You can add or delete worksheets at will. And if you'd rather start with more or less than three worksheets, you can easily change the default number.

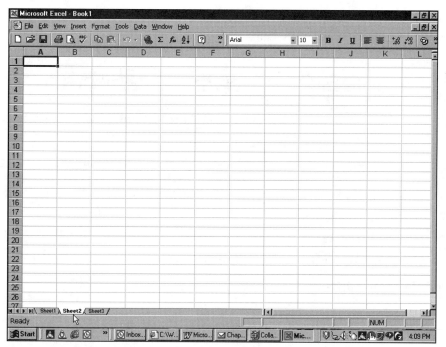

Figure 10-4: Sheet tabs.

Identifying rows and columns

Worksheets are grids of cells arranged in rows and columns. Each row has its own numerical designation, ranging from 1 to 65,536. Each column has an alphabetical designation. The first 26 columns are A through Z. After that, they go from AA through AZ, BA through BZ, and so on, until you reach the final column, which is designated IV. It doesn't go all the way to IZ because it stops at 256 total columns.

Each cell has its own distinct designation based on the row and column that contain it, with the column noted first. Thus, the cell at the intersection of Column B and Row 12 is called B12.

Tip   Although there theoretically shouldn't be any problem with cell references, if you change the cell mapping system after entering data and formulas (see the sidebar "Changing the Cell Mapping System"), it's prudent to make such decisions before beginning work on your worksheet, just in case.

Whichever cell reference style you choose to use, the purpose and function of the cells doesn't change. You enter data into the cells, and then perform calculations on that data.

Cross-Reference   We'll be covering the methods of entering and manipulating data in the rest of the chapters in this part of the book.

Changing the Cell Mapping System

Although the vast majority of people use the default cell reference style, you can use an alternative cell mapping system that uses a numerical designation for the columns. It's called *R1C1* (an abbreviation for "Row 1, Column 1"), and the columns are numbered just like the rows, running from 1 through 256 instead of from A through IV. Using the R1C1 approach, the row is noted first and the column last. Thus, the cell at the intersection of Column 2 and Row 12 is called R12C2. To use this cell reference style, follow these steps:

1. Select Tools ➪ Options from the menu.

2. Click the General tab in the Options dialog box.

3. Click the check box labeled "R1C1 reference style."

4. Click the OK button.

Moving around the grid

You can make any cell in the grid the active cell by clicking within it. Anything you type or paste goes into the active cell. In addition to the mouse method, you can use the keyboard to move around the grid. The arrow keys, Page Up, and so forth, change the active cell. If you press the down arrow key, the cell below the one you've been in becomes the new active cell; if you press the right arrow key, the cell to the right becomes the new active cell, and so on. Table 16-1 details which keys and key combinations achieve which results:

Table 10-1
Navigation Keys

Key	Action
Home	Moves to the first cell in the current row.
End	No effect unless followed by pressing one of the arrow keys (see below).
Page Down	Moves down one screen.
Page Up	Moves up one screen.
Down Arrow	Moves down one cell in the same column.
Left Arrow	Moves left one cell in the same row.
Right Arrow	Moves right one cell in the same row.
Up Arrow	Moves up one cell in the same column.
Ctrl+Down Arrow	Moves to the bottom cell in the current column if no cells in that column below the active cell have data in them. Otherwise, if starting from an empty cell or a cell that contains data but is above an empty cell, stops at the next cell with data in it. If starting from a cell with data in it, which is contiguous to other cells containing data, stops at the last contiguous cell that also contains data.
Ctrl+Left Arrow	Moves to the first cell in the current row (same as Home) if no cells in that row to the left of the active cell have data in them. Otherwise, if starting from an empty cell or a cell that contains data but is to the right of an empty cell, stops at the next cell with data in it. If starting from a cell with data in it, which is contiguous to other cells containing data, stops at the last contiguous cell that also contains data.
Ctrl+Right Arrow	Moves to the last cell in the current row if no cells in that row to the right of the active cell have data in them. Otherwise, if starting from an empty cell or a cell that contains data but is to the left of an empty cell, stops at the next cell with data in it. If starting from a cell with data in it, which is contiguous to other cells containing data, stops at the last contiguous cell that also contains data.
Ctrl+Up Arrow	Moves to the top cell in the current column if no cells in that column above the active cell have data in them. Otherwise, if starting from an empty cell or a cell that contains data but is below an empty cell, stops at the next cell with data in it. If starting from a cell with data in it, which is contiguous to other cells containing data, stops at the last contiguous cell that also contains data.
Ctrl+Home	Moves to the top left cell in the grid (A1).
Ctrl+End	Moves to the cell that intersects the last row containing data and the last column containing data in the grid .

Continued

Table 10-1 *(continued)*

Key	Action
End, Down Arrow	Does the same as CTRL+Down Arrow.
End, Left Arrow	Does the same as CTRL+Left Arrow.
End, Right Arrow	Does the same as CTRL+Right Arrow.
End, Up Arrow	does the same as CTRL+Right Arrow.

Using the Go To command

To get to a cell that is not readily visible because of the size of the worksheet, you can use the scroll bars or take the easy way and use the Go To command. To do so, follow these steps:

1. Select Edit ⇨ Go To from the menu. This will bring up the Go To dialog box (see Figure 10-5).

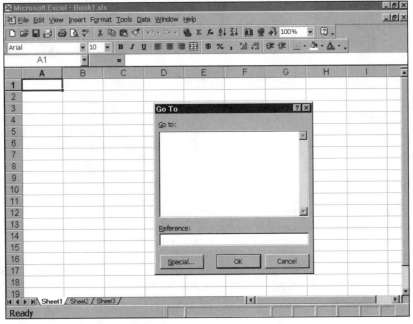

Figure 10-5: The Go To dialog box.

2. Under Reference, type in the cell designation of the desired cell.

3. Click the OK button and you'll go right to the desired cell.

Tip The Go To dialog box keeps a history of cells you've used it for. If you're using the same one over again, just select it from the list instead of typing it in again.

Adding and deleting worksheets

To add a worksheet, first click on the sheet tab of the worksheet you want to put it before, and then choose Insert ➪ Worksheet from the menu. You can add more than one worksheet at a time, too, but only as many as you currently have. Say you're starting with the default three worksheets. You can add two worksheets by clicking on the first sheet tab, and then holding down the Shift key and clicking on the second sheet tab. This selects both worksheets. Next, choose Insert ➪ Worksheet from the menu just as you would for a single worksheet. Two worksheets will be inserted. If you had selected all three of the default worksheets, three worksheets would have been inserted. Because the number of worksheets to be added is determined by the number of worksheets you select, there is no way to create more than double the number of worksheets you have at a time.

To delete a worksheet, right-click on its sheet tab, and then select Delete from the pop-up menu (see Figure 10-6). You will be asked to confirm or abort the deletion. To confirm, click the OK button. To cancel, click the Cancel button. Deleting several worksheets is just as simple. Just click on the first one you want to delete, hold down the Shift key, and click on the last one. All the ones in between will also be selected that way. Right-click on any of the selected sheet tabs, and then follow the same procedure as for deleting one worksheet.

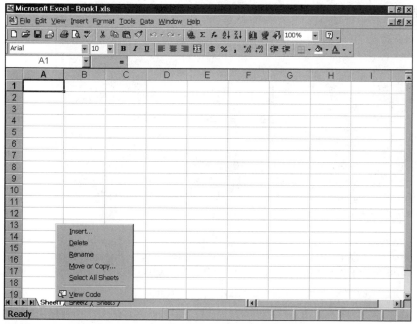

Figure 10-6: Sheet tab pop-up menu.

The one drawback to the multiple deletion technique described above is that it's only good for deleting contiguous worksheets. If you need to delete multiple worksheets that are not side by side, use the same procedure, but hold down the Ctrl key while selecting the worksheets instead of the Shift key. The Ctrl key cannot be used to select a range of worksheets, however — only individual ones. You can use both approaches together if you need to. For example, if you have seven worksheets open and you need to get rid of the first three and the sixth one, you can use the Shift key approach to select the first three as a range of worksheets, and then use the Ctrl key approach to select the sixth worksheet individually.

Changing the default number of worksheets

To change the default number of worksheets, follow these steps:

1. Select Tools ➪ Options from the menu.

2. Click the General tab in the Options dialog box (see Figure 10-7).

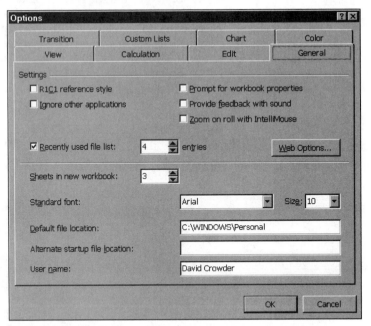

Figure 10-7: The Options dialog box.

3. Choose the number of desired worksheets in the Sheets in New Workbook text box. You can either use the up and down arrows to increase or decrease the number, or you can simply type the number directly into the box.

4. Click the OK button to complete the procedure.

Moving and copying worksheets

You can also move a worksheet to another location. However, if you want it at the end, you can't insert it there, because it has to go before another worksheet, not after. To move a worksheet within the same workbook, just click on the sheet tab and drag it to where you want it, and then release the mouse button. To copy the workbook, do the same thing, but press the Ctrl button before you drag the worksheet, and drop the worksheet before you release the Ctrl button.

To move a worksheet to another workbook you have open, follow these steps:

1. Right-click on its sheet tab.

2. Select Move or Copy from the pop-up menu (refer to Figure 10-6). This brings up the Move or Copy dialog box (see Figure 10-8).

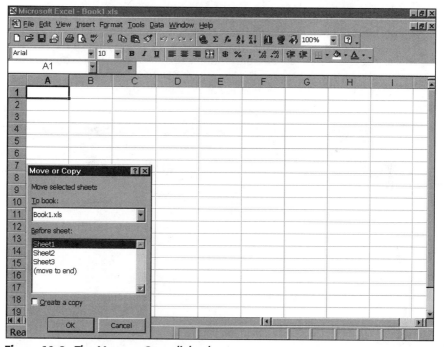

Figure 10-8: The Move or Copy dialog box.

3. Pick the workbook from the drop-down list (if you select New Book, you will create a new workbook containing only the selected worksheet).

4. Choose to place it before another worksheet or select Move to End.

5. To make a copy of the worksheet in the other workbook instead of moving the worksheet into it, just click the Create a Copy check box.

6. Click the OK button.

Caution   It's best not to move worksheets when other objects such as charts or other work-sheets depend on the data within them.

Changing worksheet names

All worksheets, when created, bear the name "Sheet#" with the "#" representing the number of the current worksheet. While this does help to differentiate among the various worksheets in a workbook, it's not terribly informative. It may not matter if you're using a single worksheet for personal use such as balancing your checkbook, but if you're using multiple worksheets or if other people need to understand your worksheet arrangements, you'll probably want to give them more descriptive names like "January Sales" or "Midwest Shipments." To change a worksheet name, double-click on the sheet tab. This will highlight the worksheet name, and you can just type the new name over the default one. The size of the sheet tab will expand to fit the size of the worksheet title. You can use up to 31 characters in a worksheet name.

If you add lots of worksheets, or the titles on them are very large, you will end up with a situation where not all of the sheet tabs are visible at once. To view the ones that are out of sight, use the arrows in the lower-left corner of the screen (see Figure 10-9). They're styled like standard database controls. The one on the far left takes you to the first sheet tab, the one on the far right takes you to the last sheet tab, and the two in the middle advance the sheet tab view by one sheet tab left or right.

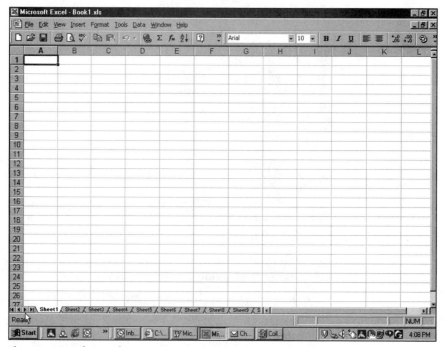

Figure 10-9: Sheet tab arrows.

You can get more viewable area for the sheet tabs by clicking on the dividing line between the sheet tabs and the horizontal scrollbar, and then dragging the divider to the right. This shortens the scrollbar, however.

Selecting and Using Ranges

Ranges are groups of cells. A range can be as little as two cells or as large as the entire worksheet. We'll be using ranges for lots of different purposes in the various chapters on Excel.

A range of cells is usually selected by clicking in the top, left cell and, while holding the mouse button down, dragging the pointer till it's in the lower-right cell of the desired range (see Figure 10-10). If you don't like dragging, you can also click in the top, left cell, move the pointer to the bottom right cell of the range, hold down the Shift key, and click in the bottom right cell.

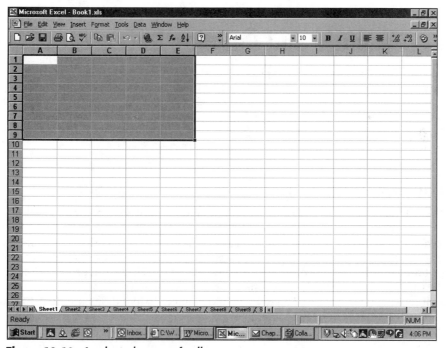

Figure 10-10: A selected range of cells.

Tip   Starting in the upper-left cell is customary, but there is no actual requirement to do so. You can start in any corner of the range.

What if the range you want to select is larger than you can comfortably select using these methods? One way to select a large range of cells is to use the keyboard combinations detailed in Table 16-1, but hold down the Shift key while performing them. You can also select an entire row by clicking on the row number to the left of the first cell in the row. Likewise, an entire column can be selected by clicking on the column designation above the top cell in the column.

Tip   To select a very large range in a hurry, click on the first cell in the range, and then select Edit ⇨ Go To from the menu. This will bring up the Go To dialog box. Under Reference, type in the cell designation of the opposite corner of the range. Hold down the Shift key and click the OK button.

There's another aspect to ranges you'll want to keep in mind. Although a "range" is normally thought of as a series of contiguous cells, there's no real requirement that they be side by side. You can select a group of noncontiguous cells by holding down the Ctrl key while selecting them. For example, you could click in cell A1 and then, while holding the Ctrl key down, click in cell D5. The two cells would each be selected and would constitute a noncontiguous range.

Using Absolute and Relative References

Cells and ranges can be referred to by three different approaches. The first two are essentially the same, but with one important difference. Using the normal cell reference method, in which the top left cell is called A1, a range that ran from that cell to D1 would be referred to as A1:D1. If it ran from A1 to H8, it would be referred to as A1:H8, and so on. You can designate an entire column or row by using it as both the start and end points of a range, as in A:A or 3:3.

Copying or moving cells

The catch comes when cells or ranges are copied or moved to another location. Any formulas that were included in one or more of those cells change their cell references to reflect their new location. Depending on your desires and worksheet planning, this may or may not be a good thing. For instance, say you have a worksheet set up to add the numbers in two cells together and put the total in a third cell. The formula in the third cell is "=B1+B2." If you copied the cell that held the totals to another location, the references to B1 and B2 would change. To avoid this problem, formulas that depend on the absolute location of cells should use the dollar sign ($) in front of the cell references. So the formula would read "=$B1+$B2" instead.

Note   If you had copied the entire range of cells to a new location, the changes in the cell references would not have affected the total, because the data on which the formula acts would have moved as well. In that case, you wouldn't want to use the $ symbol, because that locks the formula in to using the original (and now empty) cells. For more information on using formulas, see Chapter 13, "Functions and Formulas."

Using names

The third method of referring to cells or ranges is to give them a descriptive name. Actually, all cells already have a name. It's just that calling a cell N372 is not really informative, other than giving its location in the grid. If you have a very small worksheet, it doesn't really matter much, but if you're doing anything large and complex, it can help a lot to be able to refer to cells and ranges by such names as "Total" or "FebruaryCredits."

Naming a cell or range is about the easiest thing there is to do in Excel. Just click on the cell (or select the range) you want to name, and then click in the Name box (see Figure 10-11) and type in the name you want to use. Press Enter to finalize it.

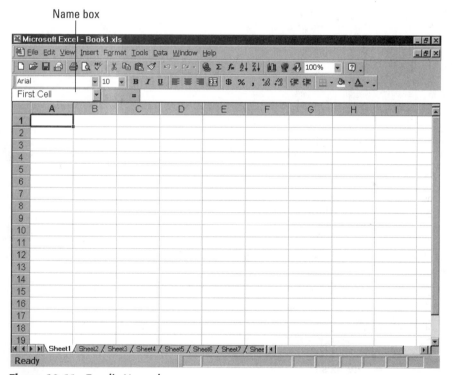

Figure 10-11: Excel's Name box.

Caution   When you use more than one word in a name, you can't use spaces. Use the underscore character (_) or a hyphen (-) instead. Names can be up to 255 characters, but ranges won't work right if you use more than 253 characters. Finally, if you use a named cell in a formula, it has the same effect as using the $ character — if you copy or move the cell containing the formula, the reference to the named cell will not change.

Saving and Closing a Workbook

To save a workbook, follow these steps:

1. Click the Save button in the toolbar. If this is the first time you've saved this workbook, you'll find yourself looking at the Save As dialog box (see Figure 10-12). If you've saved the workbook previously, it'll just save without any further effort on your part.

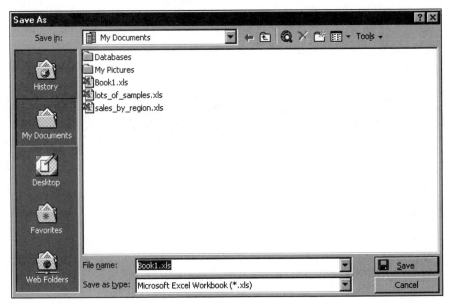

Figure 10-12: The Save As dialog box.

2. Choose the folder you want to save the workbook in.

3. Type a name in the File Name edit box

4. Click the Save button.

5. If you later want to save the same workbook under a different name, select File ➪ Save As from the menu and follow the same procedure as for a first-time save.

6. If you want to save in some format other than Excel's native one, pick the format from the Save as Type drop-down list before you click the Save button. Be aware that doing this will mean that the resultant file will have the limitations of the format it's saved in.

Note   Make it a point to save your workbooks early in the process. Otherwise, you may end up losing your work in the event of a crash.

Setting backups

It's a really good idea to have Excel create automatic backups for you. That way, every time you save your workbook, the earlier version is saved as a backup file instead of being overwritten. To do this, in the Save As dialog box, select Tools ⇨ General Options. This will bring up the Save Options dialog box (see Figure 10-13). Click the Always Create Backup check box.

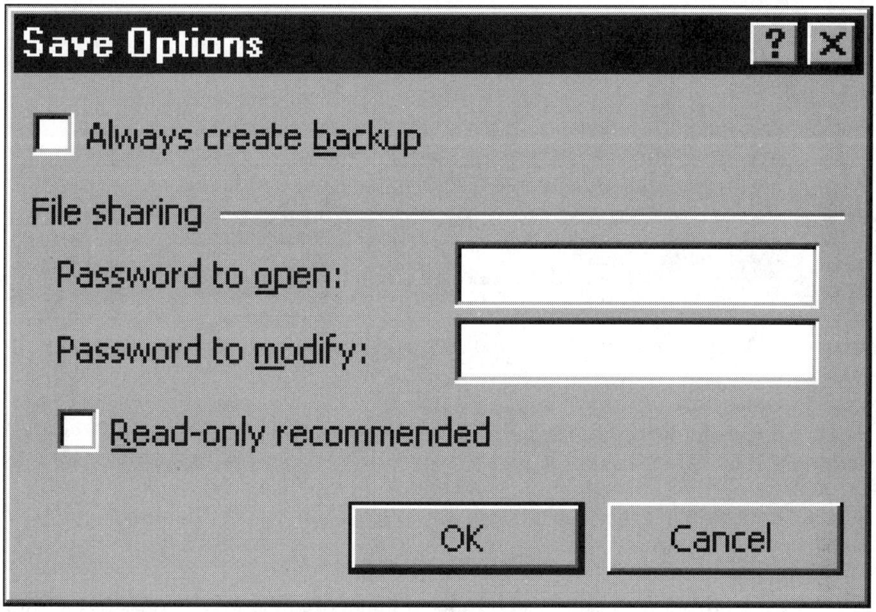

Save Options [?] [X]

☐ Always create backup

File sharing

Password to open: [   ]

Password to modify: [   ]

☐ Read-only recommended

[OK] [Cancel]

Figure 10-13: The Save Options dialog box.

Caution The backup files option is only effective for the file you set it on. You have to set the option on every single file you save, as there is no global backup option in Excel the way there is in Word.

Saving as a Web page

To save an Excel file as a Web page, select File ⇨ Save As Web Page from the menu. This brings up the Save As dialog box with Web options (see Figure 10-14).

Figure 10-14: The Save As Web Page dialog box.

There are a number of different things to consider when saving an Excel file as a Web page. The first is whether to save the entire workbook or a single worksheet (or portion of a worksheet, such as a range). Saving the workbook results in static data, whereas saving the worksheet allows you to preserve the functionality of Excel on your Web page.

Tip   The title of the Web page will be the same as the filename. If you'd rather have a different title, click the Change button and type your new title into the resultant dialog box. This will not change the filename.

To save a worksheet or part of a worksheet, click the Selection: Sheet radio button. The Add Interactivity check box now becomes active. Click it if you don't want a static Web page. Instead of clicking the Save button, click the Publish button. This brings up the Publish As Web Page dialog box (see Figure 10-15).

Caution   The interactivity of Web pages created with Excel is limited to users of the Internet Explorer Web browser, version 4.0 and later.

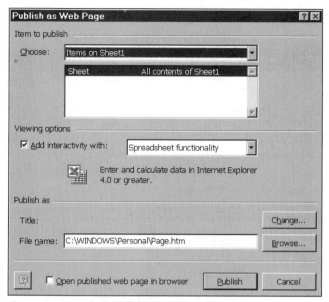

Figure 10-15: The Publish As Web Page dialog box.

By default, the entire selected worksheet is slated for publication. However, if you have cells selected when you choose Save as Web Page, the selection is the default. If you'd like to change this, make a different selection from the drop-down list under Choose. If you passed up the opportunity to choose interactivity, you can still add it here by clicking the Add Interactivity With check box. There will be various options in the adjacent drop-down list box depending on what part of the sheet you're selecting to publish. For example, normal spreadsheet interactivity, PivotTable interactivity, or Chart interactivity.

You can change the title of the Web page here if you didn't already in the previous dialog box. To do so, click the Change button and enter the new title. Finally, click the Publish button.

Tip   Click the Open Published Web Page in Browser check box if you want to view the results of your save operation immediately in Internet Explorer.

Finding Workbooks

If you have lots of workbooks scattered around your system and you're not sure which one you need or where to find it, you can use the Open dialog box to track down the one that has the information you want in it. The File Open dialog box has changed a bit from Office 97. The old familiar find options are not as readily accessible in the new version, but they're still there.

To get to the Open dialog box (see Figure 10-16), follow these steps:

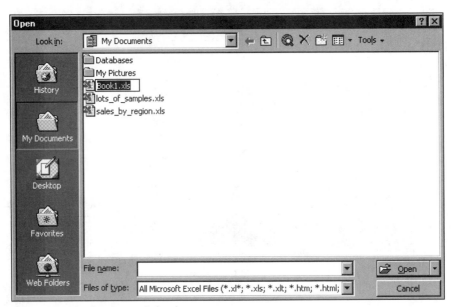

Figure 10-16: The Open dialog box.

1. Click the Open button in the toolbar.

2. Alternatively, select File ➪ Open from the menu.

3. In Office 97, the basic search options were on the Open dialog box itself and the more sophisticated ones were accessed via the Advanced button. Now, you select Tools ➪ Find from the menu in the dialog box to get to all the search options in one package.

Tip   It's faster to just use the Ctrl+F key combination to get to the file-finding tools.

4. This brings up the Find dialog box (see Figure 10-17). It's already set to search for Excel files.

5. You first need to decide whether to make the search case-sensitive or not. In case-sensitive searches, ThisProperty is not the same thing as tHIsPRopeRtY. Selecting Match Case Exactly means that the search will be case-sensitive. If you select the Match All Word Forms check box, the search will find different variations of words, such as tenses of verbs. Note that neither of these options apply to filenames, but only to other criteria in the search. Filenames are always matched without case sensitivity.

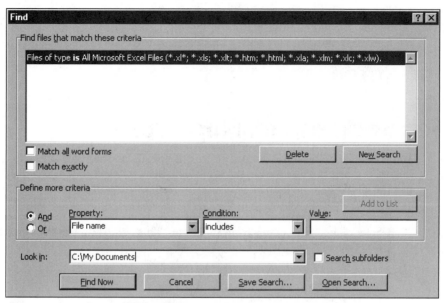

Figure 10-17: The Find dialog box.

6. Next, under Define More Criteria, you can select the properties and values you want to search for. Each criterion you input is added to the list at the top, and Find will search for the files that meet the conditions you specify.

7. The two radio buttons labeled "And" and "Or" perform Boolean logic on your options. Clicking the And radio button means that the criterion you're adding must be met in addition to any other criteria; clicking the Or radio button means that either that value or others in the search can be met.

8. In the Property drop-down list, select the item you're examining. This can be the filename, text contained within the file, or a variety of other options.

9. In the Condition drop-down list, pick what condition must be met; for instance whether the property must include, begin with, or end with the value.

10. Enter the value itself under Value.

11. Once you've defined the criteria, click the Add to List button and the search criteria appear in the list at the top of the Find dialog box.

12. If necessary, add more search criteria until you've narrowed the search sufficiently.

13. When you're ready to go, click the Find Now button.

For instance, say you're searching for a file that deals with a company named SEA. You know that the filenames of all the workbooks you've ever created for them start with "SEA," but they all have different endings. You could find all of them by selecting "File name" under Property, "begins with" under Condition, and typing "SEA" under Value.

Tip If you're not finding the files you're looking for, expand the search by using the Look in feature at the bottom of the dialog box to choose different folders. The one way to make sure you're looking everywhere is to select the root folder and click the Search Subfolders check box. That forces Find to look in every folder on your drive.

Setting Workbook Properties

You'll be doing yourself a favor if you set things up so that files are easy to find before you need to go looking for them. The best way to do this, other than by using well-planned filenames, is to use the workbook properties. These properties are a set of descriptive terms about the workbook. To set them, follow these steps:

1. Select File ➪ Properties from the menu. This brings up the Properties dialog box (see Figure 10-18).

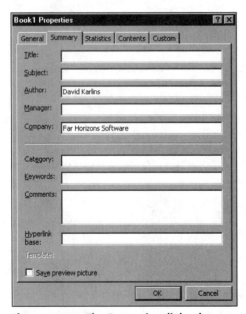

Figure 10-18: The Properties dialog box.

2. If it is not already selected, click on the Summary tab. All the information on this form can be searched for with the Find dialog box.

3. Enter Title, Subject, and any other pertinent data. Keywords and Comments can be particularly useful in finding a file later on.

4. When you're done, click the OK button to save the properties. When you save your workbook, the properties will be saved right along with it.

Summary

In this chapter, you learned how to work with workbooks and worksheets in Excel. Major points of the chapter included the following:

✦ Workbooks contain worksheets, just like ledger books contain pages.

✦ Worksheets are grids of cells arranged in rows and columns.

✦ You can change the active cell with the mouse, keyboard, or the Go To command.

✦ Worksheets can be added to or deleted from workbooks.

✦ Worksheets can be moved or copied.

✦ You can rename worksheets.

✦ Ranges are groups of cells, and there are a variety of methods for selecting ranges.

✦ Cells and ranges can be referred to by both absolute and relative references.

✦ Workbooks can be saved in other formats besides Excel.

✦ Worksheets can be saved as Web pages.

✦ You can use a variety of sophisticated search techniques to locate workbooks.

✦   ✦   ✦

Entering and Formatting Information

Although entering simple text and numbers is a piece of cake in Excel, there are some tricks that will make your life a lot easier. This chapter shows you how to use Excel's fill series to easily extend a sequential series of labels, how to enter fractions so Excel doesn't think they're dates, and how to apply number formats. It also explains your different cell editing options and how you can rearrange cells once they're in place or even add entire new rows and columns within worksheets.

Some simple planning ahead, such as labeling rows and columns that contain data, will make your worksheets easier to use and understand. You can also add pop-up comments to cells if further explanation is needed. Furthermore, you can use font faces, sizes, styles, and colors, as well as background colors and patterns to help create a graphical look that will guide viewers in understanding your data.

Excel has a large number of built-in formats for numbers, dates, and times, and you can create your own custom formats as well. If you don't want to work out all the details by hand, Excel's AutoFormat feature instantly applies consistent looks to worksheets.

Entering and Editing Data

Anything you type or paste in an Excel worksheet goes into the active cell. Text, formulas, numbers, dates, and times are common examples of the kind of data Excel is designed to handle. Just click in the cell you want to enter data into and you're ready to go. Type it in, press the Tab or Enter keys, or just click on another cell, and the data's entered.

Unless you're just whipping up a really simple quick 'n' dirty calculation for your own use, though, there's one thing you'll want to do first: label your data. At an absolute minimum, label the rows and columns of your worksheet. It's usually useful to put in an overall title at the top of the worksheet as well, although the sheet tab can function in the same capacity. Data labels serve the same function for rows and columns as the names on sheet tabs do for worksheets. Without labels, all you'll have, no matter how carefully crafted your formulas and calculations are, is a meaningless jumble of data.

Cross-Reference   See the section entitled "Copying, Moving, and Merging Cells" later in this chapter for information about creating labels that span more than one row or column.

Creating data labels

There are two basic kinds of label arrangements. The first simply uses a single line of labels, either across the top of the worksheet to designate columns; or down the side of the worksheet to designate rows. Whether the line of labels runs horizontally or vertically, it usually begins in the first column (see Figure 11-1 for an example of the horizontal labeling scheme).

	A	B	C	D	E
1	NE	NW	SE	SW	All Regions
2	$2,734,043	$6,429,834	$300,304	$3,843,900	$13,308,081
3	$1,438,293	$3,322,398	$1,248,902	$4,002,942	$10,012,535
4	$892,300	$4,925,028	$2,984,020	$3,492,348	$12,293,696
5	$372,891	$5,032,994	$4,192,858	$3,982,197	$13,580,940
6	$5,437,527	$19,710,254	$8,726,084	$15,321,387	$49,195,252

Figure 11-1: A horizontal line of labels.

This type of data labeling scheme is best used for delineating series of single values over time, by location, or by some other individual factor. One example would be to show annual sales figures by office or individual. Another would be to compare subscriptions by geographical region.

The other, more complex, label arrangement uses both row and column labels. Because the first column of the worksheet is occupied by labels, as is the first row in the range of cells holding your data, the top left cell in the range has no place in either labeling or containing data (see Figure 11-2). While some people persist in trying to find some function for the first cell, apparently feeling there's something not quite right about leaving it blank, no one has ever managed to find a way to put an unconfusing label in that cell with this type of label design. Inevitably, third parties viewing the worksheet try to fit any label in that cell into either the vertical or horizontal scheme of labels it's contiguous to, and there's no way to make it really clear to which one it belongs. Leave it blank.

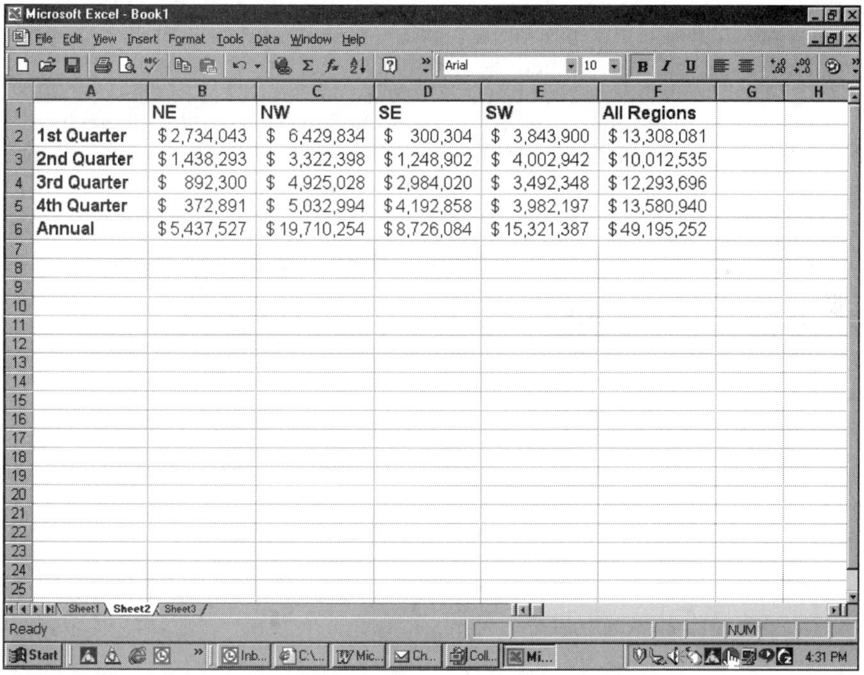

	NE	NW	SE	SW	All Regions
1st Quarter	$ 2,734,043	$ 6,429,834	$ 300,304	$ 3,843,900	$ 13,308,081
2nd Quarter	$ 1,438,293	$ 3,322,398	$ 1,248,902	$ 4,002,942	$ 10,012,535
3rd Quarter	$ 892,300	$ 4,925,028	$ 2,984,020	$ 3,492,348	$ 12,293,696
4th Quarter	$ 372,891	$ 5,032,994	$ 4,192,858	$ 3,982,197	$ 13,580,940
Annual	$ 5,437,527	$ 19,710,254	$ 8,726,084	$ 15,321,387	$ 49,195,252

Figure 11-2: A double line of labels.

Use the double-line data labeling scheme when you have multiple values to compare in various ways. Take the earlier example of comparing sales figures by office. If you wanted to add to the annual figures a breakdown of the data for each of the 12 months of the year, you'd have to have 13 rows of data instead of one. With a single value, an overall label for the worksheet will suffice, but with additional values in the worksheet, each row has to have its own label.

Note Although most of the labels in worksheets are in the leftmost column or the top row or two under the title, there's no real requirement that either labels or data must be put in the traditional places. If you have some unusual needs, feel free to put them anywhere on the worksheet.

Filling a series of labels automatically

Excel has a feature called a *fill series* that lets you fill in a series of labels without having to type out the whole thing. For instance, if your first label is 1/1/00, you can click on the fill handle (the dot in the bottom right-hand corner of the active cell or range) and drag it either across or down for several cells. As you drag the fill handle, a floating message will inform you of what value would be filled in if you released the mouse button. When you release the mouse button, the other cells will be filled in with subsequent dates. If you dragged for 5 more cells, for instance, they would be filled with 1/2/00, 1/3/00, 1/4/00, 1/5/00, and 1/6/00.

Excel recognizes many different types of series, including numbers, times, dates, and days of the week. If you have two cells beginning the series and select them both before dragging the fill handle, Excel automatically calculates the differences between them and applies that to the series it generates. For example, if your first two cells have the numbers 1 and 2 in them, the next cell will be filled with a 3. If they have the numbers 3 and 5 in them, the next cell will be filled with a 7. See Figure 11-3 for an example of a weekday fill series.

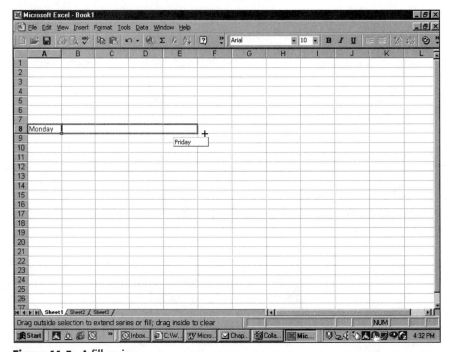

Figure 11-3: A fill series.

Entering numbers, dates, and times

Other than labels, there's not often much text in a worksheet. Spreadsheets were invented for the purpose of crunching numbers, and that's still the most common use people put them to—although today they have many other uses, too, from managing inventory to keeping track of wedding invitations!.

Cross-Reference Excel worksheets can be used to manage text-based items like mailing lists, parts inventories, and so forth. Chapter 14, "Lists and Databases," details the uses of spreadsheets for lists and databases.

Entering numbers

Entering numbers is every bit as simple as entering text, with a few caveats. Basically, just select a cell and add in the data. Excel does have some limitations and restrictions on numbers, though, that you should be aware of. First, Excel's default cell format (called "General") will only display 11 characters. In the case of numbers, this means only 11 digits will show unless you specify a fixed cell width greater than the General format's. While Excel lets you type as long a string of text as you want, it restricts numbers to 15 significant digits. Anything beyond the 15-digit limit is converted to zeroes.

Caution If you enter a number in a cell that is contained in a column with a fixed width, and that number is wider than the column width, it will not display. Instead, you will see a series of hash marks (#######) in place of the number. To solve this problem and enable the number to display properly, increase the column width so that it is at least as wide as the number. See the section entitled "Changing Column Widths and Row Heights" later in this chapter for details.

Dealing with Fractions

There's also a "gotcha!" if you work with fractions instead of decimal points. Although Excel will handle fractions properly if they're preceded by a whole number (such as 7 1/2), a fraction that stands alone (like 1/8) will be interpreted as a date (in this case, the 8th of January). To avoid this problem, you can either format the cell ahead of time to accept fractions (see the section entitled "Number, Date, and Time Formats" later in this chapter) or you can just type a leading zero (like 0 1/8).

Formatting the cell to accept fractions after the fact doesn't work, by the way—you have to plan ahead. In the case of a fraction preceded by a whole number, Excel automatically formats the cell for fractions. Regardless of the formatting of the cell, the fraction will display in decimal format in the formula bar.

Entering dates and times

Dates and times are interpreted by Excel as numbers, and you can use them just like any other number. You can subtract one date from another to see how many days apart they are, for example. To let Excel know that you're entering a date, use slashes or hyphens to separate the elements. For instance, 1-2 or 1/2 means that you're entering January 2nd (see the sidebar warning about the misinterpretation of fractions). If you just enter the month and day, but don't specify the year, it defaults to the current year. You can use any combination of hyphens or slashes. To Excel, there's no difference between 1/2-88, 1-2/88, 1-2-88, or 1/2/88.

Caution

With the year 2000 coming up, Microsoft has instituted a potentially problematical compromise about two-digit year entries. Anything from 1/1/00 through 12/31/29 is considered as a twenty-first century date and to start with 20 (12/31/29 would show up as 12/31/2029). However, anything from 1/1/30 on up is considered as a twentieth century date and to start with 19 (1/1/30 would show up as 1/1/1930). It's probably best to avoid this situation entirely and use a full four-digit year instead.

While hyphens or slashes tell Excel that the number involved is a date, colons are the key to letting it know it's dealing with time. For instance, simply entering 3: in a cell is the same thing as entering 3:00:00 A.M. Excel always defaults to A.M. settings unless you specify P.M. or use military time. To do this, type a space and either a P or P.M. following the time (it doesn't matter if the letters are uppercase or lowercase), but you can't just type the hour and a colon; you have to follow it with at least one digit. For example, 3: P doesn't set a time, but 3:1 P or 3:01 P will. Watch out that you don't assume you're typing in the tens column if you just enter a single digit for the minutes, by the way—6:5 is the same as 6:05, not 6:50. As with the year situation, it's safest to type out the whole thing and not resort to the short version.

Editing data

As you enter data or click on a cell containing data, you'll no doubt notice that the cell contents are displayed in the formula bar, even if the contents are not a formula (see Figure 11-4). Any cell contents can be edited by clicking in the formula bar and then typing the new data there, but you can also double-click on the cell and edit the contents directly in the cell. If you'd rather use function keys, you can press the F2 key to switch the active cell to edit mode. Whichever method you use, the word Edit appears in the status bar on the lower-left when you switch to edit mode.

Whether you're editing in the cell or in the formula bar, whatever you enter in one appears in the other. If you're editing in the cell, the cursor is visible there, and the data in the formula bar that is beyond the original insertion point of the changes drops down as though it were a subscript to show where the changes are being made. If you're editing in the formula bar, you have both the subscripting and the cursor to show you what's going on, but there is no indication in the cell other than the changes themselves.

Cross-Reference Chapter 13, "Functions and Formulas," deals with editing formulas.

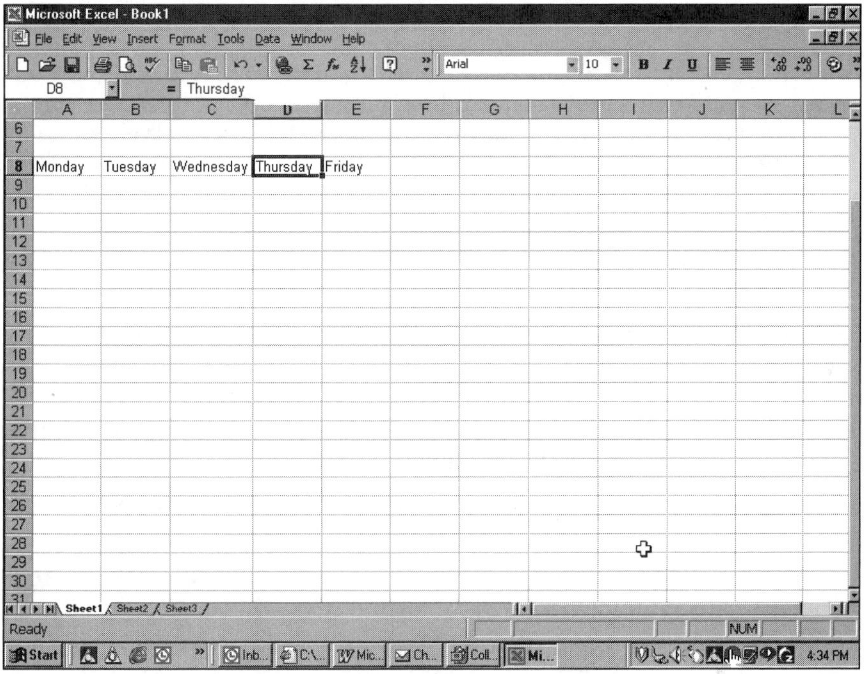

Figure 11-4: Cell contents are displayed in the formula bar.

Once you're in edit mode, the cell or formula bar acts like a miniature text editor. You can use the arrow keys to move around, Home or End to jump to the beginning or end of the data, Insert to set for overtype or insert mode, Delete or Backspace to remove characters or selections, and so forth, just as though you were typing in a word processor.

Tip The up and down arrow keys serve a special function in editing data. Pressing the down arrow key jumps the cursor to the end of the data. Pressing the up arrow key afterward returns you to the point you jumped from. If, however, the data takes up more than one line, the up and down arrow keys work normally, simply moving the cursor up or down one line. Oddly, if you press down while the cursor is on the last line, you will go to the end of the cell. Then, if you press up, you're returned to the second last line at the column you were at in the last line before pressing down.

Copying, Moving, and Merging Cells

There are a number of reasons why you would want to copy the information and formatting from one cell to another or to move a cell to another location entirely in the worksheet. The latter is the spreadsheet equivalent of a cut and paste operation in a word processor. Maybe you got partway through creating a worksheet and then decided to modify its look. Changes in one cell can be copied to others, thus saving you an awful lot of work. Or you may realize that your worksheet design is flawed and you have to rearrange the cells. Whatever your reasons, Excel provides easy-to-use tools to accomplish the tasks.

Copying cells

To copy a cell to another location in the worksheet, follow these steps:

1. Click on the cell you want to copy.

2. Click the Copy button in the toolbar. The border around the cell will change from a solid line to a moving dotted line.

3. Next, click on the cell you want to copy it to so that it becomes the active cell.

4. Click the Paste button (see Figure 11-5). The data is pasted into the new cell, including any formatting (font styles and colors, background color, etc.) you've already applied to the originating cell.

The cell you've copied from remains selected as the copy source, and you can paste into as many cells as you want, either one at a time or en masse. If you want to paste the data into more than one cell in a contiguous range, the process is the same as for pasting into a single cell, except that you need to select the destination range, instead of one cell, before you paste.

Tip   You can copy a cell into multiple, noncontiguous cells as well as to a contiguous range of cells. To do so, hold down the Ctrl key while clicking on the cells you want to paste into, and then click the Paste button in the toolbar. The results will be pasted into all the selected cells regardless of their locations in the worksheet.

Moving cells

Moving a cell is even simpler, thanks to drag and drop.

1. Click anywhere on the border of the active cell (except for the fill handle in the bottom right corner of the cell).

2. While holding down the mouse button, move the cell to the new location. As you move around the worksheet, the address of the cell under the pointer will be shown in a floating message.

3. Once you've got the cell where you want it, release the mouse button and the cell will move.

As with copy, all the original formatting comes along with the cell when you move it.

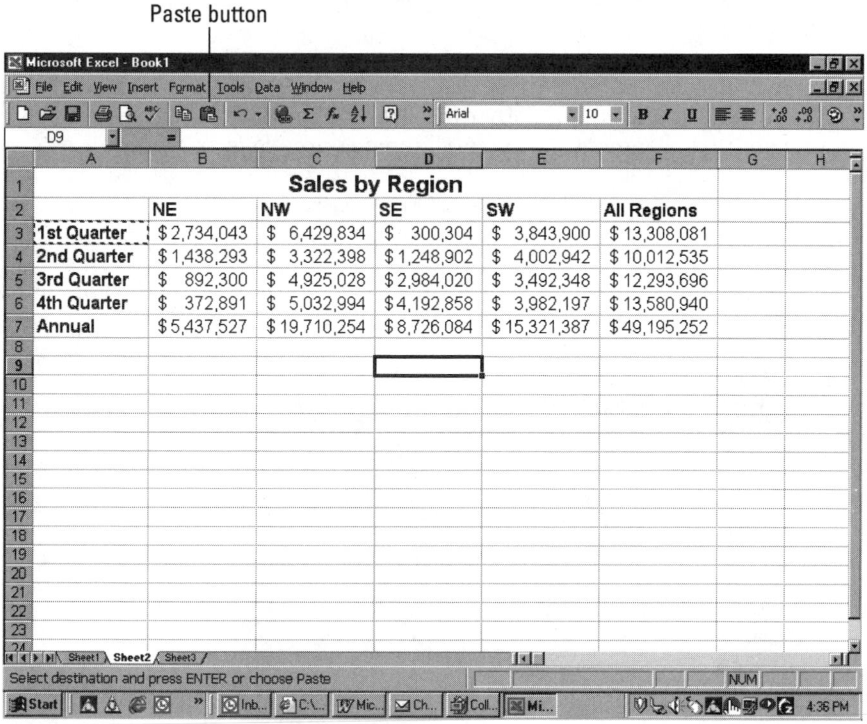

Paste button

	A	B	C	D	E	F	G	H
1			Sales by Region					
2		NE	NW	SE	SW	All Regions		
3	1st Quarter	$2,734,043	$ 6,429,834	$ 300,304	$ 3,843,900	$13,308,081		
4	2nd Quarter	$1,438,293	$ 3,322,398	$1,248,902	$ 4,002,942	$10,012,535		
5	3rd Quarter	$ 892,300	$ 4,925,028	$2,984,020	$ 3,492,348	$12,293,696		
6	4th Quarter	$ 372,891	$ 5,032,994	$4,192,858	$ 3,982,197	$13,580,940		
7	Annual	$5,437,527	$19,710,254	$8,726,084	$15,321,387	$49,195,252		

Figure 11-5: Copying a cell to a new location.

> **Tip**
> You can use the drag-and-drop technique to copy cells, too. Just hold the Ctrl key down while you're doing it and release it when you drop the cells into their new locations.

Merging cells

The capability to merge cells may seem unusual and useless, but it actually has a perfectly good function. If you want to create a data label that covers two or more rows or columns, cell merging is the way to go. Of course, you could just change the width of the column or height of the row containing a cell, but that would affect the other cells in the same column or row. It may be stating the obvious, but only contiguous cells can be merged. Merging can be done horizontally, vertically, or both at once by selecting a range of cells. (See the section entitled "Entering Data" earlier in this chapter for more information on using data labels.)

Caution   If you merge cells and more than one of the selected cells contains data, you will receive a warning that only the data in the upper-left cell will remain after the merge. Never merge cells that already contain data you are unwilling to lose. Also, when you merge cells, any formulas that rely on the existence of those cells will be affected.

There are two methods for merging cells. One is really easy, but formats the text in a way you might not want. The other is more cumbersome, but gives you full control over text alignment. The cumbersome approach is as follows:

1. Select the range of cells you want to merge.

2. Right-click on the selection.

3. From the pop-up menu, select Format Cells. This brings up the Format Cells dialog box (see Figure 11-6).

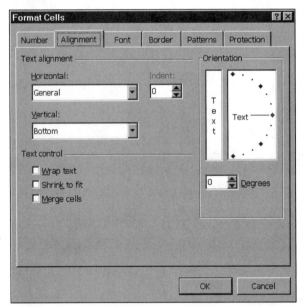

Figure 11-6: The Format Cells dialog box.

4. Click the Alignment tab.

5. Select the Merge Cells check box.

6. Click the OK button.

To unmerge a merged cell, select the merged cell by clicking on it, and then right-click on the selection. From the pop-up menu, select Format Cells. In the Format Cells dialog box, click the Alignment tab, uncheck the Merge Cells check box, and click the OK button.

The easy way to merge cells is to select the range and then just click on the Merge and Center button in the Formatting toolbar. This has the same effect as the menu approach, but forces you to accept center alignment. Fortunately, there's a really easy workaround for this problem. While the merged cells are still selected, just click on one of the other alignment buttons in the Formatting toolbar to change the alignment. If you want the merged cells left-aligned, click the Align Left button. If you want them right-aligned, well, you get the idea.

Note Merged cells lose their identity as separate cells in some ways, but not in others. The address of the merged cell as displayed in the name bar will be only the top left cell of the merged range, yet you can use the Go To command to go to the merged cell by entering the name of any of the formerly individual cells.

Adding Comments to Cells

Comments are the Post-It pads of the digital world. They're notes you can attach to cells. To add a comment to a cell, follow these steps:

1. Right-click on the cell.

2. Select Insert Comment from the pop-up menu. A yellow rectangle will appear next to the cell. Generally, it appears to the right of the selected cell, with the upper-left corner of the comment a little above the cell, but its exact location in relation to the cell depends on how much room there is on the upper-right.

Note Comments only show up within the worksheet proper, so if the cell you're commenting on is on the far right or top of the worksheet, the comment will appear on the left of or below the selected cell.

3. The comment already has your name at the top, although this can be deleted like any other text.

4. Type in your comment.

5. Click anywhere outside the comment to complete it.

The cell now has a small red triangle in the upper right-hand corner. When you move the mouse pointer over cells that have this marking, the associated comments are displayed (see Figure 11-7). Moving the pointer elsewhere in the worksheet causes the comment to disappear from view again (though it remains attached to the cell, ready to be viewed again at any time).

Caution While you type in a comment, the text will scroll if you type more than will fit in the standard-size comment window, but the text beyond the bottom will not show when the comment is displayed. Make sure you resize the comment window so all the text shows at once before you complete the comment. If you need to resize it afterward, right-click the cell and select Edit Comment.

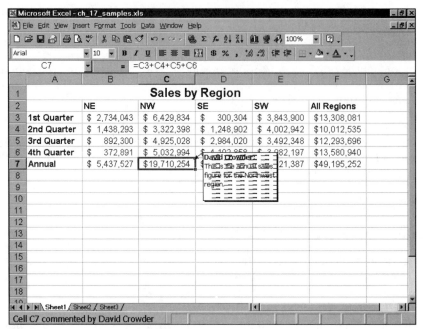

Figure 11-7: A comment attached to a cell.

Managing comments

If you right-click on a cell that contains a comment, you'll find that you have three new options in the pop-up menu: Edit Comment, Delete Comment, and Show Comment. Selecting Edit Comment allows you to make changes in the text or to move or resize the comment window. Delete Comment, of course, removes the comment entirely. Show Comment changes the behavior of the comment so that it is constantly in view instead of showing only when the pointer is over the associated cell. This causes one more change in the pop-up menu: Show Comment is now changed to Hide Comment. Selecting the latter reverses the behavior of the comment window, causing it to appear only when you hover the pointer over the cell.

Tip   When a comment is displayed constantly with the Show Comment menu option, you can just click within the comment window to get full editing capability, including moving and resizing options.

Adding and Deleting Cells, Rows, and Columns

Inserting or deleting any part of a worksheet both follow pretty much the same procedure. You'll need to consider the effect the insertion will have on other cells, because they'll need to move aside in order to make room for the new cell. You have two options regarding where the other cells end up. In the case of an insertion, they can move either to the right or down; for deletion, they can move left or up. Pick the cell where you will make the change accordingly.

Adding cells

To insert a single cell, follow these steps:

1. Decide where you want to put it.

2. Right-click on the cell currently occupying that position. To insert a range of cells, select the range you want to insert, and then right-click anywhere within the range and follow the same process as for a single cell.

3. Select Insert from the pop-up menu.

4. This brings up the Insert dialog box (see Figure 11-8), which has four options on it. The first two, Shift cells right and Shift cells down, deal with individual cells or ranges of cells. The next two, Entire row and Entire column, insert a new row or column. If a new row is inserted, the row containing the selected cell is moved down one to make room for the new row. If a new column is inserted, the column containing the selected cell is moved right one to make room. Make your selection.

5. Click the OK button.

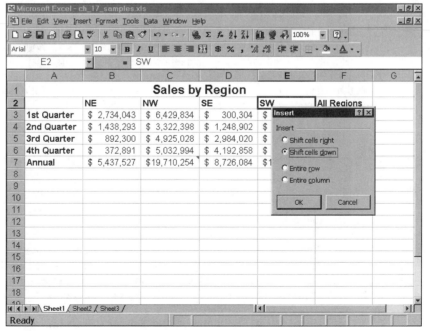

Figure 11-8: The Insert dialog box.

You can't insert anything—row, cell, or column—that would cause any cell containing data to shift past the ends of the worksheet. Of course, this is only a problem if you have data in the cells at the extreme right or bottom sides of the worksheet (column IV or row 65,536).

Deleting cells

Deleting cells, rows, or columns is done in much the same manner as inserting them, and the Delete dialog box looks just like the Insert dialog box except for the title and a small matter of phrasing.

To delete cells, row, or columns, follow these steps:

1. Right-click on the cell or range of cells.

2. Select Delete from the pop-up menu.

3. The options in the Delete dialog box are to Shift cells left or Shift cells up. To delete an entire row or column, select Entire row or Entire column. Deleting an entire row moves the rows beneath it up one; deleting an entire column moves the columns to its right left one. Make your selection.

4. Click the OK button to complete the deletion.

As with insertion, give thought beforehand to the effect that shifting cells in a particular direction will have on the cells around the deleted one(s).

Caution   When cells change their position due to inserting or deleting other cells around them, formulas that rely on their location are not affected because Excel automatically adjusts the formulas to reflect the new position. This is true even when absolute cell values are used in a formula. The new location simply becomes the new absolute cell value. However, if a cell containing data referred to by the formula is deleted, whether individually or as part of a row or column deletion, that's a different situation. In that case, the cell referred to by the formula is effectively wiped out and the formula will show a #REF error. If this happens, use Undo to reverse the deletion.

Changing Column Widths and Row Heights

The width of columns and the height of rows is changeable by a variety of methods. Some of them take place automatically as you format data, others are managed with a mouse, and some utilize menu input.

Tip   Although columns will not expand on their own to accommodate the data you put into them, rows do change their height automatically to reflect the size of the fonts you use or the fact that you've applied word wrap. You can make a column expand to fit the material it contains by double-clicking on the boundary to the right of its header. If you're more comfortable with menus, you can select the entire column and then choose Format ➪ Column ➪ AutoFit Selection. The same is true for rows, but you double-click on the boundary underneath the row header. You can also use the menu selection Format ➪ Row ➪ AutoFit.

Changing column widths

To set a new column width, follow these steps:

1. Place your pointer on the dividing line between two column headings.

2. Press the mouse button down. A floating message will give you the current width (see Figure 11-9).

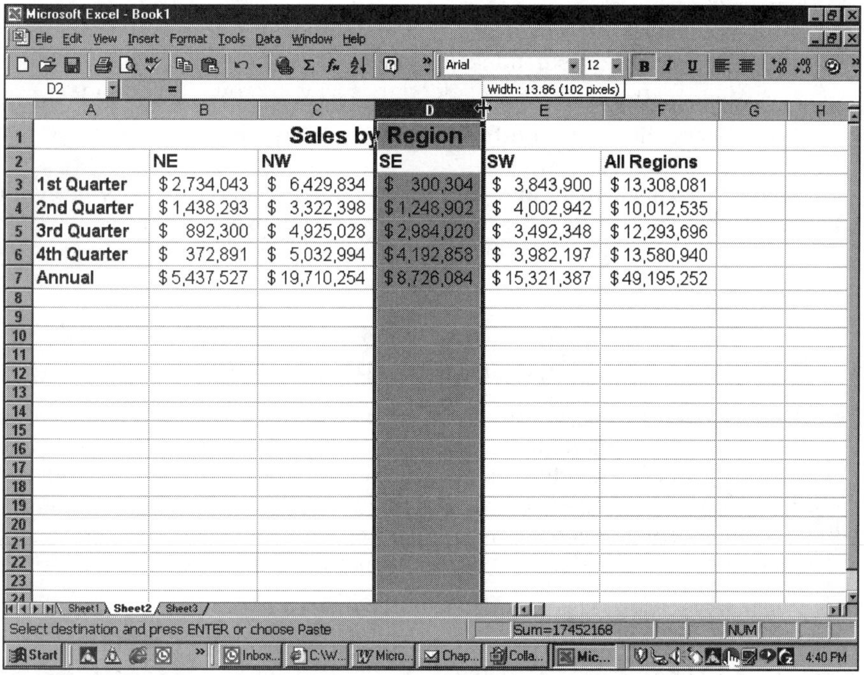

Figure 11-9: Resizing a column.

3. Next, slide the boundary left or right. The size of the column to the left of the boundary will contract or expand accordingly, and the floating message will tell you what the column size you're selecting is as you move the boundary.

4. Release the mouse button to apply the new column width.

If you want to manually enter a specific number for column width, you can right-click on the column header and select Column Width or you can select Format ⇨ Column ⇨ Width from the menu. This brings up a dialog box with only one function — to accept a new number. Do so, and then click the OK button.

Changing row heights

Row heights are handled in the same way, but you need to use the boundary between row headings instead, and slide it either up or down to decrease or increase the row height. The row affected is the one above the boundary.

1. Place your pointer on the dividing line between two row headings.

2. Press the mouse button down. A floating message will give you the current height.

3. Slide the boundary up or down. The size of the row to the top of the boundary will contract or expand accordingly, and the floating message will tell you what the row size you're selecting is as you move the boundary.

4. Release the mouse button to apply the new row height.

Manually setting a specific row height is handled similarly, but you right-click on the row header and select Row Height or select Format ➪ Row ➪ Height from the menu to bring up the Row height dialog box. Type in the new number, and then click the OK button to change the row height.

Resizing multiple rows and columns

To change the size of multiple rows at once, select the row headings of the ones you want to alter, and then click on any of the boundaries in the selection and go ahead with the normal procedure as though you were doing a single row. All the rows in the selection will be resized simultaneously. Resizing multiple columns simultaneously works the same way except, of course, you need to select the column headings and slide one of the column boundaries.

Hiding and Unhiding Columns, Rows, and Gridlines

Hiding a column or row doesn't affect anything but the visibility of cells. If you have a formula that refers to data in one of the cells in a hidden column or row, it will still work just fine. Hiding gridlines has no effect whatsoever except to improve the worksheet's appearance by removing the crosshatch of lines that defines the worksheet grid.

Hiding columns

To hide a column, right-click on the column heading and select Hide from the pop-up menu. If you're more comfortable with menus, you can click on any cell in the column and then select Format ➪ Column ➪ Hide. All the items in the column will completely disappear, from the column heading to the last cell.

Unhiding columns

How do you unhide a hidden column if you can't see it? Simple. Select the columns to either side of it, right-click on one of their column headings, and select Unhide from the pop-up menu.

Hiding rows

Hiding rows works in the exactly same way except that you need to click on the row headings involved instead of the column headings. If you're using the menu, you need to select Format ➪ Row ➪ Hide.

Hiding gridlines

To hide gridlines, follow these steps:

1. Select Tools ➪ Options from the menu. This brings up the Options dialog box (see Figure 11-10).

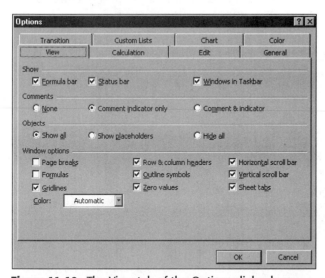

Figure 11-10: The View tab of the Options dialog box.

2. Click the View tab.

3. Uncheck the Gridlines check box.

4. Click the OK button.

To restore gridlines, reverse the operation, checking the Gridlines check box.

Using AutoFormat

If you'd rather not be bothered with making choices about font styles, borders, patterns, colors, and the like, Excel can do a pretty good job of handling it for you. The feature is called AutoFormat, and it applies a set of predefined design options to a selected range of cells.

AutoFormat is flexible in that it allows you several options within the preset choices, but if it has a weakness, it's that it's restricted to a series of common uses in worksheet design.

Applying AutoFormat

To use AutoFormat, follow these steps:

1. Select the range of cells you want to apply it to (generally, your entire active worksheet area).

2. Select Format ⇨ AutoFormat from the menu. This brings up the AutoFormat dialog box (see Figure 11-11), which shows samples of more than a dozen pre-designed formats for you to choose from.

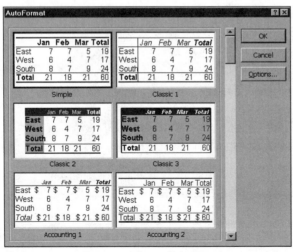

Figure 11-11: The AutoFormat dialog box.

3. To pick one, click on the sample image.

4. If you want to accept it as is, then click the OK button to implement it.

Figures 11-12 and 11-13 show two different formats applied to the same data. The first one is a simple and straightforward accounting format, while the second one is a much fancier three-dimensional approach.

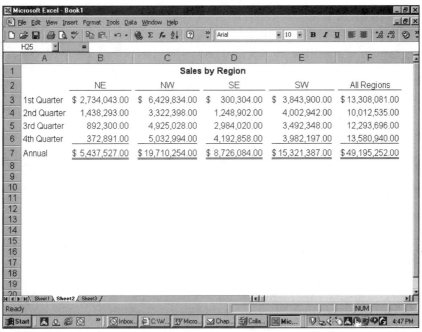

Figure 11-12: The Accounting 4 format.

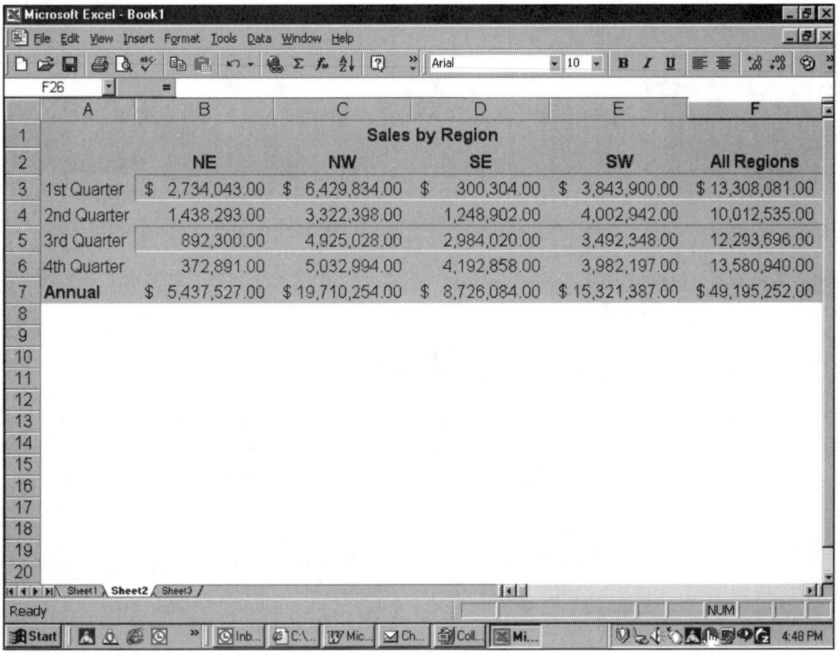

Figure 11-13: The 3D Effects 2 format.

Customizing AutoFormat

It's possible, though, that you'd like to use the basic AutoFormat but you'd rather not have all the formatting from the sample applied to your worksheet. You might, for instance, already have chosen colors, patterns, or fonts that you don't want changed, but you'd like to have the border styles applied from the AutoFormat sample. In that case, before you click the OK button, click the Options button. This adds a series of check boxes to the bottom of the AutoFormat dialog box, which allow you to customize the options that will be applied from the sample.

The new panel, labeled "Formats to apply," contains six options: Number, Font, Alignment, Border, Patterns, and Width/Height. Clicking on the check boxes to deselect them removes those options from AutoFormat; clicking on them again to select them puts the options back in. The selected sample shows the results immediately so you can judge the effect.

Removing AutoFormat

To remove the AutoFormatting from your worksheet, select the affected cells, and then select Format ⇨ AutoFormat from the menu. In the AutoFormat dialog box, scroll down to the bottom and click on the design labeled None. Click the OK button to complete the removal of the formatting. This doesn't really bring the formatting back to the way it was before the first AutoFormat, however. None of your original formatting is retained (fonts, column widths, etc.) – the None style just applies default font, color, etc.

Applying Fonts and Styles

Although you can present data perfectly well without fancy formatting of any kind, it's generally better to use it. Why? Two very good reasons. First, visual cues help to distinguish between the different parts of your worksheet and help people to understand what they mean at a glance. Second, the most attractive presentation is likely the one that will be most accepted.

Setting fonts for cells and ranges

You can apply fonts to entire cells, ranges of cells, and portions of the contents of cells. To set the font for an individual cell, click on it, and then select the desired font from the drop-down font list in the Formatting toolbar (see Figure 11-14). To set the font for a range of cells, first select the range, and then select the font.

Note   The names of the fonts in the font list will vary from one system to another, depending on which fonts the user has installed.

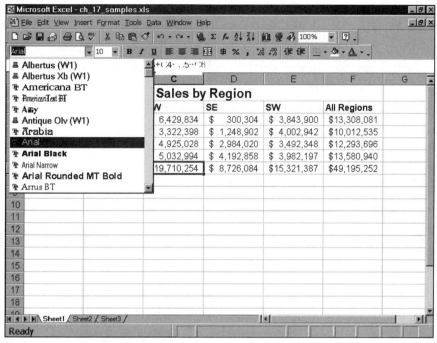

Figure 11-14: The Font list.

The font can also be set for text within cells, right down to the single character level. Double-click on the cell to enter into edit mode; then select the characters you wish to apply the font change to. Select the desired font from the drop-down list in the Formatting toolbar.

Caution

If you want to apply one font to a cell, but have some of the text within the cell be in a different font, you must set the font for the cell before you set the font of the characters. Otherwise, applying the font to the cell will override the individual character fonts within it.

Setting the size of fonts

To set the size of fonts, select the worksheet element you are going to apply the size change to, and then select the size from the drop-down Font Size list in the Formatting toolbar. As with font selection, you can apply the change to any worksheet element, whether it's an individual character within a cell, an entire cell, or a range of cells. The height of the row containing the affected worksheet element will adjust to accommodate the size of the font you choose, even if the size change is applied to only a single character within a single cell.

Tip   Instead of sizing a cell to fit its contents, you can resize the contents so it can be displayed within the cell's current width. To do this, right-click on the cell you want to adjust and select Format Cells from the pop-up menu (alternately, select Format ⇨ Cells from the main menu). This brings up the Format Cells dialog box, from which you need to select the Alignment tab (see Figure 11-15).

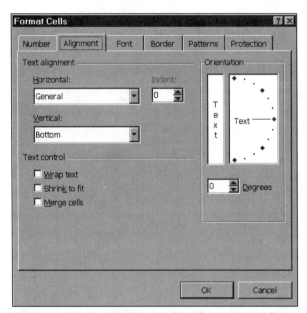

Figure 11-15: The Alignment tab of the Format Cells dialog box.

Click the Shrink to Fit check box, and then click the OK button. It will take a few moments, but the text in the cell will be squeezed to fit within the cell. (See the following section for information on applying colors to fonts and other worksheet elements.)

Adding font styles

To set fonts to bold, italic, or underline, click the Bold, Italic, or Underline buttons to the right of the Font Size list in the Formatting toolbar.

Note   If you choose to underline the contents of a cell, bear in mind that this may conflict visually with the bottom border if you're using one. For more information on borders, see the section entitled "Applying borders, patterns and colors" later in this chapter.

Changing the default font

The default font for Excel is Arial, a sans serif font also sometimes known as Swiss or Helvetica. Although Arial is good for headings, like most fonts that lack serifs (the fine details on the edges of characters), it lacks the kind of easy readability that makes for a good body font. The default size of the font is 10 points (a point is 1/72 of an inch).

To set a new default font face or size, follow these steps:

1. Select Tools ➪ Options from the menu. This brings up the Options dialog box.

2. Click on the General tab (see Figure 11-16).

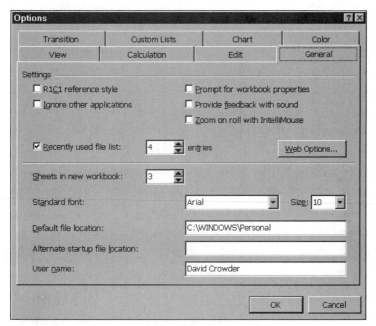

Figure 11-16: The General tab of the Options dialog box.

3. Select the new font face from the drop-down list under Standard Font.

4. If desired, select the new font size from the drop-down list under Size.

5. Click the OK button.

Aligning text horizontally

All text is, by default, left-aligned in the cell. Numbers, dates, and times are right-aligned. To change the alignment of cell contents, select the cell or cells you want to change, and then click on one of the align buttons in the Formatting toolbar. The three main alignment buttons allow you to set left, center, or right alignment (see Figure 11-17).

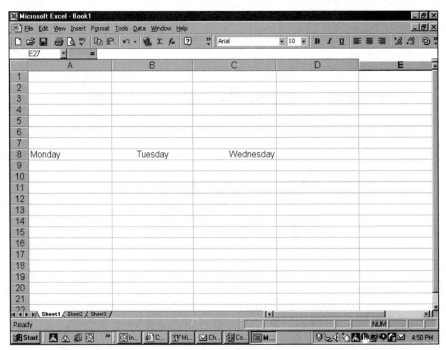

Figure 11-17: Left-aligned, center-aligned, and right-aligned cells.

In addition, there are two buttons for handling indented text: Decrease Indent and Increase Indent. Clicking on Increase Indent adds a left indentation to the cell contents; each time you click on the button, the contents are indented more (see Figure 11-18). If you want the indentation to be less, click the Decrease Indent button. As with the Increase Indent button, each click applies the action again.

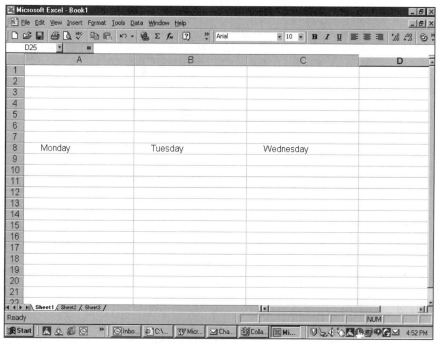

Figure 11-18: Indented text within cells.

To set more horizontal alignment options than the three basic ones and indentation, follow these steps:

1. Right-click on the selected cell or range of cells.

2. Select Format Cells from the pop-up menu. This brings up the Format Cells dialog box.

3. Click the Alignment tab.

4. Under the Horizontal setting, you'll find several options: General, Left (Indent), Center, Right, Fill, Justify, and Center Across Selection. Make your selection.

5. Click the OK button.

The first four alignment options are ones that you're already familiar with — they simply duplicate the functions of the align buttons in the Formatting toolbar. The General setting is the default left-alignment. Left (Indent) is the same as indenting. Center and Right set center-alignment and right-alignment.

Fill alignment

Fill is an unusual function, not really having anything to do with alignment at all. What it does is repeat the cell contents as many times as will fit within the width of the column containing the cell. If the contents can't at least be doubled, then nothing happens unless you expand the column width to the point where the additional characters will fit. Although this is not only useless but confusing if applied to normal text, it can be tremendously useful when you're using a cell as a buffer between other cells containing meaningful data. Simply place a single character such as an asterisk or slash in the cell, apply the Fill alignment to it, and you've got a divider cell that won't need any more attention no matter how much you change your worksheet, because the cell will fill with as many repeating characters as needed to adjust to the column width (see Figure 11-19).

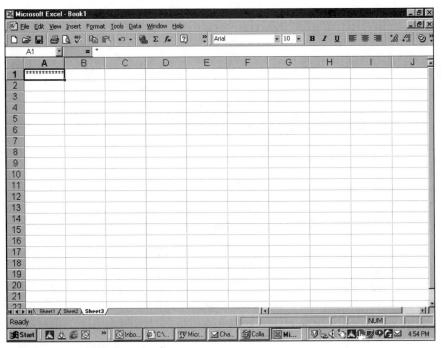

Figure 11-19: A fill-aligned cell.

Horizontal justification

Justify performs the same action as it does in word processing, making the beginning of the first word on a line meet the left margin, and the end of the last word on the line meet the right margin in multiline situations.

The effects in a worksheet cell, however, are not, generally speaking, worth the effort. While justification in a word processor takes place over the width of an entire page, it takes place in Excel within the confines of a cell. Because few cells in any worksheet are wide enough to contain more than a few words on a line, justification tends to simply put wide gaps between two or three words, thus reducing the readability of the line (see Figure 11-20). Applying justification causes all the text in the cell to be displayed by increasing the row height to the degree necessary to show it all (if you haven't changed it from its default). You can click the Wrap Text check box on the Alignment tab to achieve the same effect without justifying the text.

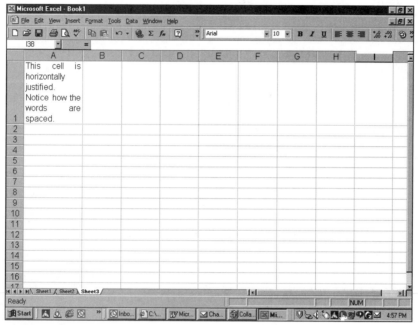

Figure 11-20: A horizontally justified cell.

Center Across Selection

The Center Across Selection option has an effect something like using the Merge and Center button. It takes several cells in a row and creates the appearance of one long cell with a single bit of centered text in the middle of it. Unlike merging cells, however, the cells involved do not lose their individual identity at all. In fact, you can still use them separately if you want to, and their separate contents will simply be centered in each cell. As with merging cells, its main utility is to create headings or titles that cover several columns.

To utilize Center Across Selection, type some text into one cell, and then select a range of cells using that cell as the starting point. Apply the Center Across Selection alignment to the range of cells and the text in the first cell will be centered across the entire range you have selected. The gridlines indicating the separate cells in the range will disappear, creating the illusion that the range is actually a single cell (see Figure 11-21).

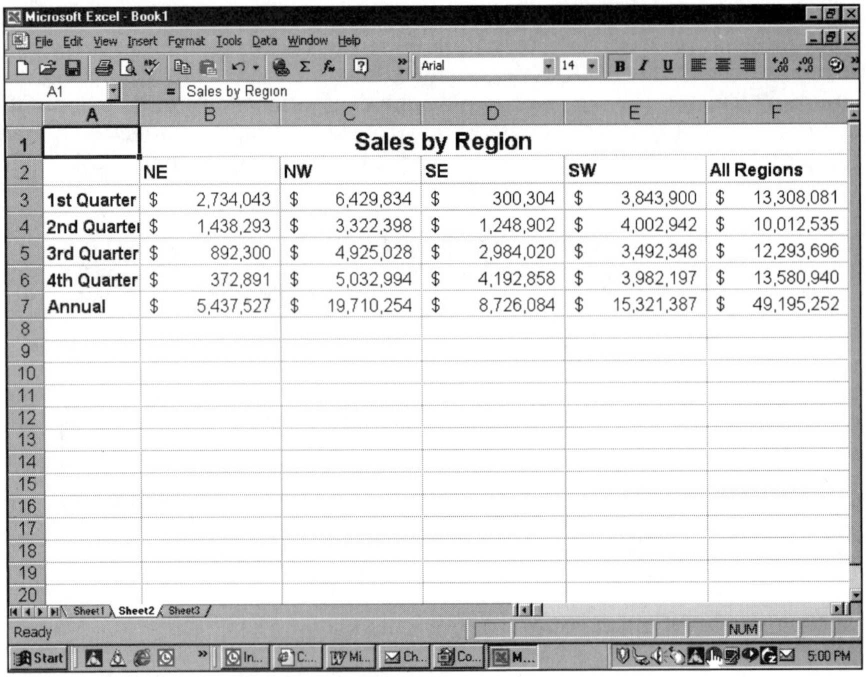

Figure 11-21: A cell centered across a selection.

Aligning text vertically

The default vertical alignment is at the bottom of the cell. To set vertical alignment options, follow these steps:

1. Right-click on the selected cell or range of cells.

2. Select Format Cells from the pop-up menu. This brings up the Format Cells dialog box.

3. Click the Alignment tab.

4. Under the Vertical setting, you'll find somewhat fewer options than for the horizontal alignments: Top, Center, Bottom, and Justify. Figure 11-22 shows the effect of the first three options. Make your selection.

5. Click the OK button.

The Justify setting works better in vertical alignment than it does in horizontal alignment, making the top and bottom lines of data line up with the top and bottom of the cell while evenly spacing all the lines (see Figure 11-23). As with horizontal justification or word wrap, vertical justification expands the row height so that all the text in the cell is displayed at once (if you haven't changed the row height from its default).

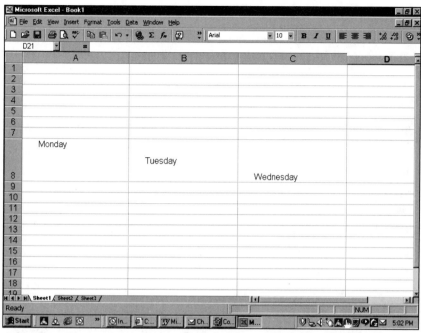

Figure 11-22: Top-aligned, center-aligned, and bottom-aligned cells.

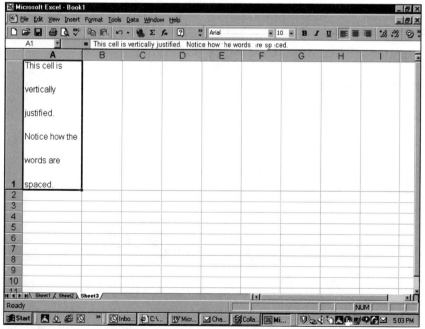

Figure 11-23: A vertically justified cell.

Rotating text

A common problem in worksheet layout and design is that the data in cells is not often as wide as the headings for the column containing the data cells. As a result, most of the cells in the worksheet are a lot of white space with a small bit of data. To solve this problem, Excel gives you two options — setting the text to vertical or rotating it.

Both are handled in the Orientation panel on the Alignment tab of the Format Cells dialog box (refer to Figure 11-15).

1. Right-click on the selected cell or range of cells.

2. Select Format Cells from the pop-up menu. This brings up the Format Cells dialog box.

3. Click the Alignment tab.

4. To set the text to vertical as shown in Figure 11-24, click within the box with the word Text printed vertically (in the Orientation area of the dialog box).

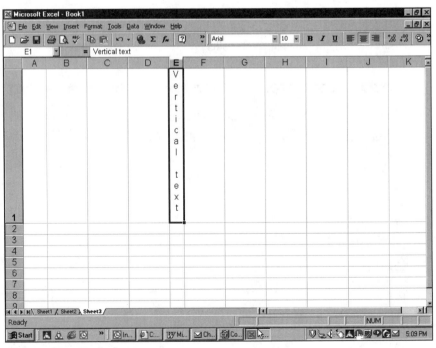

Figure 11-24: Vertical text.

5. To rotate the text as shown in Figure 11-25, you can click on one of the degree points in the rotation box, drag the rotation pointer to the setting you want, or use the arrows below it to scroll to the degree of rotation you desire. Points

below the middle of the rotation box are negative degrees and will result in left rotation; points above the middle are positive degrees and will result in right rotation. The maximum rotation in either direction is 90 degrees.

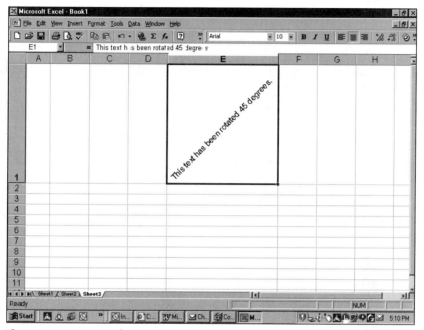

Figure 11-25: Rotated text.

6. Click the OK button.

Applying Borders, Patterns, and Colors

You can dress up your Excel worksheet with all sorts of fancy options, either just for the sake of beauty or for the more practical reason that borders, patterns, and colors can help delineate the various areas of your worksheet and set off one piece or set of data from the rest.

Applying borders

A border is a line, either around an entire cell, on one or more sides of the cell, or even through the middle of a cell. Several basic border arrangements (left border, right border, top and bottom border, etc.) are available through the Formatting toolbar. Borders are best used when gridlines are not present. Otherwise, they tend to be hard to see, as every cell is already surrounded by a thin line on all sides.

To use borders, follow these steps:

1. Select the cell or range of cells you want to apply borders to.

2. Click on the arrow to the right of the Borders button in the Formatting toolbar.

3. In the drop-down menu (see Figure 11-26), click on the border style you want to apply.

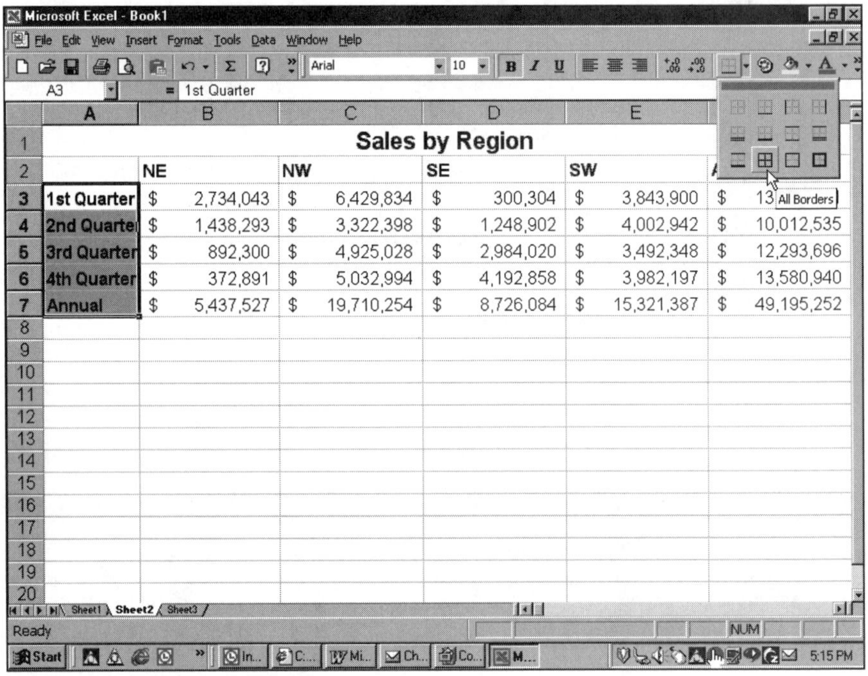

Figure 11-26: The Borders menu.

If you want more control over border styles, you can access more border options by using the following steps:

1. Select the cell or range of cells you want to apply borders to.

2. Right-click on the cell or within the range of cells.

3. From the pop-up menu, select Format Cells. This brings up the Format Cells dialog box.

4. Click the Border tab (see Figure 11-27).

5. Click on the button that shows the type of border you want to apply.

6. To select the line type, click on one of the lines in the Style box on the right of the Border tab.

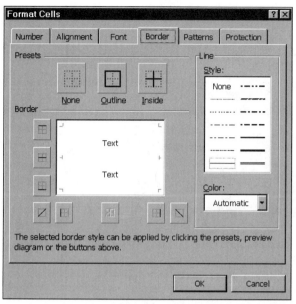

Figure 11-27: The Border tab of the Format Cells dialog box.

7. If you want to color the border, click the Color arrow below the Style box.

8. Select a color from the pop-up palette. If you don't like the color, repeat Steps 7 and 8 until you get one you like.

9. Click the OK button to finish.

Applying patterns

Patterns, properly used, can draw attention to different cells and help people to understand exactly what is most important. Improperly used, they can make your work impossible to read. A good rule of thumb is, when in doubt, use color instead. Patterns are best applied to empty cells, rather than to cells with data in them. In this way, they can show that you meant to leave a particular cell blank, serving the same function as the phrase "This page intentionally left blank" in manuals.

To apply patterns, follow these steps:

1. Select the cell or cells you wish to apply patterns to.

2. Right click on the cell or within the range of cells you've selected.

3. Select Format Cells from the pop-up menu. This brings up the Format Cells dialog box.

4. Click the Patterns tab (see Figure 11-28).

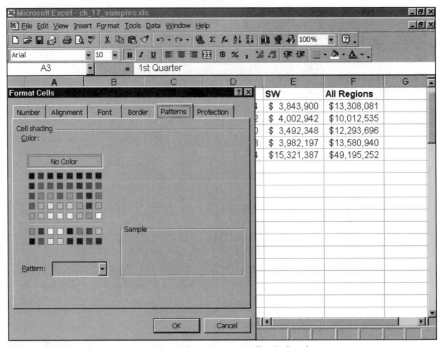

Figure 11-28: The Patterns tab of the Format Cells dialog box.

5. You can select a background color for the cell at this time by clicking on one of the color boxes in the palette. The Sample box shows the color you have chosen.

6. To access the patterns, click on the arrow next to the word Pattern.

7. Click on one of the patterns in the pop-up palette (see Figure 11-29). You will instantly be returned to the Patterns tab, where the pattern will be shown in the Sample box.

8. If you want to apply a color to the pattern, click the arrow next to the word Pattern again.

9. Click on the color you want to apply to the pattern.

10. Click the OK button.

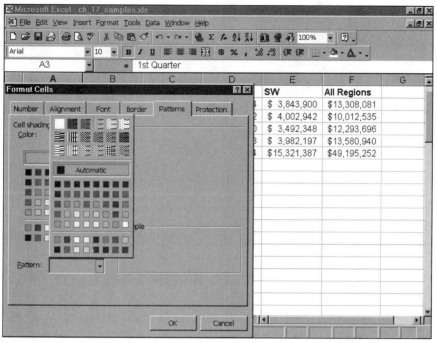

Figure 11-29: The Patterns pop-up palette.

Applying colors

You can apply colors to either the background of the cell or the fonts within a cell, or both. One way to apply background colors has already been covered in the preceding section on patterns, but Excel offers a quicker way to do the same thing.

To apply background colors to cells, follow these steps:

1. Select the cell or range of cells you want to apply a background color to.

2. Click on the arrow to the right of the Fill Color button in the Formatting toolbar.

3. In the pop-up palette (see Figure 11-30), click on the color you want to use for the background.

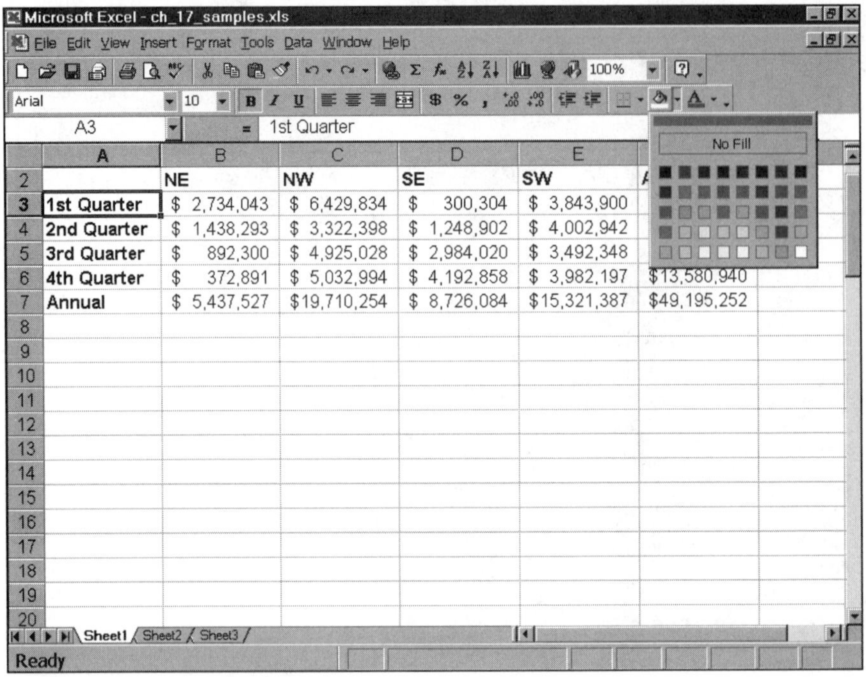

Figure 11-30: The Fill Color palette.

To apply colors to the fonts within the cell, the steps are absolutely identical, except that you click on the arrow to the right of the Font Color button instead.

Number, Date, and Time Formats

Three commonly used styles specifically dedicated to numbers have their own buttons in the Formatting toolbar: currency, percent, and comma. Additionally, you can adjust the number of decimal points via the toolbar (see Figure 11-31). Numbers, dates, and times are, by default, right-aligned, and the styles work as follows:

✦ **The currency style** takes the number in the selected cell and converts it to the local currency as set on your system. In the case of U.S. dollars, it would convert the number "2000" so it reads "$2,000.00" by adding the dollar sign, commas at each thousand break, and a decimal point followed by two zeroes. The dollar sign may not, however, be right at the beginning of the number, because it rests at the leftmost side of the cell; how close it is to the actual number depends on the length of the number and the width of the cell.

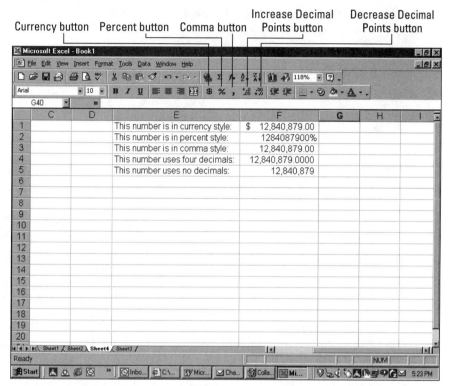

Figure 11-31: The three main number styles and the decimal buttons.

✦ **The percent style** multiplies any number in the selected cell by 100 and appends a percent sign to it. A cell containing the number 3, for example, would be converted to read "300%." Because the percent sign resides at the far right border of the cell, it immediately follows the number.

✦ **The comma style** is identical to applying the currency style for American dollars, except that it does not attach a dollar sign.

✦ **Adjusting the decimal point** has two buttons: one for adding digits to the right of the decimal point and one for removing them. Each click on either button adds or removes one digit to the right of the decimal point.

Using the Style dialog box

All these styles are also accessible by selecting Format ➪ Style from the menu. This brings up the Style dialog box (see Figure 11-32). Choose the style from the drop-down list under Style Name, and then click the OK button to implement your choice.

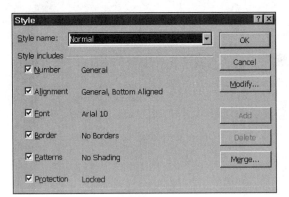

Figure 11-32: The Style dialog box.

Tip There are two variations on comma and currency styles in the Style dialog box. The comma(0) and currency(0) styles are identical to the comma and currency styles except that they do not add the two decimal points after the number. You can also select the Normal style to remove any of the other styles.

You can change any of the settings on the standard styles by clicking the Modify button, but it's better to just leave them alone and create your own if you need custom styles. Simply type the name of your new custom style into the box under Style Name, and then click the Add button. To alter the settings of your custom style, select it and click the Modify button. This brings up the standard Format Cells dialog box. Click on the various tabs and make your custom formatting selections, and then click the OK button to return to the Style dialog box. Click the OK button in it to apply your new custom style to the current selection.

Other number formats

The number style buttons on the toolbar simply provide a shortcut to using standard number formats. The Percent button, for instance, causes the Percentage Number format to be applied. Oddly enough, the Currency button doesn't apply the Currency format, but the Accounting format, as does the Comma button. You can access more detailed number formats in the Format Cells dialog box. To do this, follow these steps:

1. Select the cell (or range of cells) you want to apply the number format to.

2. Right-click on the cell or within the range of cells.

3. From the pop-up menu, select Format Cells.

4. In the Format Cells dialog box, click on the Number tab (see Figure 11-33).

5. Under Category, select the type of number format you want to apply (number, currency, accounting, fraction, etc.).

6. If the category presents options when selected, make your choices within them. Options might include such things as how many decimal places to show or what color to present negative numbers in.

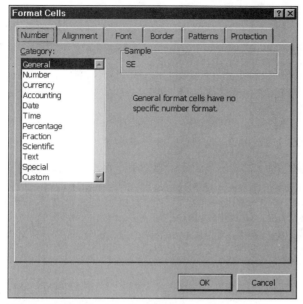

Figure 11-33: The Number tab of the Format Cells dialog box.

7. Click the OK button.

Date and time formats

Excel interprets anything typed in normal date or time formats, such as 2/2/1990 or 6:54 P.M., as dates and times and automatically formats the cell they're typed into accordingly. However, you may wish to manually change the formatting of a cell containing dates or times. To do so, follow these steps:

1. Select the cell (or range of cells) you want to apply the date or time format to.

2. Right-click on the cell or within the range of cells.

3. From the pop-up menu, select Format Cells.

4. In the Format Cells dialog box, click on the Number tab (see Figure 11-33).

5. Under Category, select either date or time.

6. Under Type, select the format you want the date or time to be displayed in.

7. Click the OK button.

Cross-Reference See the section entitled "Entering numbers, dates, and times" earlier in this chapter for more information on acceptable forms.

Custom Formats

In the rare event that the many built-in formats in Excel don't fit your needs, you can design and apply your own custom formats. The process itself is fairly simple, but the format codes are a bit disheartening at first glance. However, they follow a careful and logically designed pattern that, with a little practice, you will pick up quite easily.

Custom number formats

Number formats in Excel have four parts, divided by semicolons. The first part determines how positive numbers are displayed, the second part deals with negative numbers, the third with zeroes, and the fourth with text. You don't have to enter all the sections. For instance, if you're developing a number format in which you don't care about differences between the display of positive and negative numbers, all you have to do is enter the first section and that format will apply to all numbers.

Table 11-1 shows how the formatting codes are used in developing custom number formats.

Table 11-1 Custom Number Formats	
Formatting Code	**Meaning**
#	Placeholder for significant digits.
0	Placeholder for insignificant zeroes; adds zeroes if no number entered in that slot.
?	Placeholder for insignificant zeroes; adds spaces if no number entered in that slot.
,	Thousands separator if used in the main formatting code; divides number by 1,000 if placed to the right of the main formatting code.
.	Decimal point.
%	Percentage. Multiplies number by 100 and adds percentage sign after it.
/	Slash. Used to denote fractions.
E+,E-	Shows numbers in scientific notation. Is not case-sensitive, so can also be e+ or e-. The codes to the right of it signify the number of digits in the exponent.

Formatting Code	Meaning
[color]	Brackets surround color designations. Color comes first in section, and must be one of the following: Black, Blue, Cyan, Green, Magenta, Red, White, or Yellow.
"text"	Used to display the text within the quotation marks.
\	Backslash. Placed before a single character of text.
@	Displays text entered in the cell.
_	Underscore. Placed before a character, leaves a space the width of that character.
*	Like the Fill alignment option, fills the available space in the cell with the character following it.

Custom date and time formats

Date and time formats have only one section. They're quite a bit simpler than regular number formats, because dates have only days, months, and years to deal with and times have only hours, minutes, seconds, and fractions of seconds to consider. Table 11-2 shows how the formatting codes are used in developing custom date formats.

Table 11-2 Custom Date Formats	
Formatting Code	**Meaning**
d	Day numbering 1, 2, 3, ..., 31.
dd	Day numbering 01, 02, 03, ..., 31.
ddd	Day naming Sun, Mon, ..., Sat.
dddd	Day naming Sunday, Monday, ..., Saturday.
m	Month numbering 1, 2, 3, ..., 12.
mm	Month numbering 01, 02, 03, ..., 12.
mmm	Month naming Jan, Feb, Mar, ..., Dec.
mmmm	Month naming January, February, March, ..., December.
mmmmm	Month naming J, F, M, ..., D.
yy	Two-digit year.
yyyy	Four-digit year.

Times work in much the same manner as dates, in that they have only one section. Table 11-3 shows how the formatting codes are used in developing custom time formats.

Table 11-3	
Custom Time Formats	
Formatting Code	**Meaning**
h	Hour numbering 0, 1, 2, ..., 23.
hh	Hour numbering, 00, 01, 02, ..., 23.
m	Minute numbering 0, 1, 2, ..., 59.
mm	Minute numbering 00, 01, 02, ..., 59.
s	Second numbering 0, 1, 2, ..., 59.
ss	Second numbering 00, 01, 02, ..., 59.
ss.00	Fractions of seconds.
AM/PM	Designates normal 12-hour clock. Can also be A/P.
[h]	Elapsed time in hours.
[mm]	Elapsed time in minutes.
[ss]	Elapsed time in seconds.

Note: Each time element is separated by a colon. Thus, to set time to show hours, minutes, and seconds, you might use hh:mm:ss. The two exceptions to the need for a colon are the AM/PM designation, which is separated by a space, as in h:mm AM/PM, and the fractional seconds, which are separated by a decimal point, as in h:mm:ss.00.

Caution   If you use m or mm to denote minutes but don't include any of the variants for hours or seconds, Excel will misinterpret it to mean months instead of minutes because they use the exact same codes.

Creating custom formats

To code the custom formats, follow these steps:

1. Select the cell (or range of cells) you want to apply the custom format to.

2. Right-click on the cell or within the range of cells.

3. From the pop-up menu, select Format Cells.

4. In the Format Cells dialog box, click the Number tab (see Figure 11-33).

5. Under Category, select Custom.

6. Under Type, select the format closest in form to the new one you want to create.

7. Make the modifications to the format.

8. Click the OK button.

Now, when you want to apply the new custom format to any cell, just follow the normal procedure for applying formats, but select Custom under Category, and then your format under Type.

Summary

In this chapter, you learned how to enter and format data in Excel. Major points of this chapter included the following:

✦ Anything you type or paste in an Excel worksheet goes into the active cell.

✦ Rows and columns containing data should be labeled.

✦ Excel's fill series lets you easily extend a sequential series of labels.

✦ Excel limits numbers to 15 significant digits.

✦ Fractions must be preceded by a whole number or Excel thinks they're dates.

✦ Double-clicking on a cell causes it to enter edit mode.

✦ You can also edit cell contents in the formula bar, even if the contents aren't a formula.

✦ Cells can be copied or moved to a new location, or they can be merged together to form one large cell.

✦ Comments can be added to cells.

✦ Individual cells and even whole rows and columns can be added or deleted.

✦ Row heights and column widths can be adjusted.

✦ Rows, columns, and gridlines can be hidden.

✦ Excel's AutoFormat feature instantly applies common looks to worksheets.

✦ Font faces, sizes, styles, and colors can be changed for any Excel element — from individual characters in cells to the entire worksheet.

✦ Cell contents can be aligned horizontally and vertically, and they can even be rotated.

✦ A variety of border options can be applied to cells.

✦ Cells can contain background colors and patterns.

✦ Excel has a large number of built-in formats for numbers, dates, and times, and you can create your own custom formats as well.

✦   ✦   ✦

Charts

C harts offer a way to represent complex data in an easy-to-understand visual format. With charts, patterns that might otherwise be hidden within a bewildering array of data are easily spotted. Excel's Chart Wizard lets you easily create a wide variety of different chart types to handle various types of information. If the vast number of chart types and subtypes isn't enough for your particular situation, you can even create and save your own custom chart formats for future use.

Creating Charts with Chart Wizard

Excel's Chart Wizard makes creating charts about as easy as it can possibly get. Just let it know what it is you want to chart, and then it's just a matter of making a few selections and your chart is on the page. To make a chart with Chart Wizard, follow these steps:

1. Select the range of data you want to make a chart from (see Figure 12-1). You may not want to select all the data that's available. In this case, we've chosen only the quarterly breakdowns by region, leaving out the totals.

2. Click the Chart Wizard button in the toolbar. This brings up the first Chart Wizard dialog box, Chart Type (see Figure 12-2).

3. Under Chart type, choose the kind of chart you wish to create. The default choice is Column, but there are many others to pick from.

4. Under Chart sub-type, choose the specific variety of that chart type that you want to use. As you click on each of the visual sub-type representations, a description of the typical use of that sub-type appears below it.

5. If you want to see what your data would look like, click the Press and Hold to View Sample button. The sample that's presented gives only an approximation of the appearance of the actual finished chart, as it's crammed into a very small area, but it should tell you what you need to know in a general sense.

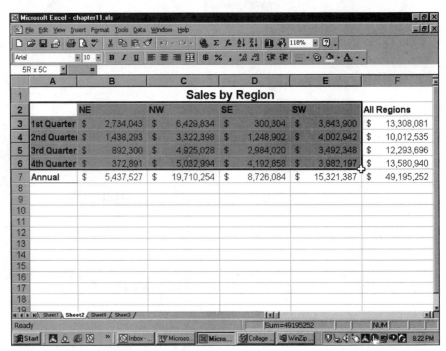

Figure 12-1: Data selected for charting.

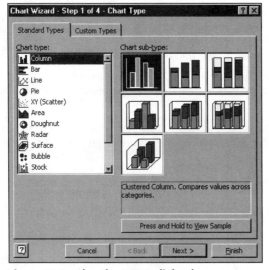

Figure 12-2: The Chart Type dialog box.

6. If you want still more options of exotic chart types, click the Custom Types tab.

7. When you've made your selections about chart types, click the Next button. This brings up the second Chart Wizard dialog box, Chart Source Data (see Figure 12-3).

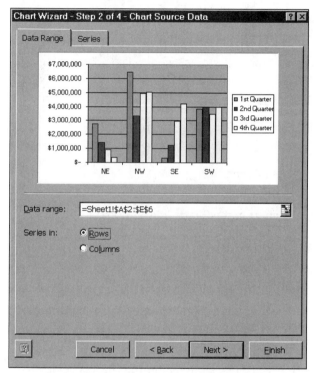

Figure 12-3: The Chart Source Data dialog box.

8. This shows a more accurate representation of how the finished chart will look. By default, the data series is taken from the rows of the selected range. If you want it taken from the columns instead, click the Columns radio button. You might want to try both to see which way your data is better presented. Just click on each radio button in turn until you're satisfied with the presentation.

9. If you want to view the range of cells from which each row or column of data is taken, click the Series tab.

10. Click the Next button to proceed. This brings up the third Chart Wizard dialog box, Chart Options (see Figure 12-4).

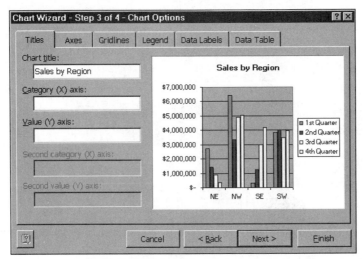

Figure 12-4: The Chart Options dialog box.

11. Type a title for the chart in the Chart Title edit box.

12. If you want any text below categories on the bottom part of the chart, type it into the Category (*X*) Axis edit box.

13. If you want any text to the left of the values that range from the top to the bottom of the chart on the left side, type it into the Value (*Y*) Axis edit box.

14. You can specify various options by clicking on the other tabs. Generally speaking, Excel does a very good job of interpreting the data you feed it and deciding what options to add for the most pleasing chart appearance, so it's not a good idea to mess with the other settings unless you have very specific requirements. They can all be altered after the chart is completed anyway (we will explore their uses for chart modification in a later section). Take the time to explore the various settings, however, because the sample chart display lets you see the effects of the different settings. Many of the options (such as data labels) merely clutter the chart to the point where it becomes useless as a conveyor of information. If you do want to add extras to the chart at this point, however, anything you put in can be removed after the chart is completed.

15. Click the Next button to proceed. This brings up the fourth and final Chart Wizard dialog box, Chart Location (see Figure 12-5).

16. This is the simplest step of all. All you need to do is to decide whether you want the chart to be included in the worksheet it draws its data from or to be created as a separate chart sheet. Unless you have a very high resolution system or a very small chart, it's usually best to make the chart on a separate sheet. If you try to put a large chart on the same worksheet as the original data, it's usually pretty difficult to fit both so that they're readable. Click the appropriate radio button, and then click the Finish button.

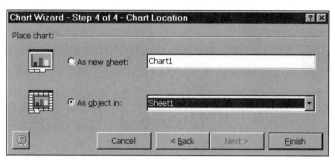

Figure 12-5: The Chart Location dialog box.

17. The chart is created. If it is on a separate chart sheet, it looks like the one shown in Figure 12-6. If it's on the original worksheet, Excel places the chart right smack in the middle of the worksheet, as shown in Figure 12-7, and you have to move it manually as well as resize it so that all the data is shown. To move it, place the pointer anywhere within the table (so long as it isn't over a table element such as the title), hold down your mouse button, and drag it to its new location. To resize it, click on any of the sizing handles around the edge and drag the handle in the direction you want to increase the size.

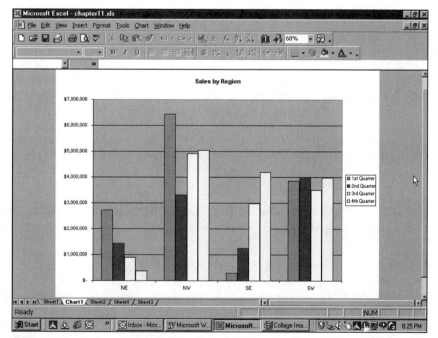

Figure 12-6: A chart as a separate chart sheet.

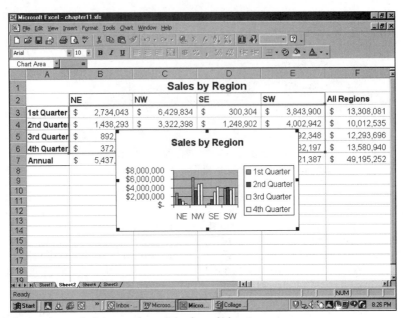

Figure 12-7: A chart on the original worksheet.

18. In both cases, the Chart toolbar will appear (we removed it from the shot for Figure 12-6 so that the full chart would be visible). You can leave the toolbar floating, or you can move it up into the main toolbar area with the other toolbars. Also, the Data menu will be replaced by a Chart menu. In the case of a chart that is placed as an object on the original worksheet, the Data and Chart menus will alternate, depending on whether you are working on the chart or the worksheet. When you click on part of the worksheet, the Data menu reappears, replacing the Chart menu, and the Chart toolbar disappears (even if you have moved it up into the main toolbar area). When you click on the chart, the Chart toolbar reappears, along with the Chart menu, which replaces the Data menu.

Creating Charts from Noncontiguous Selections

You can create charts from noncontiguous selections. For instance, you might want to choose some, but not all, rows from a set of data. You do this by holding down the Ctrl key while making the selections. The selections are supposed to still make a rectangle when they're combined into the chart. In other words, you're theoretically able to do this only if you take the same number of cells from each row, but you don't actually have to do that. You can select three cells from one row, five from another, and so on, if you want to. The chart will simply fail to show anything you don't select, but everything you have selected will be in its proper place.

However, there is one thing you definitely do have to do if you're going to make a chart out of nonrectangular data and you want it to make sense — you have to start each data series in the same column. This is because the first cell in each data series will be the first thing on the chart. Unless all the data series start from the same base, there's no way to use the chart to make valid comparisons among them.

Understanding Chart Types

There are 14 standard chart types in Excel, each with 1 to 6 subtypes in addition to the basic one. There are also 20 custom chart types, which are variations on or combinations of the standard chart types, differing mainly in color and graphical appearance. The following alphabetical list describes each of the standard chart types:

✦ **Area charts** show the relative contribution of values over a period of time or other category. The greater the area taken up by a value, the more it contributed to the overall total.

✦ **Bar charts** are perhaps the most familiar chart type. They show values by the length of horizontal bars.

✦ **Bubble charts** compare three sets of values. They are much like *XY* (scatter) charts, with *X* and *Y* coordinates representing two of the values; but the size of the bubbles is determined by the third value.

✦ **Column charts** are a variant of the bar chart type. They show values by the height of vertical bars known as columns (having nothing to do with whether rows or columns from the worksheet grid are used as the source of the data series). Column charts are the default chart type in Excel.

✦ **Cone charts** are a variant of the bar or column chart type. The only difference is that they use cones instead of bars or columns.

✦ **Cylinder charts** are a variant of the bar or column chart type. The only difference is that they use cylinders instead of bars or columns.

✦ **Doughnut charts** are pretty much the same thing as pie charts, except that they aren't limited to a single data series. Instead of slices, each different series is represented as a ring of the doughnut.

✦ **Line charts** have one *Y* value for every *X* value, like a mathematical function. A line chart is typically used to show changes over time.

✦ **Pie charts** are limited to a single data series (one row or column of data from the worksheet), and cannot display more complex series of data. The value of each element in the data series is assigned a slice of the pie, and all the slices add up to the total of the data series. However, they are visually appealing and simple to understand.

✦ **Pyramid charts** are a variant of the bar or column chart types. The only difference is that they use pyramids instead of bars or columns.

✦ **Radar charts** show data radiating outward from a central point. The center is zero, and category axes extend out from the center. Each series has a data point on each category axis and the data points of a series are connected by a line. Series can be compared by the areas enclosed by their lines.

✦ **Stock charts** are used for plotting the values of stocks. Variants require three to five different values in a given order: High-Low-Close, Open-High-Low-Close, Volume-High-Low-Close, or Volume-Open-High-Low-Close.

✦ **Surface charts** represent trends in values as a continuous curve across two dimensions.

✦ *XY (Scatter)* **charts** compare pairs of values, depicting them as sets of *X* and *Y* coordinates. One use of scatter charts might be to show the results of many trials in an experiment.

Modifying Charts

The Chart menu provides methods for modifying the data and structure of charts you've already created. The first four items on the Chart menu — Chart Type, Source Data, Chart Options, and Location — will sound familiar to you if you've used Chart Wizard. Those menu options bring up the exact same dialog boxes as you find in Chart Wizard.

The other three items are Add Data, Add Trendline, and 3-D View. 3-D View is more of a formatting issue, and will be dealt with separately in the following section on formatting charts.

Changing chart types

You can select Chart ⇨ Chart Type from the menu and choose a new chart type by simply selecting one from the listings in the Chart Type dialog box. Click the OK button and the new chart type replaces the old one.

The Chart toolbar also has an option for selecting chart types. It includes 18 different types, including all the standard types (except for stock charts) and a few of the more common subtypes. To access it, click on the arrow to the right of the Chart Type button. The listed types are represented by icons (see Figure 12-8). Click on any one of them and the old chart will be instantly changed to the new type.

If you want to try another type, repeat the process. To revert to the original chart type, just click the Undo button in the Standard toolbar.

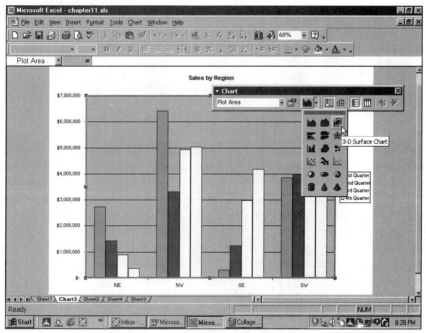

Figure 12-8: The Chart Type icons on the Chart toolbar.

Modifying and adding source data

If you want to change the source your data is drawn from in the worksheet, follow these steps:

1. Select Chart ➪ Source Data from the menu. This brings up the Source Data dialog box (see Figure 12-9), which is the same as the one in Chart Wizard. Regardless of whether the chart is an embedded object in the source worksheet or a separate chart sheet, the dialog box will appear over the source worksheet.

2. To change the entire area from which the data is drawn, enter a new range in the Data Range box.

3. If you want to work with the source data for a smaller portion of the chart, click the Series tab (see Figure 12-10). Here you can choose to make changes to the range of data from which the portions of individual data series are drawn. Select the one you want to change from the Series list, or click the Add button to make a new data series.

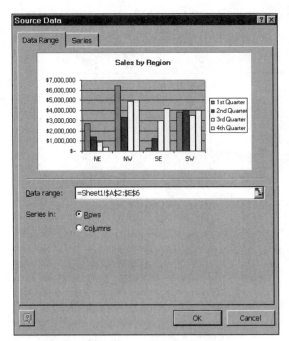

Figure 12-9: The Source Data dialog box.

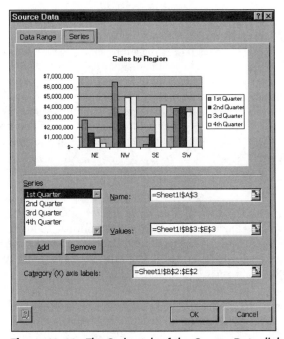

Figure 12-10: The Series tab of the Source Data dialog box.

4. To change the range of data from which the name of the series is drawn, enter the new range in the Name box.

5. To change the range of data from which the values of the series are drawn, enter the new range in the Values box.

6. To change the range of data from which the categories are drawn, enter the new range in the Category (*X*) Axis Labels box.

7. You can click the grid button next to any edit box for which you need to specify a range. This collapses the dialog box and displays only the formula describing the data range from which the chart information is taken (see Figure 12-11). With the dialog box collapsed out of your way, it is easier to find the range you want in the source data and select it. Depending on what chart element you're changing the range of the source data for, the title of the dialog box will vary somewhat; it may read "Data Range," "Name," "Values," etc.

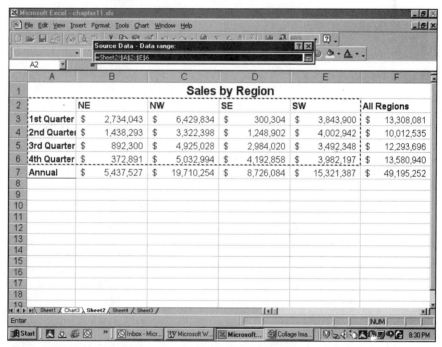

Figure 12-11: The Source Data-Data Range dialog box.

8. Initially, the dialog box floats above the worksheet, most likely obscuring part of the area you need to work with. To move it, place the pointer on the title bar of the dialog box, depress your mouse button, and drag the dialog box to a more convenient location before releasing the mouse button.

9. If you're adding a new data series, and you're working from a separate chart sheet, the Source Data Name or Source Data Values dialog box will be floating above the chart sheet, instead. Click on the sheet tab of the worksheet the source data is located on.

10. Select the cell in the upper left-hand corner of the range you wish to replace the original data source range with. Next, delineate the new data range by either depressing the mouse button and dragging the mouse till the entire new range is selected or holding down the Shift key while clicking in the cell in the lower right-hand corner of the range. Either way, the formula depicting the new range will be displayed in the Source Data-Data Range dialog box.

11. Click the grid button on the right-hand side of the Source Data-Data Range dialog box to return to the expanded Source Data dialog box. The new range will be listed.

12. Click the OK button to accept the changes.

You can also add a data series to the chart by using the Chart ➪ Add Data menu option. The process is virtually identical to the one listed above, except that you need to select the entire range including the labels and values, rather than selecting each one separately. It's up to you which approach you prefer.

Changing chart options

When you select Chart ➪ Chart Options from the menu, you get the same Chart Options dialog box as you used with Chart Wizard. It has tabs for Titles, Axes, Gridlines, Legend, Data Labels, and Data Table.

Changing titles

The Titles tab (see Figure 12-12) lets you assign different titles to the chart and all its axes individually. If any of these currently has a title, it is shown in the appropriate edit box. Those elements without titles have blank edit boxes. Edit boxes for axes that do not apply to a particular chart are grayed out. To change an existing title, highlight the previous title and type over it; to add a title where there was none before, simply type the title into the appropriate edit box. Click in one of the other edit boxes to see the changes in the chart preview box on the right-hand side of the dialog box.

If you're going to change other chart elements, click on the appropriate tab. If you're finished with your changes, click the OK button.

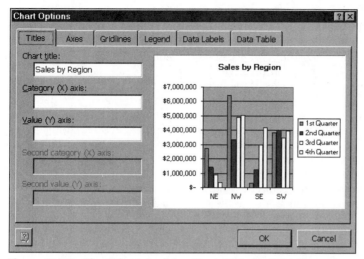

Figure 12-12: The Titles tab of the Chart Options dialog box.

Changing axes

The Axes tab (see Figure 12-13) lets you choose whether or not to show each of the primary axes, as well as any secondary axes that you may have added (if the secondary axes don't exist, they won't show here).

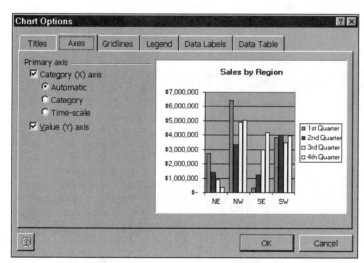

Figure 12-13: The Axes tab of the Chart Options dialog box.

To remove the horizontal axis from your chart, deselect the Category (X) Axis check box. To restore it, select that check box. The Category axis also gives you three radio buttons to choose from about how Excel interprets it. By default, the choice is Automatic. The other two are Category and Time-scale. When Excel finds the labels on your data range, it takes the labels that are normal text or numbers and assumes they are categories; if the labels are dates, then Excel assumes a time-scale is needed, instead. Time-scales cannot be used with times, only dates — you have to have days, months, and/or years as labels to trigger time-scales on the X axis. It's best to leave this setting at Automatic and let Excel do its thing. If you try to force a time-scale on a series of labels that don't fit it, the results will be arbitrary and inaccurate.

To remove the vertical axis from your chart, deselect the Value (Y) Axis check box. To restore it, select that check box. In the case of a 3-D chart, you have a Series (Y) axis and a Value (Z) axis instead.

If you're going to change other chart elements, click the appropriate tab. If you're finished with your changes, click the OK button.

Changing gridlines

The Gridlines tab (see Figure 12-14) lets you decide what kind of gridlines to show on both the Category (X) axis and the Value (Y) axis. In the case of a 3-D chart, you have a Category (X) axis, a Series (Y) axis and a Value (Z) axis. The major gridlines show where larger values cross the chart, while the minor gridlines show where smaller values cross the chart. To put any gridline in, just put a check in its check box; to remove it, deselect its check box. (As a design consideration, the fewer the gridlines, the more readable the chart. Unless you really need the minor gridlines, it's usually best to leave them out.)

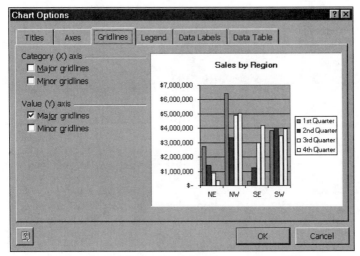

Figure 12-14: The Gridlines tab of the Chart Options dialog box.

Caution   If you're going to use shortcut keys to put in the gridlines, bear in mind that on the X axis, they're labeled Major gridlines and Minor gridlines; on the Y axis, they're labeled Major gridlines and Minor gridlines.

If you're going to change other chart elements, click the appropriate tab. If you're finished with your changes, click the OK button.

Changing legends

The Legend tab (see Figure 12-15) has one check box and five radio buttons. The Show Legend check box has only one function — to have or not have a legend on your chart. If it's checked, the radio buttons become active. They let you place the legend in different parts of your chart: bottom, corner, top, right, or left. The corner position means the upper right-hand corner. The bottom, right, and left positions place the legend in the center position on one of the edges of the chart area. The top position places the legend under the chart title.

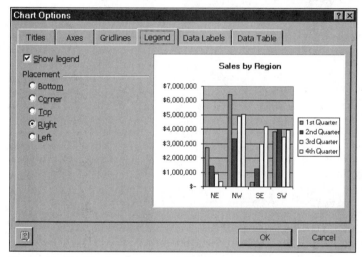

Figure 12-15: The Legend tab of the Chart Options dialog box.

Tip   Legends can also be added or removed by clicking on the Legend button in the Chart toolbar.

If you're going to change other chart elements, click the appropriate tab. If you're finished with your changes, click the OK button.

Changing data labels

The Data Labels tab (see Figure 12-16) lets you assign various data to be put into the chart alongside the representations of the data. Depending on the chart type, various options are active, while others are grayed out. The basic options, represented by radio buttons, are None, Show value, Show percent, Show label, Show label and percent, and Show bubble sizes.

There are two other options at the bottom of the tab, both of them check boxes: Legend key next to label and Show leader lines (not shown in figure). The first one puts a small colored box next to the data label keyed to the same color the corresponding data series has in the legend. The other one, which only shows up for pie charts, puts lines between the labels and the chart element they refer to (you need to move the labels away from the element before the leader lines show up).

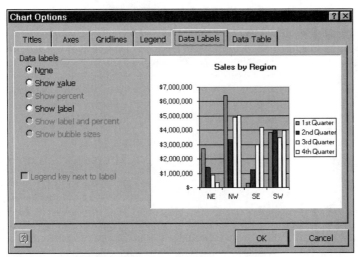

Figure 12-16: The Data Labels tab of the Chart Options dialog box.

If you're going to change other chart elements, click the appropriate tab. If you're finished with your changes, click the OK button.

Changing data tables

The Data Table tab (see Figure 12-17) has two check boxes on it. Checking the first, Show data table, places a copy of the worksheet grid you used to create the chart underneath the chart. To remove the data table, deselect its check box. The other one, Show legend keys, puts a small colored box next to each data series in the data table keyed to the same color in the legend. To remove the legend keys feature, deselect its check box. (You can also add or remove data tables by clicking on the Data Table button in the Chart toolbar.)

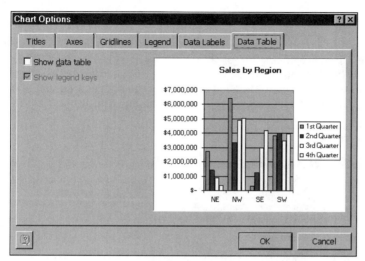

Figure 12-17: The Data Table tab of the Chart Options dialog box.

Note

Not all chart types can show data tables; if the one you're using doesn't, the Data Table tab will not be available.

If you're going to change other chart elements, click the appropriate tab. If you're finished with your changes, click the OK button.

Relocating a chart

You can change an embedded chart into a separate chart sheet and vice versa by following these steps:

1. Select Chart ➪ Location from the menu. This brings up the same Chart Location dialog box you saw in the Chart Wizard.

2. To move an embedded object onto its own chart sheet, select the As New Sheet radio button. Type the name of the new chart sheet into the edit box or accept the one Excel suggests, and then click the OK button.

3. To change a chart from being on its own chart sheet to being an embedded object on another worksheet, select the As Object In radio button. Select the destination sheet from the drop-down list, and then click the OK button. The original chart sheet will be deleted if you move its chart to another worksheet, but you can recreate it by changing the chart back to being on its own chart sheet again.

Tip

You can embed a chart on another chart sheet as well as on a regular worksheet.

Adding trendlines

Selecting Chart ➪ Add Trendline brings up the Add Trendline dialog box (see Figure 12-18). Trendlines aren't available for all charts, and won't work on most of the more exotic kinds like 3-D charts, doughnut charts, or radar charts. If your chart is one of these, the Add Trendline option is grayed out. The chart types that you can add trendlines to are normal 2-D area, bar, bubble, column, line, stock, and *XY* (scatter) charts.

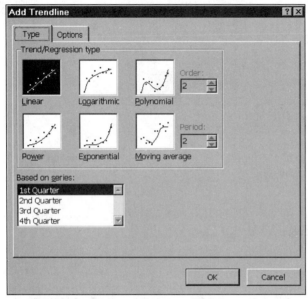

Figure 12-18: The Add Trendline dialog box with the Type tab showing.

The trendline is for the data series selected under Based on Series at the bottom of the Type tab. There are six types of trendlines you can add: Linear, Logarithmic, Polynomial, Power, Exponential, and Moving average. If you select the Polynomial type, you can also specify its Order (the default order is 2). If you select the Moving average type, you can also specify its Period (the default period is 2).

Under the Options tab (see Figure 12-19), you can set further options for your trendlines. Depending upon the trendline type you choose, some options may be grayed out. There are three sets of options:

✦ The first option on the Options tab lets you set the Trendline name. The Automatic default is composed of the type of trendline plus your data label for the affected data series. The Custom name can be anything you type into the edit box.

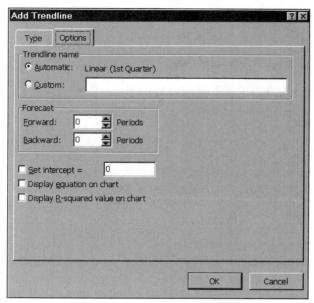

Figure 12-19: The Add Trendline Options tab.

✦ The second option lets you set the Forward and Backward forecast periods.

✦ The final set of options includes Set intercept, Display equation on chart, and Display R-squared value on chart.

Formatting Charts

While all chart items can be formatted, the options vary from one element to the next. The only thing they all have in common is patterns, although textual elements also have fonts and alignment in common, as well as (sometimes) number formatting. There are two basic methods:

✦ **Using the pop-up menu.** You can format chart elements by right-clicking on them and then selecting Format [chart element] from the pop-up menu. The actual name of the selected element will show on the menu in place of [chart element]; for instance, if you are formatting the chart title, the menu option will be Format Chart Title.

✦ **Using the Chart toolbar.** You can also format chart elements by clicking on them to select them, and then clicking on the Format [chart element] button in the Chart toolbar. As with the pop-up menu, the Format button's floating message will display the name of the selected element as you place the pointer upon it.

Tip   If you've lost your Chart toolbar, there could be a couple of reasons. If you're working on a worksheet that has a chart as an embedded object, the Chart toolbar will disappear whenever you're working on any part of the worksheet other than the chart. To get it back, just click on any part of the chart. In either an embedded object situation or with a separate chart sheet, if you've closed the Chart toolbar, you can get it back by right-clicking on any toolbar and selecting Chart from the pop-up toolbar menu.

The options in the pop-up menu vary depending on the type of chart element you've selected, but Clear is the only option in the pop-up menus that you won't find in either the Chart menu or the Chart toolbar. Clear has different results for different chart elements. Generally speaking, it deletes the item from the chart. However, in the case of the plot area in 2-D charts or the floors and walls in 3-D charts, it merely makes them invisible. They are still present, as can be demonstrated by placing your pointer over the area where they were formerly visible; the floating message will still indicate their presence.

Whichever approach you take, pop-up menu or Format button on the Chart toolbar, a dialog box with tabs reflecting the formatting options appropriate to the particular chart element will appear. Formatting options come in three basic classes: the same ones you're familiar with using in worksheets (such as formatting and coloring fonts), the ones you're familiar with for setting chart element options (such as positioning the legend), and a few new ones that are obvious in their function (such as setting the spacing between columns).

Cross-Reference   See the section entitled, "Enhancing Charts" later in this chapter for more information on using the formatting options.

Handling 3-D Chart Views

One thing that is neither familiar from worksheets nor intuitive for those who haven't worked with 3-D programs is the handling of 3-D chart views. You can open the controls for 3-D charts in two ways. You can either select Chart ➪ 3-D View from the main menu or right-click on most elements in a 3-D chart and select 3-D View from the pop-up menu. The option isn't available on the pop-up menu for all elements, even if they are part of a 3-D chart. For instance, you don't have 3-D view options for legends, axes, titles, etc. Elements such as floors, walls, plot areas, and so forth, however, do have that option in their pop-up menus.

Using the 3-D View dialog box

Whichever menu you use, you'll get the 3-D View dialog box (see Figure 12-20). You can use four controls to alter the view: Elevation, Rotation, Perspective, and Height. All four can be adjusted by typing in specific values. Elevation values range from 90 to -90, Rotation from 0 to 360, Perspective from 0 to 100, and Height from 5 to 500. The first three can also be adjusted by clicking on the arrow buttons near them.

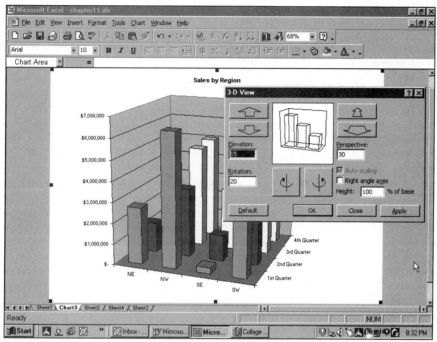

Figure 12-20: The 3-D View dialog box.

There are also two check boxes in the dialog box: Auto scaling and Right angle axes. Because perspective adjustments and right angle axes are mutually exclusive, you must clear the Right angle axes check box to make the Perspective controls appear. Auto scaling means that the fonts in the chart automatically adjust their size to accommodate changes you make in the chart. It's generally best to leave it checked.

When you've finished making your adjustments, click the OK button to apply your changes. If you want to return to the default 3-D settings, click the Default button.

Using the "Corners" method

There's an even better way to handle the view on 3-D charts; it's faster, more intuitive, and it's a lot more fun, too. Skip the menus, and move your pointer to a juncture of axes on the chart. When you get a floating message that says "Corners," you're in business. Click on that point. Now, while still on that point, press your mouse button down and hold it. Move the mouse in any direction and the 3-D chart becomes a wireframe box that responds to your every move (see Figure 12-21).

The floor of the chart is represented by the rectangle with lines across it, so you can tell which side is up. When you've got the box the way you want it, release the mouse button and you've got your reoriented 3-D chart. You can repeat this endlessly to make fine adjustments or experiment with different views of the chart.

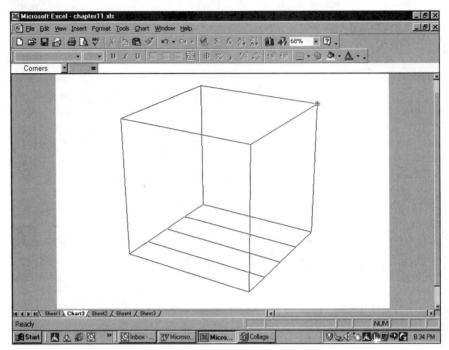

Figure 12-21: Interactive 3-D View.

Tip   If you totally botch the chart up to the point where you can't tell which side is which, just go into the standard 3-D View dialog box and click the Default button to fix it.

Enhancing Charts

The most basic approach to enhancing charts is to use the standard worksheet techniques of applying font styles, background colors, and so forth, to them. A chart title, for instance, can be changed to a larger font, italicized, and colored to make it stand out more than the usual, plain titles.

Background colors and patterns can also be applied to various chart elements with excellent effect. Figure 12-22 shows our earlier standard column chart with various effects applied.

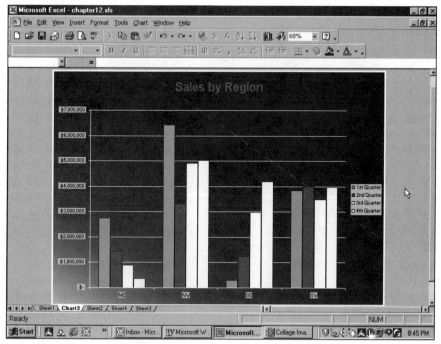

Figure 12-22: Enhanced Excel chart.

This makeover was achieved by first giving the chart area a colored fill pattern. To do this, follow these steps:

1. Right-click on the chart area, and then select Format Chart Area from the pop-up menu.

2. In the Format Chart Area dialog box (see Figure 12-23), click on the Patterns tab.

3. Click the Fill Effects button. This brings up the Fill Effects dialog box (see Figure 12-24). There are four tabs in the Fill Effects dialog box: Gradient, Texture, Pattern, and Picture. The first three have pre-designed backgrounds you can add to chart elements, and the last one lets you use your own graphics files as background elements. For this exercise, we chose to use a gradient.

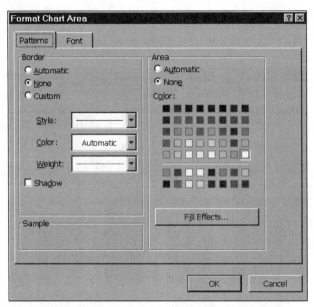

Figure 12-23: The Patterns tab of the Format Chart Area dialog box.

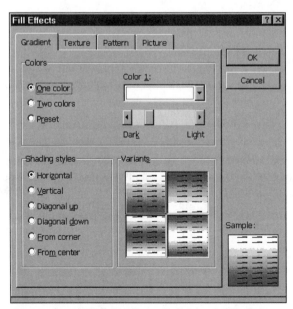

Figure 12-24: The Fill Effects dialog box with the Gradient tab showing.

4. The basic gradient options are One color, Two colors, and Preset. If you choose to use one color, then you can pick it from a drop-down list and your only other option is how dark it is. If you use two colors, you pick them both the same way, but you get no choice as to how dark they are. We chose Preset and chose Late Sunset from the drop-down list (see Figure 12-25). Under Shading styles, we picked Diagonal down and chose the upper-left example under Variants.

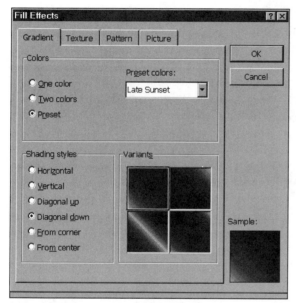

Figure 12-25: The Late Sunset gradient.

5. Click the OK button to finalize the gradient choice. This returns you to the Format Chart Area dialog box, where you also need to click the OK button. The results are a distinct improvement over the original chart, but several elements still need work. The chart title and the legend stick out like sore thumbs, and the background to the plot area is pretty dull.

6. To get rid of the plot area's background, right-click on the plot area and select Clear from the pop-up menu. The background immediately disappears. However, the gridlines and axes are now nearly invisible, because they're black against a dark background.

7. You don't have to use the chart formatting options in this case. Because all we're looking for is a quick fix for a color problem, just click on one of the gridlines so they're selected, and then click on the Fill Color arrow in the Formatting toolbar and select white from the drop-down palette.

8. Next, select the category axis and click the Fill Color button (you don't have to go through the palette this time because the Fill Color button automatically uses the last color chosen from the palette).

9. Select the value axis and click the Fill Color button.

10. Select the legend, click on the arrow to the right of the Fill Color button, and pick gold from the palette.

11. Select the chart title and select a font size of 24 from the drop-down list in the Formatting toolbar.

12. While the chart title is still selected, change the font color by clicking on the arrow to the right of the Font Color button and picking red from the palette.

13. While the chart title is still selected, change its background to black by clicking on the arrow to the right of the Fill Color button and picking black from the palette.

14. Save your workbook.

Saving Custom Chart Formats

Once you've developed a chart that you particularly like and would want to use again, you can save it as a custom chart format. To do so, follow these steps:

1. Select the chart you want to use.

2. Select Chart ➪ Chart Type from the menu. This brings up the Chart Type dialog box.

3. Click the Custom Types tab (see Figure 12-26).

4. Click the User-defined radio button.

5. Click the Add button. This brings up the Add Custom Chart Type dialog box (see Figure 12-27).

6. Type in a name for the chart under Name and a description of it under Description.

7. Click the OK button to return to the Chart Type dialog box.

8. If you want to use this as your basic chart from now on, click the Set as Default Chart button.

9. Click the OK button to finish.

Figure 12-26: The Custom Types tab of the Chart Type dialog box.

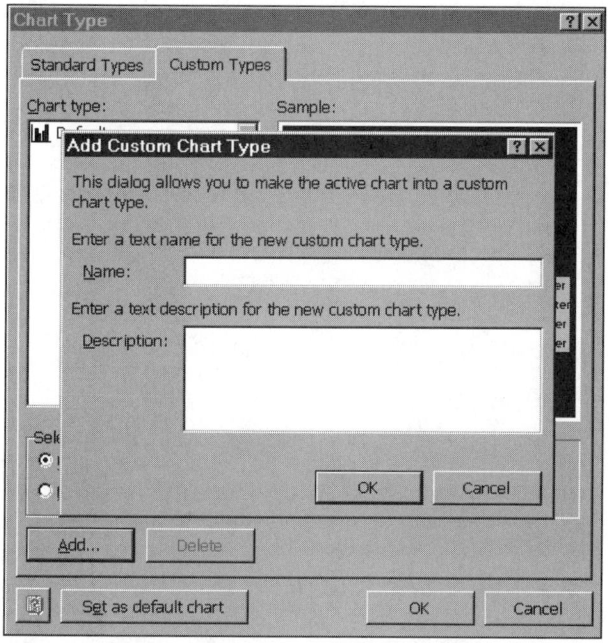

Figure 12-27: The Add Custom Chart Type dialog box.

Summary

In this chapter, you learned how to create, use, and modify charts in Excel.

✦ You create charts using Chart Wizard.

✦ Excel offers a variety of different chart types.

✦ Charts can be embedded as objects in a worksheet or they can be created as separate chart sheets. After creation, they can be changed from embedded objects to separate sheets and vice versa.

✦ You can change every aspect of a chart after it is created.

✦ The view of 3-D charts can be manipulated interactively.

✦ The appearance of charts can be enhanced by a variety of methods, some of which are specific to charts and some of which are standard worksheet approaches.

✦ You can save your own custom chart formats for future use.

✦   ✦   ✦

Functions and Formulas

Excel has built-in, ready-to-use functions for everything from Boolean logic to financial calculations. While you can build either simple or complex formulas by hand using cell references, operators, and functions, Excel provides valuable shortcuts to formula creation. Function Wizard lets you quickly and easily build complicated formulas, while the AutoSum button provides an easy way to instantly total rows and columns of data.

Once a formula has been created, it can be edited either within the cell that contains it or within the formula bar, and it can be copied or moved from one location in the worksheet to another.

Using Function Wizard

Excel's Function Wizard saves you a great deal of effort when it comes to putting functions into your worksheets. It puts a large library of functions — mathematical, financial, logical, and others — right at hand for your convenience. To use it, follow these steps:

1. Select the cell you want to put the formula's result into.

2. Click the Paste Function button in the Standard toolbar. This brings up the Paste Function dialog box (see Figure 13-1).

3. Make a selection under Function Category on the left-hand side of the dialog box. There are several categories of functions, such as Statistical, Database, Date & Time, etc. There are also two special categories: Most Recently Used and All. The Most Recently Used category keeps track of the functions you've been using lately so, if you're repeatedly using the same ones, you don't have to go hunting for them. The All category is every function in all the categories.

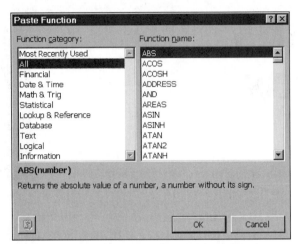

Figure 13-1: The Paste Function dialog box.

4. Once you've chosen a category, the Function Name listing will change to reflect the functions available within that category. Scroll down if necessary until you reach the name of the function you want to employ, and then click on it. A description of both the structure and usage of the selected function will appear at the bottom of the Paste Function dialog box.

5. Click the OK button to proceed. This brings up the second screen of Function Wizard (see Figure 13-2). Excel automatically guesses what range of cells you intend to apply the function to, but you can adjust the range or change it entirely to suit your desires if it guesses wrong. The result of the formula if applied to the current range is shown at the bottom of the dialog box.

6. Excel tentatively enters the function formula into the selected cell and displays it in the formula bar. Any changes you make in the range at this stage, however, are automatically reflected in both places, and you can abort the function formula entirely by clicking the Cancel button or pressing the Esc key. The formula result at the bottom of the dialog box changes along with any changes you make.

7. If the dialog box is obscuring a part of the worksheet that you want to see, you can drag it out of the way. Just click at the top of it and, while holding down your mouse button, move it to where you want it to be, and then release the mouse button.

8. If you want to keep the automatically selected range, no extra action is required. If you want to change the range, simply select a new one with your mouse on the worksheet. Continue to select cells or ranges for each value as needed for the particular function you're using.

9. When you are satisfied with the values, click the OK button to complete using Function Wizard and the function formula is finalized. The result will show up in the selected cell.

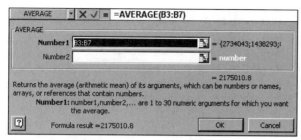

Figure 13-2: The Function Value dialog box.

Average, Maximum, Minimum, and Sum

Four functions in particular are among the most useful and the most commonly used: average, maximum, minimum, and sum.

How averages work

Averages are the arithmetic mean of a set of numbers contained within cells. For instance, if you have three cells containing the values 7, 14, and 3, their average is 8. Averages require at least two values to generate meaningful results, as the average of any single number is itself. Averages are calculated in Excel by applying the AVERAGE function to a range of cells as follows:

```
=AVERAGE(F3:F8)
```

You can also apply it to sets of numbers in which the numbers are contained in noncontiguous cells, in which case the proper form is

```
=AVERAGE(F3,G2,H9)
```

If you're using Function Wizard, it will automatically put your choices in the correct format as you select cells or ranges of cells.

Note　Although the normal usage of functions in Excel is to act on the contents of referenced cells or ranges, there's no reason why they can't be applied to actual numbers typed into a formula. You can enter the numbers either through manual editing or in the Function Wizard in place of ranges. The form is very similar to when noncontiguous cells are entered:

```
=AVERAGE(22,973,84)
```

Averages, maximums, minimums, and sums follow the same pattern in every respect, but provide different information in their results.

The MAX and MIN functions

The MAX function returns the value of the highest number in a set of cells. For example, if you had the values 229, 573, 842, and 132 in a range of cells and sought the maximum value, you'd get a result of 842. The MIN function performs the opposite role, seeking the minimum value and returning the value of the lowest number in a set of cells. If you applied it to the same example we just used for the MAX function, the MIN function would return 132.

The SUM function

The SUM function gives the total value of all the referenced cells added together. Applying it to the same range of cells as the earlier MAX and MIN examples, the result would be 1,776.

Using AutoSum

Practically everyone who uses Excel wants to total rows and columns. That makes SUM the one function used more often than any other. Microsoft has made it even easier to use by putting an AutoSum button on the Standard toolbar, symbolized by the Greek letter sigma (Σ). To use it, follow these steps:

1. Select the cell where you want the sum to show up. For best results, this should be right after the end of the cells containing the numbers you want summed. In the case of a row, this would be the first blank cell on the right side; in the case of a column, it would be the first blank cell on the bottom end. You can't use AutoSum to put a total at the left of a row or at the top of a column even if you wanted to put one in such a nonstandard location. If you'd rather have a gap between the data and the total, though, you can select a cell that's further away. For instance, if you selected a cell that was two cells below the range you were summing instead of immediately below it, the total would be the same. That's because, although the cell in between would also be added up, blank cells are considered to hold zeroes.

2. Click the AutoSum button.

3. Excel assumes that you want to add the numbers immediately above the selected cell or to its left, and automatically puts that range into the function formula. The range of cells is outlined with a moving dotted line (see Figure 13-3). If the selected cell has data both above it and to the left, Excel defaults to choosing the range of cells above it.

4. As with Function Wizard, you can change the range if it isn't what you wanted. Just click in the beginning cell of the range you really want and drag until you reach the ending cell of it.

5. Press Enter to finalize the AutoSum.

				Microsoft Excel - chapter11.xls				_|🗗|x|

Figure 13-3: AutoSum in action.

Tip

If you want to specify the range the AutoSum will act on beforehand, select it and click the AutoSum button. The total will be put into the blank cell either immediately to the right of selected data in a row or into the one immediately beneath selected data in a column. If you select only part of a possible range of data and there is no blank cell right after your selection, the results will be put into the first blank cell after the entire possible range in the same row or column as your selected data.

Working with Formulas

Formulas let you work on the data in your worksheet cells to produce mathematical and logical results. Without them, spreadsheets would be nothing more than nicely structured collections of raw data. With formulas, that data can be made to yield valuable information.

Formulas are constructed out of two basic elements: *cell references* and *operators*. Cell references are simply the locations of cells in the worksheet grid. They're used in formulas to tell Excel where to find the data to take action on. Operators are instructions for how to process the data. For example, you might use an addition operator or a multiplication operator on cells containing numbers. The operators you have at your disposal in Excel are detailed in Table 13-1.

Cross-Reference

Chapter 10, "Worksheets and Workbooks," discusses the basics of cell references.

	Table 13-1 **Excel Operators**
Operator	**Purpose**
-	Negation
%	Percentage
^	Exponentiation
*	Multiplication
/	Division
+	Addition
-	Subtraction
&	Concatenation (text addition)
=	Equality
<	Less than
>	Greater than
<=	Less than or equal to
>=	Greater than or equal to
<>	Inequality

Creating a formula

To create a formula, follow these steps:

1. Just like the formulas created by Function Wizard, all formulas you create begin with an equal sign (=). Select the cell into which you will be entering your formula and type an equal sign into it.

2. Type a reference to a cell containing data to be used in the formula. For instance, if you want to multiply the contents of cell A1 by those of A2, you would enter A1 here. You can use individual cell references, ranges of cells, and names of cells or ranges as references in a formula.

3. Enter an operator and another cell reference. To continue with the example from the previous step, you would enter the multiplication operator (*) and a reference to cell A2 here. The formula now reads =A1*A2.

4. Continue to repeat Steps 2 and 3 until you have completed your formula.

5. Press Enter to finish. The results of the formula will appear in the cell in which you entered it.

Tip

You can click on the cells you want to include in your formula instead of having to type in their references. Unfortunately, you still have to type the operators in between the cell references.

Understanding operator precedence

Operators aren't all treated the same by Excel. Some are processed before others. This is called *precedence*. The operators in Table 13-1 are listed in order of precedence. Some of them, though, have equal precedence. The multiplication and division operators (* and /), for instance, do, as do the addition and subtraction operators (+ and -). Also, the entire range of comparison operators (=, <, >, <=, >=, and <>) share precedence with one another. Other than that, the precedence runs in the order shown in the table.

For example, if you have the following formula, the multiplication will take place before the addition because multiplication has a higher precedence:

```
=B3+B4*B5
```

If you want to change the order in which operations are processed, you can use parentheses to influence the outcome. Because anything within parentheses has a higher precedence than any operator, the same formula as before can be forced to perform the addition before the multiplication by placing the entire addition operation within parentheses:

```
=(B3+B4)*B5
```

In the case of operators that have the same precedence, the decision about which operation to perform first depends on which one comes first in left-to-right positioning. In the following formula, division takes place before multiplication because the division operator comes first:

```
=B3/B4*B5
```

The Difference Between Negation and Subtraction

You probably noticed in Table 13-1 that the negation symbol and the subtraction symbol are identical (-). Although they can be made to perform identical functions, there is a distinction between them. The negation operator changes the sign of a number (positive numbers become negative and vice versa), while the subtraction operator subtracts the referenced value from the preceding value. Because the negation operator has a higher precedence, this can be a tricky problem if you have a situation in which you need to use both. In the following formula (assuming that both cells have positive numbers in them), the first value is turned to a negative and the second is subtracted from it; the effect is the same as adding two negative numbers:

```
=-B3-B4
```

If the value in the cell B3 were 5 and the value in the cell B4 were 3, you'd end up with a result of -8, as you'd be essentially adding -5 to -3. If, however, you wanted to find the negative value of the subtraction instead, you'd have to use parentheses to force the operations to take place in the desired order, as in the following example, which would yield a result of -2 by producing the negative value of the operation 5-3:

```
=-(B3-B4)
```

Displaying and editing formulas

Although the cell containing a formula normally displays not the formula itself, but the results of the formula, formulas are displayed in the formula bar anytime you click on a cell containing a formula (see Figure 13-4). You can make a cell temporarily display the formula instead of its result by double-clicking on the cell.

To make all the cells in a worksheet display their formulas as their normal behavior, select Tools ⇨ Options from the menu, and then click the View tab. On the View tab, select the check box labeled Formulas and click the OK button.

Caution

If you exercise the option to display all formulas in the cells all the time, you won't have a good-looking worksheet, because the cells have to expand to the size of the formulas in order to show them. At the very least, you'll have to reverse the option when you're ready to present your results, and that may mean last-minute design corrections or unpleasant surprises, because you won't have seen the final appearance of the worksheet or the results of the calculations beforehand.

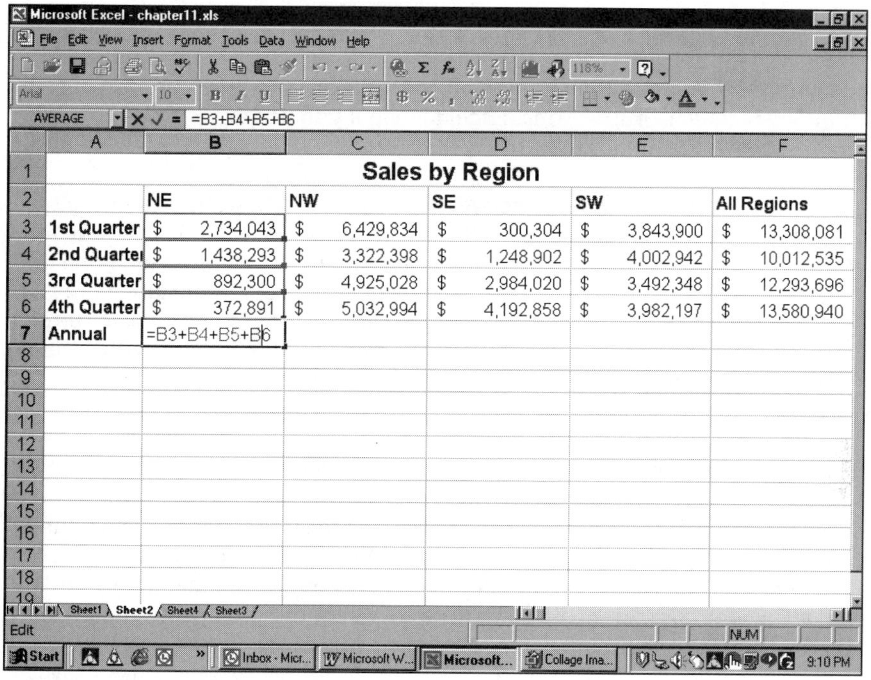

Figure 13-4: The formula bar displays the formula.

Whatever approach you take to displaying formulas, they can be edited either in the cell or in the formula bar. To edit in the formula bar, simply click within it. If the cursor doesn't land exactly where you wanted it to, move the cursor into the position where you want to edit, and add or delete to your heart's content. You can continue to put in operators by typing, and cell references either by typing or pointing with the mouse.

Tip
To replace a cell reference in the formula bar with another one, highlight the cell reference you want to replace, and then click on the cell you want to replace it with.

To edit a formula in the cell, you have to first double-click on the cell — even if the formula is already displayed within it. Setting the formula display option in the View tab does not change the editing behavior of cells, only the visibility of the formulas they contain.

Copying and Moving Formulas and Functions

You can use the standard menu or toolbar techniques to move or copy a cell containing formulas or functions. Excel also lets you use drag and drop to accomplish both procedures.

There's an important difference between the two methods other than the obvious one that when you copy a cell, the original one remains where it was, but when you move it, the original one isn't there anymore. When you move a cell, none of the cell references in a formula are affected in any way at all; they come along fully intact. When you copy it, however, that's not true. The cell references change to reflect the new position of the cell. For instance, if you move a cell two columns to the right and three rows down, all the cell references in the formula contained within it will shift by the same amount.

The only way around this is to use absolute cell references within the formula. However, there are times when you won't want to do this, because you do want the references to change. It's fine for the cell references to be locked in absolutely if you're moving only the cell containing the formula. If you're moving the cells it refers to as well, as when you reposition an entire range of data and formulas, you'll want the cell references in the formula to change along with the placement of the cells it refers to.

Caution   When you copy or move a cell or range of cells, you replace any data in the destination cells. When moving, you are warned that you're about to replace the previous contents.

Copying via the toolbar or menu

Copying formulas and functions via the menu or toolbar is done in the following manner:

1. Select the cell or range of cells you want to copy.

2. Click the Copy button on the toolbar. Alternatively, select Edit ➪ Copy from the menu or right-click on the copy source and select Copy from the resultant pop-up menu.

3. Click in the cell you want to paste the cell into (if you're copying a range of cells, click in the cell in the upper left-hand corner of the range you want to paste the range into).

4. Click the Paste button on the toolbar. Alternatively, select Edit ➪ Paste from the menu or right-click on the paste destination and select Paste from the resultant pop-up menu.

Moving is done in the exact same way, with the exception that you use the Cut button instead of the Copy button for the toolbar method. The menu differences are that you select Edit ⇨ Cut from the main menu or right-click on the selection and select Cut from the pop-up menu.

Using the Paste Special command

You can use the Paste Special command on either the regular or the pop-up menu to control which attributes of the copied or cut cell get pasted into the new location. Of particular interest with respect to formulas and functions is the Values option on the Paste Special menu (see Figure 13-5). Selecting that radio button means that only the results of the formula, not the formula itself, are pasted into the destination cell. The result, once pasted in this manner, is permanently fixed and will not change in this cell even if it changes in the original one. You can also use it to paste only the formula itself, leaving behind any cell formatting options from the original cell, by selecting the Formulas radio button. In either case, click the OK button to complete the Paste Special operation.

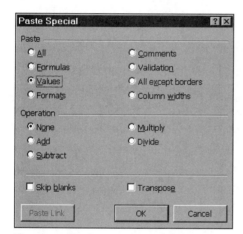

Figure 13-5: The Paste Special menu.

Using the drag and drop method

Excel's native method for copying and moving cells is easier than the standard Windows method of cut and paste—do it by dragging and dropping. To move a formula, just select the cell or cells you want to move, click on the border of the cell (anywhere except for the fill handle) and drag it to the position you want to place it in, and release the mouse button. To copy it, do the same thing, but hold down the Ctrl key while you release the mouse button, and then release the Ctrl key (if you release the Ctrl key before you release the mouse button, you'll move, not copy, the cell).

Copying as values only

If you don't want to mess with the menu or toolbar, you can still manage to paste only the results of a formula. After selecting the source cell or cells, right-click on the cell border, and then drag it to the cell you want to put it into. When you release the right mouse button, you'll get a pop-up menu on which one of the options is Copy Here as Values Only (see Figure 13-6).

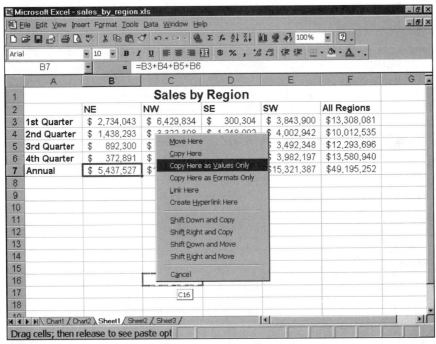

Figure 13-6: Copy as values only.

Using Range Names

While the standard cell reference method is a functional way to manage formulas, it goes all the way back to the earliest spreadsheets, and hasn't really improved since the dawn of time, relatively speaking. When compared to the other advances in Excel, it's pretty much a Stone Age method.

When you use cell references, you're forced to convert your natural thought processes into something the program can comprehend. It's far better to make the program do that kind of conversion while you're able to just move along and get your job done. The most natural way to think of formulas is to assign names to the cells and ranges of cells with which you'll be working.

For example, do you think of sales forecasts as B1+B2+B3 and so forth, or do you naturally think of them in terms of First Quarter, Second Quarter, Third Quarter, and Fourth Quarter? Is a finance charge calculated as H7*H8, or is it the average daily balance times the monthly percentage rate?

Fortunately, Excel accommodates natural human methods of expressing our thoughts and can take care of translating those into cell references without our having to specifically direct it to do so. The only real stumbling block is that Excel can't handle spaces between words, but you can just leave them out or use underscores instead. Examples would be "AverageDailyBalance" or "Average_Daily_Balance." You could also just abbreviate it "ADB," of course. One other thing to keep in mind is that, although you can use numbers in cell or range names, you can't start the name with a number. Thus, "Quarter1" is fine, but "1stQuarter" won't work.

If you're dealing with a simple one-line formula, naming the individual cells is a good solution. If you've got something more complex, though, that approach can quickly become tedious. While you could name each and every cell in an entire worksheet and painstakingly state their formulas in words, there's a much easier way to do it — name an entire range of cells and let Excel sort them out.

Say you have a worksheet like the one shown in Figure 13-7, which shows commission income by week for four salespeople. You can select the range of cells from B2 to B5 and name it "Week1," and then do the same for C2 to C5, naming it "Week2," etc. In the F column, then, all you have to do is enter the formula "=Week1+Week2+Week3+Week4" and Excel will automatically understand that you mean to add the cells from this row that fall in those ranges. Because of this, you can use the exact same formula in each row.

Tip You could do the same thing by naming a range in the rows and adding them in columns as well. An even easier approach, if your worksheet arrangement allows for it, is to name the entire row or column instead of a smaller range of cells within the row or column.

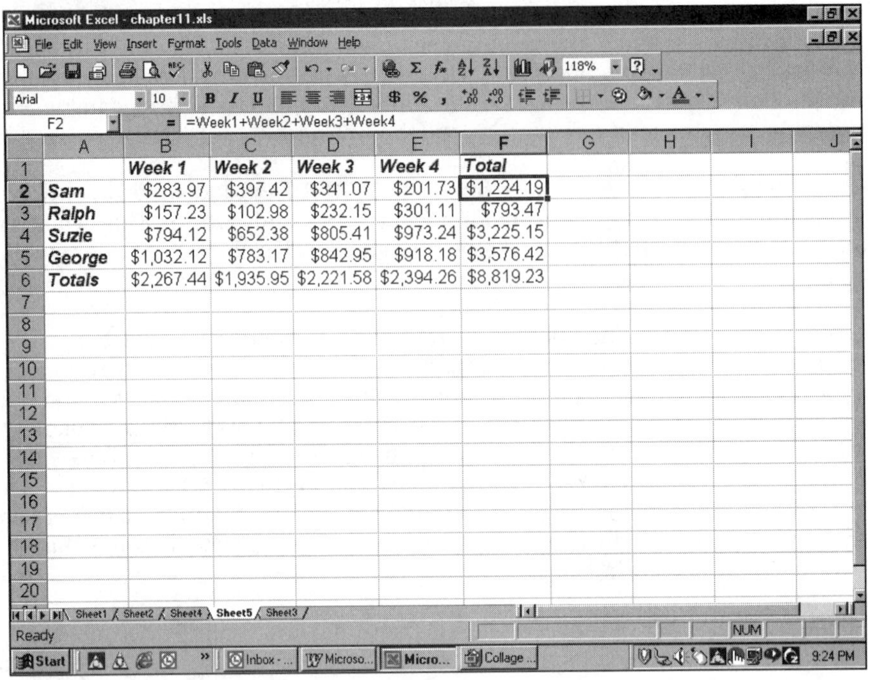

Figure 13-7: Name ranges used for formulas.

Using Arrays

Closely related to ranges are *arrays*. Arrays are sets of values, and the values can either be entered into cells on your worksheet or directly input into a formula as constants. When the values are entered into cells, the cells holding them are said to constitute an *array range*.

Array formulas are used to perform calculations on arrays or groups of arrays. For instance, the array formula in Figure 13-8 uses the MMULT function to perform matrix multiplication on a pair of arrays.

Because matrix multiplication results in an array consisting of the results of several calculations, it must be done using an array formula; a regular formula can produce only a single result, and any formula that returns an array must, by definition, be an array formula. Array formulas are entered just as regular formulas are, but instead of pressing Enter to complete them, you have to simultaneously press Ctrl+Shift+Enter.

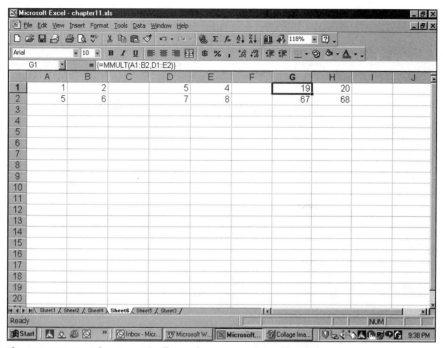

Figure 13-8: Excel automatically encloses array formulas in braces.

Using Links

The data in your worksheets doesn't have to come from within them. You can establish a link between different data sources in Office programs through linking and embedding (any other Windows programs that support linking and embedding will also work), and any change to the data in the original file will be reflected in your worksheet. To link to data in another program, follow this procedure:

1. Create and save the source file (database, document, etc.).

2. Select the item you want to put into your worksheet.

3. Copy the item (data, text, etc.). If you're using the main menu, you'd select Edit ➪ Copy. You could also simply click the Copy button on the toolbar or right-click on the selection and then select Copy from the pop-up menu.

4. Open your worksheet.

5. Select the cell where you want to create the link.

6. Using the main menu, select Edit ➪ Paste Special. Alternatively, right-click and select Paste Special from the pop-up menu.

7. In the Paste Special dialog box (see Figure 13-9), select the type of object you are going to be linking to.

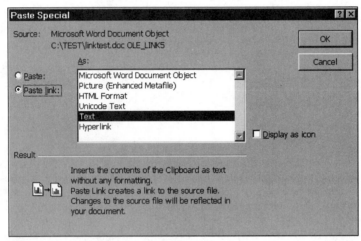

Figure 13-9: The Paste Special dialog box.

8. Select the Paste Link radio button, and then click the OK button to complete the link.

Caution

In the Paste Special dialog box, the Paste radio button is selected by default. If you don't click the Paste link radio button, it'll look as though you made the link correctly because the selected data will indeed show up in your worksheet. However, it will be a static paste, rather than an active link, and the data will fail to update in your worksheet when you change it in the original data source.331

Summary

In this chapter, you learned how to create formulas and utilize functions in Excel.

✦ Function Wizard provides a valuable and easy shortcut to formula creation.

✦ The most commonly used functions are average, maximum, minimum, and sum.

✦ The AutoSum button provides an easy way to total rows and columns of data.

✦ Formulas always begin with an equal sign (=).

✦ Formulas are constructed using cell references and operators, which tell Excel how to process the data in the referenced cells to calculate a result.

✦ Operators have a precedence that determines which operations are performed first.

✦ Formulas can be edited either within the cell that contains them or within the formula bar.

✦ Formulas can be copied or moved from one location in the worksheet to another.

✦ Cell references in formulas that are copied change to reflect the new position unless absolute references are used. Formulas that are moved retain their original cell references.

✦ Cell names and range names can be used in place of cell references in formulas.

✦ Arrays are sets of values; array formulas perform multiple calculations on arrays.

✦ ✦ ✦

Lists and Databases

Dictionaries are databases. Encyclopedias are databases. So are phone books, almanacs, tide tables, and the like. Most of these static databases are organized in some sort of simple ascending alphabetical or timeline sequence. Computerized databases, though, are capable of much greater flexibility. The order in which items occur in an Excel database is not important, as various operations (such as sorting and filtering by a number of factors) can be performed on the data.

Understanding Lists and Databases

Databases are organized collections of information. In that sense, practically every source of data you've ever used has been a database.

Defining lists

Lists and databases are the same thing in Excel. Although Microsoft defines a list in Excel as "a series of worksheet rows that contain related data," that's a pretty good thumbnail description of a basic database, and many worksheets people create fit that definition.

Records and fields

Although you're used to thinking in terms of rows and columns in Excel worksheets, the proper database parlance is to call the rows "records" and the columns "fields." Thus, every database record (a row of cells) is composed of the data in each cell in that row (the individual field entries).

While a row (or "record") can contain many different types of data, the data that goes into a particular column (or "field") is always the same kind. For instance, you might have a database that consists of weather conditions for several different cities. The first column would be the name of the city, the second the date of the report, the third the temperature, etc. In order for the database to make sense, in each row the name of the city would always have to be entered in the first column. If you entered it in the third column, then it would be impossible for you to properly utilize the information, because the database would be looking for the temperature and find the name of the city instead.

In the list shown in Figure 14-1, the database consists of a series of records, as described above.

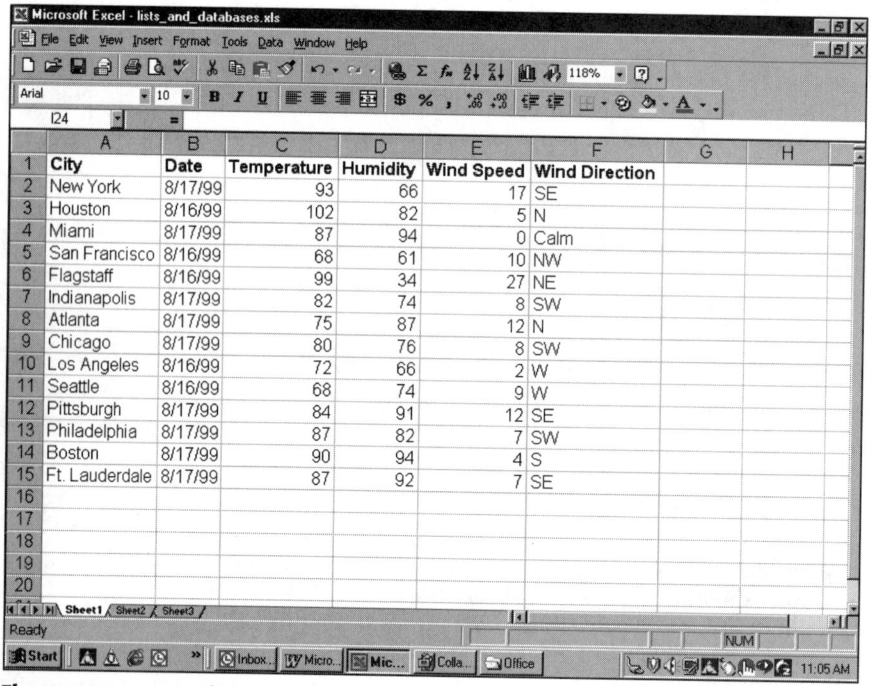

City	Date	Temperature	Humidity	Wind Speed	Wind Direction
New York	8/17/99	93	66	17	SE
Houston	8/16/99	102	82	5	N
Miami	8/17/99	87	94	0	Calm
San Francisco	8/16/99	68	61	10	NW
Flagstaff	8/16/99	99	34	27	NE
Indianapolis	8/17/99	82	74	8	SW
Atlanta	8/17/99	75	87	12	N
Chicago	8/17/99	80	76	8	SW
Los Angeles	8/16/99	72	66	2	W
Seattle	8/16/99	68	74	9	W
Pittsburgh	8/17/99	84	91	12	SE
Philadelphia	8/17/99	87	82	7	SW
Boston	8/17/99	90	94	4	S
Ft. Lauderdale	8/17/99	87	92	7	SE

Figure 14-1: A weather database.

Working with Databases

The first row of a database has to contain the labels for the fields. Microsoft advises you to format these cells as text before you type any of the labels, but there doesn't seem to be any real need for this action. Generally speaking, a column label that isn't text is pretty rare, and the General format, which is the default when you type text, seems to work just fine with all the database operations.

Note If you format the cells as text after the fact, it works without a hitch, so there's even less reason to do it beforehand. The only possible exception would be if you were using some sort of unusual label (like a date) for your fields.

Formatting labels

Microsoft suggests that you use some sort of formatting that differs from the formatting of the records as an aid to Excel in determining which parts of the worksheet contain records and which contain labels. Experimentation, however, demonstrates that this is unnecessary. As long as the labels are in the first row of the database, Excel knows they're labels. Because most people format the labels so that they stand out from the data anyway, such as by using bold or italic styles or coloring, this is an easy suggestion to accommodate, however; and there's no real reason to not do it.

There are compelling reasons, though, to actually do the formatting of the labels last instead of first. The various fields in your database are likely to have different formatting. For instance, one field may be Currency-formatted, while another is Date-formatted, etc. Because you probably don't know in advance how many records you'll be putting into the database, the only way to format all the cells in the column that you might end up using is to format the whole column at once. And, because the first cell in any column contains the field label, that's a problem, because you'll be formatting the field label at the same time as all the other cells in the column.

So go ahead and type the labels in first, so you can see exactly what formatting needs to be applied to which column, but don't bother with formatting that first row until you're done with all the field formatting for each column.

Creating a database

Here's the database creation process, step by step:

1. Type in the field labels in the first row.

2. For any field that requires formatting (such as currency or date), right-click on the column head to select the entire column.

3. From the pop-up menu, select Format Cells (see Figure 14-2).

4. From the Number tab of the Format Cells dialog box, select the desired format under Category. On the other tabs, make any other formatting selections you want (such as font style and color), and then click the OK button to complete the formatting of the column.

5. Repeat Steps 2 through 4 as many times as necessary until all the columns requiring formatting are done.

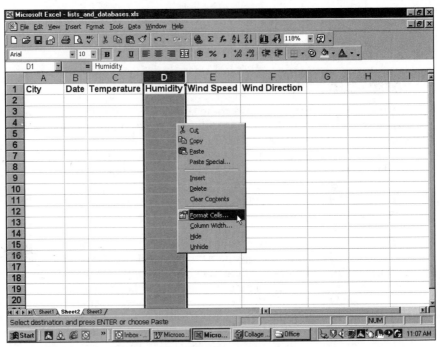

Figure 14-2: Formatting an entire column.

6. Right-click on the row heading for the labels.

7. From the pop-up menu, select Format Cells.

8. From the Number tab of the Format Cells dialog box, select either Text or General format under Category. On the other tabs, make any other formatting selections you want (such as font style and color), and then click the OK button to complete the formatting of the field labels.

9. Type in the record data starting on the second row, entering one field of data in each column (see Figure 14-3).

10. Repeat Step 9 as needed until all the records have been entered into the database.

Caution

You should have only a single database on a worksheet. Even though it's physically possible to have more than one, you run a risk of confusing Excel when it comes to manipulating the data. Because you can have multiple worksheets in a workbook, this doesn't pose any kind of practical problem.

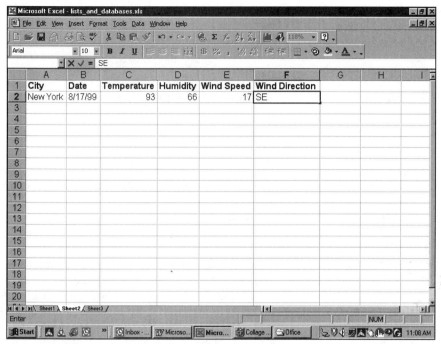

Figure 14-3: Entering the records.

Entering and Editing Records

Fortunately, you don't have to manually type in the rows and columns for the database. You can use a *data entry form* instead, which greatly simplifies the whole process and helps to prevent data entry errors as well.

Unfortunately, Excel has some wonderfully useful techniques for database entry that aren't supported in the data entry form approach, but can be used only with the type-it-in-the-cell approach. Which method you end up using for data entry will depend entirely on your particular needs and desires.

Using the data entry form

Once you've established your basic database, you can use the data entry form to delete or edit data in any field of any record. You can also use it to input entirely new records. You can use the data entry form with an existing database, or you can use it with a brand-new one, even before you put in a single record.

If you're going to use the data entry form with a new database that doesn't have any records in it yet, you have to at least have the labels in place. Beyond that, you should also have formatted the columns and the label row as detailed in the preceding section, but that's not a requirement for using the data entry form. Having at least the labels in place is required because, without some indication that you're working on a database, the data entry form won't work. If you're using it with an existing database, that problem doesn't exist, because Excel will be able to tell what you're doing.

To use the data entry form, follow these steps:

1. Select any cell within the database. This cell can be within a record or within the field labels on the top row, just as long as it's not outside the database.

2. Select Data ➪ Form from the main menu.

3. This brings up the data entry form, as shown in Figure 14-4. The form is named for the worksheet it comes from. In this case, it's named "Sheet1."

4. The form has edit boxes for each of the fields in your database. The fields that run from left to right in the worksheet run from top to bottom in the data entry box, and Excel has automatically assigned keyboard shortcuts to the field names. In the data entry box in Figure 14-4, for instance, Alt+T will take you to the Temperature field, Alt+E will take you to the Wind Direction field, etc. Most of the time, though, it's easier to just use the Tab key to move from field to field. By default, the first record is the one that is displayed (regardless of which cell in the database you selected) and its first field is always selected to start with. The current record number and the total number of records is shown in the upper right-hand corner; the "1 of 14" in the example means that the first record is shown and there are 14 in the database as a whole.

5. To edit the current record, simply tab to the field you want to change, and then enter the new data. If you change your mind about the new data and want to revert to the original data, just click the Restore button or press the Esc key. You can also revert to the original data by clicking the Find Prev or Find Next button. That will move you to either the previous or next record without implementing the changes. However, you cannot move to a previous record if the current record is the first one; nor can you move to the next record if the current record is the last one.

Caution   Pressing the Esc key when no changes have been made will close the data entry form.

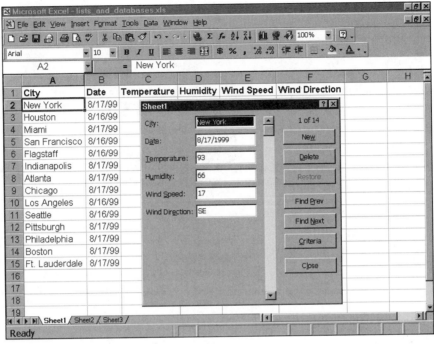

Figure 14-4: The data entry form.

6. When you're done, press Enter and the new data will replace the old in your database. The next record in the database will now be displayed. You can also implement the changes by clicking the Close button. This, however, will also close the data entry form, so do this only if you're totally finished.

Tip

You can walk through the entire database by repeatedly pressing Enter without entering any new data.

7. To permanently remove the current record, click the Delete key. When you do this, you will receive a pop-up warning message asking you to confirm that you really mean to delete the record (see Figure 14-5).

Caution

When you delete a record from the database with the data entry form's Delete button, the warning message isn't kidding about it being permanently gone. You can't even use the toolbar's Undo button to reverse the action the way you can with any of the other data entry form actions.

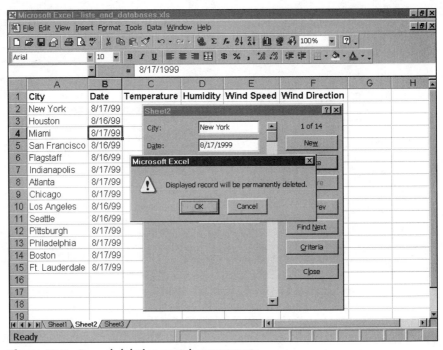

Figure 14-5: Record-deletion warning message.

8. To enter a new record, click the New button. The record number information displayed in the upper right-hand corner will change to read "New Record." All the fields will go blank and you can enter the new data. Clicking the Close button will close the data entry form and add the new record to the end of the database on the worksheet. Pressing Enter will add the new record and clear the fields so that you can enter another new record.

9. When you are finished with the data entry form, click the Close button.

Using keyboard entry

Plain old keyboard entry, just the same as entering any other worksheet cell data, seems a bit unglamorous and tedious compared to using the data entry form, but there are some real advantages to it.

With keyboard data entry, it's true that you surrender the automation of the data entry form approach, but you gain a great deal of control over the data entry process. You can control the type of data entered into any cell, you can set upper and lower limits on that data, and you can display messages about the cell. The messages come in two flavors. One is a general one that is displayed any time anyone selects that cell. The other is an error message that is displayed only when data entered into a cell falls outside the acceptable range established for that field.

All three options — setting data validation parameters, defining error messages, and defining cell entry messages — can be done in a single process. However, for the sake of clarity, they are each set out separately in the following segments.

Caution   The same problem you faced when formatting the columns exists with the row of field labels. When you've finished applying the data validation options to all the columns in your database, you have to face the fact that you've applied them to each cell in the field labels in the process. While it's probable that this won't cause any particular problem, it could interfere if you want to change the text of the labels at some point. It's best to select the row head for the field label row and clear all the data validation for that row as the last step.

Data validation parameters

To set values and parameters for data validation, follow these steps:

1. Select the column heading for the field you want to apply the data validation to.

2. Select Data ⇨ Validation from the main menu.

3. The Data Validation dialog box (see Figure 14-6) has three tabs: Settings, Input Message, and Error Alert. If it is not already selected, click the Settings tab.

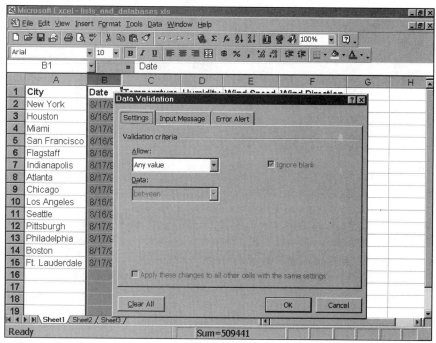

Figure 14-6: The Settings tab of the Data Validation dialog box.

4. Choose from one of the values under Allow (for a description of these values, see Table 14-1).

Table 14-1
Value Settings for Data Validation

Allowed Value	Meaning
Any Value	No restrictions.
Whole Number	Restricted to numbers without decimals.
Decimal	Restricted to numbers, but allows decimals.
List	Restricted to a preset list of options.
Date	Restricted to calendar data.
Time	Restricted to clock data.
Text Length	Restricted to specified length.
Custom	Restricted to custom formula.

5. Choose from one of the options under Data (described in Table 14-2). (The Data field is disabled for some of the Allow options.)

Table 14-2
Options for Data Validation Values

Option	Meaning
Between	The value must fall between minimum and maximum values.
Not between	The value must not be between the specified values.
Equal to	The value must be the same as the specified value.
Not equal to	The value must not be the specified value.
Greater than	The value must be more than the specified value.
Less than	The value must be less than the specified value.
Greater than or equal to	The value must be the same as or more than the specified value.
Less than or equal to	The value must be the same as or less than the specified value.

6. The parameters displayed depend on the options chosen under Allow and Data. Enter the parameters for the restrictions. In many cases, these are simply minimum and/or maximum values, such as the lowest and highest numbers or the earliest and latest dates allowed.

7. Click the OK button to finish.

Caution   The Clear All button on the bottom of the Data Validation dialog box doesn't just clear the entries on the currently selected tab. It clears all the entries on all three tabs. Don't use it unless you mean to do that. If you click Clear All by mistake, clicking Cancel will restore the cleared values if they were previously entered and "OK'd."

List, text length, and custom values

Three of the value options require further explanation. The List option draws from a predefined list of values. You can type them in directly under Source (separated by commas), or you can specify a range of cells in that space that contain the list of acceptable entries. Text length, despite the name, does not require that it be applied to text. You can also specify the length of a number with it. The Custom setting limits the entry to anything that fits a formula you've designed. As with the List parameters, you can either type it in directly (under Formula), or specify a cell reference that contains the formula.

Error messages

Any time you set validation parameters (anything other than All Values), an error message will be generated if inappropriate values are entered. The default error message has a title of simply "Microsoft Excel" and is so general as to be virtually meaningless — "The value you entered is not valid. A user has restricted values that can be entered into this cell." To change this, follow these steps:

1. Select the column heading for the field you want to create an error message for.

2. Select Data ⇨ Validation from the main menu.

3. Click the Error Alert tab (see Figure 14-7).

4. Under the Style drop-down list, you can choose from three different kinds of error alerts: Stop, Warning, and Information. Stop is the default, and presents a red circle with a white X in the middle of it when an error occurs. Warning shows a yellow triangle with a black exclamation point in the middle, and Information shows a dialog balloon with a blue "i" in the middle. Each of the three gives you the option to enter the title and text of the error message, or both. If you do not specify one of them, it will remain at the default setting. The three differ as follows:

    • **The Stop error message** presents Retry and Cancel buttons (see Figure 14-8). The effect of both is identical, with only a small technical difference. The Retry button highlights the erroneous entry, meaning that anything you type will replace it. The Cancel button deletes the erroneous entry, also leaving you free to type in a new one.

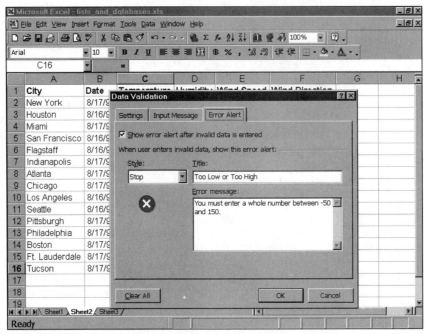

Figure 14-7: The Error Alert tab of the Data Validation dialog box.

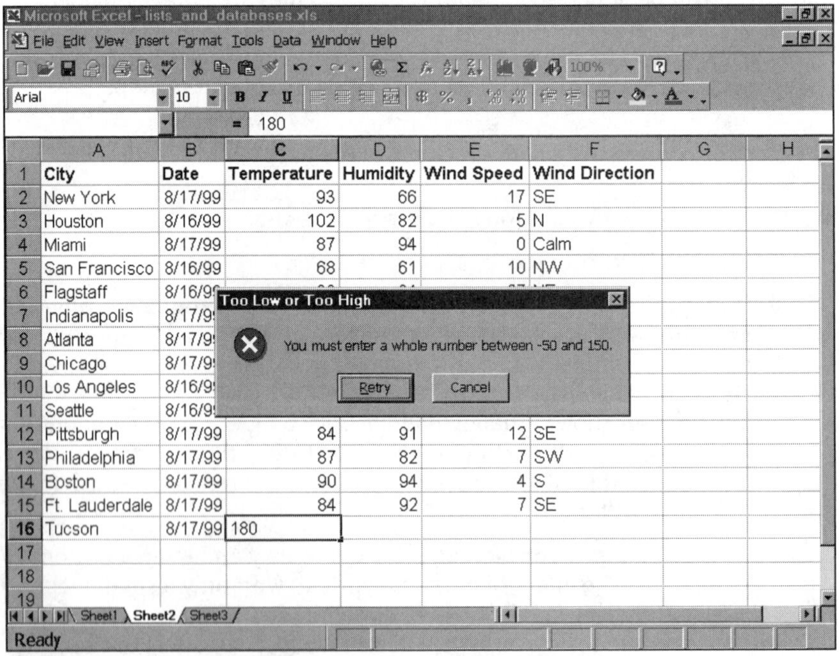

Figure 14-8: The Stop error message.

- **The Warning error message** presents three options: Yes, No, and Cancel buttons (see Figure 14-9). Clicking the Yes button enters the erroneous value even though it's supposed to be excluded. Clicking the No button is identical to clicking the Retry button for the Stop error message — it highlights the erroneous entry so you can type a new one. The Cancel button, once again, simply deletes the erroneous entry and leaves the cell selected, so you can type in a new entry if you want to or move on.

- **The Information error message** presents only OK and Cancel buttons (see Figure 14-10). Clicking the OK button enters the erroneous value, while clicking the Cancel button deletes the erroneous entry and leaves the cell selected.

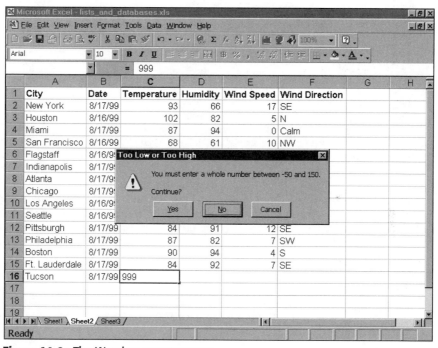

Figure 14-9: The Warning error message.

5. Click the OK button to complete the process.

Cell input messages

Cell input messages are not an integral part of the data validation process, but a fairly frivolous add-on. These messages are displayed whenever a cell containing them is selected. While they can be used to say things like, "Enter such and such a value in this cell," the purpose of the cell should already be obvious from the field label. If it isn't, give some serious thought to rewriting your field labels.

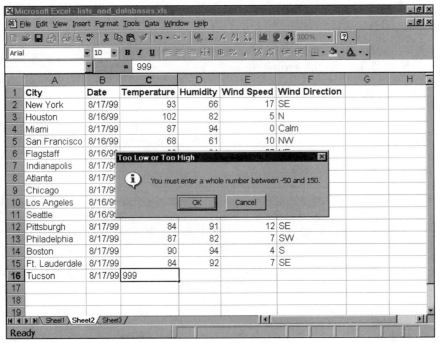

Figure 14-10: The Information error message.

In actual practice, cell input messages have limited utility and tend mainly to simply obscure part of the database from view. If you must use them, use them sparingly, or you will find that they make the database totally unworkable. However, in some cases they can serve to help idiot-proof your worksheets, as in the example in Figure 14-11.

To create a cell input message, follow these steps:

1. Select either the column heading for the field or the individual cell you want to apply the data validation to.

2. Select Data ⇨ Validation from the main menu.

3. Click the Input Message tab.

4. Enter the title and text of the error message. If you do not specify the text, no message will appear, even if you do specify a title. If you do specify a title, the title will show in the first line of the message in bold print.

5. Click the OK button to complete the process.

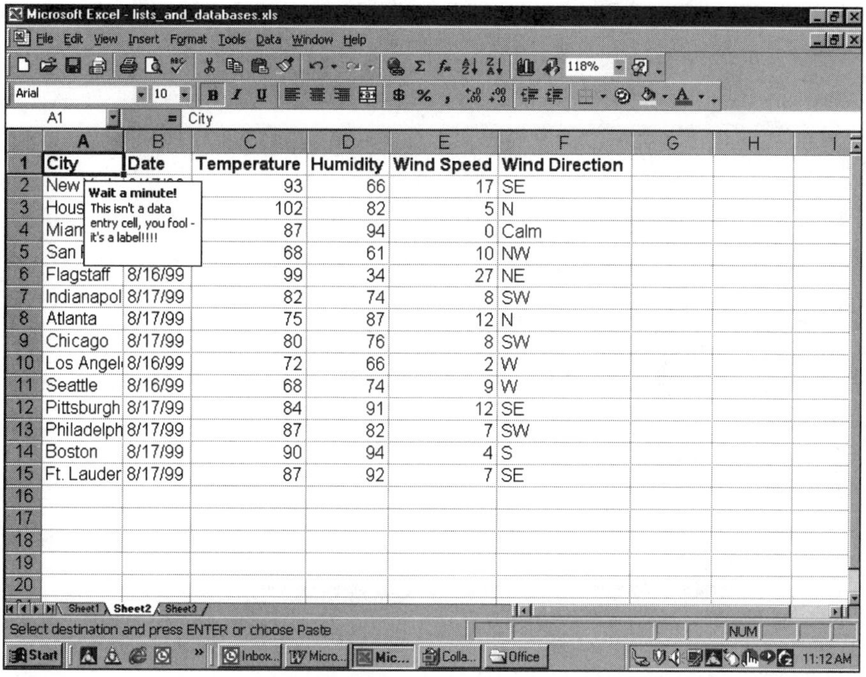

Figure 14-11: A cell input message.

Sorting and Filtering Data

The main reason why the order in which you enter the records in your database doesn't ultimately matter is that you can sort and filter them after they're entered. Sorting simply changes the order in which the records are displayed, while filtering creates a display of only those records that fit criteria you have specified.

Sorting data

The easiest way to sort is to simply select any cell in the column you want to sort by, and then click either the Sort Ascending or Sort Descending buttons on the Standard toolbar. The Sort Ascending button sorts from A to Z (it's the one with A on top and Z on the bottom). Technically speaking, it sorts from zero to Z, but that wouldn't make as good an icon. The Sort Descending button sorts from Z to A (okay, Z to zero), and it's the one with Z on top and A on the bottom. Figure 14-12 shows the weather database sorted in ascending order by city.

The drawback to this method, as with so many things that are simple to use, is that it lacks real power. Often, you'll find that you need to sort by more than one column. For instance, you might need to sort a customer database by both state and product ordered so that you can determine which products are selling best in which states. Or you may wish to sort the weather database by date *and* temperature.

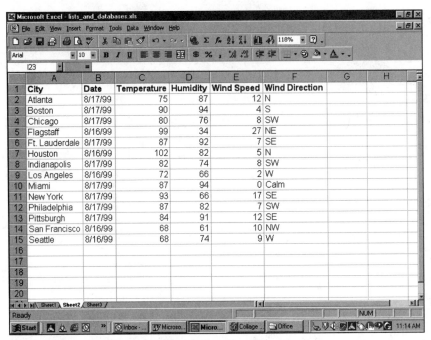

Figure 14-12: Database sorted by city.

To sort by multiple columns, follow these steps:

1. Select any cell in the database.

2. Select Data ➪ Sort from the menu. If you failed to select a cell in the database, then Excel will tell you it can't find it. In that case, go back to Step 1.

3. In the Sort dialog box, the default is to sort by the field of the active cell in ascending order (see Figure 14-13). You can click on the drop-down list to pick any field in the database, and you can select either ascending or descending order for that field by clicking on the appropriate radio button to the right of the field selection.

4. You can choose to sort by a second field by selecting a field in the topmost Then By area of the dialog box. There is also a third area for a sort field, identical to the second, which works the same way. Selecting fields in these areas increases the complexity of the sorting operation. The database will first be sorted by the top field, then by the middle field, and finally by the lower field. It is not necessary to use all three panels; you can perform a sort on just two fields if you want to.

5. To perform the sort, click the OK button. Figure 14-14 shows the weather database sorted by date and temperature (both in ascending order).

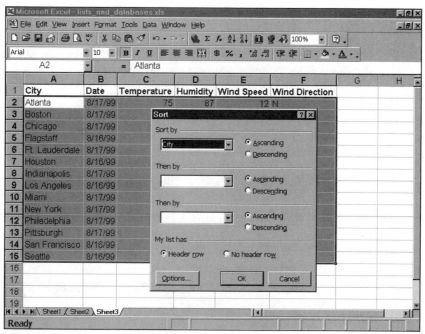

Figure 14-13: The Sort dialog box.

	A	B	C	D	E	F	G	H
1	City	Date	Temperature	Humidity	Wind Speed	Wind Direction		
2	San Francisco	8/16/99	68	61	10	NW		
3	Seattle	8/16/99	68	74	9	W		
4	Los Angeles	8/16/99	72	66	2	W		
5	Flagstaff	8/16/99	99	34	27	NE		
6	Houston	8/16/99	102	82	5	N		
7	Atlanta	8/17/99	75	87	12	N		
8	Chicago	8/17/99	80	76	8	SW		
9	Indianapolis	8/17/99	82	74	8	SW		
10	Pittsburgh	8/17/99	84	91	12	SE		
11	Ft. Lauderdale	8/17/99	87	92	7	SE		
12	Miami	8/17/99	87	94	0	Calm		
13	Philadelphia	8/17/99	87	82	7	SW		
14	Boston	8/17/99	90	94	4	S		
15	New York	8/17/99	93	66	17	SE		
16								
17								
18								
19								
20								

Figure 14-14: Weather database sorted by date and temperature.

Filtering data

Filtering your data is much more powerful than simply sorting it. Instead of being limited to three columns as you are for a sort, you can filter on any or all columns in your database. Filtering removes from view any record that doesn't match your criteria (but not from the database or worksheet). When you're done, you can restore all the records to view.

To filter your data, follow these steps:

1. Select any cell in the database.

2. Select Data ➪ Filter ➪ AutoFilter from the menu.

3. AutoFilter creates a set of drop-down menus for every field in your database, and places an arrow at the end of each field name. Clicking on these arrows shows the menu options. Figure 14-15 shows the drop-down menu for the Temperature field.

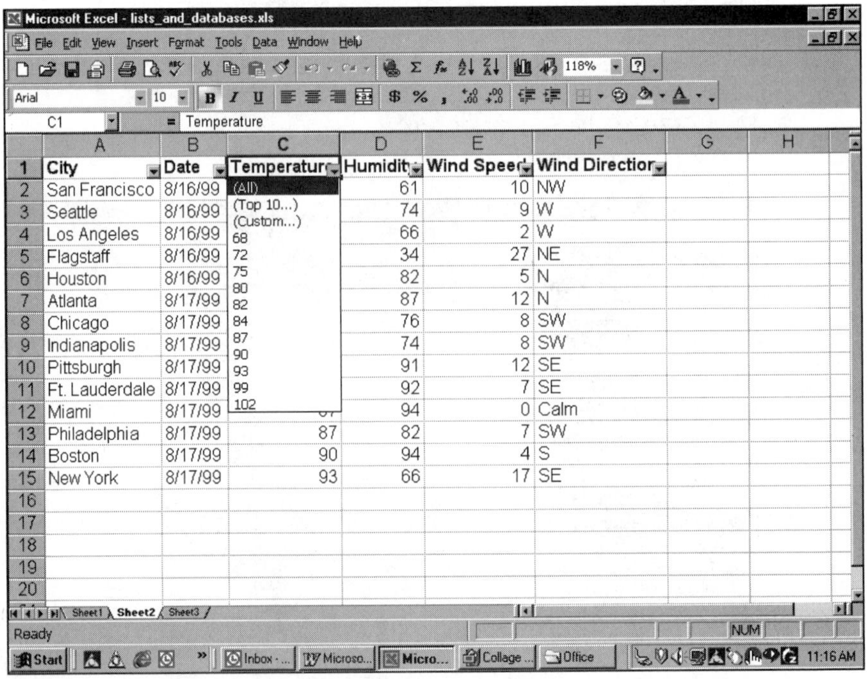

Figure 14-15: AutoFilter in action.

4. In addition to listing every value for that field in the database, the menu has options for All (the default), Top 10, and Custom. To filter for only those records that show a specific value, click on that value (for example, you could

choose to show only those records in which the temperature is 68 degrees by clicking on the number 68).

5. Selecting the Top 10 option from the drop-down menu brings up the Top 10 AutoFilter dialog box (see Figure 14-16). The default value, as the name implies, is to show the top 10 items in the list. However, you can select either top or bottom, the number 10 can be changed to any value from 1 to 500, and you can select percent instead of items. Thus, you might choose to show the top 80 percent, or the bottom 5 items. Although there is nothing to prevent you from selecting a percentage over 100, the result is the same as selecting 100.

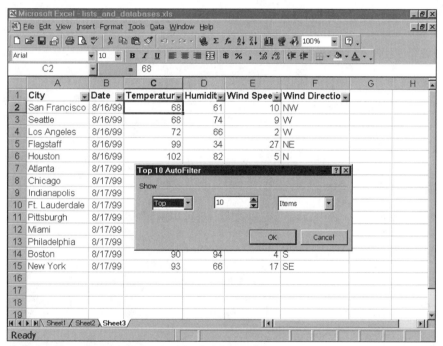

Figure 14-16: The Top 10 AutoFilter dialog box.

6. Selecting the Custom option from the drop-down menu brings up the Custom AutoFilter dialog box (see Figure 14-17). The field name is already entered, and the default is to show rows where the selected field equals a particular value (the blank box on the right side holds a drop-down list of all the values in that field). You can change the comparison operator by selecting a new one from the drop-down list where the word "equals" shows by default. The options cover just about everything you could imagine filtering by, as shown in the following list:

- Equals

- Does not equal

- Is greater than

- Is greater than or equal to

- Is less than

- Is less than or equal to

- Begins with

- Does not begin with

- Ends with

- Does not end with

- Contains

- Does not contain

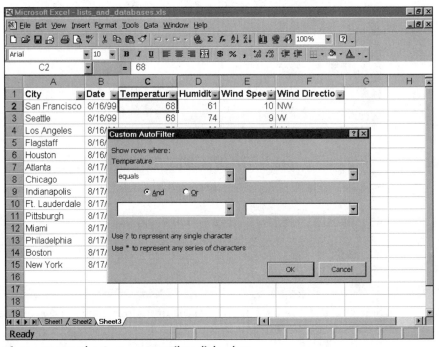

Figure 14-17: The Custom AutoFilter dialog box.

7. Once you have chosen the comparison operator, you can either select a value from the drop-down list on the right or type in a value of your own. You can either click the OK button to implement the filtering at this point, or you can specify one further criterion for filtering.

8. When you add a second criterion for filtering, you have the option of using either a logical And or logical Or. With And, both criteria must be true; with Or, either criterion can be true. Click either the And or the Or radio button to select it.

9. Select the comparison operator and value the same way you did for the first criterion, and then click the OK button to implement the filtering operation.

To restore the view so that all the rows are visible, either select All from the drop-down menus of each field used as a selection field for the filtering, or select Data ⇨ Filter ⇨ Show All from the menu. To turn off AutoFilter, select Data ⇨ Filter ⇨ AutoFilter from the menu.

Subtotaling Data

Excel's subtotal feature is accessed via the Data menu, and is used with a sorted list. It's not useful for every single type of database you can create, but only for those in which values can be kept track of for specific, repeated factors. Figure 14-18, for example, shows a database of authors, which includes the titles and prices of some of their books.

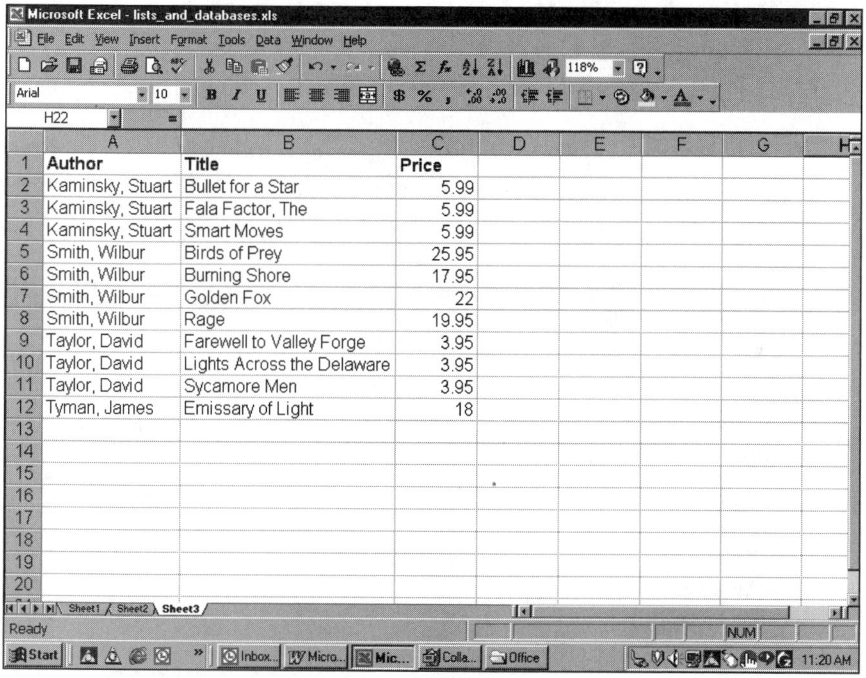

Figure 14-18: Author database before subtotaling.

To subtotal the prices of the books by author, follow these steps:

1. Sort the database by the field you want to subtotal. In this case, that would be the Author field.

2. Select any cell within the database.

3. Select Data ➪ Subtotals from the menu.

4. In the Subtotal dialog box, click on the drop-down list labeled At Each Change In and select the field that you wish to subtotal (see Figure 14-19).

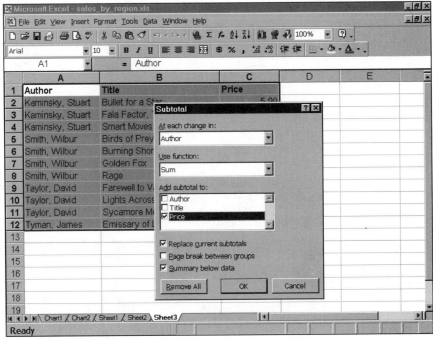

Figure 14-19: The Subtotal dialog box.

5. Select a function from the Use Function drop-down list. The available functions are as follows:

   • Sum

   • Count

   • Average

   • Max

- Min

- Product

- Count Nums

- StdDev

- StdDevp

- Var

- Varp

6. Select the fields for which you want to show subtotals in the Add Subtotal To area.

7. Click the OK button to add the subtotals. The results are shown in Figure 14-20.

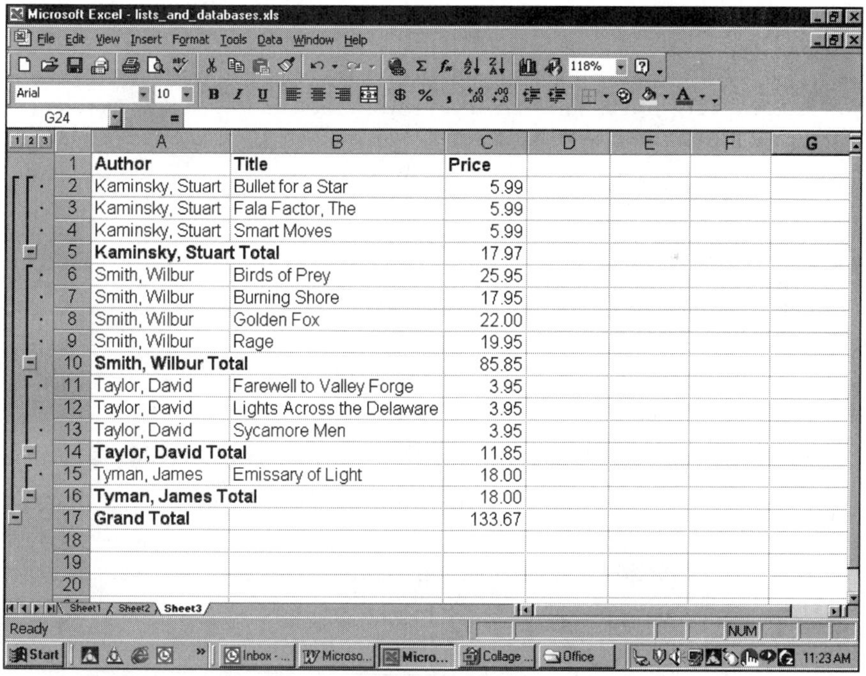

Figure 14-20: Author database after subtotaling.

You can shrink the database so that only the subtotals show by clicking on the minus signs to the left of the records.

To remove the subtotals, you can either click the Undo button immediately after adding the subtotals or select Data ➪ Subtotals from the menu, and then click the Remove All button.

Using Excel Data in a Mail Merge

To use Excel data in a mail merge in Microsoft Word, follow these steps:

1. Select the data you want to use.
2. Click the Copy button on the toolbar or select Edit ➪ Copy from the menu.
3. Switch to Word or open it if it isn't open.
4. If necessary, click the New Document button to create a blank document.
5. Click the Paste button on the toolbar or select Edit ➪ Paste from the menu.
6. Save the new document. The Excel data is now in Word format and ready for use with mail merge.

Alternatively, you can just save your workbook and open it as the data source while performing the mail merge in Word.

Summary

In this chapter, you learned how to create and manipulate databases in Excel.

✦ Databases are composed of records.

✦ Records are composed of fields.

✦ The first row of a database in Excel contains the field labels.

✦ Records can be entered either through the data entry form or by typing directly into the cells.

✦ Data validation can be used to prevent erroneous entries.

✦ Data can be sorted by individual or multiple columns.

✦ Records can be filtered so that only those that meet certain criteria are displayed.

✦ Databases can be subtotaled.

✦ Excel databases can be used in Word mail merges.

✦   ✦   ✦

Templates, Forms, and Graphics

Templates — pre-designed worksheets with the basic elements already in place — can vastly simplify your tasks. In addition to Excel's built-in templates, you can also create your own to reuse over and over again.

Forms are a specialized type of template used to duplicate the functions of regular paper forms such as order forms, invoices, and so forth. Some of the built-in templates that come with Excel are forms. Forms can contain controls that add automation, such as spinners and buttons, and you can use macros written in Visual Basic to extend the functionality of the controls.

You can spice up your worksheets and forms with graphics, either imported or created with Excel's graphics tools, such as WordArt.

Using Excel's Templates

The templates supplied with Excel utilize several utilities that are not automatically installed along with Excel. So, before you can get started with Excel's built-in templates, you'll need to load the Template Utilities add-in.

Loading the Template Utilities add-in

If you haven't already loaded the Template Utilities add-in, follow these steps:

1. Select Tools ➪ Add-Ins from the menu.

2. In the Add-Ins dialog box (see Figure 15-1), click on the check box next to Template Utilities.

Figure 15-1: The Add-Ins dialog box.

3. Click the OK button. A dialog box asking you to confirm that you would like to install the selected add-in will appear. Click the Yes button.

4. The Windows Installer will add the Template Utilities.

Excel's built-in templates

Excel comes with a few ready-to-use templates, such as an expense report, invoice, and purchase order. To use one of the built-in templates in Excel, start just as if you were going to open a new workbook:

1. Select File ⇨ New from the menu. You can't use the Ctrl+N keyboard shortcut; nor can you use the New button on the toolbar, as both of these approaches simply create a new workbook based on the Workbook template and don't give you the options of the menu approach.

2. In the New dialog box (see Figure 15-2), click the Spreadsheet Solutions tab.

3. Click on the icon for the template you want to load. A preview of the template's appearance will show on the right-hand side of the dialog box.

4. Click the OK button to load the template.

5. If the template contains macros, you will receive a warning about the possibility of macro viruses (see Figure 15-3). If the template you're using is from an untrustworthy source, it's probably wise to click the Disable Macros button. Presumably, Microsoft's built-in Excel macros are virus-free, however. If you want to be able to use the template's macros, click the Enable Macros button.

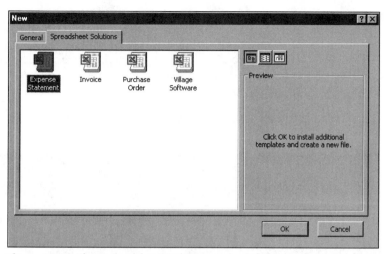

Figure 15-2: The Spreadsheet Solutions tab of the New dialog box.

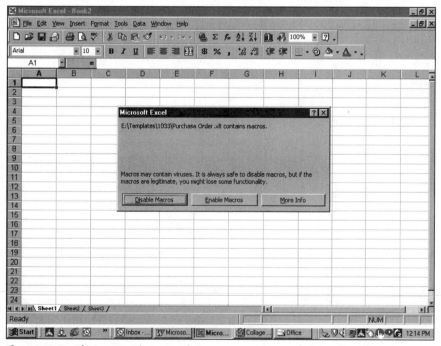

Figure 15-3: The macro virus warning.

Note
You can turn off the macro warning message by selecting Tools ➪ Macro ➪ Security from the menu. Once in the Security dialog box, click the Low radio button to disable macro checking. You should do this only if you're absolutely certain that there is no possibility of any macro virus ever being found in any Excel documents you ever load. It's a really good idea, in any case, to have anti-virus software installed on your system and to use it regularly.

6. The template is loaded into Excel, ready for use as shown in Figure 15-4.

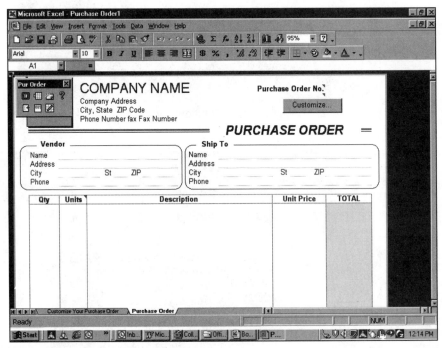

Figure 15-4: The loaded template.

7. Make any changes you want to customize the worksheet for your own purposes.

8. Save the worksheet under a new name (Excel will automatically save it as a workbook instead of as a template so you don't overwrite the original).

If you want to save the revised workbook as a new template instead of as a finished workbook, follow the instructions for saving a custom template in the following section. Make sure you use a name other than that of the original template you based your custom one on unless you want to overwrite and erase the original one.

Creating a Template

In addition to using the built-in templates that come with Excel, you can create your own as well. When should you create a template? Whenever you find yourself facing a repetitive task that will use the same setup over and over again.

In most cases, you won't want to include actual data in a template, but you'll want headings, labels, formatting, and the like, to be consistent across workbooks based on the same template, so you'll need to create those elements and apply those attributes. A good rule of thumb is to remember to create all the elements that will always be needed and none of those that won't always be.

Determining the template type

There are different ways you can use templates, and each of them has a slightly different function, as outlined in Table 15-1.

Table 15-1 Template Options	
Template Type	*Function*
Custom Workbook	The workbook is available for loading via the File ➪ New menu approach by choosing its tab and name.
Custom Worksheet	The worksheet is available for insertion from the sheet tab pop-up menu.
Default Workbook	The workbook is the default one created whenever you use the New button. You can also use the File ➪ New menu approach and choose Workbook from the General tab.
Default Worksheet	The worksheet is the default for all the worksheets on a new workbook. It's also the one that is inserted into a workbook when you select the Insert ➪ Worksheet menu command.

Saving a workbook as a template

To save a workbook as a template, follow these steps:

1. Select File ➪ Save As from the menu.

2. In the Save as Type drop-down list, select Template. This will automatically switch you to the Templates folder (in a typical installation of Office, this is C:\Windows\Application Data\Microsoft\Templates).

3. You can either accept this folder or save the template somewhere else, such as in a subfolder under Templates.

4. Type a name for your template. If you are saving the template as the default workbook, you have to use the filename book.xlt (but you only have to type "book" — the file extension will be added automatically). If you are saving the template as the default worksheet, you have to use the filename sheet.xlt (again, you don't have to type the extension). For a custom workbook or worksheet that isn't the default one, you can type any filename you desire.

5. Click the OK button to complete saving the template.

Creating your own template tab

If you save your templates in the default Templates folder, they will appear on the General tab of the New dialog box. If you want to, though, you can create your own tab in the New dialog box by creating a subfolder under the Templates folder. The tab will have the name you assigned to the subfolder. Any templates you save into that subfolder will be shown on that tab and can be loaded just like the built-in templates (see Figure 15-5).

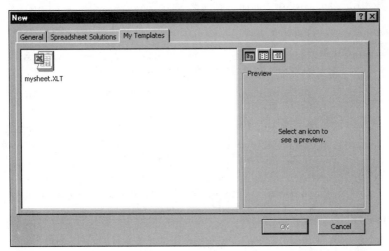

Figure 15-5: A custom template tab.

Caution   When you save a workbook as a template, you can't just type the .xlt file extension. Although it is possible to do that, and it will save under that name, it won't be saved as a template. It'll just be saved as a regular workbook with an irregular file extension. In order to save it as a template, you have to select the Template setting in the Save as Type drop-down list.

Inserting custom worksheet templates

You can't just insert a custom worksheet template into a workbook through the usual methods, because the File ⇨ New and File ⇨ Open commands open only workbooks. Also, using the Insert ⇨ Worksheet menu approach will insert only the default worksheet. To insert a custom worksheet that is not the default worksheet, follow these steps:

1. Right-click on the sheet tab of the worksheet you want to insert your custom worksheet to the left of.

2. From the pop-up menu (see Figure 15-6), select Insert.

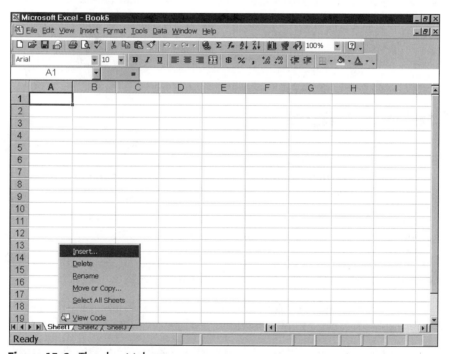

Figure 15-6: The sheet tab pop-up menu.

3. This brings up the Insert dialog box, which is identical to the New dialog box shown in Figure 15-2. Click the tab that contains the custom worksheet you want to add, and then select the desired template.

4. Click the OK button. The custom worksheet will be inserted.

5. If you want to reposition the custom worksheet, click on its sheet tab and drag it into the desired position.

The Function of Template Wizard

Excel includes an add-in called Template Wizard. You don't need it to create templates and, despite the name, its usefulness is limited to creating input forms for database entry.

Because the existing data entry form already performs this function with no effort on your part, the more complex Template Wizard doesn't have much of a place in Excel. It can be used to put data into Access and other database tables, but you're much better off using Access for that purpose.

Tip   If you want to open a new workbook that contains nothing but a custom worksheet template, use the File ➪ Open menu command and select the custom worksheet as if it were a regular workbook. Instead of the default workbook, this will open one that has only a single worksheet in it, and that worksheet will be the custom worksheet template that you just selected.

Creating Forms

One further use of custom templates is to create forms. Forms are a specialized type of template used to duplicate the functions of regular paper forms such as order forms, invoices, and so forth. Some of the built-in templates that come with Excel are forms of this sort.

Unlike normal worksheets and templates, forms often disregard the traditional grid look and opt for larger areas for data entry, as one of their advantages is that they can serve a dual purpose. They can be used for keyboard entry or they can be printed and filled out by hand. For this reason, many forms hide the cell grid entirely and opt for borders to set off key areas from one another.

Other than design considerations, forms are created pretty much like any other template. You make the basic outline, including all those elements that will remain unchanged from one form to the other, such as your company name and logo; and leave blank all those areas, such as customer name and address, that will vary from one usage of the form to the next.

Form controls

You can also add automation to your forms by using buttons and drop-down lists. You can key the buttons to macros written in Visual Basic to expand the functionality of the form as far as your programming ability can take you.

To access the form controls, you'll need to add the Forms toolbar. To do this, right-click on any toolbar and select Forms from the toolbar list as shown in Figure 15-7.

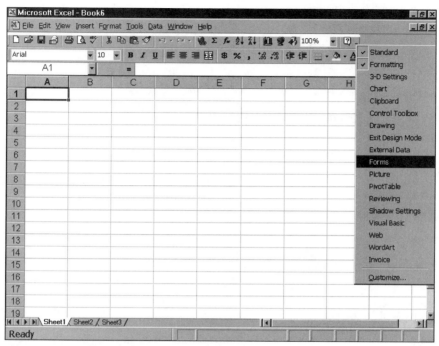

Figure 15-7: Adding the Forms toolbar.

This will give you access to the Forms toolbar. Initially, it's free-floating, as shown in Figure 15-8. You can drag it into the normal toolbar area and drop it there if you wish, or you can leave it free-floating and move it as necessary during your design activities. The decision whether to permanently dock the Forms toolbar or to just shut it down when you're not using it depends entirely on how often you plan on using it.

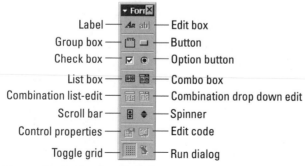

Figure 15-8: The Forms toolbar.

The controls on the Forms toolbar can greatly enhance your forms. Some of them, of course, are more useful than others, and they're not all available for the new version of Excel. Table 15-2 describes the forms controls.

Table 15-2
Forms Controls

Control	Function
Label	Used to place text on a form.
Edit box	Not available in Excel 2000. Provided for backward compatibility with Excel 5.0 dialog sheets.
Group box	Used to outline a group of controls.
Button	Used to trigger an associated macro.
Check box	Used to select an option.
Option button	Like a check box, but each option button in a group is mutually exclusive.
List box	Presents a list of options.
Combo box	A drop-down list box; the options are not visible until you click on it.
Combination list-edit box	Not available in Excel 2000. Provided for backward compatibility with Excel 5.0 dialog sheets.
Combination drop down-edit box	Not available in Excel 2000. Provided for backward compatibility with Excel 5.0 dialog sheets.
Scroll bar	Used to scroll through a series of values; displays a moving bar to indicate where in the list of values the current value lies.
Spinner	Like a scroll bar, but without the moving bar.
Control properties	Brings up the Format Control dialog box for changing control properties. Same as right-clicking on the control and selecting Format Control from the pop-up menu.
Edit code	Brings up Visual Basic for programming linked macros.
Toggle grid	Turns the visibility of all cell gridlines in the worksheet on and off.
Run dialog	Not available in Excel 2000. Provided for backward compatibility with Excel 5.0 dialog sheets.

Using a control on a worksheet

To use a control on a worksheet, follow these steps:

1. Click on the desired control in the Forms toolbar.

2. Click on the place on the worksheet where you want to put the control.

3. The control appears on the worksheet as shown in Figure 15-9. Note that controls are not contained within a cell on the worksheet, but lie on top of the cells.

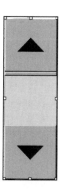

Figure 15-9: A scrollbar control.

4. Reposition and resize the control so that it is at the size and placement you desire.

Tip You can reposition a form control with fine-tuning by using the arrow keys to move it one pixel at a time.

5. On some controls that contain text, you can change the text to suit yourself, including setting different fonts, font sizes, and font colors.

6. Right-click on the control and select Format Control from the pop-up menu. Alternatively, click the Control Properties button on the Forms toolbar.

7. In the Format Control dialog box (see Figure 15-10), click the Control tab and change the settings you want to customize the actions of the control. These vary somewhat depending on the nature of the particular control (not all controls have a Control tab). For the scrollbar control in this example, the settings include the following:

   • The current, minimum, and maximum values, as well as the degree of change resulting from clicking on one of the arrows (Incremental change) or from clicking within the scroll area (Page change).

- The critical setting is the Cell link. This determines where the current value is displayed. You can either type a value directly into the edit box or select a cell by clicking on it in the worksheet itself.

- If you want, click the worksheet icon to the right of the edit box to collapse the dialog box out of the way while you're selecting cells in the worksheet.

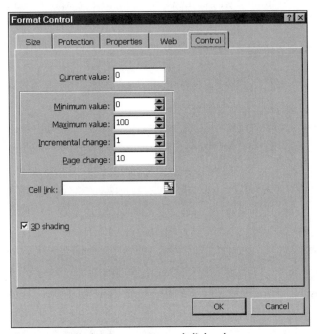

Figure 15-10: The Format Control dialog box.

8. Click the OK button to complete the process.

Using macros with form controls

Although macros can be used with all form controls, the Button control is specifically designed for working with them and has no other use but to trigger a macro. To use a Button control, follow these steps:

1. Click the Button control on the Forms toolbar.

2. Click on the place in the worksheet where you want to put the button.

3. The Button control appears on the worksheet, but is immediately obscured by the Assign Macro dialog box (see Figure 15-11).

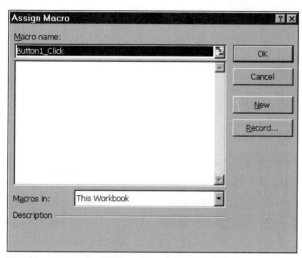

Figure 15-11: The Assign Macro dialog box.

4. The Macro name setting is based on the default name of the button. Change the name if you wish by simply typing in a new one.

5. If you want to apply an existing macro to the button, select it from the list of macro names and click the OK button.

6. If you want to program a macro, click the New button, which will launch Visual Basic, as shown in Figure 15-12.

7. If you want to record a macro, click the Record button. This brings up the Record Macro dialog box shown in Figure 15-13.

8. You can assign a keyboard shortcut for the macro (so that it runs whenever you hold down the Ctrl key and then the shortcut key) by entering the key as Shortcut key. If the shortcut key you choose for your macro is a capital letter, the keyboard shortcut will automatically be changed to Ctrl+Shift+Key.

9. Click the OK button. The Stop Recording toolbar will appear.

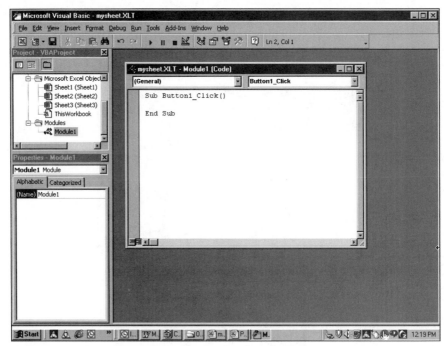

Figure 15-12: Programming a macro in Visual Basic.

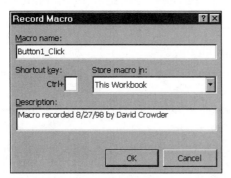

Figure 15-13: The Record Macro dialog box.

10. Perform the actions you want recorded in the macro (such as keystrokes and mouse clicks), and then click the Stop button on the Stop Recording toolbar.

11. Save the workbook. From now on, clicking on the button will automatically perform the actions you recorded.

Protecting Worksheets and Workbooks

One of the biggest frustrations with worksheets is that, once your hard work in creating them is done, it's easy for someone else — or even you — to change them by accident. All it takes is a few wrong keystrokes or someone who doesn't understand what he or she is doing and your work is trashed.

Fortunately, you can protect your work from unwanted changes. There are three levels of protection. All elements on a worksheet, such as cells and form controls, are set to protected status by default. This has no effect, however, unless the next level of protection — worksheet protection — is invoked. The third level of protection is the workbook level, which prevents anyone from doing such things as adding or deleting the worksheets that comprise the workbook.

Unprotecting cells and other elements

Because worksheet elements have protection turned on by default, setting worksheet protection means not only that no one can mess with things like button text, but that no changes at all can take place in any cell. Any attempt to alter the contents of a protected cell results in an error message. Because it's likely that, at least some of the time, you'll want some values to change (in a form, for instance), you'll need to remove protection from the cells you want people to be able to change. You can't do that after the worksheet is protected, so make sure you plan out ahead of time which elements you do and don't want to protect.

To remove protection from a cell or other element, follow these steps:

1. Right-click on the cell or other element.

2. Select Format Cells (or Format Control, Format Picture, etc.) from the resultant pop-up menu.

3. Click the Protection tab (see Figure 15-14).

4. Uncheck the Locked check box.

5. Uncheck any other protection options you don't want protected (such as Lock text, Hidden, etc.). These will vary from one element to the next.

6. Click the OK button to complete the task.

7. Repeat these steps for each element you want to unprotect.

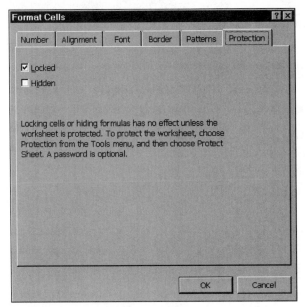

Figure 15-14: The Protection tab.

Protecting worksheets

The cell protection level cannot take effect with an unprotected worksheet. To protect the worksheet, follow these steps:

1. Select Tools ➪ Protection ➪ Protect Sheet from the menu.

2. In the Protect Sheet dialog box (see Figure 15-15), you can deselect protection for Contents, Objects, or Scenarios if you wish.

3. You can also type in a password, although this is optional. Do this only if it's absolutely necessary. If you assign a password to the worksheet, then it cannot be unprotected again without that password. If you forget it, you're out of luck. Period.

4. Click the OK button to complete the process.

5. If you entered a password, you'll be asked to confirm it by typing it in again. Do so, and then click the OK button to finish.

Figure 15-15: The Protect Sheet dialog box.

Protecting workbooks

Workbook protection has nothing to do with the protection of cells or other worksheet elements. Rather, it relates to the overall structure and content of the workbook as a whole. For instance, if someone tries to rename a worksheet in a protected workbook, he or she won't be able to.

To protect a workbook, follow these steps:

1. Select Tools ➪ Protection ➪ Protect Workbook from the menu.

2. The Protect Workbook dialog box is similar to the Protect Sheet dialog box. In it, you can select or deselect protection for Structure or Windows.

3. You can also type in a password, although this is optional. Do this only if it's absolutely necessary. If you assign a password to the worksheet, it cannot be unprotected again without that password. Again, if you forget it, you're out of luck. Period.

4. Click the OK button to complete the process.

5. If you entered a password, you'll be asked to confirm it by typing it in again. Do so, and then click the OK button to finish.

Unprotecting worksheets and workbooks

To remove the protection from either a worksheet or workbook, you just make more or less the same menu selections you made to put the protection in. The only difference is that the phrasing of the menu options changes from Protect Sheet to Unprotect Sheet and from Protect Workbook to Unprotect Workbook; otherwise, even the shortcut keys remain the same.

Caution   If you have password-protected the workbook or worksheet, you'll be asked to enter the password before the unprotection can take place. As mentioned earlier, you have to enter the right password or you can never unprotect the workbook or worksheet. Bear in mind that passwords are case-sensitive — "PASSWORD" is not the same thing as "password" or "PassWord."

Adding Graphics to Excel Worksheets

Although worksheets are usually used to hold text, dates, times, and numbers, they can also be dressed up with graphics. While an overuse of graphics can rapidly detract from the appearance and functionality of the best-designed worksheets, there are some cases where judicious use of graphical elements can vastly improve the look and understandability of your work.

Adding a corporate logo to a form, for instance, is a common graphical need in Excel. Or you might want to use the built-in drawing tools to put in callouts that emphasize or clarify the different parts of your worksheet.

There are several different ways to add graphics to your worksheets, but they break down into two categories: importing images and using drawing tools.

Importing images

There are two basic methods for importing images. One is via the standard menu; the other is via the Drawing toolbar, which is brought up by clicking the Drawing button on the Standard toolbar. The Drawing toolbar buttons offer only one way to import images, while the menu approach offers a greater variety of options. Figure 15-16 shows both methods of importing images.

File formats supported

You can import all the following file formats (among others):

- ✦ AutoCAD Format 2-D (dxf)
- ✦ Computer Graphics Metafile (cgm)
- ✦ Enhanced Metafile (emf)
- ✦ Graphics Interchange Format (gif)
- ✦ Joint Photographic Experts Group (jpeg, jpg)
- ✦ Kodak Photo CD (pcd)

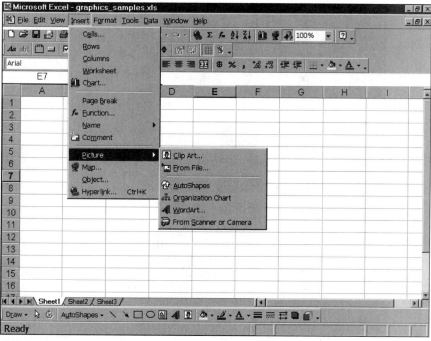

Figure 15-16: Image-importing options.

✦ Portable Network Graphics (png)

✦ Targa (tga)

✦ Windows Bitmap (bmp, dib, rle)

✦ Windows Metafile (wmf)

✦ WordPerfect Graphics (wpg)

Importing from the Clip Gallery

To import clip art from Microsoft's Clip Gallery, follow these steps:

1. Select Insert ➪ Picture ➪ Clip Art from the menu.

2. After a few moments, the Insert ClipArt dialog box appears, as shown in Figure 15-17.

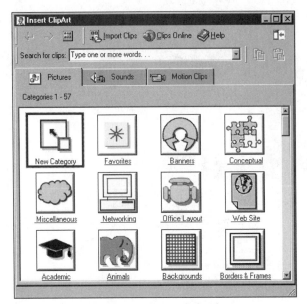

Figure 15-17: The Insert ClipArt dialog box.

3. Click on a category.

4. The images in that category will be displayed. As you place your pointer on each one, a floating message will inform you about the keywords associated with the image, the size of the image, and the fact that it's in Windows Metafile (WMF) format. Click on the image you want to import.

5. Click on the top button in the pop-up menu (see Figure 15-18) in order to import the image into Excel.

6. Close the Insert ClipArt dialog box.

Importing from other storage media

To import images from your hard drive or other storage medium, follow these steps:

1. Select Insert ➪ Picture ➪ From File from the menu.

2. Navigate to the folder containing the image you want to import.

3. Click on the filename. The Insert Picture dialog box will show the image on the right-hand side (see Figure 15-19).

4. Click the Insert button.

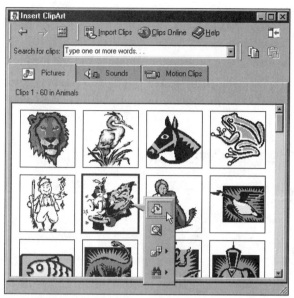

Figure 15-18: The ClipArt pop-up menu.

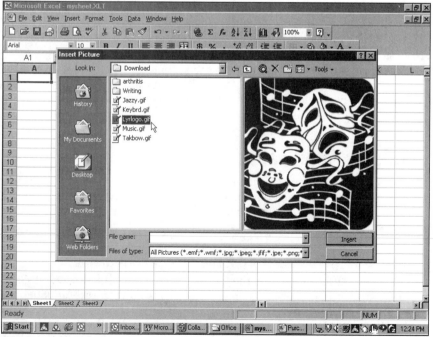

Figure 15-19: Inserting a file.

Importing from digitizing devices

To import images from a digitizing device, follow these steps:

1. Select Insert ➪ Picture ➪ From Scanner or Camera from the menu.

2. In the dialog box (see Figure 15-20), select the device you intend to use (if you have only one, it will be the only one in the list and there is no need to make a selection).

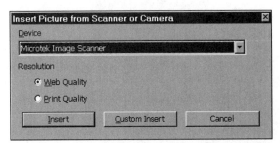

Figure 15-20: The Insert Picture from Scanner or Camera dialog box.

3. Select the image quality. Choose Web Quality for smaller file sizes and Print Quality for highest resolution (don't use Print Quality for applications that will only be viewed onscreen — even very expensive monitors won't show any significant improvement in the image as a result).

4. Click the Insert button to run the scanner or camera, and the image will be digitized and imported into Excel. If you want to use the standard controls for your device instead of letting Excel run it automatically, click the Custom Insert button instead.

Adding AutoShapes

Excel provides a rich assortment of drawing tools called AutoShapes with which you can add graphical elements to your worksheets. AutoShapes are available either via the menu or the Drawing toolbar. They're a collection of pre-designed, but adjustable, shapes ranging from simple lines to complex shapes.

Accessing AutoShapes from the AutoShapes menu

To access AutoShapes from the menu, select Insert ➪ Picture ➪ AutoShapes. To get to them from the Drawing toolbar, simply click on the word AutoShapes. The menu selection method creates a floating toolbar, while the Drawing toolbar selection method displays a menu. Figure 15-21 shows both the floating toolbar (on the upper right) and the menu versions (on the lower left). The menu version shows the AutoShapes available with the Basic Shapes selection.

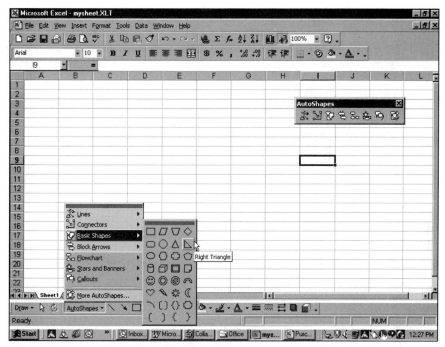

Figure 15-21: The AutoShapes toolbar and menu.

Both versions present the same options:

- ✦ Lines
- ✦ Connectors
- ✦ Basic Shapes
- ✦ Block Arrows
- ✦ Flowchart
- ✦ Stars and Banners
- ✦ Callouts
- ✦ More AutoShapes

The menu options run from top to bottom, while the same toolbar options run from left to right.

Accessing AutoShapes from the Drawing toolbar

The Drawing toolbar (see Figure 15-22), in addition to providing access to the AutoShapes menu, also has four of the most commonly used AutoShapes right on it: Line, Arrow, Rectangle, and Oval.

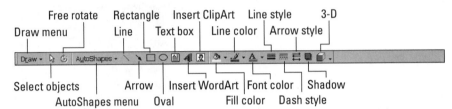

Figure 15-22: The Drawing toolbar.

Placing an AutoShape in a worksheet

To place an AutoShape in your worksheet, follow these steps:

1. Select the desired AutoShape.

2. Click on your worksheet.

3. To accept the default size, simply release the mouse button. To resize the shape, move the pointer before releasing the mouse button. In the case of lines, you need to drag the mouse from one point to another in this manner in order for them to appear. To maintain the original ratio of the shape, hold down the Shift key while resizing it.

Note   The text box is an odd object. It can either act as a stand-alone like other graphical objects, or be used in tandem with AutoShapes. When used by itself, it simply creates an area on the worksheet where you can type text. However, if you select an existing object, and then click on the text box button, you can add text directly to the object itself.

Modifying AutoShape objects

Once an AutoShape object is in place, it can be selected and modified very easily with the tools on the Drawing toolbar. Here's how they work:

Note   If the type of AutoShape doesn't support the particular option, it will be grayed out. For instance, the rectangle shape doesn't support the arrow styles, so none of them are available if you click the arrow style button while a rectangle shape is selected.

✦ The fill color and font color buttons on the Drawing toolbar are exactly like the ones on the Formatting toolbar, and you can, in fact, use the ones on either toolbar for the exact same effect.

✦ The Drawing toolbar, however, also has a line color button. It works exactly like the other two color buttons, but clicking on it establishes the color of the shape's outline.

✦ The line style, dash style, and arrow style buttons bring up menus on which you can choose line thickness, dashed and dotted lines, and several types of arrows, respectively (see Figure 15-23 for an example of the types of dashed and dotted lines available).

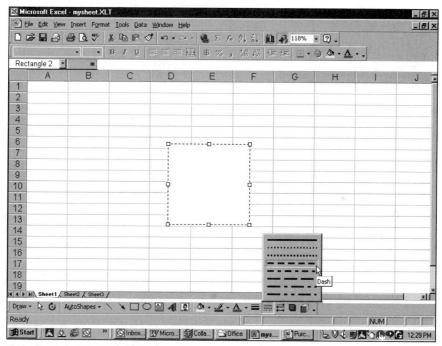

Figure 15-23: Dash style options.

✦ The shadow and 3-D options each, in their own way, give an appearance of depth to an object. The two options are mutually exclusive. An object has either a shadow or a 3-D effect, but not both.

Figure 15-24 shows the same arrow object with various modifications from the Drawing toolbar applied to it.

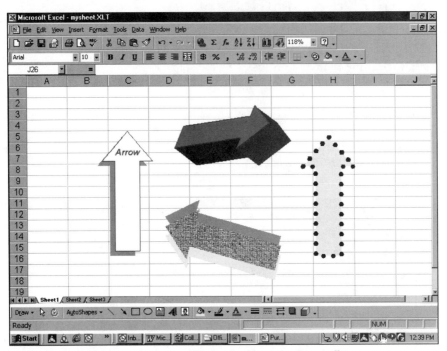

Figure 15-24: An arrow shape modified using the Drawing toolbar.

Using WordArt

WordArt is a system of presenting plain text in a colorful and vivid format. To insert WordArt images, follow these steps:

1. Click the Insert WordArt button on the Drawing toolbar.

2. In the WordArt gallery, click on the style you want to use (see Figure 15-25).

3. Click the OK button.

4. This brings up the Edit WordArt Text dialog box as shown in Figure 15-26. Type your text in the Text area of the dialog box. You can specify the font face, font size, and whether it's going to be bold or italic via the options at the top of the dialog box.

5. Click the OK button.

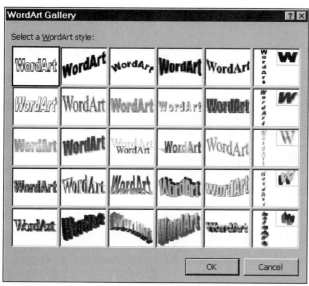

Figure 15-25: The WordArt gallery.

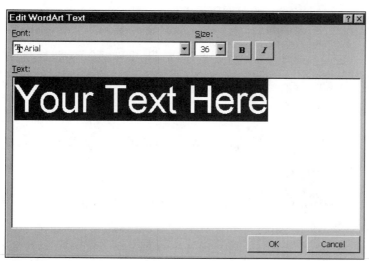

Figure 15-26: The Edit WordArt Text dialog box.

6. The WordArt now appears on the worksheet, along with its own toolbar (see Figure 15-27).

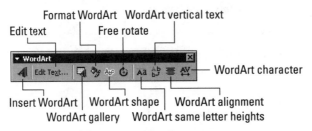

Figure 15-27: The WordArt toolbar.

Table 15-3 shows the functions of the WordArt toolbar buttons, left to right.

Table 15-3	
WordArt Toolbar Buttons	
Button	**Function**
Insert WordArt	Inserts a new WordArt object.
Edit Text	Lets you change the text in the current WordArt object.
WordArt gallery	Lets you modify the current WordArt object with the same options as you originally had when creating it.
Format WordArt	WordArt presents options for choosing colors, fill effects, precise size, protection, etc.
WordArt shape	Gives you several options about the basic shape of the WordArt object.
Free rotate	Lets you interactively rotate the object.
WordArt same letter heights	Makes all letters the same height.
WordArt vertical text	Makes the text run vertically.
WordArt alignment	Lets you alter the alignment of the WordArt object.
WordArt character spacing	Allows you to adjust the spacing of the letters in the object.

Summary

In this chapter, you learned how to create and utilize templates, forms, and graphics in Excel, and how to protect worksheets and workbooks. Key points of the chapter included the following:

✦ Excel comes with built-in templates and forms you can use.

✦ These templates require the use of add-in utilities.

✦ You can create your own templates for both worksheets and workbooks.

✦ Forms can contain controls such as spinners and buttons, which add automation.

✦ Controls can be keyed to macros written in Visual Basic.

✦ Cells are automatically protected by default, but that protection doesn't take effect until the worksheet is protected.

✦ Workbooks can also be protected.

✦ Graphics can be added to worksheets, either by importing existing files or by direct creation with Excel's graphics tools.

✦   ✦   ✦

PivotTable and PivotChart Reports

If you remember sorting, filtering, and subtotaling data from Chapter 14, "Lists and Databases," you probably think those capabilities are pretty impressive, and we're inclined to agree with you. PivotTables, though, take data tables to new heights. They allow you to interactively alter the structure of tables so that you can view the information they contain from multiple perspectives.

PivotChart reports are a combination of a regular pivot table approach and the look of a regular chart. Like pivot tables, you can dynamically alter the data, yet the presentation is in a chart format instead of a table format.

Working with PivotTable Reports

A PivotTable report is a new, interactive table created from an existing, static table. While the pivot table can be placed on the same worksheet as the original table from which it gets its data, it is generally better to put it on its own worksheet in the same workbook.

One of the great advantages to using pivot tables, other than the increased ease with which you can manipulate and study your data, is that no matter what you do in the pivot table, the structure and format of your original data remains safe, secure, and unchanged.

Creating pivot tables

The process of creating pivot tables is automated in Excel through the services of the PivotTable wizard. A pivot table is usually based on a standard Excel database list, although you can use outside data sources as well, or combine multiple Excel database lists into a single PivotTable report. Like the database lists you used in Chapter 14, the ones you use for pivot tables need to have field names in the first row so the PivotTable wizard knows how to group the data in the columns.

Pivot tables aren't very useful for simple data sources. The more complex the original data, the more you'll find pivot tables to your liking. A good rule of thumb is that you need at least four fields, at least one of which should have multiple types in it. Figure 16-1 shows an example of minimum useful source data for a pivot table.

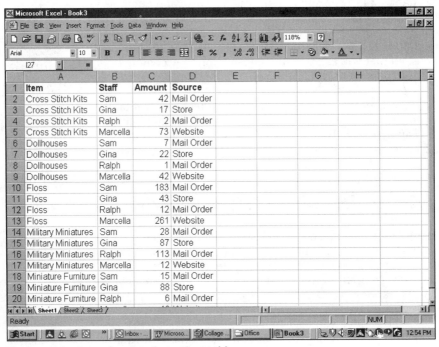

Figure 16-1: A good source for a pivot table.

To turn this data source into a pivot table, follow these steps:

1. Click on any cell in the data source.

2. Select Data ➪ PivotTable and PivotChart Report from the menu.

3. In the PivotTable wizard (see Figure 16-2), the data source is already selected because you had clicked on one of its cells. You can also select either an External data source or Multiple consolidation ranges (using identically structured Excel databases to create one pivot table).

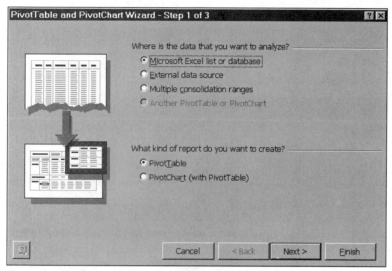

Figure 16-2: Step 1 of the PivotTable wizard.

4. Choose whether to create just a pivot table or both a pivot table and pivot chart. If you don't create a pivot chart at this point, you can do it later from your pivot table, so you aren't required to do it now.

5. Click the Next button.

6. If you're using a single data source, the next step is to simply confirm that Excel has selected the proper range for the data source (see Figure 16-3). If it hasn't, you can correct it. Click on the grid icon to collapse the dialog box out of your way.

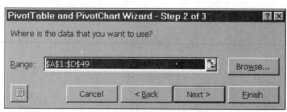

Figure 16-3: Step 2 of the PivotTable wizard for single data sources.

7. Click the Next button and move to Step 12 of this list (Steps 8 through 11 are for multiple data sources only).

8. If you're using multiple data sources, things get a little bit more complex. First, you'll need to tell the wizard whether to automatically create a page field or whether you'll do it yourself later (see Figure 16-4).

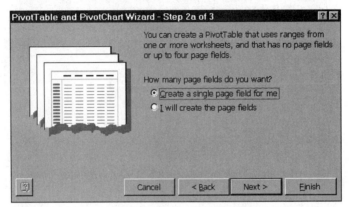

Figure 16-4: Step 2a of the PivotTable wizard for multiple data sources.

9. Click the Next button.

10. In Step 2b for multiple data sources (see Figure 16-5), you specify the range for each data source, and then click the Add button to add it to the listing. You can remove any range you've added by selecting it and pressing the Delete button. The Browse button is used to open other workbooks you want to draw data sources from.

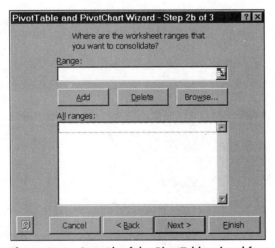

Figure 16-5: Step 2b of the PivotTable wizard for multiple data sources.

11. Click the Next button.

12. In the final dialog box of the PivotTable wizard (see Figure 16-6), you need to select whether to place the pivot table on a new worksheet or an existing worksheet. The default is for a new one.

Figure 16-6: Step 3 of the PivotTable wizard.

13. You can simply click the Finish button at this point, but you'll make it easier on yourself if you first click the Layout button. If you finish the pivot table without configuring its layout, you can still change the layout at any time, but the wizard's layout dialog box is much more intuitive and easier to use. The Options button lets you set various options for the pivot table, but that dialog box is accessible at any time after you create the pivot table, and we'll deal with it later on.

14. The PivotTable and PivotChart Wizard - Layout dialog box (see Figure 16-7) graphically illustrates the way pivot tables work. The fields from the database source are represented by buttons on the right-hand side. Simply drag the buttons to the positions you want them to occupy in the pivot table.

15. In our example, we have the fields Item, Staff, Amount, and Source. We want to begin by looking at the number of each item sold by each staff member, so we drag the Item button into the ROW area, the Staff button into the COLUMN area, and the Amount button into the DATA area. We'll also want to be able to see how these relationships are affected by the source of the orders, so we drag the Source button into the PAGE field area. Figure 16-8 shows how the PivotTable and PivotChart Wizard-Layout dialog box looks when all the fields are in place.

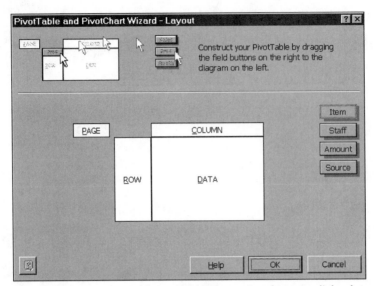

Figure 16-7: The PivotTable and PivotChart Wizard-Layout dialog box.

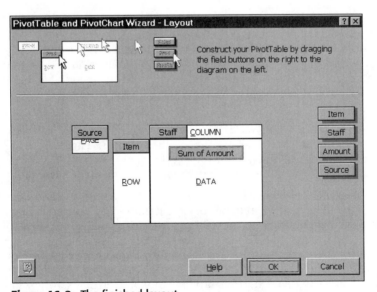

Figure 16-8: The finished layout.

16. Click the OK button to return to the PivotTable wizard.

17. Click the Finish button.

18. The pivot table is created as shown in Figure 16-9.

	A	B	C	D	E	F	G	H
1	Source	(All)						
2								
3	Sum of Amount	Staff						
4	Item	Gina	Marcella	Ralph	Sam	Grand Total		
5	Cross Stitch Kits	17	73	2	42	134		
6	Dollhouses	22	42	1	7	72		
7	Floss	43	261	12	183	499		
8	Military Miniatures	87	12	113	28	240		
9	Miniature Furniture	88	19	6	15	128		
10	Miniature Landscaping	48	18	78	72	216		
11	Model Rockets	48	1	29	6	84		
12	Model Trains	19	4	71	12	106		
13	Paint	37	26	97	15	175		
14	Rugmaking Kits	23	48	2	2	75		
15	Winter Village Miniatures	147	111	17	78	353		
16	Yarn	11	287	3	128	429		
17	Grand Total	590	902	431	588	2511		
18								
19								
20								

Figure 16-9: The pivot table on a new worksheet.

Caution

If you've applied the automatic subtotals to your data source, remove them before you use the data source in a pivot table. Pivot tables apply their own subtotals and grand totals.

Modifying pivot tables

There are three basic ways to modify pivot tables: use the built-in data limitation features; rearrange the fields; or alter the data in the original data source, and then refresh the pivot table based on those changes.

Rearranging the fields

Each of the fields in the pivot table's page, column, and row areas has a drop-down list featuring all the items in that field. Figure 16-10 shows the drop-down list for the Source field.

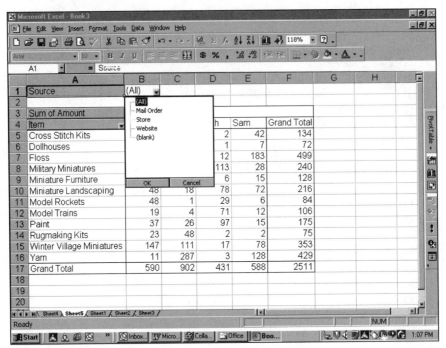

Figure 16-10: A drop-down page field list.

To limit the page display in the pivot table to a subset of the possible sources, simply select one of the fields other than All and click the OK button. The entire pivot table will adjust to show only that page of data.

The Source field used in this example is placed in the page field area of the pivot table, and your only options in that case are to choose one of the fields, or to choose all of them at once. The row and column field areas, however, allow you to choose multiple subsets simultaneously. Figure 16-11 shows the drop-down list for the row field area, which in this pivot table holds the Item field from the original data source.

Removing listed items

To remove any of the items in the listing from the display, all you have to do is uncheck the item and click the OK button. The pivot table will be redrawn without that item. You can select or deselect as many items as you want to, as long as at least one item remains selected. To restore the display, simply revisit the drop-down list and recheck the deselected items, and then click the OK button again.

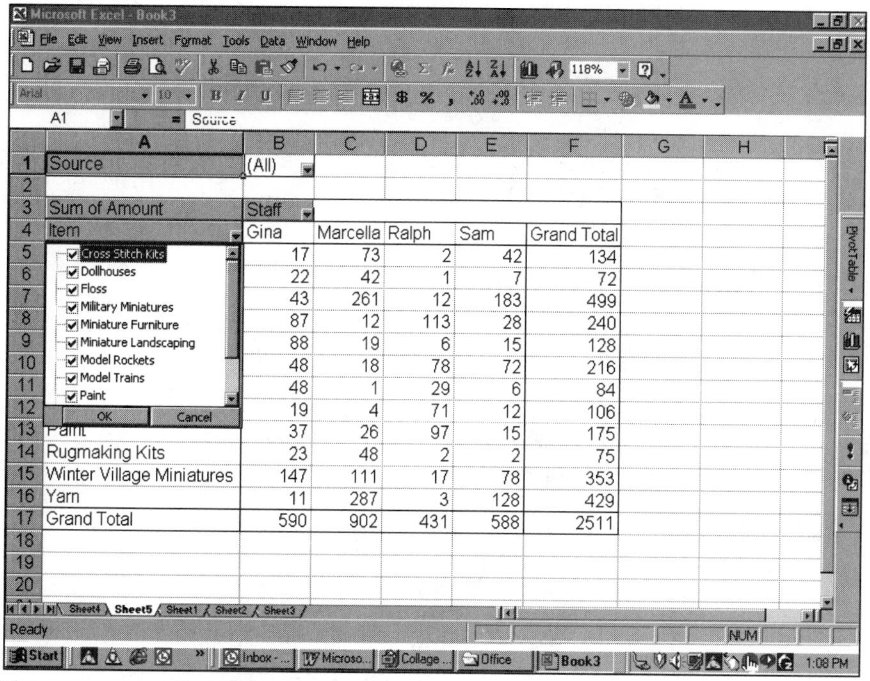

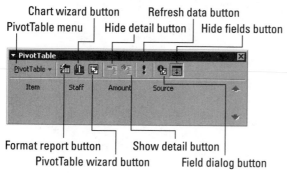

Figure 16-11: A drop-down row field list.

Restructuring the pivot table

To restructure the pivot table, you can click the Wizard button on the PivotTable toolbar (see Figure 16-12), click the Layout button, and repeat the layout process you followed when creating the pivot table. You can also simply click on the field label in the pivot table and drag it into the new position. The pivot table will automatically readjust to fit the new layout.

Figure 16-12: The PivotTable toolbar.

Caution If you drag a field off the pivot table, it will be completely removed from the pivot table. If you did not intend to do this, you can correct it by going back into the Layout dialog box and restoring the field there or simply drag the name of the field from the PivotTable toolbar back into the pivot table.

To make a pivot table change to reflect changes in the original data source, just click the Refresh Data button on the PivotTable toolbar.

Formatting pivot tables

Pivot tables are automatically formatted as they're created, and the basic formatting, such as column width and table size, alters dynamically as you choose various options while using the pivot table. You can also apply all the standard formatting methods to pivot tables that you can to any worksheet. You can, for instance, change the font color, size, and style. But pivot tables offer a special version of the AutoFormat approach that can save you lots of time and trouble.

To use AutoFormat with pivot tables, follow these steps:

1. Click anywhere within the pivot table.

2. Either click the Format Report button on the PivotTable toolbar or select Format ➪ AutoFormat from the menu. This brings up the AutoFormat dialog box (see Figure 16-13), which shows samples of pre-designed formats for you to choose from. These samples are different from the standard AutoFormats designed for use with normal worksheets.

3. To pick one, click on the sample image.

4. Click the OK button to complete the process. Figure 16-14 shows the same pivot table with a new AutoFormat applied to it.

Caution Unlike the normal usage of AutoFormat, you can't just return to the original settings by returning to the AutoFormat dialog box and clicking on the design labeled None. If you do this, you'll discover that you've removed the formatting that was applied automatically when you created the pivot table. If you want to remove an AutoFormat that you just applied, use the Undo button instead.

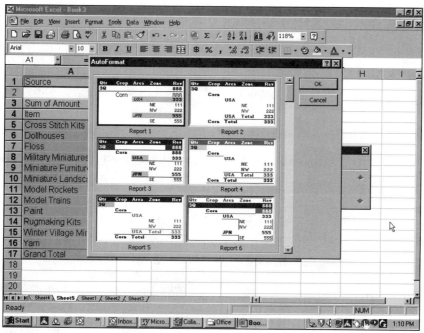

Figure 16-13: The pivot table AutoFormat dialog box.

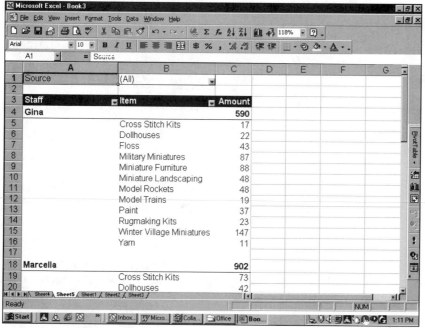

Figure 16-14: The pivot table with a new AutoFormat applied.

Working with PivotChart Reports

Pivot charts can be created at the same time you create a pivot table or afterwards from an existing pivot table. You can have a pivot table without a pivot chart, but the reverse is not true. Pivot charts draw their data from pivot tables, and if you try to create one without an existing pivot table, Excel will create the pivot table for you.

Using PivotChart reports

If you didn't create a pivot chart during the pivot table creation process, all you have to do to create one is to click anywhere within your pivot chart, and then click the Chart Wizard button (either on the Standard toolbar or on the PivotTable toolbar). A pivot chart based on the pivot table will instantly be generated and will appear on its own chart sheet, as shown in Figure 16-15.

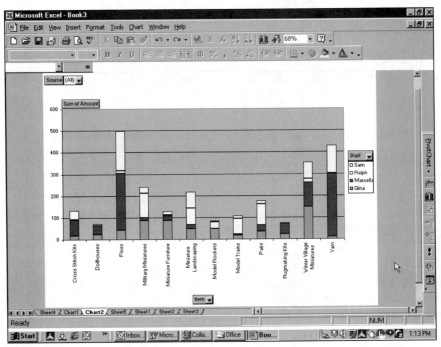

Figure 16-15: A pivot chart.

You'll recognize the similarities between the pivot chart and the pivot table it's based on. Not only do both show the same data, but the pivot chart has moveable field buttons with drop-down lists just as a pivot table does.

When a PivotChart is active, the PivotTable toolbar shows a PivotChart menu instead of a PivotTable menu, and the items on it are specifically geared toward charts. The standard Chart toolbar also appears when you create a pivot chart. Pivot charts, for all their increased capabilities, are still Excel charts, and you can use the Chart toolbar just as you would with a normal chart. You can select chart elements, change chart type, etc., as you would with any chart. The By Row and By Column buttons, however, are grayed out.

Altering pivot charts

To alter the layout of a pivot chart, you can simply drag the field buttons from place to place on the chart (from category axis to legend, for example). Figure 16-16 shows the effect of moving the Source field button from the page field area to the category axis. The category axis is the equivalent of the row area on the pivot table, and the column fields in the pivot table are the equivalent of the series fields in the pivot chart.

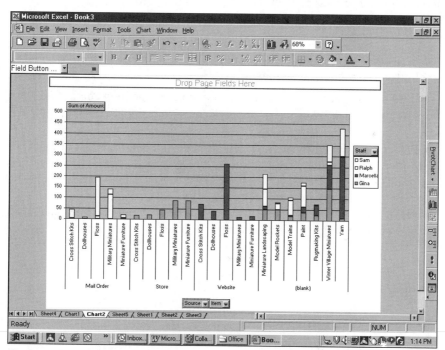

Figure 16-16: The same pivot chart with a repositioned field button.

Another way to alter the layout of a pivot chart is to just change the pivot table. Pivot tables and pivot charts exist in a totally synchronous relationship — whatever you do to one, you automatically do to the other at the same time. If you check the pivot table that's the source for your pivot chart after you alter the layout of the pivot chart, you'll see that it has changed, and if you change a pivot table that's associated with a pivot chart, you'll see that the pivot chart has changed, too.

Caution   Changing the layout of a pivot chart wipes out some of the formatting, so if you're planning on formatting the chart, don't bother with it until you're satisfied with the layout.

Summary

In this chapter, you learned how to create and use pivot tables and pivot charts.

◆ Pivot tables and pivot charts enable you to interactively restructure the presentation of data.

◆ Pivot tables are created with the PivotTable wizard.

◆ Pivot charts can be created along with pivot tables or from existing pivot tables.

◆ Both pivot tables and pivot charts can be modified by placing the field buttons in different positions.

◆ Field buttons have drop-down lists that contain the items in that field. By choosing which items are active, you can alter the display of the pivot table or chart.

◆ Pivot tables are automatically formatted during creation. The formatting can be altered by standard worksheet means or by using the AutoFormat option. AutoFormats for pivot tables are different from the ones applied to normal worksheets.

◆ Pivot tables and pivot charts are synchronized so that any change made to a pivot table changes the associated pivot chart and vice versa.

◆   ◆   ◆

Using Excel to Analyze Data

This chapter covers the many ways you can analyze data in Excel. Data tables are useful when you have a tightly limited series of fixed variables to test. Goal Seek allows you to rapidly and easily test for the results of changing a single variable. Solver, an add-in, performs the same actions as Goal Seek, but offers far more flexibility and power. Circular references — which Excel normally treats as an error — can be used with the Iteration option to allow them to be processed. The Circular Reference toolbar also lets you trace the operation of circular references so they can be corrected.

Creating and Using Data Tables

Of all the ways you can use Excel to analyze data, data tables have to be the clunkiest, ugliest approach. They're complex to set up, of limited utility, and the constraints on their construction prevent you from creating anything remotely presentable. Still, you can skip some of the official rules and manage to come up with some fairly useful output within those limitations.

Dealing with a fixed series of variables

Data tables are of value only when you have a fixed series of variables to deal with. Suppose, for instance, that you're considering how many people to put to work on a particular project. Obviously, you can't use values like 4.29 women or 17.36 men in the real world. Because you know you're dealing with whole numbers and you doubtless have some idea of the number of staff that it's remotely possible to assign to the project, you can set up a data table to test the cost of your various options.

Solving a sample problem

Suppose you have to assign somewhere between three and nine junior engineers to a project. You know the pay rate is $42.00 per hour for that rank and the project is due in two weeks. We'll leave aside the complex question of how many it'll take to actually accomplish the task for now and just look at the single variable of how much money it will take to keep a certain numbers of engineers employed on the project for its duration.

To solve this problem with a data table, follow these steps:

1. Place the data on which the formula works in a column. In Figure 17-1, this is done in B1 through B3.

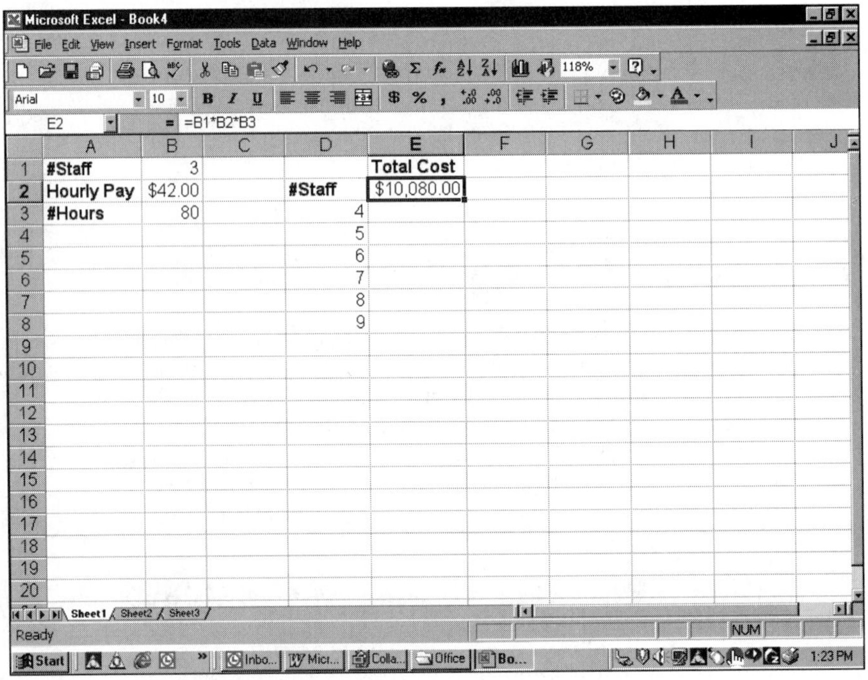

Figure 17-1: Data table layout.

2. Enter a formula to calculate the results. Our formula multiplies the number of staff members times their hourly pay times the number of hours for the project (B1*B2*B3). The formula must go into a cell at least two cells to the

right of the data column. In this example, we put it three cells over to E2 so there would be a gap between the data and the table, but this is not necessary. In fact, the formula can be placed anywhere on the spreadsheet, as long as there is an empty column to the left of it to hold variables.

3. Type the variable values in the column to the left of the formula, starting one cell down from the formula. In this case, that's D3 through D8. Because we're testing for the different costs associated with between 3 and 9 staff members, and B1 already holds the value 3, we type in only the values 4 through 9.

4. Now we're ready to create the actual data table. Select the rectangular area that includes the formula and the variables. In this example, it's D2:E8 (see Figure 17-2).

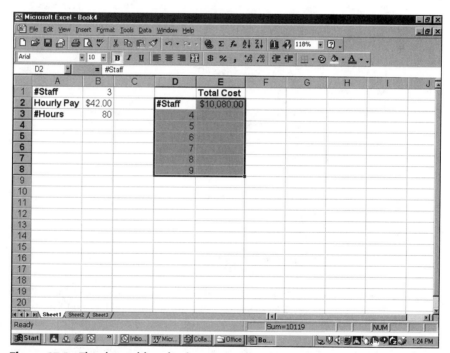

Figure 17-2: The data table selection area.

5. Select Data ➪ Table from the menu.

6. In the Table dialog box, click Column input cell (see Figure 17-3). If the data and table were in rows instead of in columns, you'd click Row input cell.

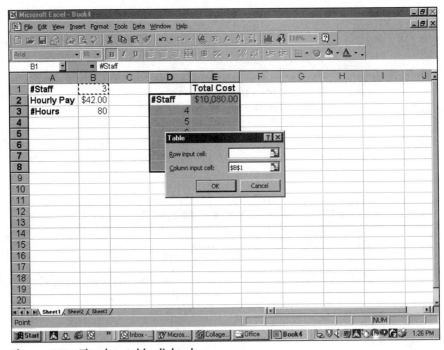

Figure 17-3: The data table dialog box.

7. Click on the cell that holds the initial value you're testing variables for. In this case, that would be B1.

8. Click the OK button.

9. The data table applies the formula to each variable and puts the outcome next to them as shown in Figure 17-4.

Tip

There is actually no requirement that you use only a single formula with a data table. You can place as many as you want to side by side, and they will all use the same variables. You could, for instance, put the formula B1*B2 in cell F2, and the amount of money required for each hour of operation would be shown in cells F2 through F8 in addition to the total cost already shown in E2 through E8. You can put all the formulas in place at once, before making the table, or you can add formulas after the initial table has been created, and then reselect the table area to accommodate the new formula and remake the data table.

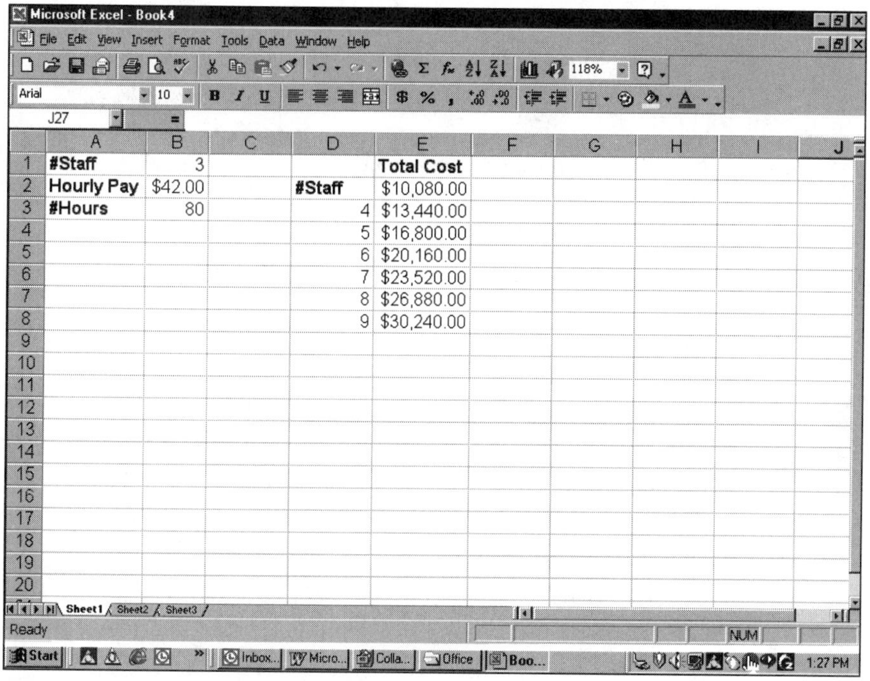

Figure 17-4: The completed data table.

Using Goal Seek

Goal Seek is a much faster way to calculate variables. It's limited to finding a single answer to a single problem, but it requires no special setup, and you don't have to jockey your worksheet layout around so that it's difficult to tell just what's what as you do with data tables.

How it works

Figure 17-5 shows a familiar situation with a couple of new twists. Once again, we're trying to figure out how to manage the project, but this time we're on a tight budget and need to show a profit. The figure in E2 is calculated by multiplying the number of staff times their hourly pay times the number of hours. The figure in F2 is calculated by subtracting this amount from the budget.

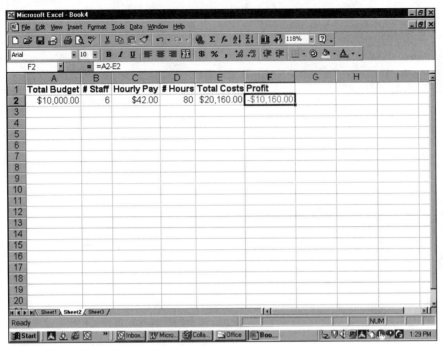

Figure 17-5: Profit/loss calculation.

Solving a sample problem

We're sure we need six people to complete the project, so we're going to use Goal Seek to find out how much the pay rate needs to be cut in order to bring it in on budget. To do this, follow these steps:

1. Click on the cell whose value you want to change. In this case, it's F2, the profit margin.

2. Select Tools ➪ Goal Seek from the menu.

3. The Goal Seek dialog box will appear (see Figure 17-6). The Set Cell value is already filled in because you had selected it before invoking Goal Seek. If you had not done so, or if you had clicked on the wrong cell, you would need to click on the desired cell at this point.

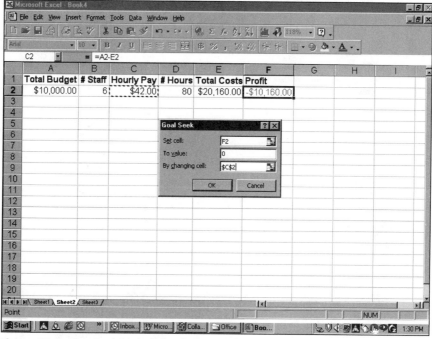

Figure 17-6: The Goal Seek dialog box.

4. Beside To Value, set the value you're solving for. Because we just want to break even, the value in this example is zero.

5. To set By Changing Cell, click on the cell that holds the value you want Goal Seek to adjust to achieve the value you specified for the profit. In this case, we want to adjust the hourly pay rate to the point where the project doesn't operate at a loss, so we select C2.

6. Click the OK button.

7. Goal Seek will now run through a series of calculations, trying out various possibilities, and rapidly find an answer. Figure 17-7 shows the Goal Seek Status dialog box after the problem has been solved. Note that the value in C2 has been changed so that the formula in F2 solves to zero.

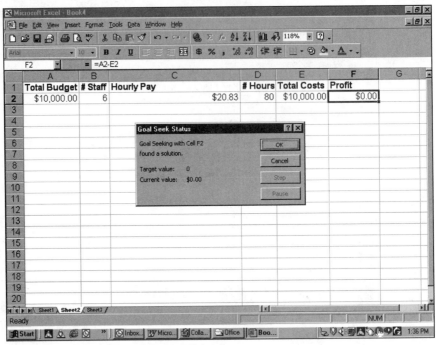

Figure 17-7: The Goal Seek Status dialog box.

8. To accept the new values, click the OK button. To reject them and return the values to the original ones that were there before you ran Goal Seek, click the Cancel button.

Note

The Step and Pause buttons aren't of much use unless you're calculating a very large value using a very slow computer, or are very fast with a mouse. Goal Seek is so fast that it'll usually find the final value before you can react. If you are quick enough, you can click the Pause button to freeze the calculation, and then use the Step button to walk through the calculation as it tries different values. When you click Pause, it becomes a Continue button, which you can click on to resume the normal mode of calculation.

Using Solver

Where Goal Seek is a great solution for single variables, more complex situations call for the power of Solver. Solver is an add-in, so you won't find it on your Tools menu unless you've already installed it.

Installing the Solver add-in

To install Solver, follow these steps:

1. Select Tools ⇨ Add-Ins from the menu.

2. In the Add-Ins dialog box, click the check box next to Solver Add-In so that it's checked.

3. Click the OK button.

4. You'll see a dialog box asking if you want to install the add-in. Click the Yes button to install it.

Solving a sample problem

Once Solver is installed, you can find it on the Tools menu. Solver works in a very similar manner to Goal Seek, but it's kind of like Goal Seek on steroids. You'll find the process quite familiar, but appreciate the extra power. To apply it to the same situation we used Goal Seek for, follow these steps:

1. Click on the cell whose value you want to solve for. This is called the *target cell*. In this case, it's F2, the profit margin.

2. Select Tools ⇨ Solver from the menu.

3. The Solver Parameters dialog box will appear (see Figure 17-8). The Set Target Cell value is already filled in because you had selected it before invoking Solver. If you had not done so, or if you had clicked on the wrong cell, you would need to click on the desired cell at this point.

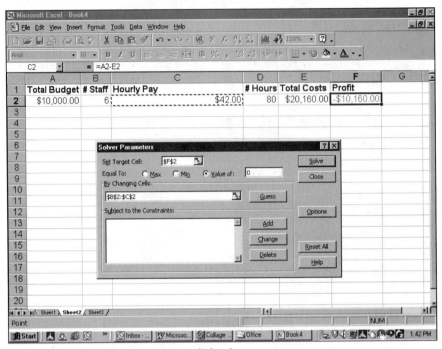

Figure 17-8: The Solver Parameters dialog box.

4. Under Equal To, you have a choice of Max, Min, and Value of. The first two, of course, are for setting a maximum or minimum value. The third is for setting a specific value that must be met, no higher and no lower. In this example, we want to just break even, so the Equal To value is set for a value of zero.

5. To set By Changing Cells, you can type in or select a range of cells. To select a series of noncontiguous cells, either type them in, separated by commas, or select them on the worksheet while holding down the Ctrl key. Alternately, you can click the Guess button and Solver will do its best to figure out which cells you're willing to change to achieve your desired results in the target cell. In this case, we're willing to adjust either the hourly pay rate or the number of staff so the project doesn't operate at a loss. Therefore, we select B2:C2.

6. So far, things have run pretty much the same as if we were using Goal Seek, but here's where they get really different. Under Subject to the Constraints, you can set limits on what Solver will do to achieve the goals. Click the Add button to put in the first constraint.

7. In the Add Constraint dialog box (see Figure 17-9), specify the cell you want to constrain changes to in the Cell Reference box, and then select a constraint operator from the drop-down list in the middle. In this case, we're simply specifying that the value in B2 has to be an integer, so we're done with the process.

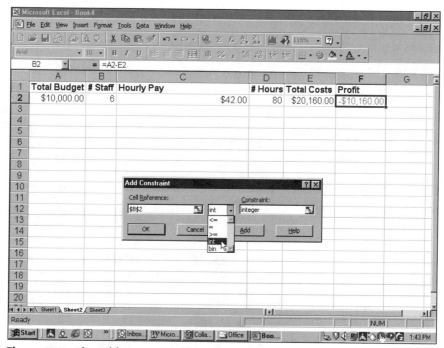

Figure 17-9: The Add Constraint dialog box.

8. If you were just adding one constraint, you'd click the OK button at this point to input the constraint to Solver. Because we're adding more, click the Add button. This has the same effect as the OK button, but leaves the dialog box open and with the values cleared for the next entry.

9. Still setting constraints on B2, we need to keep it between 3 and 9 staff members. Specify B2 again in the Cell Reference box, and then select the >= (greater than or equal to) constraint operator from the drop-down list in the middle. This time, we have to add the value we want after the operator, so we'll type a 3 in the Constraint box.

10. Click the Add button.

11. For the last constraint on B2, specify B2 in the Cell Reference box and select the <= (less than or equal to) constraint operator from the drop-down list in the middle. Type a 9 in the Constraint box.

12. Click the Add button.

13. Next, specify B3 in the Cell Reference box, and then select the >= (greater than or equal to) constraint operator from the drop-down list in the middle. No

engineer will settle for less than $10 per hour, so we'll type a 10 in the Constraint box.

14. Click the OK button.

15. The constraints are all shown in the Solver Parameters dialog box (see Figure 17-10).

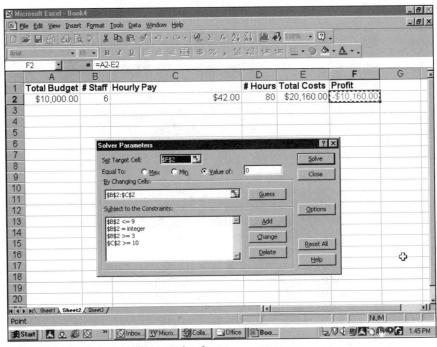

Figure 17-10: The constraints are in place.

16. You can click the Options button if you want to set more specific options, such as the amount of time you're willing to spend on the calculation.

17. To find the answer to the problem, click the Solve button.

18. Solver will now run through a series of calculations, trying out various possibilities, and rapidly find an answer. Figure 17-11 shows the Solver Results dialog box after the problem has been solved. Note that the values in C2 and C3 have both been changed within their constraints so that the formula in F2 solves to zero.

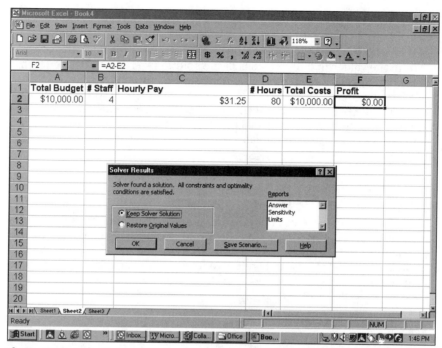

Figure 17-11: The Solver Results dialog box.

19. You can choose any or all of three reports on the Solver action by clicking on the words Answer, Sensitivity, or Limits under Reports on the right-hand side of the dialog box.

20. To accept the new values and create the reports, make sure the Keep Solver Solution radio button is selected, and then click the OK button. To reject them and return the values to the original ones before you ran Solver, click the Cancel button (the reports won't be created in this case). You can also select the Restore Original Values radio button and click the OK button to reject the new values, but that's extra work for nothing, unless you want to create the reports without actually changing the values.

Tip

You can use the Save Scenario button to keep this solution and others on hand for later review. Click that button, and then provide a name for the scenario. You can recall it by selecting Tools ➪ Scenarios from the menu and then clicking the Show button in the Scenario Manager dialog box.

Circular Reference and Iteration

Normally, formulas require a fairly simple approach in which the solution is derived from the values in different cells. If the solution were to be derived from the cell containing the formula or another cell dependent on that cell, you'd have a circular reference. A circular reference may never be able to be solved at all because the result will keep changing itself. Some specialized formulas, however, require circular references. Fractal images, for instance, are generated by repeated iterations of the same formulas. Fortunately, Excel is capable of handling both situations.

Circular references as errors

For this example, we've created a worksheet in which we've put the formula =C2 in cell A2, the value 500 in B2, and the formula =A2+B2 in cell C2. Excel is set by default to treat circular references as an error condition. Normally, setting up a situation in which a formula refers to itself will result in the warning message seen in Figure 17-12.

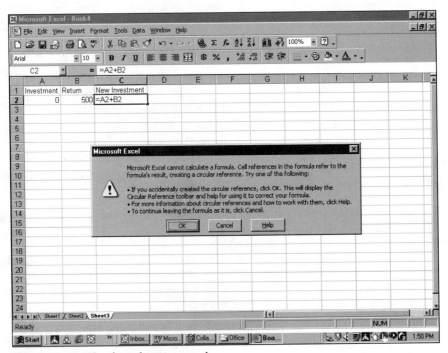

Figure 17-12: Circular reference warning.

Using circular references

If you find yourself in one of those rare situations requiring circular references, click the Cancel button. To get Excel to let you use circular references, you have to tell it you want to. To do so, follow these steps:

1. Select Tools ⇨ Options from the menu.

2. In the Options dialog box (see Figure 17-13), click the Calculation tab.

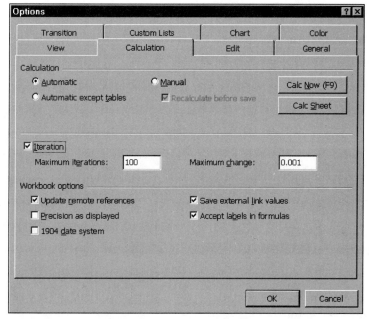

Figure 17-13: The Calculation tab of the Options dialog box.

3. Click the Iteration check box.

4. The Maximum iterations setting tells Excel how many times to repeat the formula. Type in whatever value you need.

5. The Maximum change setting is a limit on uselessly minimal iterations. Excel will halt the repetition of the formula regardless of the Maximum iterations setting if the values resulting from the last iteration have changed by less than the amount specified in Maximum change. Type in the value you need.

6. Click the OK button. Excel will now permit you to use circular references. Figure 17-14 shows the completed circular formula after 100 iterations.

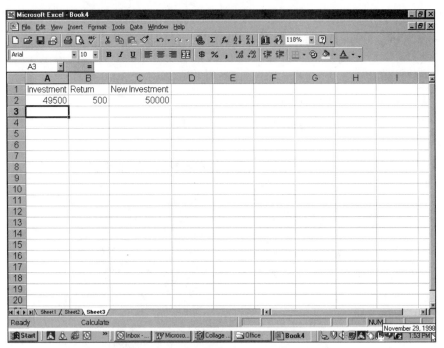

Figure 17-14: The completed circular formula.

Using the Circular Reference toolbar

If you're in a normal situation and the circular reference is an error, just click the OK button when you see the warning message. The Circular Reference toolbar will appear, as shown in Figure 17-15, and arrows on the affected cells will show which cells are involved in the circular reference.

If the problem is not readily apparent, click the Navigate Circular Reference button to view a list of all the affected cells. Clicking on any reference in that list selects that cell. Use the Remove All Arrows button to clear the arrows, and then click the Trace Dependents button to see what cells are affected by this cell. Click the Remove All Arrows button again and then click the Trace Precedents button to see which cells affect this one. Once you have traced out the route of the circular reference (which isn't always as easy as in this example), you can take action to solve the problem at its source by modifying the formula to remove the circular references.

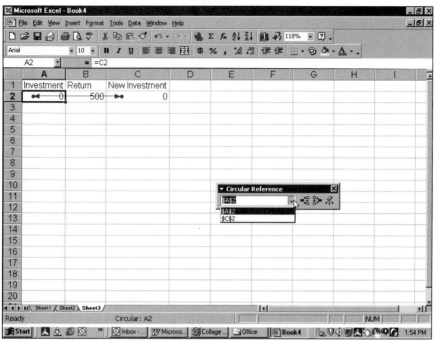

Figure 17-15: The Circular Reference toolbar.

Summary

In this chapter, you learned how to analyze data in Excel using data tables, Goal Seek, and the Solver add-in, as well as how to avoid or utilize circular references.

✦ Data tables are useful only in circumstances in which you have a tightly limited series of fixed variables to test.

✦ Data table formulas must be set up in a specific location in relation to the variables to be tested. If the original data on which the formula is based is in a column, the variables must also be in a column; if it is in a row, then the variables must be in a row.

✦ Goal Seek allows you to rapidly and easily test for the results of changing a single variable regardless of the structure of the worksheet you're using it on. Just specify the value you're seeking and the variable you're willing to change to achieve it, and Goal Seek finds the best answer automatically.

✦ Solver is an add-in that performs the same actions as Goal Seek, but offers far more flexibility and power. You can use it to alter multiple variables in the search for a particular result, and those variables can be constrained to remain within certain limitations you specify.

✦ Circular references occur when a formula is dependent upon itself, either directly or indirectly, for its answer.

✦ Although Excel normally treats circular references as an error, you can use the Iteration option to allow them to be processed.

✦ The Circular Reference toolbar provides you with the capability to trace the operation of a circular reference so that you can correct it.

✦   ✦   ✦

Excel at Work

As you've seen in the preceding chapters in this part of the book, Excel is an excellent tool for solving real-world problems. In this chapter you'll learn how to create worksheets that demonstrate cash flow management, break-even analysis, and mortgage amortization; and how to extract data from a Web page into an Excel worksheet.

Managing Cash Flow

Managing cash flow is the basic bookkeeping chore every business has to do. Keeping track of incoming and outgoing funds in Excel is an easy process. The worksheet in Figure 18-1 is designed for monthly cash flow tracking.

The final balance from the preceding month is entered in cell E3 as the current month's starting balance. Column A holds the date, and column B the description of the transaction. Column C is used to enter credits, and column D is used to enter debits. Column E contains a formula that tracks the current balance. Format column A for dates and columns C, D, and E for currency.

Entering labels and formulas

Enter the following labels and formulas into the cells as shown:

Cell	Entry
A1	Cash Flow Worksheet
A2	Date
B2	Description
C2	Credit
D2	Debit
E2	Balance
E4	=E3+C4-D4

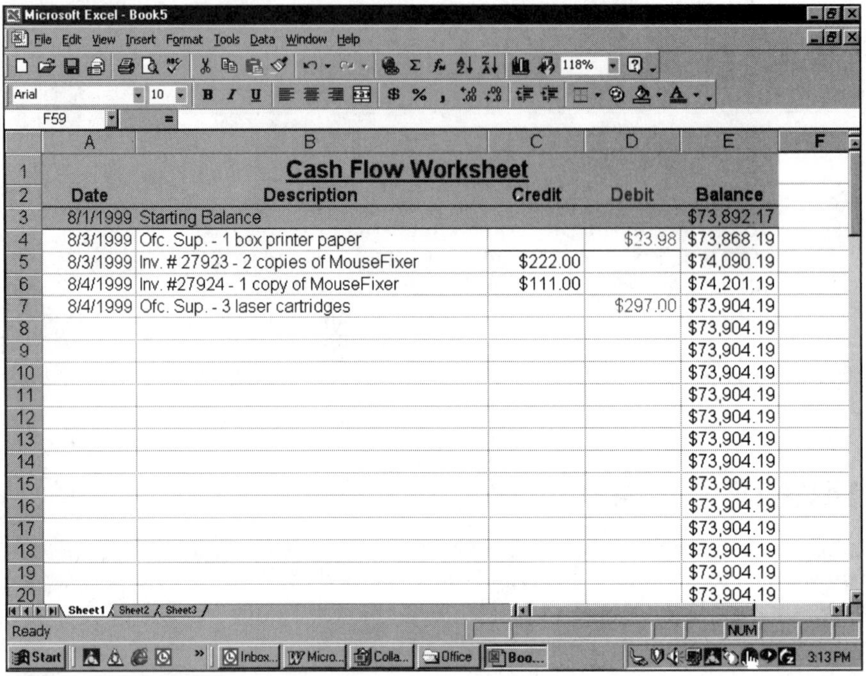

Figure 18-1: Cash flow analysis worksheet.

This worksheet is designed for 100 entries, so you'll need to copy the formula in cell E4 into the 99 cells below it. To do so, select E4 through E103, and then choose Edit ⇨ Fill ⇨ Down from the menu.

Formatting the worksheet

To format the worksheet, do the following:

✦ To help differentiate the debits from the credits at a glance, select cells D2 through D103 and set the font color to red.

✦ The headings have some cosmetic touches applied to them. To make the words "Cash Flow Worksheet" look like the ones in the example, select cell A1 and change the font to underlined, bold 14-point. Next, select cells A1 through E1 and click the Merge and Center button on the toolbar.

✦ To dress up the column labels, select cells A2 through E2, set the font to bold, and then click the Center alignment button on the toolbar.

✦ To differentiate the line that holds the starting balance from the rest of the entries, select cells A3 through E3 and give those cells top and bottom borders.

✦ To offset the heading area from the data entry cells, select cells A1 through E3 and give them a light gray background.

Protecting the worksheet

Finally, once you've entered the starting balance, you can protect it from being altered. Remember that all cells are, by default, protected, but the protection isn't active until the worksheet is protected. Select cells A4 through E103 and remove the protection from them, and then turn on protection for the worksheet.

A Break-Even Analysis

Break-even analyses are used to determine the amount of sales needed to cover operating costs. Operating costs consist of *fixed costs* and *variable costs*. Fixed costs are those like rent and salaries, which neither increase nor decrease regardless of how many sales you make. Variable costs, on the other hand, are things like packaging and shipping expenses, which increase with increased sales and decrease with decreased sales.

Determining the basic formula

The basic formula for figuring out the quantity of unit sales required to equal operating costs is fixed costs divided by selling price of the product minus variable costs, or $F/(p-c)$. The worksheet in Figure 18-2 improves on this basic formula to provide a total overview of the production/profit picture in light of the break-even concept. The heart of the break-even analysis is in cell E10, which shows the number of sales necessary to break even.

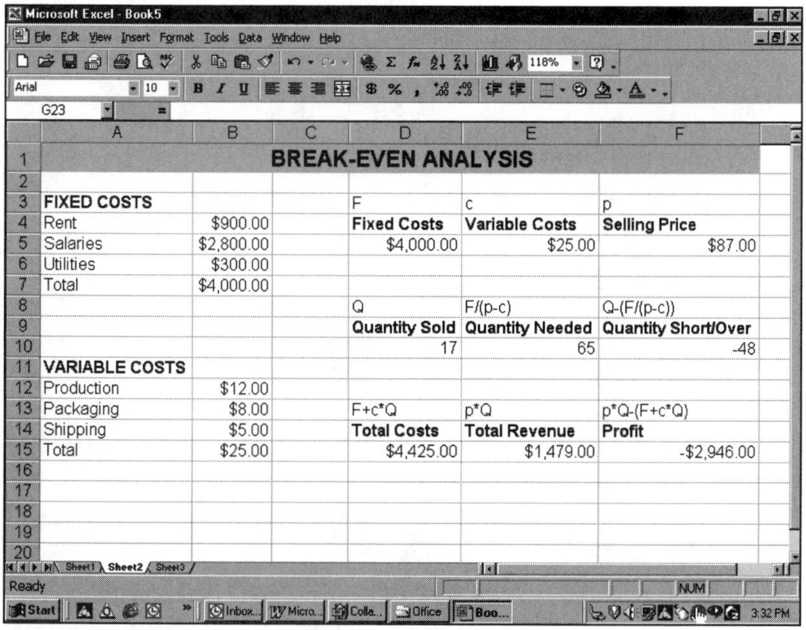

Figure 18-2: Break-even analysis worksheet.

Setting up the columns

To construct this worksheet, format column B and cells D5, E5, F5, D15, E15, and F15 for currency. Format cells D10, E10, and F10 as numbers with no decimals.

Entering the labels and formulas

Enter the following labels and formulas into the cells as shown:

Cell	Entry
A1	BREAK-EVEN ANALYSIS
A3	FIXED COSTS
A4	Rent
A5	Salaries
A6	Utilities
A7	Total
A11	VARIABLE COSTS
A12	Production
A13	Packaging
A14	Shipping
A15	Total
B4	900
B5	2800
B6	300
B7	=B4+B5+B6
B12	12
B13	8
B14	5
B15	=B12+B13+B14
D3	F
D4	Fixed Costs
D5	=B7
E3	c
E4	Variable Costs

Cell	Entry
E5	=B15
F3	p
F4	Selling Price
F5	87
D8	Q
D9	Quantity Sold
D10	17
E8	F/(p-c)
E9	Quantity Needed
E10	=D5/(F5-E5)
F8	Q-(F/(p-c))
F9	Quantity Short/Over
F10	=D10-E10
D13	F+c*Q
D14	Total Costs
D15	=D5+E5*D10
E13	p*Q
E14	Total Revenue
E15	=F5*D10
F13	p*Q-(F+c*Q)
F14	Profit
F15	=E15-D15

Note　Feel free to substitute other values for the ones in the fixed-cost cells (B4, B5, and B6), the variable-cost cells (B12, B13, and B14), the selling price (F5), and the quantity of units sold (D10). These are arbitrary values for demonstration purposes only. Do not change any of the cells containing Excel formulas, however.

Formatting the worksheet

To dress up the worksheet a little bit, make the labels in cells A3, A11, D4 through F4, D9 through F9, and D14 through F14 bold. The main heading in cell A1 can be made bold 14-point, given a gray background, and centered across the worksheet by selecting cells A1 through F1 and clicking the Merge and Center button on the toolbar.

Mortgage Analysis

Mortgage amortization is the schedule of payments required to retire the debt over a period of time. Figure 18-3 shows a typical mortgage amortization schedule. The principal (initial amount borrowed) is in cell B4, the interest rate is in cell C4, and the number of monthly payments is in D4. The formula in cell E4 applies the PMT function to these figures to determine the monthly payment. The formula is =PMT((C4/12),D4,B4). The interest rate is divided by 12 because it is an annual interest rate and we need to determine the monthly rate.

The mortgage in this example is for $100,000.00 and becomes effective on September 1, 1998, with the first payment being due on October 1, 1998. Because there is a different number of days in the payment period from month to month, we need to factor that into the interest charges (a 28-day payment has substantially smaller interest charges than a 31-day payment, even though both are a "month"). Column B gives the number of days that have passed since the prior payment was made; thus, it shows 28 days for the March 1 payment, as 28 days have passed since the February 1 payment.

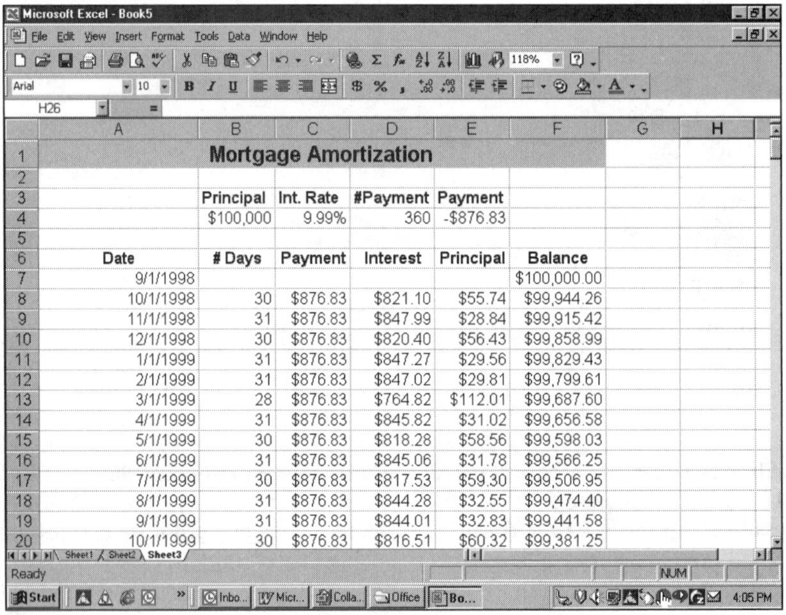

Mortgage Amortization

	Principal	Int. Rate	#Payment	Payment	
	$100,000	9.99%	360	-$876.83	
Date	**# Days**	**Payment**	**Interest**	**Principal**	**Balance**
9/1/1998					$100,000.00
10/1/1998	30	$876.83	$821.10	$55.74	$99,944.26
11/1/1998	31	$876.83	$847.99	$28.84	$99,915.42
12/1/1998	30	$876.83	$820.40	$56.43	$99,858.99
1/1/1999	31	$876.83	$847.27	$29.56	$99,829.43
2/1/1999	31	$876.83	$847.02	$29.81	$99,799.61
3/1/1999	28	$876.83	$764.82	$112.01	$99,687.60
4/1/1999	31	$876.83	$845.82	$31.02	$99,656.58
5/1/1999	30	$876.83	$818.28	$58.56	$99,598.03
6/1/1999	31	$876.83	$845.06	$31.78	$99,566.25
7/1/1999	30	$876.83	$817.53	$59.30	$99,506.95
8/1/1999	31	$876.83	$844.28	$32.55	$99,474.40
9/1/1999	31	$876.83	$844.01	$32.83	$99,441.58
10/1/1999	30	$876.83	$816.51	$60.32	$99,381.25

Figure 18-3: Mortgage analysis worksheet.

To construct this worksheet, format cells A7 through A367 for dates, cells B4, E4, and C7 through F367 for currency, and cell C4 for percentage.

Entering the labels and formulas

Enter the following labels and formulas into the cells as shown:

Cell	Entry
A1	Mortgage Amortization
B3	Principal
C3	Int. Rate
D3	# Payments
E3	Payment
B4	100000
C4	9.99%
D4	360
E4	=PMT((C4/12),D4,B4)
A6	Date
B6	# Days
C6	Payment
D6	Interest
E6	Principal
F6	Balance
A7	9/1/1998
F7	100000
B8	30
C8	=-E4
D8	=(F7)*(C$4/365*(B8))
E8	=C8-D8
F8	=F7-E8

To fill in the dates in column A, select cells A7 through A367. Next, select Edit ➪ Fill ➪ Series from the menu. In the dialog box, select the Columns, Date, and Month radio buttons and click the OK button.

For the number of days per month in column B, format cells B8 through B367 for numbers, then enter the formula =A8-A7 in B8. Next, select Edit ➪ Fill ➪ Down. The correct number of days elapsed since the prior payment for each month will appear in column B. Excel even takes leap years into account!

To extend the payments in cell C8 to the rest of the column, select cells C8 through C367. Next, select Edit ➪ Fill ➪ Down from the menu. Follow the same procedure for columns D, E, and F, except of course that you'll be selecting D8 through D367 when you fill the values for column D, E8 through E367 when you fill the values for column E, and F8 through F367 when you fill the values for column F.

Formatting the worksheet

Once again, you can dress up the worksheet's appearance by making the labels in cells B3 through E3 and cells A6 through F6 bold. The main heading in cell A1 can be made bold 14-point, given a gray background, and centered across the worksheet by selecting cells A1 through F1 and clicking the Merge and Center button on the toolbar.

Web Queries

Excel has the ability to extract data from Web pages. The Web page shown in Figure 18-4, for instance, includes a table in addition to its text.

Figure 18-4: A Web page with a table.

Although the table in the actual file is in HTML format, Excel can get at its data anyway. To do so, follow these steps:

1. Select Data ⇨ Get External Data ⇨ New Web Query from the menu.

2. In the New Web Query dialog box (see Figure 18-5), enter the address of the Web page.

3. Click the radio button labeled "Only the tables." This tells Excel to extract only those materials it finds between <TABLE></TABLE> tags or <PRE></PRE> tags in the HTML file, and to ignore everything else on the Web page.

4. Click the None radio button so the formatting of the Web page is not brought along with the data.

5. If desired, click the Advanced button to access more options, as shown in Figure 18-6. The default settings deal with handling text between <PRE> and </PRE> tags, which is considerably rarer than tables on the Web. The Disable date recognition checkbox insures that numbers that appear similar to dates on the Web page aren't turned into dates when they're imported into Excel.

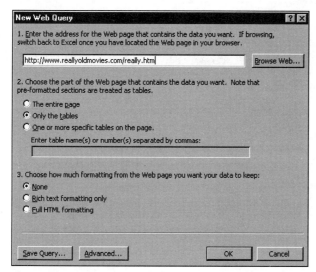

Figure 18-5: The New Web Query dialog box.

6. Click the OK button to return to the New Web Query dialog box.

7. Click on the OK button in the New Web Query dialog box.

8. The Returning External Data to Microsoft Excel dialog box appears, as shown in Figure 18-7. Click on the Existing Worksheet radio button to place the Web data in the current worksheet or click on the New Worksheet radio button to place it in a new worksheet.

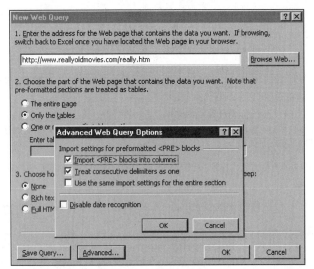

Figure 18-6: The Advanced Web Query Options dialog box.

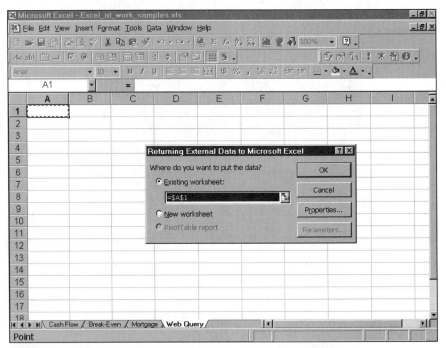

Figure 18-7: The Returning External Data to Microsoft Excel dialog box.

9. If you selected the Existing Worksheet radio button, the reference from the cell that will hold the upper left-hand entry from the Web table is shown (this will be whatever cell was selected at the time you initiated the Web query). If you prefer another cell, select it now.

10. If desired, click the Properties button to specify qualities such as data refresh options.

11. In the External Data Range Properties dialog box (see Figure 18-8), choose how often to refresh data from the Web page by setting a value in the Refresh Every box.

12. The three radio buttons near the bottom of the dialog box specify how to handle changing table size and contents. By default, this is set at "Insert cells for new data, delete unused cells." You can, however, select either "Insert entire rows for new data, clear unused cells" or "Overwrite existing cells with new data, clear unused cells."

13. Click the OK button to return to the Returning External Data to Microsoft Excel dialog box.

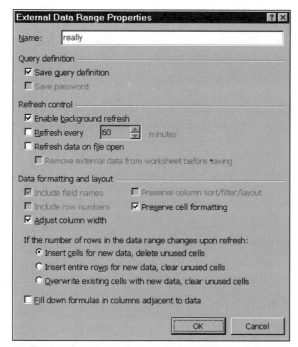

Figure 18-8: The External Data Range Properties dialog box.

14. Click the OK button in the Returning External Data to Microsoft Excel dialog box.

15. The data from the Web table is extracted and pasted into the worksheet as shown in Figure 18-9.

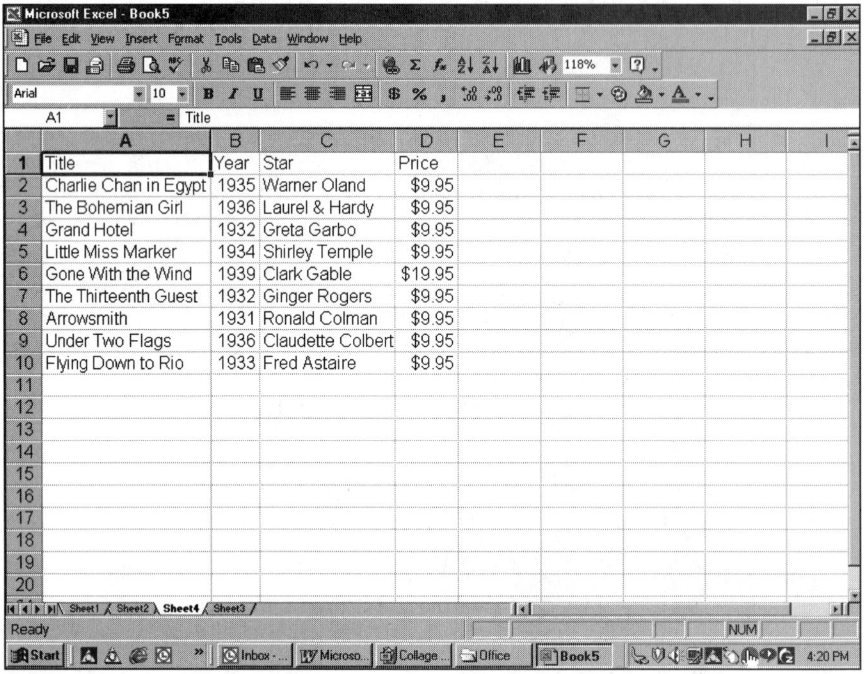

Figure 18-9: Extracted Web table data pasted into a worksheet.

Summary

In this chapter, you learned how to apply Excel techniques to solve real-world problems. Key points of the chapter included the following:

✦ Excel makes it easy to manage cash flow.

✦ You can create a worksheet that demonstrates break-even analysis.

✦ You can create a worksheet that demonstrates mortgage amortization.

✦ Extracted data from a Web page is easily inserted into an Excel worksheet.

✦　　✦　　✦

Excel Top 10

In the final chapter in the Excel portion of this book, we offer answers to ten of the most pressing questions asked about Excel. Should you find that your question or questions are not addressed in this chapter (or in any of the preceding chapters on Excel), please consult the lists of commonly asked questions and their answers presented by Microsoft on the World Wide Web at http://support.microsoft.com.

How Do I Automatically Open a Workbook When I Start Excel?

The official way to accomplish this is to place the workbook file in the XLStart folder. In a normal installation on a typical system, this folder is located at C:\Program Files\Microsoft Office\Office\XLStart.

You can also designate another folder as an alternate startup folder, and any files in it that can be opened by Excel will be opened just as though they were in the XLStart folder. To do this, select Tools ➪ Options from the menu, click the General tab, and enter the path to the folder under Alternate Startup File Location. Click the OK button, shut down Excel, wait a minute, and then start it up again, and your files will load automatically on start-up.

Tip   Be aware that Excel will open every workbook, chart, etc., that it finds in these folders, so it's a good idea to keep them pretty lean.

How Do I Remove All Worksheet Comments at Once?

Select the area of the worksheet containing the cells with comments. If you want to get fancy about it, you can specifically target just the cells containing comments. Select Edit ➪ Go To from the menu. In the Go To dialog box, click the Special button. In the Go To Special dialog box, select the Comments radio button and click the OK button. This will select every cell in the worksheet that has a comment attached.

Next, select Edit ➪ Clear ➪ Comments from the menu. That's all there is to it.

How Do I Stop AutoCorrect from Messing with My Data?

If you think AutoCorrect is a blessing, skip to the next question. If you find yourself cursing Excel every time it thinks it knows what you want to type better than you do, read on. To get to the root of the problem, select Tools ➪ AutoCorrect from the menu. This brings up the AutoCorrect dialog box, which is where the rules that affect the automatic corrections are found.

At the top are some check boxes for global corrections such as "Correct TWo INitial CApitals." Clear any check boxes for global corrections you don't want taking place while you type. At the bottom is a long list of misspellings and the corrected versions that will automatically take precedence. Scroll down through the list and look for anything you don't want done. Select it and click the Delete button. When you're finished, click the OK button.

How Do I Find a Range When I Know Its Name but Not Its Location?

If you have so many named ranges that they've gone missing in your worksheet, you have a friend in the Go To menu option. Select Edit ➪ Go To from the menu. In the Go To dialog box, all the named ranges are listed. Select the one you want to go to and click the OK button (or just double-click on the name of the range).

How Do I Clear the Formats of Cells?

You've probably noticed the hard way that when you delete the data in a cell, you don't remove the formatting from it. When you enter new data into that cell, it's going to be the same format as the old data, even though the cell looks nice and empty. To empty it of the formatting as well as the data, you need to clear it, not delete it.

To clear cells, select the ones you want to clear, and then choose Edit ➪ Clear from the menu. This presents you with a submenu where you can decide what it is you want to clear. To delete the data and clear the formats, select All. To clear the formatting, but leave the data intact, select Formats.

How Do I Find All Cells That Fit a Particular Value?

First you need to put that value into a cell in the range you want to check. You can insert a column or a row to create a new blank cell you can use. Say, for the sake of argument, that you want to find every cell that doesn't contain the word "lumber." You'd type "lumber" into a cell, and then select the range and make the cell in which you typed "lumber" the active cell.

 Note   Unfortunately, you cannot simply check an entire regular range—you can only check the row or column the cell is in.

From here, select Edit ➪ Go To from the menu. In the Go To dialog box, click the Special button. In the Go To Special dialog box, you have two options. You have to pick either the Row Differences or the Column Differences radio button. Next, click the OK button. All cells in the row or column, whichever option you chose, that do not match the value in the active cell in that row or column will be selected.

How Do I Access Lotus 1-2-3 Help?

If you're new to Excel and are used to working with Lotus spreadsheets, you'll appreciate the nice people at Microsoft who decided to make the transition a bit easier. You can access Lotus 1-2-3 help from the Help menu at any time. Just select Help ➪ Lotus 1-2-3 Help.

To turn on an easier method, select Tools ➪ Options from the menu, click the Transition tab, and click the Lotus 1-2-3 Help radio button. Click the OK button to finish the procedure. From now on, whenever you press the slash (/)key in a cell, the Help for Lotus 1-2-3 Users dialog box will instantly appear.

Note   This doesn't affect the normal usage of the slash character, by the way, as in dates— Lotus 1-2-3 Help is activated only if the slash is the first character typed in a cell.

Why Can't I Add a Data Table to My Chart?

Not all chart types can have a data table appended to them. Unless your chart type is column, bar, line, area, or stock, you're out of luck.

How Do I Keep Excel from Interpreting Numbers with Slashes As Dates?

Actually, it's numbers with colons, too. Excel thinks they're times, just as it thinks any numbers with slashes are dates. This can be a real problem when you're dealing with things like government specifications, which are heavily into slashes as separators. The solution is simple, and boils down to an ounce of prevention.

The default formatting for cells in Excel worksheets is General, and it's in that format that Excel interprets slashes as belonging in dates, and colons as belonging in times. Before you enter any number sequences containing slashes or colons, format the cells you're going to be using with the Text format instead of the General format. Excel knows that anything in a text-formatted cell isn't a time or a date.

How Do I Define the Print Area on My Worksheet?

To set the area of your worksheet that will come out of your printer if you click the Print button, select the range you want to print, and then choose File ➪ Print Area ➪ Set Print Area from the menu.

To reverse the operation, choose File ➪ Print Area ➪ Clear Print Area from the menu.

✦　　✦　　✦

PowerPoint

P A R T

In This Part

Chapter 20
Beginning a
Presentation

Chapter 21
Entering and
Formatting Text

Chapter 22
Using Templates and
Wizards

Chapter 23
Charts and Tables

Chapter 24
Adding Graphics
and Special Effects

Chapter 25
Creating and
Organizing a Slide
Show

Chapter 26
PowerPoint at Work

Chapter 27
PowerPoint Top 10

Beginning a Presentation

◆ ◆ ◆ ◆

In This Chapter

Choosing a
slide layout

Using outlines to plan
and organize

Saving a presentation

Navigating through
a presentation

◆ ◆ ◆ ◆

PowerPoint is what's called *presentation software*. It could just as easily be called *communications software* (if that wouldn't get it confused with Internet browsers and terminal programs), because the goal of a presentation is the effective communication of ideas. PowerPoint lets you present your ideas clearly and concisely, augmented by pictures, sound— even video. In this chapter, you'll look at some of the basic tools PowerPoint provides for the construction of a presentation; in later chapters in this section, you'll learn to work with the various elements of a presentation in more detail.

Choosing a Slide Layout

When you first start PowerPoint, it offers you three ways to begin a presentation: AutoContent Wizard, Design Template, or Blank Presentation (see Figure 20-1). For now, click Blank Presentation; we'll look at the other two options in later chapters.

Cross-Reference For more information on Design Templates and AutoContent Wizard, see Chapter 22, "Using Templates and Wizards."

Using AutoLayout

Once you've chosen Blank Presentation and clicked OK, PowerPoint offers you a number of AutoLayouts to choose from (see Figure 20-2). These are pre-designed slides whose placeholder contents you can replace with your own.

The New Slide dialog box shows you thumbnail-sized previews of each AutoLayout to help you make your selection. The title of each AutoLayout also tells you exactly what it's designed for, e.g., Title Slide, Chart, Organization Chart, etc.

Click on the slide you want to use, and then click OK, or double-click on the slide of your choice.

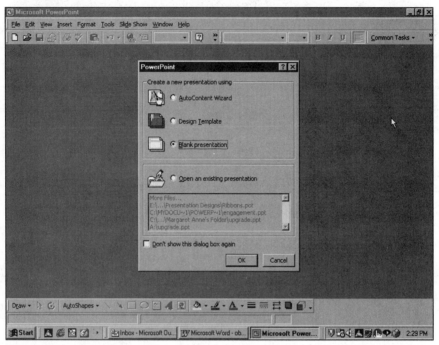

Figure 20-1: PowerPoint offers you three ways to begin a presentation.

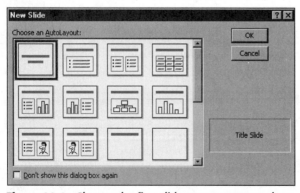

Figure 20-2: Choose the first slide you want to work on in your new presentation from the New Slide dialog box.

Working with Normal view

Once you've chosen an AutoLayout, you'll see PowerPoint's Normal view (see Figure 20-3), which actually combines three views:

✦ **Outline view.** This section, in the leftmost pane of the Normal View window, displays your presentation as an outline, with the titles of slides as the main headings and the text on the slides as subheadings. Outline View can really help you create a well-organized presentation; we'll look at it in detail in the next section of this chapter.

✦ **Slide view.** This pane shows you the slide you're currently working on. (In Figure 20-3, it's from the AutoLayout called Clip Art & Text.)

✦ **Notes view.** Notes are textual information related to the current slide. They don't appear when the presentation is displayed on a screen, but they can be printed out as handouts or to serve as speaker notes for the presenter.

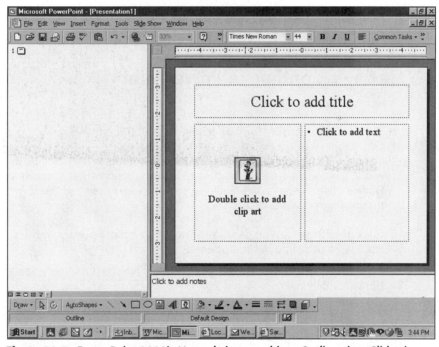

Figure 20-3: PowerPoint 2000's Normal view combines Outline view, Slide view, and Notes view.

Once you've chosen an AutoLayout for your first slide, you're on your way. Enter text, graphics, charts, and tables as you see fit; apply backgrounds, slide transitions, animation and more, and you'll soon have a presentation to be proud of. You'll learn how to work with all of these elements in later chapters in this section.

Using Outlines to Plan and Organize

PowerPoint's ability to turn an outline into a slide presentation makes it a powerful tool you can use to quickly create presentations that clearly communicate your ideas, because you can see those ideas, and their organization, as you work. You can swiftly reorganize a presentation by moving elements of the outline (and hence the slides that go with them).

You have three ways to create an Outline in PowerPoint. You can type it in, begin with an outline from AutoContent Wizard, or import an outline from another program, such as Microsoft Word.

Cross-Reference   For information on creating outlines in Word, see Chapter 5, "Outlines, Tables of Contents, and Indexes."

Creating an outline in PowerPoint

To type in an outline in PowerPoint:

   1. Turn on the Outlining toolbar. Select View ➪ Toolbars ➪ Outlining.

Note   If you don't turn on the Outlining toolbar, the buttons in it will still be available to you in the Standard and Formatting toolbars as soon as you start working in the Outline pane; however, the Outlining toolbar places them right next to the pane, making them easier to access.

   2. Click inside the Outline pane. Your insertion point appears to the right of the small icon of a slide in the upper-left corner.

   3. Type the first main heading of your outline. Notice that it appears at the same time in Slide view (see Figure 20-4).

   4. Press Return. This creates a new slide; type the second main heading of your outline.

   5. Continue adding main headings until the top level of your outline is complete.

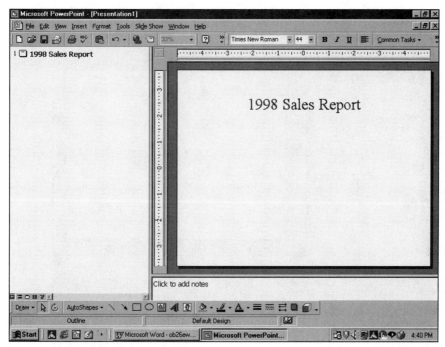

Figure 20-4: The first main heading of your outline also appears as the heading of the first slide in Slide view.

Adding subheads

To add subheads, type the text for the subheads underneath the main head, pressing Return after each subhead. Don't worry about the fact that this creates a lot of new slides.

Once the subheads are typed, select them, and then click the Demote button on the Outlining toolbar (see Figure 20-5). This turns them into subheads on the same slide as the main head above them (see Figure 20-6). You could select one or more and click Demote again to create sub-subheads; you can also turn a subhead back into a main head (creating a new slide in the process) by selecting it and clicking the Promote button on the Outlining toolbar.

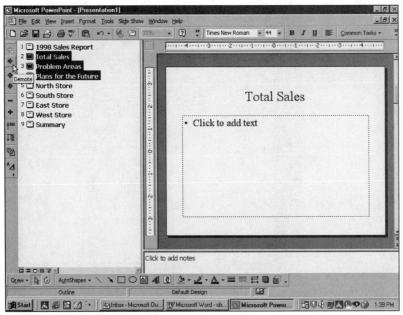

Figure 20-5: Type in subheads just as if they were main heads, then select them and click Demote.

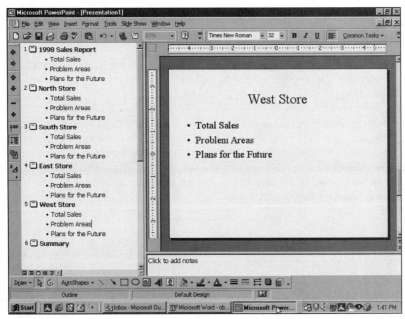

Figure 20-6: Using main heads and subheads creates outlines and slides that look like these.

Importing an outline

To import an outline created in another program, such as Microsoft Word, first make sure the outline you want to import uses heading styles. PowerPoint looks for these styles when deciding which parts of the outline are main heads and which are subheads or body text. To import an outline:

1. Choose File ➪ Open.

2. In the Files of Type box in the Open dialog box, choose All Outlines.

3. Double-click the outline you want to import. The imported outline appears in the Outline pane (if you're in Normal view) in PowerPoint; each major heading appears as an individual slide title, and each subheading appears as bulleted text on the slide (see Figure 20-7).

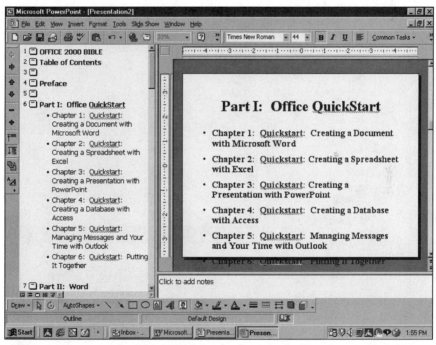

Figure 20-7: Here's what the outline for this book looks like when imported into PowerPoint. Looks like some reformatting is in order!

Tip

You can turn a Word outline (or any other Word document) into a PowerPoint presentation very easily. Open the document in Word, choose File ➪ Send To, and then click Microsoft PowerPoint. Each paragraph using the Heading 1 style becomes the title of a new slide, each paragraph using the Heading 2 style becomes the first level of text, and so on. For more information on using styles in Word, see Chapter 6, "Styles and Templates."

Reorganizing an outline

One of the greatest advantages of using the Outline pane to create your presentation is that it allows you to reorganize it so easily.

Rearranging slides

In the presentation shown in Figure 20-8, a slide entitled "West Store" appears after "East Store." To move the "West Store" slide in front of "East Store," all you have to do is highlight the text on the "West Store" slide and drag it above "East Store." A gray rectangle attaches itself to your mouse pointer to indicate you're moving text, and a horizontal line appears within the outline to show you exactly where you're about to move it to.

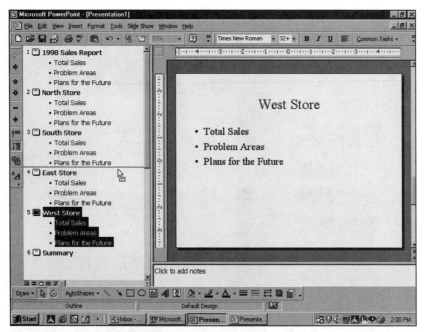

Figure 20-8: You can move slides and text around with ease in PowerPoint's Outline pane by highlighting and dragging.

Rearranging text

To rearrange items that are close to one another, you can also use the Move Up and Move Down arrows on the Outlining toolbar. Clicking these moves highlighted text up or down one line in the outline, without regard for the outline's hierarchy. For example, in Figure 20-9, after you finish relocating the "West Store" slide, you can click Move Down. This slips the selected text under the "East Store" slide title, which has the result of attaching the three subheads from the "East Store" slide to the "West Store" slide.

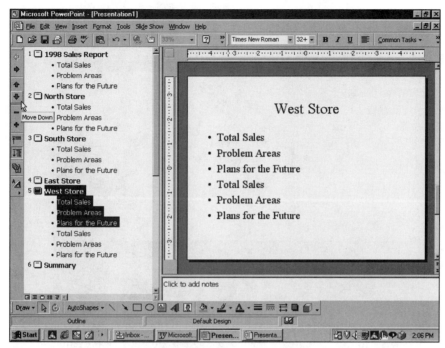

Figure 20-9: Move Up and Move Down rearranges outline items one line at a time.

Hiding subheads and text

To get a better idea of the "big picture" of your presentation's organization structure, you sometimes need to hide subheads and body text in the outline. Use the Collapse and Expand buttons to hide everything except the slide titles for the selected text; use the Collapse All and Expand All buttons to hide everything except the slide titles in the entire outline (see Figure 20-10).

Formatting text within an outline

By default, your outline appears in a simple, sans-serif screen font. However, by clicking the Show Formatting button at the bottom of the Outlining toolbar, you can see how the slide titles and body text of all your slides are formatted. Compare Figure 20-11, which shows formatting, with Figure 20-9 or 20-8, which doesn't.

Whether Show Formatting is on or off, you can format text in Outline view just as you would on the slide itself, choosing the font, size, and style. (Note that even with Show Formatting on, changes to the font color show up only in the Slide pane, not in the Outline pane, where text is always black.)

Cross-Reference For more information on working with text in PowerPoint, see Chapter 21, "Entering and Formatting Text."

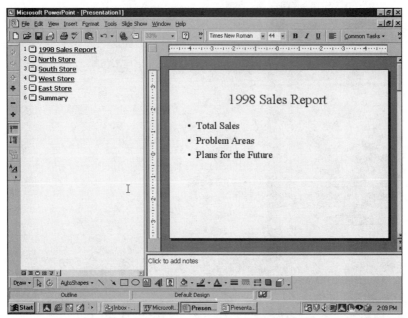

Figure 20-10: Collapse All hides everything in your outline but the slide titles, which makes it much easier to see the overall organization of your presentation and move slides around within it.

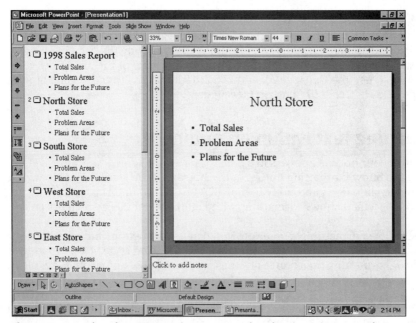

Figure 20-11: The Show Formatting command makes it easier to see how text is formatted throughout your presentation.

Saving a Presentation

As soon as you've started your presentation, you should save it — and keep saving often. Maybe your computer has never crashed or hung up, or maybe the power has never failed unexpectedly in your office, but it certainly has in mine, and nothing is more frustrating than losing hours of work because you failed to take a second or two to save it.

Of course, before you save your work you need to know how you want to save it, because PowerPoint offers you three options on the File menu:

✦ **Save.** This is the command you'll use most often; it's also the command you access by clicking the button with the image of a floppy disk on it on the Standard toolbar. Clicking this the first time opens the Save As dialog box (see Figure 20-12), which prompts you to enter a name for your file and indicate where you want to save it. Do so, and then click Save. After you've named your file, clicking Save on the toolbar overwrites the existing copy of the file with a new copy of the file that contains any changes you've made since the last Save.

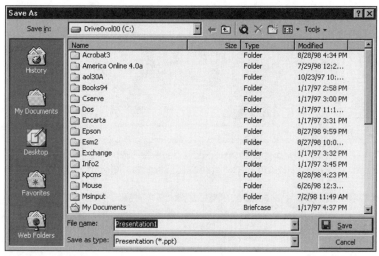

Figure 20-12: The Save As dialog box lets you name your presentation and choose a location in which to save it.

✦ **Save As.** Even if you've already saved your presentation once, this opens the Save As dialog box. You can choose to save your presentation in a number of formats (see Sidebar) using the Save as Type box. Enter a name to save your presentation under, choose the format you want, and then click Save. If you've already saved your presentation, your original file remains untouched; PowerPoint simply saves a new copy under the new name you've provided in the new format you've selected.

✦ **Save As Web Page.** Choose this if you'd like to turn your presentation into Web pages. This opens a slightly different version of the Save As dialog box, with two new options (see Figure 20-13), Publish and Change. Click Change to give your new Web-based presentation a title other than the title of the first slide, which PowerPoint uses by default. Click Publish if you're ready to go ahead and place your presentation on the Web. This saves a copy of your presentation, after which you are asked to make a number of choices to determine exactly how your presentation should be modified for viewing online.

Cross-Reference

For detailed information on the Publish command, and creating a Web site from a PowerPoint presentation, see Chapter 26, "PowerPoint at Work."

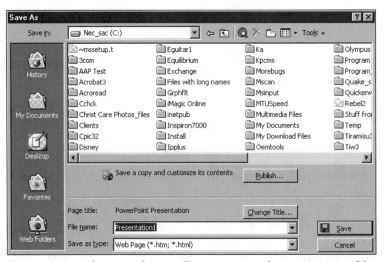

Figure 20-13: When you choose File ➪ Save As Web Page, you see this slightly modified version of the standard Save As dialog box.

File Formats for Saving Presentations

PowerPoint lets you save presentations in any one of several formats. These include the following:

✦ *Presentation (.ppt).* This is the standard format for PowerPoint presentations.

✦ *Windows Metafile (.wmf).* This saves slides as graphics.

✦ *GIF Graphics Interchange Format (.gif), JPEG File Interchange Format (.jpg),* and *PNG Portable Network Graphic Format (.png).* These save slides as graphics readily viewable by Web browsers.

✦ *Outline/RTF (.rtf).* This saves the presentation outline as an outline, but doesn't save any graphics.

✦ *Design Template (.pot).* This saves the presentation as a template, which can then be used as a guide for the creation of other presentations.

✦ *PowerPoint Show (.pps).* Presentations saved in this format always open automatically as a slide show.

✦ *Web Page (.htm).* This saves presentations in a form readable by a Web browser.

Navigating Through a Presentation

You have several ways to move from slide to slide in a presentation in Normal view. You can also use Slide Sorter view to easily find your way around. Here's how it works:

✦ The easiest way to navigate in Normal view is to use the Outline pane. Find the title of the slide you want to see and click anywhere within the title or any of the subheads that appear on that slide. The slide will automatically appear in the Slide View pane.

✦ You can also use the scrollbars to the right of the Slide View pane. Scrolling down will take you to each slide in turn; they're arranged in one long vertical column. You can also click the Next Slide and Previous Slide buttons at the bottom of the scrollbar to jump quickly, one slide at a time, up and down in the presentation.

✦ Slide Sorter view shows you thumbnail versions of all your slides (or as many as will fit on one screen) at once. To access Slide Sorter view, choose View ➪ Slide Sorter. Slide Sorter view is particularly useful when you're fine-tuning your slide show, because it allows you to set a number of properties for each slide, and easily move them from place to place. (To open any slide in Normal view, just double-click on it in Slide Sorter view.)

Cross-Reference For detailed information on using Slide Sorter view, see Chapter 25, "Creating and Organizing a Slide Show."

Summary

In this chapter you learned how to begin the process of creating a PowerPoint presentation, plus how to use Outline view to plan and organize it, save it, and move around in it while it's under construction. Highlights included the following:

✦ PowerPoint's AutoLayouts are pre-designed slides into which you can enter your own text, graphics, and other elements. Whenever you start a blank presentation, the first thing you're asked to do is choose an AutoLayout for the first slide.

✦ PowerPoint 2000's Normal view is different from previous versions of the software: it's actually a combination of three views, Outline, Slide, and Notes.

✦ Outlines are very useful for creating and organizing presentations. You can type an outline directly into the Outline Pane of Normal view. Although you create a new slide every time you press Return, you can create the different levels of the outline by highlighting text you want to turn into subheads and clicking Demote.

✦ You can import outlines from other applications that use heading styles, such as Word. PowerPoint uses Heading 1 style for slide titles; text formatted with lower heading levels appears on the slides as bulleted subheads.

✦ You can highlight and drag text within an outline to reorganize it (and your presentation), or you can use the Move Up and Move Down buttons to move text up and down a line at a time within the outline.

✦ By collapsing an outline, you can hide all text except slide titles.

✦ You can get a quick overview of the formatting applied to all your slides by clicking the Show Formatting button on the Outlining toolbar.

✦ PowerPoint lets you save presentations in a number of formats, including standard Web graphics formats, as a slide presentation that automatically launches every time it's opened, in HTML, and in Rich Text format.

✦ You can easily navigate through a PowerPoint presentation using Outline view, the scrollbars in Slide view, or by choosing View ➪ Slide Sorter, which displays miniature versions of all your slides. When in Slide Sorter view, double-click on the slide you want to edit to go directly to that slide in Normal view.

✦   ✦   ✦

Entering and Formatting Text

Many people think of presentations in terms of their visual impact, and certainly that's important, but at the heart of most presentations is text. Remember, the goal of a presentation is to communicate, and our most basic communication tools are words, which makes words rather important to any presentation. Fortunately, PowerPoint makes it easy to enter words, edit words, and (not to leave visual impact entirely out of the picture) make them look great in the bargain!

Entering and Editing Text

As described in the last chapter, one way to enter text in PowerPoint is in the Outline pane of Normal view. You can also enter text directly in Slide view by choosing an AutoLayout that includes text or drawing a text box in an existing slide. Once text is entered, you can edit it just as you would in a word processor. If you're editing in the Slide View pane, clicking on any text will automatically select its text box; if you're editing in the Outline pane, just place your insertion point where you want to make changes.

Entering text in the Outline pane

Text you type into the outline is automatically added to the slides in the presentation. By highlighting text and clicking the Demote button on the Outlining toolbar, you can create subheadings in the outline, which appear on the slide as bulleted lists underneath the slide titles (see Figure 21-1).

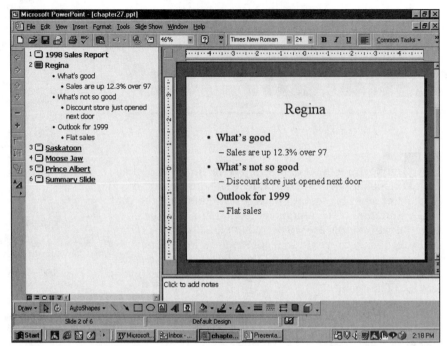

Figure 21-1: Entering text in the Outline pane of Normal view also enters text on the slides.

Cross-Reference For more information on creating presentations using outlines, see Chapter 20, "Beginning a Presentation."

Entering text in Slide view

You have two ways to enter text in Slide view: choose an AutoLayout that includes text, or draw a text box in an existing slide.

Using AutoLayout

To enter text using AutoLayout:

1. Open the dialog box containing AutoLayouts (see Figure 21-2). It opens automatically when you choose File ➪ New and select Blank Presentation from the New Presentation dialog box; it also opens when you insert a new slide into a presentation by choosing Insert ➪ New Slide, or when you choose Format ➪ Slide Layout with a slide already open.

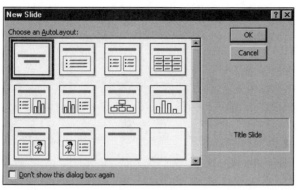

Figure 21-2: PowerPoint provides a variety of AutoLayouts, almost all of which include some text.

2. Choose an AutoLayout that includes text and click OK. This creates a new slide with placeholders where the text is to appear (see Figure 21-3).

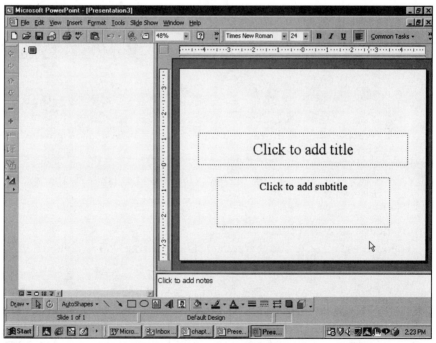

Figure 21-3: AutoLayout creates new slides with placeholders where your text will appear.

3. Click anywhere inside one of these placeholders. The instruction to "Click to add (title, subtitle, text, etc.)" disappears and is replaced with a regular PowerPoint text box, into which you can type your text (see Figure 21-4).

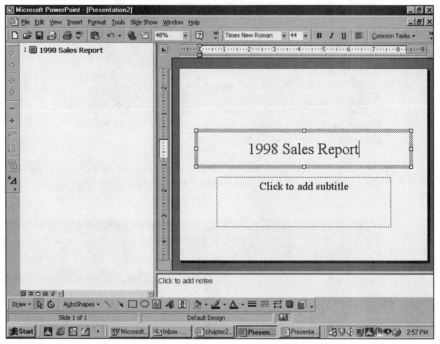

Figure 21-4: Type the text you want to appear on your slide into the boxes provided by AutoLayout.

4. When you're done entering text, click anywhere outside the text box to deselect it.

By drawing a text box

Follow these steps to add text to any slide, whether you're building it from scratch or you created it with AutoLayout:

1. Choose Insert ➪ Text Box. Your mouse pointer changes to what looks (to me, anyway) like a tiny stick drawing of a sword: a long vertical line with a short horizontal line crossing it near the base.

2. Place the pointer wherever you want the insertion point of your new text box to appear, and click once. A small text box will appear, similar to the one that appeared when you clicked inside the placeholder in Step 3 (see Figure 21-5).

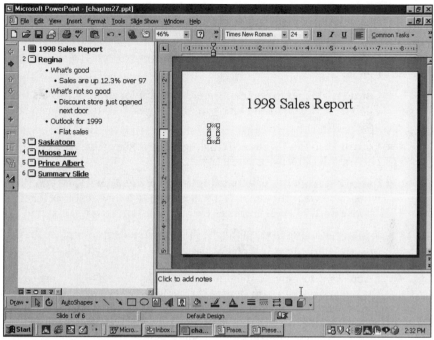

Figure 21-5: When you first create a text box, it's not very prepossessing!

3. Type in your text.

4. Again, when you're done typing in your text, click anywhere outside the text box to deselect it.

Tip

You can draw a text box larger than the one shown in Figure 21-5 by clicking, holding, and dragging your mouse pointer after choosing Insert ➪ Text Box. This can help you visualize where your text will appear, but it's not necessary; the text box will automatically expand to accommodate any text you type into it.

Editing text

Once text is entered, you can edit it just as you would in a word processor. If you're editing in the Slide View pane, clicking on any text will automatically select its text box; if you're editing in the Outline pane, just place your insertion point where you want to make changes. You can perform any of the following:

✦ **Insert new text.** Place your insertion point where you want to add new text, and then type it in. The existing text will move out of the way.

✦ **Delete one character at a time.** Place your insertion point to the left of the first character you want to delete and press Delete. Each time you press Delete, another character to the right of the insertion point will be deleted.

✦ **Delete several words at once.** Highlight the text you want to delete and press Delete.

✦ **Cut text.** This removes text from its current location but saves a copy to the Clipboard. Highlight the text you want to cut, and then choose Edit ➪ Cut or press Ctrl+X.

✦ **Copy text to the Clipboard.** Highlight the text you want to copy, and then choose Edit ➪ Copy or press Ctrl+C.

✦ **Paste text from the Clipboard into a new location.** Place your insertion point where you want the text to appear or create a new text box for it, and then choose Edit ➪ Paste or press Ctrl+V.

✦ **Replace existing text.** Highlight the text you want to replace and either type or paste in the new text. The existing text is automatically deleted.

Tip

If you want to move text from slide to slide, it's generally best to work in the Outline pane, where you can see the contents of several slides at once and easily cut and paste among them. If, on the other hand, you're concerned about how the text looks on a particular slide (where a line of text breaks, for instance), you'll probably want to work in the Slide View pane.

Importing Text from Other Applications

Sometimes the text you want in your presentation already exists elsewhere on your computer as a word processor file. You have several ways to import this text.

By copying and pasting

Probably the easiest way to place this text into your PowerPoint presentation is to open the file in your word processor, copy it to the Clipboard, and then open your PowerPoint presentation and simply paste the text wherever it's supposed to go.

By importing directly to PowerPoint

If you prefer, you can import the file directly into PowerPoint. To do so:

1. Choose Insert ➪ Object.

2. In the Insert Object dialog box, select the Create from File radio button (see Figure 21-6).

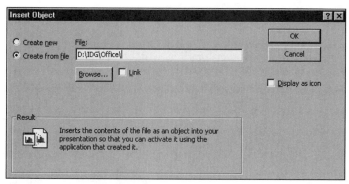

Figure 21-6: Insert existing text into your PowerPoint presentation using the Insert Object dialog box.

3. Use the Browse button to locate and select the word processor file you want to insert.

4. Click OK.

5. The file appears on the current slide (see Figure 21-7).

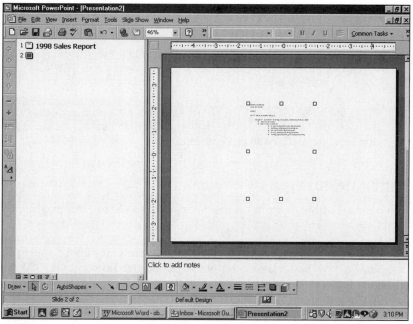

Figure 21-7: This Word file was inserted with the Insert Object command.

Editing imported text

You can't edit this text as you would text you typed into a regular PowerPoint text box. If you single-click on it, you get handles, which you can use to change its size or shape, and you can drag it around on the slide, but you can't change the contents. That's because it's really an embedded object. Because it's still in its original file format, you have to access the controls of the application in which it was created to edit it.

To do so, double-click on it. This opens a miniature window of the program in which it was created (in this case, Word). Now you can edit it using Word's controls. When you're done, click anywhere outside the object.

For detailed information on working with linked and embedded objects, see Chapter 52, "Building Integrated Documents."

Formatting Text

Formatting text can be done in either the Slide View pane or the Outline pane, although if you want to format text in the Outline pane, it's a good idea to click Show Formatting on the Outlining toolbar (the bottom-most button). With Show Formatting selected, the text in the Outline pane looks as it will on the finished slide.

To format text, you must first highlight it. Then click the button on the Formatting toolbar (shown here) that applies the formatting you want. The following sections cover each formatting option.

If you don't see some of the buttons listed here on your Formatting toolbar, click the More Buttons button at the right end of the toolbar to see the rest. If you still don't see them, click Add or Remove Buttons.

Font and size

Two menus and two buttons on the Formatting toolbar determine the font and size used for your text:

> ✦ **Font.** Use this list box to choose the typeface you want to apply to your text: that is, how you want the letters to be formed. PowerPoint 2000 makes the job of selecting a font easier by showing you the names of the fonts in the fonts themselves (see Figure 21-8).

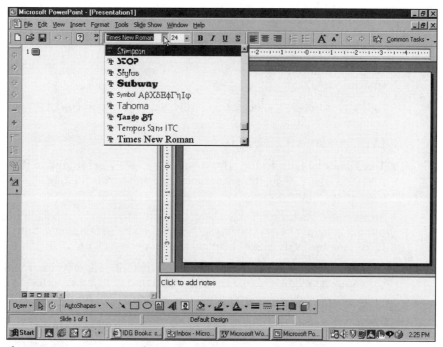

Figure 21-8: PowerPoint shows you not only the names of the fonts you can choose to apply to your text, but what they look like.

✦ **Font Size.** Choose an appropriate size from this list box. Sizes are given in points, which are 1/72 of an inch. In other words, 72-point text is one inch high; 36-point text is half an inch high, and so on. (Note that these sizes apply to printed copy; the size of type displayed on a screen may vary quite a bit, depending on the monitor being used.) You can apply a size that doesn't appear in the list by typing it directly into the Font Size box.

✦ **Increase Font Size.** This button increases the size of selected text to the next largest size in the Font Size list box.

✦ **Decrease Font Size.** This button decreases the size of selected text to the next smallest size in the Font Size list box.

Style and effects

Six buttons change the style of the text or apply special effects:

✦ **Bold.** This button makes text bold. Bold text is thicker and, therefore, darker than nonbold text.

✦ **Italic.** This button italicizes text. Italicized text is made up of thinner lines that slant to the right.

✦ **Underline.** This button underlines text.

✦ **Text Shadow.** This button adds a shadow slightly below and to the right of the text (see Figure 21-9). It makes it look as if the text is floating slightly above the surface of the slide.

✦ **Subscript.** This button makes selected text into subscript: smaller text that appears slightly below the baseline of the text surrounding it. Subscripts are most commonly used for chemical formulae (see Figure 21-10).

✦ **Superscript.** This button makes selected text into superscript: smaller text that appears slightly above the text surrounding it. Superscripts are most commonly used for footnotes and mathematical equations (see Figure 21-10).

Figure 21-9: Text Shadow adds an interesting three-dimensional element to your text.

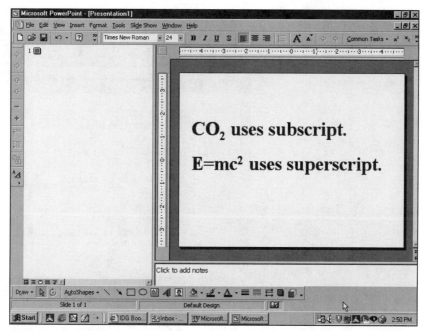

Figure 21-10: Subscript and superscript are among the styles you can apply to text in PowerPoint.

Note The Subscript and Superscript buttons are two buttons you will most likely have to add to the Formatting Toolbar by clicking the More Buttons button and choosing Add or Remove Buttons.

Alignment

PowerPoint also provides several buttons that affect the alignment of text on a slide, beginning with Align Left, Center, and Align Right, as illustrated in Figure 21-11.

✦ **Align Left.** This button aligns text flush against the left side of the text box.

✦ **Center.** This button centers text within the text box.

✦ **Align Right.** This button aligns text flush against the right side of the text box.

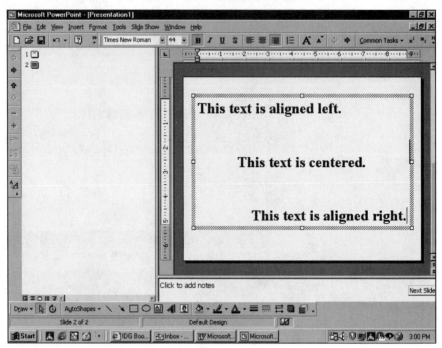

Figure 21-11: Text in PowerPoint is aligned relative to the text box that contains it, not to the outside edges of the slide on which it appears.

Promoting and demoting heads

Many slides are in point form, with a slide title followed by several subheads. The easiest way to edit these kinds of slides and adjust the size of text is in Outline view. However, Slide view has two commands that you may choose to use instead:

✦ **Promote.** This button moves text closer to the left side of the text box, and changes its style to that of the next highest level of text in the Outline hierarchy.

✦ **Demote.** This button moves text further to the right. Each time you click it, it moves the text further right and changes its style to that of the next lowest level of text in the Outline hierarchy (see Figure 21-12).

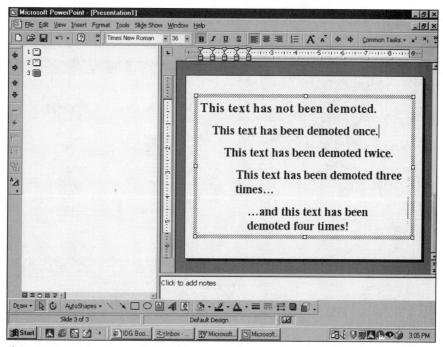

Figure 21-12: The Promote and Demote buttons on the Formatting bar move text further left or further right within the text box (and up or down a level in the Outline hierarchy, which changes the style, too).

Cross-Reference

For more information on using PowerPoint's Outline view to enter text and organize a presentation, see Chapter 20, "Beginning a Presentation."

Bulleted and numbered lists

Use the following steps to create a bulleted list inside a PowerPoint text box:

1. Click the Bullets button. A gray bullet appears in your text box.

2. Type the first list item. The bullet turns black.

3. Press Return. A new gray bullet appears.

4. Continue until the list is complete.

You can create a numbered list in exactly the same way, except, of course, you click the Numbering button in Step 1. You can even combine bulleted and numbered lists (see Figure 21-13).

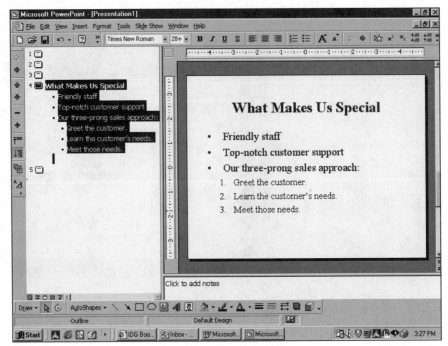

Figure 21-13: Bulleted and numbered lists are easy to create and combine in PowerPoint, to help you present your ideas more clearly.

Spacing

You can automatically increase or decrease the spacing between paragraphs (which PowerPoint defines as any text you enter prior to pressing Return) a little bit at a time, by highlighting the paragraphs, and then clicking Increase Paragraph Spacing or Decrease Paragraph Spacing. (Note that by default these commands are not on the toolbar and must be brought up by clicking More Buttons, and then Add or Remove Buttons.)

Color

You can change the color of any text by highlighting it and then clicking the Font Color button, located on the Drawing toolbar near the bottom of the Normal view screen, instead of on the Formatting toolbar.

Clicking this button applies the color currently shown on the button to the highlighted text. Clicking the down arrow next to the button opens a small menu showing standard colors and recently used colors; clicking More Font Colors from that opens palettes from which you can choose any color your computer can display to apply to your text (see Figure 21-14).

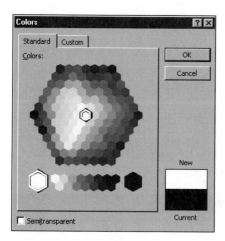

Figure 21-14: The Colors dialog box lets you choose a color for your text from a standard palette of colors like this one, or a custom palette that makes all the colors your computer can display available to you.

The Format menu

Some additional formatting options for text are available by choosing the Format menu. If the Formatting toolbar buttons don't give you enough control over the way your text looks, the Format menu may:

✦ **Font.** The Font dialog box (see Figure 21-15) puts all the controls for Font, Style, Size, Effects, and Color in one location. It also adds a new effect, Emboss, which makes letters look as if they protrude slightly from the surface of the slide (see Figure 21-16). Click Preview to see what the selections you make look like applied to the selected text, without closing the dialog box.

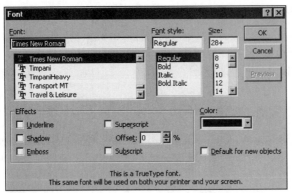

Figure 21-15: The Font dialog box includes many commands you can find on the Formatting toolbar, plus a couple of extra ones, such as the controls for subscripts and superscripts that let you set the exact location of their baselines relative to surrounding text.

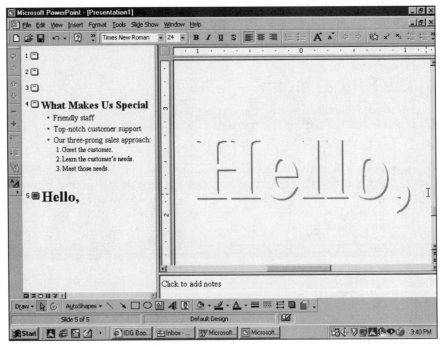

Figure 21-16: A special effect, Emboss, which isn't available from the Formatting toolbar, is also included in the Font dialog box.

✦ **Bullets and Numbering.** The Bullets and Numbering dialog box (see Figure 21-17) lets you fine-tune the look of bulleted and numbered lists. You can select from the bullets offered or find different characters (by clicking Character), or even pieces of ClipArt (by clicking Picture) to use as bullets, and set their size relative to the text and their color. Click the Numbered tab to choose from several types of numerals for numbered lists and set the size, color, and starting number.

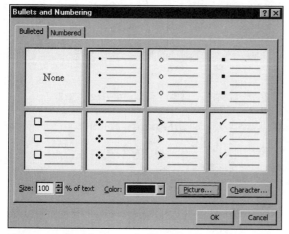

Figure 21-17: Fine-tune bulleted and numbered lists from this dialog box.

✦ **Alignment.** Choose Alignment to apply left and right alignment to text or to center it. From this menu, you can also justify text (make both its left and right edges align with the edges of the text box), an option not available from the Formatting toolbar.

✦ **Line Spacing.** Specify the spacing between lines and before and after paragraphs using this dialog box (see Figure 21-18). You can choose to measure line spacing in either lines or points.

Figure 21-18: Specify line and paragraph spacing with these controls.

✦ **Change Case.** Case refers to the way words are capitalized. PowerPoint offers you several options (see Figure 21-19): sentence case (first letter of first word capitalized), lowercase (no letters capitalized), uppercase (all letters capitalized), title case (first letter of all words capitalized), and toggle case (reverses all letters from the way they were initially typed in: capital letters become lowercase letters and vice versa).

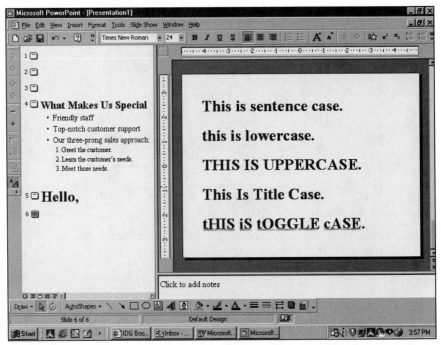

Figure 21-19: PowerPoint offers several different cases to apply to your text.

✦ **Replace Font.** This powerful tool lets you change all instances of a particular font within your presentation to a different font (see Figure 21-20). Just select the font you want to change in the top list box and the font you want to change it to in the bottom.

Figure 21-20: Oops! Don't like the font you originally used? Change it everywhere it appears in your presentation with this helpful tool.

Using WordArt

Another way to add text to a PowerPoint slide is with WordArt. WordArt, as its name implies, combines elements of both words and pictures. It can help you create very beautiful, unusual and eye-catching slides. To add WordArt to a PowerPoint slide:

1. Click the Insert WordArt button on the Drawing toolbar (near the bottom of Normal view).

2. Select a WordArt style from the WordArt Gallery (see Figure 21-21). Click OK.

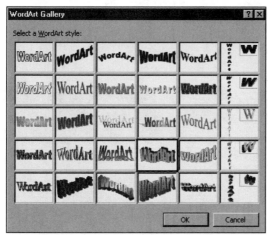

Figure 21-21: PowerPoint offers many different eye-catching WordArt styles to choose from.

3. Enter your text in the Edit WordArt Text dialog box (see Figure 21-22). Choose a font, size, and style (bold or italic). Click OK.

4. Your text appears on your slide, along with the WordArt toolbar (see Figure 21-23), which you can use to further edit its appearance—changing the font, alignment, color, character spacing, and more. You can even rotate it!

5. When you're happy with your WordArt, click anywhere outside its edges to deselect it.

Cross-Reference For a more complete discussion of WordArt, see Chapter 53, "Universal Drawing and Graphics Features."

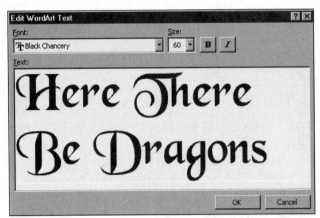

Figure 21-22: Enter the text of your WordArt, and choose a size, font, and style in this dialog box.

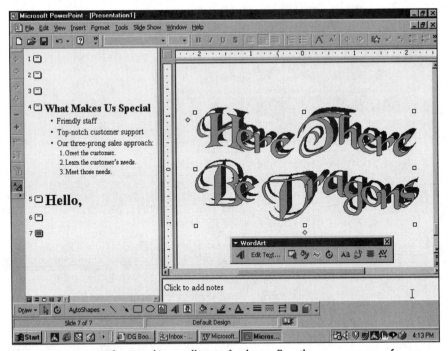

Figure 21-23: Use the WordArt toolbar to further refine the appearance of your WordArt.

Summary

In this chapter you learned about entering, editing, and formatting text in PowerPoint. Some important points included the following:

✦ You can enter text in either Outline or Slide view.

✦ You can enter text by choosing an AutoLayout that includes text, and typing your text into one of the text placeholders, or by drawing your own text box.

✦ You can cut, copy, and paste text within a text box just as you can within a word processor.

✦ You can place an existing word processor file on a PowerPoint slide by choosing Insert ⇨ Object, and then clicking Create from File and choosing the file you want to insert. You can edit that text within PowerPoint using the controls of the application in which it was created.

✦ To format text, highlight it and choose the appropriate command from the Formatting toolbar. You can set font and size using list boxes, and click buttons to make text bold, italic, underlined, shadowed, subscripted, or superscripted; to align text to the left, center, or right; to make it larger or smaller; to increase or decrease paragraph spacing; to promote or demote it (move it left or right and change its style). A button on the Drawing toolbar lets you change the color of text.

✦ You can create bulleted or numbered lists by clicking the appropriate buttons on the Formatting toolbar.

✦ For greater control over formatting, use the various dialog boxes accessed through the Format menu. For example, you can customize bulleted and numbered lists and specify the spacing between lines and before and after paragraphs.

✦ WordArt combines elements of text and pictures to let you add colorful, eye-catching text to your presentation.

✦   ✦   ✦

Using Templates and Wizards

Not everyone has the knack, the knowledge, or especially the time to design a presentation entirely from scratch. Sometimes you just want to enter your information and let PowerPoint do all the work of making it look great. Well, PowerPoint is more than equal to the task, with a number of tools to get your presentation up and running as quickly as possible.

Using AutoContent Wizard

AutoContent Wizard gets you going quickly by providing you with both a design and suggested content for a variety of common presentation types.

Whenever you start PowerPoint, AutoContent Wizard is one of the options you're presented with right off the bat (see Figure 22-1). Select its radio button and click OK. If PowerPoint is already open, you can access AutoContent Wizard by choosing File ➪ New, clicking the General tab in the New Presentation dialog box, and then double-clicking AutoContent Wizard.

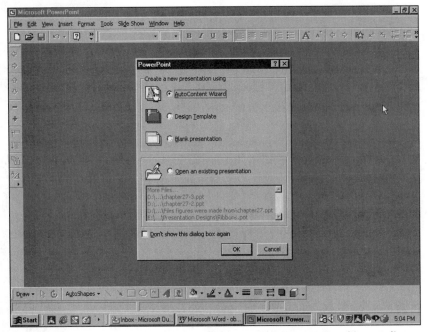

Figure 22-1: Whenever you start PowerPoint, AutoContent Wizard is standing by to help you.

From the introductory screen, click Next to open the first of three screens in which you provide AutoContent Wizard with the information it needs to help you out. The three screens are as follows:

✦ **Presentation type.** Click All (see Figure 22-2) to see all the presentation types AutoContent Wizard can help you create (everything from Recommending a Strategy to a Corporate Home Page to a Project Post-Mortem), or click General, Corporate, Projects, Sales/Marketing or Carnegie Coach to see just the presentations in those areas. (The Carnegie Coach presentations contain content designed to help you hone your own presentation and public speaking abilities.) Choose the presentation type you want and click Next.

✦ **Presentation style.** Presentations can be designed to be displayed on a computer screen, on the Web, as black-and-white handouts, as color transparencies, or even as 35mm slides. Choose the type of final product you're aiming for from this screen (see Figure 22-3); then click Next.

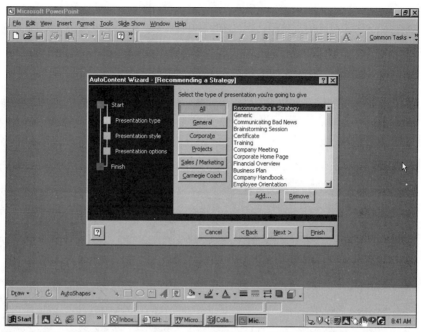

Figure 22-2: What sort of presentation would you like to create? AutoContent Wizard can help you with the most common types.

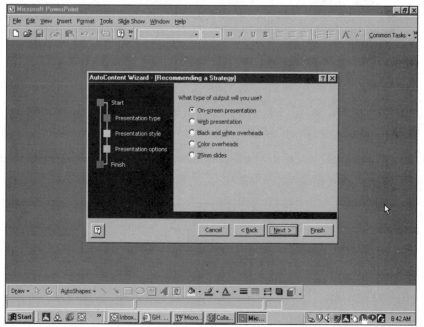

Figure 22-3: AutoContent Wizard will tailor your presentation to suit its final form.

✦ **Presentation options.** In the third and final screen (see Figure 22-4), you enter a title for your presentation and any text you'd like to appear as a footer on each slide, and decide whether you want the date the slide was last updated and the slide number to also appear in the footer.

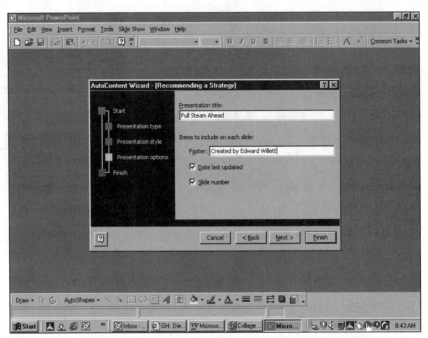

Figure 22-4: Title your presentation and design the slide footers in the third screen of AutoContent Wizard.

Once you've made all these choices, click Finish. AutoContent Wizard creates a presentation of the type you've specified with slides that are typical of that kind of presentation (see Figure 22-5). Each slide contains suggestions as to what sort of content should appear there. You can use or ignore those suggestions as you wish: At this point, the presentation is entirely yours to edit — but you're already way ahead of where you would be if you'd started from scratch!

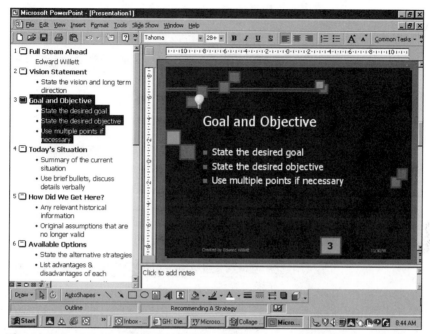

Figure 22-5: AutoContent Wizard adds suggested content to all the slides in the presentations it creates to help you with the process of adding your own content.

More About AutoLayout

As noted in Chapter 20, "Beginning a Presentation," whenever you start a new, blank presentation or insert a new slide, you're provided with a number of AutoLayout slides to choose from (see Figure 22-6). When you choose one, the new slide that appears has placeholders in it, into which you can insert your own content.

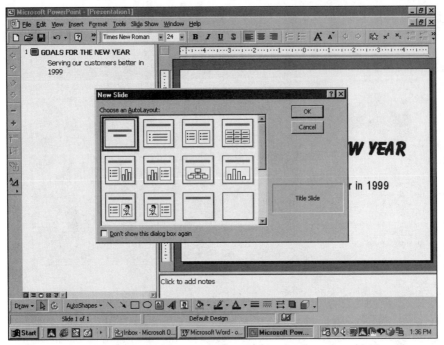

Figure 22-6: PowerPoint provides you with a wide selection of pre-designed AutoLayouts into which you can insert your own content.

Exploring the available layouts

The available AutoLayouts are as follows:

+ **Title Slide:** a large, centered text box for the title of your presentation, with a smaller text box underneath for a subtitle.

+ **Bulleted List:** a large, centered text box for the title of your slide, with a text box set up as a bulleted list underneath it. The first line of text in the bulleted list is automatically set off with a bullet, and each time you press Return a new line is begun with an additional bullet.

+ **Two Column Text:** actually, two-column bulleted list — a large, centered text box for the slide title, with two text boxes set up as bulleted lists side by side underneath it.

+ **Table:** a large, centered text box for the slide title, with a placeholder for a table underneath it. When you double-click on the table placeholder, you're prompted to enter the number of rows and columns you want in it.

✦ **Text and Chart:** a large, centered text box for the slide title, with a placeholder for a bulleted list on the left and a placeholder for a chart on the right. Double-clicking on the chart placeholder opens a datasheet for the chart and brings up the Microsoft Graph controls.

For more information on using tables and charts in PowerPoint, see Chapter 23, "Charts and Tables." For more information on Microsoft Graph, see Chapter 53, "Universal Drawing and Graphics Features."

✦ **Chart and Text:** same as Text and Chart, except the chart's on the left and the bulleted list is on the right.

✦ **Organization Chart:** a large, centered text box for the slide title, with a placeholder for an organization chart below. Double-click on the organization chart placeholder to design a new organization chart.

✦ **Chart:** same as Organization Chart, but with a placeholder for a regular chart.

✦ **Text and Clip Art:** a large, centered text box for the slide title, with a placeholder for a bulleted list on the left and a placeholder for a picture on the right. Double-clicking on the picture placeholder opens the Clip Gallery, a directory of available clip art on your computer.

✦ **Clip Art and Text:** same as Text and Clip Art, but with the picture on the left and the bulleted list on the right.

For more information on inserting pictures into PowerPoint presentations, see Chapter 24, "Adding Graphics and Special Effects." For more information on the Clip Gallery, see Chapter 53, "Universal Drawing and Graphics Features."

✦ **Title Only:** just a slide title box.

✦ **Blank:** a slide with no placeholders.

✦ **Text and Object:** a slide title at the top, with a bulleted list placeholder below it to the left, and a placeholder for an object on the right. Double-click on the object placeholder, and then choose the type of object you want to create from the Insert Object dialog box. An object is something that is created using another program; although you insert it into PowerPoint, editing it is still done using the program controls with which you created it.

✦ **Object and Text:** same as Text and Object, but with the object placeholder on the left and the bulleted list on the right.

For more information on using objects in Office, see Chapter 52, "Building Integrated Documents."

✦ **Large Object:** an object that fills the whole slide; no title.

✦ **Object:** a slide title above a large object.

✦ **Text and Media Clip:** a slide title over a bulleted list placeholder on the left and a placeholder for a media clip on the right. To insert a media clip, double-click on the media clip placeholder and choose the media clip you want from the Clip Gallery.

✦ **Media Clip and Text:** just like Text and Media Clip, but with the media clip on the left and the bulleted list on the right.

✦ **Object Over Text:** a slide title above an object placeholder above a bulleted list.

✦ **Text Over Object:** same as Object Over Text, but with the bulleted list over the object.

✦ **Text and Two Objects:** a slide title above a two-column layout consisting of a bulleted-list placeholder on the left and two small objects, one above the other, on the right.

✦ **Two Objects and Text:** same as Text and Two Objects, but with the two objects on the left and the bulleted list on the right.

✦ **Two Objects Over Text:** Same as Object Over Text, but with two small object placeholders side by side above the bulleted list, instead of a single large one.

✦ **Four Objects:** a slide title over four small object placeholders, arranged in a two-by-two grid.

Reconfiguring existing slides

AutoLayouts are good for more than just inserting new slides; you can also use them to reconfigure existing slides. To do so, bring up the slide you want to change in Normal view; then choose Format ➪ Slide Layout (or right-click and choose Slide Layout from the pop-up menu).

Figure 22-7 shows a slide created using the Title Slide AutoLayout, while Figures 22-8 and 22-9 show the same slide with the Bulleted List and Two-Column Text AutoLayouts applied, respectively.

You can experiment with as many different AutoLayouts as you like without losing any of the text you've already entered. Note, however, that if you choose an AutoLayout that doesn't contain space for text you've already entered — say you've created a subhead as in the examples above, but you try to apply an AutoLayout that doesn't include any text boxes except for the slide title — PowerPoint will simply plop a text box containing the text over whatever else might be included in the AutoLayout (see Figure 22-10).

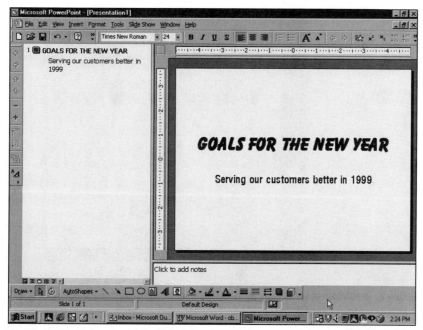

Figure 22-7: Using the Title Slide AutoLayout, I created this title slide for my presentation.

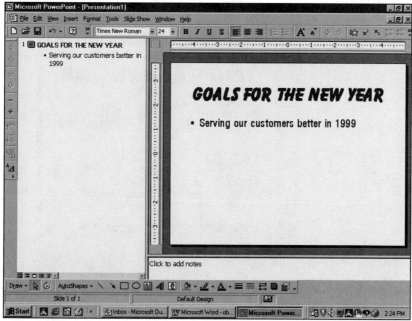

Figure 22-8: The same presentation with the Bulleted List AutoLayout applied.

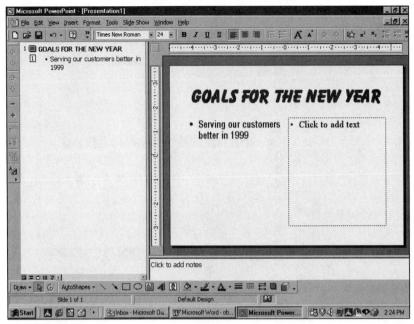

Figure 22-9: The same title slide with the Two-Column Text AutoLayout applied.

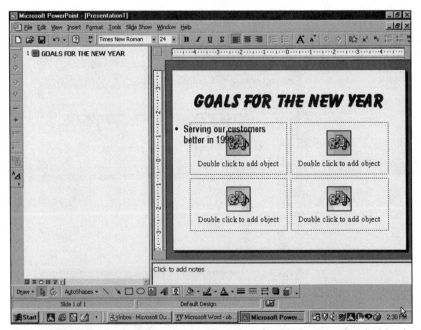

Figure 22-10: If you choose an AutoLayout that doesn't have a placeholder for text you've already entered, you'll end up with the text overlaying the AutoLayout placeholders, and you will have to do some juggling to make it all fit.

Using Masters

Maintaining a consistent style throughout your presentation is easier if you learn to use PowerPoint's four masters: Slide Master, Title Master, Handout Master, and Notes Master.

The Slide Master

On the Slide Master, you can set text characteristics such as font, size, and color, plus a background color or graphic and special effects such as shadowing and bullet style, which will then be applied by default to all the slides in that presentation.

Using the Slide Master also means that if you want to make a change to the style of, say, all the slide titles in a presentation, you don't have to change each title on each slide: You can simply make the change on the Slide Master, and all the slide titles will change appearance automatically.

You can also use the Slide Master to make anything you like appear on every slide in the presentation. A typical example would be the company logo. Rather than insert it as a separate picture on each slide, just insert it once on the Slide Master, and it will appear on each slide automatically.

Opening the Slide Master

To open the Slide Master, choose View ➪ Master ➪ Slide Master (see Figure 22-11).

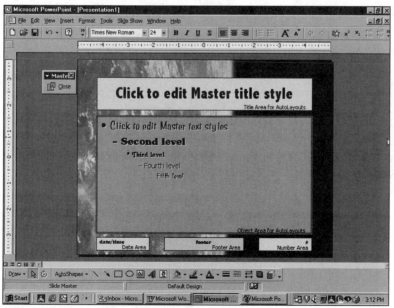

Figure 22-11: The Slide Master lets you assign slide text styles that will be used by default throughout your presentation.

Formatting with the Slide Master

To format the Slide Master:

1. Click once inside the text box containing the type of text you want to format.

2. Highlight the type of text you want to format (e.g., Second level).

3. Format the text just as you would within an ordinary text box. You can change the font, style, and alignment, and add borders and a background color to the text boxes.

4. Add any graphics you would like to appear on every slide. For example, in Figure 22-12, along with all the formatting I've done to the text, I've added a background that will now appear on every slide in the presentation by default.

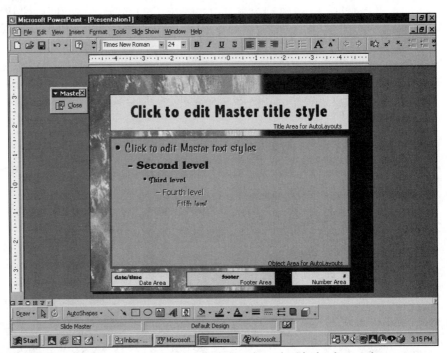

Figure 22-12: OK, so maybe I went a little overboard with the formatting possibilities . . .

5. To add text that will appear on every slide, insert a new text box by choosing Insert ⇨ Text Box, and then type in the text you want to appear. (Typing into the text placeholders that appear automatically when you view Slide Master doesn't have any effect.)

6. When you're finished making changes to the Slide Master, click Close on the small (two-command) Master toolbar.

 Cross-Reference For more information on formatting text, see Chapter 21, "Entering and Formatting Text." For more information on inserting graphics, see Chapter 24, "Adding Graphics and Special Effects."

Title Master

The Title Master is a special form of the Slide Master that applies only to the slides in your presentation that use the Title Slide layout. Use it when you want your Title slides to have a different format from the other slides in your presentation.

To access the Title Master, choose View ⇨ Master, and then choose Insert ⇨ New Title Master. Format the title and subtitle text boxes as you like. Again, you can add any graphics, media clips, or background patterns or colors you like.

Handout Master

The Handout Master works just like the Slide Master, except it lets you preformat handouts instead of slides.

Handouts can help your audience follow your presentation more easily. They can include images of slides (helpful if some of your audience members can't easily see the computer or projection screen on which you're showing your presentation, if they want to take notes, or if they want to be able to study the presentation in detail later) plus any additional information you want to supply.

To create handouts:

1. Call up the Handout Master by choosing View ⇨ Master ⇨ Handout Master (see Figure 22-13).

2. When you print handouts, you can choose from among several different layouts in the Print dialog box. To help you design your Handout Master, PowerPoint lets you preview the various layout options using the Handout Master toolbar. (If the toolbar isn't visible, activate it by choosing View ⇨ Toolbars ⇨ Handout Master.) The boxes in the main body of the Handout Master represent images of slides. Possible print layouts include two slides per page, three slides per page with room for text alongside each one, four slides per page, six slides per page, nine slides per page, or no slides per page — just the outline.

3. Make any other changes you want to the handouts — adding text that will appear on every handout, graphics, a background, etc.

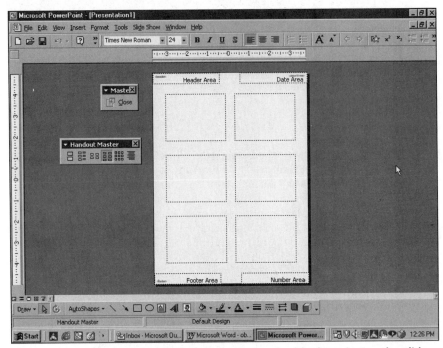

Figure 22-13: The Handout Master lets you customize handouts just as the Slide Master lets you customize slides.

4. When you're satisfied with the appearance of your Handout Master, click Close on the Master toolbar.

5. To print Handouts, choose File ➪ Print, and then choose Handouts from the Print What list box in the Print dialog box (see Figure 22-14). Choose the layout you want to use in the Handouts section of the dialog box, and whether you want slides to be arranged so they read horizontally from left to right (so that in a four-slide arrangement, Slide 1 would be in the upper-left corner, Slide 2 to the right of it, Slide 3 under Slide 1, and Slide 4 to the right of Slide 3); or vertically (Slide 1 in the upper-left corner, Slide 2 beneath it, Slide 3 to the right of Slide 1, Slide 4 beneath Slide 3). When you've made your selections, click OK to print.

Cross-Reference
For more detailed information on printing in PowerPoint, see Chapter 26, "PowerPoint at Work."

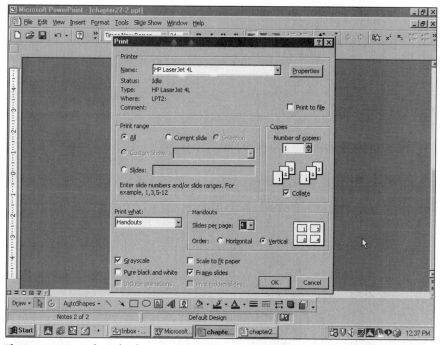

Figure 22-14: Select the layout you want to use for printing your handout in the Print dialog box.

Notes Master

Notes are even more useful than handouts. In fact, they can be used as handouts, especially if you want to provide additional information about individual slides. They're also useful for creating speaking notes for whoever will be making the presentation.

Notes pages consist of an image of an individual slide with a text area underneath. You can enter notes in Normal view in the Notes pane directly under the Slide View pane.

The Notes Master works like the other masters we've looked at: It lets you set default formats for the text you enter into notes, relocate or change the size of the slide image that appears on each notes page, and add any other graphics, fills, or backgrounds you might want.

To customize the Notes Master:

1. Open the Notes Master by choosing View ➪ Master ➪ Notes Master (see Figure 22-15).

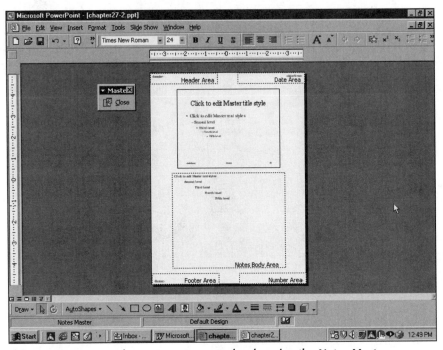

Figure 22-15: Customize your notes pages by changing the Notes Master.

2. The box at the top of the Notes Master is simply a small representation of the Slide Master. The only changes you can make to it here are to its size and position (you can change its size by clicking on it and tugging on its handles, and move it by clicking on it and then dragging it).

3. Format the text in the Notes box the way you want text to be formatted on all your notes pages. As with the Slide Master, you can format text differently depending on which level in the hierarchy it is: i.e., is it a title, a subtitle, a sub-subtitle, etc.

4. Add any graphics you want to appear on all notes pages, along with any borders, fills, or backgrounds you want on all pages.

5. When you're satisfied, click Close on the Master toolbar.

6. Print your notes pages by choosing File ➪ Print, and then selecting Notes Pages from the Print What list box in the Print dialog box.

Changing color schemes and backgrounds

Every master includes a number of ready-made color schemes you can choose from; you can also create your own. Open whichever master you want to apply a color scheme to, and then open the Format menu. You'll always see the same three options:

✦ **Master Layout.** This dialog box lets you activate or deactivate standard placeholders on the master: for example, Title, Text, Date, Slide Number, and Footer. (Note that these options change depending on which master you're working on.)

✦ **Color Scheme.** Choose this to select one of PowerPoint's standard color schemes, or design your own.

✦ **Background.** Choose this to add a background to the master, anything from a solid color to a photograph.

Changing the color scheme

To apply one of PowerPoint's standard color schemes to your master:

1. Choose Format ➪ Slide Color Scheme and make sure the Standard tab is selected.

2. From the dialog box shown in Figure 22-16, select the color scheme that appeals to you.

3. Click Apply. The colors of your master change to match the color scheme you selected.

Tip

You can also apply color schemes to individual slides or a group of selected slides. In the Outline Pane of Normal view, click on the slide or slides you want to apply the color scheme to, choose Format ➪ Slide Color Scheme, click on the color scheme you like, and click Apply. To change your entire presentation's color scheme, including the master, select any slide in the presentation, choose Format ➪ Slide Color Scheme, choose the scheme you want, and click Apply to All.

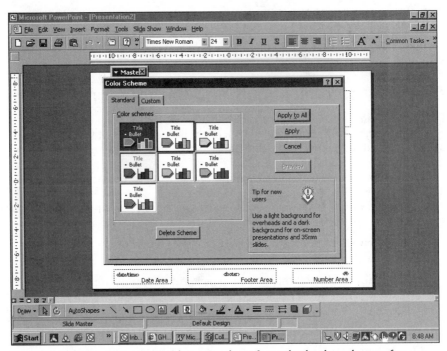

Figure 22-16: PowerPoint provides a number of standard color schemes for presentations.

Creating a custom color scheme

To create a custom color scheme and apply it to your master:

1. While viewing the master, choose Format ⇨ Slide Color Scheme and click the Custom tab.

2. From the list of Scheme Colors shown in the dialog box in Figure 22-17, click on the element of the slide whose color you want to change.

3. Click Change Color, and select the color you want from the palette provided.

4. Click OK to return to the Color Scheme dialog box.

5. Repeat the process until you've changed the colors of all the elements you want.

6. If you want to save your new Color Scheme as a Standard Color Scheme, click Add as Standard Scheme.

7. Click Apply to apply your new color scheme to your master.

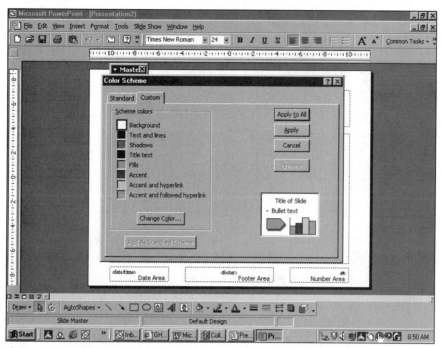

Figure 22-17: Design a custom color scheme for your presentation from this dialog box.

Changing the background

To change the background to any of your masters:

1. Choose Format ➪ Background to open the dialog box shown in Figure 22-18.

2. Choose a background color from the drop-down list at the bottom of the Background Fill area. PowerPoint displays a number of commonly used colors; if you don't see a color you want, click More Colors to open a palette from which you can choose others.

3. If you want something more complicated than just a solid color, click Fill Effects instead of More Colors. This opens the Fill Effects dialog box (see Figure 22-19), which has four tabs. In the first one, Gradient, you can choose from a variety of effects created by shading one color into another. Choose one color, two colors, or a preset effect; select the colors or the effect you want to use; choose a shading style from the list at bottom left, and then choose the variant you like from the list at lower right. When you're satisfied, click OK.

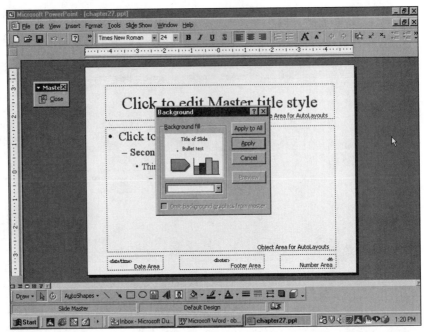

Figure 22-18: PowerPoint provides a number of standard color schemes for presentations.

Figure 22-19: Gradients can make very interesting backgrounds for your slides.

4. If you'd prefer to use a texture instead of a gradient, click the Texture tab (see Figure 22-20). Textures are small graphics that are tiled together to create the illusion of paper, rock, wood, or some other surface. Choose the texture you want from those provided and click OK. If you have a texture stored on your computer you'd prefer to use instead, clicking Other Texture lets you browse for it.

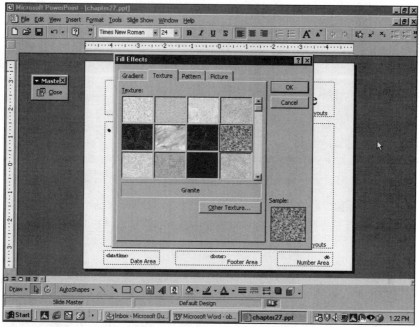

Figure 22-20: PowerPoint gives you many attractive textures to choose from for slide backgrounds.

5. Another option for your background is a pattern. Click the Pattern tab to see a display of PowerPoint's patterns (see Figure 22-21). Choose the pattern that appeals to you and the colors you want to create it with, and then click OK.

6. Finally, you can choose to use a picture as a background. Click the Picture tab (see Figure 22-22), and then click Select Picture to browse your computer for graphics files. Choose the one you want and click OK.

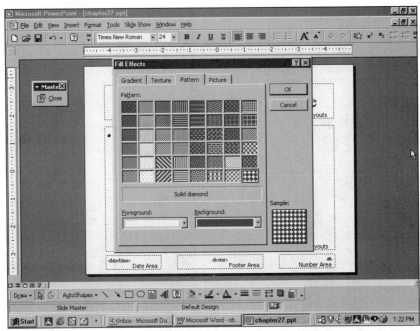

Figure 22-21: Patterns are created from two colors, foreground and background, which you can select here along with your preferred pattern.

Figure 22-22: A photograph or other picture can make an excellent background that also illustrates the content of your slide.

7. Once you've selected the background you want, and clicked OK, you'll be returned to the Background dialog box. Click Apply to apply the background you've selected to the master (see Figure 22-23).

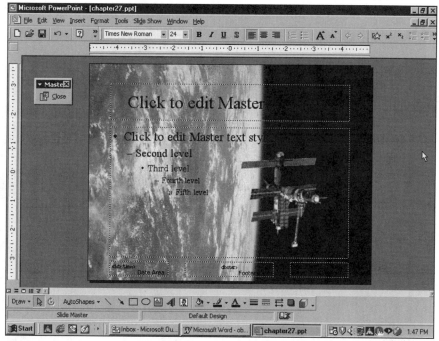

Figure 22-23: Here's what my Slide Master looks like with a photograph applied as a background.

Caution

Be careful when selecting a background fill not to use something that will make text difficult to read. Using the background in Figure 22-23, for example, is going to make it hard for me to find a good color for the text, because half of the picture is light and the other half dark. I'll have to carefully choose a contrasting color that is both legible and pleasing to the eye.

Using Design Templates

Design templates are preformatted master slides that PowerPoint provides to make it possible for anyone to create a good-looking presentation even if they don't know the first thing about design themselves.

Accessing the design templates

Whenever you start PowerPoint, Design Template is one of the first options offered to you. You can also access the design templates by choosing File ➪ New, and then clicking on the Design Templates tab of the New Presentations dialog box. You'll see an extensive list of templates (see Figure 22-24), each with a name indicative of its appearance—more or less. Fortunately, you don't have to rely entirely on sometimes cryptic titles like Lock and Key; click on any of the templates listed, and a preview of it will appear.

Figure 22-24: PowerPoint's design templates can help you create a good-looking presentation without having to design every aspect of it yourself.

Choosing an AutoLayout

When you've found a template you'd like to work with, click OK. PowerPoint asks you to choose an AutoLayout for the first slide in your presentation; once you've done that, you can begin working on the content of your presentation—the design work is already done (see Figure 22-25).

Modifying and applying the design templates

You can modify design templates by opening the Slide Master and making whatever changes you want. Another powerful feature of templates is that you can apply them to any existing presentation. To do so, choose Format ➪ Apply Design Template, and then choose the one you want from the list provided. Click Apply, and all the slides in your presentation will change to match the new template.

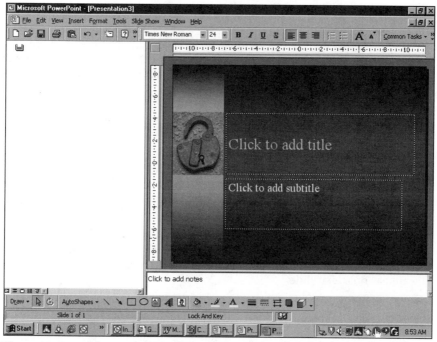

Figure 22-25: With AutoLayout, all you have to do is fill in the blanks; your background and color scheme are already taken care of.

Creating and Saving Your Own Templates

Any time you make changes to any of the masters, you're essentially creating your own template. If you come up with a design you really like, you'll probably want to save it so you can use it in future presentations.

To save your current presentation as a template:

1. Choose File ➪ Save As.

2. In the Save As Type list box, select Design Template.

3. Type a name for your new template into the File Name box.

4. Click Save.

The template, which includes all of the masters you've formatted plus all of the slides currently in the presentation, is automatically saved in the default file folder for templates. The next time you start a presentation using a design template, or choose Format ➪ Apply Design Template, your new template will appear under the General tab of the New Presentation dialog box (*not* under the Design Template tab).

Summary

In this chapter, you learned the various ways PowerPoint can help you create a great-looking presentation even if you're not an expert in visual design yourself, and how it makes it easy for you to apply changes to your entire presentation. Some of the highlights of this chapter included the following:

✦ Starting a presentation with AutoContent Wizard is probably the fastest and easiest way to get going: It provides a visual design and suggests the sort of content you should include in a variety of presentation types.

✦ You'll use AutoLayout constantly to insert new slides into presentations. Although you can choose from a wide variety of AutoLayouts, in general you add content to them by clicking once inside placeholders for text boxes and double-clicking on placeholders for pictures, tables, charts, and media clips.

✦ The Slide, Title, Handout, and Notes Masters let you set default formatting for all aspects of your presentation, including the font, style, and size of text; fills and borders for text boxes; and text, graphics, or backgrounds you want to appear on every slide.

✦ Design templates are pre-designed masters that take care of the visual look of your presentation so you can concentrate on content. You can start a presentation using a design template, or apply one to your presentation at any time by choosing Format ➪ Apply Design Template.

✦ You can save any design you're particularly happy with for future use by choosing File ➪ Save As, and then selecting Design Template in the Save as Type box. The next time you start a presentation using a design template or apply one to an existing presentation, the template you designed—which includes all of the masters you may have formatted plus all of the slides that were in the presentation when it was saved—will be available under the General tab of the New Presentation dialog box.

✦   ✦   ✦

Charts and Tables

✦ ✦ ✦ ✦

In This Chapter

Exploring chart types

Creating and editing charts

Formatting charts

Creating organization charts

Creating and editing tables

Adding Excel worksheets and Word tables

✦ ✦ ✦ ✦

Graphs created in PowerPoint bring your data to life in a presentation, making it more interesting and easier to understand. If you're familiar with creating tables in Word (a topic covered in Chapter 3, "Tables") then creating tables in PowerPoint should be a snap. Unfortunately, PowerPoint tables don't allow you to do calculations or sorting. If you want to use Word tables or Excel worksheets, however, you can import these items into PowerPoint.

Exploring Chart Types

Before creating a chart (which is also referred to as a graph), you need to decide which type to use. PowerPoint offers 18 basic chart types in addition to organization charts, which require a special feature to create and are covered in detail later in this chapter. The following list covers all the basic types of charts you can create in PowerPoint:

✦ **Column charts** – are vertical bar charts, which usually show data over time. They can be 2-D or 3-D, and the bars can be stacked or shown as a split over 100 percent. Figure 23-1 shows a column chart with the same figures graphed in 2-D and 3-D.

Note   The small boxes to the right of the charts in Figure 23-1 are called *legends*. These can also be placed inside the area of the graph. Some people call them *keys*. They show the color coding for each series displayed. Figure 23-1 has a legend identifying the colors of each of the sets of columns.

✦ **Cylinder, Cone, and Pyramid charts** – are variations of 3-D column charts.

✦ **Bar charts** – are horizontal column charts. They are not as easy to read as column charts but are useful when you have many bars of one series — it makes the labels easier to read. They can be 2-D or 3-D.

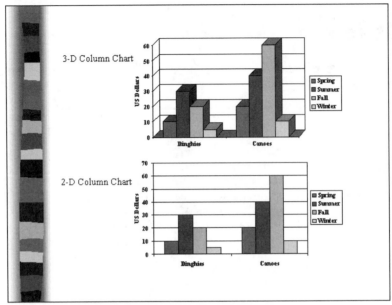

Figure 23-1: Note the difference between 2-D and 3-D. 3-D looks livelier but it is hard to read the tops of the bars.

✦ **Pie charts** – show how each item contributes to the whole. Often the data is shown as percentages, to show each slice's contribution. They can be 2-D or 3-D. A pie chart does not show comparisons over time; instead, it shows how each item contributes to the whole. For example, a pie chart could show which products among many are the biggest sellers. *Doughnut Charts* are pie charts with a hole in the center.

✦ **Line charts** – show trends more clearly as each data point is joined. A steep line indicates a big rate of change. They can be 2-D or 3-D. *Area Charts* are line charts with the area below the line filled. When the series are stacked, it shows how each series contributes to the total.

✦ **Radar charts** – are not commonly used. Each series is graphed from a central point and has its own axis.

✦ *XY (Scatter)* **charts** – are used to plot pairs of values. The two axes both show values.

✦ **Surface charts** – are 3-D charts and show the figures color-coded according to value — each range of figures appears as a different color.

✦ **Bubble charts** – show three sets of values: two are graphed against the vertical and horizontal axes; the third is represented by the size of the bubble.

✦ **Stock charts** – are used to show prices on the stock market. Up to five values can be shown — volume, opening price, closing, high, and low.

How PowerPoint Names Its Axes

Many graphs, such as column charts, have two axes. I learned them in school as the *x* and *y* axes but in PowerPoint they are known as the *category axis* and the *value axis*. Sometimes, in 3-D graphs, there is a third, or *z* axis, known as the *series axis*. Here's how they work:

✦ The *category* axis is often used to show time, such as month, quarter, or year.

✦ The *value* axis shows the volume, such as dollars, kilograms, or quantity.

✦ The *series* axis shows separate sets of data, such as the data for different products or regions. If there is no third axis, the series are often shown by using different colored columns next to one another (refer to Figure 23-1).

Creating and Editing Charts

When you create a new slide, choose an AutoLayout for a chart such as Text & Chart, Chart & Text, or Chart. Double-click on the chart placeholder. Alternatively, choose Insert ⇨ Chart or click on the Insert Chart tool on the Standard toolbar. From the chart submenu that appears you can choose any one of the 18 basic chart types discussed in the previous section.

Note

If you are using an AutoLayout for a chart, PowerPoint will place your chart in the chart area. If not, the chart will be placed in the center of your slide. Either way you can move or resize the chart however you like.

Creating a chart

Once you've double-clicked inside a chart placeholder, or chosen Insert ⇨ Chart, PowerPoint opens a special program called Microsoft Graph, which is also used by other Office applications to created charts. You can identify Microsoft Graph by the special toolbar, the different menu (including Data and Chart instead of Slideshow) and the Datasheet window, which is showing. Figure 23-2 shows all of these.

Caution

It is very easy to click in the wrong place and move from Microsoft Graph back to PowerPoint. To get back to Microsoft Graph from PowerPoint, double-click on the chart area on the slide.

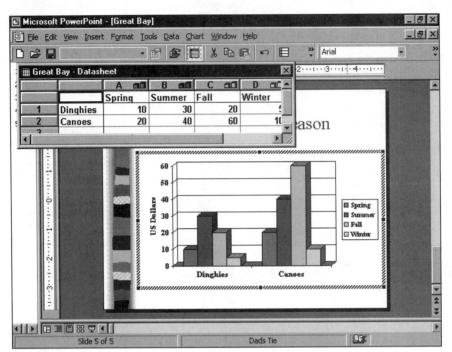

Figure 23-2: This is the charting component of PowerPoint. Notice that the menu and toolbars are different.

To complete your chart:

1. Choose Chart ⇨ Chart Type and select the type of chart you want. (Or use the Chart Type tool from the Standard toolbar, shown earlier).

2. Enter your own data in the Datasheet window to replace the sample data, using the sample data as a template. The graph changes to show your own data as soon you enter it. Here's how it works:

   • Labels typed in the top row are used for the category labels. Labels typed in the leftmost column are series labels. To enter additional series or categories, simply type the data in the next available row or column. To delete a category or series, click on the column or row header (the letter D or number 3, for example) and press Delete.

   • Move around the datasheet window using the mouse or the arrow keys. If the columns are too narrow, find the Column-width tool on the boundary between the column header and the next column header to the right, and drag to make it wider. Or choose Format ⇨ Column Width.

   • When your data is in dollars, you can type the dollar sign in front of any of the numbers. PowerPoint will insert the dollar sign on the Value axis automatically. For other currencies, highlight the data and choose Format ⇨ Number. Select currency and the currency symbol required.

- If you do not want to show all the data on the graph, you can exclude a row or a column. Select the row/column by clicking on the header and choose Data ➪ Exclude Row/Col.

- If the Datasheet window is missing and you are in Microsoft Graph (the menu shows Data and Chart instead of SlideShow), choose View ➪ Datasheet or use the View Datasheet tool on the Standard toolbar to redisplay it.

Tip You can also import data for charts from other programs — for example, from an Excel worksheet. Select Edit ➪ Import File or use the Import File tool on the Standard toolbar.

3. Make changes to your chart using the Chart ➪ Chart Options menu (see Figure 23-3). Six tabs are available:

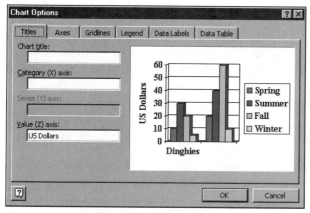

Figure 23-3: Use the Chart Options dialog box to change the look of your charts.

- **Titles**. Add a title to the chart or to any of the axes: Category, Series, or Value. A title is often required in order for the Value axis to show what unit of measure your graph is using — for example, dollars, kilograms, or thousands.

- **Axes.** Show or hide the axes and select the type of category axis — whether category or timescale.

- **Gridlines.** Show or hide major and minor gridlines on any axis. Use gridlines only when necessary — they clutter the chart.

- **Legend.** Show or hide the legend (the key) and decide on its placement. Later, you can drag the legend inside your graph. The graph can then be larger and easier to read.

- **Data Labels.** Show the data value against each point, or the label, or the percentage, if applicable.

- **Data Table.** A data table shows all the data in a table underneath the graph. Use this tab to show or hide it. A data table makes a chart look very cluttered and is hard to read in a presentation.

4. When you have finished creating the graph, click anywhere on your slide outside the graph object to go back to PowerPoint. Your graph appears on your slide. You can now move it or resize it using the white handles.

Editing charts

You can change various elements of your chart at any stage — the data, the chart type, or many aspects of the appearance.

Changing data

To change the data you need to get back to the datasheet. Double-click on the chart in PowerPoint. This takes you into Microsoft Graph. If the datasheet is not showing, choose View ⇨ Datasheet. Any changes you make to the datasheet will immediately be made to the graph. Click anywhere outside the graph to go back to PowerPoint.

Changing chart types

To change chart types — from a Bar chart to a Line chart, for example — choose Chart ⇨ Chart Type or use the Chart Type tool on the Standard toolbar. If you use the menu, choose the new chart type in the Chart Type dialog box and click OK. If the graph does not look right, look at the datasheet. You may have the wrong type of data. For example, an *XY* chart has pairs of values, not categories.

Swapping data series

If you have typed the categories and the series the wrong way, or if you decide to swap the way the data is shown, choose Data ⇨ Series in Rows or Data ⇨ Series in Columns. Or you can choose the tools By Row or By Column from the Standard toolbar. See Figure 23-4 to see the difference.

Controlling 3-D views

If you have chosen a 3-D chart, such as a column chart or pie chart, you can control the elevation, rotation, and perspective of the chart; and also the angle of the axes. Choose Chart ⇨ 3-D View. Click on each of the four direction buttons several times to see what the effect will be. Alternatively, type in figures for the elevation and rotation. You can select Auto-scaling if you have selected Right-angle axes.

Right-angle axes is the opposite of perspective. Turn off Right-angle axes and two additional buttons appear for you to change perspective. Try clicking several times on each of the buttons to see the effect.

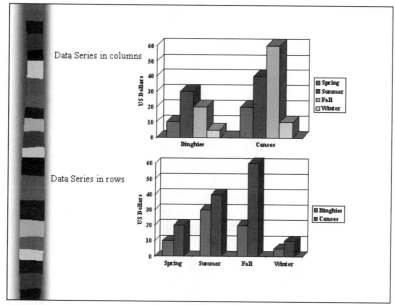

Figure 23-4: The data series are shown in columns or in rows. The two graphs compare your data differently.

If Right-angle axes is on and you turn off Auto-scaling, you can put in a height as a percentage of the base: 100% would make the height of the graph the same as the width of the base, 200% would make the height twice the width of the base, and so on.

Click Apply to see your chart change. Click OK when you have finished.

Formatting Charts

Many individual parts of your chart can be changed. The trick is to select the item you want changed and then find the dialog box. As you move your mouse over the chart, yellow boxes appear showing you what will be selected if you click: plot area, walls, a series, the legend, etc. If these yellow boxes do not appear and you are in Microsoft Graph, click once on the chart and try again. Click with the right mouse button to call up the shortcut menu. The top item will read Format [name of the chart element you're selecting]; for example, Format Plot Area, or Format Data Series. Instead of using the shortcut menu you can click on the item you want to change and choose Format ➪ Selected.

The dialog box that appears depends on the object selected.

Format data series

Be careful to check whether you have selected Format Data Series or Format Data Point. If you click a second time on a bar or a line on your graph, the individual item will be selected, rather than the whole series. If you have selected a data point instead of a data series, click somewhere else on the chart to deselect and then click just once on the series. Details of the dialog boxes vary depending on which Chart Type is selected.

Figure 23-5 shows the Format Data Series dialog box for a 2-D bar chart. (A 3-D column chart has Shape instead of Axis and Y Error Bars.) The dialog box has five tabs:

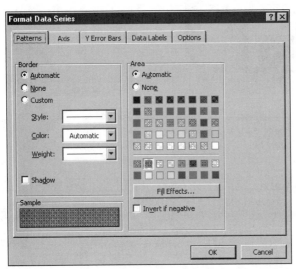

Figure 23-5: You can do several things to change the selected data series. If you select a different part of the chart, or a different chart type, the dialog box options are different.

> ✦ **Patterns** – changes the outline of the bars under the Border section, and the fill color and patterns of the bars under the Area section. For some interesting effects, click the Fill Effects button. You now have a choice of Gradient, Texture, Pattern, or Picture to fill the bars. For example, you can choose a picture to fill the bars in a series. (Pictures look best if you choose a stacked format.)
>
> ✦ **Axis** – chooses which axis you wish to plot the data against. This is used where you want two different units of measure on the same graph — for example, dollars and percentages. Use one axis for dollars and the other for percentages.
>
> ✦ **Y Error Bars** – highlights data that is out of a specified range.

✦ **Data Labels** – shows the value of each bar for this series. The placement and size of the numbers is controlled separately: When you are back in Microsoft Graph, select the labels and choose Format ➪ Selected Data Labels.

✦ **Options** – controls the look of the series: the overlap and gap between bars.

✦ **Shape** – chooses the shape of the column (only shown with 3-D column charts).

Format plot or chart area

Select either the Plot Area or the Chart Area and choose Format ➪ Selected Area. The Patterns tab lets you put a border around the graph and put in a background. A gradient fill, chosen by clicking the Fill Effects button, can be stunning.

Format legend

Select the legend and choose Format ➪ Selected Legend. The tabs for this are Patterns, Font, and Placement. Under Placement, choose where to place the legend. The shape of the legend also changes. Later, you can drag a legend to place it where you want.

Format category axis

Select the Category Axis and choose Format ➪ Selected Axis. The tabs for this are Patterns, Scale, Font, Number, and Alignment. The Scale tab lets you choose the number of categories to show. The Number tab is for number formatting, and the Alignment tab allows you to put the axis labels at an angle, which is useful if they are overlapping.

Format value axis

Select the Value Axis and choose Format ➪ Selected Axis. The tabs for this are Patterns, Scale, Font, Number, and Alignment. The Scale tab allows you to choose the minimum and maximum values for the axis, as well as the major and minor units.

 Note   This brief discussion has not covered all the numerous formatting options. Explore them all yourself and experiment to find out what you can do.

Add a trendline

A trendline is a line through your data, not necessarily linking the points, but showing the trend of the data. This feature is available only on some 2-D graphs. Select a series, right-click to call up the shortcut menu, and select Add Trendline. Choose the method you want to use to calculate the trend, and any other options (see Figure 23-6).

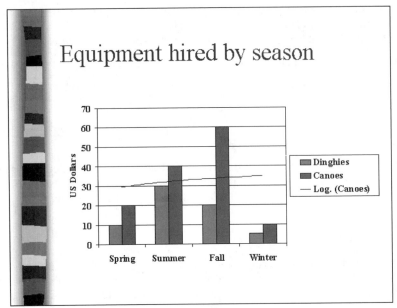

Figure 23-6: Trendlines can be inserted for a selected series on some 2-D charts.

Mixed chart types

You can mix some kinds of charts. For example, you can combine a column chart and a line chart, or a column chart and an area chart. To do so:

1. Create a 2-D column graph using all the data.

2. Select the series you want to show as a line or area chart.

3. Select Chart ➪ Chart Type and choose a line or area chart. Make sure that Apply to Selection is turned on.

4. Click OK. The selected series changes to a line or area chart. The other series continue to be displayed as columns.

Saving custom charts

Microsoft Graph provides several pre-designed graphs, called *built-in graphs,* which you can use. Also, once you have designed a good chart, you may want to save your own design to use again and again. The Chart ➪ Chart Type dialog box has two tabs: Standard Types and Custom Types. To view Microsoft Graph's pre-designed charts, select Custom Types and make sure the option Built In is selected. Try clicking on each of the chart types to see how your data will look. If you want to use one, click OK.

To save your own design:

1. Create your chart.

2. Choose Chart ➪ Chart Type.

3. Select the Custom Types tab and then Select From: User-defined.

4. Click the Add button and type a name and description for your graph. It will be added to the list of Custom Types, under the user-defined section.

To apply your custom-designed graph to your data, choose the chart type either before or after entering your data. Choose Chart ➪ Chart Type. Select the Custom Types tab, select User-defined, and select your design.

Creating Organization Charts

Anyone who has had to draw organization charts either by hand or computer will appreciate this feature. You simply add boxes where you want them and type in the information. The formatting and sizing is done for you automatically. Figure 23-7 shows an example of a simple organization chart. To create your own, use the following steps:

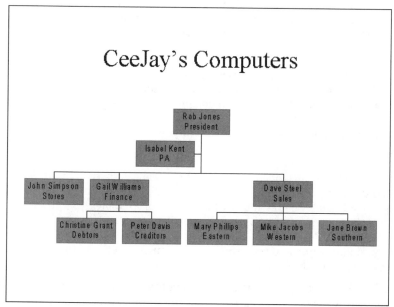

Figure 23-7: Organization charts like this are easy to produce.

1. Create a new slide and choose Organization chart from the AutoLayouts. Double-click to go to Microsoft Organization Chart. Alternatively, choose Insert ➪ Picture ➪ Organization Chart. Either way you are taken into a separate program that contains a simple chart (see Figure 23-8).

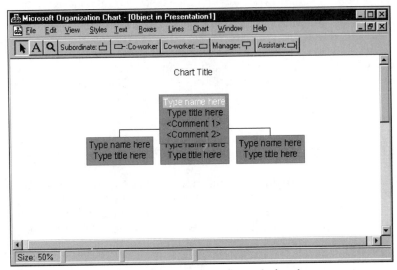

Figure 23-8: The Microsoft Organization Chart window is a separate program from PowerPoint. Make sure you choose Update on the File menu and then Exit to insert the chart into your presentation.

Caution   It is very important that once you have created your organization chart, you don't just click back on PowerPoint as you did when creating other types of charts. You must exit from Organization Chart and update your files first. See Step 8 for details.

2. Type the name of the person at the top of your organization. Press Enter and type their position.

Tip   With organization charts, one of the biggest problems is space. In a presentation, you can show only a few boxes at a time, because otherwise the text becomes too small to read. Abbreviate as much as possible. For example, type VP instead of Vice President. If any information is not essential, leave it out.

3. Click on the next box and type the information. A quick way to move from box to box is to press Ctrl+arrow.

4. To add a subordinate, click the Subordinate tool on the toolbar and click on the manager you want to assign the subordinate to. A new subordinate box appears and the chart is reorganized to fit.

Using the Right Tool

There are three tools at the start of the toolbar: Select, Enter Text, and Zoom. Here's how they work:

✦ Use Select most of the time for entering and selecting boxes.

✦ Use Enter Text and click on the page outside of the organization boxes where you want to add an annotation.

✦ Click Zoom and click on the page to zoom in. However, if you click Zoom again (it is now a different icon) and click on the chart, you will zoom to full view and not back to your previous view. You can see a list of views to select from by choosing View.

5. To add a manager, click the Manager tool and click on the subordinate you want to assign the manager to.

6. To add someone at the same level, click either of the Co-worker tools and click on the worker you want to associate the co-worker with.

7. To add an assistant, click the Assistant tool and click on the worker to whom you wish to attach the assistant.

8. Delete a box by clicking on it once (it turns black) and pressing Delete.

9. To a limited extent, you can drag boxes around. Be careful and save your work first, just in case.

10. To get back to PowerPoint, choose File ⇨ Update *presentation* and then Close Microsoft Organization Chart. If you forget to choose to update, and try and close, a reminder will ask you if you want to update the object before proceeding. Choose Yes. If you switch back to PowerPoint without having updated or exited from Microsoft Organization Chart, the area allocated to the chart will appear with diagonal shading over it. To correct this, double-click on it to take you back to Microsoft Organization Chart again. Then Update and Exit.

Tip

Limit your chart to only a few boxes per row and only a few rows. Split your chart into several separate ones with less information if you can. Otherwise, the text becomes too small to read.

Editing boxes, lines, and fonts

You can change all or some of the boxes in your chart. Drag your mouse to outline the boxes you want to select. They change color when selected. Three menus can change the look of your chart: Text, Boxes, and Lines. Browse through these to see what changes you can make. To change lines, you must have some lines selected, or more than one box. The Edit ⇨ Select and Edit ⇨ Select Levels menus help you select the boxes you want to change.

Editing the style

The Styles menu chooses a design for the chart. Be careful if you use this on an existing chart. Save before making changes as you can undo only one step, and certain steps cannot be undone.

Creating and Editing Tables

Tables are very useful for displaying numbers or text in an organized, easily understood fashion. Creating tables in PowerPoint is very similar to creating tables in Word. Both the Insert Table tool and the Tables and Borders tool are available. However, they are more limited — for example, you cannot do calculations or sorting. (If you need those capabilities, you can create tables in Word or Excel and import them into PowerPoint — a procedure covered later in this chapter.) Figure 23-9 shows a table in PowerPoint.

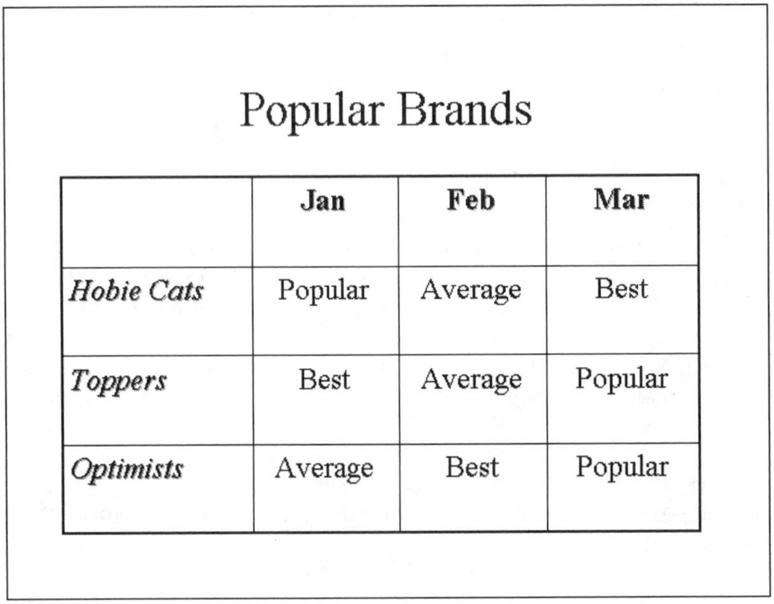

Popular Brands

	Jan	Feb	Mar
Hobie Cats	Popular	Average	Best
Toppers	Best	Average	Popular
Optimists	Average	Best	Popular

Figure 23-9: There are many ways to create a table in PowerPoint.

Creating a table

Select an AutoLayout that includes a table when creating a new slide and double-click in the table placeholder to add a table. Alternatively, choose Insert ➪ Table or the Insert Table tool from the Standard toolbar. This will place a table in the center of your slide. Double-clicking the table placeholder displays a dialog box that asks how many rows and columns you require (see Figure 23-10).

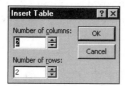

Figure 23-10: Choose how many rows and how many columns you want in your table.

Once you've decided how many rows and columns you want, the table appears on your slide with the cursor flashing in the first cell, ready for you to type in information. To move from cell to cell, use the Tab or arrow keys. When you have finished filling in information, click anywhere on the slide outside the table to deselect it.

If you draw your table using the Tables and Borders tool from the Standard toolbar, you can design a table and decide where to place the cells by dragging. Use the Draw Table tool from the Tables and Borders toolbar to draw any size table with cell locations of your choice.

Cross-Reference See Chapter 3, "Tables," for detailed information on the Table tool and the Draw Table tool on the Tables and Borders toolbar.

Editing a table

There are several ways you can rearrange your table and enhance the text.

Inserting rows/columns

✦ **To add a new row at the bottom of the table** – press Tab when you are in the last cell of the table.

✦ **To insert a row in the middle of your table** – click on any cell in the row that will be below the new row. Right-click to display the shortcut menu. Choose Insert Rows.

✦ **To add a column at the end of your table** – select the last column. To do this, place the mouse over the border at the top of the last column of your table. The cursor changes into a black down arrow. Click to select the column and right-click to display the shortcut menu. Select Insert Columns.

✦ **To insert a column in the middle of your table** – select a column and choose Insert Columns from the shortcut menu. The column is inserted to the left of the selected column.

Note The enlarged table may not fit on your slide. Use the white handles on the edge of your table to make it smaller. Otherwise, make the columns or rows smaller to fit. (See the following section.)

Changing column widths and row heights

To change column width or row height, move the mouse over the border between two columns or rows. The cursor changes shape to a Column Width tool. Drag this tool to change the width of the column or the height of the row (see Figure 23-11). If you change the size of the overall table using the white handles, the column widths and row heights will change proportionately.

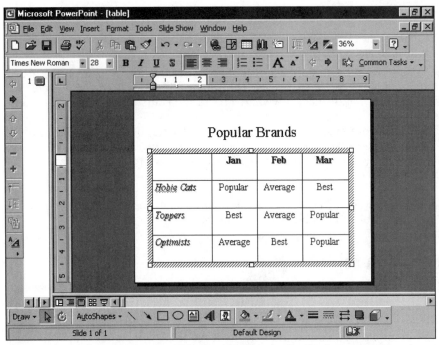

Figure 23-11: Change column widths by dragging the border between two columns.

Formatting

The text in the table can be formatted in the same way as in either Word or Excel. Use the Formatting toolbar or the Format menu for features such as font, size, and alignment. Use Format ➪ Colors and Lines to change borders, fills, and text alignment for selected cells. The Format ➪ Table menu command is used to format the whole table at once.

You can change a complete row or column by selecting it. To select a column, either drag the mouse over the cells in the column, or click with the black down arrow pointer that appears when you place the mouse at the top of the column. Select a row by dragging the mouse over the cells in the row.

Typing tabs

If you want to use tabs in a column — for example, to line up numbers — you may have found that when you press Tab, you move to the next cell. To overcome this, press Ctrl+Tab instead of Tab. You can position your tabs in the same way as in Word. To see the ruler, choose View ➪ Ruler.

Cross-Reference See Chapter 2, "Working with Text" for detailed information on setting up tabs.

Adding Excel Worksheets and Word Tables

Word tables and Excel worksheets have more power than PowerPoint tables. Create your tables in Word or Excel and you can import them into PowerPoint using one of several methods described in the following sections. Each method has its advantages and disadvantages. You can simply copy and paste, but the formatting may be lost.

Adding an Excel worksheet

If you want to import a complete table from a single worksheet in Excel, you can use the Insert ➪ Object menu command. However if you want to import only part of a worksheet, you should use Copy and Paste Special. Both methods can be used to link the table in PowerPoint to the data in Excel.

The Insert ➪ Object method

1. Create your table in Excel and save the file. You can exit from Excel if you like.

2. In PowerPoint, select the slide where you want to put the table.

3. Choose Insert ➪ Object (see Figure 23-12).

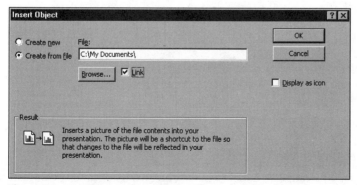

Figure 23-12: Choose Create from File and Link to insert your Excel table and keep it up-to-date with the Excel worksheet.

4. Select Create from File and then browse to find the Excel file.

5. Select Link unless you do not want the files to be linked.

6. The table is inserted onto your current slide in the center. You can move and resize it as you like. Look out for the text becoming distorted if you change the proportions of the table.

7. You can go straight to Excel to make changes by double-clicking on the table in PowerPoint. Any changes are made both in Excel and in PowerPoint.

The Copy and Paste Special method

1. Create your table in Excel and save it.

2. Select the range you wish to import into PowerPoint.

3. Copy it to the Clipboard using Edit ➪ Copy or click the Copy tool.

4. Switch to PowerPoint and select the slide on which you want to put the table.

5. Choose Edit ➪ Paste Special (see Figure 23-13). You can choose from several different formats. Read the Result box to find out how the various methods differ. One of the best methods is to choose Paste Link and Microsoft Excel Worksheet Object; your table will not only look good, but will be linked to the original file. If any changes are made to the Excel worksheet, they will be reflected in your PowerPoint table.

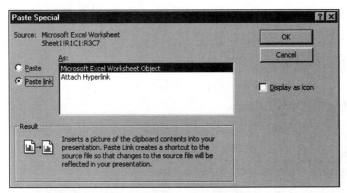

Figure 23-13: Choose Paste Special and Paste Link instead of Paste to maintain a link with your original file.

6. Move or resize the table to fit on your slide. Be careful that the text is not distorted when you change the size.

7. You can go straight to Excel to make changes by double-clicking on the table in PowerPoint. Any changes you make in Excel are made in PowerPoint.

Adding a Word table

The methods used for inserting an Excel worksheet into PowerPoint work equally well for Word tables. Either choose Insert ➪ Object or use Copy and Paste Special. However, if you would rather create your table in PowerPoint while still having all the power of Word tables at your fingertips, use the Insert ➪ Picture method, the third method listed below.

The Insert ➪ Object method

1. Create your table in Word and save the file. You can exit from Word if you like.

2. In PowerPoint, select the slide on which you want to put the table.

3. Choose Insert ➪ Object (see Figure 23-12).

4. Select Create from File and then browse to find the Word file.

5. Select Link (unless for some reason you don't want the files to be linked).

6. The table is placed at the center of your current slide. You can move and resize it as you like. Look out for the text becoming distorted if you change the proportions of the table.

7. If the files are linked you can go straight to Word to make changes by double-clicking on the table in PowerPoint. Any changes you make in Word are made in PowerPoint.

The Copy and Paste Special method

1. Create your table in Word and save it.

2. Select the range you wish to import into PowerPoint.

3. Copy it to the Clipboard using Edit ➪ Copy or click the Copy tool.

4. Switch to PowerPoint and select the slide on which you want to place the table.

5. Choose Edit ➪ Paste Special. You can choose from several different formats. Read the Result box to examine the differences between each method. One of the best methods is to choose Paste Link and Microsoft Word Document Object; your table will not only look good, but will be linked to the original file. If any changes are made to the Word file, they will be reflected in your PowerPoint table.

6. Move or resize the table to fit on your slide. Be careful that the text is not distorted when you change the size.

7. You can go straight to Word to make changes by double-clicking on the table in PowerPoint. Any changes that you make in Word are also made in PowerPoint.

The Insert ⇨ Picture method

1. In PowerPoint select the slide on which you want to place the table.

2. Choose Insert ⇨ Picture ⇨ Microsoft Word Table.

3. Select the number of rows and columns you require.

4. Even though you are still working in PowerPoint, the menus and toolbars are from Word. You can now use all of Word's tools to create your table.

5. To finish, click anywhere on the slide outside the table. The PowerPoint toolbars and menus reappear.

Summary

This chapter covered the creation of charts (graphs), organization charts, and tables in PowerPoint. Some highlights included the following:

✦ Create a chart by using an AutoLayout that includes a chart and double-clicking the chart placeholder to access Microsoft Graph.

✦ If you exit from Microsoft Graph and need to get back to edit your chart, double-click on the chart.

✦ PowerPoint offers many ways to manipulate your chart — change the chart type, whether 2-D or 3-D, switch the data from rows to columns, or format the individual series, for example.

✦ Organization charts are created in a different program. Use the Organization chart AutoLayout and then double-click on the organization chart placeholder.

✦ To get back to PowerPoint when working in the organization chart application, you must update the organization chart before exiting. Do not simply click on the PowerPoint slide.

✦ Tables can be created in PowerPoint, Word, or Excel. The choice is yours!

✦   ✦   ✦

Adding Graphics and Special Effects

Multimedia (pictures, animation, video, and sound) can bring your presentation to life. Slide transitions can be created to bring your slide onscreen with a variety of special effects. You can also work with actions, which allow you to put buttons on slides to show them in a random fashion, rather than in a linear sequence, or to run other programs, macros, sounds, or video clips.

Note All computers can show transition effects. However, you need some of the more recent features found on computers to use sound and video clips. For good-quality sound you need a compatible sound card. If you are not sure what you have in your computer, check the Windows Control Panel to see what multimedia and sound capabilities you have.

Adding Images and Multimedia

Image is another word for picture. Most of the images you use in PowerPoint will be bitmap images. (See the sidebar "Bitmap Versus Vector Graphics" for more information.) The term *multimedia* covers pictures, video, and sound in any combination. PowerPoint provides many sample images for your use. You can also create your own images using PowerPoint, a scanner, a graphics program, or a digital camera. You can edit your images to a certain extent within PowerPoint, but there is usually far more editing power in a graphics program. Most scanners also provide software with which you can edit your image.

Bitmap Versus Vector Graphics

Be aware of the difference between a bitmap and a vector graphic image. Scanned pictures, digital camera images, and photographs are all bitmap images. All of the paint type graphics programs also produce bitmaps. A bitmap image is made up of dots. Bitmap images can be saved in a variety of formats, each with its own filename extension. Some common ones you may see are .pcx, .gif, .wmf, .bmp, and .tif. There are many more. The thing to be aware of with bitmaps is that if you enlarge them, you may find that the straight lines develop jagged edges as each dot is enlarged. Another thing to be aware of is the size of the file. Bitmap files tend to be large.

Some graphics programs, especially CAD and graphic design programs, produce vector graphic images. The advantage of these files is that you can make the pictures any size and they always remain good-quality — no jagged edges. If you use the Drawing toolbar — to draw AutoShapes, for example — you are drawing vector graphics.

Adding images

Adding an image to a slide can enhance it significantly. You could add a picture that amuses — a cartoon character, for example — or a picture of the item being discussed. You may also want to put your company logo onto your slide or many slides. Be careful that you use images that are appropriate for the presentation: cartoons are suitable only under certain circumstances.

You can import an image using the following methods:

✦ Use the Clip Art Gallery, which provides Clip Art in categories and shows you thumbnails (miniatures) of your pictures so you can easily find the right image. The Clip Art Gallery also includes video and sound clips.

✦ Browse your computer's various drives to find the image you want. If you find yourself doing this often, though, you might want to move the images you're using regularly into the Clip Art Gallery. The Gallery includes a Favorites category and also lets you add your own categories: for example, you could add one for company logos and related graphics.

✦ You can also create your own illustrations and diagrams using the Drawing toolbar.

Importing images with the Clip Art Gallery

To add an image from the Clip Art Gallery to your slide:

1. Make sure you are in Normal view. If you want to use tools, rather than the menu, check that the Drawing toolbar is showing. If not, select it from the View ➪ Toolbars menu.

2. Click the Insert Clip Art tool on the Drawing toolbar, or choose Insert ➪ Picture ➪ Clip Art. The Insert ClipArt dialog box appears (see Figure 24-1). It has its own toolbar and three tabs: Pictures, Sounds, and Motion Clips. Make sure you have the Pictures tab selected.

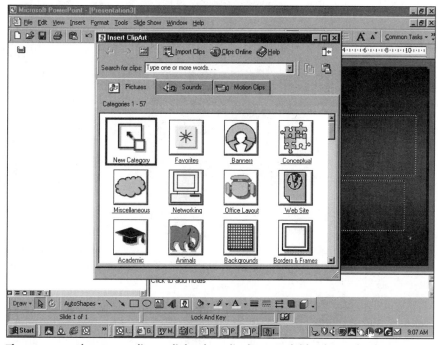

Figure 24-1: The Insert ClipArt dialog box displays available clip art by category.

3. Scroll down until you can see the category of your choice and click on it. If you change your mind about the category and want to look at another one, click on the All Categories tool on the toolbar or press Alt+Home. You'll see the categories again and can choose a different one.

4. When you place your mouse over a thumbnail of a picture, PowerPoint gives you information about its name, file type, and size. Select your image by clicking on it. A small menu appears (see Figure 24-2).

5. To see a larger version of the picture, select the second item on this menu, Preview Clip.

6. To select your picture click on the first item on this menu, Insert Clip.

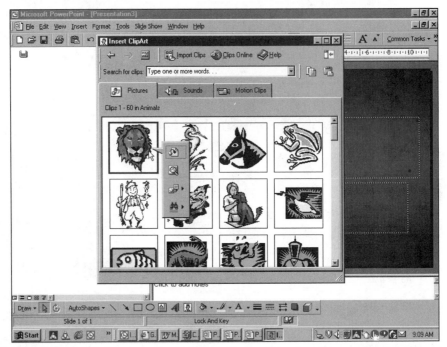

Figure 24-2: The Clip menu in the Insert ClipArt dialog box lets you preview clip art before inserting it.

7. Close the Insert ClipArt dialog box.

8. Your clip art image is placed in the center of your slide. You can move it by dragging or resize it by dragging its white handles. (If you want your image to appear on all slides, you need to put it on the Slide Master.)

 See Chapter 22, "Using Templates and Wizards," for more information about how to set up Slide Masters.

Customizing your Clip Art Gallery

You can import your own clip art from any source, such as your scanner, and choose which category to put it in. You can also create your own categories. Your most commonly used pictures can be put in a Favorites category. You can also search for related images using keywords.

 For more detailed information about how to use the Clip Art Gallery, see Chapter 53, "Universal Drawing and Graphics Features."

Importing images using the Insert File menu

Use this method to import images that don't currently appear in the Clip Art Gallery.

1. Make sure you are in Normal view.

2. Choose Insert ➪ Picture ➪ From File. The Insert Picture dialog box appears (see Figure 24-3).

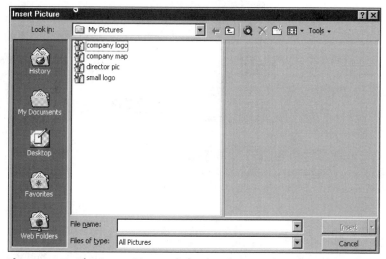

Figure 24-3: The Insert Picture dialog box lets you insert any image you have stored on your computer into your presentation.

3. Locate and select the picture of your choice and then click Insert.

4. Your picture is placed in the center of your slide. Drag it to move it, and use the white handles to resize it.

The Picture toolbar

When you have a picture on the slide and you select it (you can tell when a picture is selected because it has white handles around it), the Picture toolbar is automatically displayed (see Figure 24-4). This toolbar is for editing your picture and contains some very useful features, as described in the following list:

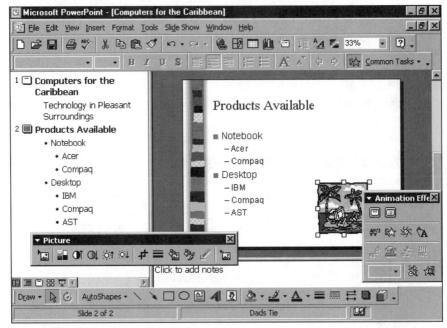

Figure 24-4: The Picture toolbar lets you fine-tune any picture you place in your presentation.

✦ **Image Control.** You can change the type of image from automatic to grayscale, black and white, or watermark. A watermark is a pale version of the image that is most often used as a background.

✦ **Brightness and Contrast.** You can adjust brightness and contrast using these four tools.

✦ **Crop.** This is used to hide part of the picture, so that only the most important part shows. To use the Crop tool, drag any of the white selection handles toward the center of the picture.

✦ **Line Style.** This adds a border to your picture.

✦ **Recolor.** This tool lets you pick out certain colors and replace them with others. For example, you could change all the red in a picture to blue. It is available only for certain types of pictures. In the Recolor dialog box, select the color to be changed in the Original color column and the new color in the second column.

✦ **Format Picture.** This opens a dialog box (see Figure 24-5) that gives you full control over the size and placement of the picture, as well as borders and other features from the Picture toolbar.

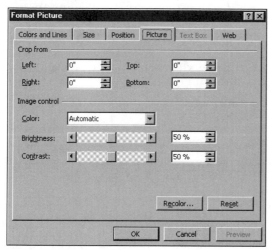

Figure 24-5: The Format Picture dialog box provides you with detailed control over the look of a picture.

✦ **Set Transparent Color.** This is a very useful tool. When you import certain images, they include a background, which hides anything underneath. For example, your company logo might include a white background. If your design template has a blue background and you place your logo on top of it, you'll see a white block behind the logo. To get rid of that white block, click the Set Transparent Color tool and then click on the white block. This will make anything that was white turn transparent and the block will disappear.

✦ **Reset Picture.** This tool changes all settings back to the original ones for this picture.

Creating illustrations and diagrams

Use the Drawing toolbar to create your own illustrations and diagrams and to edit your clip art.

Here is a summary of the main features:

✦ Open the AutoShapes menu to draw the most popular shapes: basic shapes, block arrows, flowchart symbols, lines and arrows, stars and banners, callouts and action buttons.

✦ Change the outline and fill with the tools on the toolbar or choose Format ➪ AutoShape.

✦ Add text to any shape: Click on the shape to select it and type the text.

✦ Format the text with the Formatting toolbar or select Format ➪ AutoShape and select the Text Box tab.

✦ Move the shape by dragging.

✦ Resize the shape by dragging the white handles. The yellow diamond handle adjusts the proportion of the shape.

✦ Choose Draw on the Drawing toolbar for features such as snap, order, group, nudge, and rotate.

✦ Add shadow and 3-D effects.

✦ Add AutoShape Connectors when drawing flowcharts.

Working with sound

Adding sound to your presentation can draw the attention of the audience or add humor. I wouldn't use too many sounds, though; they'll lose their impact and may become irritating. Whether or not sound is appropriate depends on the type of presentation you are giving.

Inserting sounds

PowerPoint provides you with some sample sound files. You can usually find more in the Windows\Media folder and you can use any others you may have on your computer. There are also automatic links to help you download new sound files from the Internet from within PowerPoint. Here's how the two basic methods for inserting sounds work:

✦ **From the Gallery.** To insert a sound from the Gallery, choose Insert ➪ Movies and Sounds ➪ Sound from Gallery.

✦ **From a file.** To insert a sound file that is not included in the Gallery, choose Insert ➪ Movies and Sounds ➪ Sound from File.

The sound icon

When you insert a sound, an icon appears on your slide and you are prompted with the following: "Do you want your sound to play automatically in the slide show? If not, it will play when you click it."

✦ If you answer "Yes" the sound plays when the slide appears in the slide show.

✦ If you answer "No" the sound plays only when you place your mouse over the sound icon and click on it.

You can move the sound icon around and resize it as you like.

Note You can achieve more control over the way a sound is played if you use the custom animation effects, which are covered later in this chapter.

Working with video (motion or movie)

PowerPoint uses the terms video, motion, and movie interchangeably. They all refer to the same thing. Adding a video clip adds life to your presentation. You might like to use one on the first or the last slide, or insert an animated slide that runs over and over during a coffee break until you return to continue the presentation.

Tip Some people use PowerPoint to create training modules instead of presentations, or to create continuously running demonstrations or sales presentations, which run on computers at trade shows. For such purposes, video is an excellent way of drawing attention or explaining a product. Just be aware that video files take up lots and lots of disk space.

Inserting video

PowerPoint provides you with some sample video clips. As with images and sound, there are also automatic links to help you download new ones from the Internet.

✦ **From the Gallery.** To insert video clips from the Gallery, choose Insert ⇨ Movies and Sounds ⇨ Movie from Gallery.

✦ **From a file.** To insert a file that is not included in the Gallery, choose Insert ⇨ Movies and Sounds ⇨ Movie from File.

The video clip icon

When you insert a video clip, the first frame of the video appears on your slide and you are prompted with the following: "Do you want your movie to play automatically in the slide show? If not, it will play when you click it."

✦ If you answer "Yes" the movie plays when the slide appears in the slide show.

✦ If you answer "No" the movie plays only when you place your mouse over the picture and click on it.

You can move and resize the video frame in the same way as with any other object. If you enlarge it, you'll find the resolution drops.

Note You can achieve more control over the way a video clip is played if you use the custom animation effects, which are covered later in this chapter.

Inserting a CD audio track

Another media alternative is to play a track from a music CD. You might like to have music playing while your audience is entering the room and getting settled.

You can set this feature up without the CD in the drive, but to play any music, you'll obviously need the CD. Choose Insert ➪ Movies and Sounds ➪ Play CD Audio Track. This opens the Movie and Sound Options dialog box (see Figure 24-7). Select the starting and ending tracks and the length of time you want the music to play, in minutes. You are also prompted to select whether you want to play the CD automatically or only upon a mouse click.

Figure 24-6: The Movie and Sound Options dialog box controls the way CD audio tracks are played during your presentation.

Recording your own sound

Finally, you can record your own sound if you have a microphone attached to your computer. Choose Insert ➪ Movies and Sounds ➪ Record Sound. Name your sound and then record it. Click the Stop button when you have finished.

Tip

If you find you cannot play a particular sound or video in PowerPoint, you can try playing it using the Windows Media Player. Choose Insert ➪ Object and select Create from File. Browse to find the file. It is placed on your slide as an object and is run using the Windows Media Player.

Using Slide Transitions

Slide transitions are special effects used when moving from one slide to another in a slide show. Adding slide transitions makes a presentation more interesting. You may be tempted to use a different transition for each slide, but this can confuse the audience. Your presentation is more effective if you use the same transition between each pair of slides in a series of slides. You could use one transition for each logical section. When you change to another section, change to another transition. This is a subtle way of telling the audience that you have changed to a new subject.

Note   You can assign transition effects in Slide Sorter view or in Normal view. However, in Normal view you can only add transition effects to one slide at a time.

Selecting the slides

To select the slides you want to add transition effects to:

1. Make sure you are in Slide Sorter view and that the Slide Sorter toolbar is showing. If it is not, select it from the View ➪ Toolbars menu.

2. To apply a slide transition to an individual slide, click to select the slide (a black border appears around it).

3. To apply a transition to a group of slides, click on the first slide and then hold down the Shift key and click on the last slide. The group of slides should now all be selected.

Adding transitions

There are two main methods of adding transitions. A small icon appears below a slide to show that it has a transition effect. The following sections describe how they work.

The Slide Transition tool

When you have selected the slides you want to apply a transition to, click on the Slide Transition tool or choose Slide Show ➪ Slide Transition. The Slide Transition dialog box appears (see Figure 24-7). To create a transition, use the following steps:

Figure 24-7: The Slide Transition dialog box.

1. Choose the transition effect you want from the drop-down list. When you make a selection, the Effect window shows you a preview of the effect.

2. To control the speed of the transition, choose Slow, Medium, or Fast.

3. When giving a presentation, you normally want to advance from one slide to the next by clicking the mouse. If you are creating a rolling demonstration, however, you can choose to move from one slide to the next automatically. Select Automatically After and enter the length of time the slide must be on the screen before moving on to the next slide.

4. You can choose to play a sound when the slide is shown. Choose the sound you want from the drop-down list. You can also decide whether the sound is to be played once or over and over again (loop), stopping only when you play the next sound. If you choose to loop, and want the sound to stop when the next slide appears, you have to add the sound called Stop Previous Sound to the next slide.

5. This dialog box also allows you to click Apply, which adds the transition effect only to the selected slides; or Apply to All, which adds the effect to all the slides in the presentation at once.

The Slide Effects tool

This is a shorter version of the Slide Transition tool. It adds the chosen effect but does not give you any additional options. Choose the effect you want from the drop-down list.

Using Preset Animations

You may have heard of using a build effect with a bulleted list. This is when you show a slide and reveal one point at a time in a list as you give your presentation. The list appears as one slide; sometimes the previous point fades to a softer color when you bring up the next point. PowerPoint has taken this effect many steps further with the Preset Animations. You can add sound as well.

PowerPoint lets you customize these animations to make them happen in any sequence you choose. If you have a multilevel bulleted list, with topics and subtopics, you can choose whether you want a bullet with all its sub-items to appear at once or individually, and also whether to fade the previous bullets when new ones appear.

Applying preset animations in Slide Sorter view

If you are in the Slide Sorter view, the preset animation control is restricted in some ways but more powerful in others. Many more animation effects are available in

Slide Sorter view than in Normal view or from the menu. You can also select several slides to change at once.

Note

In Slide Sorter view you cannot choose which element of the slide is to be animated. PowerPoint assumes you want to animate the main element of the slide (for example, the bulleted list or table). Also, you cannot choose any of the text animation effects, such as Laser Text Effect, that are available when in Normal view.

To add a preset animation:

1. Select the slide to be animated and click the Preset Animation drop-down list on the Slide Sorter toolbar.

2. Select the animation effect; PowerPoint immediately shows you a preview. It also puts a small icon below the slide to show there is animation.

3. If you want to see the animation again, click the Animation Preview tool. If it appears too quickly to see, click the Slide Show tool to play the current slide. Press Esc to return.

Working with preset animations in Normal view

If you want more options for animation, switch to Normal view. You can choose which element of the slide to animate. This is useful if, for example, you want to animate each column of a two-column bulleted list separately.

Applying effects

Basically, here's how it works:

✦ Select the element of the slide to be animated — for example, a bulleted list or an object such as a picture.

✦ Choose Slide Show ➪ Preset Animation. (You can also click the Animation Effects tool on the Formatting toolbar, which switches on or off the Animation Effects toolbar. However, this toolbar shows only the first eight preset effects. Animate Title, Animate Slide Text, Animation Order, Custom Animation, and Animation Preview are extra tools.)

✦ Only the animation effects available for the selected object are shown. The text-only animation effects — Laser Text, Typewriter Text, Reverse Text Order, and Drop-In Text — are available only if you have selected a text object.

✦ Some of these animation effects also have an accompanying sound: For example, the Typewriter effect also sounds like someone typing. (Removing sound from the slide is covered in the following section on customizing your animation.)

✦ You can use animation effects to bring ordinary clip art to life. Suppose you've inserted an image of a car. If you select it, choose Slide Show ⇨ Preset Animation ⇨ Drive-In. When you preview the slide in Slide Show view, the car will appear to drive onto the screen and screech to a halt.

Previewing your effects

You have several ways to preview your animation effect. On the Animation Effects toolbar is an Animation Preview tool. This puts a miniature preview window on the screen and shows a brief sample of the animation — for example, you don't hear the complete sound. The best way to preview your animation is to go to the Slide Show view. This shows the slide in full with all the sounds and movements. To return from Slide Show view, press Esc.

Creating Customized Animation Effects

You can control the way your slide is animated in many ways. You can choose the sequence in which things happen on the screen, and which elements have sounds attached to them. You can control the sequence in which the elements appear. You can decide how a multilevel bulleted list is displayed and whether lines of text must be faded once a new line appears. Use your imagination to make good use of animation effects. Here are a couple of sample ideas:

✦ On the first slide in your show, have a video playing repeatedly while a CD provides appropriate background music. When your audience is settled and you are ready to start, press Enter to move onto the first slide of your presentation.

✦ Introduce a new product with an image coming onto the screen with a drumroll.

To create customized animations it is best to be in Normal view, and then follow these steps:

1. First, design your slide with all the elements on it that you want to use.

2. Once you're happy with your slide, choose Slide Show ⇨ Custom Animation or click the Custom Animation tool on the Animation Effects toolbar. This opens the Custom Animation dialog box (see Figure 24-8).

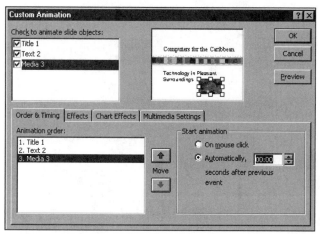

Figure 24-8: Use these controls to set the order and timing of animation events in your presentation.

3. There are four tabs: Order & Timing, Effects, Chart Effects, and Multimedia Settings. The top section lists the elements on your slide that are available for animation. Each one to be animated should have a tick in its box. Here's how to use those tabs:

- **Order and Timing.** This tab (refer to Figure 24-9) controls the order in which the objects come onto the screen. To change the animation sequence, click on the element and then on the up or down arrow to move it higher or lower in the sequence. You can also decide whether the animation starts when the mouse is clicked or automatically after a certain time. If you want it to happen immediately, choose Automatically, but leave the time as 00:00.

- **Effects.** The Effects tab of the Custom Animation dialog box (see Figure 24-9) is in three sections. The first section covers how the object comes onto the screen — the effect it uses, the direction it comes from, and the sound that plays. Below it are options covering what happens after the animation. You may like the object to fade to a color (this won't work with all objects — video, for example). This feature is often used with bulleted lists where previous bullets are faded to a softer color. The object can also disappear after the animation or be hidden by a mouse-click.

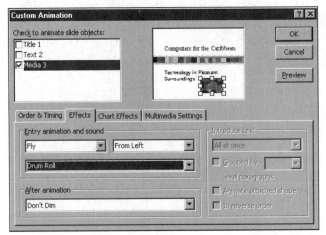

Figure 24-9: These controls fine-tune your animation effects.

The other half of the dialog box covers how text is animated. The text can come onto the screen all at once, by letter, or by word. This section is also used to specify how to bring bulleted lists onto the screen. Where there are several levels of bullets, i.e., bullets with additional points under them, a whole group can come in at once: select Grouped By and choose the level. Alternatively, the individual bullets can come onto the screen one at a time: simply unclick the Grouped By option. (Note that the Preview button does not show this effect accurately.) Bullets can also come onto the screen in reverse order.

- **Chart Effects.** You can also make charts more effective with animation, using the controls in the Chart Effects tab of the Custom Animation dialog box (see Figure 24-10). For example, you could have the bars of a bar graph appear one at a time, giving you time to explain the details of each bar, and choose whether the bars appear by series or by category.

   The first section of this tab is used to specify which parts of the chart should be animated. Your options are: all at once, by series or category, by element in series, or by element in category. In addition, you can choose to animate the grid and legend. The rest of the dialog box is identical to the Effects tab.

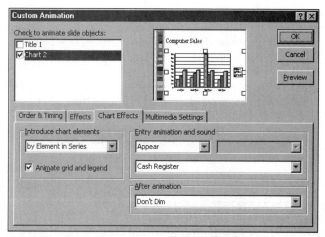

Figure 24-10: Specify chart animation effects using these controls.

• **Multimedia Settings.** The last tab of the Custom Animation dialog box is called Multimedia Settings (see Figure 24-11). This is only active when a sound or video clip is selected under the Order and Timing tab.

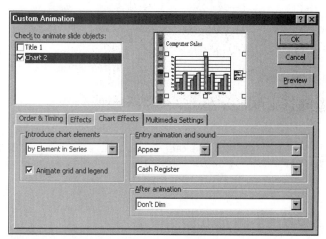

Figure 24-11: The Multimedia Settings tab controls how sound and video clips are played. Use Multimedia Settings to specify how an object should be played. For example, you can choose to have a video and a CD soundtrack play simultaneously.

Note   The More Options button offers the option of replaying a video in a loop, over and over again until stopped. You may have difficulty stopping a slide with a looping video on it using a mouse-click — it may just pause the video. If so, use the Enter key or the PgDn key to move to the next slide.

4. When you have finished with the Custom Animation dialog box, go to the Slide Show view to see how your slide works. It may take a few attempts to achieve the effect you originally imagined. There is a Preview button on the dialog box, but I find it more effective to go to the Slide Show and play the slide. The preview shows only a fraction of what is happening.

Creating Actions

Actions are links from one item on a slide that take you to other slides or initiate other actions. The following list demonstrates some of the ways they can be used:

✦ PowerPoint provides some buttons that represent commonly used actions — to go to the next slide or the start of the slide show, for example.

✦ Actions can be started from any object on the screen, not just Action buttons. You could link an action to text, an object, a table, a graph, or an image.

✦ You can decide whether the action is to be taken when the mouse moves over the item or only when you click on it.

✦ You can use actions to link to a specific slide, another PowerPoint presentation, a Word document, an Excel spreadsheet, a macro, a site on the Internet or intranet, or to run another program.

✦ Actions are useful if you are using PowerPoint to create a rolling demonstration or onscreen training course. You could insert action buttons that allow the person viewing the slide show to choose which section to cover next. In a training course, clicking on the right answer could take users to the next question; clicking on the wrong answer could take users back to the beginning of the section they are covering.

Action buttons

The standard Action buttons provided with PowerPoint are Custom, Home, Help, Information, Back or Previous, Forward or Next, Beginning, End, Return, Document, Sound, and Movie (see Figure 24-12).

Tip   Even though each of these has a name, you can use them for any function. There are no links created in advance. You can decide what action they initiate.

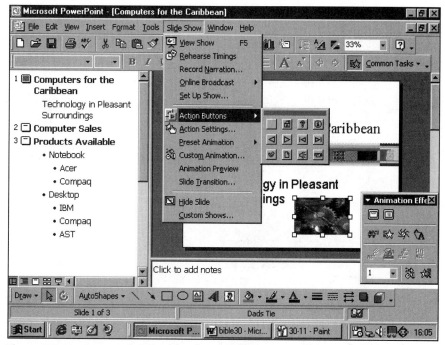

Figure 24-12: PowerPoint provides these commonly used Action buttons.

To add an action button to your slide:

1. Make sure you are in Normal view.

2. Choose Slide Show ➪ Action buttons or click the AutoShapes tool on the Drawing toolbar and choose Action buttons. A set of Action buttons is displayed.

3. Click the Action button of your choice.

4. Click on the slide where you would like to place the button. The Action Settings dialog box appears (see Figure 24-13).

5. Decide whether you want the action to be taken when you click on the button or when the cursor moves over the button. Click on the relevant tab: Mouse Click or Mouse Over. It is far safer to take an action by clicking on the button, as it is easy to move your mouse over a button by mistake!

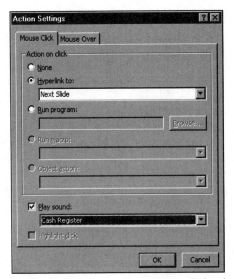

Figure 24-13: The Action Settings dialog box
lets you create a variety of useful actions.

6. Select what is to happen when you click on the Action button:

   - **Hyperlink to.** This allows you to go to a specific slide in the current slide show, e.g., first, last; to go to another slide show, run it, and return to the same place or run it and continue; to go to an URL (an Internet address); or to go to any other file.

   - **Run program.** Choose Browse to locate the program.

   - **Run macro.** This is not available from Action buttons.

   - **Object action.** This is not available from Action buttons.

7. You can also have a sound played when you click on an Action button by selecting Play Sound. Select the sound you want to be played from the drop-down list.

8. If you select Highlight Click, then when you click on the button in the slide show, the button is highlighted for a moment, to acknowledge you have clicked on it. This is only available for certain objects.

9. To test your Action button, click OK on the dialog box and run the Slide Show. Click the Action button and check what happens.

Creating a sample Action

Suppose you want to place a button on a slide that restarts the slide show by going to the first slide:

1. Go to the slide on which you want to put the Action button and make sure you are in Normal view.

2. Click the AutoShapes tool and select the Action buttons.

3. Click the Action Button: Beginning tool and then click on your slide to place it where you would like it.

4. Select First Slide from the Hyperlink to drop-down list.

5. Click Play Sound and select a sound from the drop-down list.

6. Click OK to close the dialog box.

7. Test the action button by clicking the Slide Show View tool. You should see your Action button on the screen. Click it, and you should see the Action button change color, hear the sound you selected, and be taken to the first slide in your presentation.

Action settings

If you do not use one of the built-in Action buttons, you can use other objects to link to actions. You could use some text, a video clip, a sound, an AutoShape, a macro button, etc. The dialog box is the same as the one for Action buttons, but some extra features are available, depending on which type of object you selected.

To create an action based on an object:

1. Place your object on the slide — a text box, an AutoShape, an image, a sound, a video, or a macro button — and select it. It should have white handles around it.

2. Choose Slide Show ⇨ Action Settings to open the Action Settings dialog box.

3. Decide whether you want the action to be taken by moving the mouse over the object or by clicking on the object (preferred) and select the appropriate tab.

4. Choose whether you want to create a Hyperlink, run a program, run a macro, or take an object action. If you have a sound or video clip selected, you can select Object Action and choose Play. This means that when you run the slide show and click on the video or sound clip, the video or sound starts.

5. You can also associate a sound with an object by selecting Play Sound and choosing the sound you want to be played from the drop-down list.

6. Select Highlight Click if you want the object to be highlighted momentarily when you click on it.

7. Test your action by running the slide show. Click the Slide Show View tool.

Summary

PowerPoint offers many ways to add life to your presentation:

✦ Adding an image to a slide is worth a thousand words. Choose images appropriate to the tone of your presentation.

✦ Adding sound or video uses a lot more disk space, but is very effective at drawing attention.

✦ Adding slide transitions makes the changeover from one slide to the next more interesting, but it's best to use the same transition for several slides, rather than a different transition for each slide.

✦ Preset animations let you bring elements of your slide onto the screen from different directions and with different effects, including sound.

✦ You can customize the way objects come onto the screen by choosing the sequence and timing, and also what sounds accompany them.

✦ Finally, you can create actions. These are useful for rolling demonstrations or onscreen training courses. By clicking on a specific item, for example, you can go to a particular slide, run another program, or run a macro.

✦   ✦   ✦

Creating and Organizing a Slide Show

Now that the slides you have created are ready for a slide show, PowerPoint can take you much further than simply displaying them one slide after another. You can add special effects to the way each slide comes onto the screen and hide slides you don't want to use. You can print supporting materials to hand out to the audience and record a narration to accompany the show (as well as sound and video, as covered in the previous chapter). You can use Pack and Go Wizard to put the whole show on disk so you can move it to another machine. In a corporate environment, you can give your presentation over a network, using the online meeting feature to get everyone together to confer on the presentation. Taking this concept a step further, you can even broadcast your presentation over an intranet or the Internet.

Creating a Slide Show

The slide show feature is built into PowerPoint. You do not need to do anything special to create a slide show; just create the slides and save the presentation. Slide Sorter view is used to see all the slides in sequence.

Rearranging the slide show

Click the Slide Sorter View tool, which is at the bottom of your window at the left, or choose View ⇨ Slide Sorter (see Figure 25-1).

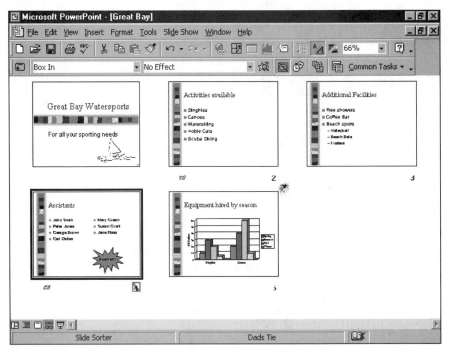

Figure 25-1: Slide Sorter view is used to change the order of your slides. Slide 4 is a hidden slide – note the icon on the slide number.

In this view, you can drag the slides from one position to another to change the sequence in which they will appear. Use the Zoom tool on the Standard toolbar to see more or fewer slides on the screen. To delete a slide, click on it and press Delete. There is no prompt to ask if you are sure, so be careful when deleting slides. If you make a mistake, click the Undo tool to get it back immediately.

If you want to move around the slide show in a different sequence, you can branch from one section to another, or even go to another program.

Cross-Reference For more information about branching from one slide to another, or to another program, see Chapter 24 "Adding Graphics and Special Effects." See the section on actions.

Hiding slides

You may change your mind and decide not to show one of the slides in your presentation. If you don't want to delete the slide, you can hide it temporarily.

Select a slide and click the Hide Slide tool on the Slide Sorter toolbar to hide it. This does not delete the slide, but prevents it from being shown when running the slide show. To unhide the slide, select it and click the same tool again. Figure 25-1 shows a hidden slide (slide 4).

If you are running a slide show and want to show a hidden slide, right-click and choose Go ➪ Slide Navigator and double-click on the slide you require. Slide numbers of hidden slides are in parentheses. A third method is to press H to go to the next hidden slide.

Adding comments

Comments can be added to slides in Normal view or Slide view. They are much like yellow sticky notes and are easy to remove. They are intended for use when reviewing the presentation. If you route the presentation to several people, they can each add their comments, and review other people's comments. Each comment starts with the author's name. Here's how it works:

✦ You can choose to run a slide show with or without comments.

✦ To insert a comment, make sure you are in Normal view or Slide view. Then choose Insert ➪ Comment. Notice that the Reviewing toolbar appears (see Figure 25-2).

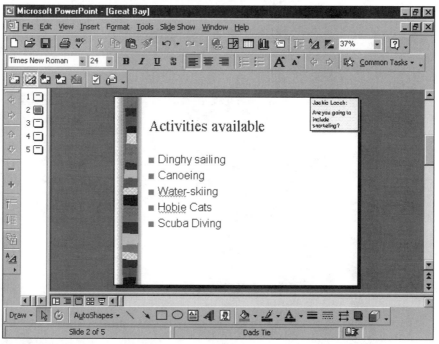

Figure 25-2: Comments are like sticky paper notes on your page. You can move them anywhere. Notice the Reviewing toolbar is showing.

✦ Type the comment and then click outside the comment area.

✦ Comments can be formatted like any other item. You can also change the shape of the comment box by going to the Drawing toolbar and choosing Draw ➪ Change AutoShape.

✦ You can move from comment to comment by clicking on Next Comment and Previous Comment on the Reviewing toolbar. Use the toolbar to add or remove comments and show or hide comments.

Adding speaker notes

Speaker notes are printed notes, which the presenter uses as a guide while speaking. Whenever you turn around to look at your slides while giving a presentation, you run the risk of losing the attention of the audience. Speaker notes help you avoid this problem, because an image of the slide is printed on the top of the note and the points you want to make are printed at the bottom. Here are some guidelines:

✦ Speaker notes can be typed when in Normal view. Click on the words Click to Add Notes and start typing.

✦ You can make this part of the screen larger by dragging the gray bar upwards. Another method is to choose View ➪ Notes Page. This shows the speaker notes as a full page.

✦ To make them readable, click the Zoom tool and select, for example, 75% (see Figure 25-3).

Figure 25-3: Use the Zoom tool to make the speaker notes page a readable size.

✦ You can also add speaker notes while running the slide show. Right-click to get the shortcut menu and choose Speaker Notes. Type your note and click Close.

✦ To print Speaker Notes, choose File ➪ Print. Under Print What, select Notes Pages. The slide prints in the top half of the page and the notes are printed underneath.

Handouts

Handouts are pages with several slides printed on them. They are intended for handing out to the audience as a reminder of what was covered in the presentation. However, they are also useful for reviewing your presentation. You can fit up to nine slides on one page (see Figure 25-4).

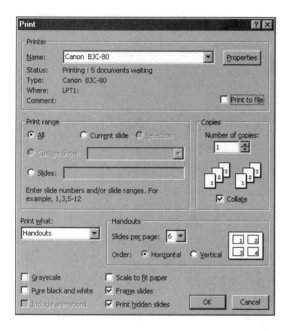

Figure 25-4: When you print handouts, you can choose how many slides per page to print.

To print handouts, choose File ➪ Print. Under Print What, select Handouts. Then decide how many slides per page you want to print and in what order.

Summary slides

A summary slide takes the titles of selected slides and puts them on one slide. This is useful for producing an introductory slide to tell the audience what subjects you'll be covering, or a closing slide to reinforce your main points. Select the slides in Slide Sorter view by holding down the Ctrl key and clicking on each slide in turn. Click the Summary Slide tool on the Slide Sorter toolbar to insert a new slide with the title Summary Slide. The titles of each of the selected slides are listed as bullets.

Playing the Slide Show

To play your slide show, simply click the Slide Show tool at the bottom left of your screen. This will run the slide show, allowing you to move from slide to slide manually. Following are alternative methods to run the show:

✦ Choose View ➪ Slide Show

✦ Choose Slide Show ➪ View Show

✦ Press F5

Note   If PowerPoint is not up and running, you can right-click on the filename and choose Show.

Moving between slides

To go to the first slide press Home. To go to the last slide press End. To end the slide show before it is finished, press Esc. To see a list of the controls you can use in a presentation, press F1 during the slide show. Table 25-1 shows the mouse and keyboard actions for moving between slides or points on a slide.

Table 25-1 Moving Between Slides	
To the Next Slide/Point	**To the Previous Slide/Point**
Enter	Backspace
Right Arrow	Left Arrow
Down Arrow	Up Arrow
N	P
PgDn	PgUp
Space	
Mouse-click	

Writing on slides (Annotations)

During a slide show you may want to write on the slide or circle an important item. To do this, right-click on the slide while running the slide show, to call up the shortcut menu. Select Pointer Options ➪ Pen or press Ctrl+P. The cursor shape changes to a pen. Drag the mouse on the screen to draw. You can hold down the Shift key while drawing to keep your lines horizontal or vertical. You can also move the mouse around until you see a button at the bottom, left corner of the screen and click the button to view the shortcut menu. The following list covers some additional features:

✦ To choose a different pen color, right-click and choose Pointer Options ⇨ Pen Color from the shortcut menu.

✦ The highlighting is temporary and disappears when you move on to the next slide. To erase it while it is on the screen, press E or right-click and choose Screen ⇨ Erase Pen.

✦ To continue with the slide show, right-click and choose Pointer Options ⇨ Automatic. When you choose Automatic, the pointer automatically disappears if it is not used for 15 seconds. You can also press Ctrl+A to change the pointer back into an arrow.

Black and white slides

When you are giving a presentation, it is handy to be able to display a plain black screen or a plain white screen. When you want the full attention of the audience, you should remove any slides from the screen and put up either a black or white screen. To do this, press B for a black screen or W for a white screen. Press the same key again to continue with the slide show.

Setting up the slide show

In a presentation, the default is to move from slide to slide manually, by pressing a key, for example. You can also create self-running presentations for use in trade shows or at kiosks. You can set the amount of time each slide must stay on the screen before automatically moving to the next slide. Choose Slide Show ⇨ Set Up Show to see the options available (see Figure 25-5).

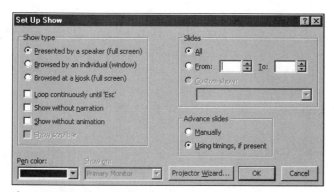

Figure 25-5: Choose the show type in the Set Up Show dialog box. The Browsed at a Kiosk option prevents the show from being modified while it is running.

There are three show types to choose from:

✦ **Presented by a speaker (full screen).** This is the normal option for a presentation. Slides are moved manually from one to the next.

✦ **Browsed by an individual (window).** This presents the show in a window instead of full-screen. A limited set of commands is available to make it easier for someone to browse the slide show (see Figure 25-6).

✦ **Browsed at a kiosk (full screen).** This prevents the slide show from being modified in any way by the audience. The audience can advance through slides. The slide show automatically restarts after 5 minutes of inactivity and repeats itself when finished.

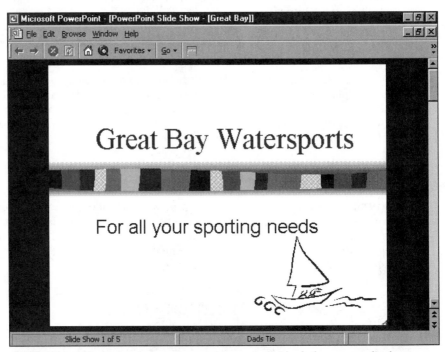

Figure 25-6: When you choose Browsed by an individual, the screen displays a special toolbar and menus.

In the Set Up Show dialog box (refer to Figure 25-5) you can also select the pen color for annotating slides. You can decide to run the show without narration or without animation. The Set Up Show dialog box is also used to select the range of slides to be shown, or a custom slide show. This is discussed later in this chapter. You can choose to run the slide show automatically or manually.

Projector Wizard automatically detects your projector, if present, and allows you to set up your computer and slide show to match the projector. Follow the instructions in the wizard.

Note To choose whether to show comments during a slide show, choose View ⇨ Comments.

Setting slide timings

To set the timings for an automatic self-running slide show, go to Slide Sorter view and select the slides you want to set a certain timing for. Click the Slide Transition tool at the left of the Slide Sorter toolbar or choose Slide Show ⇨ Slide Transition. Enter the number of seconds the slide must be displayed in the Automatically After box. Remove the Mouse Click option if you don't want the slide to move on when the mouse is clicked. If you leave both options turned on, PowerPoint will move on to the next slide either when you click on the mouse or when the time is up, whichever comes first.

Rehearsing slide timings

Rehearsing slide timings is useful for two things.

✦ You can use it to rehearse your slide show, or to find out when you are spending too much time on a particular slide or showing too many slides in too short a time.

✦ It can also be used to insert the timings for an automatically advanced slide show.

In Slide Sorter view, choose Slide Show ⇨ Rehearse Timings or click on the Rehearse Timings tool. The slide show starts and so does the timer. Show each slide for the length of time you want. At the end of the show a dialog box informs you "The total time for the slide show was xx seconds. Do you want to record the new slide timings and use them when you view the slide show?" Choose Yes.

The time now shows under each slide. If you run the slide show automatically, each slide will display for the recorded length of time. Choose Slide Show ⇨ Set Up Show and select Advance slides: Using timings, if present.

Custom slide shows

Once you have created a slide show and presented it, you often find you have to repeat the show to another audience but with some changes. Perhaps you want to hide certain slides, or change the sequence. Create a custom show for this.

Choose Slide Show ⇨ Custom Shows. Then choose New. Type a name for the custom show, click on the slides you wish to use, and click Add to put them in the list (see Figure 25-7). To transfer several slides at once to the custom show, hold down the Ctrl key and click on the slides you want. Then click Add. To change the sequence of the slides in the custom show, click on the slide in the right-hand list box and then on the up arrow or down arrow, as required. Then click OK.

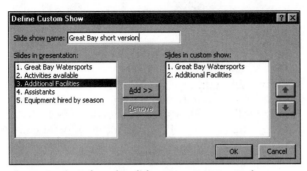

Figure 25-7: Select the slides you want to use in a custom show, and rearrange the order of them.

You can view the show by clicking the Show button. To show the custom show, choose Slide Show ➪ Set Up Show. Under the Slides section, select Custom Show and select your custom slide show.

To switch back to the full slide show, choose Slide Show ➪ Set Up Show and change the setting under Slides, back to All.

Using Recorded Narration

You can record narrations to accompany a self-running slide show. Narrations are also useful to store the verbal part of your presentation so that you can put the whole presentation on the Web, or to make the presentation available to someone who was not able to attend, or to simply store your presentation complete with the speech. You can also use the feature to store comments made during a presentation.

You'll need a microphone and sound card to create a narration, and anyone who wants to hear it must also have a sound card in his or her computer. The quality of the speech will vary from system to system. You can record your narration at various levels of quality; the higher the quality, the more disk space it will require. A noisy room may ruin a recording. And narrations are not good for people who are hard of hearing.

Tip   An alternative to recording sound is to use speaker notes to type the speech. It uses far less space and avoids the hardware and sound quality problems

You can record the narration before or during the presentation, and you can record the narration for the entire show, or for individual slides. The narration will take precedence over all other sounds attached to a slide, so only the narration will be played. When you record a narration, a sound icon appears on each slide (in views other than Slide Show view).

When you play the slide show, you can choose to run it with or without the narration. Choose Slide Show ➪ Set Up Show and select Show Without Narration if you don't want the narration to play.

Recording a narration

To record a narration, choose Slide Show ➪ Record Narration. The Record Narration dialog box appears (see Figure 25-8). Here's how it works:

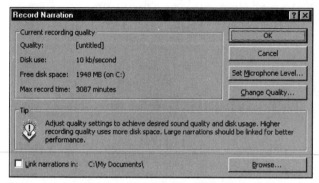

Figure 25-8: The Record Narration dialog box gives you an idea of how much space you will use on your disk. Choose Change Quality to change how much space is needed.

✦ Notice the figures regarding disk use and maximum record time. You probably don't want to fill your hard disk with a sound file.

✦ Choose Set Microphone Level to ensure the volume is appropriate.

✦ Choose Change Quality and find an appropriate combination of Format and Attributes. Choose the best quality you can use with the disk space you have available. The preset qualities are CD quality, radio quality, and telephone quality. You can save a new combination of Format and Attributes under another name.

✦ If you are recording a large narration, choose Link narrations in and select an appropriate folder. The default folder for linked narrations is the same folder as your presentation. When you link narrations, the narrations are stored in a separate file with the name: *presentation name* narration *slide number*.wav. If you don't link narrations, the audio is stored within the presentation file.

✦ Click OK and you will be prompted, "You can start recording narration on any slide. Do you want to start recording at the Current Slide/First Slide?" Make your selection for starting the slide show and record the narrations by speaking into the microphone.

✦ To pause recording narrations, right-click and select Pause Recording from the shortcut menu. To resume recording, right-click and select Resume Recording from the shortcut menu.

✦ At the end of the show, or when you stop the show, you will be prompted, "The narrations have been saved with each slide. Do you want to save the slide timings also? Yes/No." Select Yes so that the person playing back the slide show will automatically move from one slide to the next after the same length of time.

✦ When a narration is saved, a sound icon is placed in the lower right corner of each slide. This icon does not show up in Slide Show view.

✦ To remove a narration from a slide, click on the sound icon to select it and press Delete.

Rerecording narrations

To rerecord narrations, select the slide and choose Slide Show ⇨ Record Narration and click OK. Record your new narration and press Esc when you want to stop. Be careful which slide you stop on. Go on to the slide after the one you want to stop on. For example, if you want to stop on slide 8, then go to slide 9 to stop — otherwise, the new recording will not be saved to slide 8.

Using Pack and Go Wizard

Many people create their presentations on one computer, but want to run the slide show on another computer. The presentation computer might not even have PowerPoint loaded and the screen may be a different type and have projection equipment linked to it. Pack and Go Wizard puts all the files you need onto a disk(s) and compresses them. You can take the presentation to another computer and load the slide show onto the hard disk. It is automatically decompressed at the same time. When you want to run the slide show, you can use the PowerPoint Viewer, which is covered in the next section of this chapter, or you can run the slide show from PowerPoint, if it is installed.

To run Pack and Go Wizard:

1. Choose File ⇨ Pack and Go. The first of six dialog boxes appears (see Figure 25-9). Click Next.

2. You can select the currently active presentation and you can also browse to find other presentations. Click Next.

3. Select the floppy drive (A:) unless you want to send the presentation to another destination. Click Next.

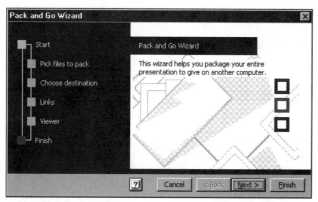

Figure 25-9: The first of the Pack and Go Wizard dialog boxes.

4. Select Include Linked Files and Embed TrueType Fonts to make sure all files and fonts are included. Click Next.

5. If you are going to run your slide show on a computer that does not have PowerPoint included, you can include PowerPoint Viewer with the presentation. To do so, select Viewer for Windows 95 or NT. Click Next.

6. The final dialog box confirms your options, states that it will compress the presentation, and will call for more than one floppy if required. Click Finish.

Here are some additional guidelines:

✦ Your slide show and the PowerPoint Viewer, if requested, will be saved on your floppy disk. If more than one disk is required, you will be prompted.

✦ To run your presentation on another computer, put the floppy in the drive and open Windows Explorer. Browse to the floppy drive and run PNGsetup. Select a folder on the computer where you would like to put the presentation. The files will be expanded and copied onto the computer.

✦ When the copying is complete, you can run the slide show either using PowerPoint or the PowerPoint Viewer.

Using the PowerPoint Viewer

The PowerPoint Viewer is provided with PowerPoint as a separate program. If you want to present a slide show on a computer that does not have PowerPoint installed, you can use the viewer instead. To take a presentation to another computer that does not have PowerPoint installed, you will need to include the PowerPoint Viewer when using the Pack and Go wizard for your slide show. The viewer can also be downloaded from the Microsoft Web site at www.microsoft. com. You are allowed to copy and distribute it freely.

To install the PowerPoint Viewer from a floppy disk containing a packed presentation, insert the disk in the drive. Choose Start ➪ Run. Browse to the A: drive and run the program called Setup. Select a folder for the viewer.

When you run the viewer, it lets you browse for a presentation. Click Open to run the slide show (see Figure 25-10). Right-click on any slide to bring up the pop-up menu, which offers you a number of options regarding the way the show is presented.

Figure 25-10: The PowerPoint Viewer lets people who don't have PowerPoint on their computers view your slide shows.

Online Meetings

You can hold a meeting using a PowerPoint presentation as your topic and collaborate with other people over a network. This is also true in the other Office programs, such as Word or Excel. Microsoft NetMeeting must be running on all the participants' computers. This program allows you to share information with people in different places in real time. It is as though you are all in the room at the same time.

In an online meeting, the host has control of the meeting. All participants can see your presentation in PowerPoint on their screens. You can allow others to edit the presentation or not. The person's initials appear next to the pointer when they are in control. You do not control your pointer when someone else is in control. You can turn on or off a whiteboard that participants can draw on, and send text messages in Chat. Everyone can work in the whiteboard and Chat.

 See Chapter 54, "Collaborating on a Network," for more detailed information.

You would normally schedule the meeting in advance, although you can set up an impromptu meeting too.

Scheduling a meeting

To set up an online meeting choose Tools ➪ Online Collaboration ➪ Schedule Meeting. This takes you to an Outlook Calendar meeting form. You can choose whom to invite, and name the topic and the time. Notice on the form that "This is an online meeting using: Microsoft NetMeeting" is turned on.

 Chapter 31, "Managing Your Time with Calendar," provides details on setting up an appointment in Outlook.

Impromptu meetings

To set up an impromptu meeting choose Tools ➪ Online Collaboration ➪ Meet Now. The Place a Call dialog box appears (see Figure 25-11); select those people you want to join the meeting. They must all be running NetMeeting. The Online Meeting toolbar appears (see Figure 25-12).

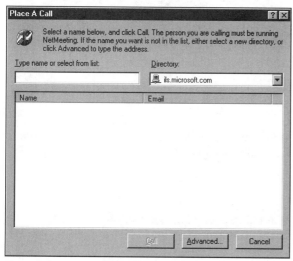

Figure 25-11: The Place A Call dialog box.

If you cancel the Place a Call dialog box—perhaps you want to phone the people to invite them—you are still ready for the online meeting.

Note If this is the first time you are running NetMeeting, a dialog box appears asking for information in the My Information and Directory boxes.

Figure 25-12: The Online Meeting toolbar has the following tools: Participant List, Call Participant, Remove Participant, Allow Others to Edit, Display Chat Window, Display Whiteboard, and End Meeting.

Running a meeting

With the Online Meeting toolbar you can display the whiteboard or the Chat window, call in participants, and allow them to edit.

Ending a meeting

To finish a meeting, click the End Meeting tool on the Online Meeting toolbar. The host is the only person who can end the meeting for the entire group. A participant can disconnect at any time by clicking the End Meeting tool.

Broadcasting Over the Internet or an Intranet

If you want to share your presentation with people in different locations, you can broadcast it over the Internet or your corporate intranet. You can include live video and audio. You use either Outlook or another e-mail program to schedule the broadcast. Each person in the audience needs a Web browser to be able to see the presentation. It is saved in HTML format, the standard format for pages on the Web.

The presentation can be recorded and saved on the Web so that it can be replayed at any stage. If you want to broadcast the presentation to more than 15 people, you need to have Internet Explorer 4.0 or higher, and a NetShow server. Speak to your system administrator if you need more information about your system and setup.

When you go through the setup to broadcast a presentation, you are asked to provide information for a Lobby Page. This is the page that is displayed before the presentation begins, and is used to show a countdown to the presentation and any last-minute messages from the presenter.

Setting up a presentation broadcast

The first step to broadcasting your presentation is to set up the Lobby Page and the Broadcast Schedule.

1. Choose Slide Show ⇨ Online Broadcast ⇨ Set Up and Schedule. Select Set Up and Schedule a New Broadcast and click OK (see Figure 25-13).

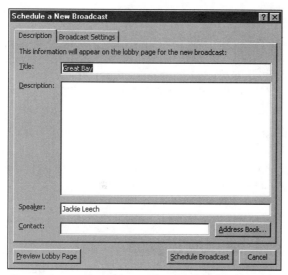

Figure 25-13: The Chat window shows everyone's messages with their names in front.

2. Type in a description of the broadcast and contact information. Click Preview Lobby Page to see what it will look like.

3. Close the Preview Lobby Page. If you need to change any of the Broadcast Settings, click on the tab. You may need help from the System administrator to enter these settings.

4. Click Schedule Broadcast and you are taken either to Outlook or your e-mail program.

   • **If you use Outlook** – use the meeting request form that appears to set up an online meeting. The link to the broadcast is already set up.

See Chapter 31, "Managing Your Time with Calendar," for more information.

   • **If you use another e-mail program** – use the new e-mail message form that appears to send out an e-mail announcing the broadcast. You will find the URL (Internet address) of the broadcast embedded in your e-mail message.

Starting a presentation broadcast

You should start the broadcast as close to the scheduled start as possible.

1. Open the presentation you want to broadcast.

2. Choose Slide Show ➪ Online Broadcast ➪ Begin Broadcast. The presentation is saved in HTML format in the location specified in the Server Options dialog box.

Viewing a presentation broadcast

It is a good idea to join the broadcast before it starts — say about 10 minutes before. The Lobby Page is opened showing you a countdown to the start of the broadcast. If there is a delay in starting the broadcast, the host can send a message that displays on the Lobby Page. If you want to continue working, you can minimize the Lobby Page.

   ✦ To view the broadcast if you are an Outlook user, you will be reminded shortly before the broadcast. Click the Join Broadcast button.

   ✦ If you are using another e-mail program, click the URL (Internet address) on the e-mail message that invited you to the broadcast.

Summary

This chapter covered various methods for presenting your slide show.

✦ You can change the sequence of the slides, hide slides, and delete slides in the Slide Sorter view.

✦ You can print notes pages and handouts as aids to the presentation. Handouts are a useful tool for proofing your slides.

✦ If you circulate the presentation among different people, they can add comments to it. You can run the slide show with or without comments, narrations, or animations.

✦ While giving the slide show, you can annotate slides temporarily. You can also display a plain black or white screen by typing B or W.

✦ You can run a slide show by advancing the slides manually or automatically.

✦ You can also choose to run the slide show at a kiosk. This option prevents people from modifying the show.

✦ A custom show using a specific selection of slides shown in a specific sequence can be set up and named.

✦ Narrations can be recorded to accompany the show. This enables you to give a presentation without being present or to archive it.

✦ Pack and Go Wizard lets you move your slide show to another machine by gathering, copying, and compressing all the necessary files.

✦ The PowerPoint Viewer allows you to run a slide show without having PowerPoint installed.

✦ Online meetings allow you to work on a presentation over a network and communicate with the meeting participants.

✦ You can also broadcast your presentation over the Internet or an intranet, using an automated system of e-mailing those you want to invite.

✦   ✦   ✦

PowerPoint at Work

This chapter gives practical examples of how to use PowerPoint to create an organization chart and a complete presentation, how to publish to the Web, and how to print.

Creating an Organization Chart

PowerPoint's organization chart feature takes the agony out of trying to draw these charts, by making it easy to add and remove people without having to totally redraw the chart. In the following example, you will create a chart for a fictitious company called CeeJay's Computers (see Figure 26-1).

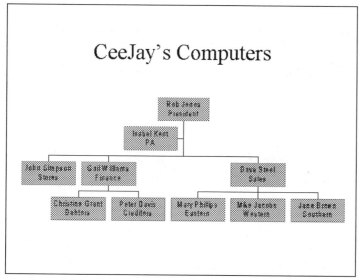

Figure 26-1: An organization chart like this is very easy to create.

1. Start a new presentation by clicking the New tool on the Standard toolbar. This creates a new, blank presentation.

2. Choose the AutoLayout called Organization Chart (see Figure 26-2).

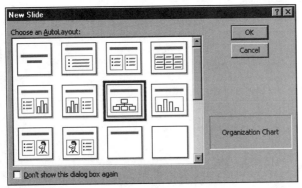

Figure 26-2: Choose the Organization Chart from the AutoLayout samples.

3. Click on the Title placeholder and type **CeeJay's Computers**.

4. Double-click on the Organization Chart area. This takes you into Microsoft Organization Chart (see Figure 26-3).

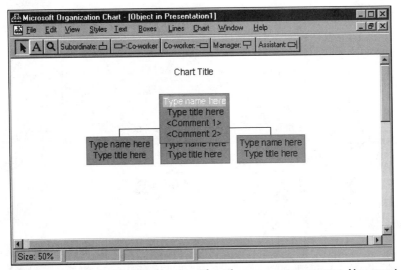

Figure 26-3: Microsoft Organization Chart is a separate program. You must update your chart and exit before returning to PowerPoint.

5. In the top box of the chart, type **Rob Jones**. Press Enter. Type **President** on the second line of the box. Press Enter, Tab, or the down arrow key to move from line to line in this box.

6. Click on the first box of the second row. Type the following names and titles in the boxes on the second row:

   John Simpson, Stores

   Gail Williams, Finance

   Dave Steel, Sales

7. You are now going to add three subordinates in the sales department. Click the Subordinate tool on the toolbar and click on Dave Steel. Repeat this two more times so there are three people under Dave Steel. Type the following information in the boxes:

   Mary Phillips, Eastern

   Mike Jacobs, Western

   Jane Brown, Southern

8. You can now add two subordinates under the Finance department. Click the Subordinate tool and click on Gail Williams. Repeat this again and fill in the following information:

   Christine Grant, Debtors

   Peter Davis, Creditors

9. Finally, add a personal assistant to the President. Click the Assistant tool on the toolbar and click on Rob Jones. Type the following in the new box:

   Isabel Kent, PA

10. To insert the chart into PowerPoint, choose File ⇨ Update <Presentation> and then File ⇨ Exit and Return to <Presentation>.

11. To make your chart larger and more readable, drag the corner handles of the chart area outward.

12. Choose File Í Save and name your presentation.

Creating a Presentation

In this section you will create a presentation with a title slide, three bulleted lists, and a column chart. You will also add some clip art to the title slide and an AutoShape to one of the slides. Then you will add sound to the title slide, and animation to your AutoShape. Notes pages will be added and you will save the presentation. Transition effects will be added before you give the slide show. The theme is a watersports company.

Creating the presentation

1. Choose File ➪ New. Click the Design Templates tab and select Dads Tie (or a different one if you prefer).

2. Choose the Title Slide AutoLayout, which is the first one.

3. Click in the top box to add the title **Great Bay Watersports**. Click in the subtitle box and type **For all your sporting needs.** Notice that the title is too big to fit on one line. It would look better if it were a little smaller. Click on the text Great Bay Watersports. To select all the text at once, you can click on the striped border around the box. The border turns fuzzy. Alternatively, you could drag your mouse over the text. Click twice on the Decrease Font Size tool on the Formatting toolbar.

4. Click the New Slide tool on the Standard toolbar. Choose the Bulleted List AutoLayout (it should already be selected). Enter the following text on the slide:

> **Activities Available** (in the Title area)
>
> > **Dinghy sailing**
> >
> > **Canoeing**
> >
> > **Water-skiing**
> >
> > **Hobie Cats**
> >
> > **Scuba Diving**

5. Click the New Slide tool on the Standard toolbar again. Choose the Bulleted List AutoLayout. Enter the following text on the slide (to put in the sub-bullets, press Tab or click the Demote tool):

> **Additional Facilities**
>
> > **Free showers**
> >
> > **Coffee Bar**
> >
> > **Beach sports**
> >
> > > **Volleyball**
> > >
> > > **Beach Bats**
> > >
> > > **Frisbee**

6. Click the New Slide tool and choose the 2-Column Text AutoLayout. Enter the following text for the title and the two columns:

Assistants	
John Smith	Mary Green
Peter Jones	Susan Grant
George Brown	Jane Ross
Grant Dalton	

Adding a column chart

You are now going to add a chart showing which equipment is popular in which season (see Figure 26-4).

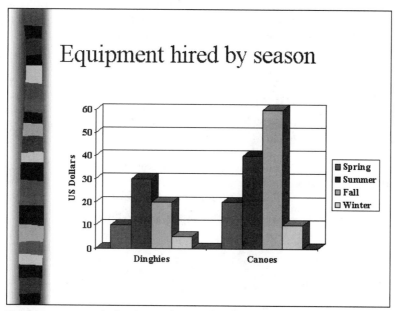

Figure 26-4: A typical column chart. Follow the instructions to create it and edit it to look like this.

1. Click the New Slide tool and choose the Chart AutoLayout. Enter the title **Equipment hired by season**. Double-click on the Add Chart placeholder to go to Microsoft Graph. Type the following labels and figures in the Datasheet window, replacing the existing data.

	Spring	Summer	Fall	Winter
Dinghies	10	30	20	5
Canoes	20	40	60	10

Note To remove the third series, click on the number 3 in the row header. This selects the entire row. Press Delete to delete the series completely. You can now close the Datasheet window if you like.

2. To change the way the data on the graph is oriented, choose Data ➪ Series in Columns.

3. To add a value axis title, choose Chart ➪ Chart Options. Type **US Dollars** in the Value (Z) axis box and click OK.

4. To change the orientation of the title, right-click on the words US Dollars and choose Format Axis Title. Click the Alignment tab and drag the red diamond up to the top of the orientation clock and click OK.

5. To get back to PowerPoint, click anywhere on the slide outside the chart area.

Adding speaker notes

Now you are going to add speaker notes for each slide. These will be printed so that you can use them as a guide when giving the presentation.

1. Make sure you are in Normal view. The Notes pane is under the chart (see Figure 26-5). To make the Notes pane larger so you can see more text, drag the border between the Notes pane and the chart upward.

2. Go to the first slide by clicking on the Slide pane and pressing Home.

3. Click on the Notes pane and type the following:

Welcome

In existence for 21 years

Continuing to provide good service

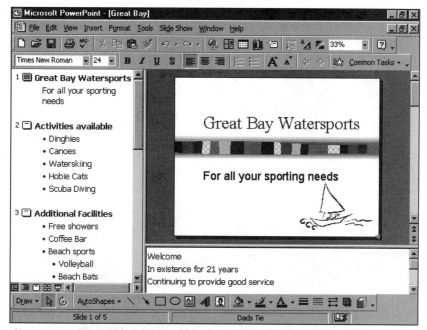

Figure 26-5: The Notes pane is at the bottom of the slide in Normal view. Make it bigger by dragging the gray bar just above it upward.

4. Go to Slide 2 and type the following on the Notes pane:

> **Many sporting activities available**
>
> **Optimist and Topper dinghies are popular**
>
> **Single and double kayaks**
>
> **Water-skiing at all levels**
>
> **4 Hobie Cats – will arrange racing if required**
>
> **Scuba – PADI courses with qualified instructor**

5. Add your own notes to the next three slides.

Adding clip art

You will now add a clip art picture to the first slide (see Figure 26-6).

1. Go to the first slide in Slide View and choose Insert ⇨ Picture ⇨ Clip Art. Scroll down and click on the Sports and Leisure Category. Scroll down and find the picture of a yacht. Click on it and choose the top menu item, Insert Clip. Close the Insert Clip Art dialog box.

2. Drag the clip art down to the bottom right corner using the four-way arrow pointer. Make it smaller by dragging the top-left white handle toward the center of the picture.

Figure 26-6: The clip art picture adds life to your slide.

Adding an AutoShape

In this section you will add a starburst to the fourth slide, entitled Assistants (see Figure 26-7).

1. Go to Slide 4, entitled Assistants.

2. On the Drawing toolbar, click on the AutoShapes menu and go to Stars and Banners. Click on the first AutoShape in the submenu. Click under the name Jane Ross. A starburst appears, but it's a bit too small. Drag the bottom-right white handle toward the bottom, right corner of your slide to make it bigger.

3. Make sure you still have the white handles on the starburst and type the following:

> **Great staff!!**

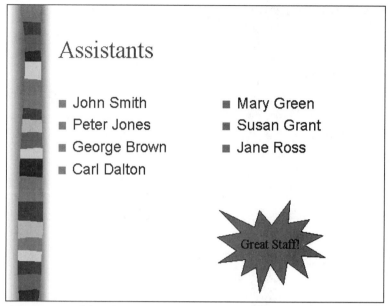

Figure 26-7: Slide 4 has an AutoShape added — a starburst.

Adding sound to the title slide

1. Go to Slide 1 and choose Insert ➪ Movies and Sounds ➪ Sound from File. Find a sound file, or go to the folder c:\Windows\Media and select the sound called Tada. Answer Yes to the prompt to play the sounds automatically.

2. The sound icon appears on your slide. Drag it into the corner of the slide, out of the way.

3. To test the slide, click the Slide Show tool. Your slide should appear and the sound should be played.

4. Press Esc to return to PowerPoint.

Adding animation to the AutoShape

1. Go to Slide 4, which has the AutoShape on it. Click on the AutoShape (the starburst) and then click the Animation Effects tool to switch on the Animation toolbar.

2. Click on Custom Animation and select the Effects tab. Make sure that Text 4, the starburst, is selected. You can see this from the miniature of the slide in the dialog box. There are handles around the starburst (see Figure 26-8).

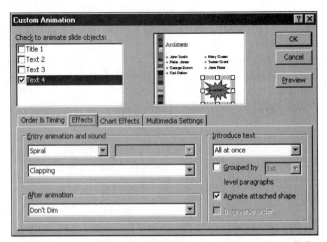

Figure 26-8: The Effects tab of the Custom Animation dialog box. Make sure that the correct item is selected. Look at the Preview window.

3. Select Entry animation as Spiral, and sound as Clapping. Click OK.

4. To test the slide, click the Slide Show tool. Your slide should appear. Click and you should see the starburst spiraling in to the sounds of applause.

5. Press Esc to return to PowerPoint.

Save the presentation

Save the presentation as you would any other file. Choose File ➪ Save and give it a name.

Adding transition effects

In this section you will add transition effects to your presentation. You will add a build to Slide 2.

1. Go to Slide Sorter view by clicking on the tool or choosing View ➪ Slide Sorter.

2. Click on Slide 1 and click the Slide Transition Effects tool and choose Dissolve (or any other effect). Repeat this for each slide in the presentation. If you want to apply the same transition to several slides at once, hold down the Ctrl key and click on each slide. Then choose the transition effect with the Slide Transition Effects tool.

3. Double-click on Slide 2 to take you back to Slide view.

4. Click the Animation Effects tool. This calls up the Animation Effects toolbar. Click the Custom Animation tool. In the dialog box, select Text 2 and make sure it is turned on. Click on the Effects tab. Under After Animation, select a pale color from the set in the drop-down list. Then click OK.

5. Save your presentation again.

Viewing the slide show

1. Go to Slide 1.

2. Click the Slide Show tool at the bottom left of your screen or choose View ➪ Slide Show.

3. To move to the next slide, press Enter or click with the mouse. Continue moving through your slide show. On Slide 2 the points should appear one at a time, with the previous points being dimmed. Slide 4 shows the starburst spiraling in with a round of applause.

Creating a Web Presentation

You can publish your presentation on the Web so that other people can view it. PowerPoint can save files in HTML format, which is the format used on the Web. You need to be connected to the Web to be able to use this. This may be a dial-up connection, or a connection via your corporate network to your corporate intranet.

There are two ways to put PowerPoint on the Web. One is to save files as Web Pages; the other is to publish them on the Web. If you publish your presentation on the Web, you will be the only person able to edit it. You can make a subset of the slides available and you can choose which browser your presentation will be formatted for. Some features are available only on the newer browsers. It is important to know which browser and what version of the browser people are going to use. If you choose a new version of the browser, and your audience has only an older version, it will not display correctly.

If you want to create a Web presentation that other people can edit, you should simply save your presentation to the Web as directed in the following section.

Saving a presentation to the Web

You can save a presentation on an Internet server in a Web folder. Use the following method:

1. Open the presentation you want to put on the Web.

2. Choose File ➪ Save As Web Page. A variation of the Save As dialog box appears (see Figure 26-9).

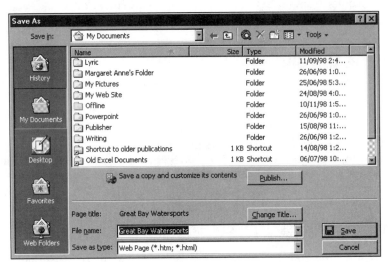

Figure 26-9: The Save As Web Page dialog box.

Note

Notice the title of the Web page. It is the name people see when they access the Web presentation and it appears in their history and favorites list if they save the page as a favorite. If you want to change the title, click the Change Title button and type the new title.

3. The name and other details are already filled in. Choose a location to save it in. Click on Web Folders and either create a new folder or use an existing one. Click Save.

Opening a presentation on the Web

To open a presentation that has been saved on the Web, you use the same procedure as opening any other presentation. Choose File ➪ Open and select Web Folders. Then open the Web folder the presentation is located in and select the PowerPoint presentation.

Publishing a presentation on the Web

When you publish a presentation on the Web, you have special features available that make it run like a slide show. You can move from slide to slide, see the notes pages, and see the outline expanded or collapsed. The Publish command opens a dialog box with four tabs. They contain options about how you want the presentation formatted. You access the Publish command from the Save As Web Page menu.

1. Open the presentation you want to publish (open Great Bay Watersports, for example).

2. Choose File ⇨ Save As Web Page.

3. Click the Publish button. The Publish as Web Page dialog box appears, as shown in Figure 26-10. Choose to publish the complete presentation and turn on Display Speaker Notes.

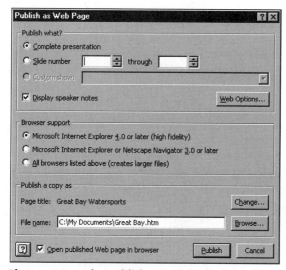

Figure 26-10: The Publish as Web Page dialog box. Decide which items you want to include – speaker notes, for example. Make sure you select a browser version that everyone likely to view the presentation uses, not necessarily the most recent one.

4. If you know who your audience will be, and that they all have Internet Explorer 4.0 or higher, then you should choose that option. If not, choose either of the next two options.

5. Click the Web Options button to customize your presentation setup further.

6. Make sure that Open Published Web Page in Browser is turned on. As soon as the Web page has been created, you will be taken into your default browser to see the results.

7. Click Publish. After a delay you will be taken into your browser and the Web page will be opened (see Figure 26-11). At the bottom of the window are tools to show/hide the outline, expand/collapse the outline, show/hide the notes pages, move from page to page, and view the screen show.

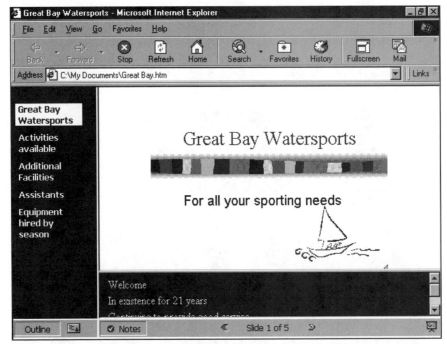

Figure 26-11: This is how your presentation may look in a Web browser. This is Internet Explorer 5. Notice the buttons at the bottom of the screen to turn on and off outlines and notes and perform other functions.

Printing

Printing the slides themselves is becoming less important now that so many people use onscreen presentations and projection equipment attached to computers. Often you want to print the slides in black-and-white and not in the colors used for the presentation. You can preview how your slides and handouts will look in black-and-white by clicking one tool. You can then change the way black-and-white prints before you print your whole presentation. If you do want to print slides in color for proofing purposes, you will save a lot of time and resources by printing handouts instead of full-page slides.

You can print slides, outlines, speaker notes, and audience handouts. You can print them in color, grayscale, or pure black-and-white. Table 26-1 shows how objects print in grayscale or pure black-and-white.

Table 26-1 Grayscale Versus Pure Black-and-White		
Object	*Grayscale*	*Pure Black-and-White*
Text	Black	Black
Text shadows	Hidden	Hidden
Embossing	Hidden	Hidden
Fills	Grayscale	White
Frame	Black	Black
Pattern fills	Grayscale	White
Lines	Black	Black
Object shadows	Grayscale	Black
Bitmaps	Grayscale	Grayscale
Slide backgrounds	White	White
Charts	Grayscale	Grayscale

Printing slides

To print your slides choose File ➪ Print. Figure 26-12 shows the Print dialog box.

You can select the range of slides to be printed. Make sure that you have chosen Slides in the Print What box. If you are printing in color, choose whether you want the animated items to print, whether you want the slides to be scaled to fit paper, rather than staying scaled as they are on the screen, and whether you want to print a frame around the slides.

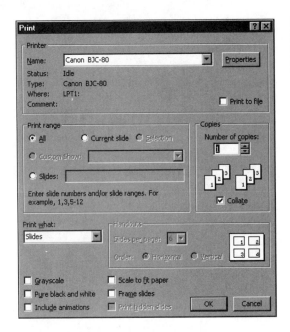

Figure 26-12: The Print dialog box has some special options for PowerPoint. The Print What list box is important.

Go to Slide 4 or go to Slide Sorter view before trying this next trick so that you can see the difference. If you print your slides in grayscale, you can preview what they will look like before going to the print menu. Click the Grayscale Preview tool on the Standard toolbar. To see how they will look in pure black-and-white, hold down the Shift key and click the Grayscale Preview tool. The name of the tool changes to Pure Black and White Preview.

You can change the way a single object prints. In Slide or Normal view, click the Grayscale Preview tool and then right-click on the object and choose Black and White. You'll find several additional options to choose from. Experiment with the starburst on Slide 4 to see the difference.

Now choose File ➪ Print and select between Grayscale or Pure Black and White.

Printing speaker notes

To print speaker notes, choose File ➪ Print and select Notes Pages under the Print What list box. You have the same options as for printing slides. Prior to printing, you can insert a header and footer by choosing View ➪ Header and Footer and selecting the Notes and Handouts tab.

Printing handouts

To print handouts, choose File ➪ Print and select Handouts under the Print What list box. You have the same options as for printing slides, plus you can choose how many slides to print on one page, and the order in which they appear on the page—horizontal or vertical. Prior to printing, you can insert a header and footer by choosing View ➪ Header and Footer and selecting the Notes and Handouts tab.

You can add a company logo, for example, by going to the Notes Master: choose View ➪ Master ➪ Handout Master

Printing an outline

Outlines print as they are displayed in the Outline pane. Whichever levels are showing will print—you can print all the text in your outline or just the slide titles. You can also show or hide formatting.

Printing files in Word

Choosing File ➪ Send to ➪ Microsoft Word takes you to the Write-Up dialog box shown in Figure 26-13. You can send notes pages and outlines to Word and touch up the formatting there. Select Paste Link if you want to keep the copy in Word up-to-date with the information in the PowerPoint presentation.

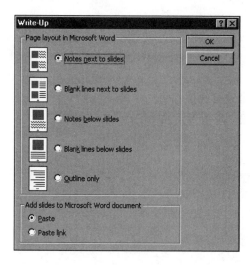

Figure 26-13: Use the Write-Up dialog box to format slides, notes pages, or your outline when you send them to Microsoft Word.

When you click OK, Word is loaded and the slides and notes pages are put in a table. Outlines are created using Outline Styles.

For more information on working with Outlines, see Chapter 5, "Outlines, Tables of Contents, and Indexes."

Creating 35mm slides

You can create 35mm slides by using a desktop film recorder, or you can create a file for a service bureau. If you have a recorder installed on your computer, you can choose File ➪ Send To and select the recorder. It is always best to speak to your service bureau to find out which way they would like to receive your files.

Summary

In this chapter you put PowerPoint to work. You created an organization chart and then a presentation using many of the features covered in this part of the book. Saving and publishing on the Web was next, followed by printing. Highlights of the chapter included the following:

✦ You created a complete organization chart and added employees and an assistant.

✦ You created a complete presentation. It included a title slide, a bulleted list, a bulleted list with two levels of bullets, a two-column bullet slide, and a column graph.

✦ Notes pages were added.

✦ An AutoShape, a sound, and some clip art were added.

✦ Animation was used to create a build on the bulleted list and to animate the AutoShape.

✦ With PowerPoint, it is easy to save a page to the Web and to publish a presentation on the Web.

✦ Finally, you learned all about printing — printing slides, notes pages, handouts, and outlines.

✦   ✦   ✦

PowerPoint
Top 10

In this chapter, you will find the answers to ten of the most common questions people ask about PowerPoint. If your question isn't answered in this chapter (or elsewhere in this book), you might try one of the lists of common questions, and their answers, maintained by Microsoft on the World Wide Web at http://support.microsoft.com.

How Do I Change an Entire Presentation's Format?

The Master Slides hold the formats for all the slides in your presentation. Any changes made to these affect all the slides based on them. There are four masters: Title, Slide, Notes, and Handouts. Changes to the Title Master change only title slides, and changes to the Slide Master change all other slides. To change the Slide Master, choose View ➪ Master ➪ Slide Master (see Figure 27-1).

You can, for example, change the font, color, or size of your titles. Click on the border of the Title area to select the complete area and make your changes. If you want to change the bullets, click in the text for one level and choose Format ➪ Bullets and Numbering. If you want a graphic to appear on every slide, insert it on the Master page.

When you have made your changes, click Close on the Master toolbar.

How Can I Copy One Object's Format to Several Others?

The Format Painter tool can quickly copy formatting from one object to another. Select the object whose formatting you want to copy. Click the Format Painter tool on the Standard toolbar. Click on the object you want to apply the formatting to.

To copy the formatting to several objects at once, double-click the Format Painter tool and then click on each object in turn. When you have finished, click the Format Painter tool again.

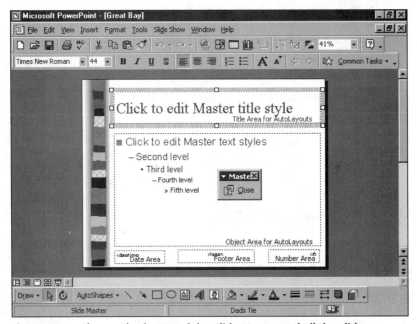

Figure 27-1: Change the format of the Slide Master and all the slides except title slides will also change. It is like a default slide format.

How Do I Download Additional Clip Art, Textures, Sounds, and Video from the Web?

Microsoft provides additional items for you to use on the Web. When you choose Insert ⇨ Picture ⇨ ClipArt or Insert ⇨ Movies and Sounds ⇨ Movie from Gallery or Sound from Gallery, you have an option on the toolbar for Clips Online (see Figure 27-2). If you have access to the Web, clicking this will take you to the Microsoft site. You can select what you want to download from here. It will automatically be placed in your Gallery.

How Can I Set the Defaults for Drawing Objects?

Suppose you decide that you want all drawing objects to have a certain thickness of border and color or fill. Draw one object with those features. Choose Format ⇨ AutoShape (see Figure 27-3). Click on Default for New Objects. This sets the default for the active presentation.

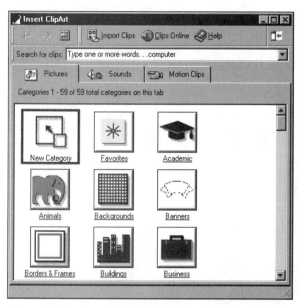

Figure 27-2: The Clips Online button will take you to the Web, if you have access, so that you can pick up additional clip art.

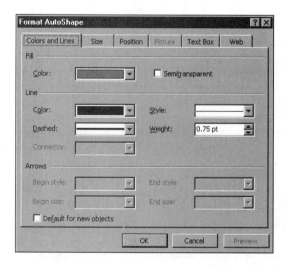

Figure 27-3: The Default check box on the Format AutoShape dialog box sets the default for your presentation.

How Can I Create a Build Effect for a Bullet List?

You have seen how a bulleted list can be built up one bullet at a time in other presentations. How do you do it in PowerPoint?

First create your slide with the bulleted list. Then click the Animation Effects tool on the Formatting toolbar. Click the Custom Animation tool on the Animation Effects toolbar. Make sure the bulleted text (often Text 2) is selected in the top of the dialog box under Check to Animate Slide Objects (see Figure 27-4). Choose an entry animation and sound, if you want. Decide what is to happen after animation; for example, perhaps you want the previous bullet to dim to a paler color.

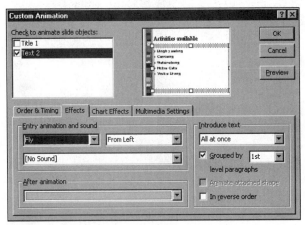

Figure 27-4: Use the Custom Animation dialog box to create a build on a bulleted list.

Then decide how you want the text to be introduced. If you have more than one level of bullet, you will find that when you play the slide show all the sub-bullets under the main headings are displayed at once. You may want each individual line to be introduced separately. In this case, choose the number of levels you have used under Grouped By.

There is a Preview button on the dialog box but this does not always completely show the build. To preview the slide, choose OK and click the Slide Show tool at the bottom of your screen.

What Are Comments and How Do They Work?

Comments are small text boxes that you can stick onto slides, rather like you would use paper sticky reminder notes on a paper document. You can pass the presentation on to other people to run on their computer so that they can add their own comments. Use the menu File ➪ Send to ➪ Routing Recipient command if you like. When you give the presentation you can hide the comments.

To add comments, choose Insert ➪ Comment (see Figure 27-5). The Reviewing toolbar automatically appears. The registered user name appears at the start of the comment. Type your comment and click on the slide afterwards.

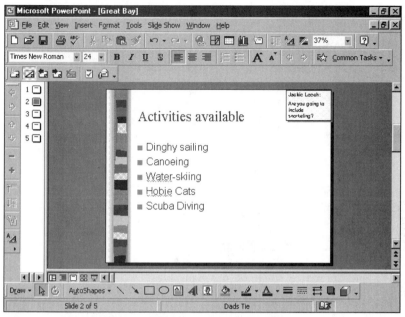

Figure 27-5: A comment is like a sticky paper note. The user's name automatically appears at the start of the comment. Other people can make their comments on your presentation.

If you don't want the comments to appear when you run the slide show, choose View ➪ Comments.

What Is a Summary Slide?

When you have created a series of slides, you can automatically create a single slide that summarizes the slides you select by including the title of each slide. Go to Slide Sorter view, hold down the Ctrl key and click on each slide you want to include in the summary.

Click the Summary Slide tool on the Slide Sorter toolbar. The summary slide is inserted before the first selected slide, with the title of each selected slide appearing as a bullet.

How Can I Save a Chart's Design for Future Use?

You can save the design of any chart you create to use over and over again. To save the design, first create your chart and then choose Chart ➪ Chart Type. Click on the Custom Types tab and click the User-defined radio button. Click the Add button and name your design and type in a description. The design is added to the list of user-defined chart types (see Figure 27-6).

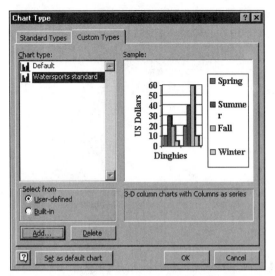

Figure 27-6: Save the special design of your own charts on the Custom Types tab of the Chart Type dialog box and you can use the same design again and again.

When you want to use your design for another graph, go to Chart ➪ Chart Type. Select the Custom Types tab and the User-defined radio button. You should see your design on the list. Select it and it will be applied to your graph.

How Do I Change an Object into a Different AutoShape?

If you have added an AutoShape and you decide you would prefer it to be a different shape, you can change it. You may have been using the flowchart shapes and want to change from one shape to another. Select the shape you want to change and click on the Draw menu tool on the Drawing toolbar. Select Change AutoShape and select the new shape you want. You can also change the proportion of the shape by dragging the yellow diamond handles.

How Can I Copy a Complete Presentation for Use on Another Computer?

PowerPoint Viewer is a program supplied with PowerPoint (or you can get it from the Web from www.microsoft.com) that lets you run a slide show on a computer that does not have PowerPoint loaded. You must install PowerPoint Viewer on the computer if PowerPoint is not loaded. (The license allows you to copy this program freely.) To copy your presentation to another computer, use Pack and Go Wizard: choose File ➪ Pack and Go. Follow the instructions on the wizard and all the necessary files will not only be copied onto your floppy disk, but compressed as well.

Run Pngsetup from the floppy disk on the other computer to copy and decompress the files.

✦   ✦   ✦

Outlook

Managing Messages and Faxes

✦ ✦ ✦ ✦

In This Chapter

Configuring and
using multiple
mail accounts

Reading messages

Addressing and
sending messages

Saving and printing
messages

Deleting messages

Configuring and
using Outlook Fax

Using remote mail

✦ ✦ ✦ ✦

This chapter covers using Outlook for both e-mail and fax messages. You can use Outlook to manage a single e-mail account or several at once. Outlook makes it easy for you to add new accounts and to modify existing ones.

You'll learn how to pick up and send messages, and how to use Outlook's interface for reading your messages. You'll also learn how to save, print, and delete them, how to enter recipient information using Outlook's contact database, and how to use remote mail to minimize online time by picking up only the headers of messages, and then deciding while offline which message bodies you want to download.

Configuring and Using Multiple Mail Accounts

Many people keep multiple e-mail accounts, perhaps one at work or school, another at a local ISP, and others at various Internet domains or with free e-mail providers. If you have more than one e-mail account, you'll be happy to know that Outlook lets you set up, manage, and access all of them. You can use them individually or all at once. Of course, Outlook e-mail also works just fine with a single e-mail account.

Note   Several Web sites offer free e-mail accounts that are Web-based. These are not compatible with Outlook or any other standard e-mail client software, but must be accessed via a Web browser (version 3 or later of either Internet Explorer or Netscape Navigator). The kind of e-mail accounts Outlook uses are the ones that use standard POP3 and IMAP4 (incoming mail) and SMTP (outgoing mail) servers. Before you sign up with a free e-mail provider, make sure that they can handle the standard e-mail protocols if you intend to use Outlook to access them.

Adding e-mail accounts

To add a new e-mail account to Outlook, follow these steps:

1. Make sure you have the following information available for any account you want to enter:

   - Your e-mail address `yourname@yourprovider.net`.

   - Your logon id. This will typically be the "yourname" part of `yourname@yourprovider.net`.

   - Your password.

   - Name of the incoming mail server. This is commonly the POP3 (Post Office Protocol, version 3) server, and it's usually pop.yourprovider.net. It may also be an IMAP (Internet Message Access Protocol) server, in which case the normal designation is imap.yourprovider.net. There are numerous variations on the exact designation for mail servers, like mail.yourprovider.net or even just yourprovider.net.

   - Name of the outgoing mail server. This is the SMTP (Simple Mail Transfer Protocol) server, and it's usually smtp.yourprovider.net, although there are variations on this just as there are with the incoming mail server designations.

2. Select Tools ➪ Accounts from the menu. Alternatively, you can access your e-mail accounts from the Options dialog box. It's a more involved process than the simple menu approach, but might come in handy if you're in the Options dialog box for some other reason and want to work with your accounts. To get to the accounts via this second approach, select Tools ➪ Options from the menu. Next, in the Options dialog box, click on the Mail Delivery tab, and then click the Accounts button. If you're running Outlook with Corporate/Workgroup support using MAPI providers, you won't have the Accounts option on the Tools menu, and to do account setup you choose Services instead. You can still use an Internet POP account (because there's a MAPI provider to do this), but not IMAP.

3. In the Internet Accounts dialog box, click the Add button (see Figure 28-1).

4. Click Mail.

5. This brings up Internet Connection Wizard (see Figure 28-2). Although this is commonly used to create a new dial-up account to access the Internet, you don't have to use it for that. You will be using it whenever you want to add a new e-mail account to Outlook. Enter the name you want to appear in the From field in your e-mail messages.

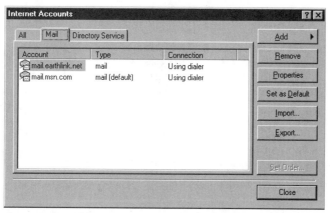

Figure 28-1: The Internet Accounts dialog box.

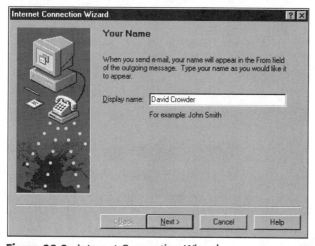

Figure 28-2: Internet Connection Wizard.

6. Click the Next button.

7. In the next screen, enter your e-mail address.

8. Click the Next button.

9. In the next screen, enter the incoming and outgoing mail server addresses and choose whether the incoming mail server supports POP3 or IMAP.

10. Click the Next button.

11. In the next screen, enter your logon ID next to Account Name.

12. Enter your password. Type it carefully, because the password will appear only as a series of asterisks (so no one looking over your shoulder can read it). But you can't read it either, and therefore won't have the normal feedback you get while typing, so you have to be careful not to make a typographical error.

13. If you don't want Outlook to remember the password for you, uncheck the Remember Password check box. Normally, you don't want to check this check box.

14. If your e-mail provider requires secure password authentication, click the radio button labeled "Log on using Secure Password Authentication (SPA)." Your administrator or ISP will tell you if you need to select this option.

15. Click the Next button.

16. In the next screen, click on the appropriate radio button, depending on whether you connect to the Internet via a normal telephone line, via a Local Area Network (LAN), or you wish to establish a connection manually.

17. Click the Next button. If your modem is not already set up, you will get a panel that asks you to choose a modem.

18. In the next screen, you are asked to choose between Create a New Dial-up Connection or Use an Existing Dial-up Connection. If you already have a dial-up connection you routinely use to the Internet, select the latter option.

19. Click the Next button.

20. Click the Finish button to complete adding the new e-mail account to Outlook.

21. You will be returned to the Internet Accounts dialog box, where your new e-mail account will be shown, identified by the name of the incoming e-mail server you entered (see Figure 28-3).

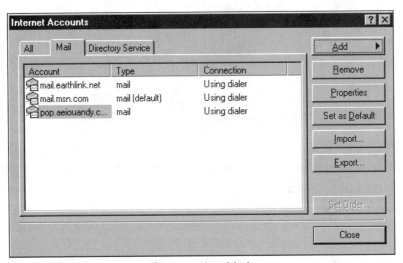

Figure 28-3: The new e-mail account is added.

22. Repeat Steps 3 through 21 for each account you wish to add at this time.

23. Click the Close button to finish.

Modifying e-mail accounts

Once an e-mail account has been created, you don't have to go through the whole Internet Connection Wizard process to change a part of it. For instance, you'll probably want to change the name of the e-mail account to something more easily recognizable than the name of the incoming e-mail server. If you're using an ISP and they have more than one telephone number you can connect with, you can change the number this way, too. Various other options allow you to adjust how you connect and what happens when you do.

1. Select Tools ⇨ Accounts from the menu.

2. In the Internet Accounts dialog box, select the account you want to change.

3. To delete an e-mail account, click the Remove button. When asked to confirm the deletion, click the Yes button.

4. To change the default e-mail account, click the Set as Default button.

5. To modify an e-mail account, click the Properties button.

6. In the Properties dialog box, if it is not already selected, click the General tab (see Figure 28-4).

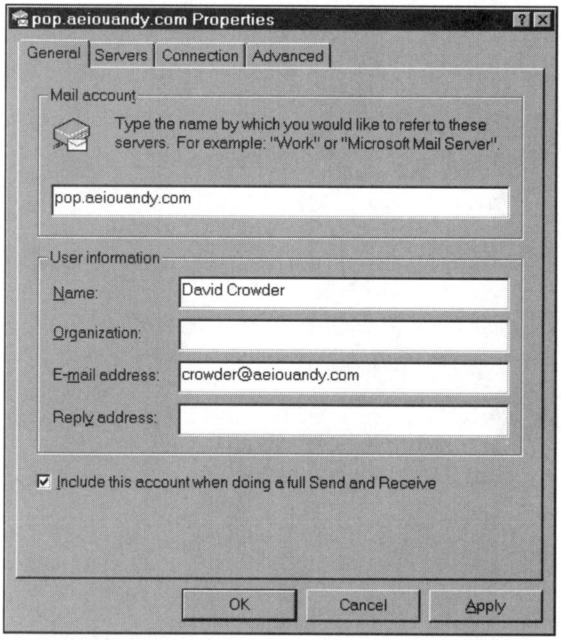

Figure 28-4: The General tab in the Properties dialog box.

7. To change the name by which the account will be referred to in the Internet Accounts dialog box and elsewhere in Outlook's menus, type the new name under Mail Account.

8. The User Information area contains basic account information that will appear in the headers of e-mail messages you send. It already includes the information you provided Internet Connection Wizard under Name and E-mail address. You can, of course, alter these. You can also add the name of your company next to Organization. If you don't want replies to come to your regular e-mail address, you can specify a different one next to Reply Address.

9. Outlook has the ability to send and receive all messages on all accounts at once. By default, all accounts are automatically set to take advantage of this ability. If you don't want messages on this account to be handled in this way, but want to send and receive them separately from the other accounts, deselect the bottom check box.

10. Click the Servers tab (see Figure 28-5).

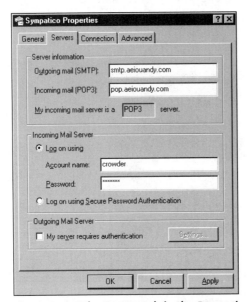

Figure 28-5: The Servers tab in the Properties dialog box.

11. Although you can change the information relating to your outgoing and incoming mail servers on the Servers tab, it would be a rare circumstance where you would need to do so. The only information you're likely to want to

change on the Servers tab is your password, if you periodically change it. Select the radio button labeled Log on Using Secure Password Authentication if your incoming mail server requires this. The Outgoing Mail Server area has a single check box, which is used only in the event that it requires a separate logon authentication from you. Checking this check box enables the Settings button, which opens a dialog box that is identical to the Incoming Mail Server area.

12. Click the Connection tab (see Figure 28-6).

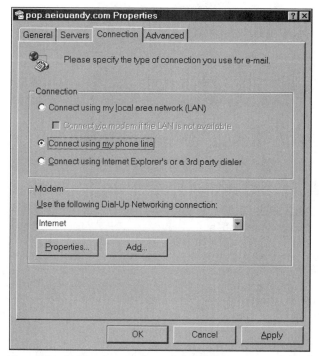

Figure 28-6: The Connection tab in the Properties dialog box.

13. The only time you will ever need to make a change in the Connection tab is if your method of connecting to your e-mail source changes. If you're using a LAN to connect to the Internet and your computer has separate modem capabilities, you may want to select the option labeled "Connect via modem if the LAN is not available." In the Modem panel, you can click the Properties button to make changes to your dial-up connection (such as changing the phone number you use to connect to your ISP). The Add button is used to create an entirely new dial-up connection.

14. Click the Advanced tab (see Figure 28-7).

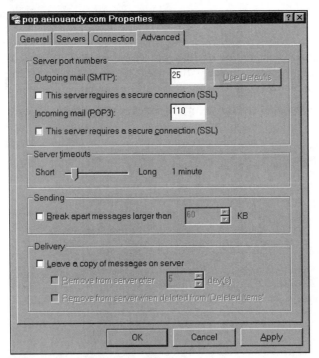

Figure 28-7: The Advanced tab in the Properties dialog box.

15. Unless you're dealing with an unusual setup, the port numbers assigned by default will not need changing. Monkey with these settings only if you know exactly what you're doing, because changing them to incorrect settings will mean you won't be able to connect. If your mail servers tend to be very slow and you constantly lose the connection to them, you may want to increase the setting under Server Timeouts. If you have problems sending large messages, you might try various settings for the Break Apart Messages Larger Than option.

16. If you're using a POP server, you have the option of choosing how to get delivery of your messages (if you're using an IMAP server, these options do not appear). Normally, messages are deleted from the incoming mail server when you download them. You can select the check box labeled "Leave a copy of messages on server" to change the default behavior, though. If you simply check this and do nothing else, your incoming mail server will eventually fill up with messages. The two check boxes below it allow you to select different options for deleting the messages from the server. The first, Remove from Server after _ Day(s), lets you set a time limit on the server's message retention. The second, Remove from Server When Deleted from "Deleted Items," ties in the deletion of messages from your local system with their removal from the server.

17. If you're using an IMAP server, there's one more tab in the Properties dialog box. Click on the IMAP tab (see Figure 28-8).

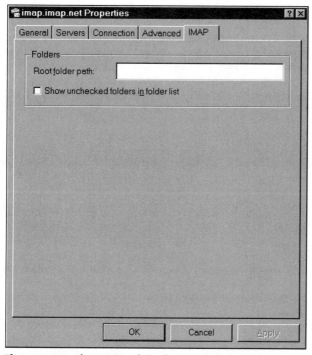

Figure 28-8: The IMAP tab in the Properties dialog box.

18. To change the Root folder path, simply enter it in the edit box. To display only the folders you have subscribed to, check Show Unchecked Folders in Folder List.

19. Click the OK button to finish.

20. If you changed the name for the e-mail account, the new name is shown in the Internet Accounts dialog box.

Reading Messages

First, unless you're running against an Exchange Server account, in order for the messages to get to you, you need to click the Send/Receive button on the toolbar. This will automatically contact every account and pick up the mail from it after it sends all queued messages (believe it or not, there is no option to just receive messages in Outlook). If you want to get the messages from just one account of several, click Tools ➪ Send/Receive in the menu, and then click on the account you want to use from the submenu.

Reading messages is basically automatic in Outlook. Any incoming mail is displayed in two windows in the Inbox. The top window shows the source, subject, and time received, while the bottom window shows the text of the currently selected message (see Figure 28-9).

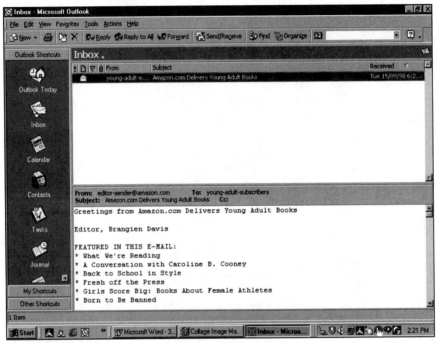

Figure 28-9: The Inbox shows message data in two windows.

To view another message, just select it. Unread messages show a closed envelope icon, while read messages show an opened envelope. You can also double-click on a message to view it in a separate window (see Figure 28-10).

Although you have several options available for message-handling in this window, the one you'll want to use for reading purposes is the ability to move among the messages either in order or by various attributes. The Previous Item and Next Item buttons allow you to do this. Simply clicking on either one will move you through the messages in the specified direction, while clicking on the options for each gives you greater latitude (you access the options by clicking on the smaller arrows next to the large arrows). Figure 28-11 shows the Previous Item button with options displayed. The options for the Next Item button are identical except that they move you in a different direction.

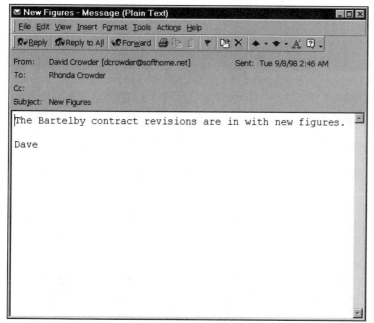

Figure 28-10: A separate message window.

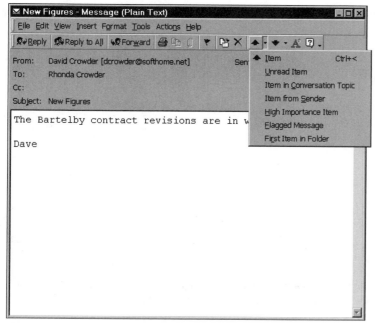

Figure 28-11: Previous Item button options.

Addressing and Sending Messages

The simplest way to prepare a message is to reply to one you've received. If you're viewing a message and click the Reply button, an e-mail message will appear, ready to go, pre-addressed to the person who sent you the original message.

Creating a new message from scratch

To create a new message from scratch, address it, and send it, follow these steps:

1. Click the New Mail Message button on the toolbar. Alternatively, you can select Actions ➪ New Mail Message from the menu or use the key combination Ctrl+N.

2. In the blank message window (see Figure 28-12), type the e-mail address of the recipient in the To field.

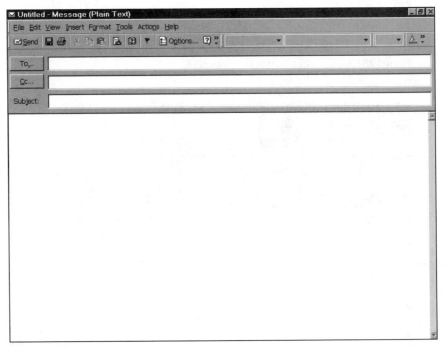

Figure 28-12: A new message window.

3. If you desire to send a copy of the message to another person besides the recipient, enter his or her address in the Cc field ("cc" is short for carbon copy).

4. If you have established a contact list, you can enter the e-mail addresses from it, instead of typing them in by hand. To do so, click either the To button or the Cc button.

Cross-Reference

For more information on establishing a contact list, see Chapter 30, "Creating and Maintaining a Contact List."

5. In the Select Names dialog box (see Figure 28-13), select the name of the recipient you want to send the message to; then click the To button.

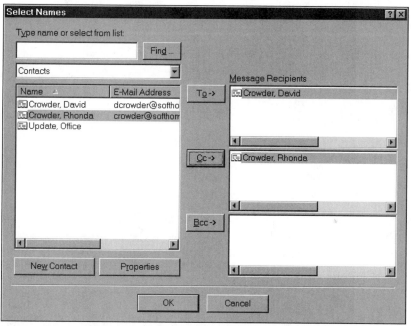

Figure 28-13: Selecting message recipients from a contact list.

6. Select the name of the recipient you want to Cc on the message, and then click the Cc button.

7. If you want to send a copy to someone but not have the person's name show in the header of the message, select the name, and then click on the Bcc button ("bcc" is short for blind carbon copy).

8. Click the OK button to return to the blank message. The names you have entered are shown in the appropriate boxes. Although they show as names, and not as e-mail addresses, Outlook knows to use the addresses from the contact lists when the message is sent.

9. Enter a topic for the message in the Subject box.

10. Type your message in the main window.

11. To send the message from the default e-mail address, just click the Send button.

12. To send from another e-mail address for which you have created an account, click File ➪ Send Using in the menu. This brings up a submenu of your accounts, as shown in Figure 28-14.

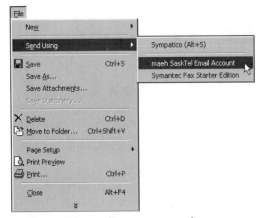

Figure 28-14: Sending a message from a specific account.

13. The default e-mail account is the first one in the listing. The others are below a separator. Click on the one you want to use.

14. The e-mail message will be placed in the queue awaiting delivery.

Tip   You can make the Bcc field visible on your e-mail messages by selecting View ➪ Bcc Field from the menu on your message before you send it. This is how you would enter an e-mail address for a blind carbon copy that wasn't in your contacts listings. To remove it from view, repeat the procedure.

Changing Outlook's message defaults

By default, Outlook checks for new messages on your incoming mail servers every ten minutes. It sends any waiting outgoing mail at that time as well. If you want to change the default behavior so that either the checking is more or less frequent, or your e-mail messages go out as soon as you hit the Send button, follow these steps:

1. Select Tools ➪ Options from the menu.

2. Click the Mail Delivery tab (see Figure 28-15).

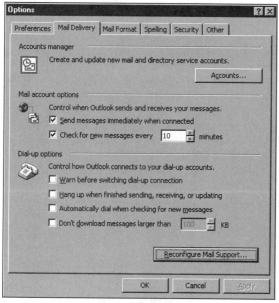

Figure 28-15: The Mail Delivery tab.

3. To change the frequency at which your messages are processed, type a new number in the Check for New Messages Every _ Minutes box. You can use the up and down arrows to scroll the values instead of typing, if you want.

4. To disable automatic message checking, deselect that check box.

5. To enable messages to go out as soon as you click the Send button, check the check box labeled "Send messages immediately when connected."

6. Click the OK button.

Note

To switch from Internet-only mail to Corporate/Workgroup mail, click the Reconfigure Mail Support button. This runs an Outlook Startup wizard; follow the instructions to make the change.

Saving Messages

Messages are automatically saved by Outlook within its own system of *items* — the Outlook equivalent of files. That's why, for instance, you will find the same messages in your Inbox when you start Outlook as were in it when you last used it. It's not just incoming messages that are affected — messages you send are saved, too, in the Sent Items folder. In addition to incoming and outgoing messages, ones you are working on but haven't sent are automatically saved every three minutes in Outlook's Drafts folder. This is a nice touch, especially if you're carefully wording an important message over a period of time, because the worst that can happen to you is to lose your last three minutes of work. Beyond this, older items in folders can be automatically moved into archive folders after a period of time (see Chapter 29, "Advanced Message Management").

Tip   You can deliberately save a message that you're working on to the Drafts folder at any time without waiting for the automatic save to take place. Just select File ➪ Save from the menu or use the Ctrl+S key combination.

To save a message outside the Outlook system, as a regular text file, select File ➪ Save As from the menu. Navigate to the disk folder you want to save the file to, and then click the Save button. The filename defaults to the message subject, and the .txt extension is selected by default. You can change either one, of course.

Printing Messages

To print a message, simply select it and click the Print button. To print multiple files, select them and click the Print button. You select a range of messages by clicking on the first message in the range, holding down the Shift key, and then clicking on the last message in the range. To select noncontiguous messages, hold down the Ctrl key while clicking on each one. When multiple messages are printed in this manner, several messages are printed on each page.

Tip   You can gain more control over the printing process by selecting File ➪ Print from the menu instead of using the Print button on the toolbar. You can also use the Ctrl+P keyboard shortcut instead.

This approach brings up the Print dialog box (see Figure 28-16). In addition to the usual capabilities such as choosing different printers if your system has more than one, or setting the number of copies, this dialog box has special features dedicated to Outlook. Here's how they work:

✦ The Print Style panel has two built-in styles. The default one is Memo Style, which is used for printing messages as text.

The Print Options panel gives you two options for this style. Selecting the top check box in this panel, Start Each Item on a New Page, will cause each message to be printed on a new page. The second one, Print Attached Files with Item(s), should be used only with attached files that are printable. It's inadvisable to select this option if the attached file is a program, for instance.

✦ The other print style, Table Style, is used to print not the contents, but the listing, of items. When you select this style, the Print Options panel changes to a Print Range panel. It also has two options. Unlike the previous panel, these options are mutually exclusive, so they use radio buttons instead of check boxes. The first one, All Rows, will cause the entire listing in the selected window to print. The second one, Only Selected rows, means that only those items you have selected will print.

✦ Once you have chosen your options in the Print dialog box, clicking the OK button causes the printing to begin.

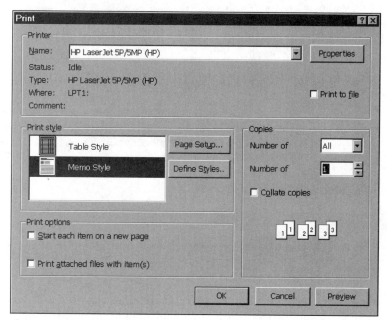

Figure 28-16: The Print dialog box.

Deleting Messages

At first glance, deleting a message seems a simple enough task. Just select it (or them), and then press the Del key. Outlook, however, has a built-in system to protect you against accidental deletion of important messages. When you delete a message, it's transferred into the Deleted Items folder.

Recovering deleted messages

To recover a message from the Deleted Items folder:

1. First open the Folder List by clicking the Folder List button (see Figure 28-17) on the Advanced toolbar (if it is not showing, you can add the Advanced toolbar by right-clicking on any toolbar and selecting it from the pop-up menu).

2. Next, select the Deleted Items folder in the Folder List, select any message in the Deleted Items folder you want to recover, and then drag it into the Inbox (or other appropriate folder, such as the Sent Items folder).

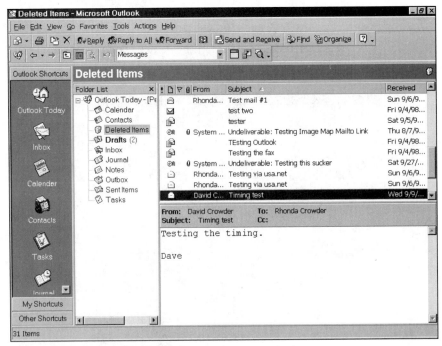

Figure 28-17: Recovering deleted messages.

Messages stay in the Deleted Items folder for two months by default. Because this can cause quite a buildup over time, you might want to either periodically manually delete the messages from the Deleted Items folder or set it to dump them every time you exit Outlook.

Cross-Reference For more information on how the Deleted Items folder works, see the section "Archiving" in Chapter 29, "Advanced Message Management."

Manually deleting messages

To manually delete messages from the Deleted Items folder, just select them and press the Del key. You'll be prompted to confirm that you really mean to permanently remove them. Click Yes to confirm.

Automatically deleting when exiting Outlook

To clear out the Deleted Items folder every time you exit Outlook, follow these steps:

1. Select Tools ➪ Options from the menu.

2. In the Options dialog box, click the Other tab.

3. Check the check box labeled "Empty the Deleted Items folder upon exiting."

4. Click the OK button.

Configuring and Using Outlook Fax

Outlook lacks a standardized fax-handling capability. Depending on your type of installation, your faxing will work differently. Internet-only installations use Symantec's WinFax Starter Edition, while Corporate Workgroup installations use Microsoft Fax.

Installing Symantec WinFax

To set up Outlook Internet-only installations for Symantec, follow these steps:

1. Select Tools ⇨ Options from the menu.

2. In the Options dialog box, click the Other tab.

3. Click the Advanced Options tab.

4. In the Advanced Options dialog box, click the Add-In Manager button.

5. In the Add-In Manager dialog box, click the Install button.

6. In the Install Extension dialog box (see Figure 28-18), select olfext.ecf (it has to have been installed with Office Setup first).

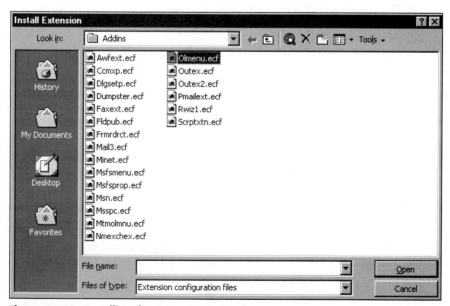

Figure 28-18: Installing the Symantec extension.

7. Click the Open button. This will return you to the Add-In Manager.

8. Back in the Add-In Manager, the Symantec WinFax Starter Edition Extension is now listed as one of the add-ins (see Figure 28-19). If the check box next to it is not checked, check it now.

Figure 28-19: The Symantec WinFax Starter Edition Extension listed as an add-in.

9. Click the OK button to return to the Advanced Options dialog box.

10. In the Advanced Options dialog box, click the OK button to return to the Options dialog box.

11. In the Options dialog box, click the OK button.

Configuring Symantec WinFax

If Outlook doesn't automatically launch the configuration setup for WinFax, exit the program and reboot your computer. Launch Outlook again. If it still won't do it, exit Outlook and use the Find feature of Windows Explorer to locate the file olfsetup.exe. In a typical installation, this is found in C:\Program Files\Microsoft Office\Office\[lang_ID] (English = 1033). Double-click on it to launch the setup program for WinFax. This will bring up Symantec WinFax Starter Edition Setup Wizard, which walks you through the following steps:

1. The opening screen is just an introduction and requires no information. Just click the Next button.

2. In the second screen, enter your Name, Company, Fax Number, Voice Number, and Station Identifier.

3. Click the Next button.

4. In the third screen (see Figure 28-20), you have several options to choose from. Check the Automatic Receive Fax check box if you're going to leave the fax on and wish to receive faxes automatically. Set the number of rings before the fax answers by either typing in a number or using the up and down arrows in the Answer After _ Ring(s) box. You'll probably want to set the Number of Retries to greater than 2 unless you know for a fact that you'll never get a

busy signal from any fax you will ever send to. The Retries Every _ Second(s) setting seems about right at 60. If this is your initial setup of WinFax, click the Setup Modem button to make sure your fax modem works with it.

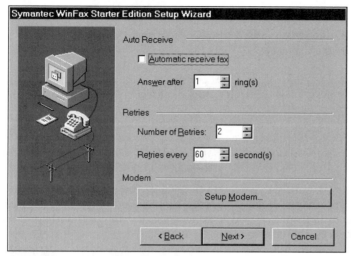

Figure 28-20: Setting WinFax options.

5. Click the Next button.

6. In the fifth screen, check the Send Cover Page check box, and then select a cover page from the supplied ones.

7. Click the Next button.

8. In the final screen, click the Finish button.

Caution

Outlook treats the fax capability as a standard e-mail account. This does not mean that you can send faxes via the Internet; it's just the way Outlook handles the fax information. Do not attempt to alter the settings in the Symantec WinFax account via the Properties button the way you would with a regular e-mail account. Any time you desire to change the fax settings, run olfsetup.exe again.

Sending a fax with Symantec WinFax

Sending a fax with WinFax is pretty much the same as sending an e-mail message. To do so, follow these steps:

1. Select Actions ➪ New Fax Message from the menu.

2. The resultant fax message form (see Figure 28-21) has To, Cc, and Subject fields like an e-mail message form. To enter a number for a fax recipient who is not in your contacts listings, the number must be entered as **fax@555-5555** — substituting the real fax number for 555-5555. If you need to dial 9 to access an

outside line, then the format would be **fax@9w555-5555** — the "w" means to wait for the dial tone after dialing 9 and before dialing the fax number.

3. If you have established a contact list, you can enter the fax numbers from it instead of typing them in by hand. To do so, click either the To button or the Cc button.

For more information on establishing a contact list, see Chapter 30, "Creating and Maintaining a Contact List."

4. In the Select Names dialog box, select the name of the recipient you want to send the fax to, and then click the To button.

5. Select the name of the recipient you want to Cc on the fax, and then click the Cc button.

6. If you want to send a copy to someone but not have the person's name show in the header of the fax, select the name, and then click the Bcc button.

7. Click the OK button to return to the blank fax form. The names you have entered are shown in the appropriate boxes. Although they show as names, and not as fax numbers, Outlook knows to use the fax numbers from the contact lists when the fax is sent.

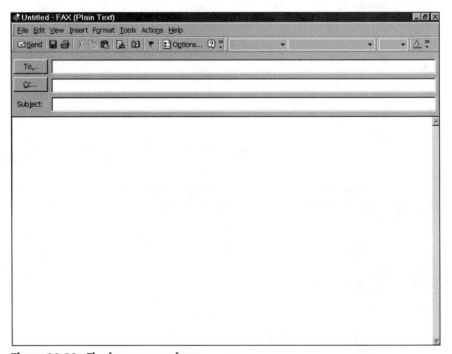

Figure 28-21: The fax message form.

8. Enter a topic for the fax in the Subject box.

9. Type your message in the main window.

10. To send the fax, select File ➪ Send Using ➪ Symantec Fax Starter Edition from the menu. If the phone line is currently available, the fax will go out right away; otherwise, it will wait until the line is free.

Caution

If you just click the Send button, and the recipient has an e-mail address as well as a fax number, Outlook will try to e-mail the message instead of faxing it.

11. If Outlook finds anything confusing about the fax number (such as with 10-digit local dialing), it will ask you to confirm the number.

Tip

To solve the annoying fax number verification routine, just add a +1 in front of every fax number. This works only for American phone numbers.

Installing Microsoft Fax

If you're using the Corporate Workgroup setup with Outlook and you're running it on Windows 95, you automatically have Microsoft Fax capabilities. However, if you don't have Microsoft Fax installed, Outlook won't be able to use it. To check whether Microsoft Fax is available, select Tools ➪ Services from the menu. If Microsoft Fax is one of the services listed in the Services dialog box (see Figure 28-22), then you're ready to go. If not, try clicking the Add button. If it's one of the services that's available, select it and click the OK button.

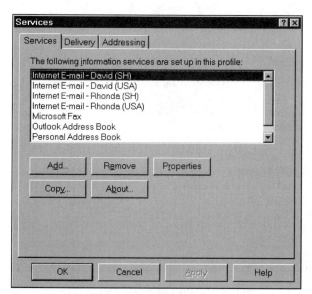

Figure 28-22: The Services dialog box.

If not, you'll need to install Microsoft Fax. To do so, follow these steps:

1. Open Control Panel.

2. Double-click Add/Remove Programs.

3. In the Add/Remove Programs Properties dialog box (see Figure 28-23), click the Windows Setup tab.

4. Check the check boxes next to Microsoft Exchange and Microsoft Fax.

5. Click the OK button.

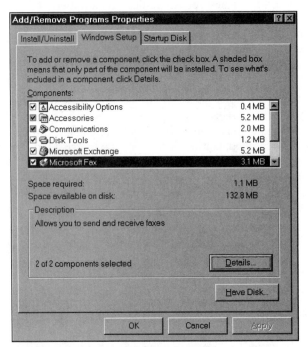

Figure 28-23: The Windows Setup tab.

Configuring Microsoft Fax

Unlike Symantec WinFax, you can configure Microsoft Fax with the Properties button just like any other service. The Microsoft Fax properties include everything from your name and phone numbers to the capability to design custom cover pages. To configure it, follow these steps:

1. Select Tools ➪ Services from the menu.

2. In the Services dialog box, select Microsoft Fax.

3. Click the Properties button.

4. In the Microsoft Fax Properties dialog box, click the Message tab if it is not already selected.

5. Under Time to Send, the default selection is As Soon as Possible. If you would rather set your faxes to go out during times when the long-distance rates are lowest, select the Discount Rates radio button, and then click the Set button to tell Outlook when those times begin and end. To set faxes to go out at a specific time, click the Specific Time radio button.

6. The Message Format panel lets you select whether or not the fax format should be editable. You can also click the Paper button to select Paper Size, Image Quality, and Orientation.

7. The lower panel is for the default cover page for your faxes. Select the one you want to use. Clicking the New button brings up the Fax Cover Page Editor (see Figure 28-24), which lets you design your own faxes. Clicking the Open button also brings up the Fax Cover Page Editor, but with the currently selected cover page open for editing. The Browse button lets you look through your drive for other cover pages.

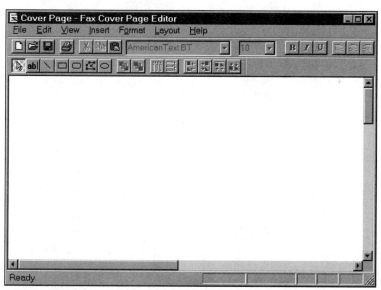

Figure 28-24: The Fax Cover Page Editor.

8. Click the Dialing tab.

9. The Dialing Properties button gives you access to your location settings. Generally speaking, you won't have much use for this, as these are already

set up in your system. The Toll Prefixes button lets you set which prefixes in your area code are long-distance.

10. In the bottom panel, the Number of Retries is set quite low at 3 by default. You'll probably want to increase this number. The Time Between Retries setting is 2 minutes by default. You might want to change it to 1 minute.

11. Click the Modem tab.

12. If you have more than one fax modem in your system, you can choose which one you want to use. Select it and click the Set as Active Fax Modem button. To allow other people in a network situation to use your fax modem, click on the check box in the lower panel.

13. Click the User tab.

14. Type your name, fax number, and other information into the appropriate boxes, as shown in Figure 28-25.

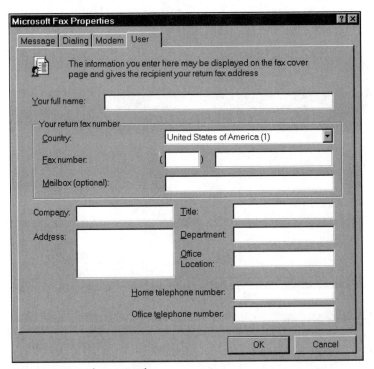

Figure 28-25: The User tab.

15. Click the OK button to finish.

Sending a fax with Microsoft Fax

Sending faxes with Microsoft Fax is very easy thanks to the Compose New Fax wizard.

1. Select Actions ⇨ New Fax Message from the menu.

2. This brings up the Compose New Fax wizard initial screen, which asks you to choose which location you're dialing from. If you have multiple locations, select the one you wish to use. Otherwise, you can avoid this screen in the future by checking the check box that says, "I'm not using a portable computer, so don't show this to me again."

3. Click the Next button.

4. The second screen (see Figure 28-26) asks you for the recipient's information. Either manually enter the data under To and Fax #, or click the Address Book button.

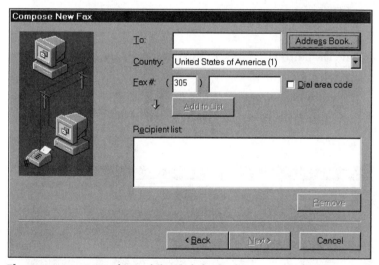

Figure 28-26: Enter the recipient's information.

5. In the Address Book dialog box (see Figure 28-27), select the recipient's fax number, and then click the To button.

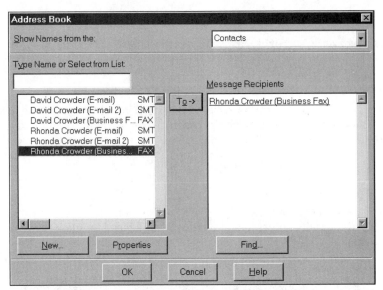

Figure 28-27: Select the recipient's fax number.

6. Click the OK button to return to the Compose New Fax wizard.

7. Click the Next button.

8. The third screen (see Figure 28-28) lets you decide which cover page, if any, will be sent. Click the No radio button to skip the cover page. Otherwise, select the one you want to use.

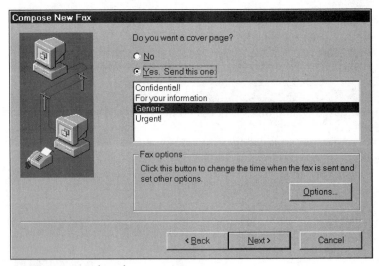

Figure 28-28: Select the cover page.

9. If you want to set a time when the fax is to be sent, click the Options button. This also allows you to set most of the same options as are found in the Microsoft Fax Properties dialog box you used during configuration. Once you have set the desired options, click the OK button to return to the Compose New Fax wizard.

10. Click the Next button.

11. The fourth screen (see Figure 28-29) is where you type the subject of the fax. Type the fax message itself under Note. By default, the message will start on the cover page. If you want it to start on the next page instead, deselect the check box at the bottom of the screen.

12. Click the Next button.

13. The fifth screen lets you attach files to the fax. Click the Add File button to select one. If you change your mind, select the file and click the Remove button.

14. Click the Next button.

15. The sixth and final screen simply tells you that you're done. Click the Finish button and your fax will be sent.

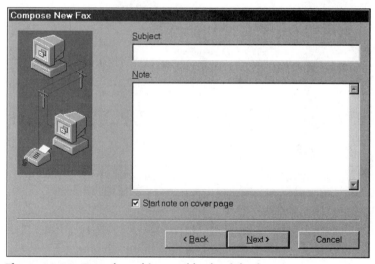

Figure 28-29: Type the subject and body of the fax.

Using Remote Mail

Remote mail lets you spend less time connected to the Internet and operate most of the time offline, logging on only to pick up mail and send it. You can save even more time by picking up only the headers of your e-mail, deciding while offline which ones you want to pick up later.

Remote mail is available only in the Corporate Workgroup option. If you have installed Outlook as Internet mail only, you won't be able to use it. To use remote mail, you must have Microsoft Exchange Server as one of your Outlook services.

Configuring remote mail

To configure Microsoft Exchange for remote mail operation, follow these steps:

1. Select Tools ⇨ Services from the menu.

2. In the Services dialog box, select Microsoft Exchange Server.

3. Click the Properties button.

4. If it is not already selected, click the General tab (see Figure 28-30).

Figure 28-30: The General tab of Microsoft Exchange Server.

5. Select the Manually Control Connection State radio button.

6. If you want to be able to select whether to work offline or not each time you launch Outlook, check the check box labeled "Choose the connection type when starting."

7. Under Default Connection State, select the radio button labeled "Work offline and use dial-up networking."

8. Click the Dial-Up Networking tab (see Figure 28-31).

Figure 28-31: The Dial-Up Networking tab.

9. Select the dial-up connection, and enter your user name, password, and domain.

10. Click the Remote Mail tab (see Figure 28-32).

Figure 28-32: The Remote Mail tab.

11. The default settings for remote mail are to Process Marked Items and Disconnect After Connection is Finished. This way, you log on, pick up message headers, review them offline, mark the ones you want, and then connect and download the marked ones. However, you can also choose to filter messages, which means that you set conditions on which ones will be downloaded. To do so, select the radio button labeled "Retrieve items that meet the following conditions." Next, click the Filter button.

12. The Filter dialog box allows you to set restrictions so that only messages from a particular person or having a particular subject are retrieved. You can also select to retrieve only those messages that are directly addressed to you or carbon copied to you. If you need more options, click the Advanced button. This adds a variety of options such as size of message, date received, etc. Once you've made your choices, click the OK button to return to the Filter dialog box; then click its OK button to return to the Remote Mail tab.

13. Click the OK button to finish.

Getting mail with remote mail

To use remote mail, you must be offline. The process involves connecting twice, the first time to retrieve the message headers, the second time to retrieve selected messages. To get your mail with remote mail, follow these steps:

1. Select Tools ➪ Remote Mail ➪ Remote Tools from the menu. This brings up the Remote toolbar, as shown in Figure 28-33.

Figure 28-33: The Remote toolbar.

2. Click the Connect button to activate the Remote Connection wizard.

3. Select which services you want to check messages on.

4. Choose to retrieve message headers only.

5. To retrieve a message, select its header and click the Mark to Retrieve button. If you want to leave a copy of it on the server, click the Mark to Retrieve a Copy button.

6. To delete a message from the server without retrieving it, select its header and click the Delete button.

7. If you change your mind about downloading a message, select its header and click the Unmark button. To clear all marks, click the Unmark All button.

8. When you're ready to retrieve the messages you've marked, click the Connect button.

Summary

In this chapter, you learned how to use Outlook for managing multiple e-mail accounts, how to read, create, address, and send messages as well as how to save, print, and delete them. You also learned how to use fax services from Outlook and how to use remote mail to save online connection time.

✦ Outlook can manage one or more e-mail accounts.

✦ New e-mail accounts are added to Outlook via the Internet Connection wizard.

✦ E-mail account properties can be modified via the Tools menu after they are established.

✦ The Send/Receive button transmits and picks up messages in a single operation.

✦ The Previous Item and Next Item buttons let you move through your messages by a variety of factors.

✦ You can enter recipient information using Outlook's contact database.

✦ Messages can be saved as separate text files.

✦ Messages can be printed individually or en masse, and you can print a list of messages.

✦ Deleted messages are moved to the Deleted Items folder.

✦ Outlook uses Symantec WinFax Starter Edition for Internet mail only installations, and Microsoft Fax for Corporate Workgroup installations (on Windows 95 only).

✦ Microsoft Fax uses the Compose New Fax wizard to make sending faxes easier (on Windows 95).

✦ Remote mail lets you minimize online time by picking up only the headers of messages, letting you decide while offline which message bodies you want to download.

✦ ✦ ✦

Advanced Message Management

This chapter shows you how to customize Outlook's interface to suit yourself, adding toolbars and menu items or modifying the existing ones. It goes on to cover the secrets of sorting messages by various parameters and grouping them by their similarities. Filtering messages is another type of message management technique that temporarily eliminates from view all the messages that don't fit your established criteria.

A different type of mail filtering allows you to set rules that automate the handling of your incoming e-mail messages. Outlook automatically archives your messages for you, but you can take control of the process and specify how and when it's done.

The chapter also shows you how to send HTML documents and virtual business cards, use "signatures" on your messages, get confirmation that your e-mail has been received and read, and how to find a particular message among many.

Customizing the Outlook Interface

You can customize the way you work with Outlook in a number of different ways. If you don't like the current menus and toolbars, you can modify the way they look and the options they contain. You can even add your own custom menus or toolbars, perhaps creating ones that contain the options you use most often when working with Outlook. You can add and delete items in the Outlook bar, and change the appearance of it.

Working with toolbars

As in any Office program, you can move Outlook's toolbars around to suit yourself. Don't like the menu bar at the top? Drag it to the bottom, or make it free-floating in the middle of your e-mail messages. If you want to see what it looks like sideways, you can always dock it on the left or right side of the Outlook window.

To move any toolbar, place your pointer at the left-hand side of it and find the spot where it turns into a four-pointed arrow. At that spot, hold down your left mouse button and drag the toolbar to another spot. When it's where you want it to be, release the mouse button at that point and the toolbar will stay there. If you want it to be a floating toolbar, just drop it anywhere but the top, bottom, or sides of the window. If you want to dock it, drag it into the sides, top, or bottom and release it. If it just sits there, free-floating, drag it farther until it docks.

Note   Floating toolbars don't have the left-hand side move handle that docked toolbars do. To drag them, grab them in their title bars (the blue area with the name of the toolbar in it) instead.

In addition to moving them around, you can actually control the contents of toolbars. You can add menus to the menu bar, buttons to the others, and even create your own custom menus and toolbars. There's no reason, by the way, why you can't add buttons to the menu bar — it's just a toolbar like the others, and you can add either buttons or menus to any toolbar, but it's probably a good idea to stick with the original design.

Customizing existing toolbar contents

To customize the toolbar contents, follow these steps:

1. Right-click anywhere on any toolbar.

2. Select Customize from the resultant pop-up menu.

3. In the Customize dialog box, click the Commands tab (see Figure 29-1).

4. The Categories listing shows first, the menus in the menu bar (from File to Help), and then lists the toolbars themselves (beginning with the Menu Bar). The Commands listing shows menus or tools associated with the selected category. Click on the items in the Categories listing to view the different commands that are available.

5. To add one of the commands to a toolbar, drag it from the dialog box onto the toolbar you want to put it on, and drop it there. Commands with an arrow to the right of them are menus that include submenus. Dragging one of these menus brings along all the options in its submenu automatically.

6. When you're done, click the Close button.

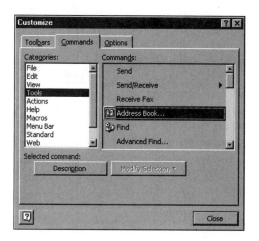

Figure 29-1: The Commands tab of the Customize dialog box.

Resetting toolbars to their default

If you decide to delete the added toolbar contents later, you can just hold down ALT and drag tools off a toolbar to remove them. You can do the same, by the way, with the default toolbar contents. To delete all of the added ones at once by resetting the toolbars to their original state, follow these steps:

1. Right-click on any toolbar.

2. Select Customize from the pop-up menu.

3. In the Customize dialog box, click the Toolbars tab (see Figure 29-2).

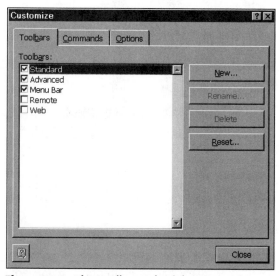

Figure 29-2: The Toolbars tab of the Customize dialog box.

4. Select the toolbar you want to reset.

5. Click the Reset button.

6. When asked to confirm your selection, click the OK button.

7. Repeat Steps 4 through 6 for each toolbar you want to reset.

8. Click the Close button to finish.

Creating a new toolbar

You probably noticed in the Toolbars tab that only two out of four buttons are active. In addition to the Reset button, there's a New button. That one comes into play when you want to create your own custom toolbar. The other two buttons are for handling custom toolbars. To create a custom toolbar, follow these steps:

1. Right-click on any toolbar.

2. Select Customize from the pop-up menu.

3. In the Customize dialog box, click the Toolbars tab (see Figure 29-2).

4. Click the New button.

5. In the New Toolbar dialog box (see Figure 29-3), the custom toolbar is automatically given a name (Custom 1, Custom 2, etc.). If you'd rather give it a more descriptive name like "Most Often Used," you can type it in now.

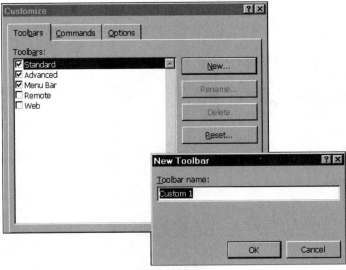

Figure 29-3: The New Toolbar dialog box.

6. Click the OK button. The new toolbar is created, as shown in Figure 29-4. It's very small at the moment, because it has no contents. The name of the custom toolbar is now listed along with the default ones, and the status of the buttons

has changed. The Reset button is no longer available (because there is no default state for a custom toolbar to be returned to) and the two buttons that were previously grayed out have become active.

Figure 29-4: The newly created custom toolbar.

7. If you want to change the name of the custom toolbar (you cannot rename the built-in toolbars), click the Rename button. This will bring up the Rename Toolbar dialog box, which is identical to the New Toolbar dialog box shown in Figure 29-3 except for the title. Type in the new name and click the OK button.

8. If you want to delete the custom toolbar (you cannot delete the built-in toolbars), click the Delete button. You will be asked to confirm the deletion. Click the OK button to do so.

9. Click the Commands tab.

10. Drag the commands you want to add onto your custom toolbar. Figure 29-5 shows a custom toolbar with a Print button, a New Fax Message text button, and a Remote Mail menu.

Figure 29-5: The finished custom toolbar.

11. When you are done, click the Close button.

Working with menu commands

The Customize dialog box has one more tab we haven't explored yet, the Options tab (see Figure 29-6). The upper section, Personalized Menus and Toolbars, has only one set of options in Outlook, those for handling the structure of menu commands.

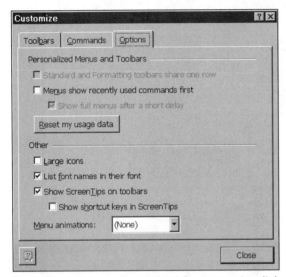

Figure 29-6: The Options tab of the Customize dialog box.

Note   The top option, Standard and Formatting toolbars Share One Row, normally found in this tab in Office applications such as Word, is grayed out here, because there is no Formatting toolbar in Outlook.

Selecting Menus Show Recently Used Commands First means that the position of menu commands will change depending on how often you access them. The commands you don't use often will not be shown unless you click on an arrow at the bottom of the menu. Show Full Menus After a Short Delay sets things up so that you don't have to manually click on the arrow at the bottom of the menu to bring up the unused commands; they show up after a couple of seconds if you keep the menu open. The Reset My Usage Data button puts the menu commands back into their original state, and clears the record of how often they've been used.

The bottom section, Other, lets you change the small icons into large icons, as well as setting font and screen tip options. The final option in this dialog box is Menu Animations. You have three options other than None—Random, Unfold, and Slide. Unfolding menus start at the upper-left corner and expand toward the lower-right corner when they appear. Sliding menus start at the top and expand downward. The Random option means you never know what they're going to do.

Customizing the Outlook bar

The Outlook bar holds, by default, three groups of shortcuts — Outlook Shortcuts, My Shortcuts, and Other Shortcuts (see Figure 29-7). If it's not visible, select View ↪ Outlook Bar from the menu. To close it, use the same menu option.

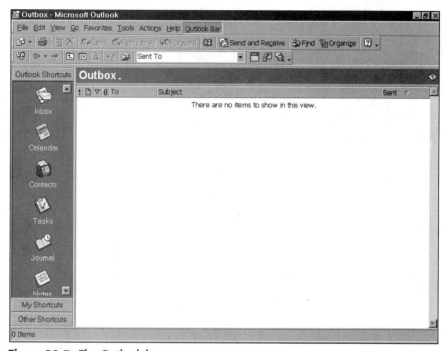

Figure 29-7: The Outlook bar.

Tip

If you're going to open and close the Outlook bar a lot, this is a classic situation where you can streamline your work by adding the Outlook Bar menu option to a toolbar with the Customize option. That way, you don't have to open the View menu first to find it.

There are three basic ways to customize the Outlook bar:

✦ Change the size of its icons

✦ Add, remove, or rename groups

✦ Add, remove, or rename shortcuts

Changing the icon size

To change icon size, right-click within a group, and then select Large Icons or Small Icons from the pop-up menu (see Figure 29-8). The change is effective only within the selected group.

| Large Icons |
| Small Icons |
| |
| Add New Group |
| Remove Group |
| Rename Group |
| |
| Outlook Bar Shortcut... |
| Outlook Bar Shortcut to Web Page... |
| |
| Hide Outlook Bar |

Figure 29-8: Changing icon size.

Note   When selecting group options, right-click anywhere within the group except on an icon. Icons have a different pop-up menu than groups do.

Adding, removing, and renaming groups

To add a new group, right-click anywhere in the Outlook bar except on an icon, and then select Add New Group from the pop-up menu. A new group heading will appear in the Outlook bar with the title "New Group." The title is highlighted and ready for editing, so all you have to do is type your title. Press Enter or click anywhere outside the title box to complete the task.

To remove an existing group, right-click within that group and select Remove Group from the pop-up menu. You'll be asked to confirm the deletion. Click the Yes button to complete the deletion.

To rename a group, right-click within it and select Rename Group from the pop-up menu. The title of the group will be highlighted. Type your new title and press Enter, or click anywhere outside the title box.

Adding, removing, and renaming shortcuts

To add a new shortcut to a group, display the group, and then right-click within that group and select Outlook Bar Shortcut from the pop-up menu. This will bring up the Add to Outlook Bar dialog box, as shown in Figure 29-9.

The Look In option has two choices — Outlook and File System. Outlook is the default options, and its folders are listed in the dialog box. If you select File System, you can choose from all the folders on your system. In either case, select the folder shortcut you want to add to the Outlook bar, and then click the OK button.

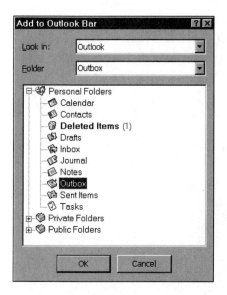

Figure 29-9: The Add to Outlook Bar dialog box.

To remove an icon from a group, right-click on the icon and select Remove from Outlook Bar from the pop-up menu. You'll be asked to confirm the deletion. Click the Yes button to complete the deletion.

To rename an icon, right-click on it and select Rename Shortcut from the pop-up menu. The title of the shortcut will be highlighted. Type your new title and press Enter, or click anywhere outside the title box.

Sorting Messages

The simplest way to sort messages is to click on the column header. To sort by sender, click on From; to sort by subject, click on Subject; etc. You can change the sort order by right-clicking on the column header and selecting either Sort Ascending or Sort Descending from the resultant pop-up menu.

To use more sophisticated sorting by multiple fields, follow these steps:

1. Right-click in the message window (but not on a message) and select Sort from the pop-up menu. This brings up the Sort dialog box (see Figure 29-10). If the message window is full of messages and there is no blank area in which you can right-click, you won't get the right menu. In that case, you'll have to take a more roundabout route to get to the Sort dialog box. Select View ⇨ Current View ⇨ Customize Current View from the menu, and then click the Sort button in the View Summary dialog box.

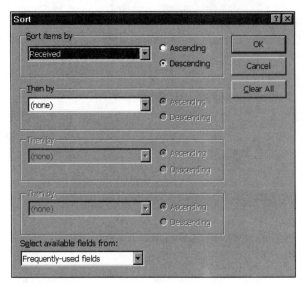

Figure 29-10: The Sort dialog box.

2. In the Sort dialog box, you can specify up to four different sequential sort parameters. The messages will first be sorted by the first field, then by the second, and so on. Select the first parameter from the drop-down list under Sort Items By.

3. Click either the Ascending or Descending radio button to set the sort order for this field.

4. If desired, select another field to sort by from the drop-down list under Then By, and choose its sort order.

5. Repeat Step 4 if desired for the remaining two parameters.

6. If the fields you want to sort by aren't available, choose a new field source from the drop-down list under Select Available Fields From.

7. Click the OK button to initiate the sort. (If you opened the Sort dialog box from the View Summary dialog box, you also have to click OK on the View Summary dialog box to initiate the sort.)

Grouping Messages

Messages can be grouped together by similarities. As with sorting, there's both a quick-and-easy and a more sophisticated and complex way to do it.

Using the Group By Box

The easiest way to group messages is to drag fields into the Group By Box. To do so, follow these steps:

1. Click the Group By Box icon on the Advanced toolbar. This opens up the Group By Box above the message field column headers. The Group By Box has the words "Drag a column header here to group by that column" in it (see Figure 29-11).

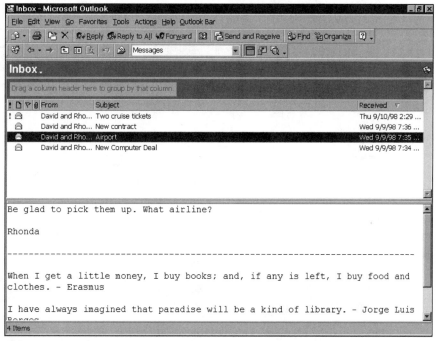

Figure 29-11: The Group By Box.

2. Drag any field into the Group By Box. The column header will move from into the Group By Box, and an arrow on the header will show the current sort direction for that field. You can change the sort direction by clicking on this arrow.

Tip You can also add fields to the Group By Box by right-clicking on a column header in the message box and selecting Group By This Field from the pop-up menu.

3. Repeat Step 2 for each field you wish to group. You can do this for up to four fields, and each field will be subordinate to the one chosen before it, so that the first field will be the main group, the second field will form a subgroup within the first group, etc. The relationships are shown by the graphical representation of the fields in the Group By Box (see Figure 29-12). You can change the relationships by dragging the field headers into new positions.

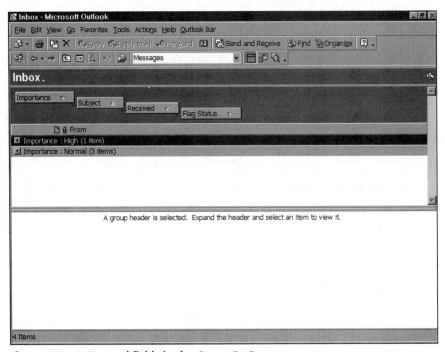

Figure 29-12: Grouped fields in the Group By Box.

4. The messages, instead of being displayed individually, are subsumed within a group heading. You can expand the group heading by clicking on the plus (+) mark to the left of the group heading.

5. To remove the grouping, just drag any field out of the Group By Box back into the column headers. You can also remove fields from the Group By Box by right-clicking on a column header in the Group By box and selecting Don't Group By This Field from the pop-up menu. If you use the latter technique, the field header will go back into the column headers at the end of the row and you'll have to manually drag it back to its former position if you want things restored to their original positions.

Using the Group By dialog box

You can also group messages by right-clicking within the message window and choosing Group By from the pop-up menu. This brings up a dialog box very much like the Sort dialog box, with four drop-down lists of fields you can group by and options for setting the sort order (see Figure 29-13).

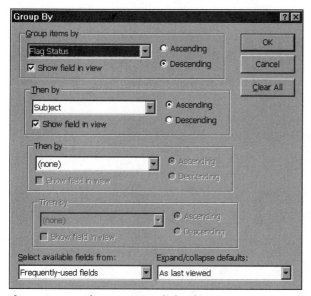

Figure 29-13: The Group By dialog box.

If the message window is full of messages and there is no blank area in which you can right-click, you won't get the right menu. In that case, you'll have to take a more roundabout route to get to the Group By dialog box. Select View ➪ Current View ➪ Customize Current View from the menu, and then click the Group By button in the View Summary dialog box.

Note
The only real advantages of using this dialog box are its Show Field in View check boxes. You may find it annoying in the Group By box approach that the column headers you move into the Group By box are missing from the column headers as a result. The Show Field in View option results in the field name being in both the column headers and the Group By box. (You'll need to click the Group By Box button on the toolbar to see the effect after the grouping is completed in the Group By dialog box). There's also an option to set the Expand/collapse defaults for groups to As Last Viewed, All Expanded, or All Collapsed.

Filtering Messages

Filters are another way to view messages. Applying a filter makes all messages not fitting its criteria disappear. They're not deleted, just temporarily invisible. Removing the filter lets you see them again. You can apply several conditions in a filter to narrow a search for a particular message. To apply a filter, follow these steps:

1. Right-click in the message window and select Filter from the pop-up menu. This brings up the Filter dialog box (see Figure 29-14). If the message window is full of messages and there is no blank area in which you can right-click, you won't get the right menu. In that case, you'll have to take a more roundabout route to get to the Filter dialog box. Select View ➪ Current View ➪ Customize Current View from the menu, and then click the Filter button in the View Summary dialog box.

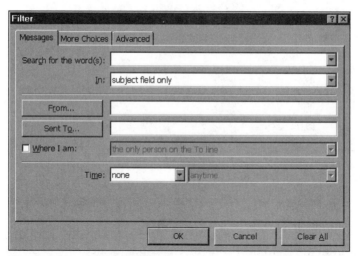

Figure 29-14: The Filter dialog box.

2. The first tab, Messages, has options to filter for particular words (and to look for them in only certain places), to filter for sender or addressee, and to filter for time settings (such as time created, sent, received, etc.).

3. Click the More Choices tab (see Figure 29-15). Here, you can filter for Categories such as personal, business, etc., or for read/unread messages, or for messages with or without attachments, or by importance or size of the message.

4. Click the Advanced tab (see Figure 29-16). On it, you select a field from the drop-down list of that name, and then set the condition it must meet, and the value concerned. The value is not always required. The field, for example, might be "Due By," and the condition "yesterday." Click Add to List to add the criterion to the filter.

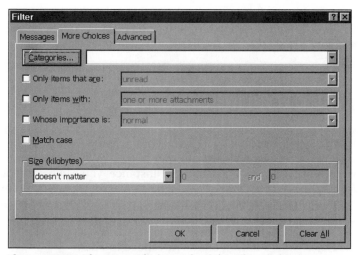

Figure 29-15: The More Choices tab of the Filter dialog box.

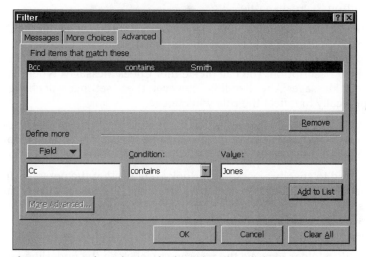

Figure 29-16: The Advanced tab of the Filter dialog box.

5. Repeat Step 4 for any other criteria you want to add.

6. If you change your mind, you can delete a criterion from the filter. Just select it and click the Remove button. To remove all criteria, click the Clear All button.

Caution

Using the Clear All button clears all three of the tabs, not just the one that's visible.

7. Click the OK button to apply the filter. (If you opened the Filter dialog box from the View Summary dialog box, you also have to click OK on the View Summary dialog box to apply the filter.)

Creating Mail-Filtering Rules

The Rules wizard can be your most useful tool in Outlook. With it, you can set up a series of rules that will automatically process your e-mail. The rules are applied in a particular order, and you can change that order at will. You can create rules to handle incoming e-mail or outgoing e-mail. For instance, you can have all messages from a particular person or address sent to a particular folder, which is very useful if you subscribe to multiple mailing lists. Outlook's rules are very flexible and powerful. To utilize them, follow these steps:

1. Click the Rules Wizard button on the Advanced toolbar.

2. When you first see the Rules Wizard dialog box, it has nothing in it. Click the New button to create a rule.

3. The first step in creating a rule is to choose what type of action to take (see Figure 29-17). Under Which Type of Rule Do You Want to Create?, pick one of the options in the top panel. It will then appear in the bottom panel under the label Rule Description. You can pick either Check Messages When They Arrive or Check Messages After Sending. However, these settings will change automatically to reflect the rule you choose.

4. Some rules require further attention. For instance, if you selected Move New Messages from Someone, you'll have to specify both who that someone is and where to move the messages to. Click on the underlined words to do so.

5. If you need to specify a person, Outlook assumes that the person is in your contacts list or Address Book. If this is the case, just select their name from the listing. Otherwise, click New and make a new entry for the person. Then choose the new entry in the left list box, click From, and click OK. The name will be entered in the rule.

6. To specify a folder to move the message to, click on the underlined word specified in the rule. This will bring up a listing of available folders. Select one and click the OK button. The folder will be entered in the rule.

7. Click the Next button.

8. The next screen of Rules Wizard lets you set more conditions if you want to. Select any you wish to add.

9. Click the Next button.

10. The next screen of Rules Wizard prompts you for the action you wish to take. It's possible, depending on what selections you've already made, that the action is already specified. If so, you don't need to do anything here. Otherwise, pick an action from the list.

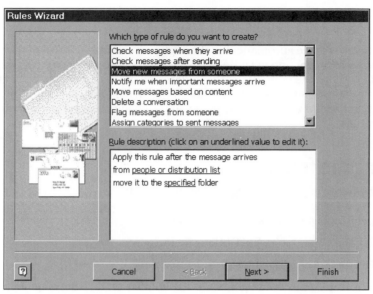

Figure 29-17: Outlook's Rules Wizard.

11. Click the Next button.

12. The next screen of Rules Wizard lets you set exceptions to the rule. For instance, you may have set up a rule that will delete any message from a particular person, but you want to see it if it has an attachment. Select the exception you want, if any.

13. Click the Next button.

14. The final screen of Rules Wizard asks you to name the rule. Give it a good, descriptive name.

15. Click the Finish button.

16. The rule now shows in the Rules Wizard dialog box. Click the OK button to exit Rules Wizard.

If you have multiple rules, they are applied in the order they're listed. You can change the order by clicking the Rules Wizard button on the Advanced toolbar; then select the rule you want to move and click either the Move Up or Move Down buttons.

Rules can be renamed or deleted by clicking the appropriately named buttons. One of the most powerful abilities, though, is to modify a rule. You can click the Modify button to change an existing rule; this will let you walk back through the wizard and change whatever settings you like.

Tip   If you want to set up two rules that are very similar, use the Copy button to make a duplicate rule; then select the copy and click the Modify button. Make the changes you want, give the rule a new name, and you're done.

Archiving

Archiving takes place automatically, although you can take control of the process. The AutoArchive function in Outlook is set by default to run every two weeks. At that time, it scans the contents of the folders and moves any items older than a set amount of time into Outlook's archive folder. Each folder has the ability to set different archiving ages and you can, of course, change how often the AutoArchive function runs.

Setting the frequency

To set the frequency of archiving, follow these steps:

1. Select Tools ➪ Options from the menu.

2. Click the Other tab in the Options dialog box.

3. Click the AutoArchive button.

4. In the AutoArchive dialog box, set the number of days between archiving. You can either type in the number or use the scrolling arrows.

5. Click the OK button to return to the Options dialog box.

6. In the Options dialog box, click the OK button to complete the process.

Setting the AutoArchive delay

To set a folder's AutoArchive delay, follow these steps:

1. Click the Folder List button on the Advanced toolbar.

2. Right-click the name of a folder in the list (Calendar is shown).

3. Select Properties from the pop-up menu, as shown in Figure 29-18.

4. In the folder's Properties dialog box (see Figure 29-19), click the AutoArchive tab.

5. Set the maximum age of messages in months, weeks, or days. Messages older than this age will be removed from the folder when AutoArchive runs. If you don't want the folder to be archived at all, clear the check box.

6. If you want to set a folder other than the default archive folder, type the filename of a personal folders file or click the Browse button and pick one.

7. Alternatively, you can select the lower radio button to prevent archiving and have old items deleted instead.

8. Click the OK button to complete the action.

9. Repeat Steps 2 through 8 for all folders you want to change.

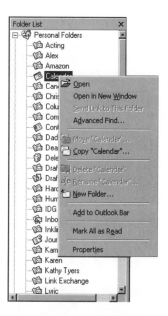

Figure 29-18: The Folder list and its pop-up menu.

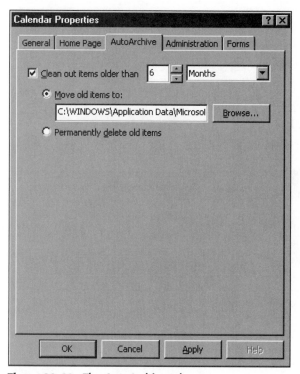

Figure 29-19: The AutoArchive tab.

Sending HTML Documents

Outlook has the ability to send e-mail in HTML format, the same as that used to develop Web pages. You should familiarize yourself with this capability even if you don't plan to use it as your default format, because you may end up using it without even intending to. When you reply to a message, Outlook automatically uses the same format that the message you're replying to used. So, if you get a message in HTML format, your reply will be in it, too.

Setting HTML as the default

To set up HTML as your default format for outgoing mail, follow these steps:

1. Select Tools ➪ Options from the menu.

2. In the Options dialog box, click the Mail Format tab (see Figure 29-20).

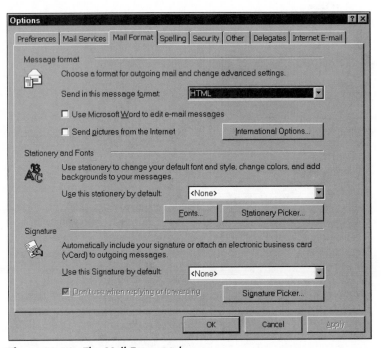

Figure 29-20: The Mail Format tab.

3. Next to Send in This Message Format, choose HTML from the drop-down list.

4. Click the OK button to complete the procedure.

Now, when you click the New Mail Message button, your message form will look just like before, except that a new bunch of options will be activated, which were grayed out when using plain text format (see Figure 29-21).

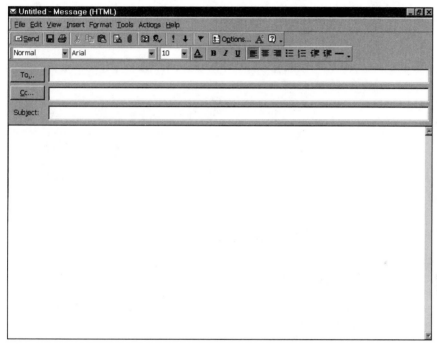

Figure 29-21: An HTML message form.

The HTML Style drop-down list

Although the majority of the buttons on the Formatting toolbar have extremely obvious uses — the Font Color button sets font color, the Italic button italicizes text, and so on — those not familiar with HTML may find the Style drop-down list a bit confusing. Table 29-1 explains the most important items on it.

Table 29-1 Most-Used HTML Styles	
Style	**Function**
Normal	Uses proportional font
Formatted	Uses fixed width font
Address	Makes text italic
Heading 1 through 6	Various sizes for text, used for separating sections. Heading 1 is the largest; heading 6 is the smallest.
Numbered List	Used to create a numbered list. Typing an entry and then pressing Enter moves you to the next line with a number in place. Pressing Enter without typing an entry after a number ends the numbering and returns you to the Paragraph style.
Bulleted List	Used to create a bulleted list. Works just like the numbered list, but uses solid circles instead of numbers to set off entries.
Paragraph	Used to put extra space between paragraphs.

Sending Business Cards

Digital business cards, or *vCards,* are the modern equivalent of the cardboard that clutters up Rolodexes all over the world. These files are imported into address books like Outlook's contacts listings. To send one via e-mail, you must have a listing in your contacts folder. Select it, and then choose Actions ⇨ Forward as vCard from the menu. This will create a new e-mail message with the vCard (.vcf file) attached to it, as shown in Figure 29-22.

All you need to do is address the message and click the Send button.

Tip   You can also save a contact as a vCard. This is useful in case you want to include it with a signature on your e-mail (see the following section). To do so, double-click on a contact to open it and select Export to vCard File from the File menu. Outlook will let you select a folder and a name for the file. The default folder is Signatures, and the default filename is the name of the contact. Click the Save button to finish.

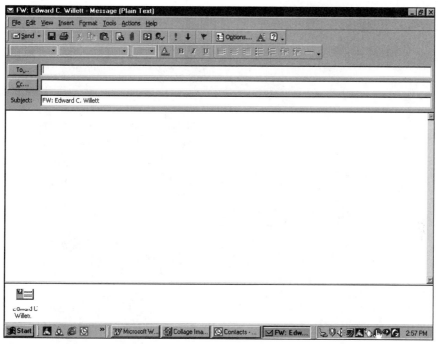

Figure 29-22: Sending a vCard.

Using Signatures and Receipts

A signature, or *sig,* is not necessarily just your name. It's a bit of text that's added automatically at the end of e-mail messages you send out. Of course, there's nothing to prevent you from using your name as the sig on your messages, but most people use quotations, statements of company policy, addresses of Web pages, and so on, instead.

Creating a message signature

To make a signature for your messages, follow these steps:

1. Select Tools ➪ Options from the menu.

2. In the Options dialog box, click the Mail Format tab (see Figure 29-23). If you already had some signatures created, you could select which one you wanted to use as your default signature from the drop-down list at the bottom of the tab.

3. Click the Signature Picker button.

4. The Signature Picker dialog box (see Figure 29-24) is blank at first, as there are no sigs yet. Click the New button.

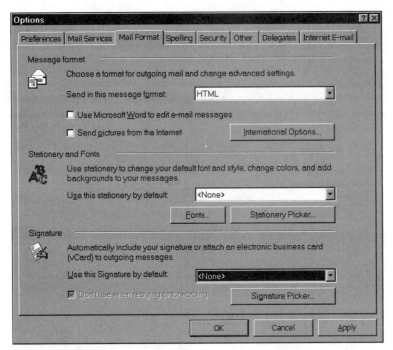

Figure 29-23: The Mail Format tab.

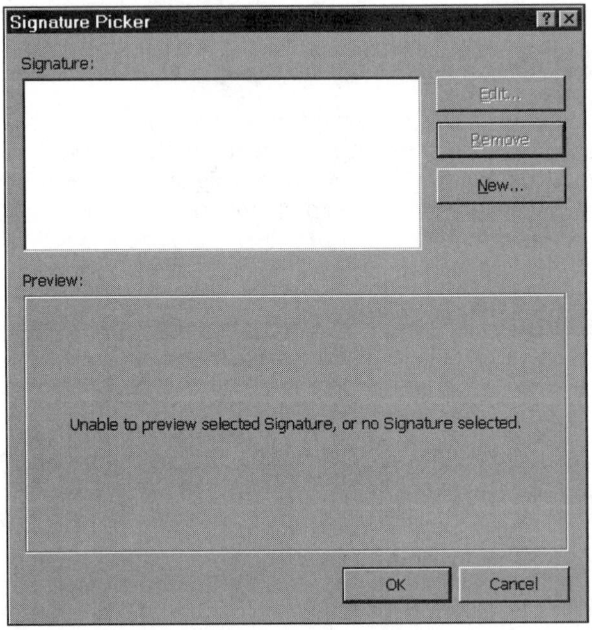

Figure 29-24: The Signature Picker dialog box.

5. In the Create New Signature dialog box (see Figure 29-25), type a name for your new sig. By default, the second option is to start with a blank signature. If you had other sigs to choose from, you could also click on the second radio button, which is Use This Existing Signature as a Template. You would then pick one from the drop-down list. In either case, you can also click on the third radio button, Use This File as a Template. You would then type the template filename or click the Browse button to locate it.

Figure 29-25: The Create New Signature dialog box.

6. Click the Next button.

7. Type your signature text into the text area at the top of the Edit Signature dialog box (see Figure 29-26). The Font and Paragraph buttons, which let you choose fonts and alignment, are not available for plain text. The Clear button erases the text area, and the Advanced Edit button invokes the appropriate editor application for the type of message the sig will be used with (e.g., Rich Text –Word, HTML – FrontPage, plain text – Notepad).

8. If you want to attach an existing vCard file as part of the sig (see the preceding section), select it from the drop-down list. It's probably not the best idea to do this, as you wouldn't give someone a physical business card every time you saw them. Nobody needs 200 copies of your vCard, either.

9. Click the Finish button to complete signature creation.

10. Back in the Signature Picker dialog box, the sig is now listed and the Edit and Remove buttons are active. Repeat Steps 4 through 9 to create more sigs.

11. Click the OK button to return to the Options dialog box.

12. In the Options dialog box, click the OK button to finish the process.

Figure 29-26: The Edit Signature dialog box.

When you send a message, if you have selected a default sig in the Mail Format tab, it will automatically be included. Otherwise, or if you want to add another sig in addition to the default, you'll have to pick one by clicking the Signature button in the message form's Standard toolbar before you send the message.

Setting up message receipts

Making sure your e-mail has arrived is much like sending snail mail with a return receipt requested form. To set things up so that you get confirmation, follow these steps:

1. Select Tools ➪ Options from the menu.

2. If it is not already selected, click the Preferences tab.

3. Click the E-mail Options button.

4. In the E-mail Options dialog box, click the Tracking Options button.

5. In the Tracking Options dialog box, click the two check boxes labeled "Request a read receipt for all messages I send" and "Request a delivery receipt for all messages I send."

6. If you don't want other people to be able to get such receipts from you, click the radio button labeled "Never send a response."

7. Click the OK button to return to the E-mail Options dialog box.

8. In the E-mail Options dialog box, click the OK button to return to the Options dialog box.

9. In the Options dialog box, click the OK button to complete the operation.

Note   Bear in mind that not all e-mail programs support sending receipts, and that someone else may use the Never Send a Response option.

Finding the Message You Want

If you have several messages in a folder, finding the specific one you're interested in can be quite a chore. There may be several on one subject, from one person, on about the same date, for instance. Outlook's Find feature makes it easy to find what you're looking for. To use it, follow these steps:

1. Click the Find button on the toolbar. The Find box will open up on top of the message window (see Figure 29-27).

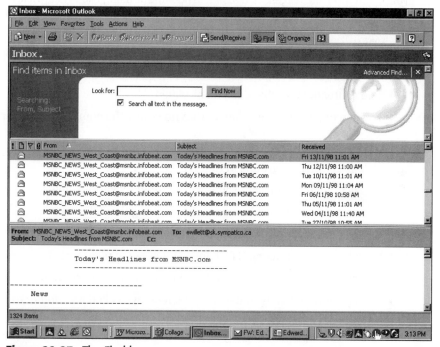

Figure 29-27: The Find box.

2. Enter the text you want to search for in the Look For edit box.

3. If you want to search in more than the From and Subject fields, click the check box labeled "Search all text in the message."

4. Click the Find Now button.

5. The Find feature will search through all your messages in the folder and filter out all that don't meet the search criteria. When the search is complete, the word "Done!" will appear next to the Find Now button.

6. Two new items now appear in the Find box—a Go to Advanced Find link and a Clear Search link. Clicking Go to Advanced Find is the same as clicking the Advanced Find button that already exists in the upper right-hand corner of the Find box. The advanced find feature is very similar to the Filter dialog box. For details about how to use it, see the earlier section on filtering messages.

7. Click Clear Search to reset the Find box to its initial state and unhide the messages the search hid.

8. Click the Find button to close the Find box.

Summary

In this chapter, you learned how to customize the Outlook interface, and sort, group, and filter messages. You also learned about using the Rules wizard to create mail-handling rules, how messages are archived, and how to send HTML documents and vCards. Finally, you learned about using signatures on your messages and how to use Outlook's Find feature to locate messages.

✦ Toolbars can be moved around the screen.

✦ The contents of toolbars can be modified.

✦ You can create custom toolbars that hold only the commands you want included.

✦ You can add shortcuts to and remove shortcuts from the Outlook bar, as well as create new groups in that bar.

✦ Messages can be sorted, grouped, or filtered by various fields.

✦ You can automate mail-handling chores using the Rules wizard.

✦ You can modify how Outlook archives old messages.

✦ E-mail can be sent using HTML format instead of plain text.

✦ You can create vCards—virtual business cards—and send them via e-mail.

✦ You can automatically add a personal message called a *signature* to the end of each e-mail message you send.

✦ You can set options so that you receive confirmations when your messages are received or read.

✦ Outlook has a Find feature that helps you locate particular messages in a folder.

✦　✦　✦

Creating and Maintaining a Contact List

This chapter covers using Outlook's contact database, beginning with using the built-in forms to enter contact data. You can also use the All Fields tab to enter more detailed data not covered in the General and Details tabs of the contact form.

Outlook has several built-in views — ways of looking at the contact information — and you can create custom views as well. Contact data can be edited either in the views or via the data entry forms.

Contact listings can be grouped the same way as messages can, and contacts can be associated with other contacts as well as items in other Outlook folders.

Adding a Contact

There are several ways to get into the Contacts folder (see Figure 30-1), but one of the easiest is to select Go ➪ Contacts from the menu. If you have the Outlook bar open, then just click on the Contacts shortcut.

Cross-Reference For more information on the Outlook bar, see Chapter 29, "Advanced Message Management."

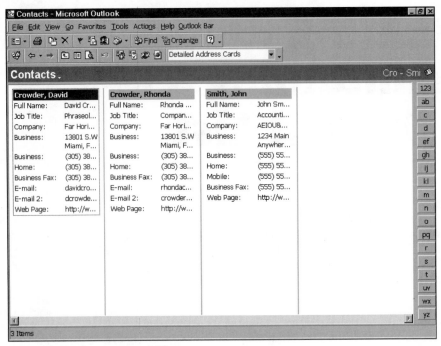

Figure 30-1: The Contacts folder.

Adding a contact listing is even easier. Just click the New Contact button on the toolbar. Where things get complex is when gathering all the information that Outlook can hold. Of course, there's no requirement that you fill in all the blanks — it's just that Outlook can cover anything you come up with. If all you've got is basic data such as name, phone number, and e-mail address, just use that. On the other hand, if you want a place to keep track of things like nicknames, birthdays, and anniversaries, and even to store digital certificates, you've got it.

To add a contact listing, follow these steps:

1. Click the New Contact button on the toolbar.

2. In the new contact form's General tab (see Figure 30-2), enter the contact's full name in normal format, like "John Smith." The name will automatically be entered in the format "Smith, John" under File As when you tab out of the Full Name box, although you can select to have it filed via the normal format instead by selecting "John Smith" instead of "Smith, John" from the File As drop-down menu.

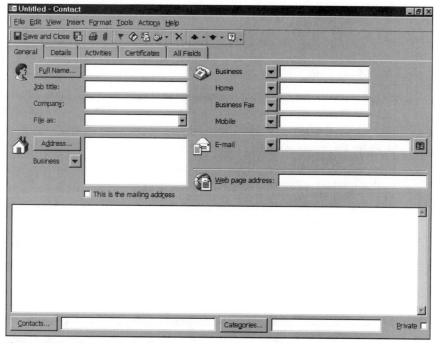

Figure 30-2: The General tab.

3. If you wish to enter more detailed name information, click the Full Name button. This will bring up a dialog box with such options as title, suffix (Jr., Sr., etc.), and middle name. Enter the data and click the OK button to return to the new contact form. Although this information does not appear in separate fields on the main form, it is included in separate field entries in the database.

4. Fill out the Job title and Company fields. When you enter a company name, three more options appear in the drop-down list under File As: to file by company name, to file by "Smith, John" with the company name in parentheses after it, or to file by company name with "Smith, John" in parentheses after it.

5. The Address field is set by default to the business address, but three different addresses can actually be entered — business, home, and other. Select which one you want to enter by clicking on the downward pointing arrow. You can enter all three if you wish. Clicking the Address button brings up an address listing where Outlook has already parsed the information you entered into its component parts, such as street address and ZIP code. You can also specify the Country/Region, which you can select from a drop-down list (Outlook does a very good job of determining the country from most addresses). After doing so, click the OK button.

6. If you have entered multiple addresses, display the one you want snail mail to go to and click the check box labeled "This is the mailing address."

7. Enter the contact's telephone numbers. Although the form lists only four numbers, several more are accessible via the arrow buttons, just as with the Address field.

8. Enter the contact's e-mail addresses. Although the form lists only one e-mail address, two more are accessible via the arrow button, just as with the Address field.

9. Enter the contact's Web page address.

10. If desired, click the Contacts button at the bottom of the form to associate this contact with other people in your listings.

11. If desired, click the Categories button at the bottom of the form to assign a category (like "competition" or "personal") to this contact.

12. If you don't want other people with access to your Contacts folder to be able to view this contact's information, check the Private check box.

13. Click the Details tab (see Figure 30-3).

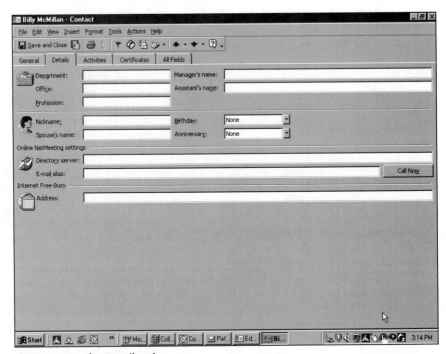

Figure 30-3: The Details tab.

14. Enter any other data you wish, such as the contact's nickname, spouse's name, etc. The only unusual elements on this form are the Birthday and Anniversary fields, which have a calendar available by clicking the downward pointing arrow. By default, the current date is shown, but other months are available by using the left- and right-pointing arrows to scroll through the year. Once you're in the right month, click on the date.

15. The Activities tab doesn't take any entries from you. It simply lists all Outlook items with which the contact is associated, such as other contacts, e-mail messages, etc.

16. If you have a digital certificate for this person and wish to use it in secure e-mail messages, click the Certificates tab (see Figure 30-4).

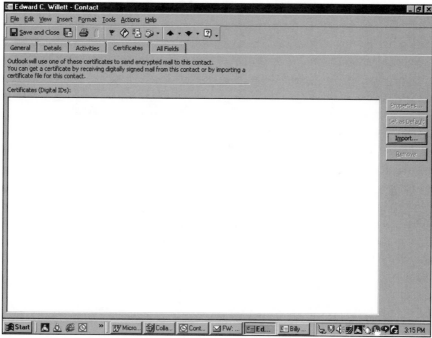

Figure 30-4: The Certificates tab.

17. Click the Import button.

18. In the Locate Security Profile dialog box, select the file and click the Open button.

19. If you want to view or change specific fields, click the All Fields tab (see Figure 30-5).

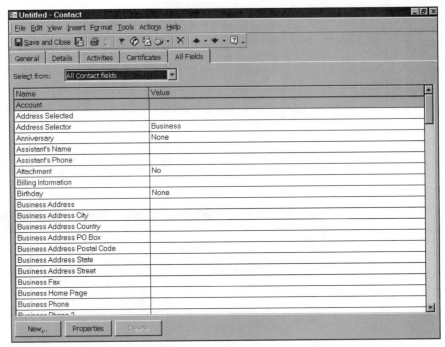

Figure 30-5: The All Fields tab.

20. The drop-down list under Select From lets you choose various types of fields to display, such as phone number, address, etc. The most all-inclusive of these options is All Contact Fields.

21. Enter data under the Value column next to the field name. Press Enter or click anywhere else on the form and the information is accepted in the field (the contact must still be saved to keep the change, though). In addition to entering new information here, you can also edit existing data. All changes you make here are instantly reflected in the appropriate fields on the other tabs.

22. Click the New button to create new fields for the database. You may, for instance, want to add a field for Pet Name or Shoe Size.

23. In the New Field dialog box (see Figure 30-6), type a name for the field.

24. Select a Type for the data (text, number, date/time, etc.) from the drop-down list.

25. Depending on the data type, you may be able to select from different formats via the drop-down list of that name.

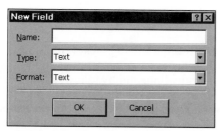

Figure 30-6: The New Field dialog box.

26. Click the OK button to complete creation of the new field.

27. Enter the data for the new field under the Value column. Unless you enter data, this field is visible only by selecting User-defined Fields in This Folder under Select From. If there is an entry under this field, it can also be viewed by selecting User-defined Fields in This Item.

28. To complete the entry of contact information, click the Save and Close button on the toolbar or use the Ctrl+S key combination.

Note

You can also add a contact in any of the contact folder views except the address card views by clicking in the first row under the column headers and then entering the data for the new contact. However, this is a comparatively awkward approach because you must scroll or tab to fill in the fields for the new contact.

Opening and Editing a Contact

You can edit contact fields directly in the address cards, detailed address cards, or phone list views (see the following section on viewing contact lists). However, not all fields are visible in these situations, and the easiest way to edit contact data is by using the same form you used to add the contact to begin with. To do so, follow these steps:

1. Double-click on the contact's listing.

2. Select the tab containing the data you want to edit. If neither the General nor Details tab has the fields you want to edit listed, select the All Fields tab.

3. Edit the data.

4. To save the listing, click the Save and Close button. To exit without saving, press the Esc key and click the No button when asked if you want to save changes.

Viewing Contact Lists

The Current View drop-down list on the toolbar offers you seven different ways to look at your contact information: with address cards or detailed address cards, by phone list, by category, by company, by location, and by follow-up flag. Table 30-1 shows the various views and their contents. The By Category, By Company, By Location, and By Follow-Up Flag views are grouped by those parameters (see the following section on grouping contacts).

| Table 30-1 | |
| **Contacts Views** | |
View	**Contents**
Address Cards	Name, follow-up flag, address, phone numbers, e-mail addresses.
Detailed Address Cards	The full listing from the General tab.
Phone List	Flag status, icon, attachment, name, company, file as, phone numbers, journal, categories.
By Category	Flag status, icon, attachment, name, company, file as, categories, phone numbers.
By Company	Flag status, icon, attachment, name, job title, company, file as, department, phone numbers, categories.
By Location	Flag status, icon, attachment, name, company, file as, state, country/region, phone numbers, categories.
By Follow-Up Flag	Flag status, icon, attachment, name, company, file as, phone numbers, categories.

You can also create your own views if you don't like any of the available ones. To do so, follow these steps:

1. Select View ➪ Current View ➪ Define Views from the menu.

2. The Define Views dialog box (see Figure 30-7) lists the currently available views. The bottom panel shows the settings for the selected view. Click the New button to create a new view; the Copy button to make a copy of a selected view that you can then modify; or the Modify button to change a selected view.

3. In the Create a New View dialog box (see Figure 30-8), type a name and select the type of view (table, timeline, etc.) that you want.

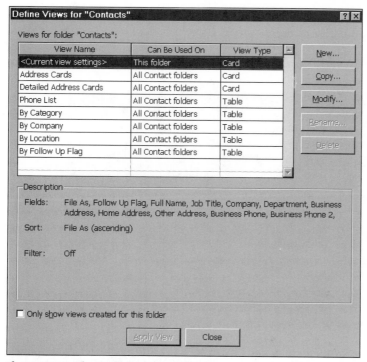

Figure 30-7: The Define Views dialog box.

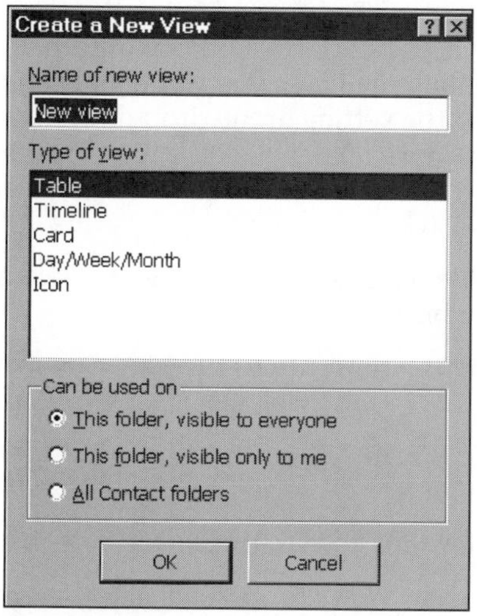

Figure 30-8: The Create a New View dialog box.

4. In the bottom panel, select the scope of the view's usability.

5. Click the OK button.

6. In the View Summary dialog box (see Figure 30-9), click the Fields button.

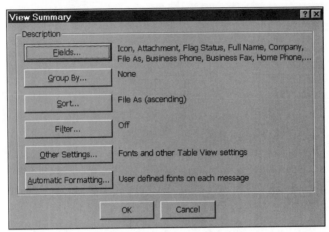

Figure 30-9: The View Summary dialog box.

7. In the Show Fields dialog box (see Figure 30-10), the left-hand panel shows the fields you can add to the view, while the right-hand panel shows the fields currently in the view. To move a field from the available panel to the show panel, select it and click the Add button. To move a field in the show panel back to the available panel, select it and click the Remove button. If the Available Fields listing doesn't contain the fields you want, you can display others to choose from by changing the setting in the drop-down list at the bottom of the dialog box. To create a new field, click the New Field button. The process is identical to the one described in the earlier section on adding a contact, and illustrated in Figure 30-6.

8. To change the order in which the fields are displayed, select a field and click either the Move Up or Move Down button.

9. When you're done, click the OK button to return to the View Summary dialog box.

10. In the View Summary dialog box, click the OK button to return to the Define Views dialog box.

11. In the Define Views dialog box, click the Close button.

12. Select your new view from the Current Views drop-down list.

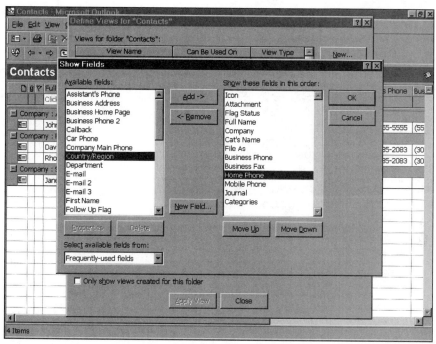

Figure 30-10: The Show Fields dialog box.

Creating Groups

Although there is no Group By Box command for contacts in the address card views, you will find that you can use it in every other view. In fact, the By Category, By Company, By Location, and By Follow-up Flag views are grouped by those parameters (see the preceding section on viewing contact lists). Figure 30-11 shows the By Company view listing with the group box open to illustrate one method of grouping.

In this method of grouping, the Group By Box button on the toolbar is pressed, opening the Group By box above the listings. Field headers are dragged into the Group By box, and the listings automatically group themselves accordingly. Up to four fields can be stacked in this manner, with each group being subordinate to the one before it. The order of the fields, and therefore the stacking of subgroups, can be changed by dragging the field headers into new positions in the Group By box.

The second method of grouping is to right-click on an empty record within the window and select Group By from the pop-up menu. In the Group By dialog box, shown in Figure 30-12, fields are chosen from drop-down lists. Once again, up to four fields can be stacked. When you're finished choosing the fields, click the OK button to implement the grouping.

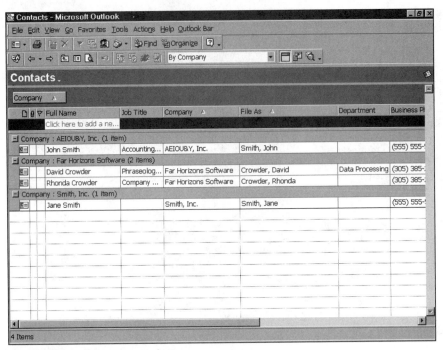

Figure 30-11: The Group By box.

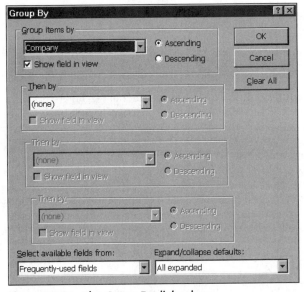

Figure 30-12: The Group By dialog box.

Both techniques are described in full detail in the section on grouping messages in Chapter 29, "Advanced Message Management."

Associating Contacts with Other Outlook Items

It's often useful to know not only who's who, but who's associated with whom or responsible for what. Outlook takes this need into account and provides a simple method for associating contacts with different items in the various folders. You can associate a contact with other contacts, with tasks, with journal entries, etc. To link a contact with an item, follow these steps:

1. Select the contact you want to associate with an item.

2. Select Actions ➪ Link ➪ Items from the menu.

3. In the Link Items to Contact dialog box (see Figure 30-13), select the folder in the top panel that contains the item you want to associate.

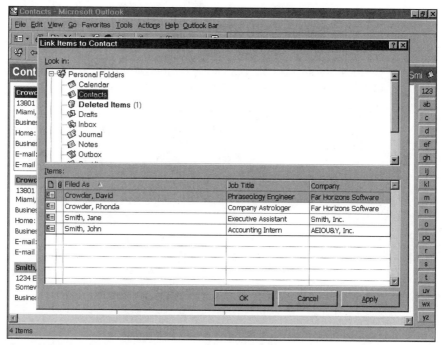

Figure 30-13: The Link Items to Contact dialog box.

4. In the bottom panel, select the item or items you wish to associate with the contact. To select a contiguous range of items, click on the first item in the range, hold down the Shift key, and click on the last item in the range. To select a noncontiguous group of items, hold down the Ctrl key while clicking on each item.

5. Click the OK button.

The associated items will now appear on the Activities tab in the form for the contact.

Summary

In this chapter, you learned how to add contacts to Outlook, what kinds of information a contact listing can contain, and how to edit the contents. You also learned about the different views of contact listings that are available in Outlook, how to group different contacts by various fields, and how to link contacts to other items in Outlook's folders.

✦ Outlook's built-in forms make entering contact data simple.

✦ The All Fields tab allows you to enter data not covered in the General and Details tabs of the contact form.

✦ Contact data can be edited either in the views or via the data entry forms.

✦ Outlook has several built-in views — ways of looking at the contact information — and you can create custom views as well.

✦ Contact listings can be grouped, just as messages can.

✦ Contacts can be associated with other contacts, as well as items, in other Outlook folders.

✦   ✦   ✦

Managing Your Time with Calendar

This chapter covers Outlook's Calendar feature, beginning with the Outlook Today view, which gives you a quick handle on your day by showing you the appointments and tasks you need to deal with and monitoring your current e-mail situation all in one place. You can customize Outlook Today to suit yourself and can make it your default opening screen in Outlook.

You will also learn how you can assign tasks to yourself or to other people (other people can assign you tasks as well), and how Calendar is used to schedule appointments, keep track of events, and invite other people to meetings.

Finally, you will learn how to import scheduling data into Calendar from other scheduling programs and send information from Calendar to other Outlook users and to users of scheduling programs that accept iCalendar format.

The Outlook Today View

Outlook Today is designed to give you a quick handle on what's facing you right now. It lists calendar events for the next several days, shows you your current e-mail message situation, and provides a list of pending tasks (see Figure 31-1). The check boxes next to the tasks are there so you can signify that you've finished them. When you check one, the task is crossed off. You can go to the Calendar, Mail, or Tasks folders by clicking on their names.

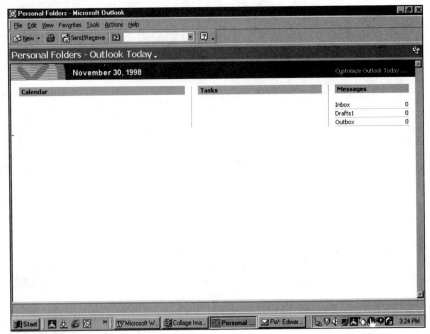

Figure 31-1: The Outlook Today view.

Customizing Outlook Today

Outlook Today's settings aren't graven in stone. You can set it up so that it's the default opening screen in Outlook, add other e-mail folders, change the number of days shown in the calendar, and control how the task list is presented. To customize Outlook Today, follow these steps:

1. In Outlook Today, click the Customize Outlook Today link. This brings up the Outlook Today options page (see Figure 31-2).

2. To make Outlook Today your default start-up screen in Outlook, click the check box labeled When starting, go directly to Outlook today.

3. To add or remove folders from the e-mail message listing, click the Choose Folders button.

4. In the Select Folder dialog box (see Figure 31-3), check a folder to include it in the e-mail messages listing or uncheck it to remove it from the listing. By default, Outlook already has the three most likely candidates included — Drafts, Inbox, and Outbox. Depending on your personal needs, however, you may want to remove one or more of these or even add the Sent Items folder or the Deleted Items folder.

5. If you don't want any folders in your e-mail messages listing, click the Clear All button.

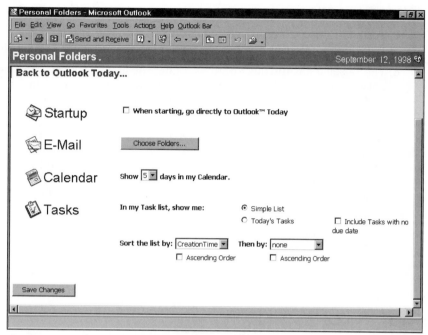

Figure 31-2: The Outlook Today options screen.

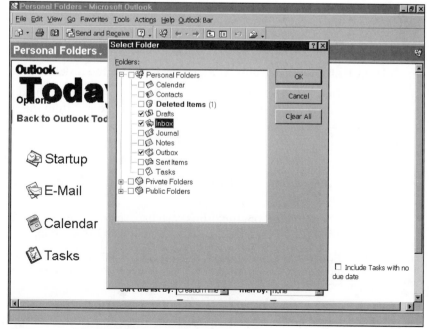

Figure 31-3: The Select Folder dialog box.

6. Click the OK button to finish the task and return to the options page.

7. To set how many days of calendar events are shown, choose a number from 1 to 7 from the list box labeled Show this number of days in my calendar.

8. The Task list has the most options. Under the In my task list, show me category, the default is All tasks. If you want to see only one day's tasks, click the Today's tasks radio button instead. Check the Include tasks with no due date check box if you don't want some of your tasks to slip by unnoticed.

9. Next, you can choose how the Task list is sorted. The default is by Due Date. However, you can also choose to sort by importance, creation time, or start date. You can add a second layer of sorting by specifying another field under Then by. The possible fields are the same for both. The default sort order is descending. If you'd prefer to change this, select the Ascending radio buttons.

10. From the Show Outlook Today in this style listbox, select the layout you want for Outlook Today. A small preview area below the listbox will help you choose.

11. Click the Save Changes button.

Adding and Editing Tasks

You can either assign a task to yourself or send a request to someone else to take on a task (of course, they can send you such a request as well). In theory, the person you send a task request to can refuse it, but in most companies, the chain of command makes this a moot point. To assign a task, follow these steps:

1. While viewing the Tasks folder, click the New Task button (see Figure 31-4).

2. In the task form (see Figure 31-5), type a name for the task under Subject.

3. Select a Due Date and Start Date. This is done by clicking on the downward pointing arrows next to those boxes and selecting dates from the pop-up calendars.

4. Select a Status for the task from the drop-down list. The options are Not Started, In Progress, Completed, Waiting on Someone Else, and Deferred.

5. Select a Priority for the task from the drop-down list. The options are Low, Normal, and High.

6. Select a % Complete from the drop-down list. The options are 0%, 25%, 50%, 75%, and 100%. You can also type any number into the % Complete box.

7. If desired, check the Reminder check box and select a date and time. The date is selected from a pop-up calendar. The time is selected from a list of half-hour increments for the day.

8. If desired, click the Speaker icon next to the time box to select a sound that will be played at the reminder time. This brings up a dialog box in which you can click on a Browse button to select a sound file.

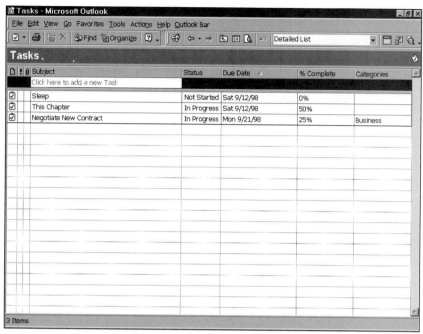

Figure 31-4: The Tasks folder.

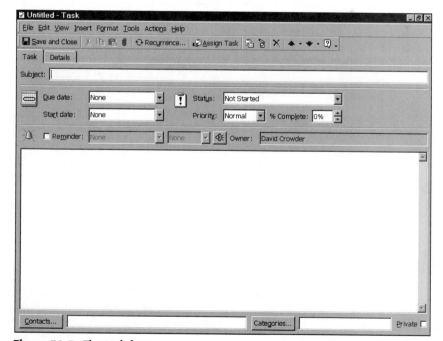

Figure 31-5: The task form.

9. You can use the buttons on the bottom of the task form to associate Contacts or Categories with this task. Note that associating a contact is not the same as assigning a task.

10. Click the Private check box if you don't want other people with access to this folder to be able to view this task.

11. At present, you are the owner of this task. If you want things to remain that way, just click the Save and Close button on the toolbar.

12. If you want to assign the task to someone else, click the Assign Task button on the toolbar. This causes some changes to the task form, as shown in Figure 31-6.

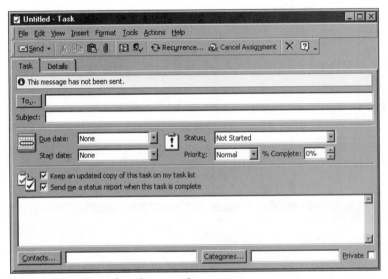

Figure 31-6: The task assignment form.

13. The Assign Task tool has vanished, and the task blank now has a To field just like an e-mail message and, as the notation at the top says, it is currently an unsent e-mail message. Click the To button to select a recipient and then click the Send button.

Note   The Details tab is used for recording such information as the amount of time spent on completing the task, the mileage run up in the process, etc.

Using Calendar

If you've ever said to someone, "Yeah, Tuesday at 4:30 will be fine," only to realize later that you already have something scheduled for that time slot, you're going to love Calendar. Calendar lets you manage your time more efficiently, scheduling appointments and events with ease.

In Outlook parlance, an *appointment* is time blocked off on your calendar for a specific purpose over a limited period of time. A *meeting* is an appointment to which you invite other people. During that time, you normally can't be doing anything else, and your calendar will show that you are busy and unavailable (unless you specify otherwise). An *event,* on the other hand, is something that takes place over a period of at least twenty-four hours, and it doesn't necessarily mean that you're unavailable during it. For example, a three-day-long seminar is an event, but you may have free periods during those days when you would be available for appointments.

Figure 31-7 shows the basic Calendar screen. Although this is a one-day view, you can also select weekly or monthly calendar views. There are actually two categories of the weekly view — you can choose either a five-day week or a seven-day week. The five-day week, of course, is for Monday through Friday, the typical work week. Each of these views is selected by clicking the appropriate button on the toolbar. The two-month calendar view in the upper right-hand side of the screen shows a highlight on the current day for the one-day view, Monday through Friday for the five-day view, and the entire week for a seven-day view. If you choose the monthly view, the entire view pane is taken up by the calendar.

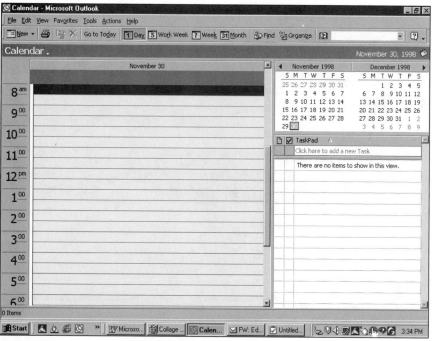

Figure 31-7: The Outlook Calendar.

Tip   You can use the two-month calendar display to move around among the months, scrolling back and forth via the left- and right-pointing arrows. To bring up the appointment listing for a particular date, click on it. To return to the current day, click the Go to Today button on the toolbar.

Creating and Managing Appointments and Events

You can add a new appointment to a particular date and time by double-clicking on the time slot in the appointment book while viewing that day. Alternatively, you can just click the New Appointment button. The only difference between the two approaches is that the first one brings up the appointment form with the correct date and time already inserted. Once you're in the appointment form, follow these steps:

1. Type a subject for the appointment into the first edit box in the Appointment tab (see Figure 31-8).

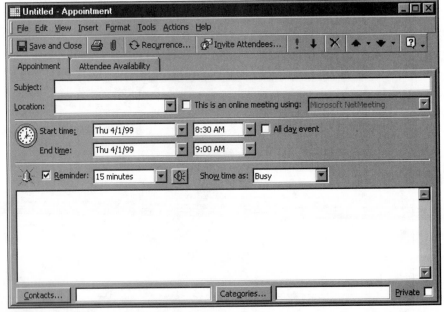

Figure 31-8: The Appointment tab.

2. Enter the location of the meeting in the second edit box.

3. If this is to be an online meeting, click on the check box to the right of the location and select the online program to be used from the drop-down list to the right.

4. If this is an event, check the All Day Event check box.

5. Set the start time and end time for the appointment. If it's an event instead of an appointment, only the starting day and ending day will be available. Otherwise, you need to set both the date and time of the appointment.

6. If you want to be reminded about the appointment ahead of time, make sure the Reminder check box is checked and select an amount of time when you will be reminded. Click the Speaker icon to select a sound file to be played at that time.

7. Under Show Time As, choose Free, Tentative, Busy, or Out of Office.

8. Add any comments in the text area.

9. If desired, specify which contacts are associated with this appointment by clicking the Contacts button at the bottom of the screen and selecting them from your contacts listings.

10. If desired, assign categories to the appointment by clicking the Categories button.

11. If you want the appointment to be private, enable the Private check box.

12. If you are dealing with other people also using Outlook on your network, click the Attendee Availability tab (see Figure 31-9). Otherwise, just click the Save and Close button on the toolbar.

13. Click the Invite Others button to bring up a contacts listing.

14. In the Select Attendees and Resources dialog box (see Figure 31-10), select a contact and click the Required button if their presence is necessary. Click the Optional button if their presence is desired, but not necessary.

15. Under Resources, enter the location and any necessary equipment.

16. Click the OK button to return to the Attendee Availability tab.

17. Click the AutoPick button and select which people you want to automatically schedule for the meeting.

18. Use the << and >> buttons to quickly find the next time slot when all the people are available.

19. Click the Appointment tab.

20. Because others from your contacts listings are being invited, the appointment blank now has a To field with their names filled in. Click the Send button to issue the appointment notification.

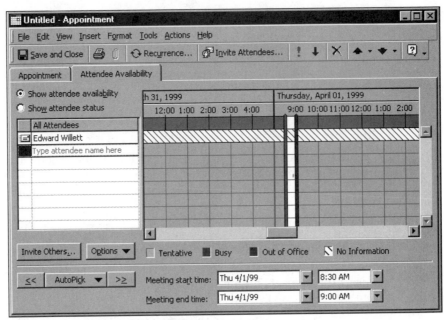

Figure 31-9: The Attendee Availability tab.

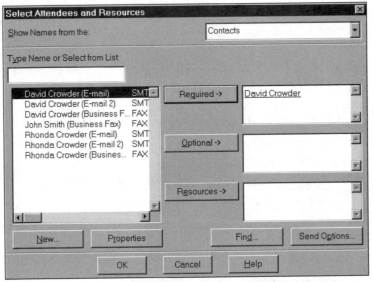

Figure 31-10: The Select Attendees and Resources dialog box.

Importing Appointments and Events

If you have scheduling data such as appointments in another program, Outlook can convert it to its own format. You can import calendar data either in the vCalendar format or from other scheduling programs such as Lotus Organizer or Schedule+. To do so, follow these steps:

1. Select File ➪ Import and Export from the menu.

2. In Import and Export Wizard (see Figure 31-11), select the action you wish to take.

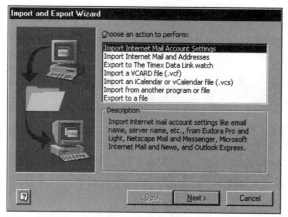

Figure 31-11: Import and Export Wizard.

3. Click the Next button.

4. If you chose to import a vCalendar file, you will be taken to a standard file Open dialog box. Select the desired file and click the Open button.

5. If you chose to import from another program or file, you'll see the Import a File dialog box (see Figure 31-12). Select the file type. Depending upon the options you choose from here on in, some options may vary from the ones illustrated.

6. Click the Next button.

7. Click the Browse button to select the file (see Figure 31-13). You will be taken to a standard file Open dialog box. Select the desired file and click the Open button.

8. Select the duplicate handling option you desire. Your options are to allow duplicate items to overwrite current ones, to allow duplicates to co-exist, or to not import duplicates.

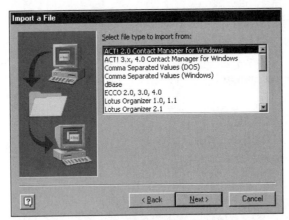

Figure 31-12: The Import a File dialog box.

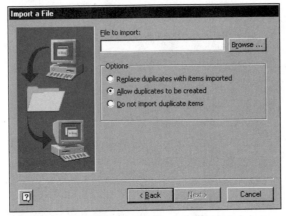

Figure 31-13: Selecting the file to import.

9. Click the Next button.

10. Make sure that Calendar is selected as the destination folder (see Figure 31-14).

11. Click the Next button.

12. The final screen of Import and Export Wizard (see Figure 31-15) shows the file you're importing.

13. Click the Finish button.

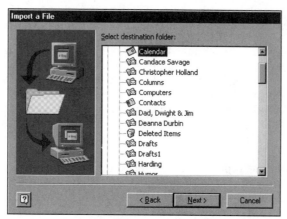

Figure 31-14: Selecting a destination folder.

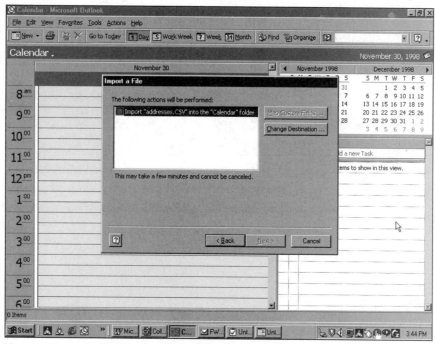

Figure 31-15: The final screen of Import and Export Wizard.

Sending Calendar Information to Other Users

Although other users on your network can view your calendar data (at least the data you haven't marked as private), you may want to send information to others who are not on your network. In that case, you can simply e-mail them the appointment. If they're using Outlook, you can just attach the appointment, but if they're not, you'll need to convert it to vCalendar format. Fortunately, Outlook takes care of that little detail for you, and it's simply a matter of making an alternate menu selection. To send calendar data to others, follow these steps:

1. If you are looking at the appointment listing on the main Calendar screen, click on the appointment you want to send. If you're looking at the appointment form itself, then the appointment is already selected and you don't need to do anything special.

2. Select Actions ➪ Forward (to send to another Outlook user) or Actions ➪ Forward as iCalendar.

3. An e-mail message will be created (see Figure 31-16) with the calendar data included as a file attachment, which shows at the bottom of the message blank. If it's in Outlook format, it'll just list the name of the appointment. If it's in iCalendar format, then the file extension .ics will be appended to the name.

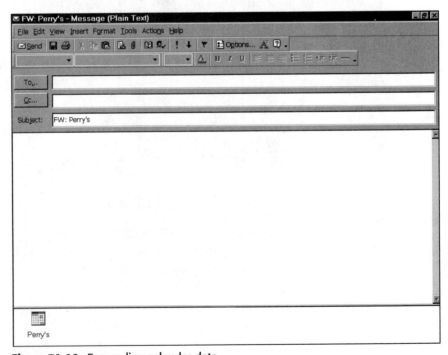

Figure 31-16: Forwarding calendar data.

4. Click the To button to select the recipient(s) from your contacts listings or type in an e-mail address if they're not among your contacts. If desired, do the same with the Cc field.

5. Type a message in the text area.

6. Click the Send button.

Summary

In this chapter, you learned how to use Outlook Today to keep track of your scheduling needs. You also learned how to handle tasks and use Calendar to manage your time.

✦ Outlook Today gives you a quick handle on your day by showing you the appointments and tasks you need to deal with and monitoring your current e-mail situation all in one place.

✦ Outlook Today can be customized in various ways, and can be designated as your default opening screen in Outlook.

✦ Tasks can be set up for yourself or for assignment to other people, and other people can assign you tasks as well.

✦ Calendar can be used to schedule appointments, keep track of events, and invite other people to meetings.

✦ You can import scheduling data into Calendar from other scheduling programs.

✦ You can send information from Calendar to other Outlook users and to users of scheduling programs that accept iCalendar format.

✦　　✦　　✦

Using Journals and Notes

This chapter covers Outlook's Journal and Notes features. The Journal automatically tracks your actions in Microsoft Office, showing them as a timeline that you can set for daily, weekly, or monthly views. You can also add items manually to the Journal timeline, and the journal entries are subject to alteration through direct editing.

Outlook's Notes are the digital equivalent of Post-it pads. Although they're created within Outlook, Notes are separate applications, which can remain open even when Outlook isn't open.

Viewing Your Journal

The Journal keeps track of your actions in Office. By default, it shows a week-long timeline onscreen (see Figure 32-1), although you can change this to a one-day or one-month view. Unlike with Calendar, there is no five-day week option; a week in Journal is seven days.

The different timelines give different levels of detail. The daily listing, for example, shows what hours a particular file was in use, while the monthly listing doesn't even give the file's name unless you specify that it should (see the following section on configuring your Journal).

You can view by type, contact, category, entry list, last seven days, and phone calls. Just select the desired view from the Current View drop-down list. Type is the default view, grouping together all Word documents, Excel worksheets, etc.

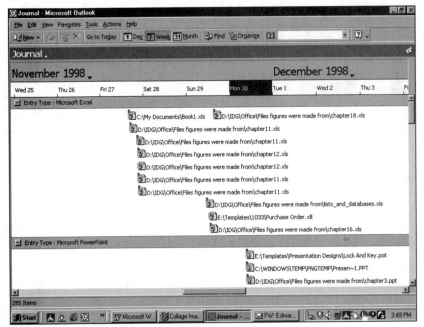

Figure 32-1: The Journal, with items viewed by type.

Configuring Your Journal

In addition to deciding which timeline view you're going to use, you can also set Journal to use specific fonts for different parts of the timeline, to show week numbers (Week 1 ends on the first Saturday of the year), and to specify the size of Item labels and choose whether or not they should be displayed during the month-long timeline view. To set these options, follow these steps:

1. Right-click anywhere in an open space—not on a journal item—and select Other Settings from the pop-up menu. If your screen is filled with journal items, use the scrollbar at the bottom of the screen to get to a view in which you've got some blank space, or switch to another timeline (daily, weekly, or monthly) in which you can find some blank space to right-click in.

2. In the Format Timeline View dialog box (see Figure 32-2), the top panel contains three buttons for font selection. The first one, Upper Scale Font, is for the top line in the Journal. In the daily view, this line shows the day, month, and year; in the weekly and monthly views, it shows the month and year only (if you're showing week numbers, they'll appear in the daily and weekly views). The second font button, Lower Scale Font, is for the second line in the Journal. In the daily view, this line shows the hours of the day; in the weekly and monthly views, it shows the day and date (if you're showing week numbers, they'll appear in the monthly view). The third one, Item Font, is for the group headings and the individual journal items within the groups.

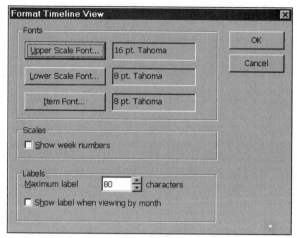

Figure 32-2: The Format Timeline View dialog box.

3. Click any font button to bring up the Font dialog box.

4. In the Font dialog box (see Figure 32-3), select the font face from the list under Font, the style (bold, italic, etc.) from the list under Font style, and the font size from the list under Size.

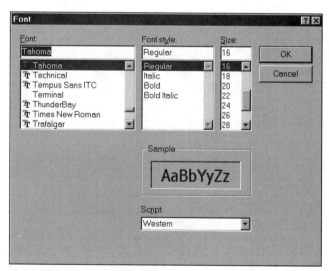

Figure 32-3: The Font dialog box.

5. Click the OK button to return to the Format Timeline View dialog box.

6. If you want to show the number of the week, check the Show Week Numbers check box.

7. The bottom panel is for label-handling options. By default, the maximum length of the label on any item is 80 characters. This number can be set anywhere from 0 to 132 characters. Either type in the desired number or use the arrows to increase or decrease the number.

8. If you want the item labels to be visible in the monthly view, as they are in the daily and weekly views, check the check box labeled "Show label when viewing by month."

9. Click the OK button to save your changes.

You might want to take a look at a couple of other settings also, such as which items are automatically added to your journal, which contacts are tracked, and how to handle a double-click on an item in the timeline. These options are handled via the Journal Options dialog box. To set them, follow these steps:

1. Select Tools ➪ Options from the menu.

2. In the Options dialog box, if it is not already selected, click the Preferences tab.

3. Click the Journal Options button.

4. In the Journal Options dialog box (see Figure 32-4), there are three different sets of check boxes. The one on the top left, labeled "Automatically record these items," shows the Outlook items that are available for automatic journal recording. Select the ones you want recorded.

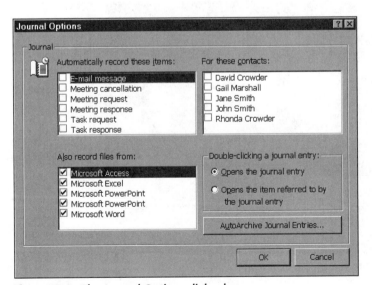

Figure 32-4: The Journal Options dialog box.

5. The check box grouping on the upper right, labeled "For these contacts," lets you choose which contacts the items are recorded for. Check the check box for each contact for whom you want the selected items made into journal entries.

6. The check box group on the lower left shows which other Office programs you want tracked. By default, none are selected. Select anything you want tracked by the journal.

7. By default, double-clicking on a journal entry opens the fully detailed entry dialog box for that item. If you'd rather open the item itself (such as a Word document), select the radio button labeled, "Opens the item referred to by the journal entry."

8. If you want the journal entries to be autoarchived, click the AutoArchive Journal Entries button.

9. Click the OK button to return to the Options dialog box.

10. In the Options dialog box, click the OK button to complete the task.

Adding and Editing Journal Entries

Because not everything is tracked automatically by Journal, you may want to manually add some entries. Or you may want to make changes to the journal entries that already exist.

The easiest way to add a journal entry for an item that is not available for automatic entry is to open the Outlook bar and drag it onto the Journal icon. This brings up a Journal Entry form (see Figure 32-5), in which you can fill out any pertinent data relating to the item.

In this example, we've decided to make a phone call to a contact, so we dragged the contact listing onto the Journal icon in the Outlook bar. The Journal Entry form shows the name of the contact, along with other information such as the date and time. To start tracking the call, click the Start Timer button. When the call is finished, click the Pause Timer button. To finish the Journal entry, click the Save and Close button. If there wasn't already a phone call group in the Journal, it's created now and the journal entry for the phone call is placed in the timeline.

To edit an existing journal entry, right-click on it and select Open Journal Entry from the pop-up menu. This brings up the same Journal Entry form, and you can change any of the data in it, including the time, date, and duration of the item. Clicking the Save and Close button puts the new information into Journal, and the journal entry is moved along the timeline to reflect the new data.

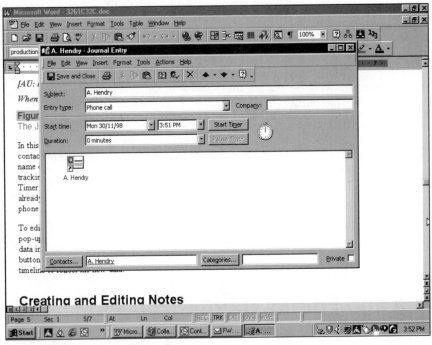

Figure 32-5: The Journal Entry form.

Creating and Editing Notes

Notes in Outlook are just like Post-it pads. They're little bits of digital paper that you scribble hasty notes on and pin up where you can find them later. There are several different ways to create notes. If you're in the Notes folder, just click the New Note button or right-click in an empty space and select New Note from the pop-up menu. Oftentimes, though, you're not there when you want to jot down a note, so it's convenient that Outlook lets you create them from any folder. The function of the New button changes to create a new item for the type of folder currently active. Thus, if you're in the contacts listings, the New button becomes a New Contact button; if you're in the Inbox, it's a New Mail Message button. Regardless of which folder you're viewing, however, you can create any type of new item, including notes, by clicking on the downward pointing arrow to the right of the New button. This brings up a listing of all the new items you can create, and you just click on Note.

Whichever method you use, you'll end up looking at a blank note (see Figure 32-6). All you have to do is start typing. Then, when you're done, you can save the note by either double-clicking on the paper icon in the upper left-hand corner of the note or just clicking anywhere outside the note.

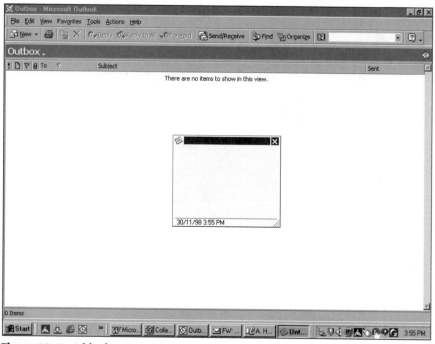

Figure 32-6: A blank note.

To delete a note, select it by clicking on it, and then press the Del key or click the Delete button on the toolbar.

Viewing Notes

Notes show up as icons in the Notes folder in Outlook. The first couple of words in the notes are shown beneath each icon so you can tell which is which. To view a note, open the Notes folder and double-click on the note's icon.

Although notes are created within Outlook, they're actually totally independent windows, and an open note will show up on your task bar along with other open applications. You can even close Outlook and the open note will still remain.

If you want to get to notes that aren't open, though, you'll have to go into Outlook and find them in the Notes folder. Figure 32-7 shows the Notes folder with a few notes in it.

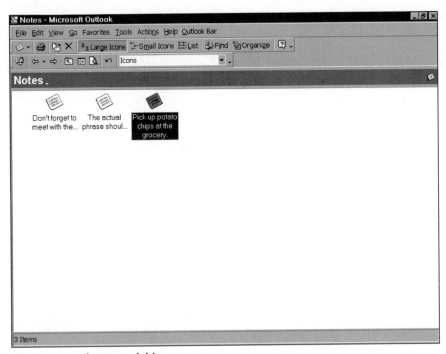

Figure 32-7: The Notes folder.

Configuring Notes

You have very few options for configuring the appearance of your notes. Essentially, you can set the color and size of the sticky pad, and you can also set the font, style, size, and color of the text you type within it. To modify these values, follow these steps:

1. Select Tools ⇨ Options from the menu.

2. In the Options dialog box, if it is not already selected, click the Preferences tab.

3. Click the Note Options button.

4. In the Notes Options dialog box (see Figure 32-8), you can select the note's color and size from the lists. Color options are Blue, Green, Pink, Yellow, or White. Size options are Small, Medium, or Large. The default options are Yellow and Medium.

5. Click the Font button to bring up the Font dialog box.

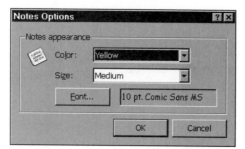

Figure 32-8: The Notes Options dialog box.

6. In the Font dialog box, select the font face from the list under Font, the style (bold, italic, etc.) from the list under Font style, and the font size from the list under Size. You can also choose to have the text be struck out or underlined, and pick a color for the text. Font color options are Black, Maroon, Green, Olive, Navy, Purple, Teal, Gray, Silver, Red, Lime, Yellow, Blue, Fuchsia, Aqua, and White.

7. Click the OK button to return to the Notes Options dialog box.

8. In the Notes Options dialog box, click the OK button to return to the Options dialog box.

9. In the Options dialog box, click the OK button to complete the procedure.

Summary

In this chapter, you learned about Outlook's automatic Journal feature and how to use Notes to remind yourself of information you may need later.

✦ The Journal automatically tracks your actions in Microsoft Office.

✦ The items in Journal are displayed in a timeline, which you can set for daily, weekly, or monthly views.

✦ In addition to the automatic tracking, you can add items manually to the Journal timeline.

✦ The information in Journal can be altered by editing the journal entries.

✦ Outlook's Notes are the equivalent of Post-it pads.

✦ Notes are separate applications that can remain open even when Outlook is shut down.

✦   ✦   ✦

Outlook at Work

This chapter provides you with some real-world examples of Outlook in action. You'll learn how to schedule meetings with other people, track telephone calls with the Journal, create a rule for sorting incoming e-mail messages based on their contents, and use the Outlook contacts listings as a source for a Word mail-merge document.

Scheduling a Meeting with Several Users

Inviting several different contacts to a meeting is similar to making an appointment with a single individual. You just have to include more names in the invitation list to begin with and track more responses as a result. Fortunately, Outlook automates the response tracking process for you. When selecting the invitees, you may wish to view the contacts listings by category, company, or location, rather than all listings alphabetically.

1. Open the Contacts folder.

2. Select those contacts you wish to schedule a meeting with. To select noncontiguous contacts, hold down the Ctrl key while clicking on their listings.

3. Click the New Meeting Request to Contact button on the toolbar.

4. The Meeting form will appear (see Figure 33-1), bearing the following notation at the top: Invitations have not been sent for this meeting. The e-mail addresses of the invitees are filled in under the To field.

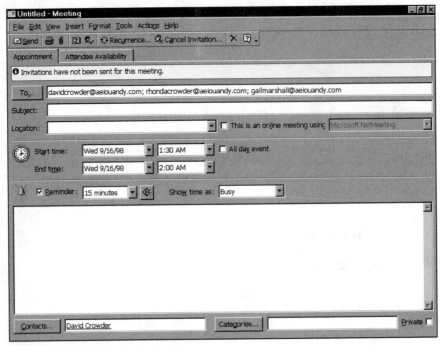

Figure 33-1: Meeting invitation form.

5. Type the topic of the meeting under Subject.

6. Enter the location of the meeting.

7. If the meeting is an online meeting, check the check box next to the Location field.

8. Set the starting and ending times for the meeting.

9. If you want a reminder to sound, set the amount of time before the meeting for it to go off. Click the Speaker icon to select a sound file.

10. Add any comments or instructions in the text area.

11. Click the Send button to send the meeting invitation to all the invitees.

To keep track of who has and hasn't responded to your meeting invitation, switch to the Calendar folder and select Active Appointments from the Current View drop-down list. Double-click on the meeting in the listing to bring up the meeting form, and then click the Attendee Availability tab. Click the Show Attendee Status radio button, and look under the Response field (see Figure 33-2).

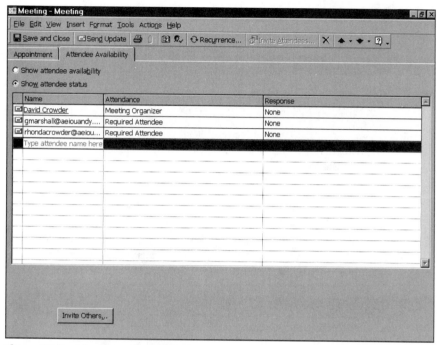

Figure 33-2: Attendee status listing.

Tracking Phone Calls

In the last chapter, you learned one way of getting Outlook's Journal to log a telephone call. Here's another way, one that takes advantage of the autodial feature.

Cross-Reference For more information on an alternative method of logging a telephone call in Outlook's Journal, see Chapter 32, "Using Journals and Notes."

1. Open the Contacts folder.

2. Select the contact you wish to call.

3. Click the AutoDial button on the toolbar.

4. In the New Call dialog box (see Figure 33-3), the selected contact's name and phone number are listed. If the contact has multiple phone numbers, select the one you want to call from the drop-down list under Number.

5. Check the check box labeled "Create new Journal Entry when starting new call."

6. Click the Start Call button. Because you're logging this call in the Journal, a Journal Entry form will come up (see Figure 33-4). The timer is already automatically running, so you don't need to do anything here.

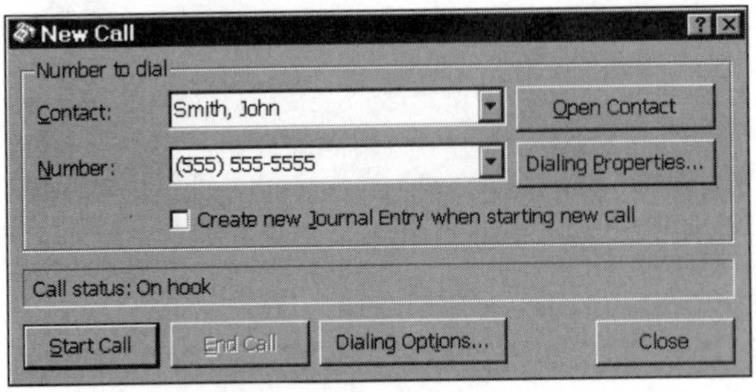

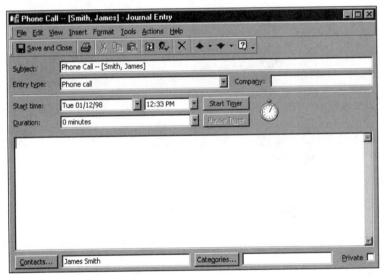

Figure 33-3: The New Call dialog box.

Figure 33-4: The Journal Entry form.

7. In a moment, the Call Status dialog box will appear (see Figure 33-5). Pick up your receiver and click the Talk button.

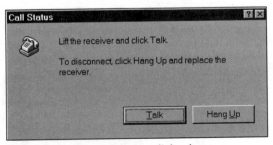

Figure 33-5: The Call Status dialog box.

8. When you're finished with your call, hang up the receiver and click the Hang Up button. This will return you to the Journal Entry form.

9. In the Journal Entry form, enter any notes you wish to make about the call in the text area.

10. Click the Save and Close button on the toolbar. This will complete the journal entry and return you to the New Call dialog box.

11. In the New Call dialog box, click the Close button.

Retrieving and Sorting Messages Automatically

You can use Outlook to totally automate the process of getting and sorting your e-mail messages. First, you need to make sure that automatic e-mail checking is activated. Select Tools ➪ Options from the menu and click on the Internet E-mail tab (see Figure 33-6). The first entry in the bottom panel sets how often to check for incoming e-mail. Make sure the check box is checked and type in how many minutes you want to elapse between checks for messages (the default is ten minutes). Click the OK button to finish the process.

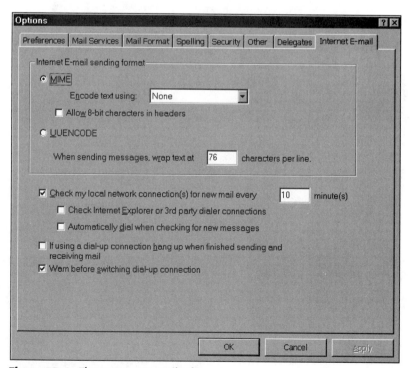

Figure 33-6: The Internet E-mail tab.

Next, you'll need to let Outlook know how you want your messages sorted. For that, you'll need to use Rules Wizard. For this example, we'll sort mail based on its content, looking for all e-mail relating to someone named Callahan at a company called AEIOU&Y, Inc.

 Cross-Reference To find out how you can use Rules Wizard to handle and sort mail from a particular person, see Chapter 29, "Advanced Message Management."

1. While viewing the Inbox folder, click the Rules Wizard button on the Advanced toolbar.

2. In the Rules Wizard dialog box, click the New button.

3. In the top panel, select Move Messages Based on Content (see Figure 33-7).

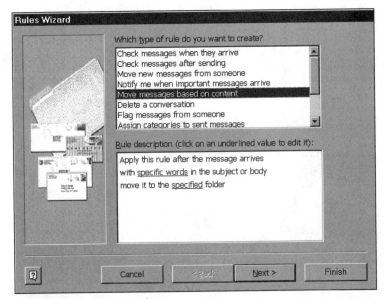

Figure 33-7: Rules Wizard.

4. In the bottom panel click on the underlined phrase "specific words."

5. In the Search Text dialog box (see Figure 33-8), enter a word or phrase you want to sort messages by under Add New.

6. Click the Add button.

7. Repeat Steps 5 and 6 until you have entered all the words or phrases you want to sort by.

8. Click the OK button to return to the Rules Wizard dialog box.

9. Click on the underlined word "specified."

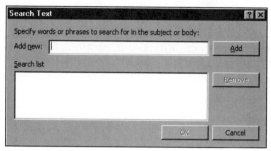

Figure 33-8: The Search Text dialog box.

10. This will bring up a listing of all the currently available folders. Because we want to sort the Callahan messages into their own folder, click the New button to create a special folder for just these messages.

11. In the Create New Folder dialog box (see Figure 33-9), type a name for the new folder.

12. Select the folder you want this one to be contained in. For instance, you may want to put it under Personal Folders.

13. Click the OK button.

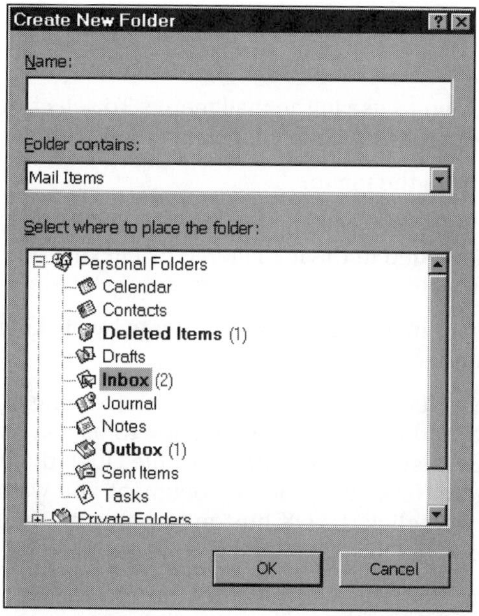

Figure 33-9: The Create New Folder dialog box.

14. You will be asked if you'd like to add a shortcut for the new folder to the Outlook bar. Click the Yes or No button, whichever you prefer. Click the OK button.

15. Unless you want to add further conditions or exceptions to the rule, just click the Finish button at this point. Otherwise, click the Next button and follow the instructions on the next screens to add more conditions or exceptions to the rule.

See Chapter 29, "Advanced Message Management," for full details on all the available screens.

16. If you opted to just use the Finish button after establishing which folder the messages would be sorted to, you'll find that the rule is named "specific words." If you want to change the name to something more recognizable, click the Rename button and enter a new name for the rule, and then click the OK button to return to the Rules Wizard dialog box.

17. Click the OK button to complete the task.

Mail Merging Outlook Contacts with Word

It's only natural that you would, from time to time, want to use your Outlook contacts listings with Word in a mail-merged document. Thanks to the integration of Office applications, you can do so easily. To use your contacts in a Word mail merge, follow these steps:

1. Open the Contacts folder.

2. Select those contacts you wish to use in the mail merge. To select noncontiguous contacts, hold down the Ctrl key while clicking on their listings.

3. Select Tools ➪ Mail Merge from the menu.

4. The Mail Merge Contacts dialog box will appear (see Figure 33-10). Choose which contacts you want included in the mail merge by clicking the appropriate radio button under Contacts.

5. Choose which fields you want included in the mail merge by clicking the appropriate radio button under Fields to merge.

6. Choose whether to create a New document or to use an Existing document by clicking the appropriate radio button. If you decide to use an existing document, you can click Browse to open a standard file Open dialog box from which you can navigate to the mail merge document you want to use. When you find it, select it and click the OK button to return to the Mail Merge Contacts dialog box.

7. To save the contact data for future use or reference, specify a file name where indicated.

8. Click the OK button to proceed.

9. Next, either the existing document will be opened or the new one will be created (see Figure 33-11). Use the Insert Merge Field drop-down list to insert contact fields as desired.

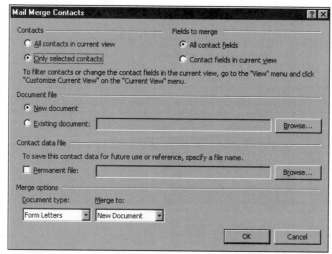

Figure 33-10: The Mail Merge Contacts dialog box.

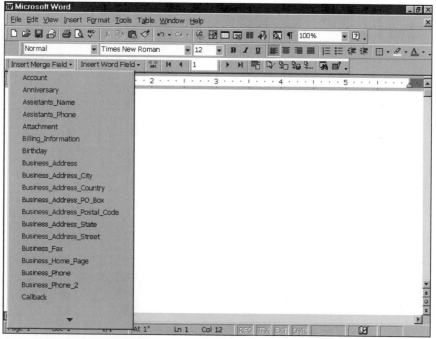

Figure 33-11: The Insert Merge Field drop-down list.

Summary

In this chapter, you learned how to apply Outlook techniques to solving real-world problems. Highlights of the chapter included the following:

✦ You scheduled a meeting with several users.

✦ You learned a new way to track telephone calls with the Journal.

✦ You created a rule for sorting incoming e-mail messages based on their contents.

✦ You used the Outlook contacts listings as a source for a Word mail-merge document.

✦   ✦   ✦

The Outlook Top 10

Here's where you'll discover the answers to ten of the most commonly asked questions concerning Outlook. Contact Microsoft on the World Wide Web at `http://support .microsoft.com` for further research on questions you may have that are beyond the scope of this chapter. Microsoft maintains a comprehensive and evolving set of questions and answers on this site.

How Can I Add a vCalendar E-mail Attachment to My Appointments List?

The vCalendar file attachment is represented as an icon at the bottom of your e-mail message. Double-click on it and it will be opened as an appointment. Click the Save and Close button to add it to your calendar.

If you've gotten the file in some other manner, select File ⇨ Import and Export from the menu. This will open the Import and Export Wizard. Select Import an iCalendar or vCalendar file (*.vcs) and click the Next button. In the file open dialog box that appears next, navigate to the location of the vCalendar file, select it, and click the Open button.

Incidentally, the same procedures apply for adding a vCard file (virtual business card) to your contacts listings, except that you're looking for a vcf file instead of a vcs file.

How Do I Use Stationery in My E-mail Messages?

You can create a new message using HTML and stationery at any time by choosing Actions ⇨ New Mail Message Using ⇨ (stationery name) or More Stationery, even if your default mail

---

In This Chapter

Adding vCalendar e-mail attachments to appointment lists

Using stationery in e-mail messages

Deciphering the gibberish in e-mail messages

Setting contacts listings to show empty fields

Finding all the messages from a single person

Setting recurring appointments

Flagging messages for follow-up action

Setting the Deleted Items folder to empty automatically

Changing the default appearance of sticky notes

Seeing the tasks in listings

format is not HTML. If you want to use Outlook's built-in stationery as your default, you have to have HTML as your default e-mail format. Furthermore, you have to have a default stationery selected, even if you want to choose from the selection of stationery instead of having one default type.

You can set both by selecting Tools ➪ Options from the menu and clicking the Mail Format tab in the Options dialog box. From the drop-down list under Send in This Message Format, select HTML. To set your default stationery, click the Stationery Picker button in the Stationery and Fonts section. In the Stationery Picker, you click on the various listings under Stationery and look at their appearances under Preview. When you find one you like, click the OK button and that one will be set as your default stationery. You will be returned to the Options dialog box, where you'll need to click one more OK button to finish.

From now on, when you start a new e-mail message, the default stationery will be there without any effort on your part. If you want to change it for a message, select Actions ➪ New Mail Message Using ➪ More Stationery from the menu. This will bring up the Select a Stationery dialog box, which is functionally identical to the Stationery Picker.

Why Do My E-mail Messages Contain a Bunch of Gibberish at the End?

If you're using the Rich Text format for your e-mail messages, then anyone who isn't using a compatible e-mail program will find a bunch of binary data under the heading "winmail.dat" at the end of the messages they receive from you. The easiest solution is to stop using Rich Text format for your e-mail. The vast majority of e-mail programs use plain text and, next to that, HTML. Not as many use Rich Text.

To change to another format, select Tools ➪ Options from the menu and click the Mail Format tab in the Options dialog box. From the drop-down list under Send in This Message Format, select either Plain Text or HTML, and then click the OK button.

How Do I Set My Contacts Listings to Show Empty Fields?

If you want your contacts listings to include empty fields in your view, open the Contacts folder, select one of the address cards views in the Current View drop-down list, and select View ➪ Current View ➪ Customize Current View. This will bring up the View Summary dialog box, where you'll need to click the Other Settings button. In the Format Card View dialog box that results, check the Show Empty Fields check box, and then click the OK button. You'll be returned to the View Summary dialog box, where you'll need to click one more OK button.

How Do I Find All the Messages I've Received from a Person?

First, open a message from that person. Then, from the menu, select Actions ➪ Find All ➪ Messages from Sender.

It may be a bit confusing at first, because you'll find yourself looking at the Advanced Find dialog box, which is not filled in with the information you're searching by. But, if you look down, you'll see that there's a listing there of all the messages you've gotten from that person.

How Do I Set an Appointment to Be a Recurring One?

Many appointments occur on a regular basis. You might, for instance, schedule an annual physical, a monthly sales meeting, etc. You can set up an appointment in Outlook so that it shows up on a regular basis.

If you're getting ready to create the appointment, open the Calendar folder and select Actions ➪ New Recurring Appointment from the menu. This brings up the Appointment Recurrence dialog box, in which you can set the appointment to recur on a daily, weekly, monthly, or yearly basis. Once you've chosen that, click the OK button and fill out the appointment form as usual; then click the Save and Close button.

If the appointment is already on your calendar and you want to modify it to be a recurring one, then you need to open the appointment and click the Recurrence button in the toolbar. This will bring up the Appointment Recurrence dialog box, which you use in just the same way as if you were creating a new recurring meeting.

How Do I Flag a Message for Follow-Up Action?

If the message is open, click the Flag for Follow Up button on the toolbar. If it's one of the listings in your Inbox, right-click on it and select Flag for Follow Up from the pop-up menu.

Either approach brings you to the same dialog box, where you can select a variety of flags, including Follow Up, Call, or Review. Use the drop-down calendar under Due By to set a date to be reminded about the flag, and then click the OK button. The message will show a flag in its listing. When opened, it will show a reminder at the top about what action you want to take and by when.

When you've followed-up, you can open the dialog box again and check the Completed check box. After that, the flag in the listings will change color from red to gray to signify that its purpose has been served, and the reminder at the top of the open message will state that you've completed the action.

How Do I Set the Deleted Items Folder to Empty Automatically?

You can set the Deleted Items folder to permanently delete all the items in it whenever you exit Outlook. To do so, you need to select Tools ⇨ Options from the menu and click the Other tab in the Options dialog box. Check the check box labeled "Empty the Deleted Items folder upon exiting," and then click the OK button.

How Do I Change the Default Appearance of Sticky Notes?

If you'd rather not have standard-sized, yellow sticky pads for your Notes in Outlook, select Tools ⇨ Options from the menu and click the Preferences tab in the Options dialog box. Next, click the Note Options button.

In the Notes Options dialog box, you can select a new color (blue, green, pink, yellow, or white) and a new size (small, medium, or large). Click the Font button to bring up a standard font dialog box. Select the font you want, and then click the OK button to return to the Notes Options dialog box. There, click the OK button to return to the Options dialog box, where you'll have to click one more OK button to complete the procedure.

Why Can't I See All the Tasks in My Listings?

Look in the upper right-hand corner of the task listings. If it says Filter Applied, that's the problem. Select Simple List in the Current View drop-down list, right-click in the task window, and select Filter from the pop-up menu (make sure you right-click in a clear area, not on a task, or you won't have the Filter option in your pop-up menu). Click Clear All and click the OK button. You should be able to see all your tasks now.

✦   ✦   ✦

Access

Creating a Database

This chapter covers how to create Access database tables, which are similar in layout to Excel worksheets. Database tables are laid out in rows and columns. The rows contain records, and the columns contain fields. Tables can be created from scratch with the help of the database wizard, or they can be imported from other database programs (you can export to other database formats, also). Access can link to databases created in other database programs as well. Once you have a database either created or linked to, you can change its look, sort and index the data, and print it.

Creating a New Table

When you first start Access, you're offered three choices — create a blank database, use the database wizards, or open an existing database (see Figure 35-1).

Fields and records

The data in Access databases is stored in tables, which look the same as spreadsheets. Like databases in Excel, they consist of columns and rows of information. The columns contain the *fields,* while the rows contain the *records.* Fields are individual bits of data such as last name, model number, serial number, etc. Records are complete collections of fields that, taken together, describe everything you need to know about a particular unit, whether that unit is an automobile, a person, or a company, for example.

Note When you create a database, you're creating one or more tables of information. If a single table will do the job, then you can use either Access or an Excel worksheet to manage the database. Where Access shines is in more complex databases requiring multiple tables. Access is a relational database management system (RDBMS), which is capable of establishing relationships among different tables.

Figure 35-1: The Access opening screen.

Starting with a blank database

If you want to create a database from scratch, go ahead and select the Blank Access database radio button and click the OK button. In the File New Database dialog box, enter a name for the database and click the Create button (Access will supply a name for the database of db1, db2, etc., but it's best to give it a more descriptive name). You'll now find yourself looking at the database window (see Figure 35-2).

Designing the new database

To utilize Design view, click the View button on the toolbar. The table now displays three columns: Field Name, Data Type, and Description (see Figure 35-3). The field name is limited to 64 characters. The data type is the kind of information that will be input into this field. The available options are shown in Table 35-1. The description is superfluous and optional. If a field name is properly chosen, it should need no further description. Good field names are things like "Last Name," "ID Number," "Home Fax," etc.

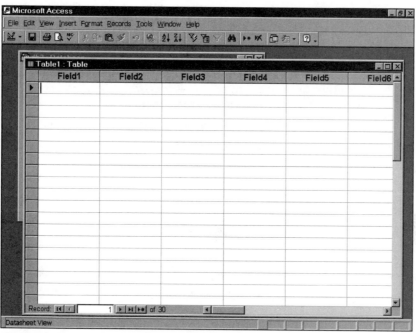

Figure 35-2: The database window and a table.

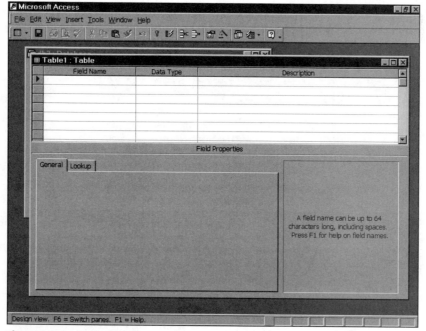

Figure 35-3: Design view.

Table 35-1
Data Types

Data Type	Description
Text	Used to put a maximum 255 characters into a field. "Text" doesn't just mean letters in this case, but can also include numbers.
Memo	Used to put larger text entries into a field, up to 65,536 characters.
Number	Used for numerical fields.
Date/Time	Used for date and time fields. Can run from the year 100 to 9999.
Currency	Used for monetary fields.
AutoNumber	Used to automatically assign a unique serial number to a record.
Yes/No	Used for binary (true/false) fields.
OLE Object	Used to link or embed objects in a field.
Hyperlink	Used to establish the URL to a resource either on the Internet or locally.
Lookup Wizard	Used to create a list of possible options in a field.

When you select a data type, several options appear on the General tab (see Figure 35-4). They vary somewhat depending upon the data type. For instance, the Currency and Number data types ask how many decimal places you want, but the Text data type does not. Also, some data types have options available under Format, while others don't. You have several options for number or date/time formats, but none for text.

Making Formatting Choices

Although you aren't required to make any formatting choices, you might want to consider some of the more important options. Caption, for instance, can help you avoid a common problem with Access databases. Access automatically uses the field name on reports. However, if you put in a caption, that will appear instead of the field name. If you have a very long field name, using a shorter caption can vastly improve the appearance of your database output.

You should also give some thought to which fields have required entry. Not all of them are critical in most databases, but some are. In a mailing list database, for instance, you should certainly require the name, address, and zip code, although a fax number would be optional.

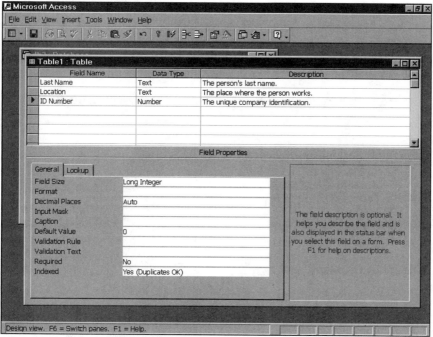

Figure 35-4: The General tab.

Assigning a primary key

You should also assign one field to be the *primary key* used in the database. While not all databases use a primary key, if you're going to create a multiple-table database, you'll have to have one. The primary key is used to tie the different records in the tables together. It should be some absolutely unique item, such as a driver's license number or company ID number. To make a particular field the primary key, click the Primary Key button on the toolbar or right-click on it and select Primary Key from the pop-up menu (see Figure 35-5).

Saving your table

To save your table, click the Save button on the toolbar. You'll then see a dialog box asking for the table name. Either accept the default one or supply your own, and then click the OK button.

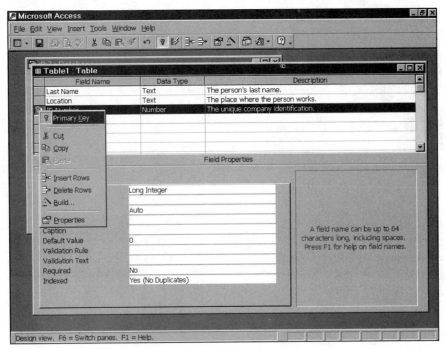

Figure 35-5: Setting the primary key.

Using a Database Wizard

A much easier way to create a database is by using a database wizard.

1. When you first start Access, choose Access database wizards, pages, and projects from the initial dialog box; then click the OK button. This will take you to the New dialog box with the Databases tab selected. If you're already in Access, you can just click the New button, and then click the Databases tab.

2. You can choose from a number of pre-designed databases, such as an inventory control, a ledger, and an expense report (see Figure 35-6). Select the one most like the database you want to create, and then click the OK button.

3. Next, you will find yourself looking at the File New Database dialog box, where you should give your database a name, and then click the Create button.

4. The Database Window will appear and, after a few moments, the database wizard will cover it. The opening screen is just a description of the database you've chosen. Click the Next button to proceed.

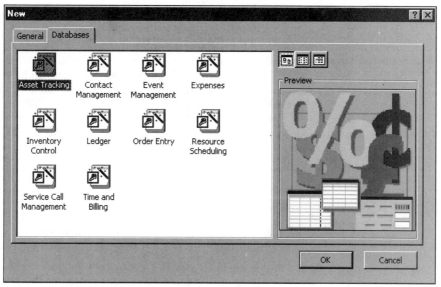

Figure 35-6: The Databases tab.

5. The next screen shows lists of tables and fields. The ones required for each table are already checked, but you can select other optional ones by checking their check boxes. When you're ready to proceed, click the Next button.

6. The next screen asks you what type of screen display you would like. Make your selection, and then click the Next button.

7. The next screen asks you what type of printed output you would like. Make your selection, and then click the Next button.

8. Next, you'll be asked to provide a title for the database. If you'd like to have an image (such as a corporate logo) included on the reports, click the check box that says "Yes, I'd like to include a picture," and then click the Picture button and select the graphics file. Click the Next button to proceed.

9. The final screen has two options on it. The first default option is to start the database as soon as it's created. If you'd rather not do so, uncheck this check box. The other option is to show a help file on database usage. If you're new to databases, check this box.

10. Click the Finish button to complete the task.

Creating a Table by Importing or Linking

In Access, you can use databases that were created outside of Access. The two ways to do this are called *importing* and *linking*. When you import an external database, you're using it as the basis for a new Access database, and the records in it are converted to Access format. When you link to an external database, the original database is used instead of creating a new one in Access. You can make changes in the linked database from within Access without affecting its format. File formats that can be imported or linked in Access include the following:

✦ dBASE databases

✦ HTML tables and lists

✦ Lotus 1-2-3 spreadsheets

✦ Microsoft Excel worksheets

✦ Microsoft Access databases

✦ Microsoft Access projects

✦ Microsoft Exchange

✦ Microsoft FoxPro databases

✦ ODBC databases

✦ Paradox databases

✦ SQL tables

✦ Text files (both CSV and fixed-width)

To import or link to databases, follow these steps:

1. Choose File ➪ Get External Data from the menu.

2. In the submenu, choose either Import or Link Tables.

3. You'll see nearly identical file-choosing dialog boxes in either case. The only difference between them is that the file Open button is labeled Link in one case and Import in the other. Navigate to the folder containing the database you want, and then select it and click the Link or Import button.

4. Different import wizards will be activated depending upon what type of database you are importing. Figure 35-7 shows a screen from the Import Spreadsheet Wizard. The wizards allow you to specify which fields you do and don't want imported, and to change the field name and sometimes the data type. Take whatever actions you desire on each screen, clicking the Next button each time you're ready to move on.

5. When you've reached the last screen of the import wizard, click the Finish button to complete the task. The database will be imported (or linked, depending on which command you chose).

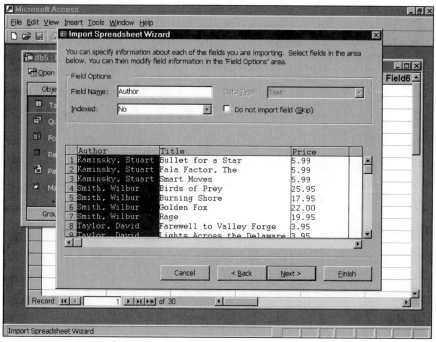

Figure 35-7: The Import Spreadsheet Wizard.

Adding and Editing Data

It's easy to add a new record to a database in Access. The last line in any Access table is always a blank record, waiting to be filled in. You have to be in Datasheet view instead of Design view. If you're not already in it, you get there by clicking the View button. Figure 35-8 shows the datasheet view for the shippers table in the Northwind sample database that comes with Access.

Note that the blank record is marked by an asterisk on the left-hand side, while the currently selected record is indicated by a rightward pointing arrow. The instant you place the cursor in the blank record, the asterisk is replaced by that right arrow. When you begin typing in the blank record, a pencil appears on the left, indicating that you're working on that record, and a new blank record instantly appears beneath the one you're working on. To continue entering data, press your Tab key to move between fields. When you've filled in the final field, the Tab key will take you to the first field in the next blank record.

To edit currently existing data, as opposed to entering new data, place the cursor where you want to make changes and use your normal editing techniques. For example, if you want to insert some text, just start typing. If you want to delete the character before the cursor, press the Backspace key. If you want to totally replace the entire contents of the field, highlight it and then type over it.

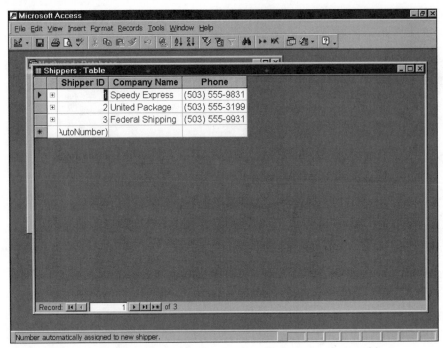

Figure 35-8: You'll always find a blank record at the bottom of any table.

Cross-Reference You can also use data entry forms to add or edit the data in a table. See Chapter 37, "Working with Forms," for more information on this topic.

Changing the Appearance of a Table

The appearance of a table is amenable to all sorts of changes. Just as in Excel, you can vary the row heights and column widths in the grid. You can also alter the appearance of the grid itself, changing line characteristics as well as foreground and background colors. The fonts can be altered to suit yourself. You can move fields around, hide and unhide them, and freeze and unfreeze them. Although these options are all available via the Format menu, it's often easier to perform them with the mouse right in the table.

Setting row heights

To change row heights, place the mouse pointer on the bottom line of any row header. When the pointer changes to a vertical double arrow with a bar across it, hold the mouse button down and move the pointer up to decrease row size; move it down to increase it. When the rows are the desired size, release the mouse button.

Note that you can't resize just one row; every row in Access is the same size. If you want precise control over the exact size, you can choose Format ➪ Row Height from the menu (or right-click on the record selector and select Row Height from the pop-up menu), and then type in the height in the Row Height dialog box. That dialog box also has a check box labeled Standard Height. Selecting this check box will return the row height to the default setting.

Setting column widths

To change column widths, place the mouse pointer on the right border of any column header. When the pointer changes to a horizontal double arrow with a bar across it, hold the mouse button down and move the pointer left to decrease column size; move it right to increase it. When the column is the desired size, release the mouse button. Unlike rows, each column can have a different size. If you want precise control over the exact size, you can choose Format ➪ Column Width from the menu (or right-click on the column header and select Column Width from the pop-up menu), and then type in the height in the Column Width dialog box. That dialog box also has a check box labeled Standard Width. Selecting this check box will return the column width to the default setting. In this case, it's not as useful as with rows, as the width of contents varies greatly across columns. However, there's also a Best Fit button that will analyze the column contents and compute a proper width for it.

Customizing datasheet properties

To change the entire datasheet at once, you can right-click on the title bar and select Datasheet from the pop-up menu (or choose Format ➪ Datasheet from the main menu). This brings up the Datasheet Formatting dialog box, as shown in Figure 35-9. Here's how to use it:

✦ **Cell Effect** has three radio buttons: Flat, Raised, and Sunken. The flat version is the default. This puts the cells of the table on the same level as the gridlines. The raised version means that the cells are raised above the gridlines, making the lines appear to be engraved between the cells. The sunken version does the opposite, making the lines appear to be higher than the cells.

✦ **Gridlines Shown** has two check boxes that let you have the vertical or horizontal gridlines either visible (checked) or invisible (unchecked). These settings affect only the flat cell effect; in either the raised or sunken effects, the gridlines are present regardless of this setting.

✦ **Background Color and Gridline Color** are the drop-down lists. The available colors are Black, Maroon, Green, Olive, Dark Blue, Violet, Teal, Gray, Silver, Red, Bright Green, Yellow, Blue, Fuchsia, Aqua, and White.

✦ **The Sample panel** lets you see the effects of your choices before you commit them to the actual table. Changes in color, gridlines, etc., show up here right away.

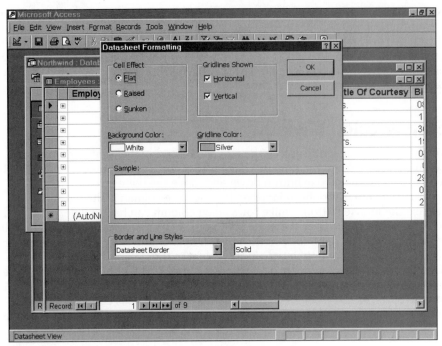

Figure 35-9: The Datasheet Formatting dialog box.

✦ **Border and Line Styles** are two complementary drop-down lists. The one on the left is where you choose which lines you want to affect. The one on the right is where you pick what the line you selected in the drop-down list on the left will look like. The options available for the lines are Transparent Border, Solid, Dashes, Short Dashes, Dots, Sparse Dots, Dash-Dot, Dash-Dot-Dot, and Double Solid.

When you're happy with your design choices, click the OK button to put them onto the table.

Customizing fonts

To change the datasheet's fonts, right-click on the title bar and select Font from the pop-up menu (or choose Format ⇨ Font from the main menu). This brings up the Font dialog box, as shown in Figure 35-10.

This is a standard font options dialog box, except that it has only two Effects options, Underline and Color. Select the font face, the style, and the size. To choose a different color for the fonts, select one from the drop-down list labeled Color. The Sample panel shows the effects of each option. When you've made your selections, click the OK button. The font setting affects the entire table. Although the row height will automatically increase or decrease to accommodate changes in font size, the column width will not.

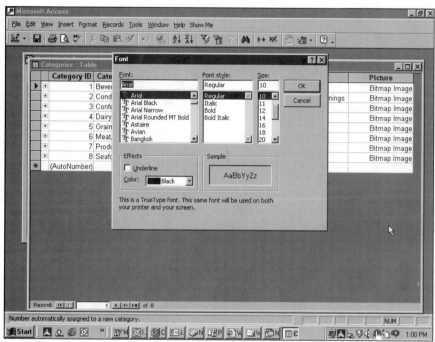

Figure 35-10: The Font dialog box.

Moving fields

You can rearrange the columns in a table by dragging and dropping them. Click on a column header so the entire column is selected. Click on it again, but this time hold the mouse button down. Drag the column to the new position (indicated by a dark vertical bar) and drop it there. If you want to move several adjacent columns at once, click on the first one and, while holding the mouse button down, move it until all the desired columns are selected. Release the mouse button, click again on any of the column headers in the selection, and then drag and drop just the same way you would with a single column.

Hiding and unhiding columns

Sometimes, possibly for display purposes, you may not want some fields to show, but you don't want to delete their data. In that case, you'll find the Hide Columns command pretty handy. To use it, right-click on a column header and select Hide Columns from the pop-up menu. The column will immediately disappear from view. How do you get it back when there's no column to right-click on anymore? Select Format ➪ Unhide Columns from the main menu. This will bring up the Unhide Columns dialog box (see Figure 35-11).

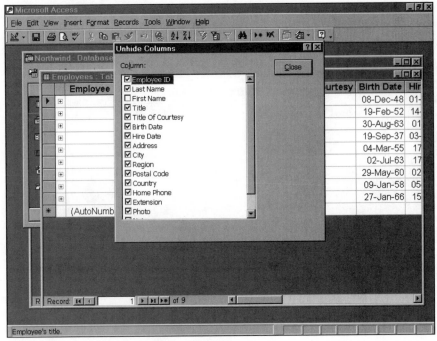

Figure 35-11: The Unhide Columns dialog box.

This dialog box has a listing of all the fields on it. The currently hidden ones show an unchecked check box. Simply check the check box again and click the Close button to make the column visible again.

Note You can also hide columns by selecting Format Í Hide Columns from the main menu. To unhide them, select Format Í Unhide Columns from the main menu. This brings up the Unhide Columns dialog box, and you can uncheck the check boxes of every field you want hidden.

Freezing and unfreezing columns

Freezing columns — making them stay put and still visible when you scroll the table — is a little bit rocky in Access. You can select any column or range of columns to freeze, but you can't unfreeze particular columns; you have to unfreeze all of them. To freeze a column, right-click on a column header and select Freeze Columns from the pop-up menu (or choose Format ➪ Freeze Columns from the main menu). The column will move to the left side of the table. When you scroll the table, that column will remain on the left side, unmoving. To freeze multiple contiguous columns, select them all first, and then freeze them. To freeze multiple noncontiguous columns, select them one at a time and freeze them individually.

When you want to unfreeze them, you'll find that there's no unfreeze command on the right-click pop-up menu, so you need to choose Format ➪ Unfreeze All Columns from the main menu.

Sorting Data

When you want to sort your data in an Access table, click anywhere in the column you want to sort the records by, and then click either the Sort Ascending button or the Sort Descending button. The records will all be sorted on the chosen field.

You can sort by one or more fields at once. Access gives the top priority in a sort operation to the leftmost field. The secondary priority is given to the field that's second from the left, and so on. You can take advantage of this default sort priority by rearranging your fields prior to sorting (see "Moving Fields," in the preceding section for details on how to accomplish this).

Say you want to sort a database by location and then by last name. Move the location field to the leftmost position, and then move the Last Name field to the second position from the left. Select both columns, and then click one of the sort buttons on the toolbar (in this case, let's make it Sort Ascending). The records will be rearranged so that those people who work at the location with the lowest alphabetical rank will be listed first. For example, the staff at the Arizona location would come before the staff at the Washington location. Within each of these locations, the staff's last names would be listed in ascending alphabetical order without regard to the names at the other location.

Adding an Index

Indexing helps Access sort databases faster. You can set up an index on a single field or on multiple fields. Indexing is most useful in fields with several totally different entries, such as a Telephone Number field. In fields that have many duplicates, such as the State field for a mailing list of local customers, indexing will do nothing to speed up sorts.

Using a single field

To create an index on a single field, follow these steps:

1. Make sure the table is in Design view. If you're in Datasheet view, you can change to Design view either by clicking the View button on the toolbar or by right-clicking on the table's title bar and selecting Table Design from the pop-up menu.

2. Click on the field you want to index.

3. In the General tab, look at the Indexed property. If it doesn't say No, then there's already an index on this field. Otherwise, select either the Yes (Duplicates OK)

or Yes (No Duplicates) option. Allowing duplicates is the normal procedure wherever two or more entries in one field could reasonably be expected to have identical values. For instance, you should allow duplicates in a Last Name field or a Zip Code field, as these aren't things that are necessarily unique to only one record. The field for a social security number, on the other hand, should not allow duplicates.

Using multiple fields

To create an index that uses multiple fields, follow these steps:

1. Make sure the table is in Design view. If you're in Datasheet view, you can change to Design view either by clicking the View button on the toolbar or by right-clicking on the table's title bar and selecting Table Design from the pop-up menu.

2. Click the Indexes button on the toolbar.

3. In the Indexes dialog box (see Figure 35-12), you'll find all the currently existing indexes for the table already listed. To add a new one, click in a blank under Index Name and type in the name of your new index.

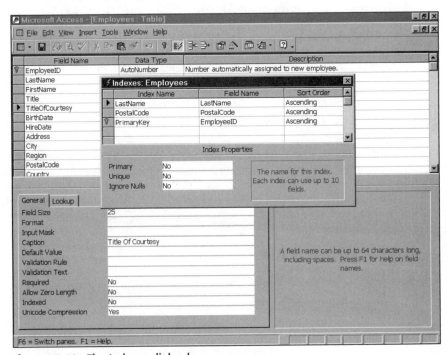

Figure 35-12: The Indexes dialog box.

4. Tab to the adjacent Field Name cell.

5. A downward pointing arrow will appear in that cell. Click on it and you'll be presented with a list of all the fields in the table. Select the one you want to index by.

6. The default sort order is Ascending. If you want to change this, click the Sort Order cell and then click the downward arrow and select Descending from the drop-down list.

7. Tab twice to get to the next blank Field Name cell (do not fill in the Index name cell for this row). Repeat Steps 5 and 6 for as many fields as you want to add to your multiple index.

Printing a Table

You need to be in Datasheet view to print a table. There are two ways to do it: one via the Print button on the toolbar, the other via the menu commands. If you just click the Print button, that's all there is to it, and the entire table will be printed right away. To give yourself more options, try the menu approach:

1. Choose File ➪ Print from the menu or use the Ctrl+P keyboard combination.

2. In the Print dialog box, select the number of copies you want printed.

3. If desired, click the Selected Record(s) radio button to print only the records you've highlighted.

4. Click the Properties button if you want to change properties specific to your printer, including the page orientation.

5. Click the Setup button to change page margins.

6. Click the OK button to print.

The printout on your printer will be the same as the view on your screen, so you might want to take advantage of rearranging fields, hiding columns, etc., before you do your printing.

Exporting Table Data

Just as you can import other database programs' output into Access, you can use Access to save a file in those programs' formats. File formats that can be exported from Access include the following:

✦ dBASE databases

✦ HTML tables and lists

✦ IDC/HTX tables and lists

✦ Lotus 1-2-3 spreadsheets

✦ Microsoft Access databases

✦ Microsoft Access projects

✦ Microsoft Excel worksheets

✦ Microsoft FoxPro databases

✦ ODBC databases

✦ Paradox databases

✦ SQL tables

✦ Text files (both CSV and fixed-width)

To export an Access database, follow these steps:

1. Select the database object you want to export.

2. Select File ⇨ Export from the menu.

3. In the Export To dialog box (see Figure 35-13), select the format you want to save the database in from the drop-down list under Save as Type.

4. Enter a filename for the database.

5. Click the Save or Save All button.

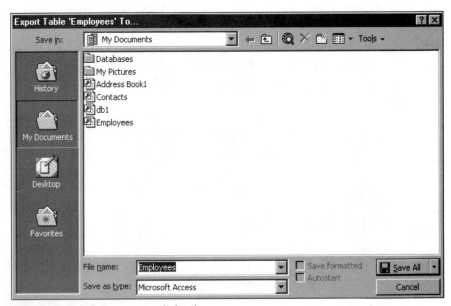

Figure 35-13: The Export To dialog box.

Summary

In this chapter, you learned how to create new database tables from scratch and via the database wizard. You also learned how to import and export different database formats, how to add and edit data, and how to alter the appearance of a table.

✦ Access tables are much like Excel worksheets.

✦ Database tables are laid out in rows and columns. The rows contain records, and the columns contain fields.

✦ The last line in any Access table is always a blank record so you can enter more records easily.

✦ The database wizard can walk you through the process of creating a new database.

✦ Access can import from or link to databases created in other database programs, and can export files in those formats as well.

✦ You can adjust the appearance of Access tables.

✦ Tables can be sorted, indexed, and printed.

✦　　✦　　✦

Charting

This chapter introduces you to Access's chart feature. In Access, charts are used with forms and reports. As with Excel, there are many different types of charts available to you, and Access has a chart wizard that can help you create charts with great ease. Once you've created a chart, you're not stuck with the initial layout or content — everything in a chart is fair game for editing and reformatting.

Types of Charts

There are 20 chart types in Access, nine of which are 3-D variations on other chart types. The following alphabetical list describes each of the standard chart types:

+ **Area charts** show the relative contribution of values over a period of time or other category. The more a value contributes to the overall total, the greater the area taken up by that value. There are also 3-D area charts available.

+ **Bar charts** are perhaps the most familiar chart type. They show values by the length of horizontal bars. There are also 3-D bar charts available.

+ **Bubble charts** compare three sets of values. They are much like XY (scatter) charts, with X and Y coordinates representing two of the values, but the sizes of the bubbles are determined by the third value. There are also 3-D bubble charts available.

+ **Column charts** are a variant of the bar chart type. They show values by the height of vertical bars known as columns (having nothing to do with whether rows or columns from the worksheet grid are used as the source of the data series). Column charts are the default chart type in Access. There are also 3-D column charts available.

+ **Cone charts** are a variant of the bar or column chart type. The only difference is that they use cones instead of bars or columns. There are also 3-D cone charts available.

✦ **Cylinder charts** are a variant of the bar or column chart type. The only difference is that they use cylinders instead of bars or columns. There are also 3-D cylinder charts available.

✦ **Doughnut charts** are pretty much the same thing as pie charts, except that they aren't limited to a single data series. Instead of slices, each different series is represented as a ring of the doughnut.

✦ **Line charts** have one *Y* value for every *X* value, like a mathematical function. A line chart is typically used to show changes over time. The lines make trends among the data much easier to spot at a glance. There are also 3-D line charts available.

✦ **Pie charts** are limited to a single data series (one row or column of data from the worksheet), and cannot display more complex series of data. The value of each element in the data series is assigned a slice of the pie, and all the slices add up to the total of the data series. However, they are visually appealing and simple to understand. There are also 3-D pie charts available.

✦ **Pyramid charts** are a variant of the bar or column chart types. The only difference is that they use pyramids instead of bars or columns. There are also 3-D pyramid charts available.

✦ **XY (Scatter)** charts compare pairs of values, depicting them as sets of X and Y coordinates.

Creating and Editing Charts

Putting the data in Access tables into chart format makes it easier to comprehend patterns and relationships than when they are viewed simply as a collection of numbers. Access provides Chart Wizard to make chart creation from raw data an easy task.

Using Chart Wizard

To use Chart Wizard, follow these steps:

1. In the Database Window under Objects, select Forms (see Figure 36-1).

2. Click the New button.

3. In the New Form dialog box (see Figure 36-2), select Chart Wizard.

4. From the drop-down list, choose which table you want to use as your data source.

5. Click the OK button.

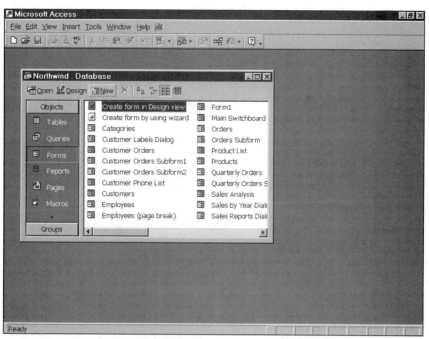

Figure 36-1: The Database Window.

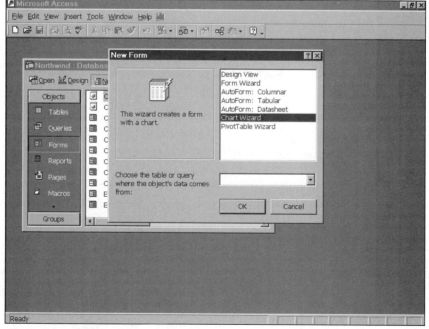

Figure 36-2: The New Form dialog box.

6. In Chart Wizard's initial screen (see Figure 36-3), choose which of the available fields you want to use for your chart. To use all the available fields, click the > button. To add an individual field to the chart, select the field, and then click the > button. Once you've added at least one field, the << and < buttons become active. They do the same thing, but in reverse, removing either all fields or individually selected fields from the chart listing and putting them back into the available fields listing.

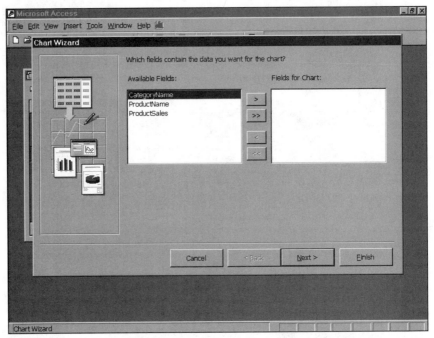

Figure 36-3: Choosing fields for the chart.

7. When you're satisfied with the field choices, click the Next button.

8. The next screen in Chart Wizard is where you choose the chart type (see Figure 36-4). There is an array of 20 chart types. You can click on each one to view the description on the right-hand side of the dialog box.

9. When you've made your selection for chart type, click the Next button to proceed.

10. The next screen of Chart Wizard (see Figure 36-5) shows you the layout that the wizard plans for your data. If you don't like the layout, drag the field buttons to new positions.

11. While in this screen, you can also double-click on any numerical field to select a new way to summarize the data. By default, this method is to use sum, but you can also choose from none, average, min, max, or count.

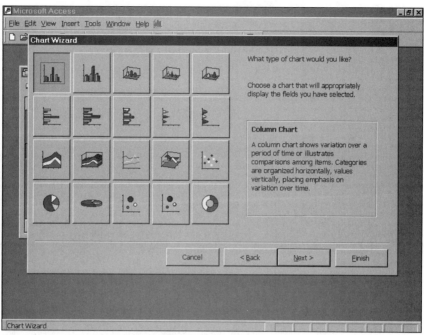

Figure 36-4: Choosing a chart type.

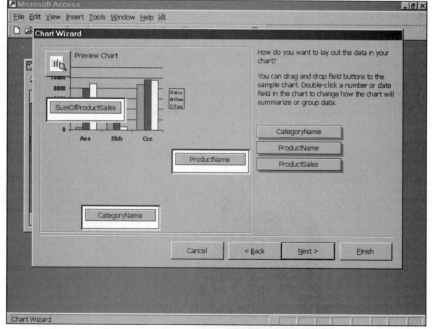

Figure 36-5: The data layout screen.

12. One other feature of this screen is the Preview Chart button. The sample shown on the screen is not based on the actual data you're using, but is just a dummy to show approximately what the chart will look like. To see the actual view of the real data, click the Preview Chart button.

13. When you're satisfied with the layout, click the Next button.

14. The final screen of Chart Wizard (see Figure 36-6) suggests a title for the chart. Type a new one over it if you want to.

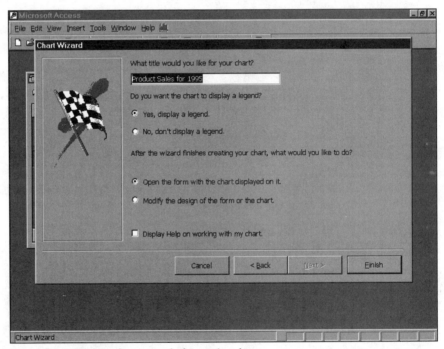

Figure 36-6: The final screen of Chart Wizard.

15. Next, you need to choose whether or not to have a legend on your chart. Click the appropriate radio button.

16. The bottom set of radio buttons allows you to choose which format your chart opens in. By default, it simply opens on a form in Form view, but you can select the radio button labeled "Modify the design of the form or the chart" to have it open in Form Design view instead.

17. Click the Finish button to complete the task.

18. Click the Save button on the toolbar to save your chart.

Note   You can use reports as well as forms to create charts.

Making your chart more readable

Although Chart Wizard is a great way to put together a basic chart in a hurry, once you've created a chart, you'll probably find that you need to make a few changes to it to get it just the way you want it.

The chart shown in Figure 36-7, for instance, is supposed to show the cost of shipping per country. However, the chart is so small that it's essentially useless; the legend is about as large as the chart itself, and the category axis fails to show all the countries involved.

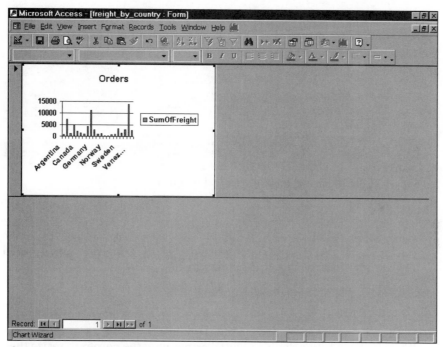

Figure 36-7: The initial chart.

To change it so that it's more useful, follow these steps:

1. Click the View button to switch to Design View.

2. Double-click on the chart to launch Microsoft Graph.

3. After a few moments, the datasheet upon which the chart is based will appear. At this point, right-click on the category axis in the chart and select Format Axis from the pop-up menu.

4. In the Format Axis dialog box, click the Scale tab (see Figure 36-8).

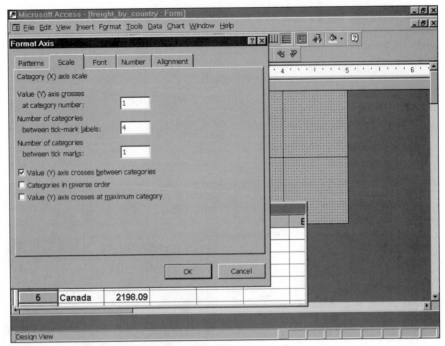

Figure 36-8: The Scale tab of the Format Axis dialog box.

5. The edit box labeled "Number of categories between tick-mark labels" is currently set at 4 in this example (this will vary from chart to chart, depending on the data used). To change the chart so that all the countries are displayed on the category axis, change this number to 1.

6. Click the Font tab and change the size to 8.

7. Click the OK button.

8. Click on the chart and place the mouse pointer over the lower right corner. When it changes to a double pointed arrow, drag the corner to resize the chart until you reach a point where the categories are readable.

9. Right-click on the legend and select Format Legend from the pop-up menu.

10. In the Format Legend dialog box, click the Font tab and change the size to 8.

11. Click the OK button.

12. Right-click on the value axis and select Format Axis from the pop-up menu.

13. In the Format Axis dialog box, click the Number tab and set the category to Currency.

14. Click the OK button.

15. Click on the chart title. You can then highlight the title text and type over it. Put in a more meaningful title like Freight by Country.

The chart, as a result of some simple editing, is now much more useful. It's readable, the dollar amounts are shown as such, the title is pertinent, and the legend no longer dominates the chart.

Formatting Charts

In addition to simple alterations of basic properties like fonts and number formats, you can do many things to totally change the look of your charts.

Choosing a new chart type

Regardless of what chart type you selected during the Chart Wizard process, you can alter it after the fact. For instance, you may want to view the Freight by Country data as a pie chart instead of as a column chart. To change the type, click the Chart Type button on the toolbar and select a new type by clicking on one of the icons in the drop-down list (see Figure 36-9).

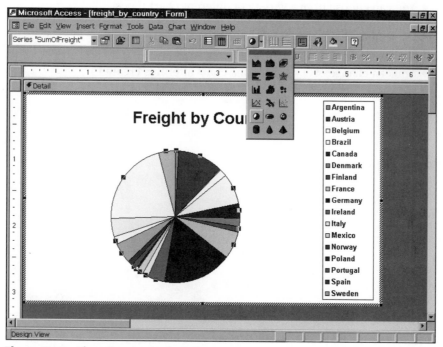

Figure 36-9: Choosing a new chart type.

Tip

You can get access to even more chart types by selecting Chart ➪ Chart Type from the menu.

Changing chart options

When you select Chart ➪ Chart Options from the menu, you get a dialog box that has different tabs for Titles, Axes, Gridlines, Legend, Data Labels, and Data Table. These options are absolutely identical with the ones used for Excel charts.

You can change any element of the chart by right-clicking on it and selecting Format from the pop-up menu, or you can select the element and then click the Format button on the toolbar. Like the chart options, these dialog boxes and processes are the same as with Excel.

Cross-Reference   For more information on chart options, the formatting dialog boxes, and processes, see Chapter 12, "Charts."

Summary

In this chapter, you learned how to create, use, and modify charts in Access.

✦ You can choose from a variety of different chart types.

✦ You create charts using Chart Wizard.

✦ Charts are used with Access forms and reports.

✦ You can change every aspect of a chart after it is created.

✦   ✦   ✦

Working with Forms

This chapter deals with Access forms. Access has a few different ways of assisting you in your form design. The simplest, AutoForm, lets you pick from three different layouts. Form Wizard gives you greater control (allowing you to use multiple tables in a single form, for one thing), but requires more effort and input on your part. The third way is via a collection of different wizards called control wizards, which provide a great deal of assistance when adding new controls to a form.

As with charts, you have full freedom to alter the content and look of a form after you create it.

Using AutoForm

AutoForm is a special tool that takes all the drudgery out of creating forms. Just tell it what table you want to use and it does the rest of the work for you.

The basic method

The basic AutoForm feature creates a simple left-aligned, one-column form. To utilize it, follow these steps:

1. In the Database Window, click either the Tables or Queries button.

2. Select a table or query you want to base a form on.

3. Click the New Object: AutoForm button on the toolbar. Alternatively, you can achieve the same effect by choosing Insert ➪ AutoForm from the menu.

The advanced method

A more sophisticated approach to AutoForm offers much better options and is almost as easy:

1. In the Database Window, click the Forms button.

2. In the Database Window, click the New button.

3. In the New Form dialog box (see Figure 37-1), select one of the AutoForm options.

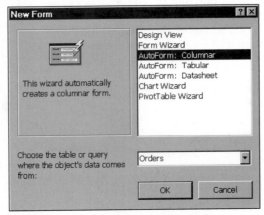

Figure 37-1: The New Form dialog box.

4. Select a table or query from the drop-down list.

5. Click the OK button to complete the task.

Choosing a layout

Three different types of layouts are available to you in the forms AutoForm can create — columnar, tabular, and datasheet. Figures 37-2 and 37-3 illustrate the differences among these three approaches.

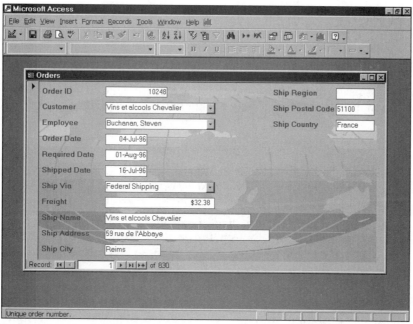

Figure 37-2: A columnar form.

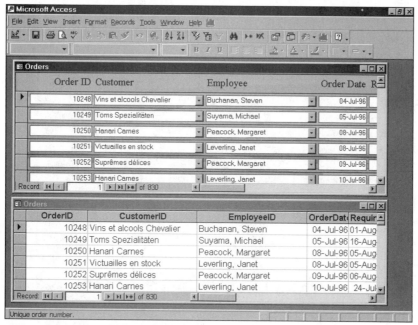

Figure 37-3: Tabular and datasheet forms.

Using Form Wizard

If you're willing to trade the ease of using AutoForm in order to get more control over the outcome of your form's design, but don't want to work up a form from scratch, then Form Wizard is just the ticket. In just a few more steps than with AutoForm, you can create a form that contains only those fields you specify, in the layout you want, with the background of your choice. To use Form Wizard, follow these steps:

1. In the Database Window, click the Forms button.

2. Double-click Create Form By Using Wizard. Alternatively, click the New button in the Database Window and, in the New Form dialog box (see Figure 37-1), select Form Wizard.

3. If you opted for the New Form dialog box approach, you can select the table you want to base the form on from the drop-down list in the New Form dialog box (although you don't have to at this stage), and then click the OK button.

4. The first screen of Form Wizard (see Figure 37-4) is where you choose which fields from which tables are included in your form. If you came to this screen via the New From dialog box and already selected a table in it, then that table will already be showing as the selected one here. Otherwise, the first table alphabetically will be the one that's showing. Either way, you can choose any table or query by selecting it from the drop-down list. When it's selected, its fields will appear under the Available Fields listing on the bottom left-hand side.

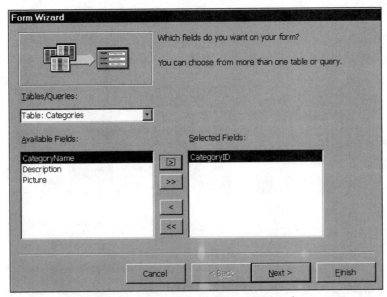

Figure 37-4: Choosing tables and fields in Form Wizard.

5. Next, you need to tell Form Wizard which fields to put on the form from those that are available. To move every field from the Available Fields listing to the Selected Fields listing, click the > button. To move one particular field, select it and click the > button.

6. Once at least one field is in the Selected Fields listing, the < and << buttons become active. They work just like the > and > buttons, but in reverse, moving fields out of the Selected Fields listing back into the Available Fields listing.

7. If you want multiple tables to appear on your form, you have to select them one at a time, as the act of selecting a table replaces any fields in the Available Fields listing with the fields from the selected table. Fields already added to the Selected Fields listing are unaffected by selecting a new table.

8. If you change your mind and don't want a particular table to be included on the form, that's no problem. Although there is no button specifically designed to remove a table from the form once it's been chosen, all you have to do to accomplish this is to move any field from that table out of the Selected Fields area. If you're not completely certain which fields belong to which tables, just clear them all out with the << button and start from scratch.

9. When you're satisfied with your field selections, click the Next button.

10. If you're using a single table on your form, jump to Step 13. If you've chosen more than one table, then you'll have to make a couple of selections (see Figure 37-5). The first selection is which table will be the main one. Select the main table from the listing on the upper left-hand side. The display area on the right side will show the basic structure of the form.

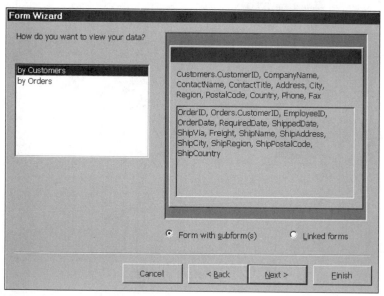

Figure 37-5: Form Wizard's multiple table options.

11. Generally speaking, you have two options about the way the tables are put together — a form with subform(s) or linked forms. However, if you've selected two tables and the one you chose for the main table on the form includes all the fields found in the other table (for instance, if you chose Orders and Customers, all the customer data is also a part of the orders table), then your only option is Single form. If you find yourself in this situation, try reversing which one is the main table. In this example, if you make Customers the main table, then Orders is a proper subtable for it.

12. When you're satisfied with the form structure, click the Next button to proceed. If you chose Linked forms, jump to Step 15.

13. The next screen (see Figure 37-6) is where you choose the layout for your form. Depending on whether you're using multiple tables or not, your layout options will be different. A single table has layout options of Columnar, Tabular, Datasheet, or Justified. A multiple-table form has layout options of only Tabular or Datasheet. Click the radio button for the one you want to use. The display area on the left side of the dialog box shows how each will look.

14. When you have selected the layout you want, click the Next button.

15. The next screen (see Figure 37-7) is where you choose the style of the form. Click on the various style names and observe the display area on the left-hand side of the dialog box to see what they look like.

16. When you have selected the style you want, click the Next button.

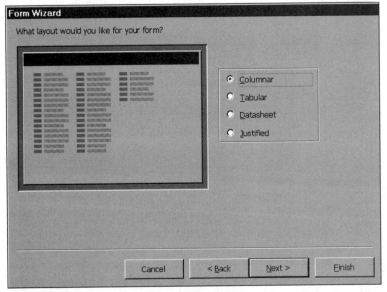

Figure 37-6: Form Wizard's form layout options.

17. The final screen of Form Wizard (see Figure 37-8) lets you assign a title to the form (or you can just accept the wizard's suggested title) and choose whether to open the form for data entry or in Design view.

18. When you're ready to complete your form, click the Finish button.

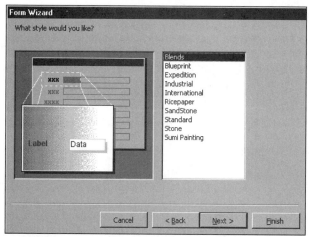

Figure 37-7: Form Wizard's form style options.

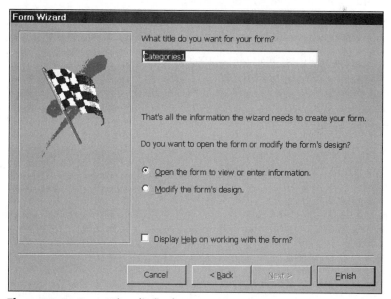

Figure 37-8: Form Wizard's final screen.

Designing a Form

If you want to take a total hands-on approach, you can skip all the assistance that Access has to offer and just create forms yourself on a blank canvas.

The easy way

The easiest way to get to the blank canvas stage is to use the following steps:

1. In the Database Window, click the Forms button.

2. In the Database Window, click the New button and, in the New Form dialog box, select Design view.

3. Select the table you want to base the form on from the drop-down list and click the OK button.

The hard way

There is another approach, which is more difficult, that we mention only for the sake of completeness:

1. In the Database Window, click the Forms button.

2. Double-click on Create Form in Design View.

3. In the blank form (see Figure 37-9), right-click on the black square in the upper left-hand corner and select Properties from the pop-up menu.

4. In the Form properties dialog box, click the Data tab (see Figure 37-10) and select the table you want to base the form on from the drop-down list next to Record Source.

5. Close the properties dialog box by clicking on the X in the upper right-hand corner of it.

Note   Whichever method you use to get to the blank canvas stage, you now need to add controls to the blank form. This process is covered in "Adding Controls to a Form," later in this chapter.

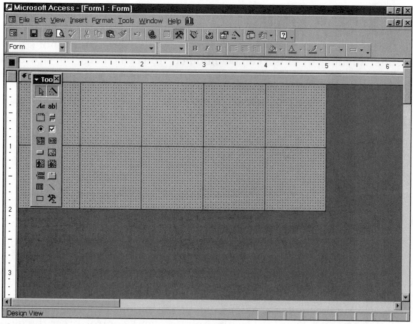

Figure 37-9: A blank form in Design view.

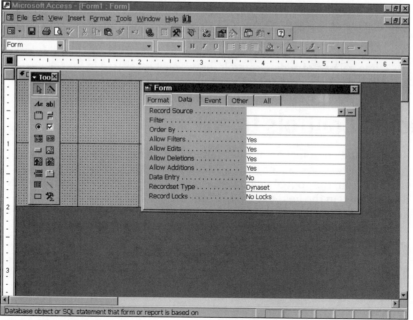

Figure 37-10: The Data tab.

Modifying a Form

Regardless of which technique you use to create a form, you're not stuck with the results. Anything in a form can be modified. You can change the size and placement of form elements (even the size of the form itself), and you can add and delete elements as well. To change anything in a form (see the following list), the form has to first be in Design view. To get there if you are in Form view, click the View button on the toolbar or choose View ➪ Design View from the menu.

+ **Increasing and decreasing height.** Once in Design view, you can place the pointer over the bottom of the form, where it will turn into a vertical arrow split by a bar. If you hold down the mouse button and move the mouse down, you will increase the height of the form. Holding down the mouse button and moving the mouse up will decrease the height of the form.

+ **Shrinking and expanding horizontally.** If you place the pointer over the right side of the form, it will turn into a horizontal arrow split by a bar. Holding down the mouse button at this point allows you to shrink the form horizontally by moving the mouse to the left, or expand the form horizontally by moving the mouse to the right.

+ **Moving the controls.** You can move the various elements (controls) on the form as well. Simply place the pointer over a control, press the mouse button down and, while holding it, move the control to the desired location (the pointer will change to a hand while you do this).

+ **Deleting controls.** To delete a control, click on it once and then press the Del key.

Note   Controls can be sized as well, just like the form itself. Because this technique is an integral part of adding controls, however, it is covered in the following section.

Adding Controls to a Form

The elements that make up a form are called *controls*. The most common control in a form is the text box, which, when linked to a data source in a table or query, displays the data from the source field on the form. Changes made in the text box on the form are reflected in the field data in the table. The form shown in Figure 37-11 is largely composed of text boxes and their associated labels.

Discovering the Toolbox

The Toolbox (see Figure 37-12) is the primary way in which you add controls to a form. Table 37-1 shows the Toolbox buttons and how they're used.

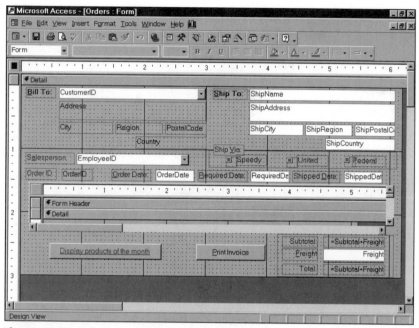

Figure 37-11: A form composed mostly of text boxes.

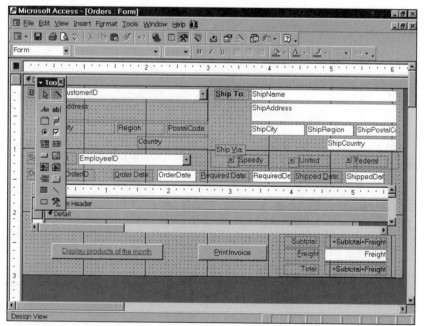

Figure 37-12: The Toolbox.

Table 37-1
Toolbox Buttons

Button	Purpose
Select Objects	Switches back to the normal mouse pointer.
Control Wizards	Some controls (such as the list box) have wizards that can help you make selections regarding their properties. This toggle switch, when depressed, causes those wizards to be activated when the control is dropped onto the form.
Label	Adds a label to a form. These labels are unbound controls, not associated with any data.
Text Box	Adds an unbound text box and its associated label to a form.
Option Group	Groups together radio buttons, check boxes, etc.
Toggle Button	Adds a toggle button to a form. Toggle buttons indicate yes/no options.
Option Button	Adds an option button (which everyone but Microsoft calls radio buttons) to the form. Option buttons are used to indicate mutually exclusive options.
Check Box	Adds a check box to a form. Check boxes are used to indicate options that are not mutually exclusive.
Combo Box	Adds a combo box to a form. Combo boxes are a combination of text boxes and drop-down list boxes.
List Box	Adds a list box to a form. List boxes present a list of predetermined options.
Command Button	Adds a command button to the form. Command buttons are used to initiate actions like printing records and opening other forms.
Image	Adds an image (gif, jpg, pcd, etc.) to the form.
Unbound Object Frame	Frame used for objects not stored in tables.
Bound Object Frame	Frame used for objects stored in tables.
Page Break	Creates a page break for multipage forms.
Tab Control	Creates multiple pages in a form, which are accessible via tabs.
Subform/Subreport	Adds subforms to a form; or subreports to a report.
Line	Adds an unbound line to the form for design purposes.
Rectangle	Adds an unbound rectangle to the form for design purposes.
More Controls	Allows access to more controls, such as ActiveX objects.

Working with text boxes

Text boxes created with Form Wizard or AutoForm are invariably *bound* to data in the associated table or query. Text boxes can also be *unbound*—that is, not linked to data—and they can contain formulas much like a worksheet cell in Excel, in which case they are said to be *calculated* controls.

Using the Field List

There are two ways to place text boxes onto a form. The first, which creates bound controls, is via the Field List. To add a text box that is bound to a field in the list, select the field and then drag it onto the form. You can add several fields at a time. To add a contiguous range of fields, select the first one. Then, while holding down the Shift key, select the last one. All the fields in between the two will be selected. Next, click within the selection and drag it onto the form. To add a noncontiguous range of fields, select the first one. Then, while holding down the Ctrl key, select the next one. Continue in this manner until you have selected all the fields you want to add. Next, click on any selected field and drag it onto the form; all the others will come along.

Using the Toolbox

The second way to add text boxes to a form is to use the Toolbox. This method adds unbound text boxes. Click the Text Box button in the Toolbox, and then click on the form at the point where you want to place the text box. The text box and a label will be created at that point.

Note

The other controls are added in the same way as unbound text boxes. Just click the button in the Toolbox, move the pointer to where you want to drop the control, and click on the form at that point.

Changing and Deleting Text Box Labels

Access always hangs a label on a text box and, in our opinion, it's always too far away from it. It's also always on the left, while you may want it above the text box. In fact, you may not want a label at all. Fortunately, you don't have to accept the default placement.

✦ If you don't want the label, just select it and press the Del key; the text box will remain. (If you select and delete the text box, though, the label will be deleted along with it.)

✦ If you want to move the label in relation to the text box, select the text box and move the pointer to the upper left corner of either the text box or its label. When the pointer changes to a pointing finger, press the mouse button and move the text box or the label until they're just where you want them.

✦ You also don't have to accept the label text that Access provides. To change it, select the label, and then click within it and you're in normal editing mode for the label text.

Using control wizards

The option group, combo box, list box, and subform/subreport controls all give you assistance in the form of control wizards that walk you through each step of getting the control up and running. The option group control wizard is typical of the kind of process you'll be using with control wizards:

1. Make sure the Control Wizards button in the Toolbox is depressed.

2. Click the Option Group button in the Toolbox.

3. Click on the form where you want the option group to be placed.

4. After a few moments, the Option Group wizard will appear (see Figure 37-13). Type the label for the first option. As you type, a pencil will appear to the left of the line you're typing on and another line will open up underneath, ready for the next label.

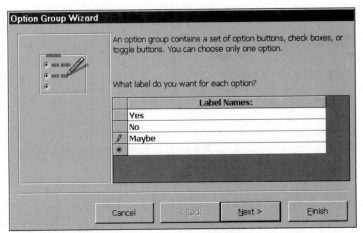

Figure 37-13: The Option Group wizard's opening screen.

5. Press the Tab key to get to the next line. Continue to type labels on each succeeding line until you have entered all the options you desire.

6. When you have entered all the labels, click the Next button.

7. The next screen (see Figure 37-14) asks you to decide if there will be a default choice and, if so, which one it will be. If you decide to have a default choice, select it from the drop-down list.

8. Click the Next button.

9. The next screen (see Figure 37-15) lets you set values for each option. If you just want to accept the default values, click the Next button.

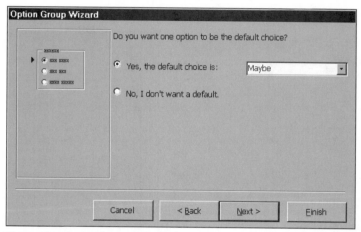

Figure 37-14: Setting a default choice.

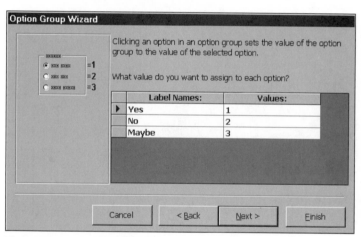

Figure 37-15: Setting the values.

10. The next screen (see Figure 37-16) lets you decide where you want the values stored. The default option is to save the values for later use. Optionally, you can decide to store the value in a particular field in the table. If this is your choice, select the field from the drop-down list.

11. Click the Next button.

12. Next, you get to choose what kind of display the option group will show: Option buttons (radio buttons), Check boxes, or Toggle buttons (see Figure 37-17). You also need to decide what kind of style (etched, flat, raised, etc.) the option group will show. The display area on the left-hand side of the dialog box will show the effect of each option.

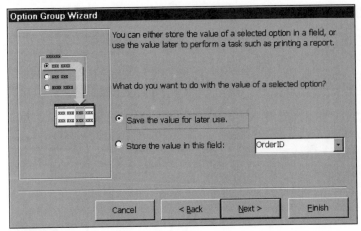

Figure 37-16: Storing the values.

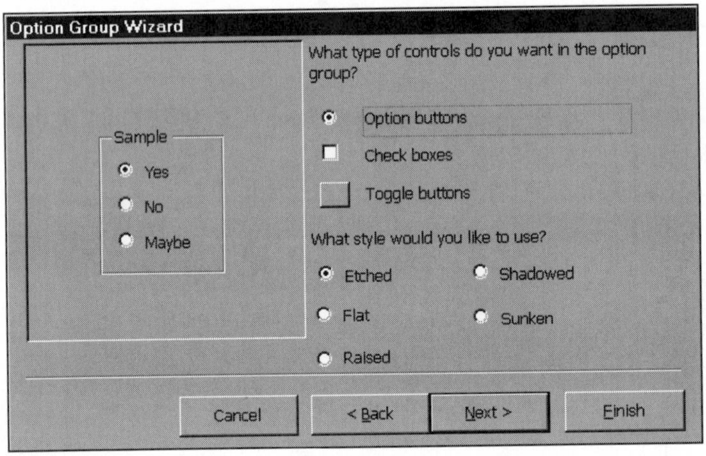

Figure 37-17: Choosing display options.

13. When you're happy with your group display options, click the Next button.

14. The final screen of the Option Group wizard (see Figure 37-18) lets you pick a caption for the option group. Type it into the edit box or accept the one that the wizard suggests.

15. When you're done with the caption, click the Finish button to complete the procedure.

Figure 37-18: The final screen.

Summary

In this chapter, you learned how to create forms with AutoForm, Form Wizard, and from scratch. You also learned how to modify forms and how to add controls.

✦ AutoForm lets you pick from three different layouts.

✦ Form Wizard gives you greater control, but requires more effort and input on your part.

✦ You can use multiple tables with Form Wizard.

✦ You can create a blank form, which you need to populate manually.

✦ No matter what technique you use, any part of a form can be modified after the fact in Design view.

✦ The Toolbox provides a great variety of controls that can be added to forms.

✦ Most forms are comprised of text boxes and their associated labels.

✦ The control wizards provide a great deal of assistance when adding new controls to a form.

✦   ✦   ✦

Using Queries

I t's Access's ability to get valuable and meaningful information from the data that makes it truly valuable. You ask Access questions about your data by using queries — a set of parameters that you create and apply to the data. Querying a database is similar to using filtering on a spreadsheet, but much more powerful.

Learning How Queries Work

There are three basic query types:

- ✦ **Select.** The most commonly used type of query is the select query, which selects and displays records based on criteria you create.

- ✦ **Action.** The next most common is the action query, which is used to simultaneously alter several records in one operation. The action can take four forms: delete, append, update, and make-table. A delete action deletes several records at once, append is used to add many records from one database to another one, update is used to simultaneously change the value of a group of records, and make-table creates a new table based on the criteria specified.

- ✦ **Crosstab.** The crosstab query is used to compare summarized values by two factors (for instance, sums of sales by salesperson for each product).

The data returned from a query is shown in a *dynaset,* which is short for a dynamic set of records. Dynasets, although they look like normal table datasheets, are impermanent — they do not create a new table. Figure 38-1 shows the dynaset resulting from a query.

Creating and Editing Queries

Although the Query wizards are very easy to use and will suffice for most of your querying needs, bear in mind that they cover only a handful of possible queries. If you want to use the full power of database queries, you'll have to design your own.

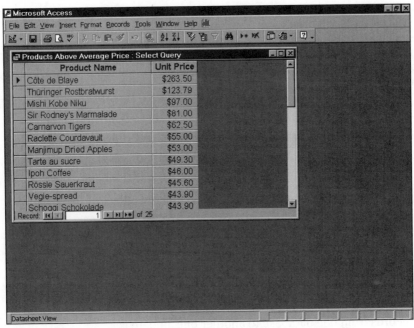

Figure 38-1: A dynaset.

Designing your own query

Fortunately, designing your own queries is a very easy process:

1. In the Database Window under Objects, click Queries.

2. Double-click Create Query in Design View.

3. The Show Table dialog box will overlay the Design view at first (see Figure 38-2). Click on the tables or queries you want to add to your query blank, and then click the Add button (you can also just double-click on the table or query to add it).

4. When you're done, click the Close button. If you want to bring back the Show Table dialog box later, you can click the Show Table button on the toolbar or select View ➪ Show Table from the menu.

5. The table is added to the query window (see Figure 38-3). By default, it's a select query. If you want one of the other types instead, click the Query Type button on the toolbar and select the desired one from the drop-down list.

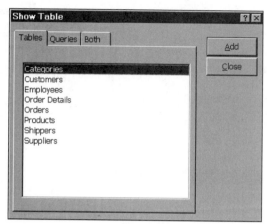

Figure 38-2: The Show Table dialog box.

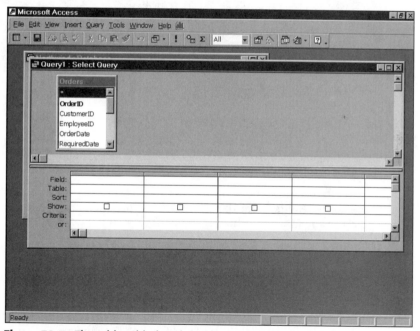

Figure 38-3: The table added to the query window.

6. To put a field from the table into the query, either select it from the table listing and drag it into the Field box or just double-click on it to add it to the next available Field box. Alternatively, you can click in the Field box and a drop-down list of all the available fields will become available (see Figure 38-4). The asterisk represents all the fields combined. Adding it is the same as adding all fields.

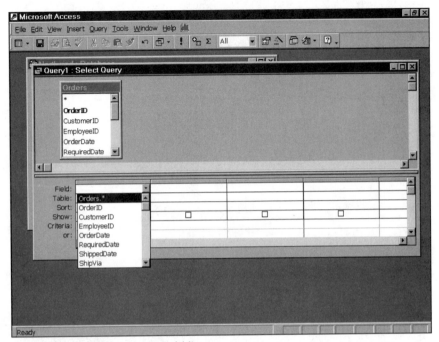

Figure 38-4: The drop-down field list.

7. Once you've entered a field in the Field box, the Table box is automatically filled in for you. If desired, you can choose a sort order — ascending, descending, or not sorted (the default) — by clicking in the Sort box and selecting one from the drop-down list.

8. By default, the Show check box is checked. If you don't want this field to show in the query results, clear the check box. In this manner, you can apply criteria to a field without having to display it in the query results.

9. Enter any criteria you want to filter the records by in the Criteria box. In the example shown in Figure 38-5, we're limiting the records to those that have "Sweden" in the ShipCountry field.

10. Add more criteria in the Or box. You can have a total of nine criteria per field.

11. Make sure to include all other fields that you want to appear in the query results. Any fields not listed in a Field box will not appear.

12. Click the Run button on the toolbar to implement the query. Figure 38-6 shows the dynaset with the query results.

Note

The dynaset, even though it's a temporary construct, has all the properties of a normal datasheet. You can resize the rows and columns, move columns, enter and edit data, sort by fields, etc., just as though it were a normal datasheet.

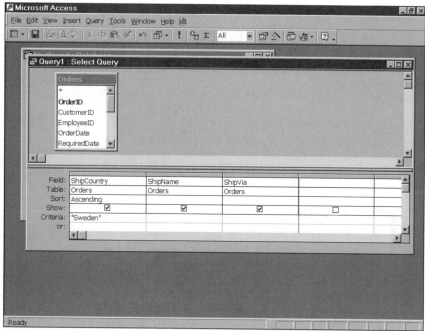

Figure 38-5: Entering criteria.

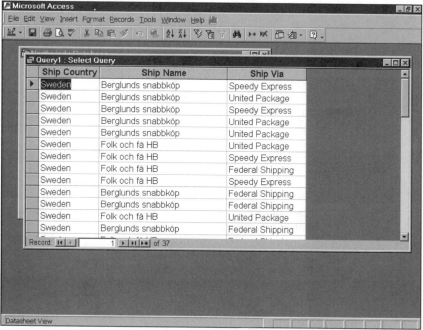

Figure 38-6: The query results.

Editing a query

To edit the query itself, click the View button on the toolbar or select View ➪ Design View from the menu to return to the Design view. Once there, you have the same capabilities you had when originally designing it. You can add more tables, add to or change the criteria used in the query, or remove fields and tables from it (if you want to add a new table, don't forget to click the Show Table button on the toolbar).

To remove a field from the Field box, simply highlight it and delete it, by pressing either the Del key or the Backspace key. Once you click anywhere else in the query window, that field will be totally removed from the query. To remove a table, click on the table and press the Del key.

Using criteria

The most important aspect of designing a query is the use of criteria. If you simply specify a particular possible value as the criteria, then — as in the use of "Sweden" in the preceding example — you'll get all the records that have that particular value. However, the possibilities inherent in the criteria values are much greater than such a simple match. For starters, you can use the Like keyword and the wildcard character (*) in your criteria. Here's how it works:

✦ The following, if entered in the criteria for ShipCountry, would return any country that started with "sw," such as Sweden or Switzerland.

   Like "Sw*"

✦ You can also specify that a term should end with a particular set of characters:

   Like "*land"

✦ Or you can combine the two approaches and look for those terms that both begin and end with particular characters. The following example will return both Spain and Sweden:

   Like "S*n"

✦ You can even specify countries that contain certain letters:

   Like "*tze*"

✦ And if that's not enough, you can specify that you want a range of letters by using brackets and the wildcard. The following example will return every country that starts with s, t, or u:

   Like "[S-U]*"

✦ In addition to the wildcard, you can also use the placeholder character (?) in your criteria. For example, you could use the following to get both England and Ireland:

   Like "???land"

✦ You can also use Boolean operators in your criteria. For instance, you could specify that you don't want any orders shipped to Sweden, and you'd get back every order that was shipped anywhere else:

Not "Sweden"

✦ You can use the And and Or operators as well:

"Sweden" And "England"

"Sweden" Or "England"

✦ When it comes to dates, you need to use hash marks (#) instead of quotation marks to set them off. Thus, you'd look for January 1, 2007, as follows:

#1/1/07#

✦ You use the Boolean operators just the same way as you would with a text field, but there's a special operator called Between And that you'll want to use to specify a range of dates:

Between #1/1/07# And #2/1/07#

✦ In addition to these approaches, you can use plain old numerical symbols as well. For instance, if you wanted to find all orders whose shipping charges were less than $100.00, you could put the following in as the criterion for the Freight field:

<100

The numerical operators you can use are shown in Table 38-1:

Table 38-1
Numerical Operators

Operator	Function
=	Equal to. Limits the return to those records equaling this value.
>	Greater than. Limits the return to those records exceeding this value.
>=	Greater than or equal to. Limits the return to those records equaling or exceeding this value.
<	Less than. Limits the return to those records below this value.
<=	Less than or equal to. Limits the return to those records equal to or below this value.
<>	Not equal to. Limits the return to those records that are not equal to this value.

You can also use the Between And operator to specify a range of numerical values, just as you can with dates.

Using Or with multiple fields

Another way to use the Boolean operators, of course, is when you specify multiple criteria in the Or boxes in the query blank, as you did in the previous step-by-step explanation. The interesting thing about this approach is that there's a hidden And operator involved in the query grid. Any time you specify criteria for two fields, you're saying "This criterion And that criterion." As long as the criteria are on the same line, you're Anding them. There's one more quirk you can use, too. You already know that you can use the Or boxes to set up several possibilities, but you can use the Or boxes across more than one field as well. If you establish a criterion for one field and want to Or it with a criterion in another field, all you have to do is to put the criterion you want to Or it with in the Or box of the second field. The query in Figure 38-7 shows this in action.

The criterion in the first column would normally limit the output of the query to those records that have a ShipCountry beginning with "s" and ending with "n." The addition of the criterion in the second column, however, because it's in the Or box, changes the situation totally. If it were in the Criteria box — on the same line as the first criterion — it would be an And situation. Therefore, the response would be limited to records that have "s*n" countries *and* also have shipping costs less than $100.00. Because it's in the Or box, though, everything's different. Now, the response is limited to records that have *either* "s*n" countries *or* shipping costs less than $100.00 *or* both.

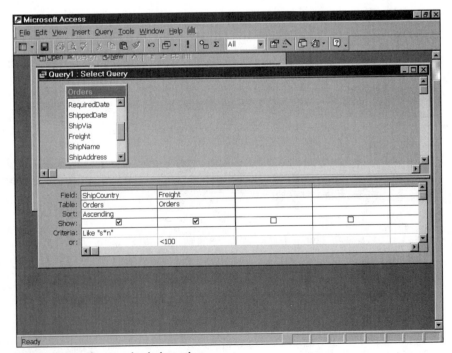

Figure 38-7: The Or criteria in action.

Using Queries to Modify Records

Once you have a dynaset, you automatically have the ability to change the records in the source table. Even though the dynaset is impermanent, each entry in it is linked to an entry in the table, and changes you make to data in the dynaset are made in the source table as well.

Changing original table values

In Figure 38-8, we've created a query that shows only the shipping carrier and the Order ID. It's limited by criteria that restricts the dynaset to showing only those orders that were shipped via Speedy Express. When you click on an entry in the Ship Via field, a drop-down list showing all the possible values of the field appears. Even though this dynaset doesn't reflect all the fields, they're still all listed for your choosing. Clicking on any of the options in the drop-down list changes the value in the original table instantly.

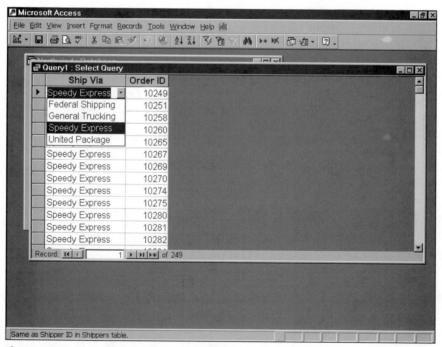

Figure 38-8: Changing a value in a dynaset.

Note   You can't change all fields. The Order ID values, for example, are generated by Access via AutoNumber and you won't be able to alter them.

Deleting groups of records

But what if you have lots of records you want to change? Suppose you're hiking all the prices of your products by 10% or you need to delete all the products under a certain price? It's possible to do this by hand, of course, but it's a tedious process fraught with opportunities for error. With action queries, it's a lot simpler. Action queries, you may recall, are the approach used to delete and update records en masse. All you have to do is specify the criteria and let Access do the work for you.

To delete a group of records, follow these steps:

1. In the Database Window under Objects, click Queries.

2. Double-click Create Query in Design View.

3. Click on the tables or queries you want to add to your query blank in the Show Table dialog box, and then click the Add button (you can also just double-click on the table or query to add it).

4. When you're done, click the Close button.

5. The table is added to the query window. By default, it's a select query. Click the Query Type button on the toolbar and select Delete Query from the drop-down list.

6. Put the asterisk field into the first Field box. To put it into the query, either select it from the table listing and drag it into the Field box or just double-click on it. Alternatively, you can click in the first Field box and select the asterisk from the drop-down list (if you're using multiple tables in your query, you'll find multiple asterisks in the drop-down list, each in the form of "tablename.*"). The asterisk represents all the fields combined. Adding it is the same as adding all fields. It's necessary to put it in because a Delete Query deletes entire records and it needs to reference all the fields in the record.

7. Put the field you want to use for the deletion criteria into the next Field box.

8. Enter the criteria by which you are judging into the Criteria box. Figure 38-9 shows how the query looks at this stage. In this example, we're deleting all records in the Products table that have a price under $10.00, so we've entered the criterion "<10" under the UnitPrice field.

9. Repeat Steps 7 and 8 for any other fields you need.

10. Click the Run button on the toolbar to delete the records that fit the criteria.

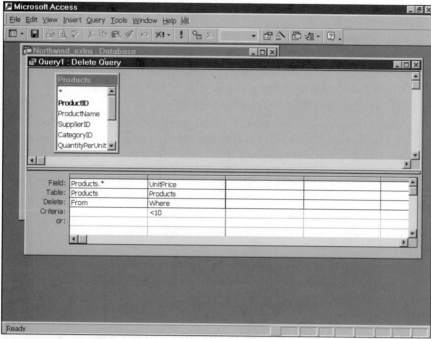

Figure 38-9: A delete query.

Changing groups of records by updating

To simultaneously change the value of a group of records with update, follow these steps:

1. In the Database Window under Objects, click Queries.

2. Double-click Create Query in Design View.

3. Click on the tables or queries you want to add to your query blank in the Show Table dialog box, and then click the Add button (you can also just double-click on the table or query to add it).

4. When you're done, click the Close button.

5. The table is added to the query window. By default, it's a select query. Click the Query Type button on the toolbar and select Update Query from the drop-down list.

6. Put the field you want to update into the query. To put a field into the query, either select it from the table listing and drag it into the Field box or just double-click on it. Alternatively, you can click in the first Field box and select it from the drop-down list.

7. Enter the criteria, if any, into the Criteria box. It is not necessary to use criteria in an Update Query if you're going to be updating all the records; only if you intend to update some and not others.

8. Enter the expression or value to which you want to change the field in the Update To box. Figure 38-10 shows how the query looks at this stage. In this example, we're updating all records in the Products table that have a price under $10.00, so we've entered the criterion "<10" under the UnitPrice field. We're doubling the price of all those items, so we've entered the expression "[UnitPrice]*2." You don't have to use an expression. We could just as easily have set a specific value instead.

9. Repeat Steps 6 through 8 for any other fields you need.

10. Click the Run button on the toolbar to update the records that fit the criteria.

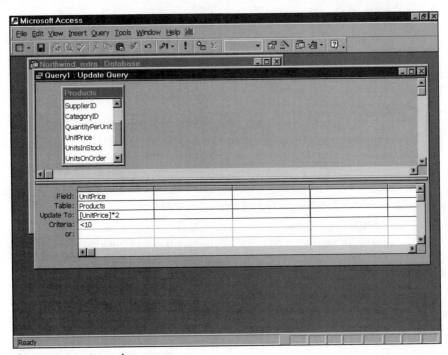

Figure 38-10: An update query.

Using the Query Wizards

The Query wizards can simplify your life by taking the drudgery out of creating queries. Four built-in queries are available via this route: simple, crosstab, find duplicates, and find unmatched. The Simple Query wizard is for a plain vanilla select query with no criteria (you can add criteria later). The Crosstab Query wizard is used to compare summarized values by two factors. The Find Duplicates Query wizard searches a table for fields that have the same value. The Find Unmatched Query wizard compares the same field in two different tables to see if there are no matching records in the two.

The Simple Query wizard

To use the Simple Query wizard, follow these steps:

1. In the Database Window under Objects, click Queries.

2. Double-click Create Query By Using Wizard to go directly to the first screen of the Simple Query wizard (see Figure 38-11).

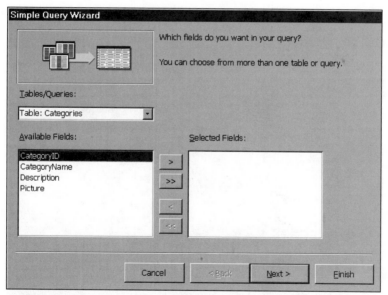

Figure 38-11: The Simple Query wizard opening screen.

3. Select the table or query on which you want to base your query. The fields from that table or query will show up under Available Fields.

4. To move a field from the Available Fields listing to the Selected Fields listing, select it and click the > button. To move all the fields at once, click the > button instead.

5. At this point, the < and << buttons become active. You can use them to move either individual fields or all fields back into the Available Fields listing.

6. Repeat Steps 3 and 4 for any other tables or queries you want to use in this query.

7. Click the Next button.

8. The next screen (see Figure 38-12) asks if you want to see all the fields (Detail) or just a Summary (depending on the fields you select, you may not get this screen).

9. If you chose a summary, you can click the newly activated Summary Options button. Otherwise, just click the Next button to proceed.

10. In the Summary Options dialog box (see Figure 38-13), you can choose to have any or all of sum, average, minimum, or maximum values calculated for selected numeric fields, as well as to have a count of the records in the table. After you've made your selections, click the OK button to return to the Query wizard and then click the Next button to proceed.

11. The final screen of the Simple Query wizard (see Figure 38-14) suggests a title for your query. You can accept this title by doing nothing, or you can type another title over it.

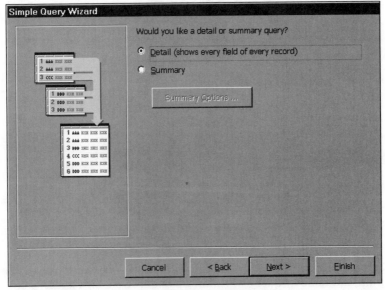

Figure 38-12: The Simple Query wizard detail screen.

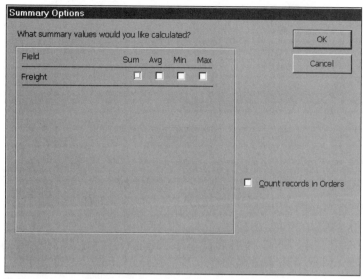

Figure 38-13: The Simple Query wizard's summary options.

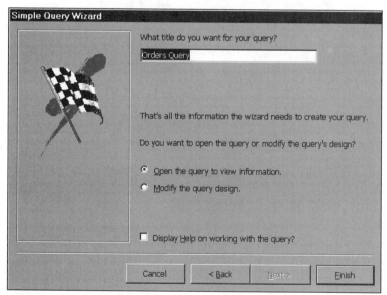

Figure 38-14: The Simple Query wizard's final screen.

12. The default option for viewing the query is to open it. If you intend to make changes to it, such as adding criteria, click the Modify Option button instead so the query will show up in Design view.

13. Click the Finish button to complete the query.

The Crosstab Query wizard

To use the Crosstab Query wizard, follow these steps:

1. In the Database Window under Objects, click Queries.

2. In the Database Window, click the New button.

3. In the New Query dialog box (see Figure 38-15), select Crosstab Query Wizard.

4. Click the OK button.

5. The first screen of the Crosstab Query wizard (see Figure 38-16) asks you to pick the table you want to use for the cross tabulation. Select one.

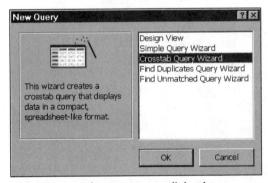

Figure 38-15: The New Query dialog box.

6. Click the Next button to proceed.

7. The next screen (see Figure 38-17) asks you to pick the row headings for your crosstab. Select a field in the Available Fields listing and use the > button to move it to the Selected Fields listing. You can have up to three row headings.

8. Click the Next button.

9. Next, pick the column heading (see Figure 38-18). Select a single field.

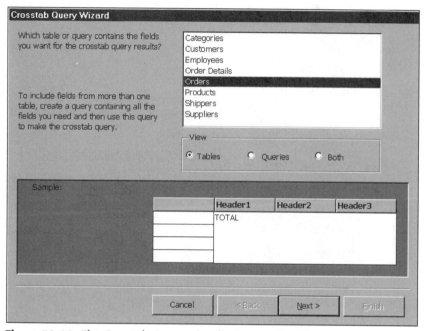

Figure 38-16: The Crosstab Query wizard's Opening screen.

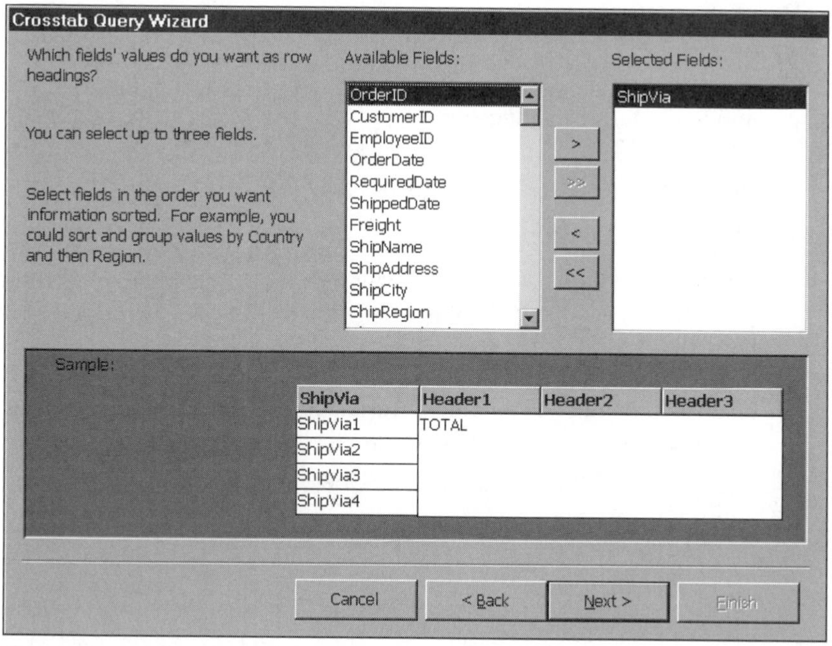

Figure 38-17: The Crosstab Query wizard's row headings.

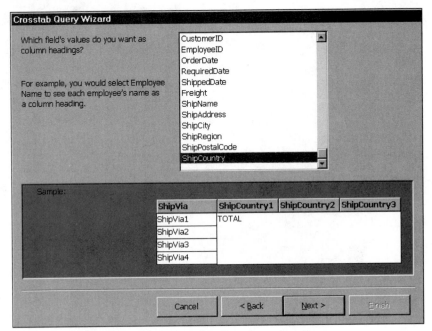

Figure 38-18: The Crosstab Query wizard's column headings.

10. Click the Next button.

11. The next screen (see Figure 38-19) asks you to decide which field's value will be cross-tabulated. Select a field and then select which function you want applied to it (for instance, you may want the field's value averaged or summed).

12. Optionally, check the check box to have each row summed.

13. Click the Next button.

14. The final screen of the Crosstab Query wizard (see Figure 38-20) suggests a title for your query. You can accept this title by doing nothing, or you can type another title over it.

15. The default option for displaying the query is to view it. If you intend to make changes to it, such as adding criteria, click the Modify Option button instead so the query will show up in design view.

16. Click the Finish button to complete the query.

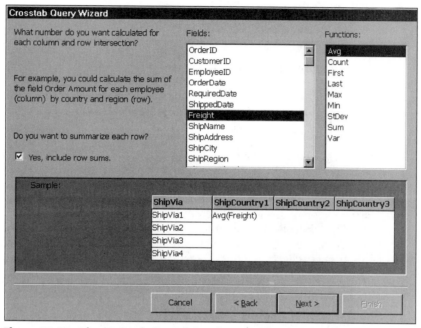

Figure 38-19: The Crosstab Query wizard's crosstab calculation.

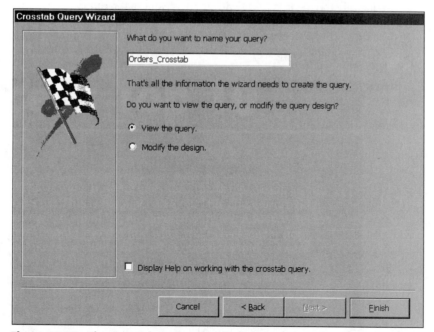

Figure 38-20: The Crosstab Query wizard's final screen.

The Duplicates Query wizard

To use the Find Duplicates Query wizard, follow these steps:

1. In the Database Window under Objects, click Queries.

2. In the Database Window, click the New button.

3. In the New Query dialog box, select Find Duplicates Query Wizard.

4. Click the OK button.

5. The first screen of the Find Duplicates Query wizard (see Figure 38-21) asks you to pick the table you want to search for duplicates in. Select one.

6. Click the Next button to proceed.

7. The next screen (see Figure 38-22) asks you to pick the fields you want to check for duplication. To move a field from the Available Fields listing to the Duplicate-value Fields listing, select it and click the > button. To move all the fields at once, click the > button instead.

8. At this point, the < and << buttons become active. You can use them to move either individual fields or all fields back into the Available Fields listing.

9. Click the Next button.

10. Next, you can choose whether to show other fields in the query besides those on which you're performing the duplicate search (see Figure 38-23). This will help you to identify the records that show up as a result of the query. For instance, if you're looking for duplicate product IDs, and you don't specify that you should also see the product name, you'll have a tougher time identifying the products in the completed query. As before, use the > and > buttons to move the selected fields.

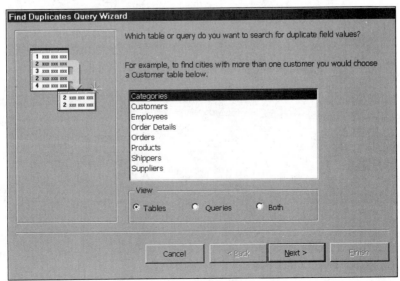

Figure 38-21: The Find Duplicates Query wizard's opening screen.

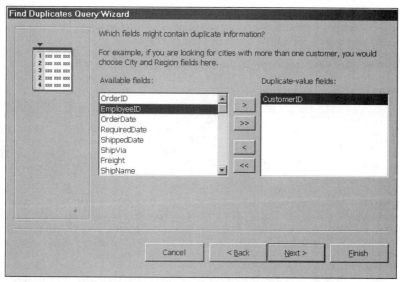

Figure 38-22: The Find Duplicates Query wizard's field options.

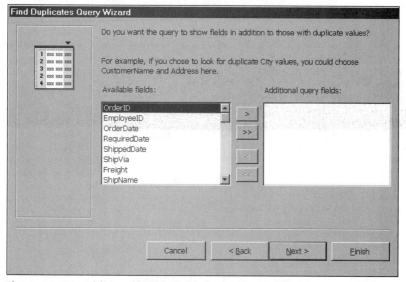

Figure 38-23: Additional visible fields in the Find Duplicates Query wizard.

11. Click the Next button.

12. The final screen (see Figure 38-24) suggests a title for your query. You can accept this title by doing nothing, or you can type another title over it.

13. The default option for displaying the query is to view it. If you intend to make changes to it, such as adding criteria, click the Modify Option button instead so the query will show up in Design view.

14. Click the Finish button to complete the query.

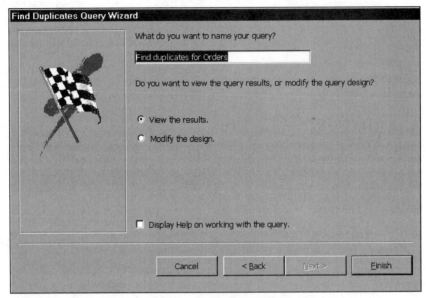

Figure 38-24: The Find Duplicates Query wizard's final screen.

The Find Unmatched Query wizard

To use the Find Unmatched Query wizard, follow these steps:

1. In the Database Window under Objects, click Queries.

2. In the Database Window, click the New button.

3. In the New Query dialog box, select Find Unmatched Query Wizard.

4. Click the OK button.

5. The first screen of the Find Unmatched Query wizard (see Figure 38-25) asks you to pick the first table to compare. Select one.

6. Click the Next button to proceed.

7. The next screen (see Figure 38-26) asks you to pick the table you want compared to the one you selected in the preceding screen. Select one.

8. Click the Next button.

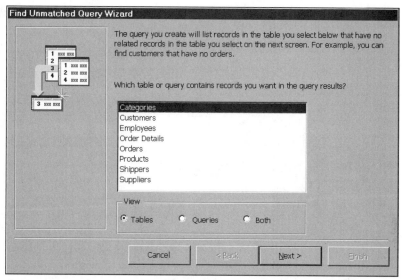

Figure 38-25: The Find Unmatched Query wizard's opening screen.

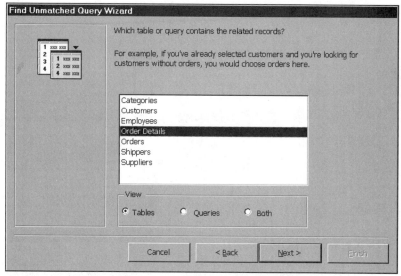

Figure 38-26: Selecting the second table in the Find Unmatched Query wizard.

9. The next screen (see Figure 38-27) is where you tell the Query wizard how to compare the two tables. Select a field in the first table's field listing that is the same as one in the second table's listing. Select the second table's matching field as well, and then click the < = > button to equate the two.

10. Click the Next button.

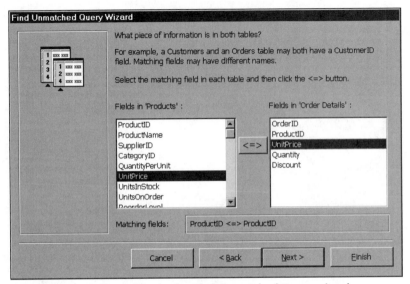

Figure 38-27: Linking tables in the Find Unmatched Query wizard.

11. Next, you can choose whether to show other fields in the query besides those on which you're performing the search (see Figure 38-28). This will help you to identify the records that show up as a result of the query. Use the > and > buttons to move the selected fields.

12. Click the Next button.

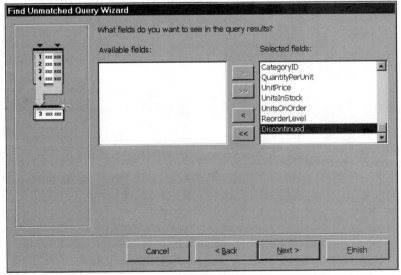

Figure 38-28: Additional visible fields in the Find Unmatched Query wizard.

13. The final screen (see Figure 38-29) suggests a title for your query. You can accept this title by doing nothing, or you can type another title over it.

14. The default option for displaying the query is to view it. If you intend to make changes to it, such as adding criteria, click the Modify Option button instead so the query will show up in Design view.

15. Click the Finish button to complete the query.

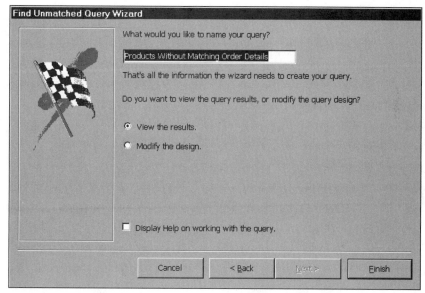

Figure 38-29: The Find Unmatched Query wizard's final screen.

Summary

In this chapter, you learned how to use queries in Access. Highlights of the chapter included the following:

✦ Queries allow you to extract meaningful data from a database.

✦ The results of queries are shown in a dynaset, which looks like a datasheet, but is impermanent.

✦ Queries can be created manually or via the Query wizards.

✦ The three basic types of queries are select, action, and crosstab.

✦ Although you can alter records in the underlying database via a dynaset, it's much easier to use action queries to change large numbers of records at once.

✦   ✦   ✦

Generating Reports

This chapter explains how to use Access reports. The three basic types of reports are columnar, label, and tabular. Access' AutoReport feature can generate columnar or tabular reports for you automatically. As usual with Office programs, you can also use a more complex wizard; in this case, it's Report Wizard, which gives you more control over the design of reports. If you want to create reports from scratch, you can still do so, taking total control over their content and appearance.

Types of Reports

There are three basic kinds of reports in Access (although some would argue that there are really only two):

✦ **Columnar.** The first kind is the *columnar* report (see Figure 39-1), which lists records by showing the fields one-by-one from the top down in a single column until all the fields are listed, at which point the next record starts.

✦ **Label.** The second kind, the *label* report (see Figure 39-2), is a variation of the columnar format, in which fields are listed in multiple columns, grouped as you specify; usually in a standard name-and-address format for mailing label purposes.

✦ **Tabular.** The third report format is called *tabular*. Tabular reports are in a table format (see Figure 39-3), with each record listed on a single line and each field beginning in a separate column.

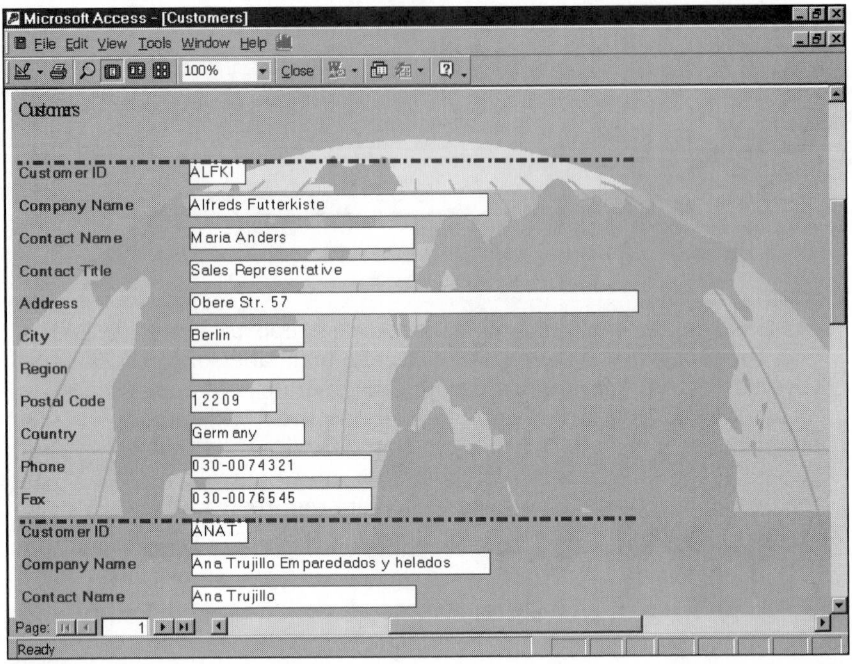

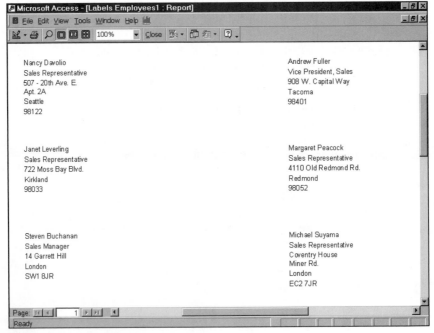

Figure 39-1: A columnar report.

Figure 39-2: A label report.

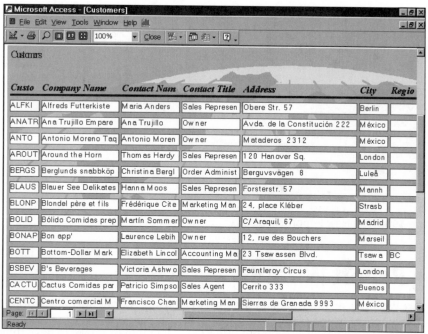

Figure 39-3: A tabular report.

Using AutoReport

AutoReport is the fastest way to generate a report. It has only two options — columnar or tabular report format. To use AutoReport, follow these steps:

Cross-Reference
The label report format is taken care of by a separate wizard, which is covered in Chapter 40, "Access at Work."

1. In the Database Window, click the Reports button.

2. Click the New button.

3. In the New Report dialog box (see Figure 39-4), select either AutoReport: Columnar or AutoReport: Tabular.

4. Select a table or query from the drop-down list.

5. Click the OK button to generate the report.

6. If you want to save the report, right-click it and select Save As from the pop-up menu. Either accept the suggested name for the report or type in your own and then click the OK button.

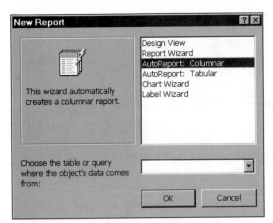

Figure 39-4: The New Report dialog box.

Using Report Wizard

Report Wizard is an intermediary step between using AutoReport and working up your own report from scratch in Design view. Whereas AutoReport gives you no options at all, but requires no input other than the table or query to base things on, Report Wizard asks more from you, but delivers more control. To use Report Wizard, follow these steps:

1. In the Database Window, click the Reports button.

2. Double-click Create Report By Using Wizard. Alternatively, click the New button in the Database Window and, in the New Report dialog box, select Report Wizard.

3. If you opted for the New Report dialog box approach, you can select the table you want to base the report on from the drop-down list in the New Report dialog box (although you don't have to at this stage), and then click the OK button.

4. The first screen of Report Wizard (see Figure 39-5) is where you choose which fields from which tables are included in your report. If you came to this screen via the New Report dialog box and already selected a table in it, then that table will already be showing as the selected one here. Otherwise, the first table alphabetically will be the one that's showing. Either way, you can choose any table or query by selecting it from the drop-down list. When it's selected, its fields will appear under the Available Fields listing on the bottom left-hand side.

5. Next, you need to tell Report Wizard which fields to put on the report from those that are available. To move every field from the Available Fields listing to the Selected Fields listing, click the > button. To move one particular field, select it and click the > button.

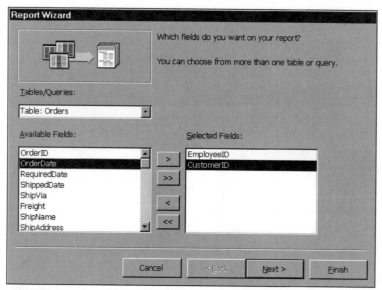

Figure 39-5: Choosing tables and fields in Report Wizard.

6. Once at least one field is in the Selected Fields listing, the < and << buttons become active. They work just like the > and > buttons, but in reverse, moving fields out of the Selected Fields listing back into the Available Fields listing.

7. If you want to select multiple tables to appear on your report, you have to select them one at a time, as the act of selecting a table replaces any fields in the Available Fields listing with the fields from the selected table. Fields already added to the Selected Fields listing are unaffected by selecting a new table.

8. If you change your mind and don't want a particular table to be included on the report, that's no problem. Although there is no button specifically designed to remove a table from the report once fields from it have been chosen, all you have to do to accomplish this is to move any field from that table out of the Selected Fields area. If you're not completely certain which fields belong to which tables, just clear them all out with the << button and start from scratch.

9. When you're satisfied with your field selections, click the Next button.

10. If you're using a single table on your report, skip to Step 12. If you've chosen more than one table, then you'll have to choose which table will be the main one. Select the main table from the listing on the upper left-hand side (see Figure 39-6). The display area on the right side will show the basic structure of the report.

11. When you're satisfied with the report structure, click the Next button to proceed.

12. The next screen (see Figure 39-7) lets you establish groupings on your report. If you don't want to add any grouping levels, just click the Next

button. Otherwise, select the field you want to group the report by and click the > button. Use the < button to remove a grouping. If you put in more than one grouping level, you can use the up and down arrow buttons to set grouping priority.

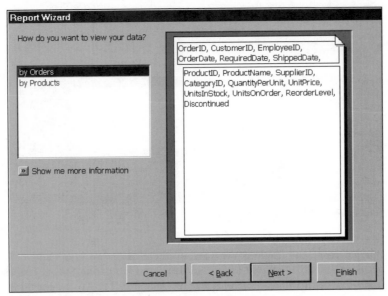

Figure 39-6: Report Wizard's multiple table options.

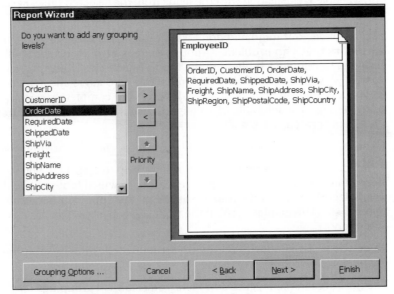

Figure 39-7: Report Wizard's grouping options.

13. Click the Grouping Options button if you want to set the grouping intervals to a custom setting. In the Grouping Intervals dialog box (see Figure 39-8), choose the desired interval for each group-level field from the drop-down list, and then click the OK button to return to Report Wizard.

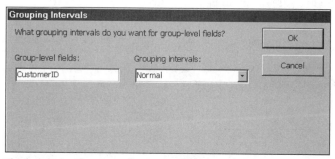

Figure 39-8: The Grouping Intervals dialog box.

14. Click the Next button.

15. Next, set the sort order for your report, if you want to. Click on the drop-down list (see Figure 39-9) to pick the field to sort by, and then click the Sort Order button to the right of the field name to select ascending or descending sort order. You can set up to four fields for sorting.

16. Click the Next button.

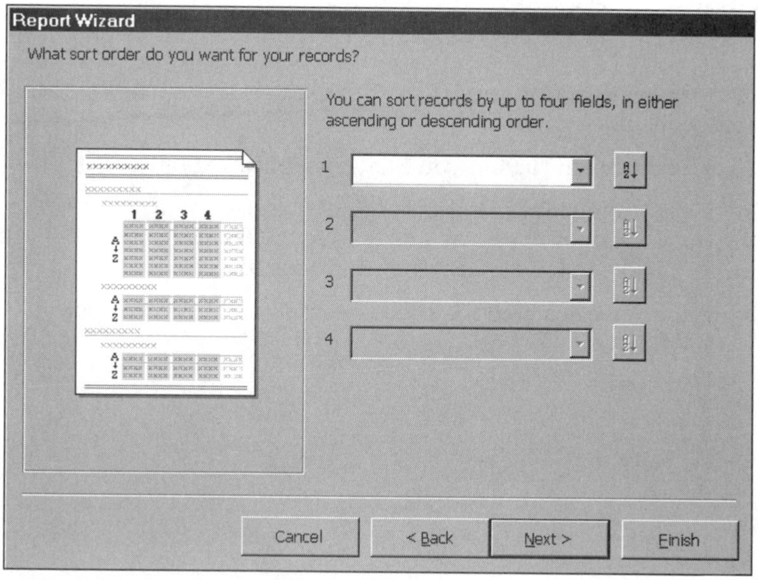

Figure 39-9: Setting sort order in Report Wizard.

17. The next screen is where you choose the layout for your report. If you're doing a basic single-table report with no grouping levels, your layout screen will look like the one shown in Figure 39-10. With multiple tables or other grouping options, more layout options are available to you, as shown in Figure 39-11. Click the radio button for the one you want to use. The display area on the left side of the dialog box shows how each will look.

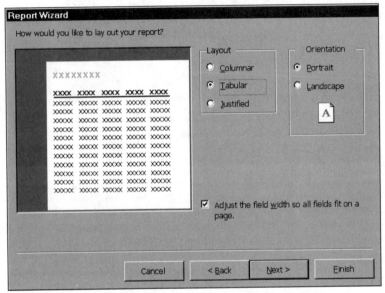

Figure 39-10: Report Wizard's simple report layout options.

18. Click the radio buttons under Orientation to select either Portrait or Landscape orientation.

19. When you have the layout you want, click the Next button.

20. In the next screen (see Figure 39-12), choose the style of the report. Click on the various names of styles and observe the display area on the left-hand side of the dialog box to see what they look like.

21. When you have selected the style you want, click the Next button.

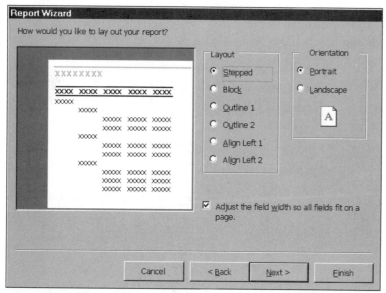

Figure 39-11: Report Wizard's complex report layout options.

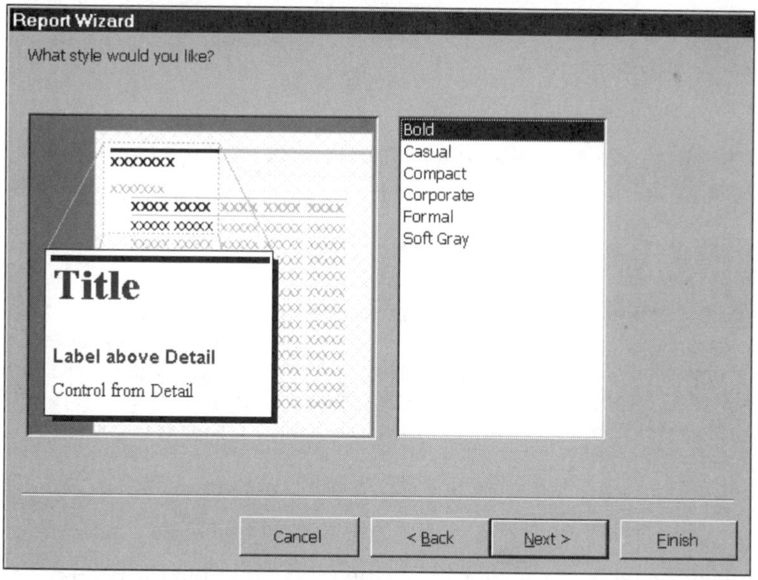

Figure 39-12: Report Wizard's report style options.

22. The final screen of Report Wizard (see Figure 39-13) lets you assign a title to the report (or you can just accept the wizard's suggested title), and choose whether to open the report in Design view or not.

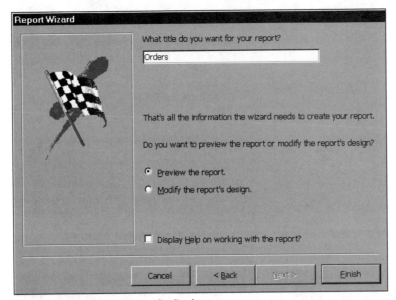

Figure 39-13: Report Wizard's final screen.

23. When you're ready to complete your report, click the Finish button.

Designing Custom Reports

Although the AutoReport approach can satisfy a quick-and-dirty report need, and Report Wizard can give you more control over the report design process, they don't cover every possible eventuality. If you're not satisfied with the results of either the AutoReport or Report Wizard approaches, you can design your own reports from scratch. To set up your own stage for report design, follow these steps:

1. In the Database Window, click the Reports button.

2. Click the New button and, in the New Report dialog box, select Design View.

3. Select the table you want to base the report on from the drop-down list, and then click the OK button. Access will create a blank report for you to work on (see Figure 39-14).

4. Access reports are created with bands. The default bands are Page Header, Detail, and Page Footer. The Detail band is where the data goes in the report. To place a field in the Detail band, drag it from the field list and drop it in place. The Page header provides a space for items that you want to show up at the top of every page of the report. You might want, for instance, to include the word "Confidential" or perhaps an image in this place. Some people use it to place labels showing the names of the fields that are shown underneath if they don't want the labels to take up precious space as a part of the Detail band. The Page footer is for items that you want to have at the bottom of every page. Generally, this is used for page numbers, although there is no requirement that you use it for that. You could, for example, put page numbers in the header and a confidentiality statement in the footer if you feel like it.

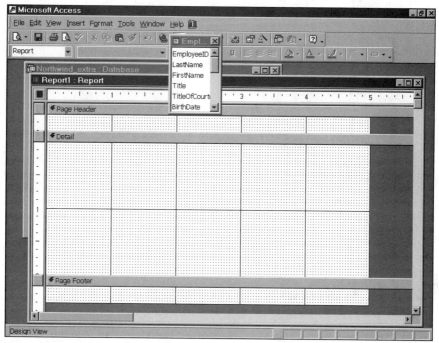

Figure 39-14: A blank report in Design view.

5. You can add another set of headers and footers to the report. These are the Report header and footer. They work just like the Page header and footer, but they print only once, on the very first page of the report. They're useful for such things as company logos and addresses. Right-click on the blank report and select Report Header/Footer from the pop-up menu to add them to the report (see Figure 39-15).

6. Right-click on the blank report and select Toolbox so that you'll have access to the controls you'll be using in the Detail section.

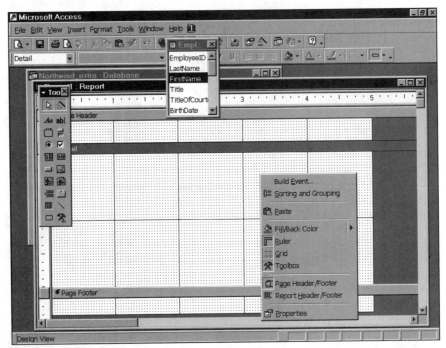

Figure 39-15: Select headers and footers from the pop-up menu.

At this point, we get into adding controls to the blank report, which is covered in the next section.

Placing Controls in Reports

The elements that go into the Detail band of a report are called *controls.* The most common control in a report is the text box and its associated label. Text boxes are linked to a data source in a table or query, and display the data from the source field on the report. The report in Figure 39-16 shows some text boxes created by dragging fields from the Field List into the Detail band.

Note   As you can see, the automatic spacing of the labels and text boxes leaves a bit to be desired from a design standpoint. Don't worry about it at this stage; every control on a report can be moved and resized, and you'll learn how to do it later in the chapter.

Bound and unbound text boxes

Text boxes created with Report Wizard or AutoReport are invariably *bound* to data in the associated table or query, as are those created by dragging a field from the

Field List. Text boxes can also be *unbound*—that is, not linked to table data—and they can contain formulas much like a worksheet cell in Excel, in which case they are said to be *calculated* controls.

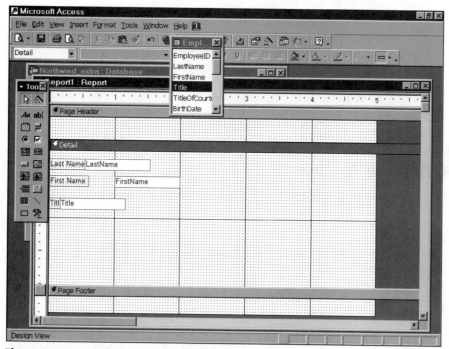

Figure 39-16: Text boxes in the Detail band.

Creating Calculated controls

Calculated controls are very useful in headers and footers—to add, for instance, the current date. To do this, simply drop an unbound text box in the header and put the value =**[Date]** into it. Likewise, the page number can be put into a footer by putting the value =**[Page]** into a calculated control. You can use the full range of Access expressions in calculated controls.

Placing text boxes in reports

There are two ways to place text boxes onto a report. Here's how they work:

✦ The first, which creates bound controls, is via the Field List. To add a text box that is bound to a field in the list, select the field and then drag it onto the report. You can add several fields at a time. To add a contiguous range of fields, select the first one. Then, while holding down the Shift key, select the last one. All the fields in between the two will be selected. Next, click within the selection and drag it onto the report. To add a noncontiguous range of fields, select the first one. Then, while holding down the Ctrl key, select the next one. Continue in this manner until you have selected all the fields you want to add. Next, click on any selected field and drag it onto the report; all the others will come along.

✦ The second way to add text boxes to a report is to use the Toolbox. This method adds unbound text boxes. Click the Text Box button in the Toolbox, and then click on the report at the point where you want to place the text box. The text box and a label will be created at that point.

Note

The other controls are added in the same way as unbound text boxes. Just click on the button in the Toolbox, move the pointer to where you want to drop the control, and click on the report at that point.

Using the Toolbox

Other than dragging fields from the Field List, you put controls into a report by using the Toolbox. Although the Toolbox contains all the buttons used in form creation, many of the controls on it are pretty useless when you're working on a report. Remember that a report is not for data entry or alteration, just for display purposes. Table 39-1 shows the only controls in the Toolbox that you're likely to use in a report.

Cross-Reference

For more information on the Toolbox and the uses of all its tools, see Chapter 37, "Working with Forms."

Moving and Deleting Text Box Labels

Access always hangs a label on a text box and, in our opinion, it's always too far away from it. It's also always on the left, while you may want it above the text box. In fact, you may not want a label at all. Fortunately, you don't have to accept the default placement. Following are some other options:

✦ If you don't want the label, just select it and press the Del key; the text box will remain (if you select and delete the text box, though, the label will be deleted along with it).

✦ If you want to move the label in relation to the text box, select the text box and move the pointer to the upper left corner of either the text box or its label. When the pointer changes to a pointing finger, press the mouse button and move the text box or the label until it's just where you want it.

✦ You also don't have to accept the label text that Access provides. To change it, select the label, click within it, and you'll be in normal editing mode for the label.

Table 39-1
Toolbox Buttons Used in Reports

Button	Purpose
Select Objects	Switches back to the normal mouse pointer.
Control Wizards	Some controls (such as the Subform/Subreport button, which are covered in the section on relational reports) have wizards that can help you make selections regarding their properties. This toggle switch, when depressed, causes those wizards to be activated when the control is dropped onto the report.
Label	Adds a label to a report. These labels are unbound controls, not associated with any data.
Text Box	Adds an unbound text box and its associated label to a report.
Image	Adds an image (gif, jpg, pcd, etc.) to the report.
Unbound Object Frame	Frame used for objects not stored in tables.
Bound Object Frame	Frame used for objects stored in tables.
Page Break	Creates a page break for multipage reports.
Tab Control	Creates multiple pages in a report, which are accessible via tabs.
Subform/Subreport	Adds subreports to a report.
Line	Adds an unbound line to the report for design purposes.
Rectangle	Adds an unbound rectangle to the report for design purposes.
More Controls	Allows access to more controls, such as ActiveX objects.

Creating Relational Reports

Relational reports use multiple tables. The structure of a relational report is a master report and a subreport. The relationship between the data in the two reports is called a one-to-many relationship. One common example of such a relationship is a salesperson who sells to different clients. The salesperson is the "one" and the clients are the "many." You often find a need in such a situation to set up a report that shows which clients the one salesperson has dealt with (or you may wish to see the many sales the one salesperson has made, or the many products the one salesperson has sold).

The master report contains data relating to the "one" end of the relationship, and the subreport contains the information on the "many" end of it. The simplest way to create a relational report is to use Report Wizard (see the earlier section on this) and use multiple tables as your input. However, if you've already got a report and want to make it into a more complex relational report, then you'll be glad to know that it's an easy matter to add a subreport to it. All you have to do is use SubReport Wizard:

1. Make sure the Control Wizards button in the Toolbox is depressed.

2. Click the Subform/Subreport button in the Toolbox.

3. Click on the report where you want the subreport to be placed. The Detail band will automatically expand to make room for it.

4. After a few moments, SubReport Wizard will appear (see Figure 39-17). You have two options in this step. You can use an existing table or query for your source, or you can use an existing report or form for it. Click the appropriate radio button. If you choose the existing report or form approach, then choose a report or form from the list in this dialog box.

5. Click the Next button.

6. If you chose to use an existing table or query for your source, then you'll see the screen shown in Figure 39-18. Otherwise, skip this step and go on to Step 12. Choose any table or query by selecting it from the drop-down list. When it's selected, its fields will appear under the Available Fields listing on the bottom left-hand side.

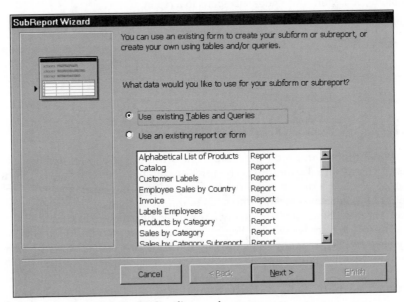

Figure 39-17: SubReport Wizard's opening screen.

7. To move every field from the Available Fields listing to the Selected Fields listing, click the > button. To move one particular field, select it and click the > button.

8. Once at least one field is in the Selected Fields listing, the < and << buttons become active. They work just like the > and > buttons, but in reverse, moving fields out of the Selected Fields listing back into the Available Fields listing.

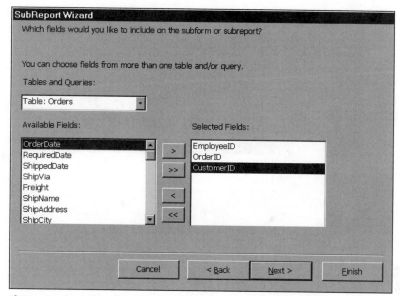

Figure 39-18: Choosing tables and fields in SubReport Wizard.

9. If you want to select multiple tables to appear on your report, you have to select them one at a time, as the act of selecting a table replaces any fields in the Available Fields listing with the fields from the selected table. Fields already added to the Selected Fields listing are unaffected by selecting a new table.

10. If you change your mind and don't want a particular table to be included on the report, that's no problem. Although there is no button specifically designed to remove a table from the report once fields from it have been chosen, all you have to do to accomplish this is to move any field from that table out of the Selected Fields area. If you're not completely certain which fields belong to which tables, just clear them all out with the << button and start from scratch.

11. When you're satisfied with your field selections, click the Next button.

12. The next screen (see Figure 39-19) is where you define the links between the master report and the subreport. The wizard will analyze the two reports and suggest fields to link them with. You can select one from the list suggested by the wizard or you can click the Define My Own radio button to choose others.

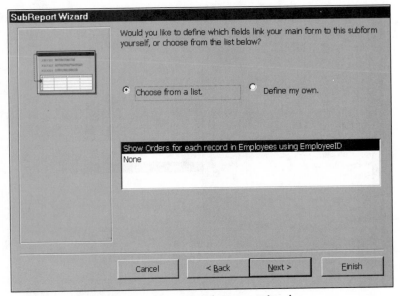

Figure 39-19: Linking the reports in SubReport Wizard.

13. If you chose to define fields yourself, then the dialog box will change, as shown in Figure 39-20. Choose fields for the master report from the Form/report fields drop-down list, and for the subreport from the Subform/subreport fields drop-down list.

14. Click the Next button.

15. The final screen of SubReport Wizard (see Figure 39-21) lets you assign a title to the report (or you can just accept the wizard's suggested title).

16. When you're done, click the Finish button to complete the procedure.

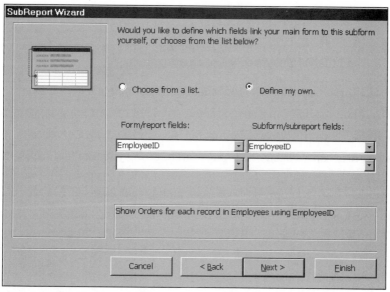

Figure 39-20: Manual linking in SubReport Wizard.

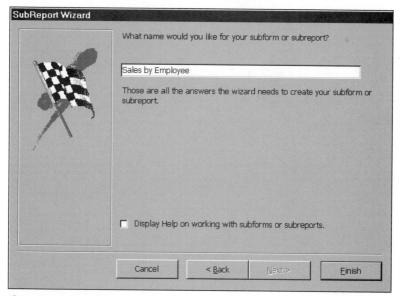

Figure 39-21: SubReport Wizard's final screen.

Summary

In this chapter, you learned about the different types of reports Access can generate and the various methods of creating them.

✦ The three basic types of reports are columnar, label, and tabular.

✦ AutoReport can generate columnar or tabular reports automatically.

✦ Report Wizard gives you more control over the design of reports.

✦ Reports can be designed from scratch, giving you total control over their content and appearance.

✦ Reports are composed of controls, mainly text boxes and labels.

✦ Relational reports, those that deal with multiple simultaneous tables, can be created with either Report Wizard or SubReport Wizard.

✦   ✦   ✦

Access at Work

This chapter gives you hands-on experience using Access in real-world situations. First, you'll learn how to use label reports to generate mailing labels, and then we'll delve into using Access to track personnel assignments. Finally, you'll learn how to create databases for the World Wide Web.

Generating Mailing Labels

One of the most common uses of databases is to generate mailing labels. Mailing labels can be generated from any table that has name and address information in it. Access provides an easy method for taking care of this important need. Label Wizard lets you set up the layout and format of mailing labels, taking into account the sizes and characteristics of major name-brand labels and even allowing you to create your own custom mailing label templates. You can also set font characteristics and even sort the order in which your database records are fed to the labels in your printer.

To use Label Wizard, follow these steps:

1. In the Database Window under Objects, click Reports.
2. Click the New button.
3. In the New Report dialog box (see Figure 40-1), select Label Wizard.
4. From the drop-down list, select the table or query you wish to use for the mailing labels.
5. Click the OK button.
6. The first screen of Label Wizard (see Figure 40-2) has a list of labels manufactured by Avery. If you use another manufacturer's labels, choose their name from the drop-down list next to Filter By Manufacturer.
7. Under Unit of Measure, select either English or Metric.
8. Under Label Type, select either Sheet feed or Continuous.

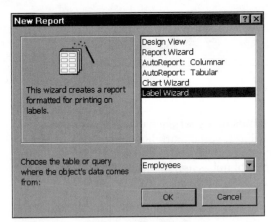

Figure 40-1: The New Report dialog box.

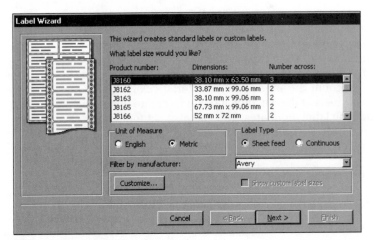

Figure 40-2: Label Wizard's opening screen.

9. If your labels aren't listed, and if none of the ones listed are the same size as your labels, click the Customize button. Otherwise, jump to Step 18.

10. In the New Label Size dialog box (see Figure 40-3), click the New button.

11. In the New Label dialog box (see Figure 40-4), enter a name for your labels.

12. Next, select the Unit of Measure, the Label Type, and the Orientation of your labels.

13. Enter the number of labels per row under Number Across.

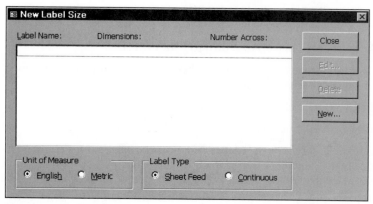

Figure 40-3: The New Label Size dialog box.

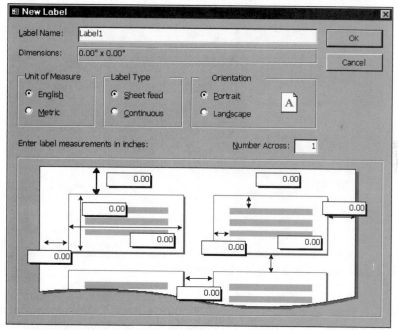

Figure 40-4: The New Label dialog box.

14. In each of the edit boxes under "Enter label measurement in inches" (or centimeters, if you chose Metric), enter the dimensions for the spacing represented by the arrows.

15. When you're finished, click the OK button to return to the New Label Size dialog box, where your new label is now listed.

16. Click the Close button to return to Label Wizard.

17. If it is not already selected, click the Show Custom Label Sizes check box so your new label will be listed.

18. Click on the label you wish to use.

19. Click the Next button.

20. In the next screen (see Figure 40-5), you choose the font characteristics for your mailing labels. Choose the font name and font size from the drop-down lists at the top of the dialog box. The particular ones available will depend on what fonts you have installed on your system.

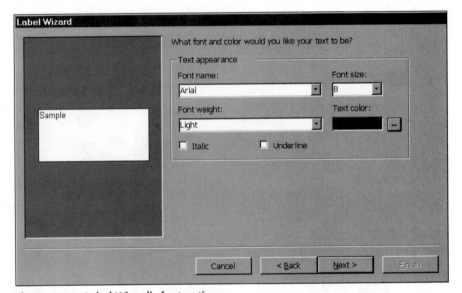

Figure 40-5: Label Wizard's font options.

21. Select the font weight (ranges from thin to heavy). Experimenting on your printer will reveal the best settings for your particular system. It's recommended that you use plain paper for testing purposes to keep costs down.

22. If you're using a color printer and want to print in a color other than the default black, click the ellipsis button to the right of the Text Color window. This will bring up a standard color picker in which you can click on the desired color. Once you've chosen a color, click the OK button to return to Label Wizard.

23. If desired, select Italic or Underline for your fonts by clicking on the appropriate check boxes.

24. Click the Next button.

25. In the next screen (see Figure 40-6), you construct the mailing label itself. Double-click on a field in the Available Fields listing to move it to the Prototype Label (or select the field and click the > button). This screen doesn't have a < button for removing a field from the label, but you can manually delete a field from the Prototype Label area. Be aware that if there are any fields to the right of the one you're deleting, they'll be deleted, too, unless they're separated by other characters like a space, or you select the field you want to delete before pressing the Delete key. However, because no field is actually removed from the Available Fields listing at any time, you can simply put them right back in.

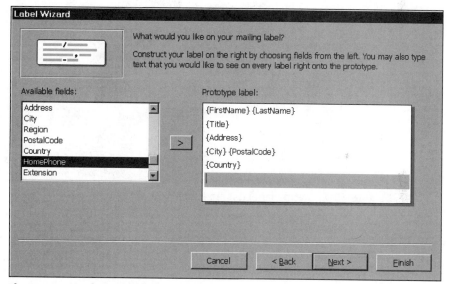

Figure 40-6: Label Wizard's label contents.

26. As you enter fields in the Prototype Label area, you can use normal editing and typing features to, for instance, put a space between the fields for first name and last name, so that the label will have a normal appearance. Make sure to press Enter at the end of each line of information, or you'll have all your data on a single line. There are no restrictions on what you may type into a mailing label, and you can enter any text you want to in addition to the fields.

27. When you're finished designing the label, click the Next button.

28. In the next screen (see Figure 40-7), you have the option to sort the records before they're printed on the labels. The fields in the selected table are listed under Available Fields. To move every field from the Available Fields listing to the Sort By listing, click the > button. To move one particular field, select it and click the > button.

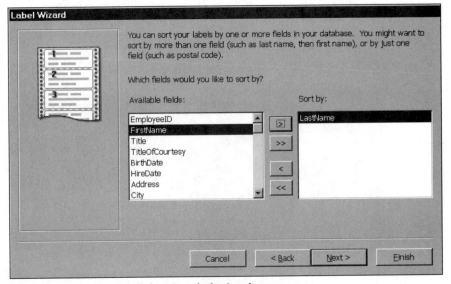

Figure 40-7: Sorting label data in Label Wizard.

29. Once at least one field is in the Sort By listing, the < and << buttons become active. They work just like the > and > buttons, but in reverse, moving fields out of the Sort By listing back into the Available Fields listing.

30. When you're satisfied with your sort options, click the Next button.

31. The final screen of Label Wizard (see Figure 40-8) lets you assign a title to the label report (or you can just accept the wizard's suggested title), and choose whether to open the report in print preview or in Design view.

32. When you've made your selections, click the Finish button. Figure 40-9 shows the finished mailing labels.

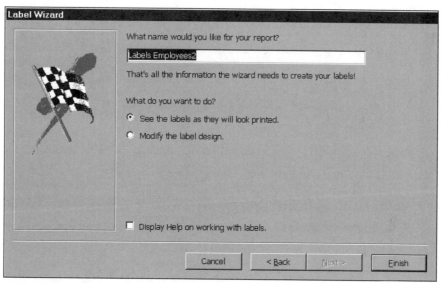

Figure 40-8: Label Wizard's final screen.

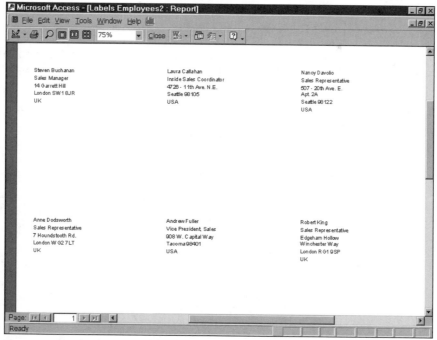

Figure 40-9: The finished mailing labels.

Tracking Personnel Assignments

Individual personnel assigned to accomplish several tasks is another classic case of a one-to-many relationship. It practically cries out for a relational database. Here's the basic procedure:

✦ To set it up, we'll need one table for employee data and another for assignment data.

✦ To make the process of adding, editing, and deleting records easier, we'll use forms.

Creating the database

First, create the database:

1. Select File ⇨ New from the menu.

2. In the New dialog box, click the General tab and then choose Database.

3. Click the OK button.

4. In the File New Database dialog box, navigate to the folder you want to store the database in and give it a filename.

5. Click the Create button.

6. In the Database Window, choose how you want to enter data into the database. For this exercise, double-click Create Database in Design View.

Entering field names and data types

Enter the following field names and data types into the new database:

Field Name	Data Type
First Name	Text
Last Name	Text
Title	Text
Department	Text
ID Number	AutoNumber
Extension	Number

Right-click the ID Number field and select Primary Key from the pop-up menu. Finally, click the Save button and give the table the name "Employees." Figure 40-10 shows how the table looks at this point.

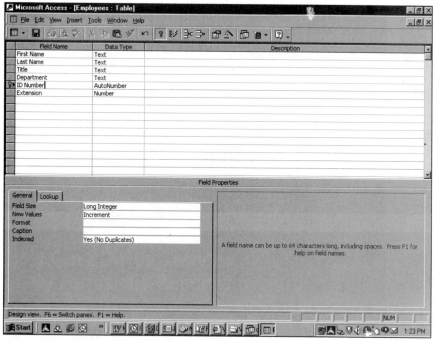

Figure 40-10: The Employees table.

Creating the second table

In the Database Window, double-click on Create Table in Design View to start the second table. Enter the following field names and data types into it:

Field Name	Data Type
Task Description	Text
Date Assigned	Date/Time
Date Due	Date/Time
Assigned To	Number
Completed	Yes/No

Right-click the Task Description field and select Primary Key from the pop-up menu. Next, click the Save button and give the table the name Assignments. Figure 40-11 shows how the table looks at this point.

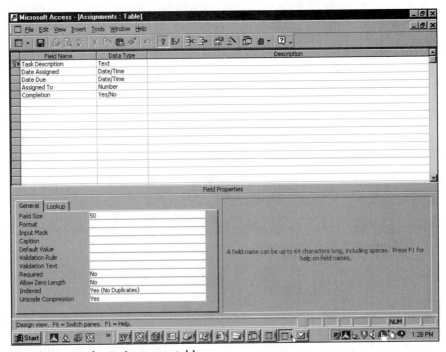

Figure 40-11: The Assignments table.

Establishing relationships

The two tables need to be related to each other in order for relational forms to be built that utilize fields from both tables. To do so, follow these steps:

1. With the Database Window active, click the Relationships button.

2. The Show Table dialog box will appear automatically.

3. In the Show Table dialog box (see Figure 40-12), select each table and click the Add button; then click the Close button.

4. The fields from the two tables are now shown in the Relationships window (see Figure 40-13). Click the Assigned To field and drag it onto the ID Number field.

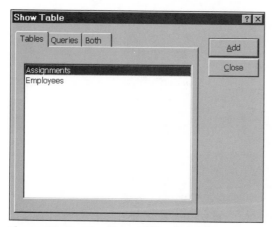

Figure 40-12: The Show Table dialog box.

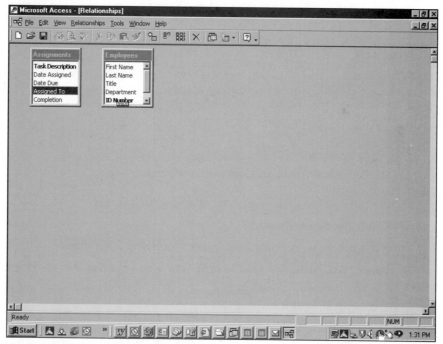

Figure 40-13: The Relationships window.

5. The Edit Relationships dialog box will now appear (see Figure 40-14) with the relationship between the two fields already in place. Click the Create button.

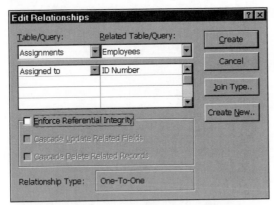

Figure 40-14: The Edit Relationships dialog box.

6. The connection between the two fields in the separate tables is now indicated by a line connecting them. Click the Save button to save the relationship.

Making the forms

Now that the relationship between the two tables has been established, we can go ahead and build relational forms that access the data in both tables. We'll need one form for each of the tables for data entry purposes and a third form for generating reports.

The data entry forms

To make the data entry forms, follow these steps:

1. In the Database Window under Objects, click Forms.

2. Click the New button.

3. In the New Form dialog box, select AutoForm: Columnar.

4. Select Assignments from the drop-down list of tables.

5. Click the OK button. An assignments form like the one shown in Figure 40-15 will appear after a few moments.

6. Click the Save button. A Save As dialog box will appear with the name "Assignments" already in place. Click the OK button to save the form under that name.

7. Close the form.

8. Repeat Steps 2 through 7 using the Employees table instead of the Assignments table. A form like the one shown in Figure 40-16 will appear.

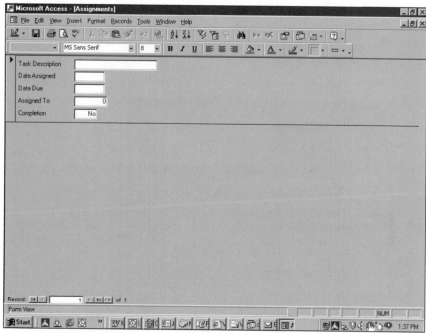

Figure 40-15: The Assignments form.

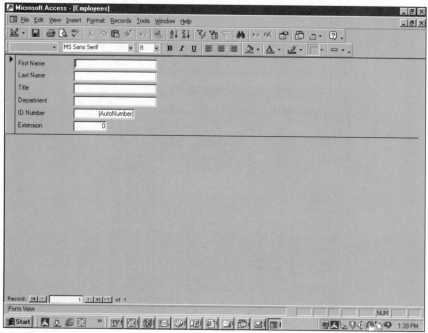

Figure 40-16: The Employees form.

The relational form

Next, we'll make the relational form that will display the data from both tables:

1. In the Database Window under Objects, click Forms.

2. Click the New button.

3. In the New Form dialog box, select Form Wizard.

4. Click the OK button.

5. Select Table: Assignments from the drop-down table listing.

6. Click the > button to add all its fields to the Selected Fields listing.

7. Select Table: Employees from the drop-down table listing.

8. Select the First Name field and click the > button to add it to the Selected Fields listing.

9. Repeat Step 8 for the Last Name field.

10. Click the Next button.

11. In the next dialog box, select By Employees for the view.

12. Click the Finish button. Figure 40-17 shows the completed form.

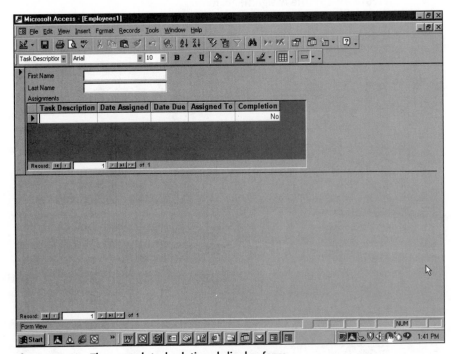

Figure 40-17: The completed relational display form.

Making the report

There's one more item we need now that all the forms have been created—a relational report to show which employees have been assigned which tasks. To make the report, follow these steps:

1. In the Database Window under Objects, click Reports.

2. Click the New button.

3. In the New Report dialog box, select Report Wizard.

4. Click the OK button.

5. Select Table: Assignments from the drop-down table listing.

6. Click the > button to add all its fields to the Selected Fields listing.

7. Select Table: Employees from the drop-down table listing.

8. Select the First Name field and click the > button to add it to the Selected Fields listing.

9. Repeat Step 8 for the Last Name and Title fields.

10. Click the Next button.

11. In the next dialog box, select By Employees for the view.

12. Click Next three times to get to the screen that offers you layout options. Choose Outline 1.

13. Click the Finish button. Figure 40-18 shows the completed report.

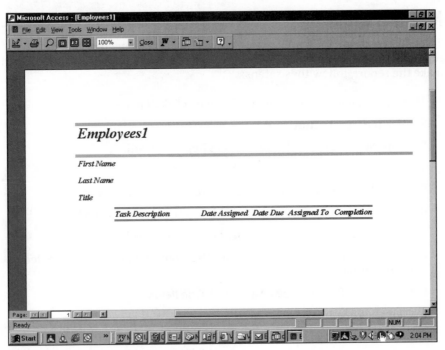

Figure 40-18: The completed relational report.

Creating HTML Data Access Pages

Access greatly simplifies the formerly daunting task of creating databases for the World Wide Web. Page Wizard lets you quickly determine what data you want to include on your Web page and what you want it to look like. To use it, follow these steps:

1. In the Database Window under Objects, click Pages.

2. Click the New button.

3. In the New Data Access Page dialog box, select Page Wizard.

4. Click the OK button.

5. In this first screen of Page Wizard (see Figure 40-19), choose which fields from which tables are to be included in your page. Choose any table or query by selecting it from the drop-down list. When it's selected, its fields will appear under the Available Fields listing on the bottom left-hand side.

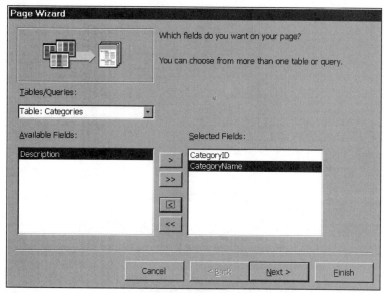

Figure 40-19: Choosing tables and fields in Page Wizard.

6. Next, you need to tell Page Wizard which fields to put on the page from those that are available. To move every field from the Available Fields listing to the Selected Fields listing, click the > button. To move one particular field, select it and click the > button.

7. Once at least one field is in the Selected Fields listing, the < and << buttons become active. They work just like the > and > buttons, but in reverse, moving fields out of the Selected Fields listing back into the Available Fields listing.

8. If you want multiple tables to appear on your report, you have to select them one at a time, as the act of selecting a table replaces any fields in the Available Fields listing with the fields from the selected table. Fields already added to the Selected Fields listing are unaffected by selecting a new table.

9. When you're satisfied with your field selections, click the Next button.

10. The next screen (see Figure 40-20) lets you establish groupings. If you don't want to add any grouping levels, just click the Next button. Otherwise, select the field you want to group by and click the > button. Use the < button to remove a grouping. If you put in more than one grouping level, you can use the up and down arrow buttons to set grouping priority.

11. If you've added one or more grouping levels, click the Grouping Options button if you want to set the grouping intervals to a custom setting. In the Grouping Intervals dialog box (see Figure 40-21), choose the desired interval for each group-level field from the drop-down list, and then click the OK button to return to Page Wizard.

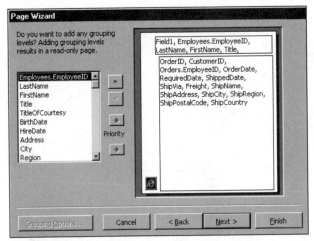

Figure 40-20: Page Wizard's grouping options.

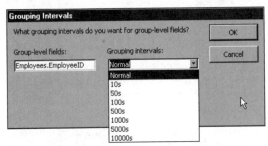

Figure 40-21: The Grouping Intervals dialog box.

12. Click the Next button.

13. Next, you can set the sort order for your page if you want to. Click on the drop-down list (see Figure 40-22) to pick the field to sort by, and then click the Sort Order button to the right of the field name to select ascending or descending sort order. You can set up to four fields for sorting.

14. Click the Next button to proceed, and the final screen of Page Wizard (see Figure 40-23) suggests a title. You can accept this title by doing nothing, or you can type another title over it.

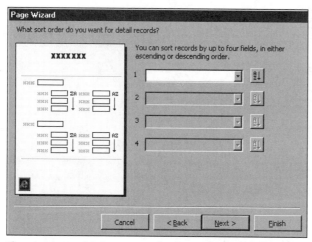

Figure 40-22: Setting sort order in Page Wizard.

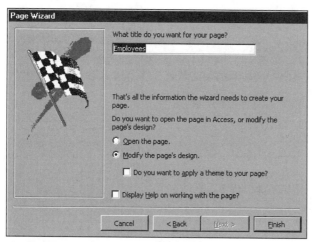

Figure 40-23: Page Wizard's final screen.

15. When you're ready to complete your report, click the Finish button. Figure 40-24 shows the completed page.

16. To view your page in Internet Explorer, select File ⇨ Web Page Preview from the menu.

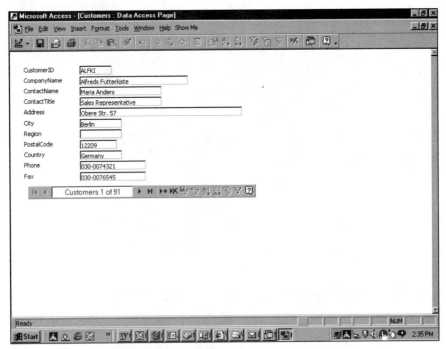

Figure 40-24: The finished data access page.

Summary

In this chapter, you learned how to put Access to work doing practical tasks.

✦ You generated mailing labels.

✦ You built a personnel assignment tracking system.

✦ You created an HTML data access page.

✦   ✦   ✦

Access Top 10

If you have some burning questions that keep arising as you use Access, this is the place to look. This chapter provides the solutions to ten of the most commonly encountered Access dilemmas. Should you not find what you're looking for here, Microsoft keeps an up-to-date set of questions and answers on the World Wide Web at http://support.microsoft.com. Don't despair: First look here and then go online to find the answers you need.

How Do I Eliminate the Dialog Box When I Start Access?

If you don't want to use the dialog box that Access starts with, you can customize Access so it won't appear. Select Tools ⇨ Options from the menu. On the View tab, uncheck the Startup dialog box check box, and then click the OK button.

How Can I Divide Sections of My Forms and Reports?

Use the rectangle and line buttons in the Toolbox to add those elements in Design view. Once they're there, you can stretch and size them by clicking on the corners and dragging them until they're the size you want (or, in the case of a rectangle, the shape and size you want).

How Do I Create a Tabbed Form or Report?

Click the Tab Control button in the Toolbox and click on a blank form or report in Design view. Click on the tabs to bring one or the other to the top and drop controls on them just as you would on a form or report. Any control you drop on one tab is invisible when the other tab is selected. To add more tabs, right-click on the tab control and select Insert Page from the pop-up menu. To remove tabs from the control, right-click on it and select Delete Page from the pop-up menu.

Why Can't Others Modify a Database While I'm Working on a Report?

Access 2000 automatically locks a database for the exclusive use of one person whenever they're working on anything involving Visual Basic for Applications. Even if you're not specifically writing VBA code, the forms, reports, etc., generate it while you're modifying them.

Why Can't Netscape Navigator Users View My Access Databases on the World Wide Web?

The capability to view forms created from Access databases that are then placed on a Web site is limited to users of Internet Explorer 3 or later with the HTML Layout ActiveX control.

How Can I Speed Up Queries?

One of the easiest ways to speed up queries is to index, index, index. When a field is indexed, Access doesn't have to search through it, but can just go right to the index. Just as you use the index in this book instead of looking at every page to find what you want, it's a lot faster.

Tip   It's best to put indexes on fields you're likely to use in a query. For example, it's very unlikely that you'll run many queries on street addresses, but quite likely that you'll run them on states or perhaps on zip codes.

To see if a field is indexed, put the table into Design view, select the field, and look at the General tab. Next to the word "Indexed," there are three possible values: No, Yes (Duplicates OK), and Yes (No Duplicates). If the value is No, select one of the other options from the drop-down list for the indexed property.

How Do I Spell-Check My Data?

In either Form or Datasheet view, click the Spelling button on the toolbar (the one that has a checkmark and the letters "ABC" on it). You can also start the spell-checker from the Database window—just select the table, query, or form and click the Spelling button. The object will be displayed and the spell-checker will launch.

The spell-checker will run through your data and when it finds something that isn't in its dictionary, it'll stop and present it to you along with a list of suggested replacements. At that point, you can decide to ignore the word or add it to the dictionary if it's spelled properly. If it's spelled improperly, you can select one of the suggested replacements or type in your own correction and replace the word.

How Do I Make Databases Readable by Earlier Versions of Access?

Open the database and Select Tools ➪ Database Utilities ➪ Convert Database ➪ To Prior Access Database Version from the menu. In the file Save dialog box that appears next, give it a name, and then click the Save button.

What Do I Do If I Suspect My Database Is Corrupt?

If your database is acting quirky, select Tools ➪ Database Utilities ➪ Compact and Repair Database from the menu. This will solve most database damage problems.

How Do I Change the Name of a Field?

If you're in Table Design view, all you have to do is highlight the field name you want to change and type over it. If the field name is a single word, then you can highlight it by double-clicking on the field name, but if it has spaces in it, you'll have to click and drag to cover it all. Save the table and you're done.

In Datasheet view, you can double-click on the field name regardless of whether it has spaces in it or not and the whole thing will be selected, ready for typing over. When you're done, either press the Enter key or click anywhere outside the field name. Changes to field names in Datasheet view do not require a separate save action to take effect.

✦   ✦   ✦

Web and Desktop Publishing Tools

◆ ◆ ◆ ◆

An Introduction to FrontPage

Microsoft FrontPage 2000 is the new kid on the block in Office 2000. Bundled with Office 2000 Premium, FrontPage gives you powerful Web page publishing features that allow you to create sophisticated and attractive Web sites.

What Is FrontPage?

Web pages differ from other documents you create in Office 2000 in that they are designed to be interpreted by Web browsers. The most popular browsers are Microsoft's own Internet Explorer (IE), and Netscape's Navigator (often referred to as just Netscape, for short). These two browsers take text, graphics, and even interactive elements like input forms, sound and video, and present them in the form that you're used to seeing when you visit a Web site on the Internet.

The Hypertext Markup Language (HTML)

Web browsers interpret and display Web page content by reading a programming language called Hypertext Markup Language, or HTML. Back in the Dark Ages, folks who wanted to create Web pages had to master the intricacies of HTML, memorizing hundreds of coding commands to control the display of their Web pages. Today, you can create very complex Web pages without even being aware of HTML using FrontPage.

Publishing Web pages

The Web pages you create in FrontPage 2000 can be published on computers with Web server software, and accessed by others. You can publish your Web pages to an internal server called an *intranet,* where they can be accessed by your co-workers (who have been given access to the server by your server administrator if prompted). Or, these pages can be published to the Internet, where the whole world can access them. Finally, you can simply share Web files you create in FrontPage for others to view on their computers, by opening these files with IE or Netscape.

Note   You'll find the FrontPage interface very friendly and familiar now that you've mastered other components of Office 2000. The difference is that the files you create in FrontPage are not optimized for hardcopy printing, but rather for viewing on a computer using a Web browser.

Navigating Through FrontPage Views

When you launch FrontPage 2000, you'll see a Views list on the left side of the screen, and a big open space on the right. The Views list is where you select from many different ways to look at the files you create in FrontPage. The area on the right is your workspace. Even before you start creating Web pages and organizing them into a Web site, you can introduce yourself to the different views in FrontPage 2000:

✦ **Page view.** Most of us spend the vast majority of our FrontPage work time in Page view. This is where you edit individual Web pages. The workspace doesn't look that different from Word 2000, so you'll soon feel right at home here if you've worked with Word. Figure 42-1 shows FrontPage's Page view.

✦ **Folders view.** Think of Folders view as a directory of the files you create in FrontPage. After you start saving Web pages, you'll see them listed here.

✦ **Reports view.** FrontPage can generate reports that provide interesting information on the state and status of your Web site. Here's where you'll find them.

✦ **Navigation view.** Navigation view is going to be your second most popular view, after Page view. This is where you organize all your different Web page files into an integrated Web site.

✦ **Hyperlinks view.** Hyperlinks (or links, for short) are text or graphics that, when clicked on, jump a visitor to another Web page. Links can become broken or out of date when Web pages change, and this view checks up on them for you.

✦ **Tasks view.** Finally, FrontPage allows the organizationally fixated among us to create lists of things to do. If you're designing a site yourself, a notepad might do. But if you're collaborating with other Web authors, the Tasks view will help keep you all on the same page.

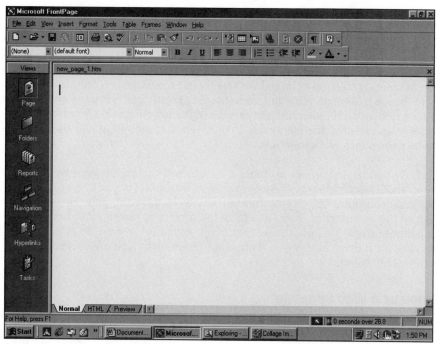

Figure 42-1: The FrontPage Page view is where you will design your Web pages.

Creating a Web Site

There are two ways to go about creating a Web site in FrontPage 2000. You can start by creating individual pages, or you can start by designing a Web site. Either way works, and there are times and places when one approach works best. If you are creating a single Web page, there is no need to worry about how it will connect with other pages at your Web site. But if you are designing a multipage Web site, it often works best to design the whole site first, and then provide page content.

To use an architectural analogy, if you were designing an office building, you would almost always want to start by laying out the design of the building, and then worry about furnishing the individual suites and individual offices. When you design Web sites with FrontPage, you will learn to develop site design skills.

Creating a new Web

The word *web* has many meanings, and is used in referring to the World Wide Web and a Web site. But FrontPage uses the term a bit differently. A FrontPage Web is a collection of files including Web pages that function together as a Web site. The first step in creating a group of linked Web pages in FrontPage is to create a Web. A useful image to keep in mind in understanding FrontPage Webs is a spider's web, with its network of connected points. One of the functions of a FrontPage Web is to organize and save all the elements of your Web site, including files that are needed to make the pages work together.

You have two basic options in creating a Web. You can create your Web on a Web server that is accessible to the Internet or an intranet. Or, you can create your Web on a local computer drive (your hard drive). Webs saved to your hard drive cannot have all the advanced features available in FrontPage, like the ability to collect data from input forms. And, of course, they can't be visited by anyone else. But you can use your local drive to design a Web, and then publish it to a Web server when one becomes available.

Choosing a Web template

Before you create your new Web, you will be asked to choose from one of the Web templates or wizards. Those include the following:

- ✦ **One-Page Web.** A new Web with a single blank page.
- ✦ **Corporate Presence Web.** A complex Web with dozens of pages that can be converted into a Web site for a corporation.
- ✦ **Customer Support Web.** A Web site that includes input forms for customer questions and feedback.
- ✦ **Discussion Web wizard.** A wizard that leads you, step-by-step, through the process of creating a Web site where visitors can post questions and get answers.
- ✦ **Empty Web.** Just a Web site, no pages.
- ✦ **Import Web wizard.** This wizard leads you through the process of assembling a Web from pages created outside of FrontPage.
- ✦ **Personal Web.** A nifty little four-page Web site that works well for sharing your interests.
- ✦ **Project Web.** A very specialized Web site template for project managers.

Some of these templates are quite complex, and require a pretty high level of expertise with FrontPage to customize. These Webs, which include the Corporate Presence Web, the Customer Support Web, the Discussion Web wizard, and the

Project Web, also require a FrontPage Server Extensions-equipped Web site. The Empty Web, One-page Web, and Personal Web, however, all work well without FrontPage Server Extensions on a Web server. We'd advise holding off on the complex Web templates until you've worked your way through this part of the *Office 2000 Bible.*

Cross-Reference For more on FrontPage Server Extensions and FrontPage-friendly Web sites, see the next section in this chapter.

Publishing your FrontPage Web to the Internet or an intranet

If you have access to a Web server, you can publish your FrontPage Web there, and it can be visited by anyone who has access to that server. While FrontPage Webs can be saved or transferred to any server, it is much easier to save them to servers that have a set of files provided by Microsoft called FrontPage Server Extensions.

Finding a server

Where do you find such servers? Server administration and setup is quite a bit beyond the scope of this part of the *Office 2000 Bible.* Web administrators who are working with FrontPage 2000 will find a detailed discussion of server issues and FrontPage Server Extensions in the *FrontPage 2000 Bible.* If your office network is running on Microsoft Windows NT 4.0 or higher, your network administrator can install FrontPage Server Extensions and you can then easily save your FrontPage Web to your local intranet.

Publishing on the Internet

If you want to publish your Web site on the Internet, hundreds of Web site providers are competing to sell you FrontPage-compatible Web server space. The going rates for enough server space for a small business, school, organization, or individuals start as low as $25 per month. Links to these providers are available at http://www.ppinet.com/resource.htm.

When you contract for server space from a Web site provider, or when you get permission from your Internet or intranet provider to publish a FrontPage Web at a server, you'll need the following information:

✦ A URL (Uniform Resource Locator — the address of your Web site).

✦ A user Name that you will use to log on to your site.

✦ A user Password that you will use to gain access privileges to your site.

Make sure you get all three of these elements from your Web site provider.

Publishing Your Site the Easy Way

It is possible to save your FrontPage Web site to Web servers that do not have FrontPage Server Extensions, but it's much more of a hassle than using sites that have FrontPage Server Extensions. In order to publish your site the easy way, you'll need to work with a Web server that has these files installed.

Experienced FrontPage Web administrators will provide you with the three items listed in this chapter (URL, Name, Password) without prompting. But if your Web site provider or server administrator insists on giving you an FTP (File Transfer Protocol) address, or wants to give you information other than that listed above, he or she either is not actually providing you with a FrontPage-compatible Web server, or is unfamiliar with the elements required to establish a FrontPage Web site.

Insist on getting all three of these pieces of information from your Web site provider before you beat your head against a wall trying to log onto FrontPage without the required information.

Establishing a Web on your server

If you have access to a Web server, either on your intranet or the Internet, follow these steps to establish a new FrontPage Web on your server:

1. Start FrontPage 2000.

2. Select File ➪ New ➪ Web from the FrontPage menu.

3. Specify the location of the new Web in the New dialog box, entering the URL for your site, as shown in Figure 42-2.

4. Select one of the Web site templates from the left side of the New dialog box, or select Empty Web to design a web from scratch. We'll explore Web templates in the following section, "Choosing a Web Template."

5. Click the OK button in the New dialog box.

6. After FrontPage connects to your server (which might take a minute), enter the name and password that were given to you by your server administrator. Then click the OK button in the Name and Password required dialog box.

You're in! Once you complete those steps, you've established a Web at your server, and you can begin to construct your Web site in FrontPage 2000.

Note   What if you don't yet have access to a Web server? You can still learn FrontPage, and construct a Web site on your own local drive.

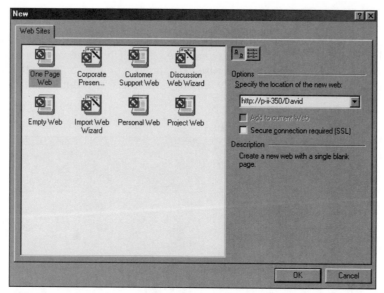

Figure 42-2: New FrontPage Webs on the Internet require a URL address.

Publishing your FrontPage Web to your local drive

You don't need access to a Web server to create FrontPage Webs. You don't even need a modem or a network connection. Of course, nobody will be able to visit your Web site, but you can still learn to design one. And later, when you are ready, you can buy Web space on the Internet and publish your Web there for all the world to see. Follow these steps to create a Web on your local drive:

1. Start FrontPage 2000.

2. Select File ➪ New ➪ Web from the FrontPage menu.

3. Specify the location of the new Web in the New dialog box, entering a folder on your computer (you can create a new folder; for example, C:\webs).

4. Select one of the Web site templates from the left side of the New dialog box, or select Empty Web to design a web from scratch. We'll explore Web templates in the section below, "Choosing a Web Template."

5. Click the OK button in the New dialog box.

That's it! You can now begin to design a Web right on your own computer.

Creating a home page

Once you have created a Web, the first step in designing your Web site is to create a home page. If you used the Personal Web template, or the One-Page Web template, your Web opens up with a home page. Figure 42-3 shows a new Web generated by the One-Page Web template, with a lonely looking home page in the middle of Navigation view.

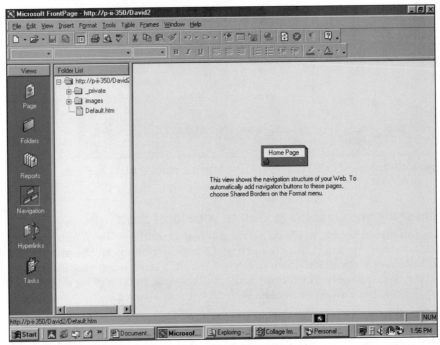

Figure 42-3: A brand-new Web site, ready to be designed.

If you created your new Web from the Empty Web template, you can click the New Page button on the FrontPage toolbar to create a new page. The first page you create will be your home page.

Adding pages to your Web site

You can add Web pages to your Web site in Navigation view by clicking the New Page button on the toolbar. As you click the New Page button, new pages appear as child pages of the selected page.

If you click on one of your child pages, and then click the New Page button, the new pages will become child pages of child pages. You can construct many levels of Web pages. Figure 42-4 shows a Web site with three levels of pages.

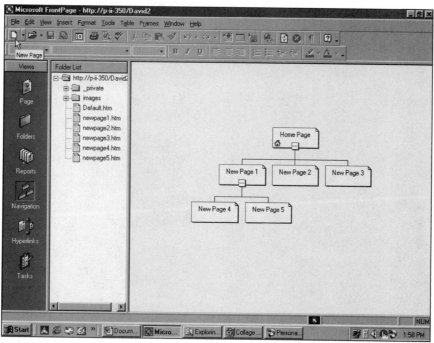

Figure 42-4: The site is growing!

Tip   While designing Web structure is always a process of trial and error, it's helpful to envision your entire Web site as you construct it in Navigation view. What options do you want to provide for visitors as they enter your site? Many site designers recommend providing between three and five options at each page so as to not overwhelm visitors. FrontPage eliminates the drudgery of coding HTML for your Web pages, and allows you to focus on the essential issues, like how to lay out your Web site.

Naming pages in Navigation view

As you generate new pages, they arrive with uninspiring page names, like New Page 6. To rename your pages, right-click on a page and select Rename from the context menu. Type a new name, as shown in Figure 42-5, and press Enter. A quick trick for renaming many pages is to use the Tab key to jump from one to another, which automatically allows you to rename pages.

As you generate new pages in Navigation view, they appear as HTML files in the Folders list on the left side of the Navigation view window. The page names, sometimes called page titles, change when you rename them. But the files retain the boring filenames they were given when FrontPage generated them. This can make it confusing if you need to locate a page in the Navigation flowchart and all you know is its filename. The solution is to right-click on a page in the Folder list, and select Find from the context menu. The page associated with the file will be selected in Navigation view.

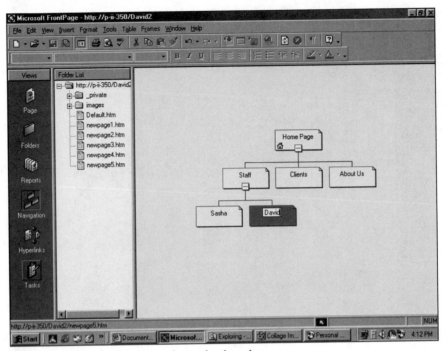

Figure 42-5: Renaming a page in Navigation view.

Defining site flow

Once you have defined your Web structure, you can change it. Simply click and drag on a page in Navigation view to move it to another location or level in the flowchart. Figure 42-6 shows a page being moved.

You can delete pages from your Web by right-clicking on them in Navigation view and selecting Delete from the context menu. If your site is large, you can use the horizontal or vertical scrollbars to move around within it. And you can simplify your view by clicking on the "–" symbol on parent pages to shrink the flowchart, and display only the parent page. To expand the flowchart, click on the + sign under a parent page.

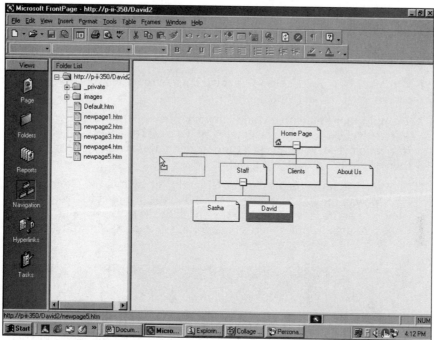

Figure 42-6: You can rearrange pages in Navigation view by clicking and dragging.

Designing Web Site Elements

Once you have designed your site structure, you have created a building without furnishings. You need to add content to the pages you have created. Of course, the main content you need to add is text, graphics, and other elements that make the pages worth visiting. But there are also elements of your Web site that can be added globally. They include themes, which assign a universal color and design scheme to a Web; and shared borders that place navigation links on each page in the Web site.

Selecting and assigning a site theme

Themes are collections of design elements that are assigned to *every* page in a Web site. You can remove a theme from a page, or even use different themes for different pages in a Web site. But generally, the point is to use the same theme throughout a site to give it a distinct and consistent look and feel.

Themes include background colors, font size, style, and color, and graphic elements. They are assigned in the Themes dialog box.

Follow these steps to assign a theme:

1. With your Web open, select Format ➩ Theme from the FrontPage menu. You can do this from any view.

2. To apply your theme to all pages in your site, click the All Pages radio button. Alternatively, if you have selected a single page (or pages) in Folders, Page, or Navigation view, you can click the Selected page(s) radio button to apply the theme to only the selected page(s).

3. Click on one of the themes in the list on the left side of the Themes dialog box. A preview of the theme will be displayed in the Sample of Theme area on the right side of the dialog box. Use the check boxes to experiment with Vivid Colors, Active Graphics, and a Background Picture, as shown in Figure 42-7.

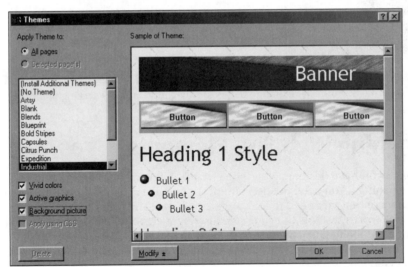

Figure 42-7: Themes provide uniform graphic elements and color schemes for your Web pages.

Note

The Apply Using CSS check box allows those of you who are familiar with Cascading Style Sheets to connect one to your Web site. A full discussion of Cascading Style Sheets in FrontPage is beyond the scope of this book. You can, however, tweak and change the effects of a theme by using the Modify button in the Themes dialog box to access buttons that let you change colors, graphics, or inline styles. You'll learn about these options later in this part of the *Office 2000 Bible*.

4. When you have settled on just the right theme to suit your image, click the OK button to apply the theme to your Web site (or selected pages).

You could sneak a peek at your Web pages now by double-clicking on one in Navigation view to open it in Page view. However, you will appreciate the impact of themes more after you add shared borders in the next section of this chapter.

Adding shared borders

Shared borders are actually separate HTML Web pages that are attached to a border of every page in a Web site. Like themes, shared borders are most effective when applied to every page in a site. Combined with navigation links, shared borders provide a consistent navigational tool in every page of your site.

To apply shared borders to your Web site:

1. Select Format ⇨ Shared Borders from the FrontPage menu (you can be in any view).

2. Select either the All Pages or Selected Pages radio button to apply the shared borders to either only selected pages, or to the entire Web.

3. Top and Left shared borders are the most widely used. Start experimenting by selecting them. Later, you can elect to deselect one or both of these shared borders, and apply bottom or even right shared borders.

Tip

Most Web designers shy away from right-side shared borders. Visitors tend to look up, left, or possibly down for navigational links. And the right side of a Web page is sometimes out of the browser window and requires horizontal scrolling to view.

4. If you select Top and/or Left shared borders, you can select the Include Navigation Buttons check boxes for one or both of these shared borders. To explore the full effect of shared borders, try Top and Left borders with navigation buttons in each, as shown in Figure 42-8.

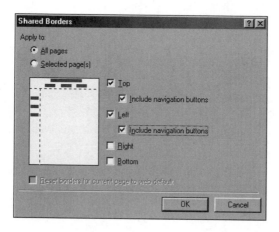

Figure 42-8: Shared borders with navigation buttons provide convenient links throughout your Web site.

5. When you have selected shared borders, click the OK button.

Assessing your site in Page view

By now, you have not only constructed the framework of a Web site, you've furnished it with matching accessories. You're still missing any real content in your site, but at this point it will be fun to explore how your site is shaping up. To view your Web pages in Page view, follow these steps:

1. Double-click on a page in Folders view or Navigation view. The page opens in Page view.

2. One easy way to open other pages in Page view is to return to Navigation view and double-click on them. You can toggle between open pages in Page view by using the Window menu. Your pages don't have any content yet, but they have design elements such as background and text colors and navigational buttons, as shown in Figure 42-9.

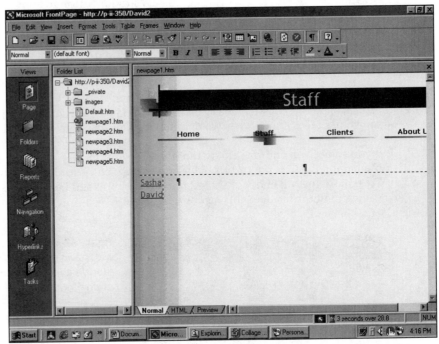

Figure 42-9: Page view illustrates the look and feel of your new Web pages.

3. Page view provides a close approximation of how your page will look when viewed with a Web browser. You can get a somewhat more accurate picture of the page through the eyes of a browser by clicking the Preview tab in Page view.

4. If you're curious about the HTML code that FrontPage generated as you designed your page elements, you can click the HTML tab. There won't be too much HTML code yet, because you haven't added much content to your page. But you can see what HTML code looks like, as shown in Figure 42-10.

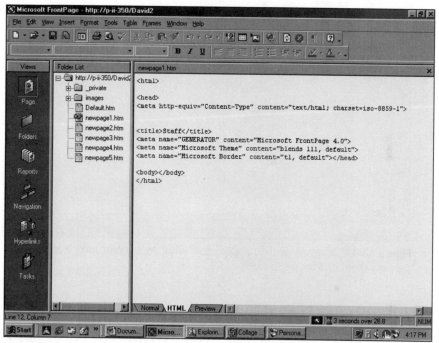

Figure 42-10: A peek behind the curtain — FrontPage-generated code can be viewed in the HTML tab.

5. To get the most accurate picture of how your Web site will look and work, you need to preview your site in a Web browser. If you have a Web browser installed (Internet Explorer comes with FrontPage), click the Preview in Browser button on the Standard toolbar. Here, you can begin to test your Web site. Pretend you are a visitor, and test the navigation links in the shared borders, as shown in Figure 42-11.

Some pages will not have navigation buttons because there are no pages that fit the logic of navigational links assigned by FrontPage. You'll learn to edit these links in Chapter 45, "Managing Your Web Site."

So far, you've created a full-fledged Web site with consistent design elements and navigation links throughout the site. All that's missing is some content!

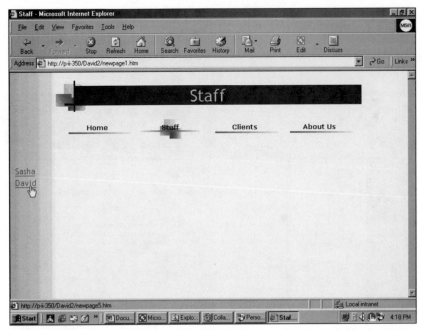

Figure 42-11: The only way to really know what your pages look like is to preview them in a browser.

Adding content to your pages

Start by opening a page in Page view, and just typing text. Before moving on to the next chapter, feel free to experiment by adding some text to your pages.

Cross-Reference Chapter 43, "Designing Web Pages with FrontPage," is devoted to adding, editing, and formatting text in Web pages.

To enter text in Page view, make sure you have selected the Normal tab. You can't edit page content in the Preview tab. Figure 42-12 shows a bit of text being added to a Web page.

Tip As you begin to experiment with adding content to Web pages, avoid for now the shared borders that are separated from the page by dotted lines in Page view. Shared borders can be edited, but the process is more complex and will be explored later in chapter 45, "Managing Your Web Site."

After you enter text on your Web pages, click the Save tool on the toolbar to save your changes. Changes to a Web are saved by saving individual pages (you don't save a Web; you save pages within it to update files).

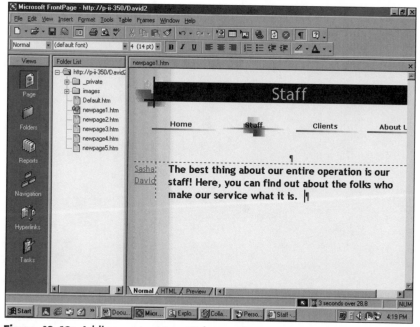

Figure 42-12: Adding content to a Web page is as easy as typing!

Summary

Now that you've created a Web site structure, and begun to add content to pages, you're ready to explore Page view in detail. That's the subject of the next chapter.

✦ You've seen how FrontPage generates not just Web pages, but entire Web sites.

✦ The first step in designing a Web site is to create a FrontPage Web, either on your local drive, or on a Web server.

✦ You can design Web page structure in Navigation view.

✦ Themes provide consistent graphic and design elements for all pages in your Web site.

✦ Shared borders can be assigned to each page in a Web, and can include navigational links to help visitors get around your Web site.

✦ You can view your Web pages in Page view. The Normal tab allows you to edit page content. The HTML tab reveals the HTML code generated by FrontPage, and the Preview tab gives a close approximation of how your page will look in a Web browser.

✦ The most accurate way to see how your Web site will look to visitors is to actually preview it in a Web browser.

✦   ✦   ✦

Designing Web Pages with FrontPage

◆ ◆ ◆ ◆

In This Chapter

Creating new Web
Pages in Page view

Adding and
formatting text

Using tables as
layout tools

Adding graphic
images

◆ ◆ ◆ ◆

In the previous chapter, you learned to design Web sites
using FrontPage's Navigation view, as well as global Web
components such as themes and navigation bars. In this chapter, you'll learn to add text and graphical content to your Web
page, and to edit and format Web page content.

Creating Web Pages in Page View

In the previous chapter, you learned that it is easy to generate
new Web pages in FrontPage's Navigation view. While Navigation
view is a great place to organize your Web site, and assign global
features such as themes and navigation bars, you can't edit the
content of particular Web pages in Navigation view.

Page view is where you will spend most of your FrontPage time.
It is in Page view that you add, edit, and format the actual content of your Web pages. You can also create new pages directly
in Page view. These pages will not be automatically linked to
your Web site, and won't have navigation bars included.

Web sites and Web pages

In the last chapter, you learned to design not just a single Web
page but a Web *site*, with a coherent flow between pages. We
thought it important to start with this approach for the following reasons:

 ✦ Coherently linked Web pages make it easier for visitors
   to navigate your online material.

 ✦ Breaking your material into bite-sized Web pages makes
   it faster to download into your visitor's Web browser.

With that said, there are times when all you need is a single Web page. For example, you may be creating a Web page that will be plugged into another Web site that someone else is designing. Even if your Web site consists of just a single Web page, you should still start by creating a FrontPage Web site, as you learned to do in the last chapter. That way, you can include the more sophisticated features of FrontPage, which are covered in the following chapter. And, on an even more basic level, you can rely on FrontPage to organize all your graphics and other embedded files, making it easier to transfer those files from one Web site to another.

Note   If you really know how to manage Web site files, you can override FrontPage's logic, skip the step of creating a Web site, and just design a page by going right to Page view and designing your page.

Exploring Page view

You can open an existing Web page in Page view by double-clicking on it in any other view, including Navigation view. When you do, you'll see your page open in Page view. If you assigned a theme, shared borders, or navigation links to your Web page, you'll see those elements in Page view, as shown in Figure 43-1.

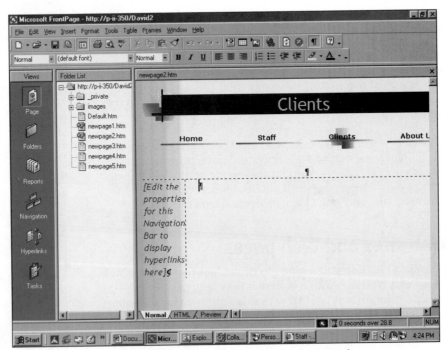

Figure 43-1: Page view is where you edit the content of your Web pages.

The Standard and Formatting toolbars at the top of the Page view window will look somewhat familiar to you. Many tools (New Page, Copy, Cut, Paste, and others) have the same function as they do in other Office 2000 applications. And as in other Office 2000 applications, these toolbars are detachable, and can be moved off the top of the window by clicking and dragging on the toolbar, but not on a button. Detached toolbars can be re-anchored at the top of the window by dragging them back to the top of the screen.

Note

You can experiment with the buttons described in the following sections to apply formatting to your Web page text. If you've wrestled with HTML coding to apply formatting, you'll be pleasantly surprised by the control you have with WYSIWYG (what you see is what you get) formatting in Page view. If you haven't formatted Web page text before, you'll note that not as many formatting options are available in HTML (Web pages) as are available in other applications for printing.

The Standard toolbar

While the Standard toolbar (see Figure 43-2) includes some buttons you already know from other Office 2000 applications, many are unique to FrontPage.

Cross-Reference

We'll explain what each tool does, and return to many of them in more detail, later in this chapter.

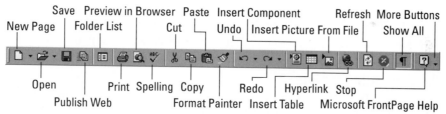

Figure 43-2: Page view's Standard toolbar will look pretty familiar to Office 2000 users.

✦ **New Page.** Creates a new Web page with themes and shared borders, but is otherwise blank.

✦ **Open.** Opens existing Web pages.

✦ **Save.** Saves your Web page.

✦ **Publish Web.** Publishes your Web site from your local computer to an intranet or Internet location.

✦ **Folder List.** Displays (or hides) a list of folders and files associated with your Web site.

✦ **Print.** Prints your Web pages to your printer.

✦ **Preview in Browser.** Displays your Web page in your default Web browser.

✦ **Spelling.** Checks spelling for your Web page.

✦ **Cut.** Cuts selected text or objects and saves them to the Clipboard.

✦ **Copy.** Copies selected text or objects and saves them to the Clipboard.

✦ **Paste.** Pastes contents of the Clipboard at the insertion point.

✦ **Format Painter.** Copies a selected format and displays the (paintbrush) format pointer that can be used to apply that format to other text or objects.

✦ **Undo.** Undoes your last command or keystroke.

✦ **Redo.** Cancels your last undo.

✦ **Insert Component.** Opens the Insert Component submenu.

✦ **Insert Table.** Opens the Insert Table grid.

✦ **Insert Picture From File.** Opens the Picture dialog box.

✦ **Hyperlink.** Allows you to insert or edit a link to another Web page or a location on a Web page.

✦ **Refresh.** Reloads your Web page and displays the currently saved version.

✦ **Stop.** Stops refreshing a page.

✦ **Show All.** Shows paragraph and line breaks.

✦ **Microsoft FrontPage Help.** Displays FrontPage online help.

✦ **More Buttons.** Allows you to customize the Standard toolbar.

The Formatting toolbar

Most of your Web page text formatting is controlled from the Formatting toolbar in Page view. You can see the Formatting toolbar in Figure 43-3.

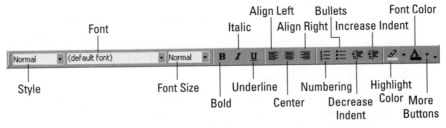

Figure 43-3: Page view's Formatting toolbar acts a bit differently than it does in Word.

The Formatting toolbar in Page view is similar to the Formatting toolbars you've seen in other Office 2000 applications. But here, again, there are some subtle twists and differences, so we'll review these tools as well.

✦ **Style.** The styles in the list are HTML styles, not customizable in the way styles are in Word. You can assign formatting without worrying about what HTML tag is used for the style.

✦ **Font.** This drop-down list assigns fonts to selected text.

✦ **Font Size.** This drop-down list assigns font size to selected text. The limited selection of sizes reflects the limitations of HTML.

✦ **Bold.** Assigns boldface to selected text.

✦ **Italic.** Assigns italics to selected text.

✦ **Underline.** Underlines selected text.

✦ **Align Left.** Left-aligns selected paragraph(s).

✦ **Center.** Centers selected paragraph(s).

✦ **Align Right.** Right-aligns selected paragraph(s). HTML does not support full justification.

✦ **Numbering.** Assigns sequential numbering to selected paragraphs.

✦ **Bullets.** Assigns indenting and bullets to selected paragraphs.

✦ **Decrease Indent.** Move selected paragraphs to the left (undoes indenting).

✦ **Increase Indent.** Indents entire selected paragraph(s).

✦ **Highlight Color.** Adds a background highlight to selected text.

✦ **Font Color.** Assigns colors to selected text.

✦ **More Buttons.** Allows you to customize the Formatting toolbar.

Assigning font attributes

Just as you can in Word (or PowerPoint), you can assign font attributes to selected fonts using the Formatting toolbar. For example, you can select a color to assign to text by clicking on the down arrow next to the Font Color button. This opens the (detachable) Font Color palette, shown in Figure 43-4.

After you assign a color to the Font Color button, you can assign that color to selected text by simply clicking on the button. You can also assign default font colors for a page. You'll learn to do that in the next section, "Defining Page Properties."

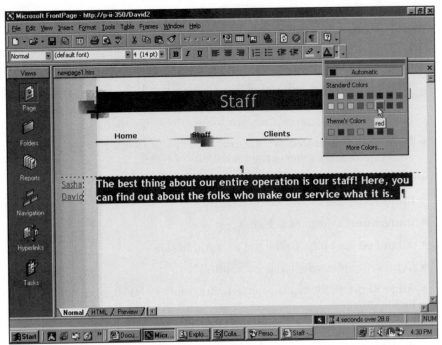

Figure 43-4: The detachable Font Color palette lets you choose a color to assign to text.

Defining page properties

Page properties include background and default font colors, margins, page titles, and other attributes that apply to an entire Web page. These attributes are available in the Page Properties dialog box.

Dealing with themes

Because themes define some page properties, if you have a theme assigned to a Web page, you won't be able to control all page properties. At least when you first explore the available page formatting features, it might be helpful to remove themes from your Web page. To do that, right-click anywhere in a Web page in Page view, and select Theme from the context menu. Choose the Selected Page(s) radio button and then select (No Theme) from the list of themes on the left side of the Themes dialog box, as shown in Figure 43-5. Then click the OK button in the Themes dialog box.

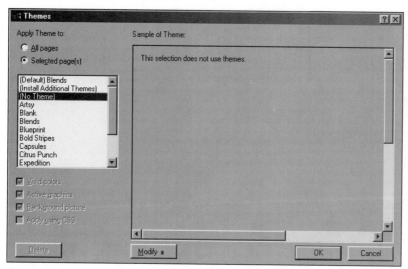

Figure 43-5: You can remove a theme from a selected page.

Once you have removed your theme, you can apply all the properties in the Page Properties dialog box. They are divided into six different tabs, but the page properties associated with page appearance are in the General, Background, and Margins tabs. We'll investigate those tabs in detail here, and briefly look at the other tabs with more esoteric page property options. You can access the Page Properties dialog box by right-clicking anywhere in an open page in Page view, and selecting Page Properties from the context menu.

The General tab

The main features of your Web page that are defined in the General tab of the Page Properties dialog box (see Figure 43-6) are page title and background sound. The page title displays in the title bar of a visitor's Web browser. Your Web page may be called index.htm or default.htm (these filenames designate home pages that typically open first when a visitor comes to your Web site), or your page filename may be something like newpage4.htm. No matter, you can create a title like David's Web Site, and that page title will display when visitors come to your Web page.

Your FrontPage Web page can also have a sound file associated with it. The sound will play when your page is opened in a browser.

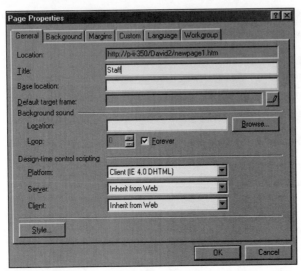

Figure 43-6: Add a page title and background sound in the General tab.

The key features of the General tab are as follows:

+ **Title.** Here you can enter a page title, like Home Page or any other text, that will display in the title bar of visitors' browsers.

+ **Background Sound Location.** Use the Browse button to locate sound files on your system that will play when the page is opened. WAV format sound files are the most widely recognized by browsers.

+ **Background Sound Loop.** The Loop spin box defines how many times the sound will play. The Forever check box plays a background sound over and over, as long as the page is open.

Other features of the General tab are used for complex linking involving frames. Base Location allows you to define a starting point in your Web hierarchy. The location field designates the location of the page on your local computer or Web site. This field is always grayed out. The fields in the Design-time control scripting area are for programmers.

The Style button at the bottom of the General tab opens the Modify Style dialog box. Here you can use the Format button to define font, paragraph, numbering, and border defaults for your page.

The Background tab

The Background tab, shown in Figure 43-7, is available in the Page Properties dialog box if you do *not* have a theme assigned to your page. If you have a theme assigned, the theme color scheme overrides the Page Properties dialog box settings, so you can't assign colors here until you remove the theme.

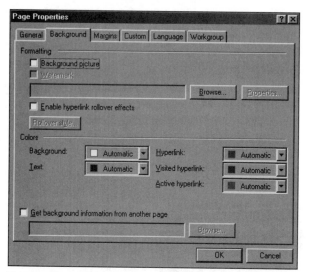

Figure 43-7: Assign background color and default text colors in the Background tab.

The Background tab lets you define both the page background and default text colors. It's handy to define the two at the same time. For example, if you create a dark blue page background, you'll probably want to change your default text color to white, yellow, or another bright, light color that can be read against a dark background.

The Background tab has the following options:

✦ **Background picture check box.** This allows you to define a graphic image to tile in the background of your Web page. Tiled images repeat horizontally and vertically as necessary to fill all the space behind your Web page.

✦ **Browse button.** You can locate a background image on your local computer or Web site by using the Browse button and navigating to the image file.

✦ **Watermark check box.** This freezes the background image on the browser screen so that as visitors scroll up and down your Web page, the background image stays in the same place.

✦ **Background drop-down list.** This allows you to select a color from a color palette to assign to your Web page background. Background images override background colors, so if you want the selected background color to work, deselect the Background picture check box.

✦ **Text drop-down list.** This opens a color palette from which you can assign a default text color for your page.

✦ **Get Background information from another Page check box.** This allows you to link the current page to another page's background and colors. For example, you can use the Browse button here to select the home page for your Web site as a source of background and color for your page. Then, when you make changes to colors and background at your home page, the current page will change as well.

✦ **Hyperlink drop-down boxes.** These allow you to define colors for links on your page.

The Margins tab

The Margins tab has two check boxes and two spin boxes, as shown in Figure 43-8. The Specify Top Margin check box allows you to define an area at the top of the page that will be clear (except for any page background).

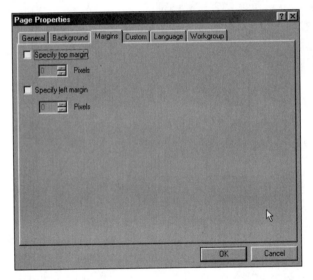

Figure 43-8: Margins are a page design tool that create space to the top or left of your Web page objects.

The Specify Left Margin check box allows you to define a left margin. Both spin boxes are used to set the margin size in pixels. Figure 43-9 shows a Web page in a browser with a defined 72-pixel left margin, a dark page background color, and light text and hyperlink colors.

The other page properties tabs

The Custom and Workgroup tabs are for programmers, or for teams working together to design Web pages. These features are covered in advanced-level books devoted to FrontPage 2000, but are not really essential for designing Web sites. The Language tab allows you to set page defaults for Albanian, Zulu, and dozens of other languages.

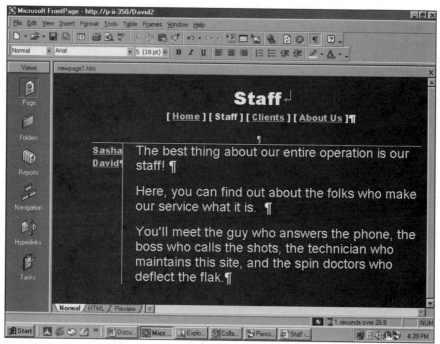

Figure 43-9: Background colors, default text, and margins are all defined page properties.

Adding and Formatting Text

The basic text editing and formatting tools you learned to use in Word are available in FrontPage 2000. You no doubt figured that out already. Type, cut, paste, or click the Spelling button to check your spelling. Click the Bold button on the Formatting toolbar to assign boldface to selected text.

One thing you might not have expected is how easy it is to take text, graphics, and even tables from other Office applications. In this section, you'll learn to do that.

Getting text without typing

You can copy text from Word (or Excel, Access, and PowerPoint for that matter) right into FrontPage's Page view. Simply select the text in another Office application and click the Copy button in that application's toolbar to save the text to the Clipboard. Then, open or switch to FrontPage's Page view and paste the text at the cursor insertion point.

Much, but not necessarily all, of your formatting will be saved when you paste text. You may be using formatting in your other application that's not available in HTML pages. But FrontPage will do its best to keep your font type, size, color, and attributes when you paste in text from other applications.

Editing text

The editing tools at your disposal in Page view include the following:

✦ **Edit ➪ Find and Edit ➪ Replace** lets you find and/or replace text in Page view. Can you Find and Replace globally, for an entire Web site? Yes, you can — just select the All Pages radio button in the Replace dialog box, as shown in Figure 43-10.

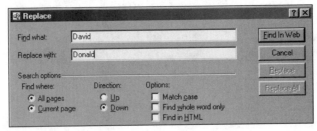

Figure 43-10: You can replace within one page or throughout an entire Web site.

✦ **The Spelling tool in the Standard toolbar** allows you to check spelling for the open page in Page view. Want to spell-check your entire document? This too can be done. Click the Spelling tool while in any view except Page view, and you get the option of selecting the Entire Web radio button, as shown in Figure 43-11. The Add a Task for Each Page with Misspellings check box creates a link in Tasks view to each page that needs fixing.

Figure 43-11: You can spell-check your whole Web site at once.

Formatting text

All the formatting tools in FrontPage Page view work in ways very similar to how they work in other Office applications. As mentioned earlier, the main difference is that different options are available when you are creating Web pages in FrontPage than when you are creating documents to print in other applications. Following are some general guidelines:

✦ **Font sizes.** When you select font sizes from the Font Size drop-down list, you'll notice a rather limited selection. This is because as yet, Web browsers like Netscape Navigator and Internet Explorer don't interpret many font sizes.

✦ **Font colors.** On the plus side, you can assign font colors with the Font Color button and every browser will interpret those colors, so long as you stick with the basic colors available on the font color palette. First select the text. Then choose a font color from the palette that appears when you click on the down arrow next to the Font Color button, as shown in Figure 43-12.

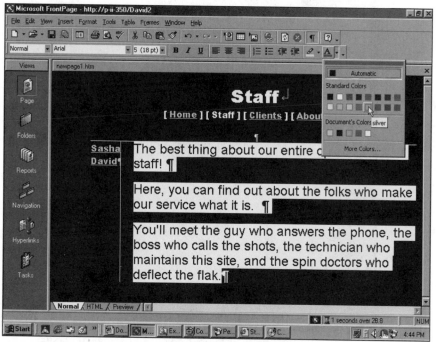

Figure 43-12: Assigning color to Web page text is easy.

Formatting paragraphs

The following list details the general capabilities and restrictions you'll encounter when formatting paragraphs with FrontPage:

✦ **Indenting.** FrontPage lets you indent selected paragraphs using the Increase Indent tool.

✦ **Alignment.** You can also left-align, center, and right-align paragraphs using the toolbar buttons (but you can't justify text margin to margin).

✦ **Numbered and bulleted lists.** Automatic numbering or bullets are assigned by selecting text and clicking either the Numbering or Bullets button. If you are adding to a numbered or bulleted list, each time you press Enter, you create a new bulleted or numbered item, as shown in Figure 43-13. Remove bullet or numbering formatting from a selected paragraph by clicking the respective button again on the Formatting toolbar.

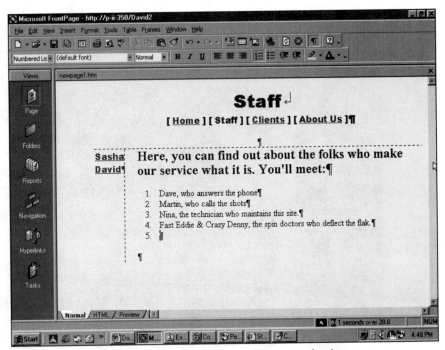

Figure 43-13: Numbering just keeps going, and going, and going.

✦ **Spacing.** There is no reliable way to control spacing between paragraphs. By default, most paragraphs have a line of spacing between them. You can create line breaks without vertical spacing by holding down the Shift key and pressing Enter to create a forced line break.

While not all browsers will recognize the additional formatting features available in the Paragraph dialog box, you can apply them, and visitors using IE 4 and higher will see these formatting effects. Right-click on selected paragraphs, and choose Paragraph from the context menu. The Paragraph dialog box, shown in Figure 43-14, allows you some control over line and paragraph spacing. The Preview area of the dialog box demonstrates the effect of the formatting you apply, assuming that your page is viewed by a visitor with a browser version current enough to recognize these formatting features.

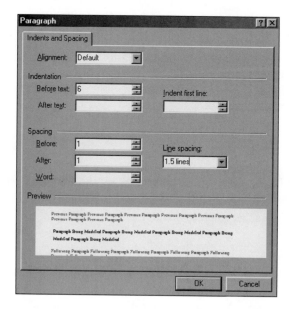

Figure 43-14: Options available in the Paragraph dialog box may or may not be viewable by your visitors' browsers.

Using Tables As Layout Tools

Tables serve two purposes in Web page layout. You can create Excel or Word-type tables to display information in rows and columns. Or, you can use tables to lay out text in newspaper style columns.

In either case, the easiest way to create a table is to click the Insert Table tool on the Standard toolbar and click and drag in the Table grid to define the number of rows and columns in your table. In Figure 43-15, we've created a four-row by three-column table. Here's how it works:

✦ **Adding text.** You can add text to a table by clicking in a cell and typing.

✦ **Inserting objects.** You can also insert any other object (such as a graphic image) into a table cell. You can apply the same editing and formatting techniques to table text as you do to text outside a table.

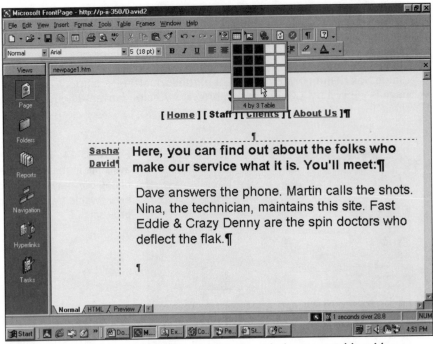

Figure 43-15: You can design tables graphically with the Insert Table grid.

✦ **Selecting rows or columns.** You can select a row or column of a table by clicking in a cell, and then choosing Table ➪ Select ➪ Column or Table ➪ Select ➪ Row from the menu.

✦ **Deleting cells, rows, or columns.** You can delete selected cells (or rows or columns) by choosing Delete Cells from the Table menu.

Once you create a table, right-click in the table and select either Table Properties or Cell Properties from the context menu.

✦ **Formatting cell properties.** If you want to format the properties of specific cells, make sure you have the cell(s) to which you want the properties applied selected when you choose Cell Properties.

✦ **Formatting table properties.** Table properties include table alignment, border size (if any), table size, and cell spacing. Cell properties include alignment, size, and background and border colors.

Defining table properties

Formatting assigned in the Table Properties dialog box applies to all cells in the table, and governs the overall appearance of the table. Right-click anywhere in a table, and choose Table Properties from the context menu to open the Table Properties dialog box, shown in Figure 43-16.

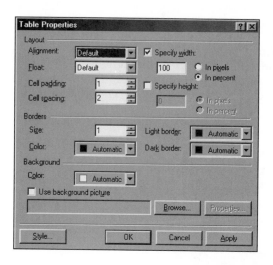

Figure 43-16: Define global table formatting in the Table Properties dialog box.

✦ **Alignment** defines where the table is located. Left alignment aligns the table to the left; right to the right; and center aligns the table in the center.

✦ **Float** lets you wrap text next to the table.

✦ **Size** (in the Borders area) sets the width of the outline placed around the table. A setting of 0 means that no border is displayed in a browser.

✦ **Cell Padding** specifies the space, in pixels, between the contents of a cell and the border.

✦ **Cell Spacing** defines the spacing between cells.

✦ **Specify width and Specify height** sets overall height and width of a table. The height and width can be set in either pixels or as a percentage of the browser window. If the Specify Width check box is not checked, the table will adjust its width depending on its content. If the Specify Height check box is not checked, the table will be whatever minimum height is required to display everything in your cells.

✦ **Color and Use background picture** (in the Background area) define the background color (or image) for your entire table, much as you learned to assign a background to an entire page. Click the Use Background Picture check box and use the Browse button to locate an image to tile as the background for the table, or choose a background color from the Color drop-down list.

✦ **The Borders area** lets you assign colors to the table's border. There are three settings: Color, Light Border, and Dark Border. The Color setting lets you set a single color for the entire border. The Light Border and Dark Border settings allow you to specify colors for the top-and-left and bottom-and-right edges of the border, respectively. This can help you give your table a 3-D look. Setting either of these overrides the Color setting for its respective area.

✦ **The Style button** in the Table Properties dialog box opens the Modify Style dialog box. Use the Format button in the Modify Style dialog box to assign default font, paragraph, border, or numbering styles to your table.

Defining cell properties

The Cell Properties dialog box, shown in Figure 43-17, provides quick access to all of the formatting options available to individual cells within the table. To open this dialog box, select the cells to which you want to apply attributes, and then select Table ➪ Properties ➪ Cell, or right-click within the selected cells and select Cell Properties from the pop-up menu.

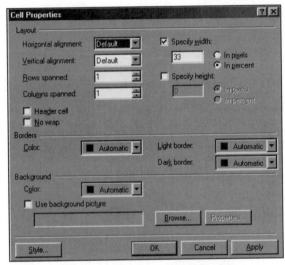

Figure 43-17: The Cell Properties dialog box.

✦ **Horizontal Alignment** defines where the text or graphic is placed horizontally within the cell. The options are default, left, right, center, and justify.

✦ **Vertical Alignment** determines where the text or graphic is placed vertically within the cell. The options are default, top, middle, baseline, and bottom. Baseline makes the bottom of all letters in the cell line up, no matter what the size. The default setting is middle, but you may find you usually want to select top alignment for cell text.

✦ **Header Cell** formats the cell as a table header that appears in bold by default.

✦ **No Wrap** forces text to remain on one line.

✦ **Specify width and Specify height** set the width and height for the cell. Note that the greatest width setting in a column applies to all cells in that column, and the greatest height setting in a row applies to all cells in that row.

✦ **Columns spanned** specifies the number of columns spanned by a cell.

✦ **Rows spanned** specifies the number of rows spanned by a cell.

✦ **The Background area** lets you assign colors or images to the background of selected cells.

✦ **Border colors** set the colors for the border of an individual cell, rather than the table as a whole. Light Border refers to the bottom and right edges of the cell, and Dark Border refers to the top and left edges of the cell; this is the opposite of their positions for the table's outline. If the table border is set to 0 width, these settings have no effect.

Converting tables to text and text to tables

You can easily convert a table into text. You won't lose any of the objects (text, graphics, etc.) in the table. Those objects become normal page objects, laid out in paragraphs. To convert a table to text, click anywhere in the table and select Table ⇨ Convert ⇨ Table to Text.

Using tables for columns

Because HTML does not yet support multicolumn layout for Web pages, the workaround used by most Web designers is a table. You don't get nice desktop publishing features like autoflow between columns. But if you are willing to manually cut and paste your text into two columns, you can create two- or three-column layouts using one-row tables, like the one in Figure 43-18. You'll learn how to add images in the next section of this chapter.

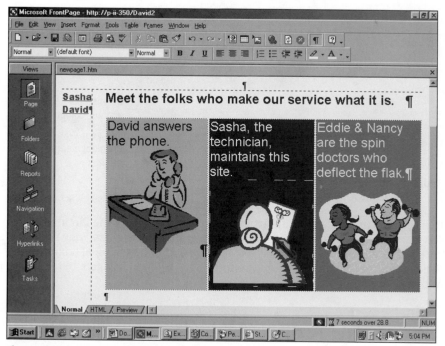

Figure 43-18: Using cells for column layout.

Adding Graphic Images

Perhaps you've heard a bit, or quite a bit about Web-compatible graphics. Or perhaps you've heard nothing about Web graphics. In either case, you'll like the way FrontPage handles graphic images.

The easiest way to get graphics into your Web page is to either insert them as files, or copy them in through the Clipboard. Once you copy or insert a graphic of *any* file format, FrontPage will handle the process of saving that image as a Web-compatible GIF, PNG or JPEG (also know as JPG) file.

Inserting graphic files

Insert a graphic image file by placing your insertion point and clicking the Insert Picture From File button on the Standard toolbar. The Picture dialog box appears, as shown in Figure 43-19.

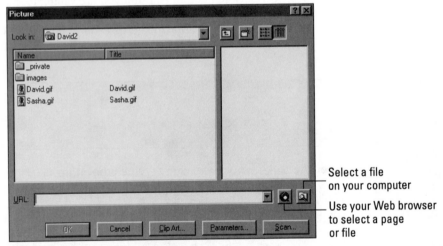

Select a file on your computer

Use your Web browser to select a page or file

Figure 43-19: The Picture dialog box.

To insert clip art, click the Clip Art button on the bottom of the Picture dialog box. You can search the Web for a graphic image by clicking the Use Your Web Browser to Select a Page or File button, or you can find a file on your local computer by clicking the Select a File on Your Computer button. Then navigate to the file on the Web or your computer.

Once an image is already saved to your Web, it will appear in a list of graphics in the Picture dialog box, and you can insert it again by double-clicking on the image file in the list.

Copying a graphic

You can copy a graphic image by creating or opening it (or a file that contains it) in any application. Copy the graphic to the Clipboard, and then paste it into a Web page open in Page view.

Saving graphics

When you save your Web page, FrontPage will convert all the graphics on your page to Web-compatible formats, and prompt you to save these embedded files. The Save Embedded Files dialog box will appear, as shown in Figure 43-20.

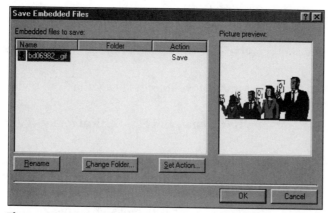

Figure 43-20: FrontPage prompts you to save all graphics on your page.

Editing pictures in FrontPage

When you select an image in Page view, the Picture toolbar appears at the bottom of the window. The tools on the Picture toolbar give you quite a bit of power to tweak the appearance of your graphic image right in FrontPage. For more serious graphic editing, you'll need an image editor like Microsoft PhotoDraw. Figure 43-21 shows the tools on the Picture toolbar.

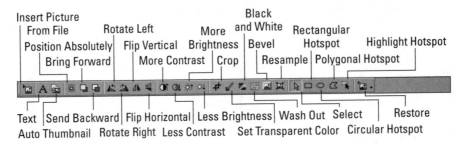

Figure 43-21: Edit pictures right in FrontPage with Picture tools.

The picture tools let you add images and text to, and change the appearance of, a picture.

✦ **The Insert Picture From File button** lets you insert a new image.

✦ **The Text button** adds text to your image.

✦ **Auto Thumbnail** generates a small version of your image.

✦ **Position Absolutely** allows you to lock the position of your image to any spot on your page.

✦ **Bring Forward and Send Backward** move selected images in front of or behind other objects on the page.

✦ **Rotate Left, Rotate Right, Flip Horizontal, and Flip Vertical** rotate or flip your selected image.

✦ **More Contrast, Less Contrast, More Brightness, and Less Brightness** work like the contrast and brightness dials on your monitor or TV to change the brightness and contrast of your image.

✦ **Crop** creates a marquee around your image with movable corner and side handles. Click and drag on these handles to crop your picture, and then click the Crop button again to finalize your cut.

✦ **Set Transparent Color** displays an Eraser tool. Point and click at any one color in your image to make that color disappear, allowing the page background to show through.

✦ **Black and White** converts images from color to black-and-white.

✦ **Wash Out** applies a watercolor-like effect to images.

✦ **Bevel** adds a 3-D frame around an image, suitable for navigation buttons.

✦ **Resample** saves your image as a smaller file if you've reduced the size of your image on the page.

✦ **Select** deselects other tools and displays the arrow pointer.

✦ **Rectangular Hotspot, Circular Hotspot, and Polygonal Hotspot** create clickable links called *image maps*.

Image maps are discussed in Chapter 44, "Adding Advanced Elements to Web Pages."

✦ **Highlight Hotspots** helps identify hotspots.

✦ **Restore** undoes changes to your picture, as long as you haven't saved the changes.

Changing image properties

Earlier, we promised that if you *did* know about different Web-compatible graphics formats, you would like how FrontPage handles images. Up to now, we've relied on FrontPage to save images and assign a format. But you can choose from the three widely recognized Web graphics formats (GIF, JPEG, or PNG). And you can assign other graphic properties to your pictures.

Assigning attributes to Web graphics can get quite complex, but the basic picture tools and image properties you'll find in this chapter will give you the control you need to insert and format very nice graphic images on your Web pages.

The General tab

To define image properties, right-click on a picture and select Picture Properties from the context menu. The General tab of the Picture Properties dialog box includes options to set the following image options:

✦ **Picture Source** is the filename for the picture.

✦ **The Type radio buttons** (in the Type area) let you manually select a file type. Note that only the GIF file format allows you to apply transparency to an image. The GIF format allows for interlacing as well, which causes an image to fade in to a browser window.

✦ **The Text field** is the other widely used feature in the General tab, which allows you to define the text that will display either a) when a visitor has graphics turned off in his or her browser; or b) when a visitor points at a graphic. Figure 43-22 shows alternative text being defined for an image.

The alternative text you define acts as kind of a caption for visitors who point at a picture when they visit your Web site, as shown in Figure 43-23.

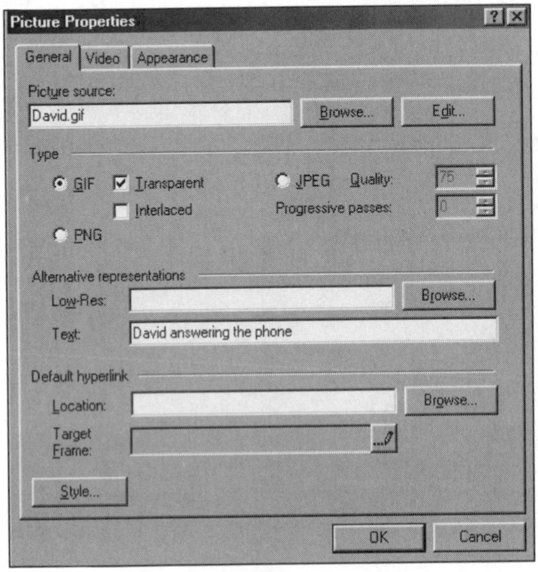

Figure 43-22: Defining alternative text.

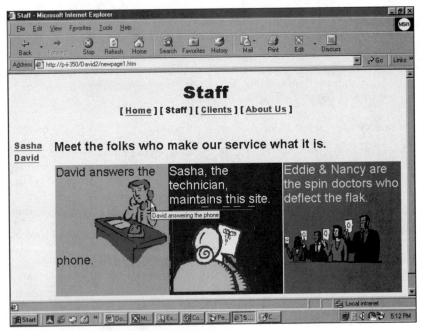

Figure 43-23: Viewing alternative text.

The Appearance tab

Other formatting features are available in the Appearance tab of the Picture Properties dialog box, but you can do most of these things right in Page view. You can click and drag on the handles around a picture to resize it, as shown in Figure 43-24. You can also use the Align Left, Center, and Align Right buttons to align a selected picture. Aligning a picture allows text to flow around the image.

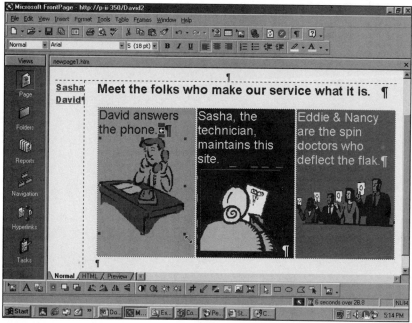

Figure 43-24: Resizing a left-aligned picture.

Summary

In this chapter, you learned some of the ways you can format your Web pages in FrontPage:

✦ Assigning page formatting, such as background colors, default text color, and page margins

✦ Formatting Web page text with font type, font color, font size, and paragraph attributes such as alignment and spacing

✦ Using tables as layout tools for grids, as well as laying out text in columns

✦ Inserting and editing graphic images

✦   ✦   ✦

Adding Interactive Elements to Web Pages

FrontPage includes built-in features that allow you to include interactive elements in your Web pages. Interactive elements respond to visitors. For example, a hyperlink responds by jumping the visitor to another place in your Web site, or to another Web site. Search boxes respond by helping a visitor find information he or she is looking for. And hit counters change each time your page is visited.

Hyperlinks and Image Maps

Hyperlinks (or links, for short) are text or graphic images on your Web pages that provide links to something else. Here are some general guidelines:

- ✦ **Other Web pages.** Hyperlinks usually lead to another Web page, either in your own Web site or another site in your intranet or on the World Wide Web.

- ✦ **Within a Web page.** Hyperlinks can also be used to navigate within a Web page. You can define bookmarks on your Web page to allow visitors to jump around within a single page.

✦ **Hyperlink formatting.** Earlier versions of Web brow-sers relied on underlined, blue text to identify which text served as a hyperlink. Some Web designers still like to stick to underlined, blue text to tell visitors that text functions as a hyperlink. However, modern brow-sers respond to hyperlinks by displaying a finger when a visitor moves his or her cursor over the link. Therefore, you can pretty safely get away with more creative formatting for hyperlinked text.

Cross-Reference

In Chapter 43, "Designing Web Pages with FrontPage," you learned to define default colors for hyperlinks as part of defining page properties.

✦ **Images as links.** Images can serve as links in two ways. An entire picture can be defined as a link. Or, parts of a picture can be defined as hyperlinks. This second type of image link is called an *image map,* and is often used as a navigation tool for a Web site. Figure 44-1 shows a cursor responding to a section of an image map.

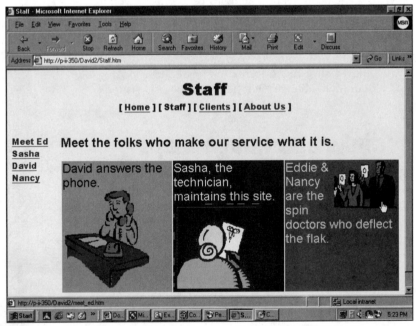

Figure 44-1: Image maps allow visitors to follow links by clicking on sections of a picture.

Creating hyperlinks to Web sites or e-mail addresses

The easiest way to create a link in Page view is to simply type a Web address or an e-mail address. For example, if we type **Email me at dkarlins@aol.com** in a Web page and then press Enter or the space bar, FrontPage automatically turns that text into a link to our e-mail address, as shown in Figure 44-2.

When visitors click on this link, their e-mail program will launch automatically, and the e-mail address in the link will be placed in the To field of a new e-mail message.

In the same way, you can create a link to another Web site by typing the URL for that site. Most browsers don't require the http:// preface anymore, so you can just type an address like **www.ppinet.com**, and as soon as you press the spacebar or Return, your text will be converted into a link, like the one shown in Figure 44-3.

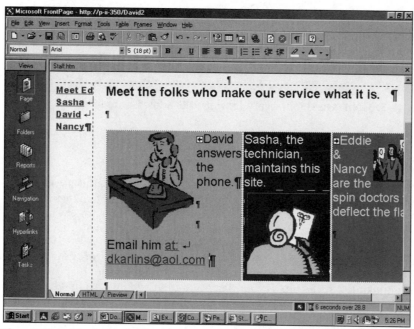

Figure 44-2: Type an e-mail address and it automatically becomes a link.

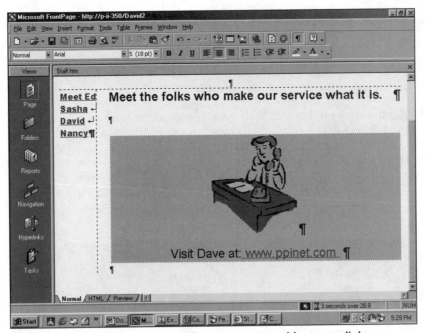

Figure 44-3: FrontPage automatically converts URL addresses to links.

Creating bookmarks

The target of a link can be a Web page (or an e-mail address). But it can also be a set location on a Web page. These spots on a page are called *bookmarks*. You can define bookmarks on long Web pages to make it easier for visitors to move around them without having to use the vertical scrollbar to look for material on the page.

One frequently useful design technique is to include one or more Top links on your page that allow a visitor to jump to the top of your page. To do this, you have to first define a bookmark at the top of your page, and then add links to that bookmark in your Web page. To create a top bookmark, and links to it, follow these steps:

1. Click at the top of your Web page and select Insert ⇨ Bookmark from the menu.

2. If you have text selected, that text will be the default bookmark name. If you don't, you can type a bookmark name, as shown in Figure 44-4.

3. Click OK in the Bookmark dialog box. The new bookmark is displayed as a small blue flag, or, if the bookmark is assigned to selected text, that text will be underlined with a dotted line, as shown in Figure 44-5.

Figure 44-4: Defining a bookmark.

With bookmarks defined, you can create links to them from other locations on your page. You'll learn to do that in the next section.

Bookmarks   Bookmarked text

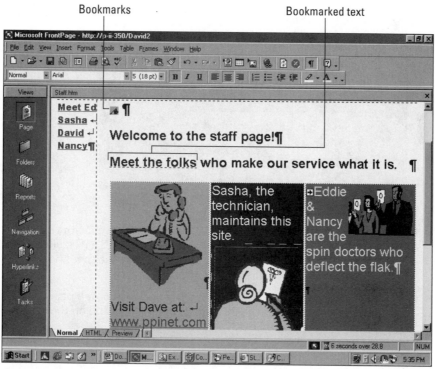

Figure 44-5: Bookmarks can lead to text or a blank spot on your Web page.

Assigning links to text

You don't have to type an URL or e-mail address to create text links. You can make any text on your page a link to any location in your Web page or the Web. So, for example, you can type **Click here to learn more about our company**, and then make that text a link to any Web site or location in a Web page. Here's how to assign a link to text:

1. Click and drag to select the text to which you will assign a link.

2. Click the Hyperlink button on the Standard toolbar. The Create Hyperlink dialog box opens, as shown in Figure 44-6.

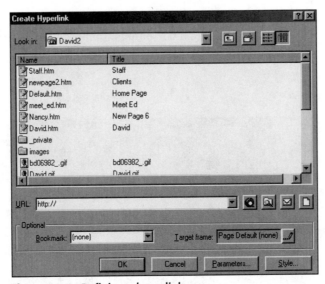

Figure 44-6: Defining a hyperlink.

3. Define the target for the hyperlink by clicking on a page in your Web site in the list at the top of the dialog box, or by typing an URL (Web site address) in the URL field. If you want to link to a bookmark, choose that bookmark from the Bookmark drop-down list as shown in Figure 44-7.

4. Click OK in the Create Hyperlink dialog box. Save your Web page, and test your new links by clicking the Preview in Browser button on the Standard toolbar and following the links.

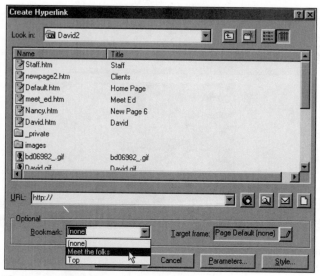

Figure 44-7: Linking to a bookmark.

Assigning links to pictures

Assigning links to pictures works just like assigning links to text, except that you select the picture, not text, before clicking the Hyperlink button and defining a target for your hyperlink.

When visitors point at a linked image, a finger appears telling them that it is a link, as shown in Figure 44-8.

You can make graphic links even more intuitive by right-clicking on an image, choosing Picture Properties from the context menu, and entering alternative text that can serve as a helpful hint when visitors point at a linked graphic.

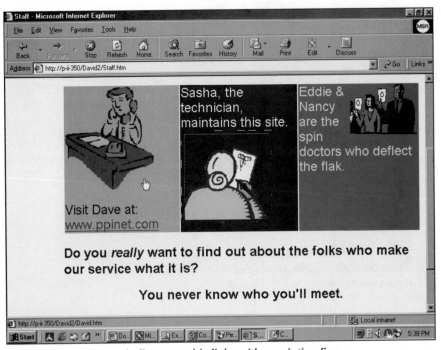

Figure 44-8: Browsers indicate graphic links with a pointing finger.

Creating image maps

Image maps divide sections of a graphic image into different links. So, for example, you could post a picture of your staff, and let visitors connect with anyone on the staff by clicking on their faces.

Cross-Reference In Chapter 50, "Using PhotoDraw," you'll learn to design logos and graphics that can serve as image maps. Here, you'll learn to assign links to parts of an image.

To assign hotspot links to parts of a picture, follow these steps:

1. Click anywhere in the picture to which you want to add hotspot links. The Picture toolbar at the bottom of the window becomes active.

2. Click the Rectangular Hotspot, Circular Hotspot, or Polygonal Hotspot button on the Picture toolbar.

3. If you selected the Rectangular or Circular Hotspot buttons, click and drag to draw a rectangle or circle around part of your picture. Figure 44-9 shows a rectangular hotspot being drawn. You can use the Polygonal Hotspot tool to draw an outline around an irregularly shaped part of your picture. Do that by clicking to set outline points, and double-clicking to end the outline.

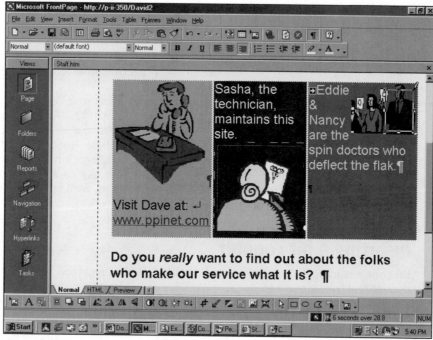

Figure 44-9: Drawing an image map hotspot.

4. As soon as you complete your hotspot shape, the Create Hyperlink dialog box opens. Here, you can define a target for your link by selecting a page in your Web site, or entering an URL in the URL field. You can also use the Bookmark drop-down list to link your hotspot to a bookmark, if your target page contains bookmarks.

5. After you define the target for your hotspot, click the OK button in the Create Hyperlink dialog box. Define additional hyperlinks as needed for your image.

Tip
As with regular picture links, you can make navigating with your image map more intuitive by assigning alternative text to the picture. You can't assign different alternative text to each hotspot, so you should come up with a generic message like "Click on a face to meet that staff person" or "Click on a button to visit that Web page."

Including FrontPage Components

FrontPage comes with many built-in, preprogrammed components that add sparkle and interactivity to your Web pages. FrontPage components include the following:

✦ **A Hit Counter** tells how many times your page has been visited.

✦ **A Search Form** lets visitors search your site for topics of interest.

✦ **Marquees** display scrolling text across your page.

✦ **Banner ads** alternate images in a slideshow type of effect.

There are more components built into FrontPage. But you'll find the four components we explore here very useful additions to almost any Web site.

Note

Some FrontPage components require that you publish your Web site to a server with FrontPage 2000 Server Extensions. In Chapter 42, "An Introduction to FrontPage," you learned how you can publish your Web to a server with or without FrontPage Server Extensions. You can still design these FrontPage components without publishing them to a Web server with FrontPage Server Extensions, but you can't make them work until you publish your site to a Web server with FrontPage Server Extensions. In the following sections, we'll let you know which components require FrontPage Server Extension to work.

Inserting a hit counter

Hit counters indicate how many hits your Web site has received. Hits pretty much correspond to visits (if a visitor refreshes his or her browser window, that counts as an additional hit). Hit counters can be used to brag about how many visitors have been to your Web site, or to simply track Web traffic for your own information. In most cases, the bragging use of hit counters strikes visitors as annoying, although there are probably occasions when it is appropriate to display "XXX people have visited our Web site!"

Figure 44-10 shows a hit counter subtly stashed at the very bottom of a Web page, where it quietly keeps track of visitors.

To insert a hit counter follow these steps:

1. Click to place your insertion point where you want the hit counter to appear.

2. Select Insert ➪ Component ➪ Hit Counter. The Hit Counter Properties dialog box appears, as shown in Figure 44-11.

3. In the Hit Counter Properties dialog box, click a radio button to select a style for your hit counter.

4. Use the Reset Counter check box to enter a starting number other than zero (which is the default).

5. Use the Fixed Number of Digits check box to enter a set number of digits for your counter.

6. When you have defined your hit counter, click the OK button in the dialog box. Your hit counter will display when you preview your Web page in your browser. You will see a code "[Hit Counter]," as shown in Figure 44-12.

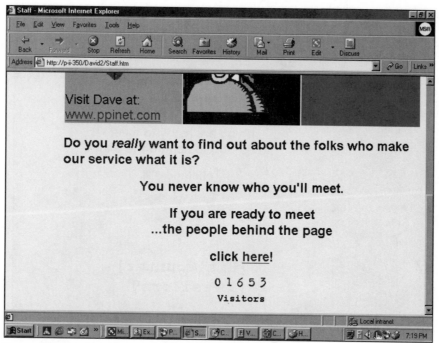

Figure 44-10: A hit counter is a useful tool for analyzing traffic at your Web site.

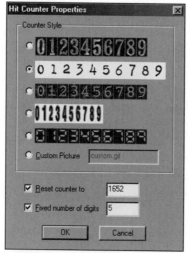

Figure 44-11: Defining a hit counter.

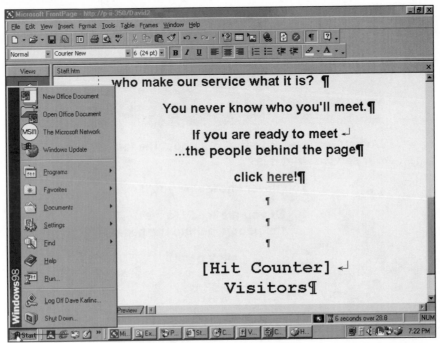

Figure 44-12: Hit counters don't show up in FrontPage, but they display in browsers.

Including a search form

It's hard to think of a more useful feature of a large Web site than a Search Form. As a designer, you will do your best to include easy-to-find intuitive navigation links to different pages in your Web site. But some visitors will arrive knowing exactly what they're looking for, and a Search Form allows them to jump right to Web pages that address their interests.

Search forms accept input from a visitor, and then list Web pages that match that content. When more than one page is relevant to a visitor's inquiry, FrontPage will do its best to list pages in order, with the page that matches best listed first.

Follow these steps to create a search form:

1. Click in Page view to set the insertion point for the search form.

2. Select Insert ➪ Component ➪ Search Form. The Search Form Properties dialog box displays with the Search Form Properties tab selected, as shown in Figure 44-13.

Figure 44-13: Defining a search form.

3. The four fields in the Search Form Properties tab are pretty standard, and there's usually no need to change them. You can, if you want to, change the Label for Input from "Search For" to "Look For" or some other prompt. And if you want to encourage visitors to type in long, long strings of text to search for, you can expand the size of the input box by entering a larger value in the Width in Characters field.

4. Click the Search Results tab of the dialog box, shown in Figure 44-14. The Word List to Search field defaults to All, which means all pages will be searched except for ones in the _private folder in your FrontPage Web (FrontPage creates a _private folder when you generate a new Web). Alternatively, you can enter a folder name here to confine search results to pages in that folder. The three check boxes in this tab allow you to include additional information in the list of matching pages. Display Score uses a scoring system understood only by a secret cabal of programmers, but the higher the score, the closer the match. The Display File Size and Display File Date check boxes display the size and date of matching files when a list is generated. If you click the Display File Date check box, the Date Format and Time Format fields become active, and you can define how you want to display the file date.

5. When you complete the dialog box, click OK to place the search box in your Web page. To test your search box, save your page, and preview it in your browser.

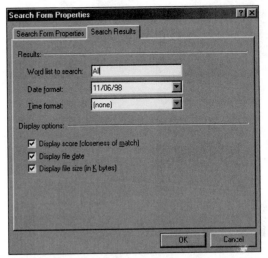

Figure 44-14: You can include file time and date, and closeness of match, in search results.

Displaying text as a scrolling marquee

Scrolling marquees present text scrolling across your screen. To create a scrolling marquee, follow these steps:

1. Click in Page view to set the insertion point for the marquee.

2. Select Insert ➪ Component ➪ Marquee. The Marquee Properties dialog box displays, as shown in Figure 44-15.

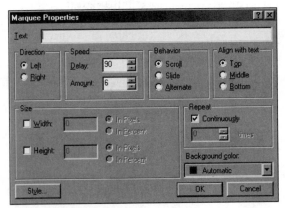

Figure 44-15: Designing scrolling text.

3. You can tweak many scrolling text properties. The Background Color drop-down menu lets you select a background for the scrolling text. The three radio buttons in the Behavior area are pretty safe to experiment with, but there is quite a bit of potential for disaster when you start fiddling with the other options. We'd advise sticking with entering some text in the Text field, and going with the default settings. For the young and adventurous, go ahead and experiment, and remember that you can always delete a messed-up marquee and start from scratch with the default settings.

4. After you enter text in the Text field, click the OK button. You can see how your scrolling text will look by clicking the Preview tab in Page view.

5. You can resize your scrolling text marquee by clicking and dragging on the side or corner handles, as shown in Figure 44-16.

Note   Scrolling marquees are one FrontPage component that do not require you to save your site to a Web server. It's not necessary to preview your Web page in a browser to see how marquees will look. You can test them out in the Preview tab of Page view.

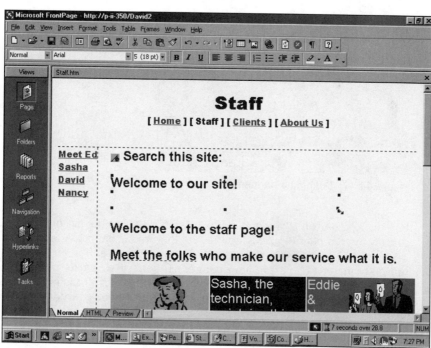

Figure 44-16: Resizing a scrolling text marquee.

Presenting a banner ad

Banner ads alternate two or more images in a space, creating an animated presentation for visitors to your Web site.

The first step in preparing a banner ad is to have some images that you want to display. You don't need to insert pictures into your page in order to include them in your banner ad, but you do need to have them available in file form.

Cross-Reference Chapter 43, "Designing Web Pages with FrontPage," discusses how to insert images into your Web page.

With your images picked out, select Insert ➪ Component ➪ Banner Ad Manager. The Banner Ad Manager Properties dialog box appears, as shown in Figure 44-17.

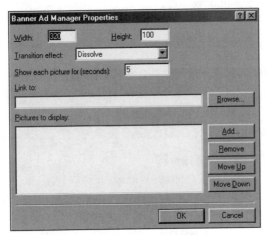

Figure 44-17: Defining a banner ad.

Use the Add button in the dialog box to add images to the list of those that will display in your banner ad. Using the Add Picture for Banner Ad dialog box, shown in Figure 44-18, you can pick images from your Web site. Or, you can use the Clip Art button to include clip art in your banner ad. You can also use the Use Your Web Browser button or the Select a File on Your Computer buttons in the lower right corner of the dialog box to include files from the Web or your local computer.

You can edit your display list using the Remove, Move Up, or Move Down buttons in the Banner Ad Manager Properties dialog box. You can also make the whole banner ad function as a link by entering a target for the link in the Link To field.

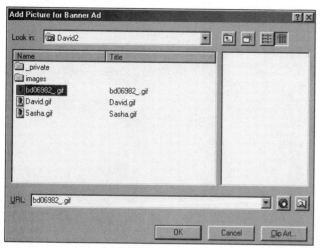

Figure 44-18: Selecting images to include in your banner ad.

Define the size of your banner ad in the Width and Height fields. Choose a transition effect from the drop-down list. Then, select a number of seconds to display each image. When you have defined your banner ad, click OK in the dialog box. Banner ads don't require FrontPage Server Extensions. You can preview your banner ad in a browser.

Summary

In this chapter, you learned some of the ways you can add advanced features to Web pages in FrontPage.

✦ Text and graphic hyperlinks make your page dynamic, and allow visitors to jump around your Web site, or around the World Wide Web.

✦ Hyperlinked hotspots can be assigned to images to create image maps, providing intuitive graphical links for visitors to your site.

✦ Hit counters keep track of how many times your site is visited. You can put them at the top of a page to brag about how many visits you get, or discreetly place them at the bottom of a page to collect data for your own use.

✦ Search forms allow visitors to find exactly what they are looking for at your Web site.

✦ Banner ads and scrolling marquees can present animated pictures and text.

✦   ✦   ✦

Managing Your Web Site

C H A P T E R

45

I n Chapters 42 through 44, you learned techniques that will allow you to create quite a nice Web site. In Chapter 42 you learned to use one of FrontPage's templates to design a Web site, to publish that site to your local drive or to a Web server, and to add themes and shared borders. In Chapter 43 you learned to customize the look and content of Web pages. And in Chapter 44 you added advanced elements such as hit counters, scrolling marquees, and even a rotating banner ad. Wow! You've come a long way. In this chapter, you'll learn to use FrontPage to manage your Web site, and in the process to customize it to give it a unique look and feel.

Customizing FrontPage Themes

Themes attach similar graphic design elements to every page in your Web site. While themes are great for instant style, an obvious drawback is that they are prefabricated. Is there a way to combine the ease of universally assigned themes with the freedom to present your own customized image? The happy answer is yes! FrontPage 2000 has dramatically improved the usefulness of themes by making them fully customizable. Here are some general guidelines for theme design:

Cross-Reference

See Chapter 42, "An Introduction to FrontPage," for more information on how to assign one of FrontPage's diverse collection of themes to your Web site.

+ The first step in designing your own, custom-built theme is to assign a theme that is close to the look you desire. To do that, open your FrontPage Web, and from any view (including Page view), select Format ⇨ Theme.

+ Your list of themes will vary depending on whether you elected to install all of FrontPage's themes, and also depending on whether or not you downloaded additional themes from the FrontPage Web site, or from folks who sell additional themes. (You can find links to both the

---

In This Chapter

Customizing FrontPage Themes

Defining shared borders and navigation bars

Checking the status of your Web site and its links

Editing your site globally

Publishing your site to an intranet or the Internet

♦ ♦ ♦ ♦

FrontPage 2000 site and to vendors of additional themes at `http://www.`
`ppinet.com/resource.htm.`) So, with that variable in mind, you'll see a
Themes dialog box that looks something like the one shown in Figure 45-1.

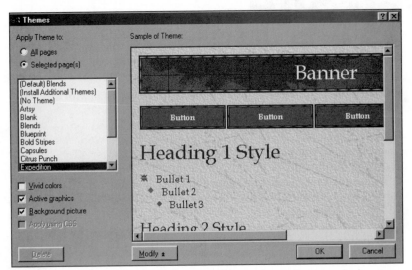

Figure 45-1: Your selection of themes will vary depending on which ones
you install or purchase.

✦ When you click on a theme in the list on the left side of the Themes dialog
box, you can see a preview of the theme in the Sample of Theme window on
the right.

✦ You can do some basic customizing of the theme by making selections in the
Vivid Colors, Active Graphics, and Background Picture check boxes. As you
select or deselect these check boxes, the Sample of Theme window will reflect
changes to the page attributes.

Note The fourth check box in the Themes dialog box, Apply Using CSS, allows you to
attach page attributes from an HTML-coded Cascading Style Sheet file. But you'll
find that you can assign many of the same features using the theme options that
we are about to explore in this chapter, without programming.

✦ Once you settle on a theme that approximates (even roughly) the look you
want for your Web pages, click the Modify button in the Themes dialog box.
This button adds five additional buttons to your dialog box: Colors, Graphics,
Text, Save, and Save As.

In the following sections, you'll learn how to modify (and save) your theme using
these new tools.

Modifying theme colors

Clicking the Colors button in the Themes dialog box (after clicking Modify) opens the Modify Theme dialog box, with three tabs shown in Figure 45-2. These three tabs provide three different ways to change the colors in your theme.

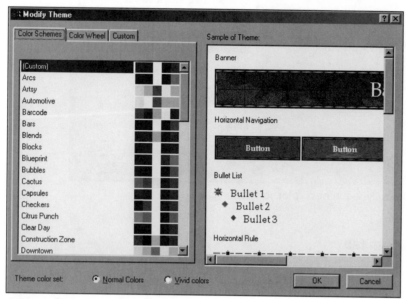

Figure 45-2: You can customize the color scheme in your theme.

The Color Schemes tab

The Color Schemes tab allows you to substitute the color scheme of a different theme for the selected theme. So, for example, if you like the graphics and fonts of the Citrus Punch theme, but you prefer the color scheme in the Cactus theme, you can assign the Citrus Punch theme, but select the Cactus color scheme.

The Color Wheel tab

Switching color schemes from one theme to another gives you some, but not complete, control over your theme colors. For even more options, click the Color Wheel tab in the Modify Theme dialog box. Here, you can click a location in the Color Wheel to generate a new set of colors matched in sync with the color you click on in the wheel. Figure 45-3 shows a color scheme being substituted.

You can also adjust the colors in your theme color scheme by moving the Brightness slider. And, you can toggle between intense colors and muted colors by using the Normal Colors or Vivid Colors radio buttons at the bottom of the dialog box.

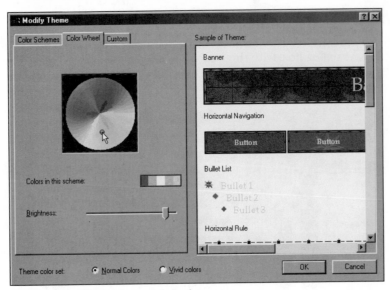

Figure 45-3: Fine-tuning a color scheme.

The Custom tab

Finally, you can modify the colors of different text elements in the Custom tab of the Modify Theme dialog box. First, pull down the Item list and select the item you want to assign a color to. Then, click on the Color drop-down list and select a color to assign to that text element, as shown in Figure 45-4.

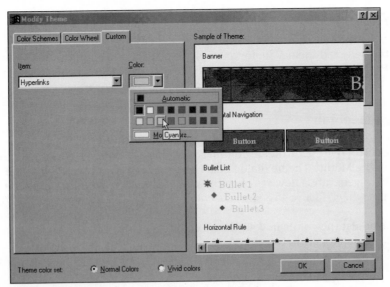

Figure 45-4: You can assign colors to any text element.

When you have finished modifying the color scheme of your customized theme, click the OK button in the Modify Theme dialog box.

Modifying theme graphics

Themes assign many graphics to your Web pages, e.g., a background image, a graphic to use for bullets, horizontal rules, and navigational icons. You can substitute your own graphics images for those that come with a theme, and you can customize the font of the text that gets added to these images. To do all this, click the Graphics button (after clicking Modify) in the Themes dialog box. A Modify Theme dialog box opens, as shown in Figure 45-5.

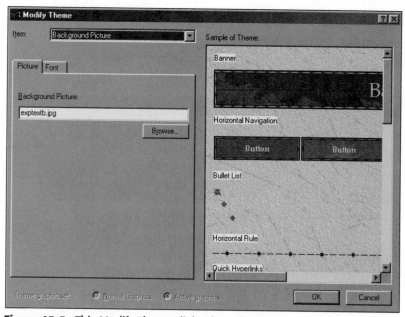

Figure 45-5: This Modify Theme dialog box allows you to substitute your own graphics for theme elements.

The Image tab

Some graphic elements have both images and text. For example, navigation buttons have button graphics and text that displays links generated by navigation bars. Those elements allow you to assign graphics by clicking the Browse button next to an image, and to assign text to that element in the Font tab of the dialog box.

The Font tab

The Font tab, shown in Figure 45-6, allows you to assign fonts, font sizes, and horizontal and vertical alignment. Remember, you already assigned font colors in the Colors tab.

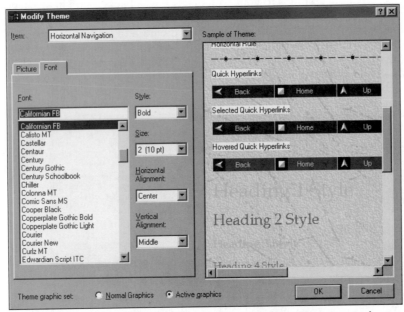

Figure 45-6: You can change the text attributes assigned to generated theme items.

After you assign pictures and fonts to your theme elements, click OK in the dialog box.

Changing theme styles

You can assign fonts to any of the HTML styles available in the Style drop-down list in Page view. To do this, click the Text button in the Themes dialog box. Select a style from the Item drop-down list, and then a font from the Font list. Figure 45-7 shows a font being assigned to the Heading 1 style.

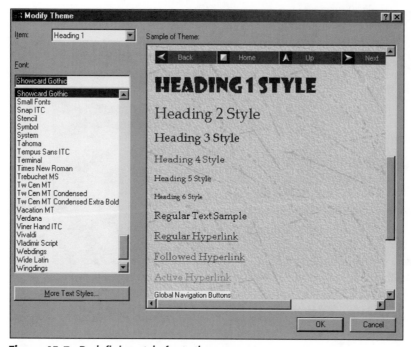

Figure 45-7: Redefining style fonts the easy way.

You can see additional styles by clicking the More Text Styles button. After you've assigned custom fonts to different styles, click the OK button to close this dialog box and return to the Themes dialog box.

Saving a custom theme

By now, you've assigned custom graphics, custom color schemes, and custom text, so you've actually defined a brand-new theme of your own. To save this new theme, and add it to the list of available themes, click the Save As button in the Themes dialog box.

The tiny Save Theme dialog box appears, as shown in Figure 45-8. Enter a new descriptive theme name in the Enter New Theme Title field, and click OK.

Once you have saved a theme, it appears in your Themes list.

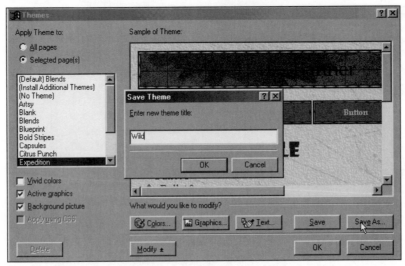

Figure 45-8: Once you've defined custom theme attributes, you can save your new theme.

Navigation Bar and Shared Border Properties

Along with themes, the most powerful shared elements of a Web site are navigation bars and shared borders. Navigation bars can be located in shared borders, but they're not the same thing. Shared borders are actually embedded pages that appear on *every page* of your Web site. Navigation bars provide automatically generated links to other pages in your site.

In the following sections of this chapter, you'll explore how to customize these two universal elements of a Web site.

Changing navigation bar links

You can change the logic of how navigation links get generated in navigation bars. You can define navigation bars by selecting Insert ➪ Navigation Bar. The Navigation Bar Properties dialog box appears, as shown in Figure 45-9.

If you've ever designed a family tree, you can follow the metaphor here. Parent pages are pages one step up on the flowchart hierarchy. Child pages are one step below in the flowchart. These relationships are defined in Navigation view.

Cross-Reference   For more information on Navigation view, see Chapter 42, "An Introduction to FrontPage."

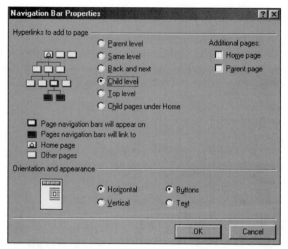

Figure 45-9: Navigation bar options use the metaphor of a family tree.

✦ **Parent Level** links display only a link to the page above the page being viewed.

✦ **Same Level** links display other Web pages on the same level of the Navigation view site flowchart.

✦ **Back and Next** display the nearest link to the left and to the right of the current page.

✦ **Child Level** links generate links only to pages directly below the current page in the Navigation view flowchart.

✦ **Top Level** links display links to all pages in the top level of the flowchart.

✦ **Child Pages** under home links display the child pages of the home page.

✦ **The Home Page check box** adds a link to the site home page on every page in the site. This is a very useful option. Allowing visitors to navigate directly to your home page is usually the most-appreciated navigational link you can provide.

✦ **The Parent Page check box** adds a link to the parent page on each page. This is redundant if you selected the Parent Level radio button, but if you're using other linking logic, it can be helpful.

Tip

Which type of navigational link is best? Probably the most useful navigation links for many sites are generated by selecting the Child Level radio button, and both the Parent Page and Home Page check boxes.

✦ **The Orientation and Appearance area** has two sets of two radio buttons that let you choose between lining up your links horizontally or vertically, and using Buttons or Text. Your selections are previewed in the small preview page in the lower left corner of the dialog box.

Customizing shared borders

Shared borders can hold navigation bars, but they can also contain any other object, like graphics or text. To define shared borders, select Format ➪ Shared Borders. It might be easier to do this if you are in Page View, so you can immediately see the impact of the borders you create.

Assigning shared borders

The Shared Borders dialog box, shown in Figure 45-10, has check boxes that allow you to assign shared borders to the Top, Right, Left, or Bottom of your pages. If you select Top or Left, you can use the check boxes that appear to assign navigation buttons to either or both of these borders.

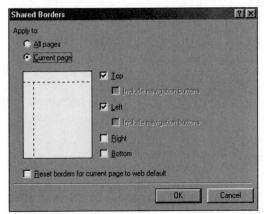

Figure 45-10: You can define as many as four shared borders for pages in your Web site.

Assigning navigation bars to shared borders

Why can't you assign Navigation bars to the right or bottom shared borders? Actually, you can. You just have to do it manually, by clicking in the generated border and using the Insert ➪ Navigation Bar menu command. Figure 45-11 shows a navigation bar in a bottom shared border.

Note   Shared borders can include any Web page element, including text and graphics. Shared borders act as a consistent element of each page in your Web site.

Editing shared border content

To edit the content of a shared border, click in the border, and edit as you would any other Web page. When you save the Web page, the embedded shared border page is saved as well. How many shared border elements can you find in Figure 45-12?

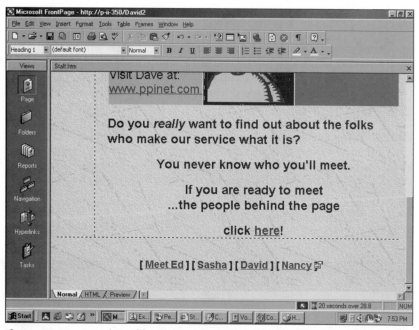

Figure 45-11: Any shared border can have a navigation bar.

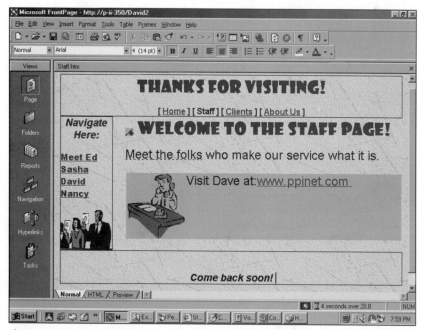

Figure 45-12: Top, left, and bottom shared borders include images, text, and a navigation bar.

Checking Up on Your Site

The Reports view provides a list of many useful statistics about your Web site. Additional reports update you on the status of navigational links, slow pages, and new files. You can select a report by choosing View ➪ Reports from the menu, and then selecting one of the available reports. Following are brief descriptions of how you can use these reports:

✦ **The Site Summary report** gives you an overview of your site. The rows in the Site Summary are themselves links to other views. One of the most useful things about the Site Summary view is you can get a quick idea of the size of your Web site, which is helpful when you are looking for server space for your site.

✦ **The All Files report** is shown in Figure 45-13. This report shows you detailed information about each file in your Web site.

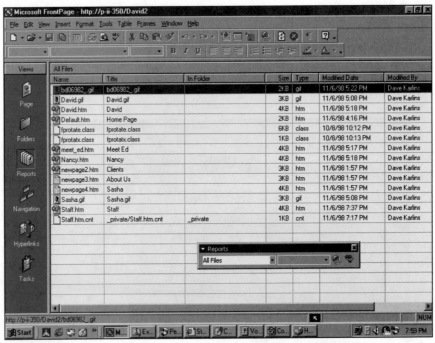

Figure 45-13: The All Files report tells you everything you need to know about files in your Web site.

✦ **Recently Added Files, Recently Changed Files, Older Files, and Slow Pages** are rather subjective categories. What's recent? What's old? What's slow? You define criteria for these reports by selecting Tools ➪ Options and selecting the Reports View tab, as shown in Figure 45-14.

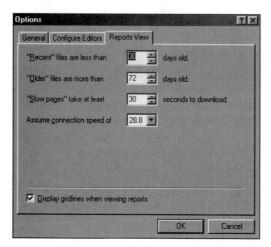

Figure 45-14: The Reports View tab of the Options dialog box lets you define what files to display as Recently Added, Recently Changed, and Older. Slow pages are calculated based on the modem speed you enter in the Assume Connection Speed Of spin box.

✦ **The Unlinked Files report** shows files in your Web site to which there are no links. These stranded Web pages are sometimes called *orphan pages*.

✦ **The Broken Hyperlinks report** shows you hyperlinks in your Web site that are either invalid or untested. You can right-click on one of these untested hyperlinks and choose Verify from the context menu to test the link. If the link is to an Internet or intranet site, you must be logged on to the Internet or your intranet to test the link. After an unverified link is tested, and FrontPage determines that the link works, you'll see an OK mark in the Status column, as shown in Figure 45-15.

✦ **The Component Errors report** tests FrontPage components.

For more information on exploring FrontPage components for errors, see Chapter 44, "Adding Interactive Elements to Web Pages."

✦ **The Review Status and Assigned To reports** are for workgroups collaborating on a Web site. The Review Status report allows you to log pages that need to be reviewed, and track whether pages have been reviewed. The Assigned To report is similar to the Review Status report, but it tracks who is assigned to which page.

✦ **The Categories report** sorts components of your Web site by category, such as Business, Competition, Expense Report, etc.

✦ **The Publish Status report** lists which pages are marked to be published to your Web server when you publish your Web.

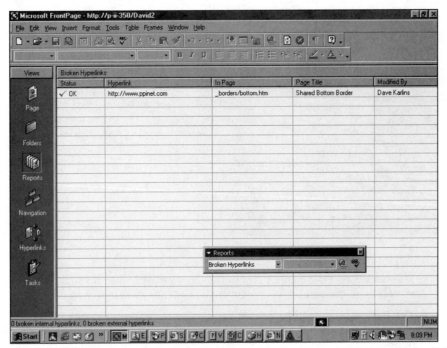

Figure 45-15: You can test unverified links in the Broken Hyperlinks report. If the links pass, the status bar registers OK. If not, right-click and select Edit Page to correct the link.

Global Site Editing

Most of the work you do to edit the content of your Web site takes place in Page view, and is done on a page-by-page basis. But there are editing tools in FrontPage that work across an entire Web. Here, we'll look at two of them: spell-checking and search and replace.

Spell-checking your entire site

To spell-check your whole Web site, select Tools ➪ Spelling from a view other than Page view. Here's how it works:

Note   Why not spell-check in Page view? If you select Tools ➪ Spelling in Page view (or click on the Spelling tool on the Standard toolbar), you will spell-check only the open page.

✦ When you select Tools ⇨ Spelling (in a view other than Page view), the Spelling dialog box has two radio buttons: one to check Selected Page(s), and one to check the Entire Web. To spell-check your entire Web site, use the Entire Web option.

✦ You can also select the Add a Task for Each Page With Misspellings check box. This handy option creates a list of pages that need their spelling corrected.

✦ After you've selected these options, click the Start button to begin the check of your spelling. After FrontPage checks all your pages for spelling problems, it produces a list in the Spelling dialog box, as shown in Figure 45-16.

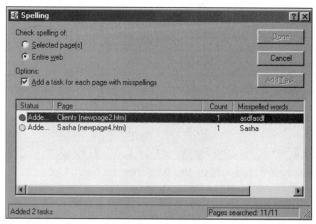

Figure 45-16: FrontPage's spell-checker creates a list of pages with potential spelling mistakes.

✦ If you did not select the Add a Task check box, you can click the Add Task button to add the selected page to your task list.

✦ If you would rather correct your spelling on the spot, you can just double-click on the page in the list in the Spelling dialog box. This opens a conventional Spelling box, as you are used to in other Office applications. Use this Spelling dialog box to correct (or ignore) questionable spellings.

Tracking tasks for your entire site

In the previous section, you learned that you can add pages that require spelling corrections to your Tasks list. To see this tasks list, click Tasks in the view bar. Figure 45-17 shows a Tasks view.

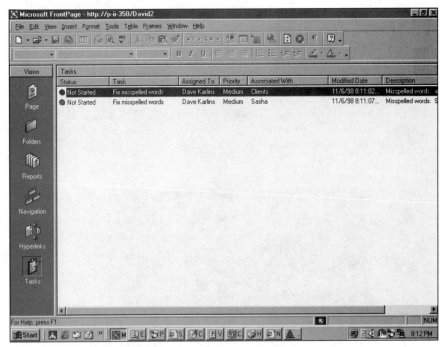

Figure 45-17: Tasks view with two tasks – fixing spelling on two pages.

You can also add your own tasks to the Tasks view list. Select Edit ➪ Task ➪ **Add Task** to define a new task. The New Task dialog box appears, as shown in Figure 45-18.

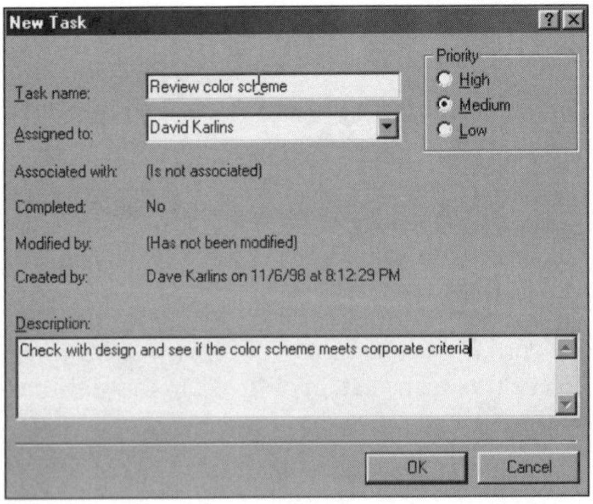

Figure 45-18: You can add your own tasks to the Tasks view list.

As you complete tasks, you can click on them in the Tasks view list, and select Edit ➪ Task ➪ Mark as Completed. Use the command Edit ➪ Task ➪ Show History to toggle between showing and hiding completed tasks. Tasks like correcting spelling, that were generated automatically by FrontPage, can be launched by selecting Edit ➪ Task ➪ Start.

Replacing throughout a site

You can use Search and Replace throughout your site. This comes in very handy when the corporate president you gushed over on every single Web page gets axed, and a new one has taken his or her place. Here's how it works:

1. To replace text throughout a site, select Edit ➪ Replace in any view.

2. In the Replace dialog box, enter text to find in the Find What box, and replacement text in the Replace With box.

3. Choose the All pages radio button to replace the text in every page.

4. The Up and Down radio buttons determine the direction that the search and replace will occur throughout your Web pages.

5. The Find Whole Word Only and Match Case check box options work as they do in the Replace dialog box in Word and other Office applications. But the Find in HTML check box allows you to search and replace HTML code if you are so inclined.

6. After you define your replace options, if you are replacing in an entire Web, click the Find in Web button (or the Find Next button if you're only searching the current page). FrontPage will generate a list of pages at the bottom of the Replace dialog box with the text to be replaced. (see Figure 45-19).

7. Double-click on a page to make the changes in that page. Or, select a page in the list and click the Add Task button to add a task for the selected page to your task list.

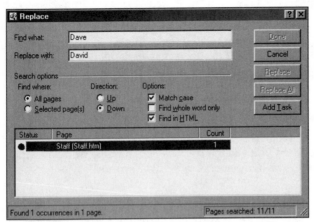

Figure 45-19: Replacing for an entire site generates a list of pages that need fixing.

Publishing Your Site to a Web Server

At the beginning of this part of the *Office 2000 Bible,* we encouraged you (strongly) to always begin your work by creating a FrontPage Web. Even if your Web site is only one Web page, working from within a Web allows you to use the full power of FrontPage to manage your files.

Assuming that you've been working with a Web all along, publishing your Web to a Web site is a breeze. Select File ➪ Publish Web to open the Publish Web dialog box. You enter an URL, get prompted for a log-on name and a password, and you're in. We'll walk through that process in a bit more detail in the following sections.

Local drives versus Web servers

One of the most frequently asked questions posted to the FrontPage Forum at www.ppinet.com is "How do I get my Web from my local computer to another computer?" The simplest way to do this is to simply enter a: in the Specify the Location to Publish Your Web To field in the Publish Web dialog box. You'll be prompted to create a Web on your A drive floppy disk, and then all your files will be transferred. It's a bit crude, but if all you want to do is bring the Web you created at home into the office, it works.

You can also publish a Web site to other folders by specifying other folders on your hard drive or network. Again, FrontPage will create a Web folder that can hold your FrontPage Web.

If you want to share your Web site with others, however, you'll want to publish it to a Web server. To do that, enter an URL in the Specify the Location to Publish Your

Web To field in the Publish Web dialog box. You'll be prompted for a name and a password in the Name and Password Required dialog box, as shown in Figure 45-20.

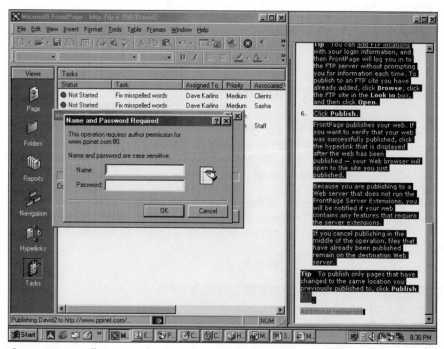

Figure 45-20: All you need to know to publish your Web site is your log-on name and password.

If your Web site supports FrontPage 2000, you can just enter a password and name in this dialog box, and that's it! Your entire site will be transferred to your new Web server.

 Note   When you arrange for space on a Web server, either from an Internet service provider or from your local intranet administrator, you must get a log-on name and a password from your administrator.

If you don't yet have a FrontPage-compatible Web site provider, read on.

Publishing to FrontPage-friendly sites

Hundreds of Web site providers are engaged in cutthroat competition to publish *your* Web site. If you want to shop for one of them online, click the WPP's button in the Publish Web dialog box. This will take you to a Web site that lists Internet service providers (ISPs) that support FrontPage. You can compare prices and features. Try e-mailing your prospective site host with a question, and see how quick, accurate, and friendly a response you get.

After you contract for your site (and many providers let you do this online, instantly with a credit card or a promise to pay after a short, free trial period), you'll get an URL address, a log-on name and a password. With just that information, you're ready to publish your site to the Internet.

If your local intranet supports FrontPage, your intranet administrator can also give you an URL, a log-on name and a password.

Other publishing options

You may find yourself in a position where you want to publish your Web site to a site provider that does not support FrontPage. These sites have not added the programs called FrontPage Server Extensions. Therefore, they do not support the Publish features in FrontPage. They also don't support other advanced elements of FrontPage Web sites; such as input forms, for example.

If you know that you will be publishing your site to a Web provider that does not have FrontPage Server Extensions, select Tools ➪ Page Options and click the Compatibility tab. Deselect the Enabled with Microsoft FrontPage Server Extensions check box, as shown in Figure 45-21.

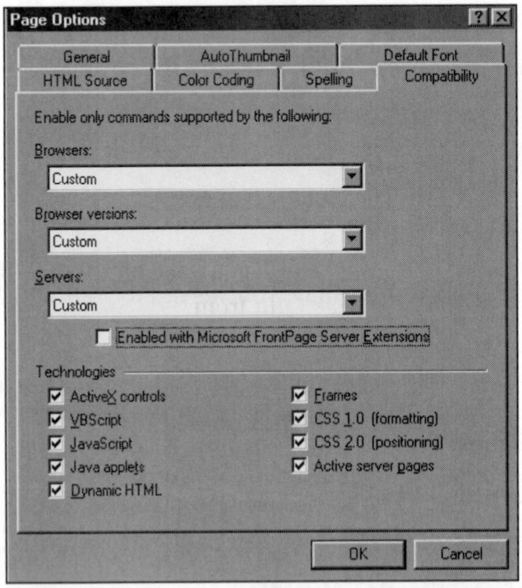

Figure 45-21: By deselecting Enabled with FrontPage Server Extensions, you can publish a Web on a Web server without the extensions, but you won't be able to apply some features that require the extensions.

If your Web server does not have FrontPage Extension files, you can use File Transfer Protocol (FTP) to publish your Web. To do that, you will need to get an FTP server name and directory path from your server administrator. Then, in the Specify the Location to Publish Your Web To field, enter the location of an FTP Web server and click the Publish button in the dialog box.

So, in short, you lose a couple things by going with a Web provider that doesn't have FrontPage Server Extensions: You can't use all the features you find in FrontPage. But if you still want to publish your FrontPage Web to a non-FrontPage enabled server, you will need to get instructions from your server administrator on how to transfer your files using their protocols. You can find your files using the All Files report.

Summary

In this chapter, you learned some of the ways you can orchestrate your entire Web site:

✦ You can create customized themes, save them, and apply them to your Web site to create a unique atmosphere for your entire Web site.

✦ You can assign customized navigation bars.

✦ You can edit the content of shared borders to create embedded pages in the top, bottom, left, or even right side of all pages in your Web site.

✦ You can check the status of your Web site using the selection of reports available in Reports view.

✦ You can globally spell-check, and search and replace throughout your Web site.

✦ You can publish your site to another Web server. This is easy if your Web site has installed FrontPage Server Extensions to make it FrontPage-friendly. You can even shop for a FrontPage-friendly server right from the Publish Web dialog box.

✦　　✦　　✦

FrontPage at Work

◆   ◆   ◆   ◆

In This Chapter

Creating a FrontPage
Web site in a day

Scanning a photo
into your Web page

Organizing Office
documents into
a Web site

Taking a quick look
at HTML code

◆   ◆   ◆   ◆

In the previous four chapters you learned about the specific components of FrontPage, the basics of designing and adding interactive elements to Web pages, and how to manage your Web site. This chapter provides practical step-by-step instructions about how to put FrontPage to work in everyday situations — making a Web site in a day, scanning photos into your Web pages, building a Web site from Office documents, and experimenting with HTML.

Whipping Up a Web Site in a Day

Scenario: You need to throw up a quick Web site that represents your department or organization. And you need it by tomorrow morning! No problem.

Corporate Presence Web Wizard

The solution lies in FrontPage's Corporate Presence Web Wizard. Don't feel constricted by the word "Corporate" in the title; you can use this Web wizard to present anything from an environmental activist group to a bank that specializes in accounts of a billion dollars or more. Your Web won't be the most original ever designed, but it will be a functional, easy to navigate, attractive, and informative Web site. And, if you've got some ideas about the image and material you want to present, you can do it in a day.

Note   The one assumption we'll start with here is that you have a Web server to publish your Web site to. Without that, the assignment to create a site in a day is still possible; you'll just have to publish the site to a local drive Web, where it can be seen only on your computer.

To use Corporate Presence Web Wizard, follow these steps:

1. Open FrontPage, select File ⇨ New ⇨ Web, and click Corporate Presence Wizard in the New dialog box, as shown in Figure 46-1.

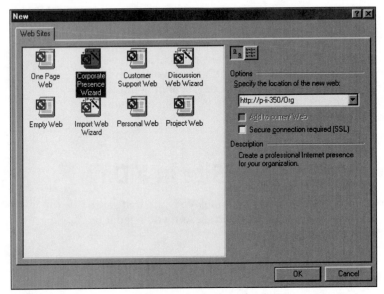

Figure 46-1: Start your instant Web site by selecting Corporate Presence Wizard.

2. After you select Corporate Presence Wizard, enter the location for the Web in the Specify the Location of the New Web box (either a URL if you have one, or enter a folder name to be created on your own computer).

3. Then, click the OK button in the New dialog box.

4. Click the Next button to move to the next window of Corporate Presence Web Wizard. This window provides six check boxes that allow you to define what elements you want to include in your new Web site (see Figure 46-2):

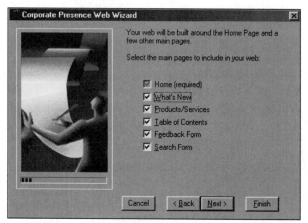

Figure 46-2: Corporate Presence Web Wizard will ask you some questions, and then generate a Web site for you.

- **Home.** Every Web site needs a home page, a page where visitors first arrive when they visit your Web site. That's why this check box is grayed out — a home page is required. If you wanted to create a *really basic* Web site, you could just select this option.

- **What's New.** This page tells visitors what is new at your organization or your Web site.

- **Products/Services.** Think large here; services can include information, advice, or even people.

- **Table of Contents.** This might be overkill in a small site, but if you're planning on dozens of pages, you may want to include this option.

- **Feedback Form.** This page collects comments and (hopefully, constructive) criticism. You need a FrontPage-friendly Web server (with FrontPage Server Extensions) to implement this part of a Web site.

- **Search Form.** Even if your site is only a few pages, this can be helpful.

5. Select as many elements as you need in this dialog box, and then click the Next button. The next set of options is shown in Figure 46-3. It asks what you want to include on your home page.

6. Depending on what pages you chose to include in your Web site, the wizard will prompt you with options for each of those pages. Make selections, and use the Next button to move on to the next wizard dialog box.

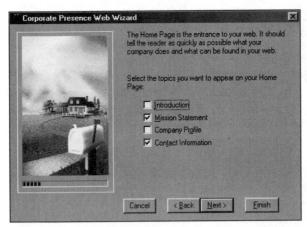

Figure 46-3: FrontPage will even help compose the text on your home page.

7. After you supply information for your Web pages, you'll be prompted with a dialog box that has a Choose Web Theme button (not shown). Click that button to open the Choose Theme dialog box, and pick a theme from the list. You can see a preview of the theme in the Sample of Theme area of the dialog box, as shown in Figure 46-4.

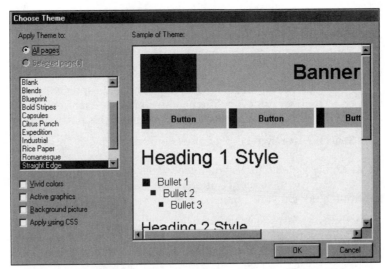

Figure 46-4: If you're in a hurry, themes provide instant atmosphere.

8. After you select a theme, click OK in the Choose Theme dialog box to return to the wizard and click Next.

9. The final dialog box in the wizard has one option, the Show Tasks View After Web is Uploaded check box (see Figure 46-5). Use this option to display Tasks view with a list of work to do after the wizard does its thing to generate most of your Web site.

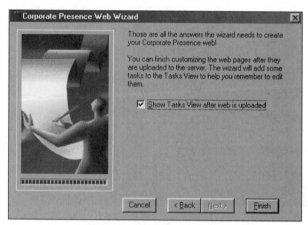

Figure 46-5: The Tasks view list will come in handy after FrontPage generates a framework for your Web site.

10. Click the Finish button to generate your Web.

Completing the tasks on your list

After FrontPage creates your Web, you'll see a list of work to do in Tasks view, as shown in Figure 46-6.

Double-click on each task, one at a time, and select Start Task in the Task Details dialog box. Web pages will open. Comment text (which isn't visible in a browser but is visible in FrontPage Page view) will prompt you with advice on how to complete the generated Web pages, as shown in Figure 46-7.

After you've finished all the tasks in Tasks view, your site will be ready to show off! Of course, you'll want to follow up by viewing your site in a browser, noting things you'd like to add or improve. But you've created a full-fledged Web site in a day, if not less.

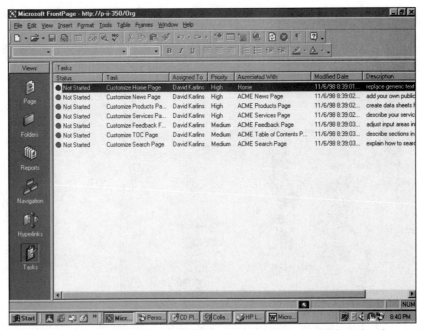

Figure 46-6: Your site is almost done! FrontPage has created a list of tasks yet to do.

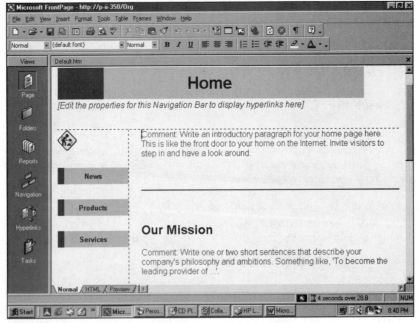

Figure 46-7: Comment text prompts you with advice about how to complete your Web pages.

Scanning a Photo into Your Web Page

Got a photo you'd like to include in your Web page? Got a scanner? If the answer to both these questions is yes, you can drop a scanned photo right into FrontPage. And the Picture toolbar in FrontPage actually includes most of the tools you'll need to tune the brightness, contrast, and other attributes of your scanned photo.

Here's the routine:

1. With your photo on your scanner, select Insert ➪ Picture ➪ From File, and click the Scan button in the Picture dialog box.

2. If you've already used your scanner, you can click the Acquire button in the Camera/Scanner dialog box. If you have more than one digital camera or scanner connected to your system, click the Source button, select a source from the Select Source dialog box, and click Select. Then, click Acquire.

3. A dialog box for your scanner (or camera) will appear. Click Prescan, and then draw a marquee around your photo in the Preview window, as shown in Figure 46-8.

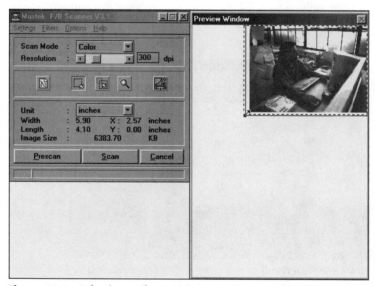

Figure 46-8: Selecting a photo to scan.

4. In the scanner dialog box, you should consider the following options:

   - You can choose a resolution of 72 dpi, as that's the resolution of the monitors people will likely be using to view your Web graphic.

   - You'll probably want to choose Color from the Scan Mode options, as most Web graphics are in color (if not, choose grayscale).

5. After you set scan options, click the Scan button to load the image on your scanner into FrontPage. Then, click OK in the Picture dialog box to place the scanned photo on your Web page.

6. With your image scanned into Page view, select it and experiment with the following options to enhance it:

   • Often scanned photos are too dark. Click the More Brightness button a few times on the Picture toolbar, and see if that helps.

   • If you overdo brightness, click the Less Brightness button to darken the picture.

   • Try making your image smaller by dragging in on a corner handle. Smaller photos often look better and load faster.

   • Check the time displayed in the lower right corner of the Page view window. How many seconds will your page take to download? Try making the picture smaller (if you haven't already) and then click the Resample button. Did this decrease your download time? It often does.

   • To assign a hyperlink to your photo, click the Hyperlink button on the Standard toolbar with the photo selected, and assign a link.

7. Save your Web page. You'll be prompted to save the embedded photo as well (see Figure 46-9).

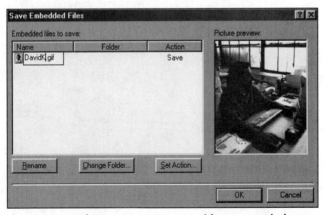

Figure 46-9: When you save a page with a scanned photo on it, you are prompted to save the embedded picture file as well.

Organizing Office Documents into a Web Site

In other parts of this book, you learned that nearly every Office 2000 application easily saves files as Web pages. You may have saved a Word file as an HTML Web page. You may have saved an Excel workbook as a Web page. Perhaps you've even got a PowerPoint slideshow saved as an ActiveX object that will play like a video in a Web page.

For example, in Word and Excel you can select File ⇨ Save as Web Page, and then enter a filename to save your files as HTML pages. In any case, you can incorporate all these files into a FrontPage Web site. There are different ways to do this, but one reliable approach is to break the process into three parts:

✦ Create Web-compatible files in Office applications by saving files as HTML pages, GIF or JPEG files, or other Web-compatible files.

✦ Create a FrontPage Web (it can be blank), and then import the files into a FrontPage Web.

✦ Organize the Web pages in Navigation view, and add other objects (such as GIF or JPEG files) in Page view.

Let's walk through this process step by step:

1. With your Office files saved as HTML files, or other Web-compatible file types, use the File ⇨ New menu option in FrontPage to create a new, empty FrontPage Web. Select the Empty Web template in the New dialog box, as shown in Figure 46-10.

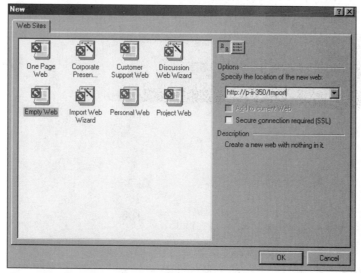

Figure 46-10: Start importing Web elements by creating an empty Web.

2. Name your empty Web in the Specify the Location of the New Web field, and then click OK in the New dialog box to generate an empty Web with no Web pages.

3. Select File ➪ Import to open the Import dialog box.

4. Click Add File to begin to add files to your Web site. Navigate to the file you want to include in your Web site in the Add File to Import List dialog box, as shown in Figure 46-11.

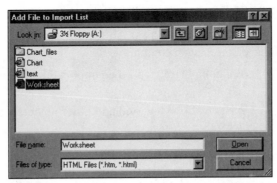

Figure 46-11: Adding an HTML page to a Web.

5. Click Open to add the file to the list of files you will import into your Web site.

6. Add additional files to your site. The list of files to import will display in the Import dialog box, as shown in Figure 46-12.

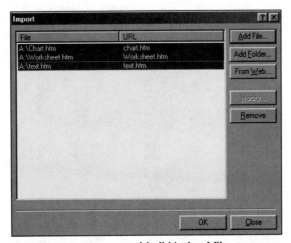

Figure 46-12: You can add all kinds of files to your Web site.

7. When you've completed your list of files (you can always add more later), click the OK button. Your selected files will be imported into your Web site.

8. Use Navigation view to organize the new files in your Web site. Click and drag files from the Folder list in Navigation view into the flowchart to connect them to the Web site, as shown in Figure 46-13.

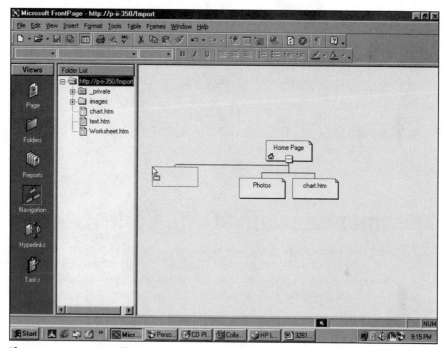

Figure 46-13: HTML files imported into your Web site can be moved into the Navigation view.

9. Objects such as images can be added to Web pages. In Page view, use the Insert Picture From File button on the Standard toolbar, and select the image from the list that appears in the Picture dialog box. Graphics that have been imported into your Web will appear in the list, as shown in Figure 46-14.

10. Save your Web pages with the new images (or other objects).

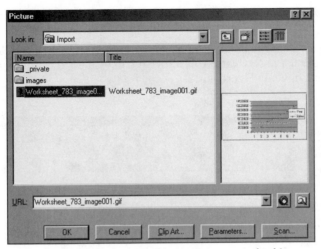

Figure 46-14: Imported graphics are easy to embed in a Web page.

Experimenting with HTML Code

FrontPage automatically generates HTML code when you create Web pages. That code is interpreted by Web browsers. You don't need to know HTML to create Web pages in FrontPage. That's part of its attraction! But you can enter your own HTML code, or you can examine the code FrontPage generates to teach yourself HTML.

The HTML tab in Page view

You have a couple of ways to look at HTML code, or *tags*, in Page view. One is to look at the HTML tab in Page view. This view presents pure HTML, as shown in Figure 46-15.

You can examine the HTML generated by FrontPage in the HTML tab, and probably figure out what some of the tags mean. For example, text turns boldface on () before the word text, and then turns it off ().

The Normal tab in Page view

You can also view HTML tags on the Normal tab in Page view, along with the WYSIWYG (What You See Is What You Get) view. To do that, in the Normal tab of Page view, select View ➪ Reveal Tags from the menu. You'll see the WYSIWYG view, but with HTML tags visible, as shown in Figure 46-16.

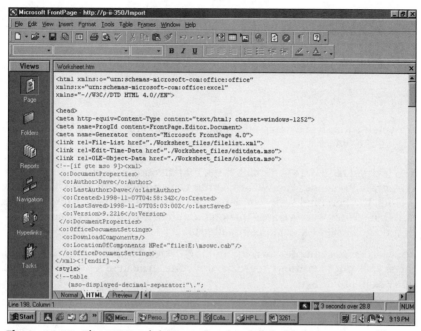

Figure 46-15: The HTML tab in Page view is a full-fledged HTML text editor.

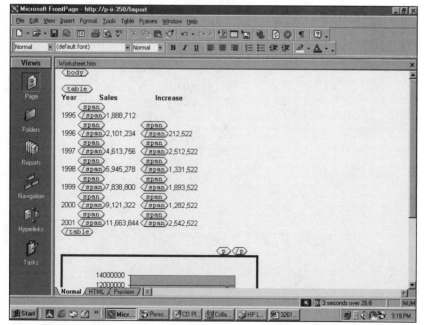

Figure 46-16: You can display HTML tags along with your formatted page on the Normal tab in Page view.

Tip   That's about all the HTML we'll explore now. If you want to teach yourself HTML, there are many fine books on that subject, including *HTML For Dummies* (a good place to start).

Summary

In this chapter, you learned some additional tricks and techniques for using FrontPage at the office.

✦ You learned to generate a quick but sophisticated Web site by using Corporate Presence Web Wizard. Other ways to whip up a quick Web site include the Personal Web template, the Customer Support Web template, and Discussion Web Wizard (this one requires a Web server that has FrontPage Server Extensions installed).

✦ You learned to scan photos right into FrontPage. No, FrontPage won't replace those $500 photo editing programs, but you can scan in a photo, and touch it up right in FrontPage.

✦ You learned to organize Office documents into a Web site. The New dialog box also has an Import Web wizard, but it's just as easy to use the Import dialog box (File ➪ Import) to assemble your Web site elements. If you've created HTML Web pages, or images in other Office applications, use FrontPage to orchestrate them into a coherent Web site.

✦ FrontPage generates HTML code. If you aspire to expert Web designer levels, you'll want to, some day, learn this coding language. As you do, you can edit in the HTML tab of Page view, and then toggle over to Normal view to see the results of your coding.

✦   ✦   ✦

The FrontPage Top 10

In this chapter we look at answers to ten commonly asked
questions about FrontPage 2000. If your question isn't posed
(let alone answered) in this chapter, you might try one of the
lists of common questions, and their answers, maintained by
Microsoft on the World Wide Web at `http://support`
`.microsoft.com`. Or, you can check into one of the online
communities of FrontPage users, including the FrontPage
Forum at `http://www.ppinet.com`.

How Do I Configure My Browser for FrontPage 2000?

You never really know what your Web pages will look like until
you preview them in a Web browser. Why is that? Isn't FrontPage
a WYSIWYG (What You See Is What You Get) page editor? And
what's with the Preview tab in Page view?

Features and standards

There are a couple reasons to check out your Web pages in
a browser.

+ Some features just don't look the same in a browser as
  they do in Page view, even when you use the Preview
  tab. Table content can end up formatted differently. And,
  shared borders don't always have quite the same width
  in a browser as they do in Page view, for example.

+ Then there is the question of different browser standards.
  There has been much discussion in the past about differ-
  ent browser standards used by Internet Explorer and
  Netscape Navigator. With the latest versions of these
  browsers, the features we've covered in this part of the
  Office 2000 Bible will look pretty much the same.

Caution

If you experiment with FrontPage components that go beyond what we've explored here, you'll begin to run into incompatibility issues with Netscape Navigator. For example, ActiveX components are not supported in Netscape as of this writing.

Browser resolution

While the two dominant browsers will both interpret your FrontPage Web pages, a bigger compatibility issue is browser resolution. Visitors who view your Web pages will be using resolutions of 640 □ 480 (pixels), 800 □ 600, 1,024 □ 768, and other resolutions. In general, your pages will look OK if viewed by a browser with a larger screen (higher resolution), but can often look pretty bad when viewed in a browser with a lower resolution than what you designed the page for.

An example is shown in Figure 47-1. Here, a Web page is being viewed in a browser with an 800 □ 600 pixel resolution.

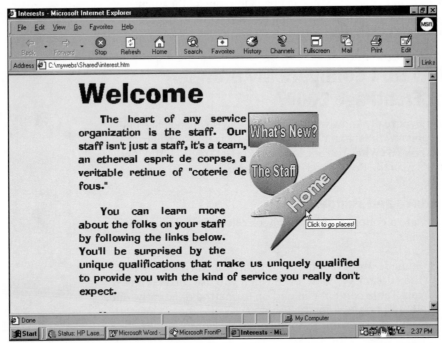

Figure 47-1: Viewed with a resolution of 800 □ 600, it's not necessary to scroll horizontally to see the entire Web page.

When this same page is viewed in a browser with a resolution of 640 × 480 pixels, the page doesn't work very well. The fully justified text doesn't space well at this resolution (see Figure 47-2).

Figure 47-2: The only way to know how your page will look at a different browser resolution is to test it.

Browser settings

You can quickly preview your page in your default browser settings by clicking the Preview in Browser button on the Standard toolbar. If you haven't saved your page since you last changed it, FrontPage will prompt you to save changes (because only the latest saved version of a page appears in a browser).

However, if you want to control your browser settings, select File ⇨ Preview in Browser from the menu. The Preview in Browser dialog box appears, as shown in Figure 47-3.

To experiment with different resolutions, use the 640 ☐ 480, 800 ☐ 600, or (if available in your system) the 1,024 ☐ 768 option.

Caution

You'll also notice a check box for the option Automatically Save Page. This is a somewhat dangerous option, because it causes your pages to be saved automatically without a prompt whenever you preview them in your browser. Saving a page when previewing means you can't close it without saving and revert to the previously saved version of the page.

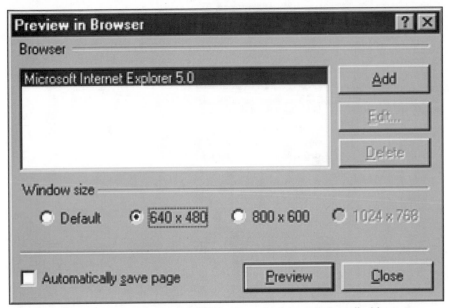

Figure 47-3: The Preview in Browser dialog box displays your installed browsers, but it also lets you define the window size in which you preview your page.

How Do I Delete a Web?

Webs take up a lot of disk space. If you created one or more as experiments to teach yourself FrontPage, or you created a Web you don't need anymore, you can delete that Web by following these steps:

1. Open the Web you want to delete.

2. In Folders view, right-click the root folder of the Web and click Delete.

3. The Confirm Delete dialog box offers you two options. You can Remove FrontPage information from this Web only, or you can delete this Web entirely. The first option, Remove FrontPage information, is much safer.

Caution

If you select the second radio button in the Confirm Delete dialog box, you run the risk of deleting other files unrelated to FrontPage!

4. After selecting the *first* radio button in the dialog box, click the OK button to delete the Web.

How can I display submenu toolbars?

Like other Office 2000 applications, the FrontPage menu structure is designed to remove clutter. However, one person's clutter is another person's vital menu options or tools. You can create your own floating toolbars from FrontPage submenus. The following example creates a floating toolbar for the Insert Component submenu:

1. Select Insert ⇨ Component. Click on the gray bar above the submenu. It turns blue, and displays a message, as shown in Figure 47-4.

2. Click and drag to move the submenu into the workspace, creating a new floating toolbar.

3. Click the Close button (X) on the floating toolbar to close it.

Figure 47-4: Submenus can be detached to create floating toolbars.

How Do I Change Page Names and Page Titles?

A page name is the URL or filename used by a browser to locate the page. A page title displays in the browser title bar.

The page title

You can easily change the page title by selecting File ➪ Properties from the menu, with a page open. The Title field in the General tab of the Page Properties dialog box lets you enter a new title, as shown in Figure 47-5.

The page name

Changing a page name is not as necessary, and it's a bigger hassle. The hassle is that if you have links defined to your page, or if visitors know your page address, those connections will be broken when you change the page's name. And, because it is the page title that displays in browser title bars, it sometimes isn't that important what the page name is.

However, if you do want to change the page name, you can do that in the Folders view. Right-click on a filename and select Rename from the context menu, as shown in Figure 47-6.

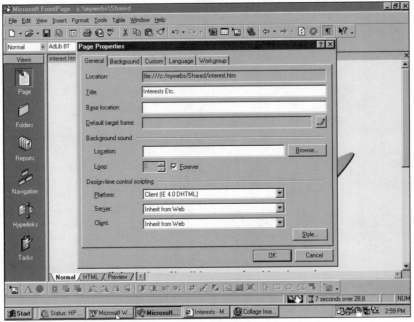

Figure 47-5: You can change a page title without disrupting page links.

Revising the links

FrontPage will prompt you if renaming a page will invalidate existing links. The Rename dialog box (see Figure 47-7) asks if you want to update any pages that have links to the renamed page.

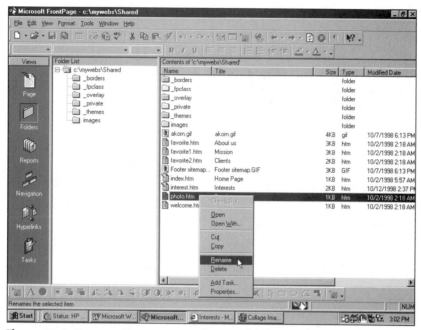

Figure 47-6: You can rename a page, but you'll have to adjust any links defined to that page.

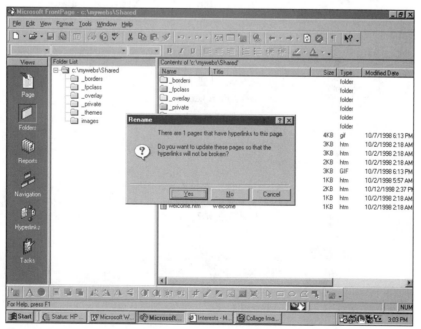

Figure 47-7: When you rename a page, you need to revise links to that page.

When you select Yes in the Rename dialog box, FrontPage edits links so they remain valid.

How Do I Tell Visitors There's Something New on My Page?

At any place in a Web page, you can place the date the page was last changed. Here's how:

1. Click in a Web page (in Page view) to place your insertion point.

2. Select Insert ⇨ Date and Time, as shown in Figure 47-8.

3. The first radio button in the Date and Time Properties dialog box inserts a timestamp that is updated whenever the page is edited. The second option inserts a timestamp that is updated whenever the page is changed automatically (this applies if you have placed a component on the page that automatically updates; such as a counter, for example).

4. Select a date format from the Date Format drop-down list. Select a Time format (or None) from that drop-down list, and click OK to place the date on your page.

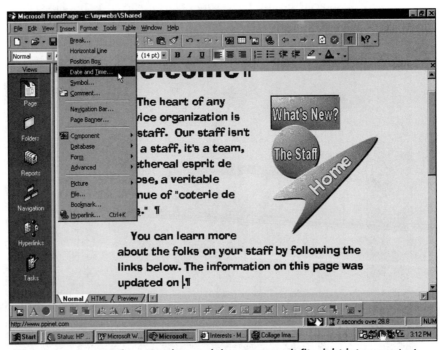

Figure 47-8: You can format a date and timestamp so it fits right into page text.

How Do I Include a Search Form on My Web Site?

Search boxes are one of the handiest ways to help visitors locate information in your Web site. They do, however, require that your Web page be published to a Web server with FrontPage Server Extensions. You can still create a search box without publishing your Web to a FrontPage-ready server, but it won't work until you do publish to a FrontPage-ready server.

Create a search box by following these steps:

1. Place your insertion point in a Web page (in Page view) where you want the Search box to appear.

2. Select Insert ➪ Component ➪ Search Form.

3. The Search Form Properties dialog box has four options in the Search Form Properties tab. The default settings work fine for almost any search box.

4. The Search Results tab of the dialog box has some options you may want to set. Leave the Word List to Search field set to the default (All) to search all folders in your site except those that start with an underscore (such as _Private). Or, enter a folder to restrict the search to that folder. The three display option check boxes allow you to include a score (a somewhat arbitrary number that tries to define how close of a match a page is to a requested search), the file date, and the file size of pages that match the search criteria.

5. When you've selected your search box options, click OK.

How can I work with a server without FrontPage Server Extensions?

You can configure FrontPage so it displays only options available without access to a Web server that has FrontPage Server Extensions installed:

1. Choose Tools ➪ Page Options, and click the Compatibility tab.

2. Deselect the Enabled with Microsoft FrontPage Server Extensions check box (see Figure 47-9).

3. Click OK.

When you let FrontPage know that you aren't going to publish your site to a server with FrontPage Server Extensions installed, features that require those extensions are grayed out on menus.

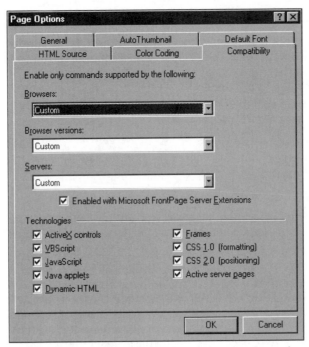

Figure 47-9: You can set FrontPage to function for Web servers without FrontPage Server Extensions installed.

What Kinds of Add-Ins Are Available for FrontPage 2000?

With the increasing popularity of FrontPage as a Web design tool, third-party software publishers have created a nice array of handy programs that work with FrontPage to allow you to add Java applets, use additional themes, and even turn your FrontPage Web site into an online shopping center.

Following are a few of these add-in products you might want to check out:

✦ **StoreFront for FrontPage.** This product let's you create your own Web store. Last time we checked, they were charging $200 for a license that allowed you to create as many stores as you want. Find them at `http://www.storefront.net/frontpage`.

✦ **ThemePack.** These folks offer themes that you can plug right into your existing list of themes. They sometimes offer free samples at `http://www.themepak.com/index.asp`.

✦ **Microsoft Corporation.** You'll find a nice list of free downloads from a little start-up in the Northwest called Microsoft Corporation. Go to `http://www .microsoft.com/msdownload/default.asp`.

✦ **Microsoft PowerPoint Player.** You can download the Microsoft PowerPoint Player to let visitors see embedded PowerPoint animations even if a visitor's browser will not interpret PowerPoint files. Get it at `http://www.microsoft .com/powerpoint/internet/player/default.htm`.

✦ **Bug List.** Think you found a bug in FrontPage 2000? It's possible. See if it's listed at Clay Niemann and Armadillo Consulting & Graphics' Bug List at `http://www.dillonet.com/fp98bug/buglist.htm`.

✦ **JBOTS.** The folks at JBOTS sell Java scripts for FrontPage. Check out the collection at `http://websunlimited.com/fpjbotsv2/fp-jbots.htm`.

How Do I Back Up My Web Site?

Yes, you do need to back up your Web site. Even more so than other files, Web files are fragile. Web servers crash. Anyone who has maintained a Web site for a while knows this happens, and it's not fun.

To create a backup of your Web site, follow these steps:

1. With your Web open, select File ➪ Publish Web.

2. In the Publish Web dialog box, enter a location and name for your backup Web (like "backup").

3. Click the Publish button.

After you create a backup folder with your Web, you can publish the Web in that folder onto your server if something goes wrong with the version of your Web on your server.

Can I create a single Web page without using FrontPage Webs?

We've cautioned against creating a single Web page outside of a FrontPage Web because when you do, you disconnect many of FrontPage's friendliest features. But if you want to keep track of your own embedded files, and really don't want to mess with FrontPage, simply click on Page view when you start FrontPage. You can design a single page.

This option is for folks who understand Web file structure, and purposely want to invalidate many of the safety-net features built into FrontPage. (You folks know who you are: You rewire your houses yourselves and disconnect the seat belt warning tones in your cars.)

✦   ✦   ✦

An Introduction to Publisher

Once upon a time, it took designers, typesetters, and complex mechanical equipment to turn out a published document, especially if it featured pictures, fancy typefaces, and color. Today, thanks to computers, every desktop is a full-featured print shop, with designers, typesetters, and printing equipment within arm's reach — at least, it is if it has a computer with desktop publishing software installed.

You can achieve a lot of desktop publishing effects with Word and PowerPoint, but if you really want your publications to look their best, you need a dedicated desktop publishing program — and if you have Office 2000 Premium, then you have one, because it includes one of the most popular personal desktop publishing programs available, Microsoft Publisher.

The Publisher Workspace

Publisher shares a basic look with other Office applications, but it's still worthwhile taking a quick look at the Publisher workspace before you begin trying to use the application.

When you first start Publisher, you'll find yourself in something called the Publisher Catalog. Here you'll find dozens of pre-designed publications that you can adapt to your own use. For now, though, click the Blank Publications tab, followed by Full Page, and then click Create. This opens Publisher's workspace.

At the left is the Quick Publication wizard, which provides design help even when you start with a blank page, like this one. For the moment, click Hide Wizard, so the workspace looks similar to that shown in Figure 48-1. (In the figure I've added a text frame — more on that later — to bring up the Formatting toolbar.) The various components of the workspace are labeled in this figure.

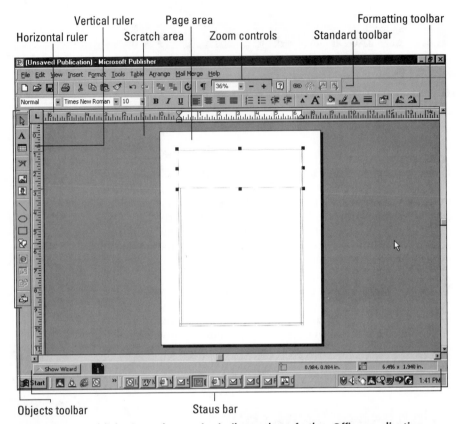

Figure 48-1: Publisher's workspace is similar to that of other Office applications.

The main features of the workspace are the *page area* (the white rectangle) and the *scratch area*. The page area is where you'll place the text, graphics, etc., that you want to appear in the final publication; the scratch area is a virtual desktop where you can drag items when you want to get them out of the way or store them for later use.

Framing the top and left sides of the workspace are the *vertical* and *horizontal rulers*, which help you position items precisely.

Like most Office applications, Publisher displays the Standard and Formatting toolbars by default. The Standard toolbar is directly under the Menu bar and the Formatting toolbar is directly under that.

Publisher also has a special toolbar called the *Objects toolbar*, which runs vertically down the left side of the workspace. These tools let you create what Publisher calls *objects,* which include text frames, picture frames, WordArt, tables, lines, and shapes.

Among the tools on the Standard toolbar are the *Zoom controls*. The Zoom list box lets you choose how large you want the display of your page to be; in addition to specific percentages of full size, it offers you the option of viewing the whole page, the full width of the page, or to zoom in to a selected object. You can zoom in and out a step at a time by using the Zoom In and Zoom Out buttons, marked with a plus and minus sign, respectively.

At the bottom of the workspace is the *Status bar*, which provides precise information about the location of the pointer and the dimensions of objects currently selected. It also shows an icon for each page in the publication; you can jump from page to page just by clicking on its icon.

Using the Publisher Catalog

As noted earlier, by default, whenever you start Publisher, you're shown the Publisher Catalog. The catalog has three tabs: Publications by Wizard, Publications by Design, and Blank Publications.

Publications by Wizard

No Office application boasts more wizards to help you create attractive, effective publications than Publisher, as you can see in Figure 48-2.

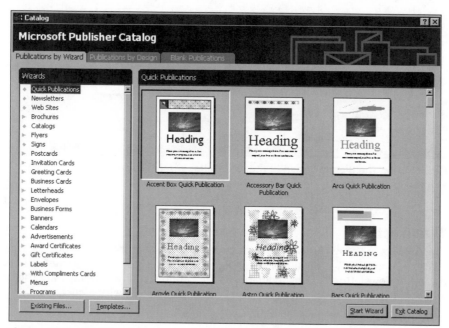

Figure 48-2: Publisher has more wizards than a whole shelf full of fantasy novels.

The available wizards are listed in a menu down the left-hand side; choose a wizard to see previews of the publications of its type. Double-click on the design you like to start the wizard.

How they work

Once you've answered the questions in a wizard, Publisher opens a default version of your choice of design in its regular workspace, and then provides you with a menu, which allows you to back and change your answers to the wizard's questions, if you decide you made the wrong choice (see Figure 48-3). If you prefer, you don't need to use the wizard at all; you can plunge right in and start making changes to the publication Publisher has already created.

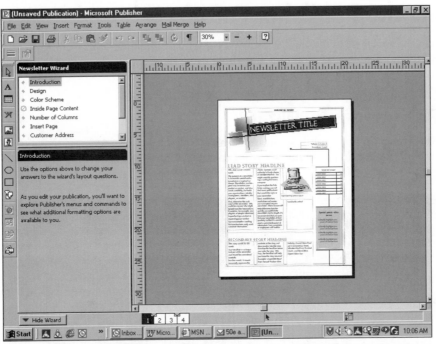

Figure 48-3: The Blends design of the Newsletter wizard. The wizard itself appears as a menu down the left side of the screen.

Wizard options

The options in the wizard will vary from publication to publication, but the ones in Figure 48-3 are fairly typical. For example, clicking Design offers you a menu of all of the other newsletter designs available in the catalog, so if you really hate the one you chose now that you see it up close, you can change it with a click.

Choosing a color scheme

One option you'll see in most wizards is Color Scheme. Publisher comes complete with a number of preset color schemes designed to ensure that all the colors in your publication work well together. Click on each one in turn to see how your publication looks with a new set of colors (see Figure 48-4).

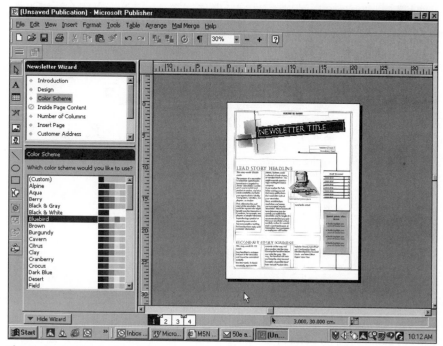

Figure 48-4: Most wizards let you choose a color scheme for your publication from a menu like this one.

Other wizard options

Other tasks wizards can typically help you with include changing the number of columns, adding a page, setting up for one-sided or two-sided printing, inserting personal information, and even converting your publication into a Web page (or pages).

Note   About the only thing a wizard can't help you with is creating and inserting your own content: text, graphics, tables, etc. That you'll still have to do yourself, and we'll look at the basics of each of those tasks later in this chapter.

Publications by Design

If you click the Publications by Design tab in the Publisher Catalog instead of the Publications by Wizard, you'll see a list of Design Sets down the left side, with previews of individual items on the right (see Figure 48-5).

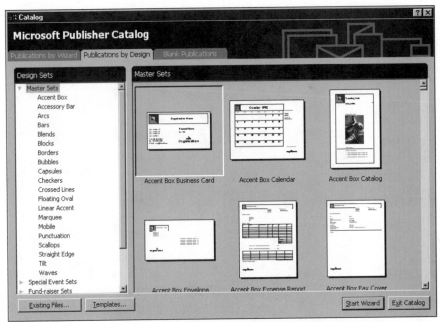

Figure 48-5: The Publications by Design tab offers you templates of sets of various types of publications, all done in matching designs.

These design sets each contain a selection of publications whose designs are complementary — in other words, color schemes, graphic elements, fonts, etc., are generally the same from publication to publication, whether you're creating a calendar, a catalog, a card, or another type of publication.

These publications are really the same as those you can access through the Publications by Wizard tab; they're just arranged differently. If you double-click on one, it will open just like a publication you choose from the Publications by Wizard tab, with the appropriate wizard appearing down the left side of the workspace.

Blank publications

If you prefer to start your publication from scratch, click on the Blank Publications tab in the Publisher Catalog, and then choose the type of blank publication you'd like to create from the previews provided (see Figure 48-6).

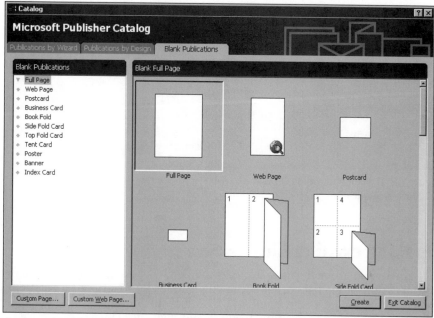

Figure 48-6: The Blank Publications tab offers you a variety of blank publications, from an ordinary full page or Web page to a tent card, poster, or banner.

You can also create a custom blank page by clicking the Custom Page or Custom Web Page button. Click the radio buttons in the Choose a Publication Layout area of the resulting dialog box to specify the size of your publication or how it will be folded; you can also create custom labels or envelopes. Figure 48-7 shows the dialog box for creating a blank page of a specific size. Similarly, Custom Web Page lets you create a Web page of a specific size.

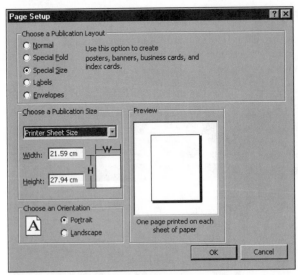

Figure 48-7: With this dialog box, you can tell Publisher to create a publication of any size.

Opening existing files

You can also open existing files from the Catalog by clicking the Existing Files button in the bottom left corner of the Publications by Wizard or Publications by Design tabs. This opens the standard Office 2000 file browsing window; locate the publication you want to open, highlight it, and then click Open.

The Basics of Working with Text

The primary components of any publication are text and graphics, so in the rest of this chapter, we'll look at how you insert and manipulate text and graphics in Publisher — beginning with text.

Typing in text

Follow these steps to type new text into a Publisher publication:

1. Click the Text Frame Tool at the top of the Objects toolbar.

2. Your pointer changes to a crosshairs; use this to draw a box where you want the text to appear.

3. Type your text into the frame just as if you were typing a document in Word (see Figure 48-8).

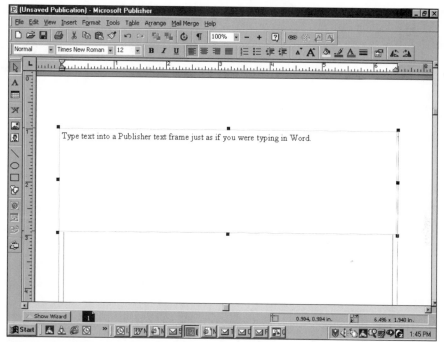

Figure 48-8: Typing text into a Publisher text frame is as easy as typing in Word.

If you run out of space, you can resize your text frame by clicking and dragging the handles that surround it. A text frame can hold more text than is visible, so if you reduce the size of the frame, some text will disappear, but it isn't lost; expanding the text frame will make it visible again.

Inserting a text file

Sometimes you want to insert a whole text file from Word or some other application. To do so:

1. Draw a text frame as before.

2. Choose Insert ➪ Text File from the menu bar.

3. Locate the file you want to insert and click OK.

4. Publisher inserts the file into your text box (see Figure 48-9).

Note   Notice the small box in the lower-right corner of the text frame with the letter A, followed by three dots, in it. That indicates that more text is contained in the text frame than is currently visible.

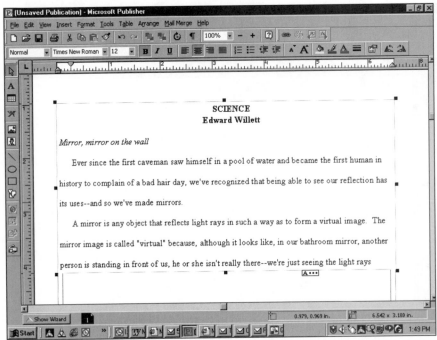

Figure 48-9: This Word file, inserted into a Publisher document, keeps all its original formatting.

Autoflow and linked frames

When you insert text into an existing text frame, you'll sometimes get a message warning you that the inserted text won't fit. You're asked if you'd like to use autoflow. If you choose Yes, Publisher will jump to every other text frame in the publication in turn, asking if you'd like to insert the remaining text into that frame. If you don't place all the text in existing frames, it eventually asks you if it should insert new pages and frames to accommodate the text.

Text inserted into multiple frames using autoflow results in a series of linked frames. When frames are linked, changing the formatting in one frame — making text larger, for instance, or reducing line spacing — results in adjustments in all of the linked frames. You can also select all the text in all of the frames simply by choosing Edit ➪ Select All.

You can tell when frames are linked because a small image of a chain link with an arrow beside it appears in the lower-right corner of the first frame (see Figure 48-10); a similar image appears in the upper-left corners and bottom-right corners of frames further down the chain. Clicking these images takes you automatically to the next or previous frame in the chain.

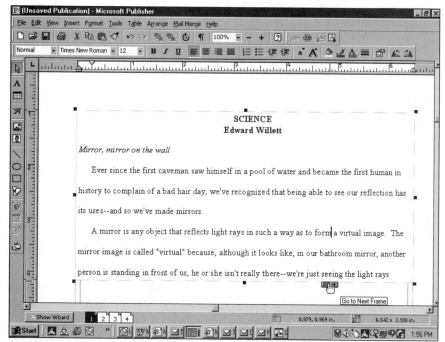

Figure 48-10: This little icon at the bottom of a text frame indicates it's just one frame in a chain. Clicking on it takes you to the next frame in the chain.

You can unlink text frames at any time by clicking the Disconnect Text Frames button on the Standard toolbar. You can also link text frames together by selecting the first frame you want to link, clicking the Connect Text Frames button, and then clicking the next frame.

Formatting text

Once you've inserted text into a text frame, you can format it just as you would in Word. Many of the tools on the Formatting toolbar are, in fact, identical, so choosing font, style, size and alignment, etc., will seem very familiar.

Note You can set the formatting for a text frame before you begin typing in it, or you can apply formatting to highlighted text.

Formatting toolbar buttons

Briefly, from left to right, the Formatting toolbar buttons for text are as follows:

✦ **Style.** Choose the style you want from the list box. You can create your own style or import them from another program by choosing Format ➪ Text Style.

✦ **Font.** Choose the font you want to use from this list. Font names are shown in their respective fonts by default, which makes it easier to pick the one you want.

✦ **Font Size.** Choose the size you want your text to be, in points, from this list. Remember that a point is approximately 1/72 of an inch, so 36-point letters, for example, are half an inch high.

✦ **Bold, Italic, Underline.** Click these buttons to apply their respective effects. Click them again to cancel their effects

✦ **Align Left, Center, Align Right, Justify.** Specify the alignment of your text within the text frame with these buttons.

✦ **Numbering, Bullets.** Create numbered or bulleted lists by clicking these buttons. Specify the formatting of the lists by choosing Format ➪ Indents and Lists.

✦ **Decrease Indent, Increase Indent.** Clicking the Decrease Indent button moves text closer to the left margin; clicking Increase Indent moves it away from the left margin. Adjust indents with more accuracy by using the sliders on the horizontal ruler or by choosing Format ➪ Indents and Lists.

✦ **Decrease Font Size, Increase Font Size.** Clicking these buttons changes the text size to either the next smallest size in the Font Size list or the next largest.

✦ **Fill Color, Line Color, Font Color.** Fill Color determines the color that fills the text box; you can also choose patterns as fills or create gradient fills. Line Color and Font Color determine the color of any lines used in the text frame border and the color of the text itself, respectively. Each offers options for choosing colors from the Color Schemes mentioned earlier, or for picking your own colors from those available on your computer.

We'll look at some of these options in greater detail in Chapter 49, "Advanced Publisher Techniques."

✦ **Line/Border Style.** This lets you specify the location and appearance of border lines around the text frame.

BorderArt, which we'll look at in Chapter 49, "Advanced Publisher Techniques," lets you create a variety of fancy graphical borders.

✦ **Text Frame Properties.** Clicking this opens the dialog box shown in Figure 48-11. Here you can set the internal margins of the text frame, as well as the number and spacing of columns. You can also have text in the frame wrap around other objects and, if the frame is part of a linked series, automatically include messages telling readers that the text is continued from or on a particular page.

✦ **Rotate Left and Rotate Right.** This rotates the entire selected text frame 90 degrees left or right with each click. If you really need upside-down text in a publication, these buttons can provide it for you in a hurry.

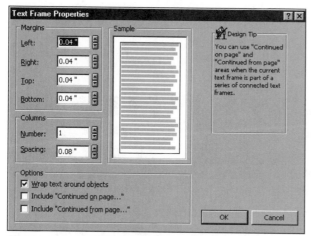

Figure 48-11: Each Publisher text frame has its own specific margins and column layout.

Format menu options

For more detailed formatting, choose Format from the menu bar and select the item you want to fine-tune. Options under the Format menu include the following:

✦ **Font** opens a dialog box that lets you choose font, font style, size, and color all in one place. In addition, it offers a variety of underlining styles and some formatting styles that aren't available on the Formatting toolbar, including Superscript, Subscript, Emboss, and Engrave.

✦ **Character Spacing** lets you set scaling, tracking, and kerning. Scaling lets you stretch or condense characters. It doesn't change their height, only their width. This can create interesting special effects or let you cram a bit more text than you'd normally be able to into a narrow text box (see Figure 48-12). Tracking adjusts the overall spacing of a block of text, while kerning adjusts the spacing between adjacent characters.

✦ **Line spacing** lets you adjust the amount of space between lines and between paragraphs.

✦ **Align Text Vertically** lets you choose whether text in a particular text frame should be snuggled up against the top margin, against the bottom margin, or centered between the two.

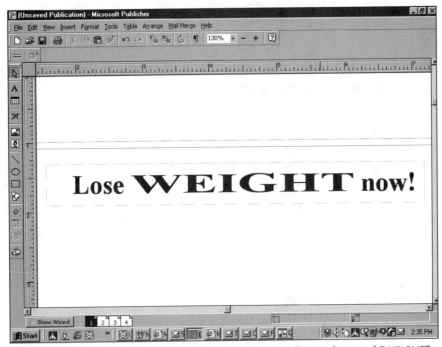

Figure 48-12: Scaling your text can create interesting effects. The word "WEIGHT" in this figure is scaled to 200 percent.

The Measurements toolbar

One of the new features in Publisher 2000 is a toolbar that lets you control many aspects of the spacing and positioning of text frames with handy control boxes.

To view the Measurements toolbar, choose View ➪ Toolbars ➪ Measurements or click View Toolbar on the dialog boxes just mentioned that relate to spacing, such as the Line Spacing dialog box or the Character Spacing dialog box.

The Measurements toolbar is shown in Figure 48-13. Any changes you make with the Measurements toolbar controls show up immediately on the screen, which makes this a very useful mechanism for fine-tuning your publication. Here's how it works:

✦ The two leftmost controls, labeled x and y, control the horizontal and vertical position of the text box, measured from the zero points of the horizontal and vertical rulers to the left and top edges of the text box. Of course, you can always drag a text box around on the page to reposition it, but if you want precise positioning, these controls can give it to you. You can either type in the coordinates you want or click the little up and down arrows beside each control.

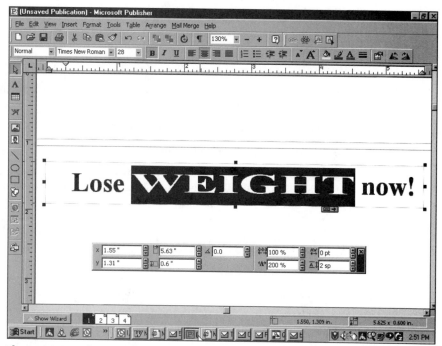

Figure 48-13: The Measurements toolbar lets you fine-tune your publication by entering precise values for a number of parameters.

✦ The next two controls to the right control width and height of the text box.

✦ The next one to the right, which appears in a column by itself, controls rotation.

✦ In the right section are spacing controls for the text itself: tracking, left top; scaling, left bottom; kerning, right top; and line spacing, right bottom.

The Basics of Working with Graphics

Images for your publication can come from several sources: the Office Clip Gallery, a file on your computer, or a scanner or digital camera. Once they're inserted into your publication, you can manipulate them in a variety of ways.

Inserting a picture file

To insert a picture file:

1. Click the Picture Frame tool on the Objects toolbar.

2. Your pointer changes to a crosshairs; use it to draw a frame approximately the size you want the inserted picture to be.

3. Double-click inside the frame or choose Insert ⇨ Picture ⇨ From File.

4. Locate the picture file on your computer; click Insert.

5. The picture is inserted into the frame you drew for it. The frame is automatically resized so the picture isn't distorted; the width of the frame will remain the same, but the height may change.

Inserting a Clip Gallery image

To insert a Clip Gallery image:

1. Click the Clip Gallery tool on the Objects toolbar.

2. Your pointer changes to a crosshairs; draw a frame approximately the size you want the inserted Clip Gallery image to be.

3. Clip Gallery opens automatically. Find the image you want and double-click on it to insert it into your publication.

4. The Clip Gallery picture is inserted into the frame. Again, the frame's height will change to prevent the picture from being distorted.

Inserting a scanner or camera image

To insert an image from a scanner or digital camera:

1. Click the Picture Frame tool on the Objects toolbar.

2. Draw a frame approximately the size you want the inserted picture to be.

3. Choose Insert ⇨ Picture ⇨ From Scanner or Camera ⇨ Select Device to choose the camera or scanner you want to acquire the picture from.

4. Choose Insert ⇨ Picture ⇨ From Scanner or Camera ⇨ Acquire Image to open the device's software and acquire the picture.

5. The picture is inserted into the frame you drew for it. Again, the frame is automatically resized so the picture isn't distorted.

Formatting pictures

Once you've inserted an object, you can manipulate it in a variety of ways:

✦ **Recolor it.** Choose Format ➪ Recolor Picture to open the dialog box shown in Figure 48-14. You can recolor the whole picture or leave the black parts black and just recolor the colored parts. Choose the color using the Color control; you can also apply tint and shade fill effects. You can undo changes to the color of a picture by clicking Restore Original Colors.

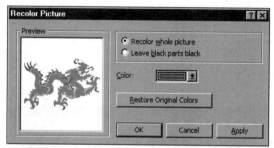

Figure 48-14: Recolor a picture, or restore it to its original color, using these controls.

✦ **Resize it.** Choose Format ➪ Scale Picture to open a small dialog box in which you can change both the height and width of the picture by entering a percentage of its original size. (Be aware that if these two percentages don't match, your picture will be distorted.) You can return a picture to its original size by checking the Original size check box.

✦ **Apply a fill or a border.** Just as with a text frame, choose Format ➪ Fill Color or Format ➪ Line/Border Style, or by clicking the appropriate buttons on the Formatting toolbar.

✦ **Change the picture frame properties.** Choose Format ➪ Picture Frame Properties or click the Picture Frame Properties button on the Formatting toolbar. This opens the dialog box shown in Figure 48-15, where you can set margins for the picture frame and also determine whether, if the picture is placed over a text frame, text will wrap around the outside of the picture frame or tuck in closely around the picture itself. The difference is demonstrated in Figure 48-16. You can also set these wrapping options by clicking the Wrap Text to Frame or Wrap Text to Picture buttons on the Formatting toolbar.

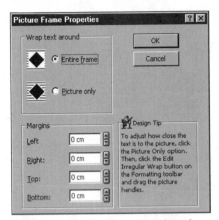

Figure 48-15: Set the properties of a picture frame using this dialog box.

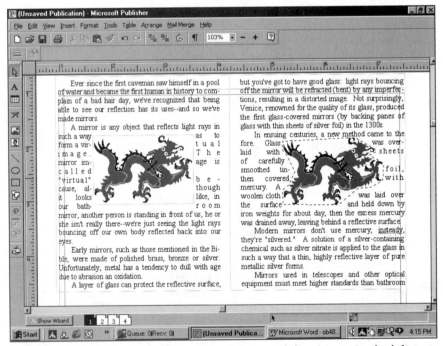

Figure 48-16: Two versions of how text wraps around the picture. On the left, text wraps around the picture frame; on the right, it wraps around the picture itself.

✦ **Crop the picture.** Click the Crop Picture button on the Formatting toolbar. Place the pointer over one of the handles of the picture frame and the pointer changes to a cropping tool that looks just like the one on the Tool button.

Drag to crop the picture. Although portions of the picture will be hidden by cropping, the information is still there; you can uncover it again simply by moving the edges of the frame back to their original locations with the Cropping tool.

✦ **Rotate or flip the picture.** The Rotate Left and Rotate Right buttons work exactly the same on picture frames as they do on text frames. Flipping, however, is a little different. The easiest way to grasp the concept is to think of your picture as being painted on a piece of transparent glass. When you flip a picture you also reverse it. Figure 48-17 shows the original picture at the left, the same picture flipped horizontally in the middle, and the result of flipping vertically on the right.

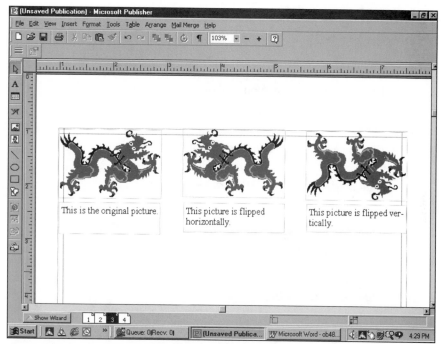

Figure 48-17: Flipping a picture can give it a whole new look without changing the amount of space it takes up.

Drawing lines and shapes

Publisher also lets you draw basic shapes with four simple drawing tools on the Objects toolbar: the Line tool, the Oval tool, the Rectangle tool, and the Custom Shapes tool. The Line tool also lets you draw arrows and adjust the shape of the arrowheads.

Custom Shapes provides you with a small menu of a variety of starbursts, arrows, and other useful shapes. If the shape includes a small gray diamond, its shape is adjustable; click and drag on the diamond to see what effect it has.

You can apply different line styles and fills to shapes and rotate them as well.

Working with Tables

The third most common type of object you're likely to want in a Publisher publication is a table.

Inserting a table

To insert a table:

1. Click the Table Frame tool on the Objects toolbar.

2. Draw a frame, just as you did for text and graphics.

3. The Create Table dialog box opens (see Figure 48-18). Enter the number of rows and columns you want in your table.

4. Choose a design you like from Table Format menu.

5. Click OK. Publisher creates a table with the number of rows and columns you indicated, sized to fit in the frame you drew.

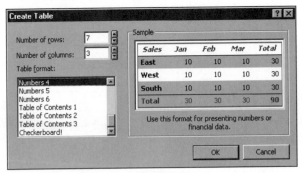

Figure 48-18: The Create Table dialog box gives you a number of table designs to choose from.

Entering data into a table

Once you've got your blank table, entering information into it is simply a matter of clicking on the cell you want to enter information into, and then typing away. The same formatting tools are available to you for formatting text within a table that are available when you are working in a text frame (see Figure 48-19).

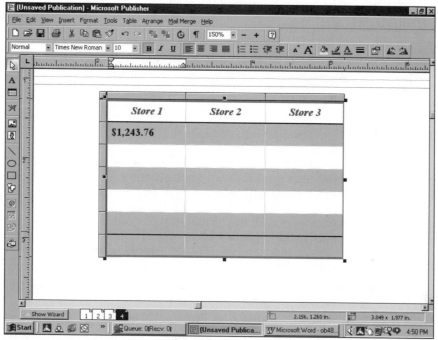

Figure 48-19: To enter data into a Publisher table, just click and type.

Editing a table

Publisher tables don't offer as many options as, say, Word tables when it comes to making changes to a table. In fact, there are only a few, all accessed by choosing Table from the menu bar:

✦ **Insert Rows or Columns** opens a dialog box in which you can specify whether you want to insert rows or columns, how many, and whether the new rows or columns should appear before or after the currently selected range of cells.

✦ **Delete Rows or Columns** deletes the rows or columns containing the currently selected cells.

✦ **Merge Cells** turns any currently selected cells into one big cell, erasing the borders between them.

✦ **Cell Diagonals** splits currently selected cells into two divided by a diagonal line, which can slant either up or down.

✦ **Table AutoFormat** lets you change the format of your table.

✦ **Select** lets you select the entire table, the current rows or columns, or just the cell in which the cursor is currently located.

✦ **Fill Down and Fill Right** fill a column or row of selected cells with the contents of either the topmost or leftmost cell in the selected range.

✦ **Grow to Fit Text,** when checked, makes the table automatically increase row height to make room for whatever text you enter into it.

Summary

With Publisher, Office 2000 users have access to one of the best personal desktop publishing programs on the market today. In this chapter we took a brief look at the basics of using Publisher. Highlights included the following:

✦ Publisher's workspace is similar to that of other Office applications; the biggest difference is the Objects toolbar down the left side, which is where you'll find the tools you need to insert text, graphics, and other basic elements of desktop design into your publications.

✦ The Publisher Catalog is packed with preset designs for everything from letterheads to newsletters. Wizards make it easy to customize any of the publications to meet your personal needs.

✦ If you prefer to start from scratch, the Catalog also offers a number of standard blank publications, and lets you design your own blank pages.

✦ Entering text into a Publisher publication is as easy as drawing a text frame with the Text Frame Tool, and then typing away. Formatting text in Publisher is almost identical to formatting it in Word.

✦ Inserting images is just as easy. Draw a picture frame, and then fill it with Clip Gallery art, a picture file from your disk, or an image from a scanner or digital camera. Pictures can then be resized, recolored, and cropped to your heart's content.

✦ Publisher's tables are simpler than Word's, but still a useful way to present data. Publisher has a number of preset designs to choose from; all you have to do is set the number of rows and columns.

✦   ✦   ✦

Advanced Publisher Techniques

Now that you know the basics of creating your own publications in Publisher, it's time to look at some more advanced techniques that can add extra pizzazz to your creations, and take a look at how you can use Publisher to design Web pages. You'll also learn all about printing: both printing to your personal printer and preparing your publication for printing by a print shop.

Adding Special Effects

Why settle for ordinary text in ordinary text frames when you can dress up your text in a number of ways? With its border art, drop caps, and WordArt tools, Publisher can give your publication the added oomph it needs to catch and hold your reader's attention.

BorderArt

Adding an ordinary border to a text or picture frame in Publisher is the same as adding a border in Word: click the Line/Border Style button on the Formatting toolbar, click More Styles, choose a size and color of line and which sides of the frame to apply it to in the Border Style dialog box, and then click OK.

But while you're in the Border Style dialog box, you'll see a tab labeled BorderArt. Click it, and the border possibilities suddenly expand exponentially (see Figure 49-1).

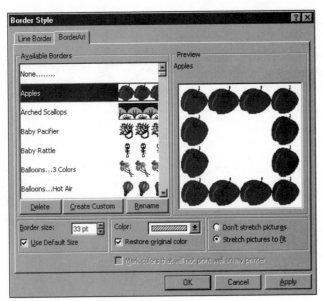

Figure 49-1: You're not limited to ordinary lines when you create borders in Publisher.

Publisher comes with a number of decorative borders, which you can peruse and choose from in the Available Borders area of this dialog box—literally everything from apples to zigzags.

Each border has a default size, indicated in the Border Size area; if you think the border is too thick or too thin, though, you can change it by setting the width of the border yourself in points. You can also modify the color, and choose whether or not to deform the individual pictures that make up some borders (such as the apples in the figure) to make a more continuous border.

Figure 49-2 shows how the appropriate border can dress up text.

You're not limited to the available borders; you can also create your own border using any graphic image. Click Create Custom in the Border Style dialog box, and then choose a picture file from your computer or from the Clip Gallery. Publisher converts it into a border, which you can then name what you wish (see Figure 49-3). That border will continue to appear in your list of available borders until you choose it and click Delete.

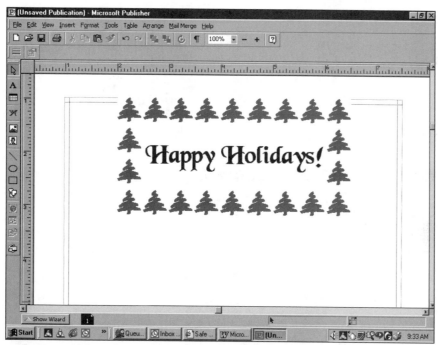

Figure 49-2: Happy Holidays looks a lot more festive with a few Christmas trees around the edges.

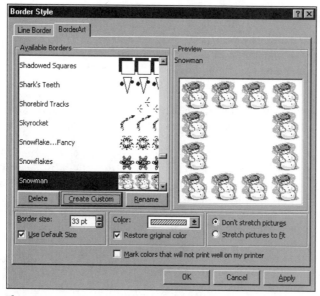

Figure 49-3: You can create your own borders from any image in the Clip Gallery or on your computer.

Drop caps

A *drop cap* is a large initial letter in a piece of text, reflecting the style of the illuminated manuscripts of the middle ages, when books often began with large, lavishly decorated initial letters.

To apply a drop cap to the beginning of a particular paragraph, click anywhere in that paragraph; then choose Format ➪ Drop Cap. This opens the dialog box shown in Figure 49-4.

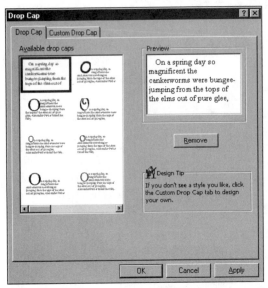

Figure 49-4: Create a fancy initial letter for a paragraph with the Drop Cap dialog box.

As with borders, Publisher has several available styles of Drop Caps ready and waiting for you. Click on the one you like and then click OK. The drop cap is added to your paragraph (see Figure 49-5).

If you don't see a drop cap you like in the Drop Cap dialog box, click the Custom Drop Cap tab and you can design your own, using the tools shown in Figure 49-6.

This dialog box is divided into two sections, one in which you choose the appearance of the initial letter, and one in which you determine its position and size.

In the Choose Letter Position and Size area, you can choose to make your drop cap drop into the paragraph until its top is even with the top of the first line of text, or have it rise above the paragraph (as in Figure 40-5), so that the bottom of the drop cap is level with the bottom of the first line of text. Or you can compromise, and have it rise a specified number of lines above the paragraph.

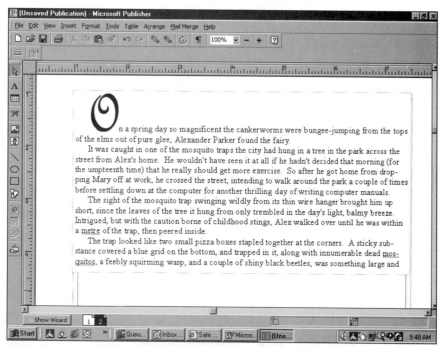

Figure 49-5: Drop caps are an ornamental touch that can bring your text alive.

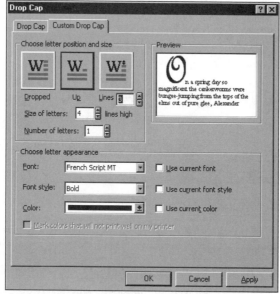

Figure 49-6: Don't like Publisher's available Drop Caps? Design your own!

You can also set the size of the drop cap, in lines, and how many letters you want in the drop cap style. (Typically just one, but some of the preset drop caps include two letters, and you might want to set the entire first word in drop-cap style.)

In the Choose Letter Appearance area, you choose a font for the drop cap, a style (regular, italic, bold, or bold italic), and a color. If you wish, you can automatically use the font, style, and color of the rest of the paragraph.

When you're happy with your drop cap, click OK.

WordArt

Another form of fancy text is WordArt, which applies special formatting to text — shapes, shadows, etc., that you can't apply through the ordinary formatting tools.

To create a WordArt object:

1. Click the WordArt Frame tool on the Objects toolbar and draw a frame the size and shape you want. Your screen will change to look like the one shown in Figure 49-7.

Figure 49-7: WordArt is really a separate program that opens whenever you create a WordArt frame.

2. Type the text that you want to apply WordArt formatting to in the Enter Your Text Here window. Press Return to add a second line of text and any additional lines of text after that.

3. From the drop-down list in the upper-left corner, choose a shape for your text (see Figure 49-8).

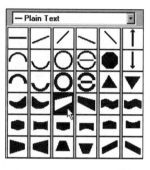

Figure 49-8: WordArt lets you fit text into any of these shapes.

4. Choose a font and font size from their respective list boxes. Choosing Best Fit from the Font Size list box automatically sets the font size at the one that best fits into the frame you've drawn.

5. The set of five buttons to the right of the Font Size list box apply various styles. From left to right, they are Bold, Italic, Even Height (which makes all letters the same height), Flip (which stacks letters on top of one another so they run top to bottom instead of left to right), and Stretch (which expands text in all directions to the edges of the WordArt frame). Apply any of these styles you like by clicking the appropriate buttons.

6. The next button to the right sets alignment: center, left, right, stretch justify (which justifies text by horizontally stretching the letters), letter justify (which justifies text by adding spaces between letters), and word justify (which justifies text by adding spaces between words). Choose the alignment you want.

7. Use the next button over to adjust the spacing between characters, using the dialog box that it opens. You can set spacing anywhere from very loose to very tight, or set a custom spacing based on a percentage of normal. Click OK when you're satisfied.

8. The Special Effects button, to the right of the character spacing button, lets you rotate text or adjust the WordArt shape you picked from the list box in Step 3. When you've made the changes you want in the Special Effects dialog box, click OK.

9. The next button to the right determines the color and pattern that will fill the letters of your WordArt. Choose one of the patterns from the Style area of the dialog box, as shown in Figure 49-9, and then choose a background and foreground color for the pattern. You can see what effect your changes will have in the sample window. When you're satisfied, click OK.

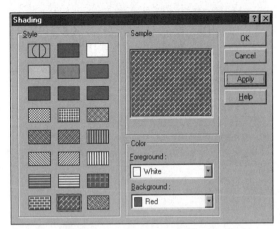

Figure 49-9: Choose a pattern to fill your letters with, and the colors to use, from this dialog box.

10. The next button lets you attach a shadow to your WordArt. Choose one of the shadows from the dialog box shown in Figure 49-10 and then click OK.

Figure 49-10: Shadows can add an intriguing 3-D look to your WordArt characters.

11. Finally, the Border button lets you choose a border, not for the WordArt frame itself (although you can add one to it after it's created just as you can to a text frame or picture frame) but for the individual characters. You can choose to outline them in a variety of thicknesses of lines, of whatever color you choose. When you're satisfied, click OK.

12. To close the WordArt controls and see your WordArt creation within your publication, click anywhere outside the WordArt frame (see Figure 49-11).

You can edit your WordArt at any time by either double-clicking on the frame to bring up the tools you worked with to create it, or by right-clicking and choosing Change Object ➪ Microsoft WordArt ➪ Open from the pop-up menu. This opens a special dialog box that lets you edit all aspects of your WordArt object (see Figure 49-12).

Figure 49-11: When you're done creating your WordArt, you'll have a block of decorative text perfect for sprucing up an ordinary publication.

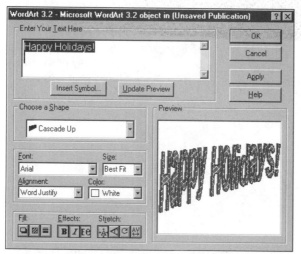

Figure 49-12: Once you've created your WordArt object, you can edit it easily from this handy dialog box.

Using Linked and Embedded Objects

Sometimes you may want to insert an object into a Publisher document that you can't create with Publisher's own tools. An Excel spreadsheet is a good example. Another is an image that you may have created using a specialized graphics program. You can insert these objects and continue to edit them if the program they were created in supports linking and embedding. First, a couple of definitions:

✦ A *linked* object is one that appears in your publication but isn't really part of it: it's stored somewhere else. All that's really included in your publication is the object's name and location; when you display or print the page that includes the linked object, Publisher fetches the object from wherever it is and dutifully includes it. One advantage of linking over embedding is that any changes made to the object in the original program (e.g., Excel or Word) will automatically be reflected in the Publisher publication in which it is included.

✦ An *embedded* object is created and edited with another program, but all the data for it is contained within your publication. Whereas a linked object has little effect on the amount of disk space your publication takes up, an embedded object may have a much greater effect.

Embedding a new object

To insert a new embedded object into your publication:

1. Choose Insert ➪ Object from the menu bar. This opens the Insert Object dialog box shown in Figure 49-13.

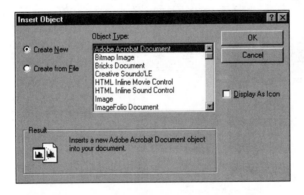

Figure 49-13: You can insert any of the objects listed here into your publication.

2. Choose the type of object you'd like to embed from the Object Type list. If you want to simply display an icon representing the object, check Display as Icon; otherwise, the entire object will be displayed.

3. Click OK. Figure 49-14 shows an embedded Microsoft Graph chart. Notice that Publisher's toolbars have vanished, replaced by the Microsoft Graph toolbar.

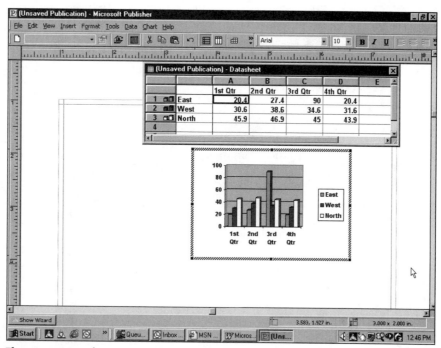

Figure 49-14: When you create a new embedded object, Publisher's controls are sometimes replaced by controls specific to that object.

Once you've finished creating your embedded object, click anywhere outside the object's frame; Publisher's controls will reappear and you can continue creating your publication as normal. Whenever you want to edit the embedded object, just double-click on it, and its controls will reappear.

Embedding an existing object

To insert an object that already exists as a file created by another program:

1. Choose Insert ➪ Object.

2. This time, click Create from File.

3. Locate the file you want to insert as a new object.

4. If you want the object to be linked, check Link; otherwise, the object will be embedded.

5. Click OK. The file you selected is inserted into your publication (see Figure 49-15).

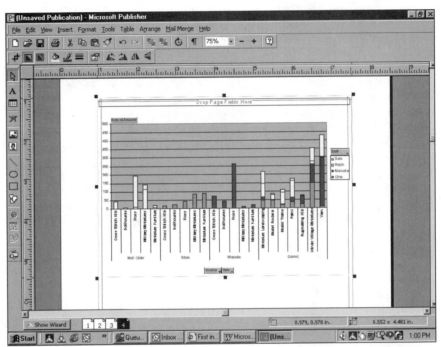

Figure 49-15: This Excel chart was inserted as a linked object from its workbook file. Any changes to the chart in that workbook will be reflected in this Publisher publication from now on.

Mail Merging in Publisher

Another useful tool in Publisher 2000 is the mail merge capability. You can create a database in Publisher specifically for that purpose, or you can use a database you created in another program.

Creating a Publisher database

To create a database file in Publisher, choose Mail Merge ➪ Create Publisher Address List. This opens the New Address List dialog box shown in Figure 49-16.

By default, the dialog box includes fields for the most common fields used in address lists. If these fields suit your purpose, just type the information into the blanks. Click New Entry to create a new entry.

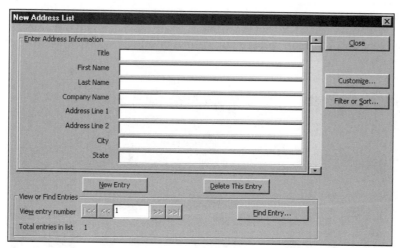

Figure 49-16: Create a database to merge with a publication here.

When you've finished, click Close, and save your database using the Save As dialog box that opens. You can locate a specific entry using the View Entry Number controls, or conduct a search for a specific entry by clicking Find Entry.

If the fields included by default don't suit you, you can customize fields by clicking Customize. You can add new fields, delete fields, or rename fields. Once you've created a database, you can edit it at any time by choosing Mail Merge ➪ Edit Publisher Address List.

Preparing your publication for merging

Obviously, to conduct a mail merge you not only need data, but a place to put it within your publication. Use the following steps to set up your publication for merging:

1. Draw a new text frame.

2. Choose Mail Merge ➪ Open Data Source. This offers three options: Merge from an Outlook contact list, Merge information from another type of file, and Create an address list in Publisher. (If you've already created an address list in Publisher, choose Merge information from another type of file.) Database formats that Publisher can use include Microsoft Access, Word, and Excel databases.

3. Choose the file you want to use as a data source and click OK.

4. The Insert Fields dialog box opens, listing all the fields contained in the data source. Click on each field in turn that you want to insert and click Insert, in the order you want to insert them. When you're done, click Close.

5. There is now a field code in your text box for each field you chose. Format those codes as you want them to appear in your final merged document (see Figure 49-17). Be sure to include any spaces or punctuation you want between the codes.

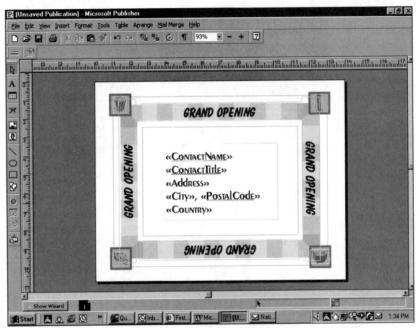

Figure 49-17: Before merging, your document will consist of field codes like these, which in this figure have been formatted for a post card announcing a grand opening.

Filtering

If you don't want to use all the information in your data source, you can filter it out by choosing Mail Merge ➪ Filter or Sort, and, under the Filter tab of the Filtering and Sorting dialog box, entering the fields you want to use as the basis of your filtering, and then comparing them to a particular value. For instance, you could filter the database so that only people whose first names are John, or whose postal codes exceed a certain number, will be merged.

Sorting

You can also have Publisher sort the records in the data source in a particular order before merging by clicking the Sorting tab in the Filtering and Sorting dialog box. You can sort by up to three fields in either ascending or descending order.

Merging

The next step is conducting the merge itself. To do so, choose Mail Merge ➪ Merge. In the publication, Publisher replaces the field codes with data from the database file, and provides you with a dialog box that lets you preview each entry in turn (see Figure 49-18).

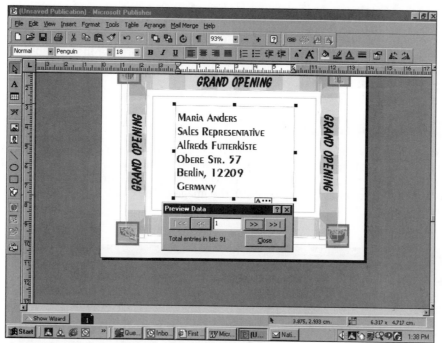

Figure 49-18: You can preview the results of your merge, and make changes to formatting as necessary, using this dialog box.

Print merge

Finally, choose File ➪ Print Merge to print your merged publication. The Print Merge dialog box varies slightly from the regular Print dialog box we'll look at later in this chapter. It asks you which entries you want to print, if you want to skip over rows on a sheet of labels, and if you want to print lines that contain empty fields. Generally it's a good idea to avoid printing those lines, because you will prevent awkward gaps in your printed document.

Designing Web Sites with Publisher

You can turn any publication you've created with Publisher into a Web page by choosing File ➪ Create Web site from current publication. You'll be asked if you want to run the Design Checker (more on that a little later). After you choose File ➪ Create Web site from current publication, you'll discover that you can save your publication as a Web page just by choosing File ➪ Save as Web Page. Several of the Publisher Catalog wizards also help you create Web pages.

Once you've created a Web page, several new tools become active on the Objects toolbar. These tools let you create a hot spot, insert a form, or insert a specific fragment of HTML code. You can also insert hyperlinks and change background and text colors.

Creating a hot spot

A *hot spot* is a specific area within a Web page that a viewer can click on to activate a hyperlink. Hot spots are generally used in conjunction with graphics. To create a hot spot, click the Hot Spot tool and draw a frame around the area that defines the hot spot. For example, in Figure 49-19, the image of the clock face is being turned into a hot spot.

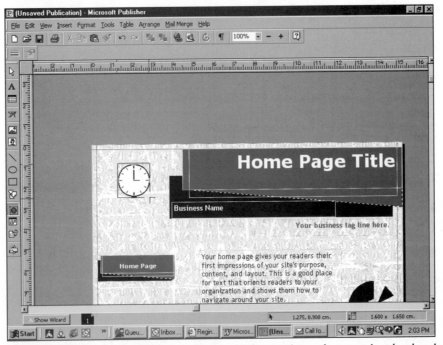

Figure 49-19: You can turn any part of your Web page into a hot spot just by drawing a frame around it with the Hot Spot tool.

As soon as you release your mouse button, the Hyperlink dialog box pops up (see Figure 49-20). It gives you four options:

✦ **A Web site or file on the Internet.** Enter the URL in the blank provided or click Favorites to choose it from the Favorites list maintained by your browser.

✦ **Another page in your Web site.** You can choose from First, Previous, Next, or Specific. For Specific, you enter the page number.

✦ **An Internet e-mail address.** Enter the address in the blank provided.

✦ **A file on your hard disk.** Type its path or browse for it. Make your selection and click OK.

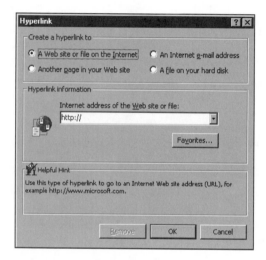

Figure 49-20: The Hyperlink dialog box lets you create links to other Web sites, files, or an e-mail address.

Inserting hyperlinks

To insert an ordinary hyperlink, simply click on the object you want the hyperlink to be attached to, or highlight the specific text, and then press Ctrl+K or choose Insert ➪ Hyperlink. The Hyperlink dialog box will open; make your selection, enter the necessary information, and click OK.

Adding a form control

Form controls are objects that enable the viewer of your Web page to make choices and/or enter data that you can later retrieve (you'll have to talk to your Internet Service Provider or network manager about how exactly).

To add a form control, click the Form Control tool on the Objects toolbar, and then choose the type of form control you want to add and draw a frame as you would for any other object.

Publisher can create five form controls: a single-line text box, a multiline text box, a check box, an option button, and a list box. It can also create a Command button that you can define as either a Submit button (which submits the data entered in the form controls) or a Reset button (which erases everything and has the submitter start over.) These controls are illustrated in Figure 49-21.

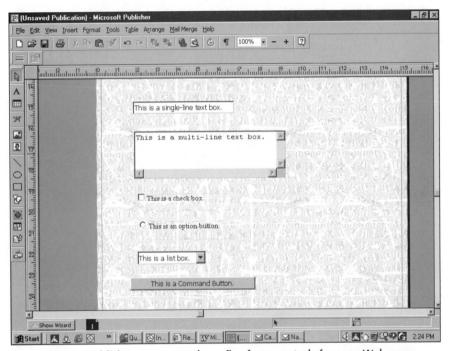

Figure 49-21: Publisher can create these five form controls for your Web page.

Each can be edited by double-clicking on it. You can set a variety of options, including how the data contained in the form is labeled when it's submitted to you and the default text that appears.

When you create a Command button, you're given options as to how data contained in forms is to be submitted to you: as a file on your Web server you can retrieve, as an e-mail message, or via a program that's provided by your Internet Service Provider. Again, you should talk to your ISP or network manager to determine what settings to use.

Inserting an HTML code fragment

Sometimes you want to insert a specific piece of HTML code into your Web page. Publisher now lets you do that without having to open your Web page in a text editor. Simply click the HTML Code Fragment button on the Objects toolbar, draw a frame, and type your HTML code into the dialog box that opens. Click OK when you're done. The HTML code will appear just as typed within the frame in Publisher, but any hyperlinks, images, etc., that it specifies will appear when the Web page is viewed in a browser.

Changing the color and background scheme

To change the color and background scheme of your Web page, choose Format ⇨ Color and Background scheme. The dialog box that appears has two tabs. The first, Standard, shows a number of preset color schemes (see Figure 49-22). (These correspond to the color schemes available for non-Web publications by choosing Format ⇨ Color Scheme.)

Figure 49-22: Choose a standard color scheme and modify the background of your Web page here.

Choose the color scheme you like; the Preview area shows you how your Web page will look with the new colors. You can also change the background, either applying a solid color or, by clicking the Browse button, using any image on your computer.

To customize your color scheme, click the Custom tab and select the new colors you want to replace the current colors in the scheme. You can save the modified scheme; once you do, it will be added to the list of available schemes on the Standard tab.

Previewing your Web page

To see what your Web page will look like once you've published it to the Web, choose File ➪ Web Page Preview. This opens the page in your default browser.

Using the Design Gallery

No matter what kind of publication you're working on, from a postcard to a Web site, Publisher has already done a lot of the design work for you. The results are stored in the Design Gallery, where you can find everything from logo designs to order forms to newsletter mastheads.

To insert an object from the Design Gallery, click the Design Gallery Object button at the bottom of the Objects toolbar. This opens the Design Gallery, which looks a lot like the Publisher Catalog. It has the following three tabs, like the Publisher Catalog:

✦ **The Objects by Category tab** (see Figure 49-23) lists all the categories of objects in the Gallery; click on the category and then choose the object you want from those displayed.

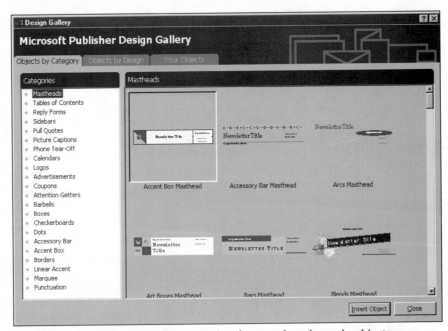

Figure 49-23: The Design Gallery contains dozens of ready-made objects you can use in your own publications.

✦ **The Objects by Design tab** shows the same objects, but organizes them differently: by related designs, rather than by category.

✦ **The Your Objects tab** shows objects you've created and added to the Design Gallery (see Figure 49-24). To add an object, select it and choose Insert ⇨ Add Selection to Design Gallery. You'll be asked to give the object a name and assign it to a category. Once you've done that, the object will remain in the Design Gallery until you remove it, and you can add it to any future publications by choosing the Design Gallery Object button and clicking on the Your Objects tab.

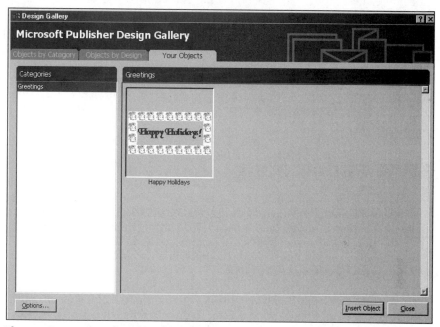

Figure 49-24: Now that this object has been added to the Design Gallery, it will be readily available for use in future publications.

Grouping by Design

Sometimes you'll create designs that are made up of many different objects—several text boxes mixed with graphics, for example. You can make it easier to move that design or resize it by grouping all its constituent objects together.

To do that, select them, either by drawing a box around them with your mouse pointer or clicking on each in turn while holding down Shift. A blue border will appear around the outside of the entire group, with a button at the bottom with what looks like two pieces of a jigsaw puzzle in it. Click that button, and the two pieces of puzzle lock together. Similarly, all the objects in the group are locked together.

Now whenever you click on one of them, the whole group will be selected, and can be moved or resized as you wish. (Note, however, that if you resize a group, the text in it doesn't resize as the graphics do; you'll have adjust font sizes manually to make them fit the resized group.) A border can be added only to the active object in the group selection.

Saving and Printing

To save a Publisher publication, choose File ➪ Save and assign the publication a name. By default, Publisher saves publications in their own file formats, but you can also save them in a variety of other file formats, including word processor formats, PostScript (if you have a PostScript printer), or as a Publisher template—in which case it will be accessible through the Publisher Catalog and can be used as the basis for future publications.

In any format except Publisher's own, you run the risk of losing formatting, so unless you have a really good reason to do otherwise, it's probably best to leave your publications in the default format.

Using the Design Checker

Before you print your publication (or, in the case of a Web page, save it to your Web server), it's a good idea to run Publisher's Design Checker.

Choose Tools ➪ Design Checker, and then choose whether to have Design Checker examine a particular selection of pages or all pages. You can also click Options (see Figure 49-25) to choose which problems Design Checker looks for.

The options are different for Web pages and regular publications. For Web pages, by default, Design Checker will alert you to empty frames, frames containing text in the overflow area (which means it's not visible), pictures that have been distorted during scaling, objects that aren't entirely on the page, text that might be converted into a graphic, blank space at the top of pages, pages that have no hyperlinks to the home page, and pages that will take a long time to download.

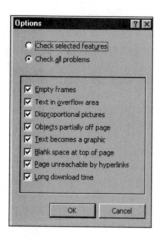

Figure 49-25: Choose the options for the Design Checker in this dialog box.

For regular publications, Design Checker looks for empty frames, objects that are hidden by other objects, text in the overflow area, objects in nonprinting regions of the page, distorted pictures, and extra spaces between sentences.

Printing

When you're satisfied your publication is as near perfect as you can make it, you're ready to print. Printing is pretty much the same as in any Office application — choose File ➪ Print, and then select a printer, a range of pages to print, and the number of copies you want.

The Print dialog box contains an additional button, Advanced Print Settings. These options include what resolution to print linked graphics at, whether to allow the printer to substitute its own fonts for fonts included in the publication, whether to allow bleeds (images that extend to the edge of the paper — as most printers won't print right to the edge, you have to make your page size slightly smaller than your paper size, and then trim the paper to achieve this effect), and whether to improve screen and print color matching. (Color printers can't, as a rule, exactly match screen colors, but checking the box for color matching may help.)

Preparing for Outside Printing

Sometimes you want to be able to send your publication to a print shop for printing on a professional press, rather than on your own printer. Publisher can help you prepare your files for that purpose.

Choose File ➪ Pack and Go ➪ Take to a Commercial Printing Service. (The other option here, Take to Another Computer, can split your file over multiple disks, embed necessary fonts, and include linked graphics, making it easy for you or someone else to work on your publication on another computer.) This opens a wizard that takes you step by step through the process of preparing your files for outside printing, including embedding TrueType fonts, including linked graphics, creating links for embedded graphics, compressing your publication, and adding an unpacking utility for decompressing it when it gets to its destination.

Summary

In this chapter you learned some more advanced aspects of working with Publisher. Highlights included the following:

✦ You can add fancy borders to any frame in Publisher by choosing Format ⇨ Line/Border Style ⇨ More Styles, and then clicking on the BorderArt tab. You can even create your own border from any graphic image.

✦ Drop Caps, created in text frames by choosing Format ⇨ Drop Cap, can dress up your text and can be customized to use the size and font you prefer.

✦ WordArt is another way to create eye-catching text. Color, shape, and even 3-D effects are possible. Use the WordArt Frame tool on the Objects toolbar.

✦ You can create a variety of objects in other programs, such as Word or Excel, and then embed them in or link them to your publication. Choose Insert ⇨ Object to link or embed an object. Linked files have the advantage that changes made to them in their originating program are automatically reflected in your publication.

✦ You can conduct mail merging in Publisher either by using a database you create within Publisher, or by using a database created in Access, Excel, or other programs.

✦ Publisher is also a powerful Web-site designing tool. You can turn any publication into a Web site; you can also add such Web-specific objects as form controls, hot spots, and HTML code fragments, using the controls on the Objects toolbar. Hyperlinks can be added to text or graphics by pressing Ctrl+K.

✦ The Design Gallery contains dozens of useful pre-designed objects you can place in your publication; you can also save objects you create into the gallery so they're only a click away the next time you need them.

✦ If you want to send your publication to a commercial printing service, choose File ⇨ Pack and Go ⇨ Take to a Commercial Printing Service, and a wizard will lead you through the necessary steps.

✦　　✦　　✦

Using PhotoDraw

Graphics are a vital part of both desktop publishing and Web page design, but in order to create good graphics, you need to have a good graphics program. Office 2000 provides one: PhotoDraw 2000. Whether you're creating your own picture, scanning one in or taking it with a digital camera, or using existing clip art you've found on one of your disks or on the Web, PhotoDraw can help you polish it up so it shines like a new penny on your document or Web page.

This chapter explains the basics of working with PhotoDraw without going into great detail; the best way to see what PhotoDraw can do for you is to experiment with it.

The PhotoDraw Workspace

When you start a new, blank picture in PhotoDraw, you'll see two different areas, the picture area (the white space shown in Figure 50-1) and the scratch area (the gray space). The picture area contains the image you're working on; if you print, whatever is in the picture area is what will appear on paper. The scratch area is like a virtual desktop, where you can drag and drop items that you may want later but you don't want to appear in your picture just yet.

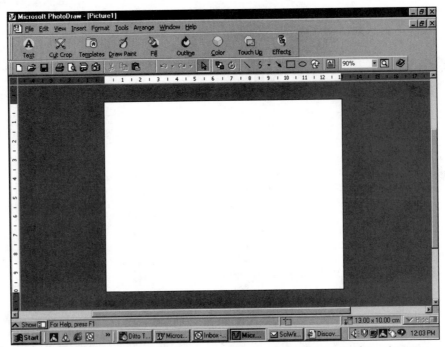

Figure 50-1: The white space area is where you create and manipulate pictures; the gray scratch area is where you can store images and objects for later use.

The rest of the workspace should be familiar to anyone who has worked with other Office programs. We'll look at these areas in more detail later in the chapter, but in brief, the similarities and differences are as follows:

✦ **Visual menu.** For one thing, there's a different-looking toolbar, one with extra-large icons on it. This is the Visual menu, which provides easy access to all the tools PhotoDraw puts at your disposal for creating and improving graphics. We'll look at each of these buttons in detail a little later on in the chapter.

✦ **Formatting toolbar.** Like other Office applications, PhotoDraw also has a Formatting toolbar, but it doesn't appear by default. To call it up, choose View ➪ Toolbars ➪ Formatting. It contains a mixture of the text formatting buttons common to all Office applications and buttons that you'd usually find on the Drawing toolbar; most of its tools appear elsewhere in PhotoDraw as well, which is why the Formatting toolbar isn't open by default.

✦ **Picture List.** The Picture List shows you thumbnail images of all the images you're currently working on, and lets you move objects from image to image easily. You can access this by choosing View ➪ Picture List, or by pressing F3.

✦ **Workpane.** The Workpane opens automatically whenever you select a tool from the Visual Menu. Figure 50-2 shows what the workspace looks like with both the Picture List (on the left) and the Workpane (on the right) opened. You can access this by choosing View Workpane or by pressing F2.

Note

You can close either the Picture List or the Workpane by clicking the Close button in the upper-right corner of each, or by clicking the Hide buttons beneath them on the Status bar.

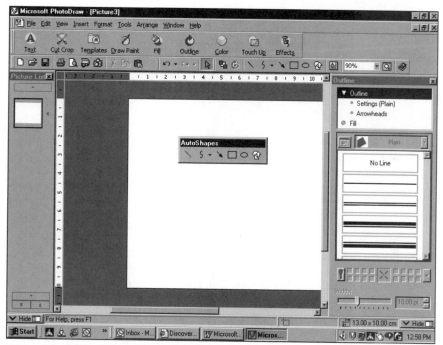

Figure 50-2: The Picture List (left) and Workpane (right) are two other basic elements of the PhotoDraw workspace.

Using PhotoDraw's Templates

The first time you start PhotoDraw—and every time you start it thereafter, unless you click the Don't Show Me This Dialog Box Again check box—you're presented with five ways to begin working with the program: Blank picture, Design template, Download from digital camera, Scan picture, or Open an existing picture (see Figure 50-3).

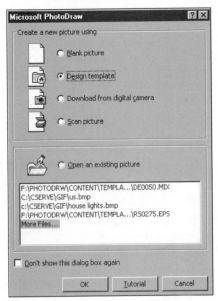

Figure 50-3: Every time you start PhotoDraw you're presented with several different ways to use it.

If you want to make things as easy as possible for yourself, and take full advantage of PhotoDraw's built-in design expertise, then your best bet is to click the Design template radio button. This opens the Templates Workpane and a preview window from which you can choose whatever template is closest to what you have in mind. In Figure 50-4, a selection of Web Graphics templates are displayed.

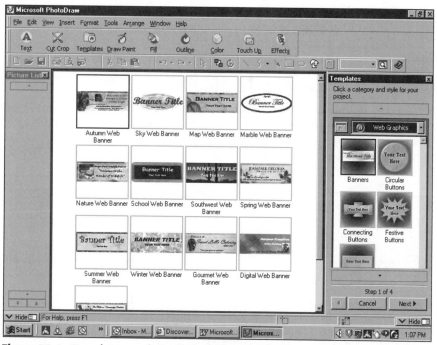

Figure 50-4: Templates are beautifully designed graphic images that you can use as is or as a starting point for your own graphics.

The Templates Workpane is really a kind of wizard, which you follow step by step to create your own graphic. In Step 1, seen in Figure 50-4, you choose the template you want from one of four main categories and several subcategories. The categories, which you access from the drop-down list near the top of the Workpane, are as follows:

✦ **Web Graphics.** This includes the banners in Figure 50-4 as well as a variety of buttons.

✦ **Business Graphics.** These include templates for bulletins, certificates, flyers, icons, labels, and logos.

✦ **Cards.** These include templates for announcement, direct mail, and invitation cards as well as postcards and tent cards.

✦ **Designer Edges.** No need for your graphic to have boring straight edges when you can choose from a variety of edges made to look like torn paper or frames or any number of artistic shapes.

✦ **Designer Clip Art.** This is special clip art designed to be easily manipulated by PhotoDraw. It appears as simple line drawings of everything from animals to sports activities, but a little tweaking can make any one of these drawings into an eye-catching illustration.

> **Note** If you can't see all of the template categories in the Template Workpane, scroll up and down through the display by clicking on the rectangles containing up- and down-pointing diamonds at the top and bottom of the display.

Working with regular templates

Once you've chosen a category (e.g., Web Graphics), a style (e.g., Banners), and a template (e.g., Southwest Banner) for your graphic, click Next at the bottom of the Workpane. This takes you Step 2 of the template process: replacing any elements of the template you don't want to keep with your own text or images (see Figure 50-5).

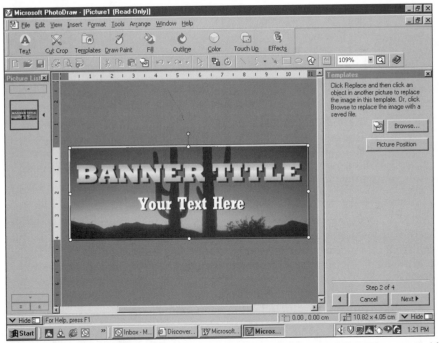

Figure 50-5: PhotoDraw's templates allow you to replace any of their elements with others you like better.

Each template is made up of one or more objects. For example, the Southwest Banner template shown in Figure 50-5 consists of three objects: a background image and two text boxes.

To replace an object with some other object, first click on it to select it. (You can tell when an object is selected in PhotoDraw because it is encased in a frame with little white circles at each corner and in the middle of each side of the frame. A green circle also appears just above the frame.) Then you can either browse your computer for an image file you like better, by clicking on the Browse button in the Workpane, or, if you have more than one picture open, you can replace the object in the current template by clicking the Replace Tool button, clicking on the thumbnail of the other picture in the Picture List, and then clicking on the object from that picture you want to use to replace the selected object in the template.

When you're happy with the objects in the template (in this example, none of them were changed) click Next.

Now you can replace the text in the text boxes with your own. To do so, click on the text box whose text you want to replace, and then type your text in the window in the Workpane (see Figure 50-6). You can also change the font, by picking the one you want from the drop-down list in the Workpane, and adjust the point size and style (regular, bold, italic, or bold italic) the same way.

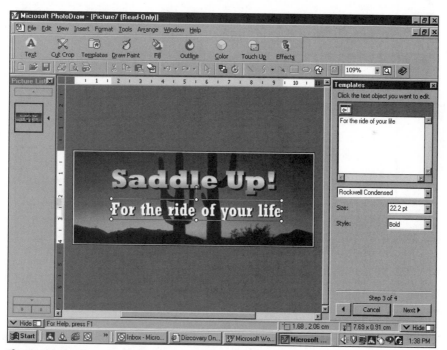

Figure 50-6: Change the template text to suit your needs.

Clicking Next again just brings up a message telling you to click Finish; click Finish and the Workpane disappears, leaving your new design in the middle of the work-space, ready for further editing, if you wish.

Working with Designer clip art

All of the templates except for the Designer Clip Art templates will take you through pretty much the same steps. Designer clip art is a little different.

Designer Clip Art templates, to begin with, look like rather badly rendered line drawings (see Figure 50-7). That's because they're really just skeletons you can use as the basis for your own fully fleshed-out clip art.

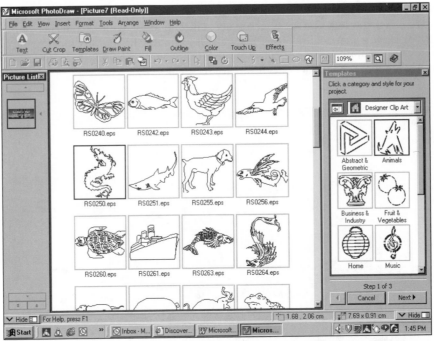

Figure 50-7: Designer Clip Art templates don't look like much when you first start working with them.

When you choose a style of Designer clip art and click Next, your next option (see Figure 50-8) is a little different; instead of replacing objects within the image, you're asked to choose a line style to replace the simple thin line that currently defines the clip art (although you can stick with that if you choose). You can select from artistic brushes (a variety of brush strokes and artful squiggles), plain lines (the kind of lines you usually use for borders in Office), and photo brushes, which are made up of a series of semi-photographic images — chain links, for example, or stars. You can control the color and width of artistic brushes and the width of photo brushes (but not the color) with the controls at the bottom of the Workpane.

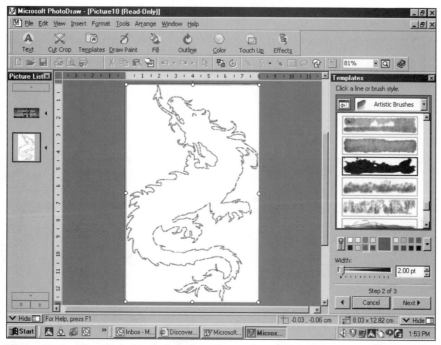

Figure 50-8: Alter the edges of your Designer clip art using these controls.

Click Next, then Finish, and continue editing your image using PhotoDraw's usual tools.

Sources of Pictures

Pictures created with templates are only one sort of picture you can edit in PhotoDraw. As noted earlier, when you first start PhotoDraw, you're also given the opportunity to open an existing image, scan one in, or download one from a digital camera.

You can also open any of those sorts of images at any time from within PhotoDraw.

Opening or inserting an existing image

Actually, you have two ways to place an existing image into PhotoDraw: you can either open it by itself in a new picture area, or you can insert it into the picture area in which you're currently working. In addition, you can browse for the image using either the usual Office Open File dialog box, or a special PhotoDraw dialog box that shows you thumbnail previews of images before you insert them.

To open a file using this visual method of browsing for images:

1. Choose File ➪ Visual Open.

2. By default, PhotoDraw opens the My Picture file folder; however, you can search elsewhere using the Look In drop-down list to the left of the dialog box. Whenever a file folder you click on contains images, PhotoDraw displays them on the right (see Figure 50-9). You can limit your search to specific types of images by using the Files of Type drop-down list.

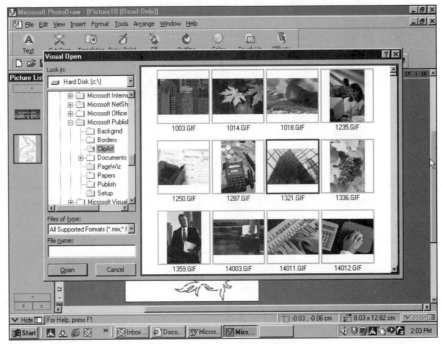

Figure 50-9: PhotoDraw's Visual Open dialog box lets you see previews of images before you open them.

3. Click on the image you want to open, and then click Open.

To insert one picture into the same picture area as another, so you can combine them, choose Insert, and then one of four options:

✦ **Clip Art.** This opens the Clip Gallery and allows you to choose images from it just as you would in any other Office application.

✦ **From File.** This opens the usual dialog box for browsing your computer's drives; if you know the exact location and name of a file, this is the way to go.

✦ **Visual Insert.** This works just like Visual Open, letting you browse for picture files and showing you a preview of each one you find.

✦ **PhotoDraw Content.** This is really just Visual Insert again, except it takes you directly to the PhotoDraw-supplied images from your PhotoDraw CD.

Scanners and digital cameras

A scanner is a device for converting images into digital form. Flat-bed scanners, probably the most common, look like photocopy machines; you place the photograph, drawing, or other item to be scanned face down in them and activate the scanner. A bright light shines on the subject and sensors translate the light reflected back to them from the subject into digital form, allowing you to re-create the image on your computer. There are also sheet-fed scanners, into which you feed images much as you do into a fax machine; and even hand-held scanners, with which you run over an image by hand.

Digital cameras are just like ordinary cameras, except instead of capturing an image to film, they capture it in a digital form, storing it on a floppy disk or in their own internal memory. You can then download that information to your computer, where you can manipulate it, print it, publish it to Web pages, or insert it into a document.

In general, scanners and digital cameras come with their own software, but PhotoDraw also contains generic software that you can use if you want. This simplifies the process while limiting the amount of control you have over it.

Use the following steps to scan a picture into PhotoDraw, for example:

1. Place the item to be scanned into the scanner.

2. Choose File ➪ Scan Picture, or click the Scan Picture button on the Standard toolbar. This opens the Scan Workpane (see Figure 50-10).

3. If you have more than one scanner attached to your system, choose the one you want to use from the Source drop-down list in the Scan Workpane.

4. Choose whether you want to perform an automatic scan, using PhotoDraw's default settings, or take more direct control of the scan using your own scanner's software, by clicking the appropriate radio button.

5. Choose a resolution and whether you want PhotoDraw to automatically correct brightness and contrast.

6. Click Scan.

   Downloading from a digital camera is much the same process; begin by choosing File ➪ Digital Camera or clicking the Digital Camera button on the Standard toolbar, choose the digital camera you want to download information from, and then use either PhotoDraw's automatic downloading function or your camera's own software to download the image you want into PhotoDraw.

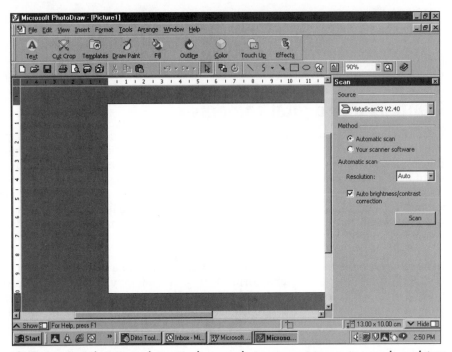

Figure 50-10: PhotoDraw lets you choose what you want to use to scan in a picture and whether to use your scanner's software or PhotoDraw's.

Creating Pictures from Scratch

If you just can't find a picture that really suits your needs, you can always create one from scratch. Several of the tools on the PhotoDraw Visual menu let you do this. Generally you'll begin by clicking Draw Paint.

Using the Draw Paint tools

Clicking the Draw Paint button gives you three further options: Draw, Shapes, and Paint. Click Draw or Shapes, and you'll see the Workpane shown in Figure 50-11, along with the floating AutoShapes toolbar; if you click Draw, the Curve button of the AutoShapes toolbar is preselected, whereas if you click Shapes, the Rectangle button is preselected.

Use the AutoShapes tools (Line, Curve, Arrow, Rectangle, Ellipse, and AutoShapes) to create a shape. (Clicking the Curve and AutoShapes buttons gives you several more options.) The shape will appear in your picture space in the color and type of line you chose in the Workpane. Again, as when you were choosing a line for a template image, you have the choice of plain lines, artistic brushes, and photo brushes.

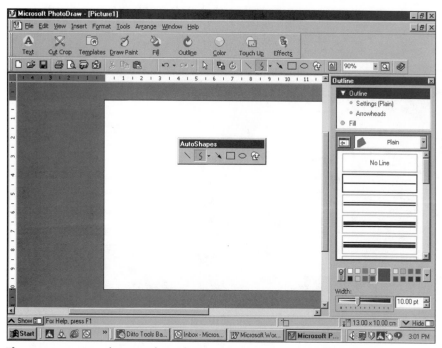

Figure 50-11: Use these tools to draw your own images in PhotoDraw.

The image shown in Figure 50-12 was drawn using a five-point-star AutoShape and the Chain photo brush.

Further refinements of the outline can be made by clicking on one of the subheadings under Outline in the list box at the top of the Workpane. Settings (Photo Brushes) opens controls that let you choose a different outline, change its width, set its transparency (so you can print text over it, for example) and choose whether to put it on top or beneath other objects within the image.

If you're working with arrows, you can choose from a variety of shapes of arrowheads and change their sizes by clicking Arrowheads in the list box at the top of the Workpane.

You can manipulate the shape of your object by clicking Edit Points. Every shape is made up of a number of points, which are placed automatically in places where the line making up the shape changes direction. By clicking and dragging on those points or changing the way in which lines are drawn between them, you can change your object's shape.

For example, in Figure 50-13, two sides of the star have been flattened out by dragging the points that define them away from the center of the image.

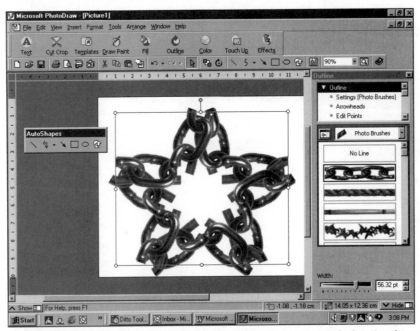

Figure 50-12: A simple shape becomes a striking illustration with the simple application of one of PhotoDraw's photo brushes.

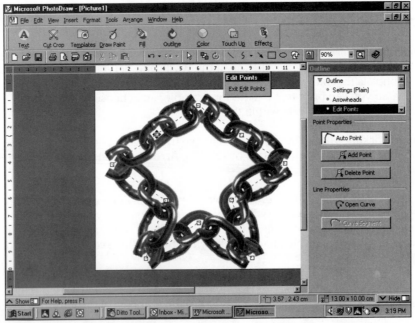

Figure 50-13: Change a shape by manipulating the points that define it.

If you choose Draw Paint ⇨ Paint from the Visual menu, the Outline Workpane will open again, and your cursor changes to what looks like a targeting reticule. Choose the type of brush you want to use, set the width and color (if it's an artistic brush), or just the width (if it's a photo brush), and paint away by clicking and dragging (see Figure 50-14). The line you draw will appear as a thin, black line until you release the mouse button, at which time the brush shape you chose will be applied to it.

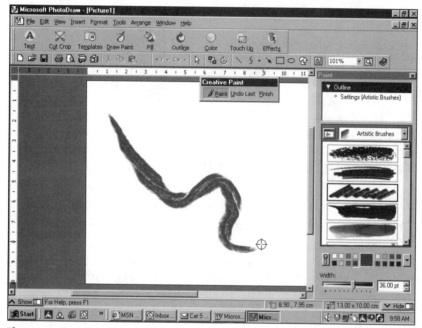

Figure 50-14: Paint freehand with your mouse using the Paint tools.

If you create a line you're not happy with (which is quite likely, as painting with a mouse isn't the easiest thing in the world), click Undo Last on the small floating Creative Paint toolbar to erase it. (You can continue clicking Undo Last to back up several steps in the painting process.) When you're done painting, click Finish on the floating toolbar.

Adding fills

Once you've drawn a picture using either the Draw, Shapes, or Paint tools, you may want to fill it with one or more colors or patterns. To do that, select the image and then click the Fill button on the Visual menu. You have five options: solid color, texture, designer gradient, two-color gradient, and picture.

Whichever one you choose, you'll open the Fill Workpane, where a drop-down list continues to make all five options available. In Figure 50-15, the Solid Color option is selected.

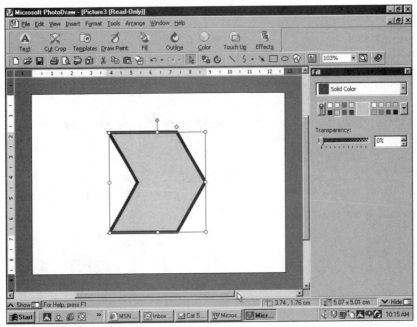

Figure 50-15: Flesh out your images with colorful fills.

For a solid color, simply choose the color you want (you can access more colors by clicking the button with the down-pointing arrow at the right of the small color palette, or pick a particular color out of your image to use as a fill by clicking the Eyedropper button and then clicking on a color in the image). You can also set the transparency. (Basically, the more transparent a color is, the fewer pixels within the area of the fill are assigned that color, which allows any other color in the same area to show through. Against a white background, the color appears to get dimmer as you increase the transparency.)

Choose Texture from the drop-down list at the top of the Workpane, and you can fill your image with one of several interesting textures, ranging from wood-like grain to clouds to money (see Figure 50-16). If you have a particular texture you like somewhere on your hard drive — maybe you've used it in a Web page — you can browse for it. Again, you can set transparency and alter the color. You can also scale the texture, making it finer or coarser as you wish.

Gradients are fills that use two or more colors flowing into each other more or less smoothly. If you choose Designer Gradient from the drop-down list of fills, you can choose from one of several interesting pre-designed gradients, ranging from rainbows to stripes (see Figure 50-17). Again, you can adjust the transparency; you can also adjust the shape, making the gradient appear in a spiral, for example, or as though applied to a cone, and change the angle of the gradient, so that instead of appearing to flow horizontally, as in Figure 50-17, it appears to flow from the corners.

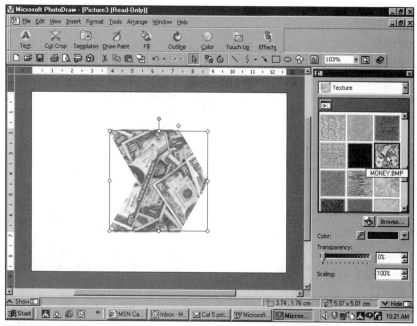

Figure 50-16: Texture is another way to make images interesting.

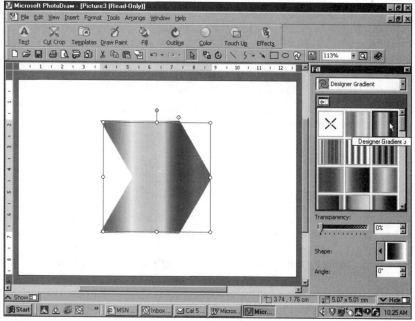

Figure 50-17: Designer Gradients add complex color and patterns to your images.

Two-color gradients are similar, except you design them yourself, choosing two colors, each with its own level of transparency, a shape, a center for the shape, and an angle.

Finally, you can fill an image with any picture (see Figure 50-18). PhotoDraw provides you with several, but you can also use any picture file already on your computer. Set the color and the transparency, and click Picture Position to move the fill picture around on the shape, so just the section of the shape you want to appear shows.

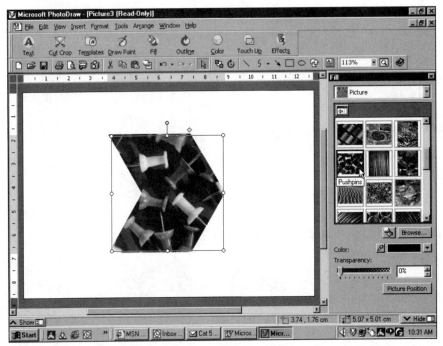

Figure 50-18: PhotoDraw provides you with several interesting pictures you can use as fills.

Working with multiple images

Many of the images you create using PhotoDraw will actually consist of several objects grouped together, as you saw when you were working with templates. When you have more than one object overlapping, you can rearrange their order respective to each other by clicking the Order button on the Standard toolbar. Click Bring to Front or Send to Back to send the selected object all the way to the top or all the way to the bottom of the stack of objects; click Bring Forward or Send Backward to move it just one step closer to the top or bottom.

Editing and Enhancing Pictures

Whether you've scanned in a picture, loaded it off a disk, downloaded it from the World Wide Web, or drawn it yourself, chances are good you're going to want to make some changes to it. As you've already seen, you can change the lines that make up some images, and you can add fills to just about anything, but PhotoDraw also lets you add text, cut and crop pictures, change their color, touch up photographs, and add a variety of special effects.

Adding text to an image

One common way to change an image is to add text to it. The banner templates we looked at earlier in the chapter, for example, combine a background image with text in the foreground. You might also want to add text as a label, to identify the picture for viewers, or to make a point.

To add text, click the Text button in the Visual menu and choose Insert Text. This opens the Text Workpane, and inserts a text box into your image containing the words "Your text here" (see Figure 50-19). To change that text, replace the matching phrase in the window in the Workpane with the text you want to appear in the image, and choose your preferred font, size, and style.

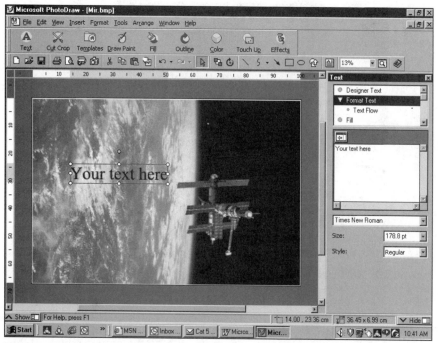

Figure 50-19: Insert any text you want into your images using the Text Workpane.

Once you've inserted text, several more options open up; you can format it, bend it, give it a 3-D effect, or apply one of several designer styles to it. You can access these options both from the list box at the top of the Workpane and by clicking the Text button in the Visual menu. The menu in the Workpane also contains Fill and Outline options, which let you access the Fill and Outline tools discussed earlier — which means you can fill the characters in your text with solid colors, gradients, or even pictures, just as you can any other image, and change their edges from plain lines to artistic brushes to even photo brushes. The possibilities are almost endless.

In addition to size and style, text formatting options include Text Flow. Clicking on this provides options for alignment, orientation (horizontal or vertical), and whether you want to apply smoothing.

You can bend any text into one of a variety of shapes, from a simple curve to a full circle (see Figure 50-20). Just click on the option you want from the menu. You can control the amount of the bend using the slider at the bottom of the Workpane.

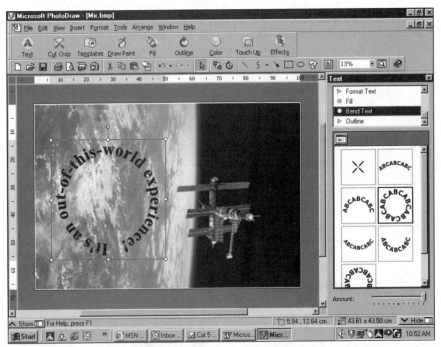

Figure 50-20: Twist your text into a complete circle, if you want, using the Bend Text controls.

You can also apply spectacular 3-D effects to your text. Choose from the menu provided (see Figure 50-21); you can fine-tune the 3-D effect using the Beveling and Extrusion controls.

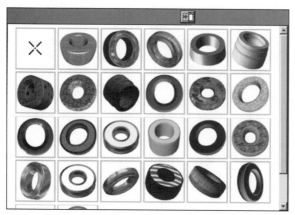

Figure 50-21: PhotoDraw lets you apply any of these amazing 3-D effects to text (and other images).

All these text tools make it possible for you to achieve just about any effect you can imagine with your text, but if you'd prefer to leave the design work to someone else, you can also choose from one of several eye-catching designer text styles (see Figure 50-22).

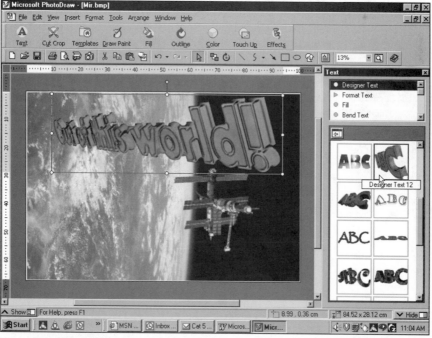

Figure 50-22: PhotoDraw's designer text styles really are out of this world!

Cutting and cropping

Sometimes you don't want everything that appears in an image; sometimes you want only part of it. You can achieve that either by cutting out the part you want and working on it separately, or by cropping away the rest of the picture until only the part you want is left. PhotoDraw lets you do both. It also lets you erase portions of a picture. To access the cutting and cropping tools, click the Cut Crop button on the Visual menu, and then choose from Cut Out, Crop, or Erase. Each opens a different Workpane.

Choosing Cut Out opens the Cut Out Workpane, which lets you select a portion of your image to cut out, much like you might cut a portion out of a picture on paper using scissors. There are four ways of cutting: by shape, by drawing, with the edge finder, or by color.

Cutting by shape

When you choose to cut by shape, you're presented with a menu of several different shapes. They look a lot like cookie cutters, and they work the same way: clicking on one creates a cutter in that shape. You just position that cutter over the portion of the picture you want (see Figure 50-23), adjust the size, click Finish, and presto!, you've got a portion of the picture cut out in an eye-catching shape. Options allow you to give the cut-out area a harder or softer edge, to cut out the opposite area (that is, to create a hole in the picture in the shape of the cut-out), and to automatically paste the cut-out area into a new picture.

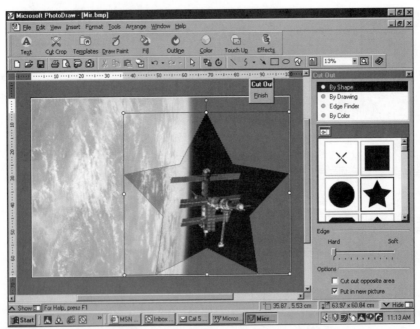

Figure 50-23: The Cut Out tools let you cut portions out of pictures in a variety of interesting shapes.

Cutting by drawing

Cutting by drawing is straightforward; click your mouse on the picture where you want the cut-out to start, and then draw a series of straight lines, clicking each place where you want to change direction. Finish back where you started (it's marked with a big yellow diamond), click again, and the area you've surrounded with the lines you've drawn will be cut out.

To adjust the drawing, place your cursor along any one of its edges. That edge will change from dashed to solid purple. Click and drag it to adjust its placement.

You can smooth out the otherwise naturally jagged lines of your cut-out with the control in the Workpane and, again, you can also choose to cut out the opposite part of the picture and/or to paste the cut-out area into a new picture automatically.

The Edge Finder

The Edge Finder is particularly useful for cutting out an object that has a distinctly different color than its background. Click anywhere along the edge of the object to start the process; a rectangle appears, which you can open up to take in as much of the object's edge as you can (see Figure 50-24). When you have to change direction, click again, just like when you were cutting by drawing. Eventually return to the big yellow diamond marking your starting point and click a final time, and the edge of the object will be defined. Click Finish, and the object is cut out. You can set the width of the Edge Finder rectangle in the Workpane.

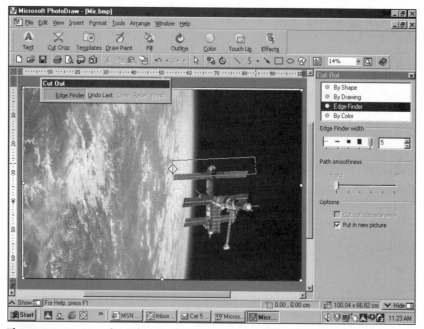

Figure 50-24: Use the Edge Finder to cut out an object in an image that is distinct from its background.

Cutting by color

Finally, you can cut out sections of a picture by color. This is particularly useful for removing solid-color backgrounds — for example, the black space in the image we've been working with in this section. Click in the color you want to cut out, and then click Finish on the floating toolbar. You can choose how exactly you want to match the color; whether you want to cut out the color only in the area where you click or throughout the picture; whether you want a hard or soft edge; whether to cut out the opposite part of the picture instead; and whether you want to paste the cut out portion into a new picture automatically.

Cropping

The Cropping Workpane looks pretty much the same as the one for cutting by shape; you'll see the same shapes, and they work the same way. The difference is that the portion outside the shape is cropped away, instead of being left behind while the portion you cut out is pasted into a new picture or dragged away.

Erasing

Erasing works exactly the same as cutting — you'll see the same menus, letting you erase by shape, by drawing, with the Edge Finder, or by color. The difference is that the area you select is discarded instead of just being cut out and saved for use elsewhere.

Adjusting color

PhotoDraw makes it easy for you to adjust every aspect of color within an image. Click the Color button on the Visual menu, and you'll see several options: Brightness and Contrast, Tint, Hue and Saturation, Colorize, Color Balance, Negative, and Grayscale. Clicking any one of these opens the Color Workpane, from which you can access all of them. If you've ever adjusted the color on a TV screen or on your computer monitor, you'll be familiar with most of these controls:

✦ **Brightness and Contrast.** These are controlled using sliders, or, if you prefer, you can click a button to let PhotoDraw adjust them automatically — but be prepared to adjust them right back again. PhotoDraw's notion of proper brightness and contrast may not correspond to your own!

✦ **Tint.** Sliders also adjust tint; one adjusts hue (from red to violet), while the other adjusts the amount, or intensity, of the selected hue. Again, you can let PhotoDraw adjust tint automatically; if you click the Automatic button, you must then click on an area of the picture that should be white or light gray. PhotoDraw will adjust the overall hue to make that happen.

✦ **Hue and Saturation.** Hue is a little different from tint; tint leaves existing colors but mixes them with the tint color, whereas hue changes existing colors into entirely new colors. Saturation corresponds to intensity; you can also adjust brightness.

✦ **Colorizing.** This has the same effect you might get if your image were made of cloth and you dipped it into a dye: the color is applied equally to the whole picture. Again, you can choose a color and the intensity of the effect.

✦ **Color Balance.** This lets you adjust the shades used in the palette of colors that makes up the picture. You can add a cyan or red tint with the topmost slider, a magenta or green tint with the second, and a yellow or blue tint with the third.

✦ **Negative.** Choose this from the Color menu, click the Negative button in the Workpane, and all the colors in your picture will be reversed: that is, they'll change to the complementary color of the original color. The effect is exactly like that of a photographic negative (see Figure 50-25).

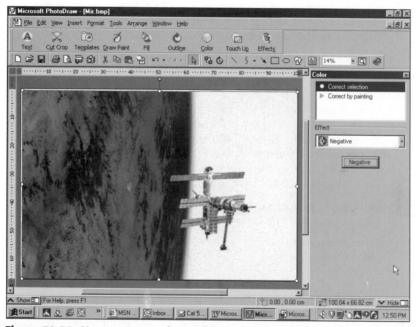

Figure 50-25: You can turn an image into a negative of itself with the click of a button.

✦ **Grayscale.** This turns a color image into a black-and-white image.

✦ **Restore.** This removes all changes and returns your image to the way it looked when you last saved it to disk.

Tip

You don't always have to apply an effect from the Color menu to the entire image. Some effects—Brightness and Contrast, Tint, Hue, and Saturation, Colorize, and Color Balance—can be applied selectively to the image. Choose Correct by Painting instead of Correct Selection from the list box at the top of the Workpane, and then choose a brush and paint in the color effect with your mouse wherever you want it to go. Other areas of the picture will remain untouched.

Using Touch Up

The Touch Up button on the Visual menu provides tools for fixing up flawed images — or just improving ones that aren't quite up to snuff. Here's how they work:

✦ **Red Eye.** This is a specialized tool for removing that red glow that sometimes appears in people's eyes in flash photographs. Click on the eye you want to correct, and then click Fix on the floating toolbar. A slider in the Workpane lets you adjust the amount of correction.

✦ **Remove Dust and Spots.** This works similarly to Red Eye; click on the spot you want to remove, and PhotoDraw fills in that space with whatever surrounds it.

✦ **Despeckle.** If a picture has a lot of dust and spots, choose Despeckle and use the slider to determine how aggressively you want to remove spots. (Be careful; if your image is very grainy and you use a high level of despeckling, you may despeckle all the detail out of your image and end up with a blur.)

✦ **Remove Scratch.** This works similarly to Remove Dust and Spots; you use your cursor to draw a line over the scratch, and PhotoDraw fills it in automatically. You can choose the size of line you want to draw over the scratch.

✦ **Clone Paint.** This lets you use existing parts of the picture to paint over another portion of it. For example, if the lawn in your picture has a big patch of bare ground in it, you could clone the grass surrounding it, and then paint that grass over the bare ground. You can choose the size of brush you want to use for painting; then click on the area you want to clone, and paint over the area you want to cover up with the pointer (see Figure 50-26).

✦ **Smudge.** This works exactly as if the picture were freshly painted; it blurs colors together and creates a smudge. You can choose a variety of brush types.

✦ **Erase.** This works exactly like an eraser; choose a brush type, run it over the picture with your mouse, and the areas over which the cursor passes are erased.

Applying effects

Effects can both improve the look of a picture and completely alter its appearance. Here's how:

✦ **Shadow** applies a shadow to an image or text. You can choose a type of shadow from the menu provided, and then adjust it further by changing its position relative to the image, its color, its transparency, and hardening or softening its edges.

✦ **Transparency** alters the transparency of the entire image. (You set the level of transparency with a slider.)

✦ **Fade Out** applies a gradation of transparency across the image. You select the starting and ending level of transparency, and then choose the shape, angle, and center of the effect — just like applying a gradation using Fill.

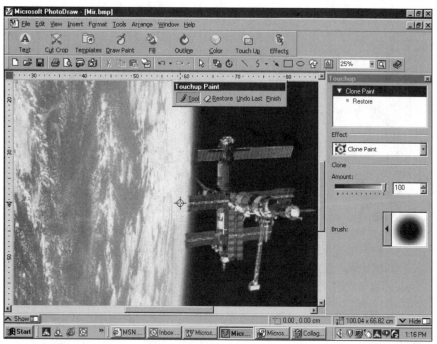

Figure 50-26: Using Clone Paint, portions of the space station's solar panels disappear.

✦ **Blur and Sharpen** does exactly what it sounds like. A slightly fuzzy picture can be effectively sharpened using this sliding control, or one that's a little too harsh can be softened.

✦ **Plug-Ins** are add-ons to PhotoDraw that provide additional effects.

✦ **Distort** can change your picture in a number of ways that may be highly effective — or may just make it impossible to tell what your picture is supposed to look like. Experiment by clicking each one in turn. In Figure 50-27, Kaleidoscope distortion has been applied. You can apply more than one distortion by clicking Lock Distort after applying the first one, and then choosing another. The first distortion will remain in place and the second distortion will be applied in addition. You can apply additional distortions by clicking Lock Distort after each one.

✦ **3-D** applies the same 3-D effects already described in the section of this chapter on inserting text to images.

✦ **Designer Effects** offers a huge number of interesting effects (see Figure 50-28), which can do everything from making your picture look like it was painted in watercolor to turning it into stained glass. Experiment with all these effects to see what is possible. (Many effects, in turn, have a variety of settings that can be changed, which means the possibilities, if not endless, are at least astronomical.)

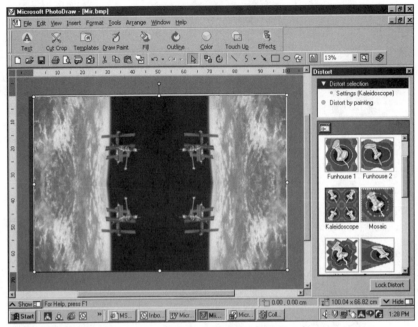

Figure 50-27: Distort your picture to make it more effective.

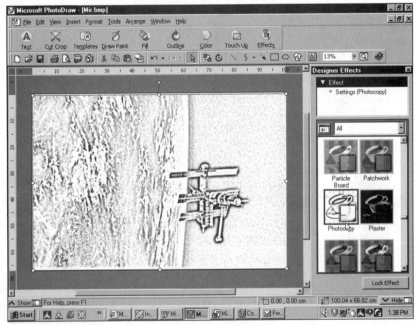

Figure 50-28: Designer Effects can alter your picture's appearance in a vast number of fascinating ways. This is just one.

Saving PhotoDraw Images

There are three options for saving PhotoDraw images, each accessible under the File menu. Save saves the image you're working on in whatever format it was originally created in, if it's an existing image you've opened to work on in PhotoDraw. If you've added objects to it—text, for example, or an additional image—you'll get a warning message telling you that saving it in the original format will flatten out all the objects so you won't be able to edit them individually again.

To avoid that, or to specify a different file format, choose Save As. PhotoDraw can save images in a number of formats, including GIF, JPEG, and Portable Network Graphics (PNG), the three most commonly used formats for Web pages; as well as PC Paintbrush (PCX), Windows Bitmap (BMP), Tag Image File Format (TIF), and Targa (TGA) Formats. If you want to be able to work on individual objects within the image again, however, you'll want to save it in the MIX format, which is used by PhotoDraw and Picture It, another Microsoft picture-editing application; or, you can save it in both formats so you can, for example, post it to the Web but continue to make changes to it in the future.

The third Save option, Save for Use In, opens a wizard (see Figure 50-29) that helps you save your picture in the most appropriate format for use on the Web, as a thumbnail image on the Web, in an Office document, in an onscreen presentation, or in a publication. Choose the appropriate radio button, and then follow the wizard's instructions to save your image.

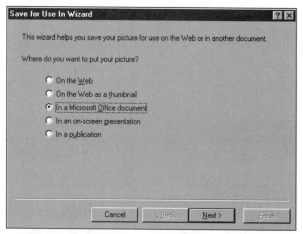

Figure 50-29: PhotoDraw can guide you through the process of saving your image in the most appropriate format.

Once the image is saved, you can insert it into any Office document by using the appropriate Office application's Insert Picture from File command and locating the saved image on your hard drive.

Summary

In this chapter, we took a brief look at Microsoft PhotoDraw and how it can help you create more effective images for your Office documents. Among other things, you learned:

✦ PhotoDraw offers templates for many common design needs that can save you time and effort.

✦ Images you work on in PhotoDraw can be drawn from PhotoDraw's own collection of Designer clip art, from the Clip Gallery, from elsewhere on your computer, from a digital camera, or from a scanner.

✦ You can also create your own images using PhotoDraw's Draw, Paint, Text, and Fill controls.

✦ PhotoDraw offers a number of methods of cutting and cropping images, in a variety of shapes.

✦ PhotoDraw gives you full control over the color of any image, and also provides you with tools for touching up scratched or dirty photos.

✦ With Effects, you can alter your image's appearance in an enormous number of ways, from adding shadows to turning them into watercolor paintings. You can even sharpen blurred images and soften harsh ones.

✦ PhotoDraw lets you save your images in any one of several popular picture formats; however, if you want to work on the separate objects that sometimes make up an image, you need to save it in PhotoDraw's own MIX format.

✦   ✦   ✦

Integrating and Automating Office Applications

◆ ◆ ◆ ◆

◆ ◆ ◆ ◆

Using Binder

Y ou'll often find yourself working on projects that require documents created in a variety of Office applications. You could use linking and embedding (discussed in the next chapter) to create the whole thing in, say, Word, adding bits and pieces created in other applications as necessary, but this will greatly increase the size of your document and slow down your computer.

Cross-Reference For a full discussion of linking and embedding, see Chapter 52, "Building Integrated Documents."

For very complex joint documents, a better option is to use the Binder, a special tool supplied with Office that lets you attach a variety of documents together; just like in school, where you probably carried notes for many different classes in the same binder.

Creating a Binder and Adding Documents

To create a binder, choose Start ➪ Programs ➪ Office Tools ➪ Microsoft Binder. A blank binder appears — not that it's much to look at (see Figure 51-1).

Once you've opened a binder, you can add documents to it. There's more than one way to do this.

Dragging documents into the binder

One of the easiest methods is to simply drag files into the binder. You can do this by arranging your desktop so the My Computer window and the binder are side by side. Find the Office file you want to add to the binder on your computer, and then just click and drag it into the white space down the left side of the binder window (see Figure 51-2). You can also do this from Windows Explorer or from your desktop.

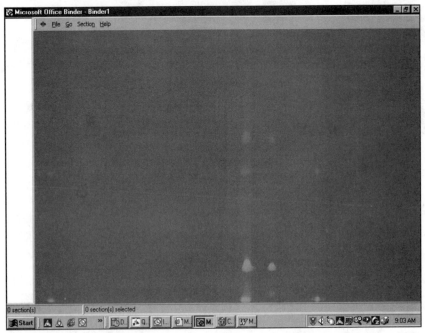

Figure 51-1: A blank binder presents one of the duller screens Office has to offer.

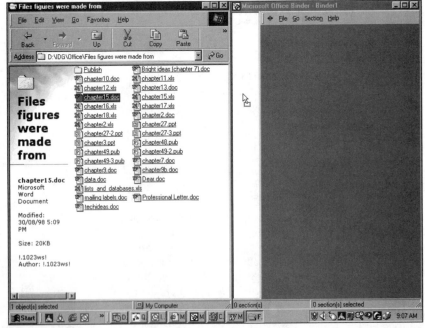

Figure 51-2: You can drag and drop Office files from your computer into your binder.

Adding existing documents using the Section command

You can also add files to the binder using the Section command on the menu. If that seems a little counterintuitive it's only because, in binder-speak, each file you add is a section. It makes sense, because essentially what you're creating with Binder is one large document, which consists of documents you originally created separately. Use the following steps to add an existing file to the binder using the Section command:

1. Choose Section ➪ Add from File.

2. In the Add from File dialog box, a standard browsing dialog box, choose the file you want to add.

3. Click Add.

The left pane of the binder now displays an icon for the document, while the document itself appears in the binder's main pane (see Figure 51-3). Notice that when you add a file to the binder, the application that created that file is automatically activated, too.

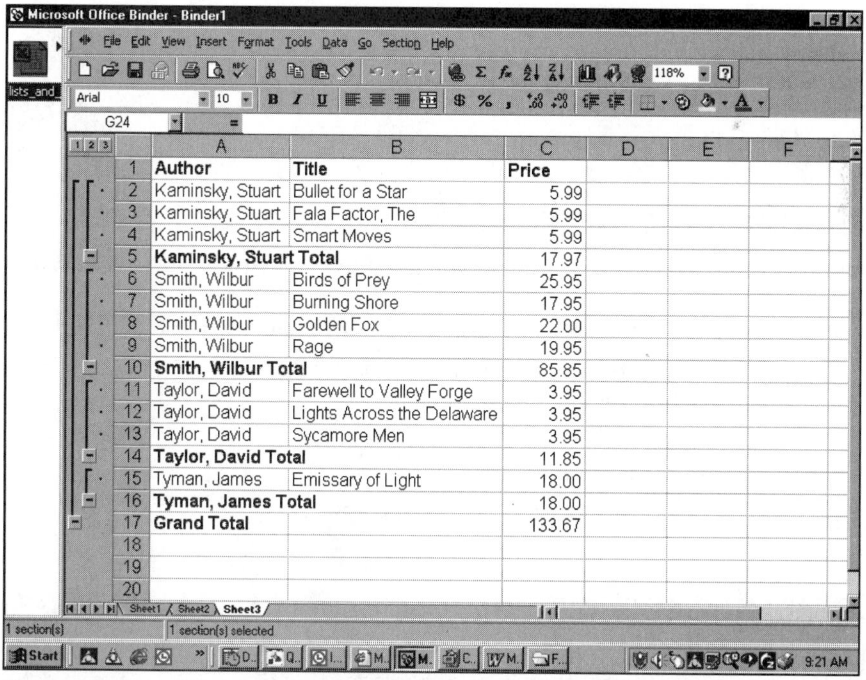

Figure 51-3: Adding an Office document, such as this Excel workbook, to the binder places an appropriate icon in the left pane and opens the Office application that created the document in the binder's main pane.

Creating new documents in Binder

You can also create brand-new Office documents in Binder. To do so:

1. Choose Section ➪ Add.

2. In the Add Section dialog box, which is similar to the New dialog box you see whenever you create new documents in Office applications, click the tab for the type of publication you want to add, e.g., General, Letters & Faxes, Reports, etc.

3. Click the icon for the type of template you want to use to create the new document.

4. Click OK. An icon for the selected template appears in the left pane; the template itself, along with the appropriate application, opens in the main pane.

Working with Documents in a Binder

In general, you can edit the sections in a binder just as you could when they were separate documents outside the binder. To provide yourself with a bit more room to do so, click the Show/Hide Left Pane button just to the left of the File command on the menu bar. This hides the left pane. To show it again, click the button again.

You can perform a number of actions on the sections within the binder to organize them as you see fit.

Selecting sections in Binder

Before you can do anything, though, you need to know how to select sections:

✦ Selecting a single section is easy — just click on its icon in the left pane.

✦ To select a range of contiguous selections, click the icon for the first section, move to the last one, and Shift+click.

✦ To select noncontiguous selections, click the icon for the first section, then Ctrl+click the icons for the other sections.

✦ To select all selections, choose Section ➪ Select All.

Organizing sections

Now that you know how to select sections, you can begin organizing them. Binder lets you delete, duplicate, rename, and rearrange them.

✦ To delete a section, highlight it, right-click, and choose Delete from the pop-up menu, or choose Section ➪ Delete.

✦ To duplicate a section, highlight it, right-click, and choose Duplicate, or choose Section ⇨ Duplicate. This opens the dialog box shown in Figure 51-4, where you can choose which of the current sections you want the duplicated section to follow.

Figure 51-4: Decide where you want a duplicated section to appear in the binder.

✦ To rename a section, highlight it, right-click, and choose Rename; or choose Section ⇨ Rename. You can then type the new name directly over the old one in the left pane.

✦ Finally, to rearrange sections, click them and drag them to where you want them in the left pane. If you prefer, you can choose Section ⇨ Rearrange. This opens the Rearrange Sections dialog box shown in Figure 51-5. Highlight the name of the section you want to move, and then use the Move Up and Move Down buttons to reposition it within the list.

Sometimes when you're reorganizing sections, you may want to hide some of them so that only the most crucial ones are displayed in the left pane. To hide a section, highlight it and choose Section ⇨ Hide. You can unhide it by choosing Section ⇨ Unhide Section. (Hiding a section also prevents it from being printed when you choose the Print All Visible Sections option.)

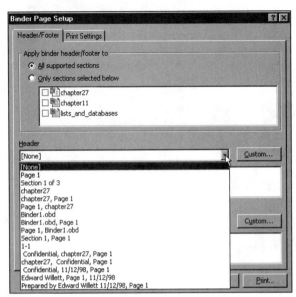

Figure 51-5: Use this dialog box to reposition sections within the binder.

Opening sections in their original programs

Sometimes you'll want to move outside the binder and work on a section in the program in which it originated. You don't have to close Binder to do so; just highlight the section and choose Section ➪ View Outside. The file is opened in the original program. If you return to the binder while you are viewing a section outside the binder, the section isn't visible; instead you get a message telling you it's being viewed outside Binder. To return the section to the binder, close it in the original program.

Saving and Updating Binder Files

Once you've created and organized a binder, you'll want to save it. You save a binder just as you do any other Office creation: choose File ➪ Save Binder, find a folder for it, and give it a name.

Note   By default, binders are saved to the My Documents folder. You can change this default location by choosing File ➪ Binder Options, and then entering a new default location in the default binder file location field.

Updating original files

It's important to understand that when you save a binder, you're making copies of the original files that make up the sections. That means that any changes made to the originals won't be reflected in the versions in the binder, and any changes made to the documents inside the binder won't be reflected in the originals. To save changes made in the binder to one of the original files, choose Section ➪ Save As File, and then locate the original version and overwrite it with the version you're saving.

Saving a binder as a template

If you create the same binder document over and over, just changing the files it contains, you might want to save a template version. The template will store the overall structure of the binder, plus header and footer settings and print settings. To turn a binder into a template:

1. Open the binder you want to convert into a template.

2. Choose File ➪ Save Binder As.

3. From the Save As Type drop-down list, choose Binder Templates. (By default, Binder saves templates into the appropriate Templates folder. If you save it in a different folder, it won't appear on the Binders tab when you choose File ➪ New Binder.)

4. Type a name for the template into the File Name box.

5. Click Save.

Printing Binders

One of Binder's most powerful features is its ability to print all the sections it contains as a single document, with headers and footers and consecutive page numbers.

Setting up your binder pages

To set up your current binder for printing, choose File ➪ Binder Page Setup. This opens the dialog box shown in Figure 51-6, with the Header/Footer tab selected.

Figure 51-6: Set up headers and footers using this dialog box.

To set up headers and/or footers:

1. In the top section, decide whether you want the header and footer applied to all sections, or just to those you specify by checking the boxes beside their names in the list.

2. Choose the header and footer you want from the drop-down lists provided.

3. If you don't want to use any of the headers or footers provided, you can create your own. To do so, click the Custom button. This opens the Custom Header dialog box shown in Figure 51-7.

4. Enter the text you want in each of the three fields: one for the left side of the page, one for the center, and one for the right. You can format the text by clicking the Font button in the upper-left corner, which opens a dialog box that lets you set font, style, and size.

5. You can also click one of the buttons at the top to enter a preset field. From left to right, these buttons will automatically insert the page number, section number, number of sections, section name, binder name, date, and time. You can put more than one of these fields in each of the boxes.

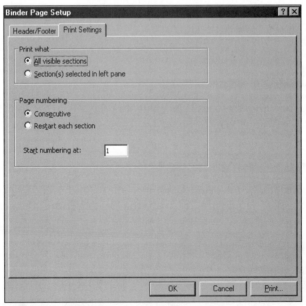

Figure 51-7: Create custom headers and footers for your binder document here.

6. Click OK to return to the Binder Page Setup dialog box.

7. Next, click the Print Settings tab. This opens the dialog box shown in Figure 51-8. Here you have three choices to make: do you want to print all the sections that aren't hidden, or just sections you've selected in the left pane; do you want page numbering to be consecutive or to restart with each new section; and what number do you want page numbering to start with?

8. Click OK.

Previewing binders

To preview a binder before printing, choose File ⇨ Binder Print Preview. Binder will show you an onscreen preview of what your document will look like on paper. What this preview looks like depends on what type of section you're viewing; Binder uses the same Print Preview as the application in which the section was created. Suppose, for example, you're viewing a section created in Excel. Print Preview will look like the screen shown in Figure 51-9. Move from section to section with the floating toolbar. (Binder cannot show you a print preview of PowerPoint presentations. To preview those, you'll have to open them in PowerPoint itself.)

Cross-Reference

For information about how to use Print Preview with different section types, refer to the chapters of this book that discuss the various Office applications in detail.

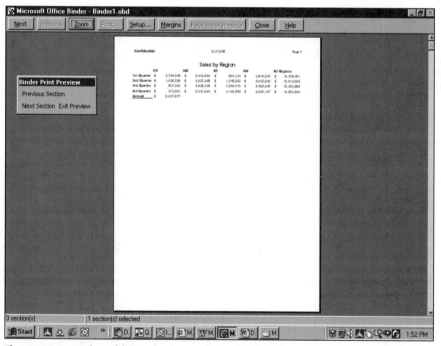

Figure 51-8: Make additional print setting selections here.

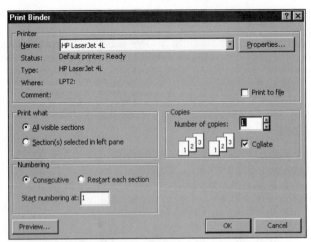

Figure 51-9: Print Preview shows you exactly what your document will look like when printed.

Printing your binder

Finally, you're ready to print. To do so, choose File ➪ Print Binder. In the Print Binder dialog box (see Figure 51-10), you have a couple of specialized options. You have to choose whether to print all visible sections or just the sections selected in the left pane. You also get the opportunity to change your mind about page numbering — you can change it from Consecutive to Restart Each Section and back again, and change the starting page number.

Otherwise, this is like other print dialog boxes you've seen. Choose a printer, enter the number of copies you want to make, and decide whether you want copies collated; then click OK.

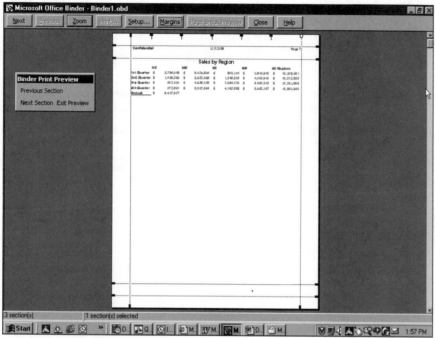

Figure 51-10: Make your final printing selections here.

Summary

Binders, just like binders you kept notes in at school, help you organize many different files into one large document. Some aspects of Microsoft Binder we discussed in this chapter included the following:

✦ You can add documents (called *sections*) to a binder just by clicking on them in the My Computer window and dragging them into the left pane of the binder. You can also choose Section ➪ Add from File and browse for files you want in the binder.

✦ You can work in the binder right from the very beginning, creating and editing new documents inside it. To start a new Office document in the binder, choose Section ➪ Add and then choose the type of document you want to create.

✦ You can select sections in the left pane just by clicking on them, and then rename them, delete them, or duplicate them by right-clicking and making the appropriate choice from the pop-up menu.

✦ To open a binder section in the program where it originated, choose Section ➪ View Outside.

✦ You can give your binder document consistent headers and footers over all the sections, and consecutive page numbers. Choose File ➪ Binder Page Setup.

✦ Chose File ➪ Binder Print Preview before printing to see exactly what your binder document will look like on paper.

✦   ✦   ✦

Building Integrated Documents

Each Office application is so powerful in its own right that you can usually find some way to make it do whatever you want it to. Forcing Excel to print a letter, however, or trying to make a Word table work like a spreadsheet isn't very efficient. That's where linked and embedded objects come in: you can use them to create an Office document in one application that contains objects you created in other applications. Not only that, you can arrange things so that changes made to those objects in their original applications are automatically reflected in the document in which they all appear together.

Inserting Objects from Other Applications

There's more than one way to insert an object created in another application into your current Office document.

Copy and paste

One simple method to move an object from application to application is simply to copy and paste it. For example, if you highlight a range of cells in an Excel spreadsheet, select Edit ⇨ Copy, go to Word, and select Edit ⇨ Paste, the spreadsheet will be pasted into Word as a Word table. The trouble with this is that you no longer have an Excel spreadsheet, which means you can't manipulate the information in that object the way you could before, even though you might still like to.

Using Paste Special in Word

A better choice is to select Edit ⇨ Paste Special in Word. This opens the dialog box shown in Figure 52-1. Choose the format in which you want to paste the object from the Clipboard, and then click OK. By default, Paste Special creates an embedded object, but you can make it a linked object by choosing Paste Link.

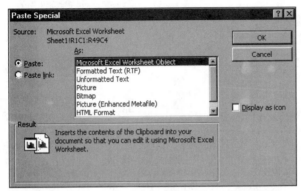

Figure 52-1: The Paste Special dialog box determines how an object created in another application is pasted into the current one.

Choosing a paste method

You have several ways to paste your copied object into the new application:

✦ **Object.** This creates an embedded or linked object, depending on whether you have the Paste or Paste Link radio button selected. If you want to be able to edit the object using the tools of the application that created it, this is the choice to make.

✦ **Text.** You can insert many objects as either formatted (RTF) or unformatted text. If it's primarily the words in the object you're interested in, then choose one of these options.

✦ **Picture.** You can insert the object as a high-quality picture—the equivalent of a screenshot—of itself, in either Picture (the best choice for high-quality printers and also the one that takes up the least disk and memory space), Bitmap, or Picture (Enhanced Metafile) format. The only editing you'll be able to do to the object if you make this choice is the kind of editing you can do to an inserted piece of clip art: resizing, recoloring, etc.

✦ **HTML.** This inserts the object in HTML—extremely useful if you're building a Web page.

Using the Insert Object command

You can also insert objects into Office applications by choosing Insert ➪ Object from the menu. This opens a dialog box similar to the one shown in Figure 52-2, from Word.

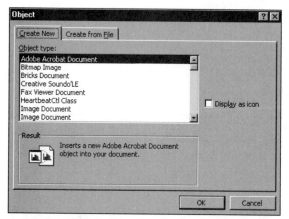

Figure 52-2: The Insert Object command lets you insert a variety of objects created in other programs into an Office application.

By default, the Create New tab is selected. Choose the type of object you'd like to insert from the Object Type list. If you wish, you can display the object as an icon that has to be double-clicked in order to view the object. When you've made your selection, click OK, and a new object of the type specified will be embedded in your Office document.

Clicking the Create from File tab changes the look of the dialog box to that shown in Figure 52-3.

Click Browse to locate the file you want to insert as a new object. By default, this will create an embedded object, but you can make it a linked object by checking the Link to File box.

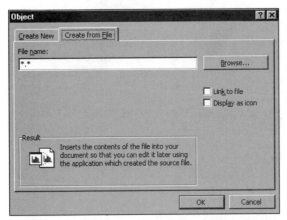

Figure 52-3: Use these tools in your Office application to create an embedded or linked object that already exists as a separate file elsewhere.

Using special commands

Some Office applications have built-in commands for creating commonly used embedded objects:

✦ **In Word.** The Standard toolbar includes a button for creating an Excel spreadsheet. Click it and choose the number of rows and columns you want. (You can add more columns and rows later using the Excel controls.)

✦ **In PowerPoint.** You can insert a Word table by choosing Insert ➪ Picture ➪ Microsoft Word Table. Choose the number of rows and columns you want from the little dialog box that opens.

Working with Embedded Objects

Once you've inserted an embedded object into an Office document, it appears to be part of the document. But there's a big difference: If you click on the object once, you can move it around and possibly resize it, but you can't edit it. To do that, you have to double-click on it. When you do, the menus and controls of the current application change to those of the application that created the object, so you can use the controls of the object's native application to edit it.

Figures 52-4 and 52-5 illustrate this. Figure 52-4 shows an embedded object, part of an Excel worksheet, as it looks embedded in a Word document; Figure 52-5 shows what it looks like when you double-click on the embedded worksheet to edit it.

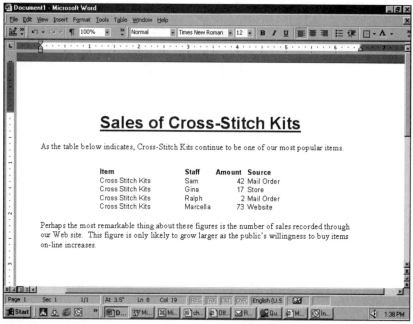

Figure 52-4: This embedded Excel spreadsheet looks like an ordinary Word table.

Figure 52-5: This looks like an ordinary Word table, until you double-click on it to edit it.

Working with Linked Objects

Linked objects, like embedded objects, look like they're part of your Office document—but they really aren't. They're simply displayed in it. They really still live somewhere else, associated with the program that created them.

If you're working with dynamic data that changes all the time, linked objects are great, because it doesn't matter if someone changes some figures in the Excel spreadsheet you've linked on page 3 of your report—the link ensures that your report reflects those changes.

Caution   Linked objects require two documents in two different files, the source document and the destination document. If you want to send a document containing linked objects to someone else, you also have to send the source document for those objects–and make sure that the recipient stores the source document in exactly the same drive and file folder as you had it stored. If the source document isn't where the destination document expects it to be, the link won't work.

Moving and resizing linked objects

You can move or resize a linked object just as you can move or resize an embedded object. You can also edit it in its source application by double-clicking on it, with one difference: When you double-click an embedded object, the menus and toolbars of the originating program are displayed in the destination document's application. Double-clicking a linked object opens the source document in the originating application: In the case of our previous example, it would open the source document in Excel in a new window.

Editing and updating links

If you have a lot of linked objects in the same document, the easiest way to work with them is to choose Edit ➪ Links. This opens a dialog box similar to the one shown in Figure 52-6. (Its appearance varies slightly among the various Office applications.)

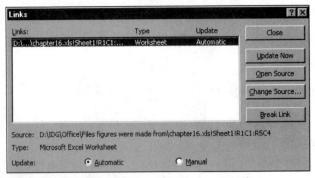

Figure 52-6: Edit your links using these controls.

The list box lists all the linked objects in the current document (in this case, only one). Down the right side are additional controls:

✦ **Update Now** updates the linked object in the destination document to match the source.

✦ **Open Source** opens the source file in its originating application.

✦ **Change Source** lets you browse your computer for a different source file. Obviously, changing source files is likely to completely change the appearance of your current document. You can also use Change Source to find a source file that has been relocated, thus repairing the severed link.

✦ **Break Link** turns the linked object into a picture, severing its connection with the source file.

You can also choose to either automatically update the linked object whenever you open the destination document or whenever the source file changes, or you can choose to update the linked object only when you click Update Now.

Using the Locked and Save picture options

Some applications include two additional options in this dialog box: Locked and Save Picture in Document. If Locked is available, you can select it to deactivate the Update Now button and prevent the linked object from being updated automatically.

Save Picture in Document is normally checked. If you uncheck it, you can save a graphic — from PhotoDraw, for example — as a linked object, instead of inserting it into your document. This can save disk space.

Other Methods of Sharing Data

The four main Office applications also offer additional ways to share data. We'll look at collaborating on a network (including the Internet) in a separate chapter, but there are several other ways in which Office applications work together.

For a full explanation of how you can collaborate on a network with Office 2000 applications, see Chapter 54, "Collaborating on a Network."

Sending a Word document to PowerPoint

Word lets you send the currently active document to PowerPoint as the basis of a new presentation. It automatically turns each paragraph of the document into a new PowerPoint slide (see Figures 52-7 and 52-8). To send a document to PowerPoint, choose File ➪ Send To ➪ Microsoft PowerPoint.

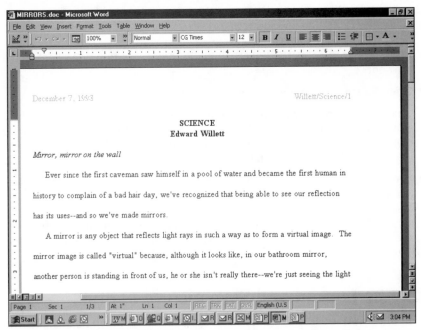

Figure 52-7: This ordinary Word document can be sent to PowerPoint.

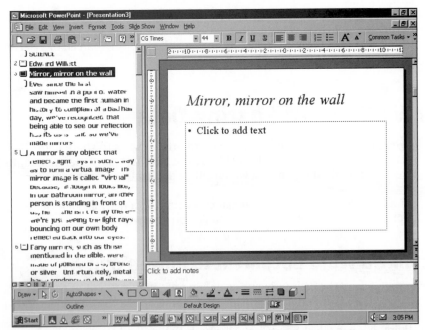

Figure 52-8: When a Word document is sent to PowerPoint, it becomes a presentation in which each paragraph forms a new slide.

Analyzing Access data in Excel

Access is a great application for storing and retrieving, but when you want to analyze data, Excel wins out. For that reason, Office makes it easy to analyze Access databases in Excel.

To do so, open the Access table you want to analyze, and then choose Tools ⇨ Office Links ⇨ Analyze it with MS Excel. Excel opens and the table is converted into a spreadsheet, where you can play with the data to your heart's content.

Publishing Access reports with Word

Access has a disadvantage when it comes to designing reports for its data: its tools are awkward. For that reason, Access also makes it easy to publish reports in Word.

Open the report you want to publish in Word in Access, and then choose Tools ⇨ Office Links ⇨ Publish it with MS Word. Access opens Word and converts the report into a new document in RTF format.

Merging Access data in Word

Access also lets you easily merge data from a database table with a Word document. To do so:

1. In Access, open the table you want to merge, and then choose Tools ⇨ Office Links ⇨ Merge it with MS Word. This opens the wizard shown in Figure 52-9.

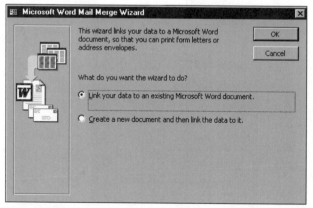

Figure 52-9: Use this wizard to merge Access data in Word.

2. Choose either to link your data to an existing Microsoft Word document — a form letter, for instance — or to create a new document and then link the data to it. If you choose to use an existing document, you'll be asked to select it.

3. Access opens Word and either displays the existing document you chose, or a blank document that you can create and format. You can't see it, but the Word document and the Access document are linked.

4. From here on, the process of using the Access data is the same as creating any other mail merged document in Word.

Cross-Reference   To review mail merging procedures, see Chapter 4, "Forms, Fields, and Merging."

Sending a PowerPoint presentation to Word

Just as you can turn a Word document into the basis of a PowerPoint presentation, you can turn a presentation into a Word document, which can be a great way to create a hard-copy version of it.

To do so, open the presentation you want to turn into a Word document, and choose File ➪ Send To ➪ Microsoft Word. This opens the Write-Up dialog box shown in Figure 52-10.

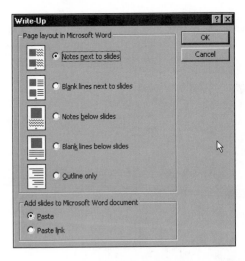

Figure 52-10: Turn your PowerPoint presentation into a Word document, laid out just the way you like it.

Choose how you want to lay out the pages (you can position slides two to a page, with notes or blank lines beside them; one to a page, with notes or blank lines below them; or send the outline only, without any slide images), and whether you want to paste (embed) the presentation into Word or paste it as a linked object.

Click OK. PowerPoint creates a new document in Word and pastes the presentation into it.

Summary

In this chapter, you learned ways to build documents using more than one Office application at a time. Key points included the following:

✦ There's more than one way to insert an object from one application into another. You can copy it and select Paste Special, choose Insert ➪ Object from the menu, or, in some applications, use built-in tools.

✦ When you use Paste Special, you can choose to insert an object in a number of formats, which vary depending on what kind of object you copied. Typical options include inserting the object as text, as a picture, as a linked or embedded object, or as HTML.

✦ Embedded objects can be edited using the program that created them by double-clicking on them.

✦ Linked objects can be edited in the same way. The difference is that linked objects are created from a source file, and if that source file is changed in the originating program, the display in the destination document also changes. This is useful for keeping documents up-to-date when data is changing rapidly.

✦ You can edit all the linked objects in your document by choosing Edit ➪ Links. You can choose to update links automatically or manually.

✦ Other ways to share data in Office include sending Word documents to PowerPoint presentations (and vice versa) and sending Access data to Excel for analysis or to Word for publication or mail merging.

✦   ✦   ✦

Universal Drawing and Graphics Features

Not all embedded objects you may place in your Office documents are created by one of the main Office applications. In fact, the most commonly embedded objects are those you insert using one of the supplementary programs that comes with Office: programs that you call up whenever you want to insert a chart, for example, or a bit of WordArt. Separate from the main applications, yet integrated with them, these programs enhance Office's capabilities and provide you with lots of highly useful tools for making better documents.

In this chapter we'll take a brief look at some of these programs, plus a powerful graphics editor you may not even realize you have!

Using Microsoft Map

Computer mapping is a powerful tool for analyzing data on a geographic basis. Fully grasping the pattern of sales across the country, for example, can be very difficult if you're looking at a spreadsheet with possibly hundreds of rows and columns. That same data might become crystal-clear if you're looking at in the form of a color-coded map. According to MapInfo, a company that specializes in computer mapping (and whose maps are generally compatible with Microsoft Map's), more than 85 percent of business information has a geographic component, ranging from a zip code to a latitude/longitude coordinate. That makes analyzing data by geography a particularly useful tool.

You can insert a number of maps into Office applications using Microsoft Map. Because most maps use data from a spreadsheet, Microsoft Map is most readily accessed in Excel, but you can insert a map into any Office application by using the Insert ➪ Object command and choosing Microsoft Map from the list of objects available.

(If Microsoft Map is not available, you may have to install it from your Office CD. Run Setup, choose Add or Remove Features, and locate Microsoft Map under Microsoft Excel for Windows in the list of features. Click on it and choose Run from My Computer, and then click Update Now.)

Adding the Map button to an Excel toolbar

Even in Excel, Map does not appear on any of the toolbars by default. However, you can add a Map button by choosing Tools ➪ Customize. Click the Commands tab, and then choose Insert from the list of Categories and scroll down until you see the Map command (see Figure 53-1). You can then drag the Map button onto whichever toolbar you would like it to appear on.

Figure 53-1: If you plan to do a lot of mapping, you might want to add the Map button to one of your Excel toolbars.

Creating a map

To create a map based on a spreadsheet that contains geographic data:

1. Highlight the data you want to use to create the map. One column of that data must include geographic information, such as the names of countries; additional columns that provide data about those geographic areas you want to include in the map must also be highlighted.

2. Next, click the Map button and draw a frame for the map where you would like it to appear on the sheet.

3. Map will attempt to map the geographic data you've selected with one of its available maps. If more than one map matches the data, you'll be asked to select the one you want to use (see Figure 53-2).

4. If Map cannot match a map to your data, you'll be asked to select from the complete list of maps installed, which include maps of Canada, the U.S., Mexico, Australia, the U.K., Europe, Southern Africa, and the world. Additional maps are available from Microsoft and from MapInfo. To prepare maps you purchase or create with MapInfo for Windows, run the Data Installer (find the program Datainst.exe on your hard drive or Office CD).

Note

Microsoft Map also comes with sample demographic data for each map. Locate the workbook mapstats.xls on your hard drive or Office CD to view this data, which includes figures such as total population, total male population, total female population, and total employed population.

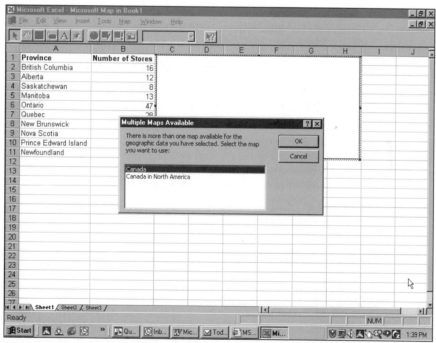

Figure 53-2: Map attempts to map the geographic data in your spreadsheet — in this case a list of Canadian provinces — with one of its available maps.

5. When you've found the map you want to use, click OK. The map will be drawn and the Microsoft Map Control dialog box opens (see Figure 53-3). In addition, Excel's menu and toolbars are replaced with the Microsoft Map menu and toolbar.

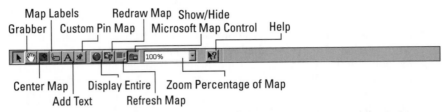

Figure 53-3: Control the way your data is displayed in Microsoft Map with this new toolbar.

Using the Map Control dialog box

Use the Microsoft Map Control dialog box to change the way the map displays your data. There are six options:

✦ **Value Shading** is the default format, applied in Figure 53-3. Excel looks at the range of values being displayed, in this case 2 to 47, and then breaks that into subranges, each of which is assigned a shade of gray. The geographic regions are then shaded according to which subrange their values fall into.

✦ **Category Shading** applies a different color to each category. For example, you could categorize the provinces as Western, Central, or Maritime, and color all of the provinces in each region the same.

✦ **Dot Density** randomly distributes dots within a geographic region to indicate the value: the more dots, the higher the value. The legend tells you the value each dot represents. In this example, each dot would represent one store, but if the number were higher, each dot might represent 10 or 100 stores.

✦ **Graduated Symbol** applies a differently sized symbol to each geographic area, depending on its value: the bigger the symbol (by default a dot), the higher that area's value.

✦ **Pie Chart** turns the data for each geographic region into a pie chart. In our example, this wouldn't do much good, as there's only one value, but if there were several values included in the data, the pie charts would show their relationship to the whole for each region.

✦ **Column Chart** turns the data for each region into a column chart. Although you can mix several of these formats — for instance, you can show Dot Density, Category Shading, a Graduated Symbol, and a Pie Chart all at once — you can't show both a Pie Chart and a Column Chart.

To set a format, drag it into the Microsoft Map dialog box into the dotted rectangle labeled Format. Then drag the column of data you want to apply that format to down from the top of the dialog box into the dotted rectangle labeled Column.

To fine-tune any format, double-click on its icon after you've dragged it into the white area of the dialog box.

Using the Map toolbar

You can further fine-tune your map using the Map toolbar. This contains several buttons, described as follows:

✦ **Grabber.** Click this and your mouse pointer turns into a hand icon that you can use to position the map within its frame. This is useful if your map is partially hidden by the legend or label.

✦ **Center Map.** Click this and the mouse pointer changes again; place it where you want the center of the map to be and click once.

✦ **Map Labels.** This opens a small dialog box that lets you create labels for whatever map features are displayed. Choose the feature you want to apply labels to, and then whether you want to create labels from the names Map already has stored for the displayed features, or from one of your sets of data values. As you run your mouse pointer over the map, Map temporarily displays the label for the feature you're pointing at (see Figure 53-4, where the label for Quebec is being displayed); click once to insert the label; then, while it's still selected, click and drag it to where you want it. To format the label, right-click on it and choose Format Font.

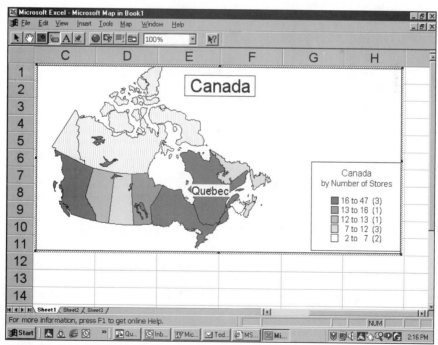

Figure 53-4: Add labels with the click of a mouse.

✦ **Add Text.** Click this, and then place your mouse pointer where you want the text to appear and click once. Type in the text — the frame expands automatically to accommodate it — and then drag it where you want. Again, right-click and choose Format Font to set font, size, color, etc.

✦ **Custom Pin Map.** This lets you stick virtual pins and labels into your map. You'll be asked to supply a name for the custom pin map (or, if one already exists that you want to edit, you can choose to call it up instead). Your mouse pointer changes to an image of a stickpin; click that wherever you want the pin to appear, and then type in a label for it and format it as before (see Figure 53-5).

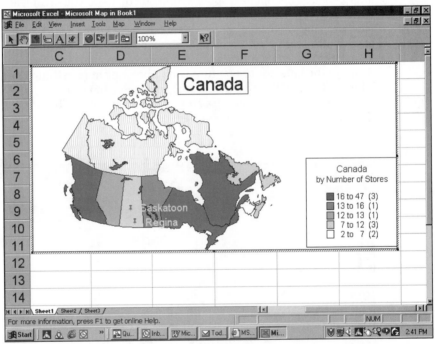

Figure 53-5: This custom pin map highlights the location of two major cities.

✦ **Display Entire.** This centers the map and zooms out (or in) so all features are visible.

✦ **Redraw Map.** This redraws the map. This is a good idea if you've used the Grabber to move it around; it minimizes the distortion which otherwise might occur because you're using a flat image to represent a rounded surface.

✦ **Map Refresh.** This redraws the map, making changes to it to reflect any recent changes in the data it's based on.

✦ **Show/Hide Microsoft Map Control.** This shows or hides the Map Control dialog box.

✦ **Zoom Percentage of Map.** This lets you choose what percentage of full-size you want the map displayed at — all the way up to 1,000,000 percent.

✦ **Help.** Click this and point your mouse pointer at any button and click once to get more information about it.

Other map options

To add additional data to your map, choose Insert ⇨ Data and specify the range of cells you want to draw data from (you can either type in cell coordinates or simply select the cells you want to use).

To add additional features to your map (the names of lakes or cities, for example), choose Map ⇨ Features. This opens the Map Features dialog box (see Figure 53-6), which lists the features available for the current map. Click the Visible check box for each feature you want to show. (For some features, you can also choose the color you want the feature to appear in.) To add any other available features, even if they're on a different map, click the Add button.

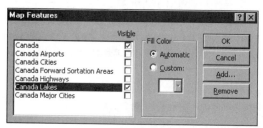

Figure 53-6: Each map can display a variety of features.

Using WordArt

WordArt is a program, used primarily in Word, PowerPoint and Excel, for creating fancily formatted text: text with 3-D effects, for example, or made to look like a brick wall or some other texture.

Creating a WordArt object

To create a WordArt object in Word, PowerPoint, or Excel:

1. Choose Insert ⇨ Picture ⇨ WordArt. This opens the WordArt Gallery dialog box shown in Figure 53-7.

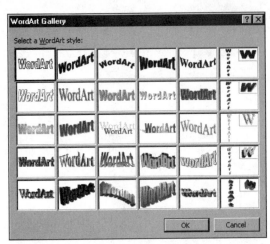

Figure 53-7: Choose from this dialog box the style of WordArt object that's closest to what you want.

2. Choose the style of WordArt object that appeals to you; then click OK.

3. In the Edit WordArt Text dialog box (see Figure 53-8), type in the text you want. Choose the font you want to use from any of those available in the Font drop-down list (there may only be one), and choose a size and style (bold, italic, or both).

Figure 53-8: Type the text you want to make into a WordArt object into this dialog box.

4. Click OK. Your text appears in the style of the WordArt object you chose (see Figure 53-9).

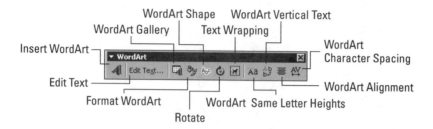

Figure 53-9: Notice the WordArt toolbar.

Editing and formatting WordArt

Now you can edit the WordArt object further using the WordArt toolbar that has also appeared. (Exactly which tools you see depend on which application you're using.) This toolbar features a number of commands:

✦ **Insert WordArt.** This inserts a new WordArt Object.

✦ **Edit Text.** This reopens the Edit WordArt Text dialog box shown in Figure 53-8.

✦ **WordArt Gallery.** This opens the dialog box displaying all the WordArt styles, so you can apply a different style to your text if you wish.

✦ **Format WordArt.** This opens the Format WordArt dialog box (see Figure 53-10), which has several tabs. (Again, the tabs you'll see depend on which application you're using.)

  • *Colors and Lines* contains controls for changing the appearance of the WordArt characters' fill. You can apply a solid color; choose a preset one- or two-color gradient (or create one); choose from a variety of textures ranging from stone to wood grain; or even use a picture. In addition, you can change the color, weight, and dash of the lines (if any) outlining the letters in the WordArt object.

  • *Size* lets you set the height and width of the WordArt object and rotate it by a specified number of degrees. You can also change the size of the WordArt object by scaling it to a certain percentage of normal height or width.

  • *Layout* determines how the object will interact with the Office document: should it be In line with text (as though it were just one large text character itself), or should text wrap itself Square to the edges of the WordArt frame or Tight to the image itself (rather than the frame)? Or should the object appear Behind text or In front of text? Layout also lets you set the alignment (left, right, or center) of the WordArt frame.

  • *Web* lets you enter alternative text to be displayed while the WordArt object is being loaded into a Web browser.

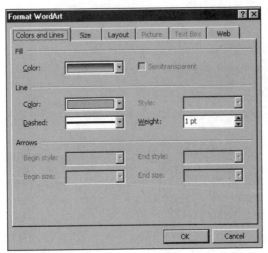

Figure 53-10: You can completely redesign your WordArt object using the Format WordArt dialog box.

✦ **WordArt Shape.** This lets you change the shape the text in your WordArt object takes (see Figure 53-11).

✦ **Text Wrapping.** Like the Layout tab of the Format WordArt dialog box, this lets you set the way surrounding text will interact with your WordArt object. Clicking Edit Wrap Points lets you manually adjust the normally invisible border around the image that text wraps to when Tight is selected.

✦ **WordArt Same Letter Heights.** This makes all letters in your WordArt object the same height and aligns the tops and bottoms of all letters.

✦ **WordArt Vertical Text.** This makes letters appear vertically, stacked one over the top of the other and reading from top to bottom. Clicking this button again makes the WordArt text horizontal again.

✦ **WordArt Alignment.** This determines how text is positioned within the WordArt frame. It can be aligned left, right, or center, like ordinary text. Three types of justification are also possible: *word justify*, which justifies the text by adding space between words; *letter justify*, which justifies the text by adding space between letters; and *stretch justify*, which justifies text by making the letter wider.

✦ **WordArt Character Spacing.** This determines the spacing between letters in the WordArt text. You can set it for very tight, tight, normal, loose, or very loose; or set a percentage of normal. You can also change kerning (the amount of space between pairs of letters).

Figure 53-11: Choose the shape you want your WordArt text to take from this menu.

Once you're satisfied with your WordArt object, click anywhere outside its frame to deselect it. After that you can move it and resize it anytime by clicking on it once, and then dragging it from place to place or clicking and dragging on its handles, or you can edit it by double-clicking on it.

Using the Clip Gallery

The ClipGallery is a virtual art gallery that stores and organizes the pictures, animation clips, videos, and sounds on your computer for easy access by Office applications.

Accessing the Clip Gallery

To access the Clip Gallery in Word, Excel, or PowerPoint, choose Insert ⇨ Picture ⇨ Clip Art. (To open the ClipGallery from Access, choose Insert ⇨ Object, and then choose Microsoft Clip Gallery from the list of available objects.) The Insert ClipArt dialog box opens (see Figure 53-12).

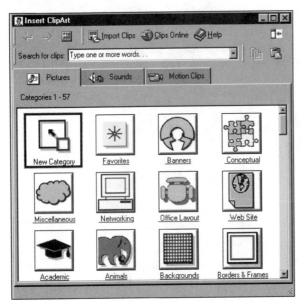

Figure 53-12: The Clip Gallery keeps picture, motion clips, and sounds organized.

Choosing an image

Everything in the Clip Gallery is assigned to a particular category; the available categories are displayed. Click on the category you want, and the images in that category are displayed (see Figure 53-13).

Place your mouse pointer on any image and you'll see a pop-up label telling you the name of the clip and its size, and a pop-up menu with four icons on it (see Figure 53-14). From top to bottom, these options are as follows:

 ✦ **Insert clip.** Click this icon to insert the clip into your Office document.

 ✦ **Preview clip or Play clip.** If you're looking at a picture, click this to see a larger version of it. If you're looking at a sound or motion clip, click this to hear or view it.

 ✦ **Add clip to Favorites or other category.** Click this if you'd like this clip to appear in your Favorites category, where you can store clips you use a lot, or in some other category. Choose the category you want from the list provided, and then click Add.

 ✦ **Find similar clips.** This searches Clip Gallery for clips that closely match this one. In the case of pictures or animations, you can look for clips with the same artistic style or general color or shape, or that have one or more of the same keywords assigned to them; only the keywords option is active with sound clips.

Figure 53-13: Clicking on an Insert ClipArt category displays the images contained there.

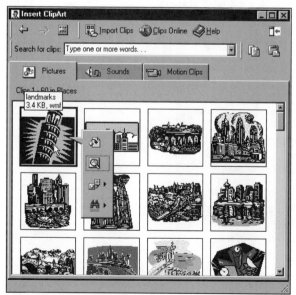

Figure 53-14: When you click on a Clip Gallery clip, you see four options.

Searching for clips

You can search for clips by keyword by typing a word related to the kind of clip you're looking for in the Search for Clips field (where it says "Type one or more words"). Words you've used to search with recently are stored and can be called up by clicking the down-arrow control on the right end of the Search for Clips field.

Use the copy and paste buttons to the right of the Search for Clips field to copy or paste text within the field. You can also use these buttons to copy selected clips to the Clipboard, from which you can paste them into a document or into another category.

A few more buttons across the top of the Clip Gallery round out the controls available. At the left are Back and Forward arrows, which you can use to retrace the steps you've followed in looking for clips. To the right of those is the All Categories button, which shows you all the available categories.

Importing clips

Next comes the Import Clips button, which you can use to import clips from your computer that aren't yet included in the Clip Gallery. Clicking on it opens the dialog box shown in Figure 53-15.

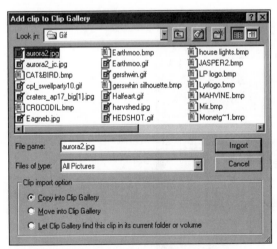

Figure 53-15: You can import clips you have stored on your computer into the Clip Gallery.

You can choose to copy the clip to the Clip Gallery, move it to the Gallery, or simply let the Gallery find it where it is (but if you ever move the clip to another location, you'll get an error message if you try to insert it using the Clip Gallery).

Once you've located the clip (or clips) you want to import and clicked Import, you'll see the Clip Properties dialog box (see Figure 53-16). Here you'll see key features of the clip, and you can give it a description and assign it to whichever categories you like. You can also attach keywords to it for search purposes.

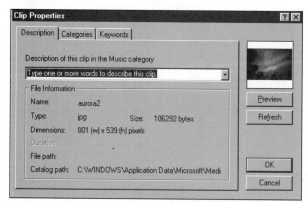

Figure 53-16: Label and organize new clips with this dialog box.

Using Clip Gallery Live

The remaining button (aside from Help) at the top of the Clip Gallery is Clips Online. Microsoft maintains an area on its Web site where new clips for the Clip Gallery are constantly being posted. If you have an Internet connection, clicking this button will take you to that Web site, called *Clip Gallery Live*.

After being presented with an agreement regarding fair use of the Clip Gallery Live clips (which you must accept), you'll be taken to the home page of Clip Gallery Live, where you'll see the latest news about new clips at the site. Choose one of the categories of clips available, or search for clips just as you would in the Clip Gallery on your own disks; eventually you'll end up with a selection of clips similar to those shown in Figure 53-17. You can check the boxes next to several clips and then download them all at once, or download any individual clip at once by clicking the little icon of an arrow pointing at a disk drive.

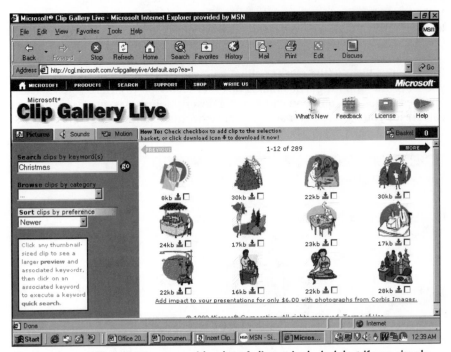

Figure 53-17: Office 2000 comes with a lot of clip art included, but if you simply can't find what you need, Clip Gallery Live is well worth visiting.

Using Microsoft Photo Editor

If you have one of the Office editions that includes PhotoDraw 2000, you'll probably want to use that full-featured program to edit photos and other artwork. But even if you don't have PhotoDraw, Office provides a powerful tool for editing and altering photographs: Microsoft Photo Editor.

Cross-Reference   For complete information about how to use PhotoDraw, see Chapter 50, "Using PhotoDraw."

To use Photo Editor, choose Start ➪ Programs ➪ Office Tools ➪ Microsoft Photo Editor. Once you're in Photo Editor, open the photo you want to work on by choosing File ➪ Open and browsing for the file you want. Once you open a photo, Photo Editor will look something like Figure 53-18 (although if you have this particular photo on your hard drive I'll be a little concerned, as it's a photo of my wife!).

Another way to get a photo into Photo Editor, of course, is to scan it in (assuming you have a scanner). To scan an image, choose File ➪ Select Scanner Source and choose the appropriate piece of hardware from the list; then choose File ➪ Scan Image. Your own scanner software will take over at that point; scan the picture as you usually would, and it will automatically appear in Photo Editor.

Figure 53-18: Edit your photographs with Microsoft Photo Editor.

Once you have a photo in Photo Editor, you can manipulate it in a number of ways, using both the tool buttons on the toolbar and the commands in the menus.

Using the Photo Editor toolbar

The first few buttons on the toolbar are much the same as you'll see on the Standard toolbar in any Office application, with one addition: New, Open, Save, Print, Scan (which lets you initiate a scan without opening a menu), Cut, Copy, Paste (all three commands apply to the entire picture unless a smaller section is first selected), Undo, and Redo. The more specifically photo-related tools available to you on the toolbar include the following:

✦ **Select.** Click this and then use your mouse pointer to draw a frame around an area of the picture you want to select. Once you've drawn the frame, you can move it by clicking and dragging it (see Figure 53-19). As long as a specific area is selected, it's the area affected by any further manipulation. If no area is selected, the entire picture is affected. To work on a selected section without seeing the rest of the picture, select an area and choose Cut; then choose New and paste the selected area into the blank picture New creates.

Figure 53-19: If you want to work on only part of a photo, or want to crop it, use the Select tool.

✦ **Zoom.** Click this and your mouse pointer turns into a magnifying glass. Place it on an area of the picture you want to enlarge and click to zoom in. The Zoom control shows you what percentage of full size the picture is being displayed at, from 10 percent all the way up to 1,600 percent. You can also use the Zoom control to choose a specific percentage, or to fit the picture to the window.

✦ **Smudge.** Click this and your mouse pointer turns into a pointing finger. Place the finger where you want to smudge colors, and then click and move the finger around with your mouse. Smudge has the same effect you might get if the picture had just been painted with watercolors and you were running a wet brush over it: the colors blur and run together.

✦ **Sharpen.** This increases the difference between adjacent gray values in a picture—at least, that's how Microsoft describes it. The visual effect is sharper edges, almost as if an out-of-focus picture were being brought into focus. Again, your mouse pointer becomes a finger, which you can use to sharpen any area of the picture you choose.

✦ **Image Balance.** This opens a dialog box with three sliding controls in it: one for Brightness, one for Contrast, and one for Gamma (which controls the contrast in dark areas of the picture). You can control these three values for all colors, or for red, green, and blue individually. By adjusting these sliders, you can dramatically alter the look of your picture.

✦ **Set Transparent Color.** This lets you choose a color to make transparent by clicking the Set Transparent Color tool on it — which means, when you integrate the photo you're editing into an Office document, the background color will show through anywhere the transparent color is used. This allows text or other images to show through your photo, and can be used to create a variety of effects.

✦ **Rotate 90°.** This rotates the picture 90 degrees clockwise with each click.

Using the Photo Editor menu commands

Additional photo editing commands are included in the Photo Editor menus:

✦ To return a picture to the way it was before you started editing it, choose File ➪ Revert.

✦ To add a ruler to the left and top edges of your photo, choose View ➪ Ruler (see Figure 53-20). Under the View menu you can also set the measurement units for the ruler to inches, centimeters, or pixels.

Figure 53-20: Rulers can help you make your photo editing more precise.

✦ To crop and mat a photo, choose Image ➪ Crop. This opens the Crop dialog box shown in Figure 53-21. The Mat margins in the upper-left corner create white space around the photo, like a frame. In the middle section, choose how much of the picture you want to crop off on each side, and whether you want to crop it in a rectangular or oval shape. If you choose to crop it into a rectangular shape, you can choose the shape of the corners — round, square, or cut (angled), fillet (which takes a little semi-circular shape out of the corners), or ear (which gives the corners a dog-eared look). In Figure 53-22, the picture has been given a rectangular mat with filleted corners.

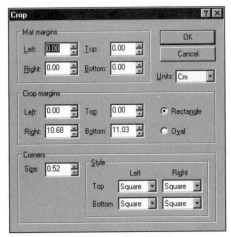

Figure 53-21: The Crop dialog box.

✦ Choose Image ➪ Resize to resize your photo. You can set exact dimensions for the height and width or enter the dimensions as percentages of the original size. Check the Allow Distortion box if you're willing to let the proportion of height to width change, which has the effect of stretching or squashing your picture in one direction or the other; check Smooth to smooth the edges off of ragged pixels that might otherwise appear when you enlarge a photo.

✦ Choose Image ➪ AutoBalance to have Photo Editor adjust the contrast, brightness, and gamma of your photo automatically.

✦ Effects is the most interesting menu. These effects do everything from removing speckles to turning your photo into what appears to be a pen-and-ink sketch (see Figure 53-23). Each effect can be further fine-tuned and adjusted. Experiment with them all to see what's possible.

Figure 53-22: An interesting framing effect achieved by using the Crop dialog box.

Figure 53-23: This is just one of the many effects you can apply with Photo Editor.

When you're happy with your image, you can save it in any one of several popular graphics formats. Choose File ➪ Save As, and select the format you want from the list of those provided: Graphics Interchange Format (GIF), Windows Bitmap (BMP), JPEG File Interchange Format (JPG), Tag Image File Format (TIF), Portable Network Graphics (PNG), or PC Paintbrush (PCX). Click More to make further adjustments to the number of colors used and, in the case of JPG files, to the quality (and size) of the final file.

Give your file a name and then click OK.

Using Microsoft Graph

One of the most commonly used special graphics programs in Office is Microsoft Graph. It's discussed in detail in the context of Excel in Chapter 12, "Charts." It's also discussed more briefly in the context of Word in Chapter 7, in the context of PowerPoint in Chapter 23, and in the context of Access in Chapter 36.

Using Microsoft Equation Editor

Microsoft Equation Editor is a fairly esoteric program, in that its use is primarily limited to those who work with complex mathematical equations. Equation Editor lets you create equations using a wide range of mathematical symbols, and can be used in Word, PowerPoint, and Excel.

To open Microsoft Equation Editor, choose Insert ➪ Object and select Microsoft Equation 3.0 as the object type. This creates an object frame in your document and opens the Equation toolbar (see Figure 53-24). (It's a fairly safe bet that if you only recognize two or three symbols on this toolbar, you're unlikely to ever need to use Microsoft Equation Editor!)

This toolbar consists of an upper and lower row. The upper row contains mathematical symbols, while the lower row contains mathematical templates. Each template consists of a predetermined set of symbols and unfilled slots. Once you choose a template, the insertion point automatically moves to the slot that would ordinarily be filled first. Equation Editor adjusts spacing, formatting, and so on, to adhere to standard mathematical layout. Once you've created the equation, you can use the Format, Style, and Size menus to adjust its appearance.

Click anywhere outside the equation's frame to close Microsoft Equation Editor and return to your Office application.

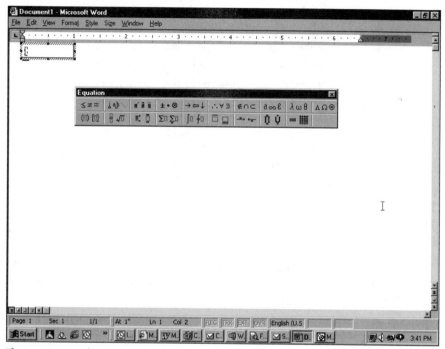

Figure 53-24: The Microsoft Equation Editor toolbar has 19 function buttons.

Summary

In this chapter, you learned how to use some of the supplemental programs that give added functionality to all Office applications. Highlights included the following:

✦ Microsoft Map helps you understand Excel data that has a geographic component by presenting the information graphically on a map of the region involved. You can add the Map button to your toolbar by choosing Tools ➪ Customize and looking under the Insert category on the Commands tab.

✦ Map lets you choose from a variety of formats for displaying data on your map; you can also add a number of features, such as city names, and create labels for both geographic regions and the data being displayed.

✦ WordArt is a powerful tool for creating eye-catching text that features 3-D effects, unusual shapes, and colorful fills. You can access it in PowerPoint, Word, and Excel by choosing Insert ➪ Picture ➪ WordArt.

✦ Once you've chosen the type of WordArt you like from the WordArt Gallery, you can easily customize it using the WordArt toolbar.

✦ Microsoft Clip Gallery organizes images, sounds, video, and animation clips by category and keyword, so you can easily find, preview, and insert them.

✦ You can add clips from your computer to the Clip Gallery by clicking the Import Clips button, and find more clips at Microsoft's Clip Gallery Live Web site by clicking the Clips Online button.

✦ Microsoft Photo Editor is a powerful photo-editing tool provided with Office that you access by choosing Start ➪ Programs ➪ Office Tools ➪ Microsoft Photo Editor. The toolbar and menus provide commands for everything from resizing a picture to applying special effects to making certain colors in it transparent.

✦ Microsoft Graph, used to create graphs, is one of the most commonly used programs in Office. For a detailed discussion of it, refer to Chapter 12, "Charts."

✦ Microsoft Equation Editor is only likely to be of use if you're a mathematician, but if you need mathematical symbols to construct equations, you'll find it invaluable. Access it by choosing Insert ➪ Object and selecting Microsoft Equation 3.0 as the object type.

✦   ✦   ✦

Collaborating on a Network

In most business environments, very few things are done by an individual. Projects are planned, discussed, dissected, and carried out by teams of people working together. If one of the final products of a project is to be an Office document, it's helpful if all members of the team can share information, files, and ideas online, either via the company's internal computer network or, if team members are more far-flung, via the Internet.

Office makes it possible!

Sharing Office Documents

If your computer is hooked up to a local network of some type, chances are good you have a choice of saving your files either to your own computer or to a location somewhere on the network.

Access to various folders on the network is overseen by whoever looks after the network; it's quite likely that many people not in your workgroup may have access to a particular folder. However, in most Office applications you can control who has access to files you place in network folders. You can also allow or deny access by network users to your own computer's hard drive.

Setting file-sharing options when saving

Whenever you save a Word or Excel document, you have the option of restricting access to it.

Clicking the Save button to save your document for the first time, or choosing File ➪ Save As if the document has already been saved, opens the Save As dialog box shown in Figure 54-1. Choose Tools ➪ General Options, as shown, to open the Save dialog box shown in Figure 54-2. (Note that this dialog box varies somewhat between Word and Excel. The examples given are from Word.)

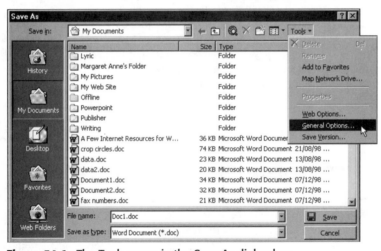

Figure 54-1: The Tools menu in the Save As dialog box.

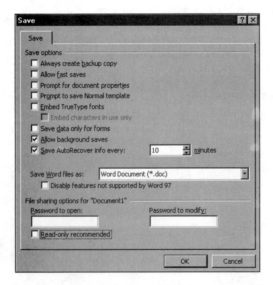

Figure 54-2: The Tools menu leads you to the Save dialog box, where you can restrict access to any file.

At the bottom of this dialog box is an area where you can set file-sharing options for your document. Three levels of security are provided here:

✦ **Read-only recommended.** If you check this, users opening this file will get a message suggesting they open it as a read-only file. If they do, they won't be able to change the original document; instead, any changes they make must be saved as a new document, under a different name.

✦ **Password to modify.** If you enter a password here, anyone can open the file, but only someone who knows the password can modify it. (Passwords can be up to 15 characters long and contain letters, numbers, and symbols, and are case-sensitive. As you type them in, only asterisks are displayed.) Users who don't know the password can open the file only as read-only — and that includes you, if you forget your password, so don't!

✦ **Password to open.** If you enter a password here, only someone who knows the password will be able to open the file.

Protecting documents

In addition, you can fine-tune the level of access you want to allow people to have to a particular file by applying protection within the application that created it.

Protecting documents in Word

To protect a document in Word:

1. Choose Tools ➪ Protect Document. This opens the Protect Document dialog box shown in Figure 54-3.

Figure 54-3: Protect Word documents using this dialog box.

2. If you want to enable the Track Changes command, so that other users can change the document but all changes they make will be tracked so you can review them later, click the Tracked Changes radio button.

3. If you don't want to let users change the document but you do want to allow them to insert comments, click the Comments radio button.

4. If you want to protect a document from changes everywhere except form fields, click Forms. To protect only certain sections of the document from changes, click Forms, then Sections, and uncheck the names of sections to which you're willing to allow changes. (Of course, you must first break the document into sections.)

5. You can reinforce your document protection by entering a password that users must know before they can unprotect the document. The password is optional, however.

6. Click OK.

Protecting documents in Excel

To protect an Excel worksheet or workbook:

1. Choose Tools ➪ Protection.

2. From the submenu, choose which part of your Excel document you want to protect: a particular worksheet or the workbook. You can also choose to protect and share your workbook (more on sharing workbooks a little later in this chapter).

3. If you choose Protect Sheet, you'll see the dialog box shown in Figure 54-4. Here you have four options:

   - *Contents* prevents changes to cells and charts in a worksheet.

   - *Objects* prevents users from moving, deleting, resizing, or editing graphic items on a worksheet.

   - *Scenarios* prevents changes to the definitions of scenarios in the worksheet.

   - *Password.* You also have the option of entering a password users must have before they can unprotect the worksheet.

Figure 54-4: Set protection for Excel worksheets here.

4. If you choose Protect Workbook, you'll see the dialog box shown in Figure 54-5, where there are three options:

- *Structure* prevents users from adding, deleting, moving, hiding, or unhiding worksheets.

- *Windows* prevents users from moving, hiding, unhiding, resizing, or closing workbook windows.

- *Password.* Again, you can enter a password users must have before they can unprotect the workbook.

Figure 54-5: Protect elements of your workbook here.

5. Protect and Share Workbook brings up a dialog box with only one box you can check, to prevent those sharing the workbook from turning off change tracking. You can enter a password they'll have to have before they can do so.

Protecting files in Access and PowerPoint

We'll look at protecting Access files in detail later in this chapter. You need to use file system features to protect PowerPoint files; talk to your system administrator.

Allowing access to other network users

If you want other users on your network to be able to access files you've saved on your computer, and you're using Windows 95 or 98, you need to turn on File and Print Sharing. To do so:

1. Choose Start ➪ Settings ➪ Control Panel.

2. Double-click the Network icon.

3. In the Network dialog box (see Figure 54-6), click the File and Print Sharing button.

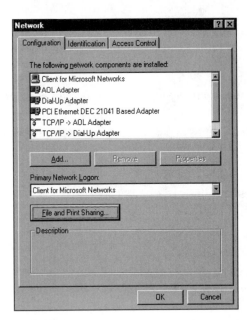

Figure 54-6: You can change your Network settings to let others on a network have access to your computer.

4. Check the box labeled "I want to be able to give others access to my files."

5. Click OK, and then click OK again.

6. Go to My Computer, and locate the folders you want to make accessible to others. Right-click on each folder and choose Sharing from the shortcut menu, and then click the Sharing tab. This opens the dialog box shown in Figure 54-7. (Note that the options on the Sharing tab vary depending on the settings you made on the Access Control tab of the Network Control Panel. Those shown assume you've selected Share-level access control, the default, from that tab.)

7. Click the Shared As radio button.

8. Choose a name for the folder shared and type it into the Share Name field. You can use the current name or give it another name. If you want to add a longer description, type it into the Comment box.

9. Set the level of access you want to allow. *Read-only* lets users open and copy documents in the folder, but not change or move them. *Full* lets users do anything they want to the documents in the folder. *Depends on password* determines the level of access depending on which password (entered below) users provide.

10. Click OK.

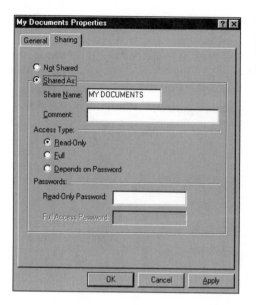

Figure 54-7: Determine how much access you want to allow to a particular folder on your computer using these controls.

Holding Online Meetings

Online meetings let you share data and hold discussions with people at several different sites, just as if they were all in the same conference room, except perhaps for the lack of coffee and doughnuts (maybe in the *next* version of Office...). There's even a whiteboard!

Online meetings can be held over a corporate intranet or over the Internet. You can start them from any Office application, or you can start them from the program Windows provides for conducting online meetings, called Microsoft NetMeeting, which you can open by choosing Start ➪ Programs ➪ NetMeeting. NetMeeting provides all sorts of tools for holding meetings — you can even set up online videoconferencing with it — but for the purposes of this book, we'll concentrate on starting meetings from Office applications.

Cross-Reference To learn how to schedule an online meeting in advance using Microsoft Outlook, see Chapter 33, "Outlook at Work." For more information about NetMeeting, consult Windows Help.

Starting a meeting

Use the following steps to start a meeting from an Office application and share an Office document with the other meeting participants:

1. Open the document you want to share.

2. Choose Tools ➪ Online Collaboration ➪ Meet Now. If you haven't held an online meeting before, Microsoft NetMeeting will ask you to provide information about yourself and choose a directory. If you're not sure which directory to use, check with your system administrator.

3. The Place a Call dialog box opens (see Figure 54-8). Find the name of the person you want to invite to join the meeting, select it, and click Call. (They have to be running NetMeeting, too.)

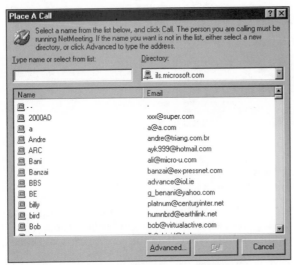

Figure 54-8: Hook up with other NetMeeting users by choosing them from the appropriate directory.

4. The Office application will now open an Online Meeting toolbar (see Figure 54-9), which includes the tools you'll need to run the meeting. To invite another person to join the meeting, click the Call Participant button, just to the right of the list of current participants.

Cross-
Reference

For an explanation of the other buttons on the Online Meeting toolbar, see "Hosting an online meeting," which follows.

Figure 54-9: The Online Meeting toolbar includes the tools you need to run or participate in an online meeting.

Joining an online meeting

If someone else starts an online meeting in Office and invites you to join, you'll see a Join Meeting dialog box (assuming you have NetMeeting running). Click Ignore to decline and Accept to join. If you accept, the Online Meeting toolbar and the document the host has open will appear on your screen. (Only the host has to have the application and the document installed.)

Hosting an online meeting

If you called the online meeting, then you're the host, which gives you a few more options than ordinary participants have. Here's how it works:

✦ You're the only person who can invite new people to join the meeting. Click the Call Participant button, just to the right of the list of current participants on the Online Meeting toolbar.

✦ You're also the only person who can remove a participant, by choosing his or her name in the list of participants in the Online Meeting toolbar, and then clicking the Remove Participants button (the second button from the left).

✦ By default, you're also the only person who can make changes to the document being viewed. However, you can allow other people to make changes by clicking the Allow Others to Edit button on the Online Meeting toolbar (the third button from the left). When you activate that button, other people in the meeting are able to take turns in control of the document by double-clicking anywhere in it the first time, and then simply clicking in it thereafter.

Note

While other people in the meeting are in control, you lose control of your mouse pointer. You can tell who is in control at any given time because their initials appear beside the mouse pointer.

✦ As the host, however, you can stop others from editing the document at any time by clicking the Allow Others to Edit button again if you're in control of the document, or pressing Esc if you're not.

✦ The host is also the only one who can activate two other buttons on the Online Meeting toolbar: Display Chat Window and Display Whiteboard (which are the fourth and fifth buttons from the left).

Using the Chat window

The Chat window (see Figure 54-10) is where you talk to other participants in an online meeting. Type your message into the Message field at the bottom of the window, select the recipient, and then click the Send button to the right of the

Message field. Your message is displayed, and will also appear in the Chat windows of all the meeting participants you sent the message to, who can also post their own messages. You can vary the way messages are displayed by choosing Options ➪ Chat Format.

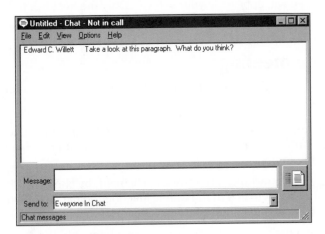

Figure 54-10: Talk to other online participants in the Chat window.

The discussion in the Chat window can be saved and/or printed at any time by choosing the appropriate commands under the File menu, so you can have a permanent record of what was said.

Using the whiteboard

The whiteboard (see Figure 54-11) is very much like a whiteboard in an ordinary conference room, except you have the advantage of computer tools to help you illustrate your points. To completely clear a page, delete a page, or add a new page before or after the current page, click the Edit menu. You can save and print whiteboard pages from the File menu. The whiteboard also provides you with several very useful drawing tools:

Note   If you want everyone in the meeting to be able to use the whiteboard simultaneously, you have to be sure that the Allow Others to Edit button is activated.

✦ **Selector.** Click this button, and then click on an object in the whiteboard or draw a frame around it to select it.

✦ **Text.** Click this button, and then click anywhere in the whiteboard and start typing. A Font Options button will become active at the bottom of the whiteboard, which you can use to format your text. That's how the text was typed in Figure 54-11.

✦ **Pen.** Use this to draw on the whiteboard just as you would on a regular whiteboard. In Figure 54-11, the pen was used to draw the arrow and write "Look." Choose the color you want the pen to write in from the palette.

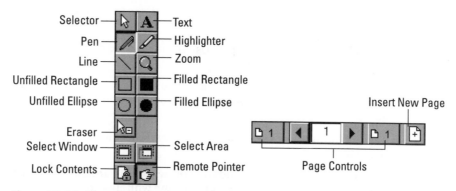

Figure 54-11: The whiteboard serves the same purpose in an online meeting as a blackboard does in an ordinary meeting.

✦ **Highlighter.** Use this like a highlighting pen; in Figure 54-11, it was used to highlight the text in yellow.

✦ **Line.** Use this to draw straight lines, like the one joining the rectangle and the oval in Figure 54-11.

✦ **Zoom.** Use this to enlarge the whiteboard image, as shown in Figure 54-12. (Note that the Text button is not available in enlarged view.)

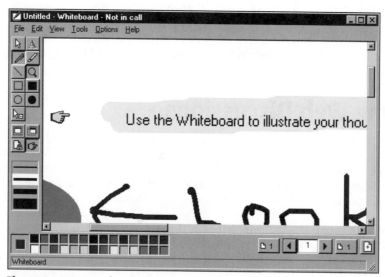

Figure 54-12: Use the Zoom button to get a closer look at what's on the whiteboard.

✦ **Unfilled Rectangle/Unfilled Ellipse**. Use these to draw the outlines of rectangles and ellipses.

✦ **Filled Rectangle/Filled Ellipse.** Use these to draw solid rectangles and ellipses in the active color.

✦ **Eraser.** Click on this, and then click on any object you want to erase, and away it goes. You can also drag a rectangle around multiple objects to erase them all.

✦ **Select Window.** Click on this, and the next window you click on is captured to the whiteboard.

✦ **Select Area.** Click on this, and then draw a frame around any area of the current screen you want to capture to the whiteboard.

✦ **Lock Contents.** Click this if you don't want any other participants in the meeting to be able to alter the contents of the whiteboard.

✦ **Remote Pointer.** This is an icon of a pointing finger you can activate and drag around the whiteboard to point out various objects to meeting participants. In Figure 54-11 it appears next to the text.

✦ **Page Controls.** These controls let you move from page to page on the whiteboard, or directly to the end or beginning of the range of pages.

✦ **Insert New Page.** Click this to add a new page to the whiteboard.

Sending files to other participants

As host, you can send the Office file that's currently open to the other participants in an online meeting by choosing File ➪ Send To ➪ Online Meeting Participant.

Creating Web Discussions

Office's Web Discussions feature lets users carry out a discussion of documents published to a Web server that is running Office Server Extensions (check with your network administrator to find out where to publish your documents to enable discussions). Documents can be published to a Web server by choosing File ➪ Save As, and then clicking on the Web Folders tool in the Places bar of the Save As dialog box.

The remarks are threaded, which means that the response to any remark is nested directly under it, much like you see in Usenet newsgroups. This makes it much easier to follow the flow of conversation.

Discussions can also be carried out in any frames-capable browser. When Office Server Extensions are installed on a Web server, an Office Server Extensions Home Page becomes available to users. This allows them to search and navigate published documents, and to receive e-mail notifications when published documents are changed or discussed. Internet Explorer 5 offers the most integrated experience: It displays a Discussions button on its toolbar and allows inline discussions—discussions that actually appear in the document under discussion.

You can start a discussion from inside Excel, PowerPoint, or Word. To do so:

1. Choose Tools ➪ Online Collaboration ➪ Web Discussions. This opens the Discussion Options dialog box shown in Figure 54-13.

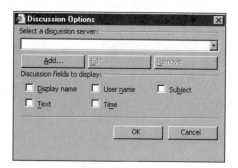

Figure 54-13: Start a Web discussion of the current document from this dialog box.

2. Click Add and enter the name of the discussion server given to you by your network administrator. The next time you start a discussion you'll be able to choose the server from the list, and edit or remove it by clicking those respective buttons.

3. Check the boxes for the discussion fields you want to appear in the discussion window, and click OK.

4. The Discussion toolbar appears (see Figure 54-14). Click the Discussions button, and then choose the type of discussion you want to start. In Word and in Internet Explorer 5, you can create a discussion that appears in the document, relating to some particular aspect of it (choose Insert in the Document); in other applications, you have to initiate a general discussion about the document that isn't displayed within it. (Choose Insert About the Document in Word or IE5 if that's the kind of discussion you want to begin.)

Figure 54-14: Use the Discussion toolbar to create or reply to discussion items.

5. Type the subject of the discussion under Discussion subject, and then type your remarks under Discussion text.

6. Click OK. The discussion pane appears, where you can read your own remarks and others as the discussion continues.

Once a discussion is begun, anyone who has access to the document can add to the discussion by opening the document and choosing Tools ➪ Online Collaboration ➪ Web Discussions. Use the Discussion toolbar buttons to create new messages, navigate through messages, reply to messages, and edit messages.

Sharing Excel Workbooks

One of the most common types of Office documents shared on a network is an Excel workbook, because workbooks frequently contain budgetary or sales information that is constantly being updated by a variety of users. Excel lets multiple users share and edit a single workbook simultaneously; it also lets you combine several workbooks into a single workbook.

Creating a shared workbook

To create a shared workbook:

1. Choose Tools ➪ Share Workbook. This opens the dialog box shown in Figure 54-15.

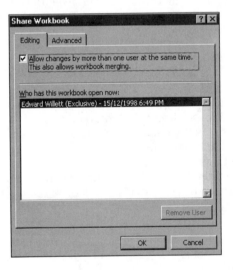

Figure 54-15: The Editing tab of the Share Workbook dialog box shows you who currently has the workbook open.

2. If you want more than one person to be able to edit the workbook at the same time, or to combine several workbooks into one shared workbook, check the box at the top of the dialog box.

3. To fine-tune the way the workbook is shared, click the Advanced tab (see Figure 54-16). In the Track Changes section, choose the number of days you want to track changes — if at all.

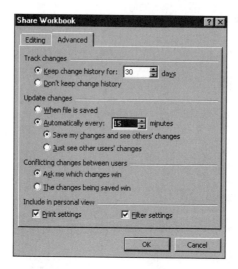

Figure 54-16: The Advanced tab lets you choose your method of tracking, updating, and dealing with conflicting changes.

4. In the Update Changes section, choose when you want changes made to the workbook to be updated: whenever the file is saved, or automatically how ever often you specify. If you choose to automatically update changes, you can choose to save your changes and see everyone else's changes at the specified interval, or just see everyone else's changes at the specified interval without saving yours.

5. Sometimes two or more users will make conflicting changes to the workbook — changes that are mutually exclusive. You can decide how to deal with those changes either by having Excel ask you which change should take effect, or by replacing any conflicting changes with your own changes every time you save.

6. Click OK.

Reviewing changes

Once a workbook is being shared, you can review changes in it by choosing Tools ➪ Track Changes ➪ Accept or Reject Changes. Choose the changes you want to review in the Select Changes to Accept or Reject dialog box shown in Figure 54-17. You can filter the changes you want to look at using the three fields. The *When* field lets you look for changes made on a specific date; the *Who* field lets you look at changes made by everyone, everyone but you, only you, or only any other user who has made changes; and the *Where* field lets you specify a range of cells to look for changes in.

Any changes found are brought to your attention in the Accept or Reject Changes dialog box (see Figure 54-18). You can choose to accept or reject any or all of the changes brought to your attention.

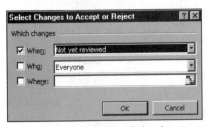

Figure 54-17: Use this dialog box to select the changes you want to review.

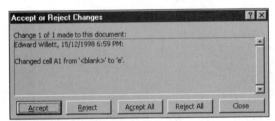

Figure 54-18: Changes made to the workbook are brought to your attention here.

Tip

You can merge different versions of the same shared workbook into a single workbook by choosing Tools ➪ Merge Workbooks. Track Changes must be turned on (and the workbook must be shared) for this to work.

Sharing Access Databases

The information in the typical Access database is valuable not only to people working in Access, but also to people working in all other Office applications. Typically, the Access database changes constantly as changes are made to the data in it; by drawing on it, network users can ensure that their own Office projects always contain the most up-to-date information.

If you don't need any extra security on your Access database, you can share it just as you would any other file in Office (see the first part of this chapter). If you do need extra security, however, Access can provide it in several different ways: passwords, permissions, user groups and accounts, and encryption.

Using passwords

A password is the easiest way to protect a database. Every time a user tries to access a password-protected database, he or she will be asked to provide a password. Without it, the database can't be opened.

To set a password for a particular Access database:

1. Choose File ➪ Open.

2. In the Open dialog box, find the database you want to assign the password to and select it.

3. Click the down arrow next to the Open button and choose Open Exclusive. This ensures that no one else can open the database while you are assigning a password to it.

4. The database opens. Now choose Tools ➪ Security ➪ Set Database Password.

5. In the Set Database Password dialog box (see Figure 54-19), enter the password once in the Password field, and then enter it again in the Verify field (all you'll see are asterisks). (Remember, passwords are case-sensitive, limited to 15 characters, and contain letters, numbers, and/or symbols.)

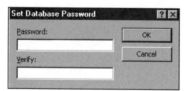

Figure 54-19: Enter your database password in this dialog box.

6. Click OK.

Caution Once the password is set, it doesn't matter if you're the user who created the database and assigned the password to it: If you forget or lose the password, you won't be able to open the database!

To remove the password, open the file exclusively again, and then choose Tools ➪ Security ➪ Unset Database Password. Enter the password and click OK.

Creating user and group accounts

If a password doesn't provide enough security, you might want to set up user accounts and groups, which will require users to supply both an account name and a password before they can access a database. This is called user-level security.

To set up user and group accounts:

1. Open a database.

2. Choose Tools ➪ Security ➪ User and Group Accounts. This opens the dialog box shown in Figure 54-20.

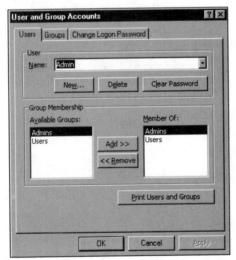

Figure 54-20: Add new users and new user group accounts here.

3. By default, Access creates two groups: Admin and Users. Admin users can perform administrative functions such as adding users and groups; users can access only the database itself.

4. By default, Access creates an Admin user called, unimaginatively, Admin. Choose it from the Name drop-down list, and then click the Change Logon Password tab. Type the password you want to use in the New Password and Verify fields. (Once you've closed the database and Access, the next time you open it you'll have to log on using this account name and password.)

5. Click the Users tab.

6. To create a new account, enter the name of the user in the Name box, and then select the group you want to add him or her to; click the New button. This opens the dialog box shown in Figure 54-21.

Figure 54-21: The name and personal ID of each user are entered here.

7. Enter the name of the user and the personal ID — a string of four to 20 characters of your choice that Access combines with the user's name to identify that user in the group.

8. Click OK to create the new account.

9. To create a new group, click the Groups tab, click the New button, and enter a name and personal ID for the new group.

10. To delete a user, click on the group he or she is a member of in the Available Groups list; then locate the name in the Name list and click Delete. To delete a group, click the Groups tab, highlight the group you want to delete, and click Delete.

Securing the database

Access makes securing the database easy by providing a wizard. Choose Tools ⇨ Security ⇨ User-Level Security Wizard, and follow the instructions, providing information as needed. At one point you'll be asked to choose which objects in the database should be secured. All secured objects will thereafter be accessible only by users in the Admin group until you grant other users permissions.

The Wizard makes a backup copy of your database, and then encrypts the original.

Assigning permissions

To assign permissions, choose Tools ⇨ Security ⇨ User and Group Permissions. This opens the dialog box shown in Figure 54-22.

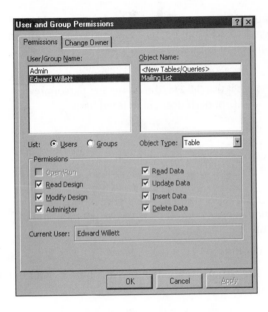

Figure 54-22: You can limit the access of certain users or groups of users to specific databases and objects by setting up permissions.

To assign permissions from this dialog box:

1. Click the Users radio button if you want to assign permissions to individual users, or the Groups radio button if you want to assign permissions to groups.

2. Select the name of the user or group you want to assign permissions to.

3. Select the object you want to assign permissions for from the list of objects, and select the object type from the drop-down list.

4. Use the check boxes to set permissions for that user or group: check boxes to grant permission for the action described to be performed, uncheck boxes to deny that permission.

5. When you've set permissions for all the users and groups, click OK. You'll have to close and open the database again for the permissions to fully take effect.

6. Click the Change Owner tab to assign ownership for the database or objects in it to someone other than the Admin user.

Encryption

Encryption doesn't actually limit access; it simply makes it impossible to view the file in any other program except Access, and even in Access you'll have to decrypt it first. It's usually used in conjunction with a password or user-level security (remember, the User-Level Security Wizard encrypts the database as part of securing it).

To encrypt a database:

1. Open Access without opening a database.

2. Choose Tools ➪ Security ➪ Encrypt/Decrypt Database.

3. Locate the database you want to encrypt in the Encrypt/Decrypt Database dialog box (which looks just like a Save As dialog box).

4. Click OK.

5. Another dialog box opens that looks much like the first; in this one, specify the name and location of the encrypted file.

6. Click Save.

You can save the encrypted file over the original by specifying the same filename and location.

To decrypt a file, follow the same procedure, but choose an encrypted file to be decrypted in Step 3.

Summary

In this chapter you learned some of the ins and outs of sharing Office information over a network. Highlights included the following:

✦ You can add a level of protection to Word and Excel documents when you're saving them by choosing Tools ➪ General Options from the Save As dialog box and specifying passwords for opening and/or modifying the file.

✦ You can add additional protection to Word and Excel files by choosing Tools ➪ Protect Document in Word and by choosing Tools ➪ Protection in Excel.

✦ In Windows 95 and 98, by activating File and Print Sharing under Network in the Control Panel, you can allow other network users to access your computer's hard drive — but you can still control which folders they're allowed to poke around in.

✦ You can initiate an online meeting in any Office application by choosing Tools ➪ Online Collaboration ➪ Meet Now. Choose a directory and the people you want to meet with; provided they're running NetMeeting and they agree to the meeting, you can add them to the online discussion of whatever Office document you have open.

✦ As host of the meeting, you can initiate Chat and even call up a virtual whiteboard that everyone can have access to. You can also allow other participants in the online meeting to edit shared documents and send the files to them by choosing File ➪ Send To ➪ Online Meeting Participant.

✦ Provided Office Server Extensions are installed on your network Web server, you can initiate Web Discussions (a threaded series of messages) of documents in Word, Excel, and PowerPoint by choosing Tools ➪ Online Collaboration ➪ Web Discussions. You can initiate discussions in Internet Explorer 5 by clicking the Discussion button. In Word and IE5, discussions can be inserted into a document near the content they're focused on. In other applications and frame-capable browsers, discussions are displayed in a separate pane from the document.

✦ You can create a shared workbook in Excel by choosing Tools ➪ Share Workbook.

✦ Access databases are one of the most commonly shared types of Office files. You can make them freely available or create very tight security for them by using the commands under Tools ➪ Security on the menu.

✦   ✦   ✦

Creating Macros

Macros can help make you more productive by automating tasks that you carry out frequently. Suppose you've developed a procedure to, for example, change the formatting of a document from what's standard for interoffice memos to what's standard for documents released to the public on business letterhead. You could create a macro for that procedure and even turn it into a button on a toolbar or a menu item, so all you have to do is click once, and all the tasks you used to have to perform step-by-step are carried out for you.

Recording and Running Macros

The simplest way to create a macro is by recording it: You turn on the macro recorder, perform the procedures you want to make part of the macro, and then turn the macro recorder off.

The first step in creating such a macro is to think very carefully about what you want to do and the sequence of commands you'll have to issue to achieve that goal. You might even want to jot them down on a piece of paper.

Recording a macro in Excel

Suppose, for example, that you want to create a macro that will automatically apply a green fill and an 18-point bold italic, Times New Roman font in blue to Excel cells. Here's how you'd do it:

1. Open an Excel worksheet.
2. Choose Tools ➪ Macro ➪ Record New Macro. This opens the dialog box shown in Figure 55-1.

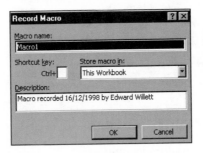

Figure 55-1: You need to make a few decisions about your macro before you begin recording it.

3. In the Record Macro dialog box, enter a name for your macro and choose where it should be stored: in the currently open workbook, in a new workbook, or in a personal macro workbook, the last of which is a workbook that exists just to store your macros and which ensures that they're available every time you run Excel (otherwise they're available only when you open the workbook they're stored in). You can also choose a shortcut key that, pressed with Ctrl, will activate the macro at any time. Finally, you can add additional information about the macro to the description field.

4. When you click OK, recording begins immediately, and the Stop Recording toolbar opens (see Figure 55-2). It has just two buttons: one on the left, which stops recording; and one on the right, which lets you choose whether you want to use absolute or relative cell references when recording.

Note

By default, Excel uses absolute references, which means that, if you record cells being selected, the next time you run the macro those exact same cells will automatically be selected. If you click this button and switch to relative references and record cells being selected, the next time you run the macro the cells that are selected will be based on whatever cell is currently active. It will also have the same position relative to it as the cells you originally selected had to the active cell at the time of recording, even if the actual location within the worksheet is completely different. Because we want to create a macro that will format a single cell or a range of cells, we're not going to record cell selection.

Figure 55-2: The Stop Recording toolbar button on the left stops recording, and the one on the right lets you choose absolute or relative cell references.

5. Carry out the actions you want to record. In this case, you'd click Fill Color and choose green from the color palette, click Font and choose Times New Roman, choose size 18 from the Font Size list, click the Bold and Italic buttons, and then click the Font Color button and choose blue from the color palette. (In this particular case the order is arbitrary—the macro will work just as well regardless of what order these steps are recorded in.)

6. Click Stop Recording.

Recording macros in other applications

Although the procedure is basically the same, recording a macro is slightly different in Word and PowerPoint than in Excel, and creating a macro in Access is a whole different ballgame.

Word

In Word, the Record Macro dialog box looks like the one shown in Figure 55-3. Instead of simply assigning a shortcut key, you're given the option of assigning your macro to either the keyboard or a menu (we'll look at how to do both of those a little later in the chapter). The macro can be saved to either the normal.dot template, which means it will be available to all documents based on the Normal template (the default template), or just to the current document.

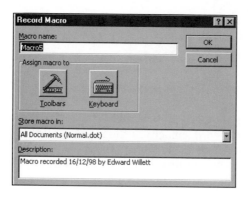

Figure 55-3: Word's Record Macro dialog box differs slightly from Excel's.

The Stop Recording toolbar looks a little different, too (see Figure 55-4). Although it has two buttons, the second one is Pause Recording. This allows you to halt recording temporarily while you carry out steps you don't want to record, and then resume recording.

 Figure 55-4: The Pause Recording button is a useful addition to Word's macro-recording controls.

Note   Also notice that while you're recording a macro in Word, your mouse pointer changes: a small image of a tape cassette is attached to it.

PowerPoint

In PowerPoint, things are even simpler. The Record Macro dialog box has only three fields: one for naming the macro, one for choosing which of the open presentations it should be stored in, and one for providing a description (see Figure 55-5). There's no provision at the time of recording for assigning the macro to a shortcut key or toolbar. The Stop Recording toolbar is simpler, too: it consists only of a Stop Recording button.

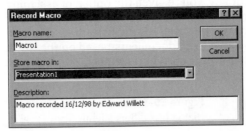

Figure 55-5: PowerPoint's Record Macro dialog box is particularly straightforward.

Access and Outlook

Access and Outlook don't allow you to record a macro as the other applications do; Outlook macros must be created in the Visual Basic Editor (see the Introduction to Visual Basic later in this chapter), while Access macros can be created in the Visual Basic Editor or using an entirely different method. Access macros are also covered later in this chapter.

Editing macros

Editing macros requires a thorough knowledge of Visual Basic for Applications (see the introduction to Visual Basic later in this chapter). To edit a macro, choose Tools ⇨ Macro ⇨ Macros. This opens a Macros dialog box similar to the one shown in Figure 55-6. (This is the Word version, but Excel and PowerPoint's dialog boxes are similar.) Choose the macro you want to edit, and then click Edit to open the Visual Basic Editor and display the Visual Basic code for the macro. Click Step Into to see each Visual Basic command in the macro highlighted in the Visual Basic Editor as it's carried out.

Running a macro

To run any macro, especially one that hasn't been assigned a shortcut key, tool button, or menu item (see the next section of this chapter), choose Tools ⇨ Macro ⇨ Macros, highlight the macro you want to run, and then click Run.

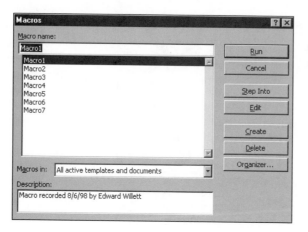

Figure 55-6: You can edit macros in Visual Basic by finding them here, and then clicking Edit.

Assigning Macros to Keys, Toolbars, and Menus

A successfully recorded macro is really just another command — in fact, the built-in commands in Office applications are, strictly speaking, just a permanent set of macros — and, just like other commands, can be assigned a shortcut key or attached to a toolbar button or menu item.

Assigning shortcut keys to macros

As noted earlier, you're given the opportunity to assign a shortcut key to macros in Excel before you even record them, in the Record Macro dialog box. You can do the same thing in Word, but the procedure is a little different.

To assign a macro to a shortcut key in Word before you record it:

1. Choose Tools ⇨ Macro ⇨ Record New Macro.

2. In the Record Macro dialog box, click the Keyboard button in the Assign Macro to area. This opens the Customize Keyboard dialog box shown in Figure 55-7.

3. Click inside the Press New Shortcut Key box, and then press the key combination you'd like to use as a keyboard shortcut for your new macro. If you choose a combination that's already assigned to a command, Word tells you that. You can overwrite the existing keyboard shortcut if you wish, or you can find another shortcut that's not yet assigned.

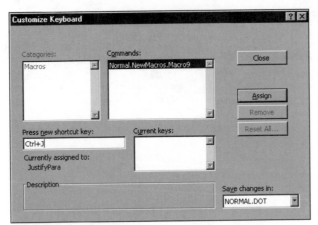

Figure 55-7: You can assign a Word macro to a keyboard shortcut in this dialog box.

4. When you're happy with your shortcut, click Assign, and then record your macro as usual. Once it's recorded, you can run it at any time by pressing the assigned shortcut keys.

PowerPoint does not let you assign a shortcut key to a macro.

Assigning macros to toolbars and menus

Once you have recorded macros in Excel, Word, or PowerPoint, the process of attaching them to toolbars and menus is straightforward: it's exactly the same procedure you follow for customizing any other tools.

In all three applications:

1. Choose Tools ➪ Customize. This opens the Customize dialog box, which is almost identical in Word, Excel, and PowerPoint.

2. If you want to create a brand-new toolbar to contain your macros, click the Toolbars tab, and then click New. Enter a name for the toolbar. In Word, you can also specify which documents you want to have access to the new toolbar (documents based on a particular template or just the current document). Click OK. A tiny floating toolbar with no buttons on it appears.

3. To place your macro on the new toolbar or on an existing toolbar, click the Commands tab and scroll down through the Categories list until you find Macros. Highlight that, and all the macros you've created will be displayed.

4. Click on the macro you want to assign to a toolbar and drag it to the toolbar you want to add it to. In Figure 55-8, for instance, three macros were dragged onto the new toolbar created in Step 2, and a fourth is in the process of being dragged.

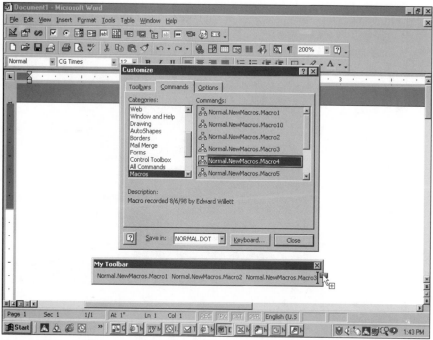

Figure 55-8: Add your recorded macros to toolbars or menus from here.

5. Once you've installed a macro onto a toolbar, you can customize its appearance by clicking on it, and then clicking Modify Selection (see Figure 55-9). (Each time you want to customize a different tool, you have to click on it, and then click Modify Selection again.) Here you can choose whether you want the new command displayed as text only in both toolbars and menus, as an image on toolbars and text on menus, or as both an image and text; assign a new button image, edit the current one pixel by pixel or paste in a new one you've copied from another command (click the button you want to copy, click Copy Button Image; click the button you want to use the copied button's image with; and click Paste Button Image). You can also make the macro button the beginning of a new group of commands on the toolbar you've dragged it onto.

6. In Word only, you can click Keyboard to reopen the Customize Keyboard dialog box and assign a new shortcut key to the macro.

7. Adding a macro to a menu follows exactly the same procedure as adding it to a toolbar; simply drag it onto any menu in the location you want (see Figure 55-10), and then modify its appearance using the Modify Selection button.

8. When you've successfully installed your macros onto their toolbars and menus, click Close.

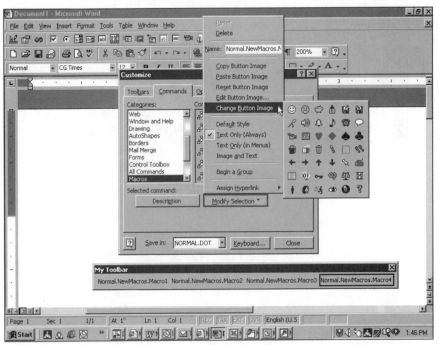

Figure 55-9: Modify the way your macro's button is displayed from this menu.

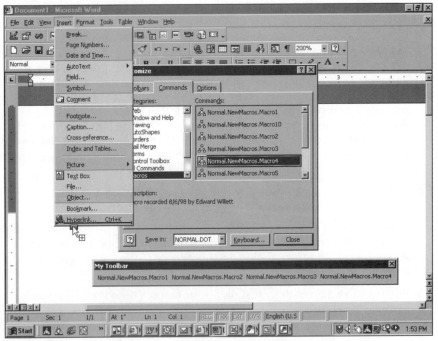

Figure 55-10: You can drag a macro onto a menu just as you can drag it onto a toolbar.

Using Macros in Access

As already noted, you can't record macros in Access the same way you can in other Office applications. That's because Access macros are typically more complex than those in other applications — which is why Macros get their own button under Objects in the database window (see Figure 55-11).

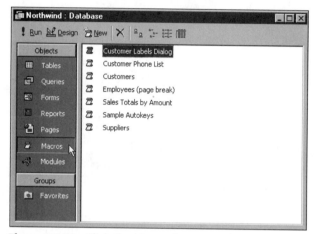

Figure 55-11: Click the Macros button under Objects to see a list of all macros created for the current database.

Creating an Access macro

Rather than record macros in Access, you create them by assembling a list of actions from a list. To create an Access macro:

1. In the database window, click Macros, and then click New. This opens the window shown in Figure 55-12.

2. Choose the first action you want to perform as part of the macro from the drop-down list in the Action column, and click on it.

3. In the Action Arguments section, enter any additional information that is required.

4. Enter any comments you want to make about the action in the Comment column. You don't have to enter comments, but they make macro maintenance easier.

5. Move to the second row of the Action column and choose the second action you want to perform.

6. Repeat Steps 2 – 5 until you've finished your macro.

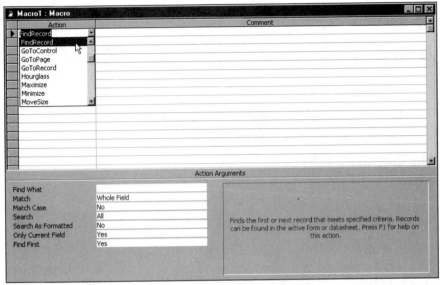

Figure 55-12: This is where you assemble your Access macros.

7. When you're done creating your macro, close the Macro window. Access asks if you want to save changes; click Yes.

8. Provide a name for your macro and click OK.

9. Click the Macros button under Objects in the database window again, and you'll see your new macro listed with the others in the database.

Tip   You can also create macros that carry out actions on specific objects in the database by arranging your windows so you can see both the Macro window and the database window, and then dragging objects from the database window to the Action column. In Figure 55-13, for instance, we've dragged the Summary Sales by Year report from the database window to the Action column. Access automatically entered the OpenReport action and the correct name of the report in the Action Arguments section.

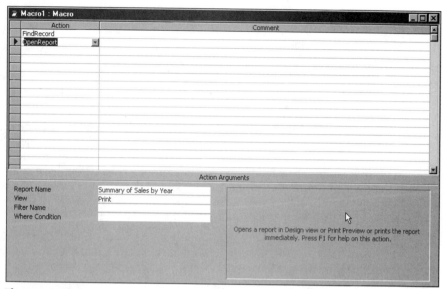

Figure 55-13: You can speed macro creation by dragging objects from the database window to the Action column.

Creating macro groups

If you have a lot of macros, grouping similar ones together can help you keep them straight. To create a macro group instead of a single macro, follow the steps just outlined, but click the Macro Names button on the toolbar when the Macro window is open. This adds another column to the Macro window. You can enter a name for a macro and then select a list of actions for that macro to carry out; and then enter a name for a new macro, selecting another list of actions for that macro to carry out, etc. When you save, you'll be specifying the name for a macro group, instead of a single macro.

Running an Access macro

Once you've created your macro, you can run it directly by clicking the Macros button under Objects in the database window, and then double-clicking on the name of your macro or clicking it once and clicking Run. If the database window isn't visible, you can run a macro from anywhere in Access by choosing Tools ➪ Macro ➪ Run Macro, choosing the name of the macro you want to run in the Macro Name dialog box.

It's rather unusual for a macro to be run directly, however, except to test it; most macros created in Access are run from forms or reports or even from other macros. To run a macro from a form or report:

1. Open the form or report in Design view.

2. Right-click on the object that you want to use to activate the macro, and choose Build Event.

3. If an event is already attached to that object, you can insert a command to run a macro in the Action column. If no event is attached to that object, you'll be asked to choose which Builder you want to use; choose Macro Builder and build the macro as before. If an event already exists, you'll see something similar to Figure 55-14; right-click where in the order of events you want the macro to run and choose Insert Rows; then enter the name of the macro you want to run under Macro Name in the new row.

4. You can also add a macro that already exists to an object. Right-click on the object, choose Properties, and then click on the Event tab. You can assign any existing macro to any one of several possible events for that object.

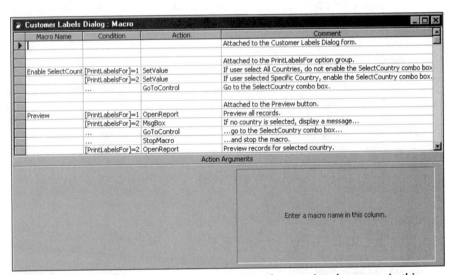

Figure 55-14: Make a form or report run a macro by entering the macro in this builder.

Note   You can also add Access macros to toolbars and menus just as you did in other Office applications.

Introduction to Visual Basic for Applications

Visual Basic is a powerful programming language that you can use to create new procedures for all of your Office applications — once you learn how to use it. Learning to use it effectively is outside the scope of this book — entire books are devoted just to that — but what follows is a brief introduction to some of the basic concepts behind VBA.

VBA is an object-oriented programming language, which means that you program in it by scripting a series of events, each of which is triggered by something that happens to an object (such as text boxes, command buttons, or sections of a form). This is consistent with all programming under Windows, which also involves responding to a series of events.

VBA offers you a great deal more control than regular macros do, especially in such areas as handling program errors, creating new functions, and performing applications at the level of the operating system. VBA programming consists of units called *procedures*, each of which consists of a group of statements and methods that perform a desired operation; procedures, in turn, are grouped into *modules*.

And that's about as far as we're going to delve into VBA in this book. For more detailed information, consult a good reference book such as the *Visual Basic for Applications Bible* by D. F. Scott, published by IDG books, or *Microsoft Office 2000 Visual Basic Programmer's Guide,* published by Microsoft.

To get a taste of VBA, open Word, Excel, PowerPoint, or Outlook and choose Tools ➪ Macro ➪ Macros, choose a Macro, and then click Edit. You'll see a display something like the one in Figure 55-15.

Examining the innards of macros to see how they're put together is one good way to begin to grasp how Visual Basic for Applications programs are constructed.

If you're really the hands-on type, VBA will let you tweak Office to your heart's content; but if you're a more typical user, you'll probably never go near it.

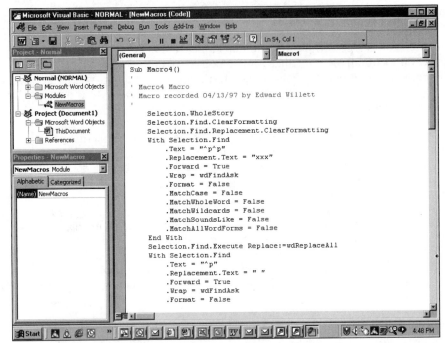

Figure 55-15: The Visual Basic Editor is a powerful application for creating programs in Visual Basic.

Summary

In this chapter you learned procedures for creating macros in Office applications. Highlights included the following:

✦ You can automate procedures you perform regularly by choosing Tools ⇨ Macro ⇨ Record New Macro (in Word, Excel, and PowerPoint), and then performing the series of actions you want to automate.

✦ Recorded macros are essentially identical to any other command in Office, and can be added to toolbars and menus by using the Tools ⇨ Customize dialog box. Word and Excel also allow you to create keyboard shortcuts for macros.

✦ You can run a macro either by clicking the toolbar button or menu command you created for it (or pressing the keyboard shortcut), or by choosing Tools ⇨ Macro ⇨ Macros, selecting the macro you want to run, and clicking Run.

✦ You can't record a macro in Access; instead, you have to build it. Click Macros under Objects in the database window, and then click New. You can choose from a series of available actions to create a macro that does what you want it to.

✦ Macros in Access can be run from toolbars or menus as in other Office applications; they can also be activated from forms or reports.

✦ Macros in Access and in other Office applications can also be created using Visual Basic for Applications, a powerful programming language included with Office. You can access the Visual Basic Editor by choosing Tools ➪ Macro ➪ Visual Basic Editor, but you might want to get a good reference book on the topic first.

✦   ✦   ✦

Using ActiveX

In Chapter 4 we looked at creating forms in Word. In Chapter 15 we discussed the use of forms in Excel, and Chapter 37 was devoted to forms in Access. In each of these programs, one of the things you can do when creating a form is insert special controls such as check boxes, list boxes, and radio buttons.

You've seen those same sorts of controls throughout Office's dialog boxes, wizards, and templates, and if you've browsed the Web very much at all you've probably even come across them on Web pages.

They are called *ActiveX controls,* and in addition to letting you insert them into forms, Office lets you insert them into any other Office document (although obviously it has to be a document that's going to be viewed on a computer, not just on paper).

What Is ActiveX?

ActiveX was designed by Microsoft to make it easy to add interactive content to online documents, particularly on the Web, but also on your computer. Even novice Web page designers, for instance, can add list boxes, command buttons, and even controls that play movies.

ActiveX controls can be written in a variety of programming languages and are designed to work with a variety of computer programs, two characteristics that make ActiveX very attractive to programmers. As a result, there are literally thousands of ActiveX controls available, many of which you can download free from the Web.

Using ActiveX Controls in Office Documents

In Access, ActiveX controls are available in Design view by choosing View ➪ Toolbox.

Cross-Reference For detailed information on Active X in Access, see Chapter 37, "Working with Forms."

To insert ActiveX controls in Word, Excel, or PowerPoint, choose View ➪ Toolbars ➪ Control Toolbox (shown in Figure 56-1).

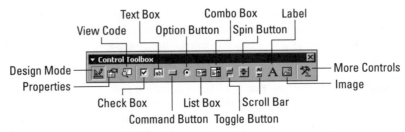

Figure 56-1: The Control Toolbox contains the most commonly used ActiveX controls.

In Word, simply clicking on one of the control buttons automatically inserts that control in your document wherever the insertion point is currently located. In Excel and PowerPoint, clicking on one of the control buttons changes your mouse pointer to a crosshairs; position it where you want the control to be inserted and click.

In either program, the control when it first appears will look something like the check box shown in Figure 56-2.

The controls in the Control Toolbox include the following:

✦ **Check Box.** This lets users turn an option on or off.

✦ **Text Box**. This provides a box into which users can type text.

✦ **Command Button**. Command buttons cause some action to be performed when they are clicked.

✦ **Option Button**. Option buttons let users select one option from a group of options.

✦ **List Box**. List boxes contain a list of items.

✦ **Combo Box.** A Combo box combines a text box with a drop-down list box, so users can either type in information or select an item from a list.

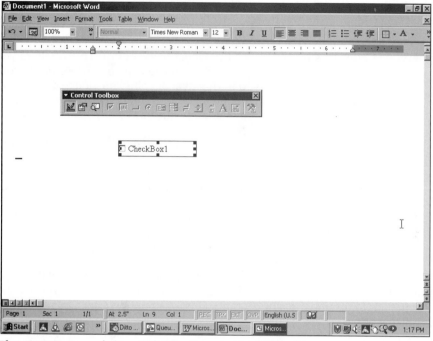

Figure 56-2: A newly inserted ActiveX control looks like this.

✦ **Toggle Button**. Toggle buttons remain depressed when clicked, and then release when clicked again. They're used for turning things on and off.

✦ **Spin Button**. Spin buttons are usually attached to a cell (in Excel) or to a text box. Clicking the up arrow increases the value in the cell or text box; clicking the down arrow decreases it.

✦ **Scroll Bar**. Scroll bars let the user scroll through a range of values by clicking on the scroll arrows or dragging the scroll box.

✦ **Label**. A label is text added to a document to provide information about a control or the document in general.

✦ **Image**. This button embeds a picture in the document.

✦ **More Controls.** Clicking this opens a menu of all the ActiveX controls currently available on your system. Many of these may not work in your Office document, but you may be able to use them in a Web page (see the next section of this chapter on using ActiveX controls in Web design).

There are three other buttons in the Control Toolbox:

✦ **Design Mode.** This button toggles Design Mode on and off. You must be in Design Mode to edit ActiveX controls. (The small toolbar that opens once you're in Design Mode also contains a button for toggling Design Mode off.)

✦ **View Code.** This button opens the Visual Basic Editor. This is where you can make modifications to the function of the control. For example, you can attach one or more macros to it. However, a solid knowledge of Visual Basic for Applications is necessary. Find a good reference book on the topic or refer to the Help files that are included with the Visual Basic Editor.

See Chapter 55, "Creating Macros," for a very brief introduction to Visual Basic for Applications.

✦ **Properties.** For those unwilling or unable to delve into Visual Basic, this button offers you many ways to fine-tune a control. The Properties sheet lets you view all the properties associated with the control in either alphabetical order or categorized by function. Figure 56-3 shows the Categorized tab of the Properties sheet for the check box created earlier.

To change a property, click in the right-hand row alongside the name of the property you want to change. Depending on the property, you may be able to type in new information (for example, a new caption), choose an option from a menu, or open a new dialog box.

It bears repeating that to make good use of ActiveX controls, you need a strong grounding in Visual Basic for Applications. This brief overview tells you how to insert them into your documents, but their true power lies in customizing them in the Visual Basic Editor to carry out all sorts of specialized tasks. For those who have the time and desire to create their own Office tools, ActiveX and VBA are an unbeatable combination.

Figure 56-3: Set the properties of an ActiveX control on the Properties sheet.

Adding Controls to Web Pages with Word

As noted throughout this book, Office 2000 makes it easy to turn any Office document into a Web page; all you have to do is save it as one. Not only that, but as much as possible, Office 2000 maintains all formatting, so that an Office document you save as a Web page can be brought back into Office still looking pretty much the same, with data and formatting intact.

You can add ActiveX controls to documents you're saving as Web pages, just as you can to other Office documents. However, there is a potential downside: Not all browsers support ActiveX, so you could conceivably be creating pages that some visitors to your site won't be able to view properly.

For that reason, Word, in addition to the ActiveX controls in the Control Toolbox, also provides you with a collection of HTML controls, which look and function much like ActiveX controls (although they're not as powerful because they can't be as extensively modified as Visual Basic allows with ActiveX), but are accessible by all browsers.

To access the Web Tools toolbar in Word, choose View ⇨ Toolbars ⇨ Web Tools. That opens the Web Tools toolbar shown in Figure 56-4.

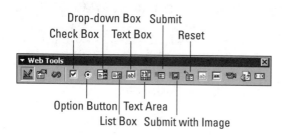

Figure 56-4: Choose the perfect HTML control for your Web page from this toolbar.

Many of the controls available here overlap those in the Control Toolbox, but not all of them. Controls you can insert include the following:

✦ **Check Box.** This lets viewers select or clear one or more options.

✦ **Option Button**. This differs from a check box in that, while you can have multiple check boxes checked, only one option button in a group of related option buttons can be active at a time. Use it when you want viewers to make a selection among mutually exclusive possibilities.

✦ **Drop-down Box**. This shows a list of options in a drop-down list box.

✦ **List Box**. This displays a list of options in list format. If there are more items in the list than there is room for in the box, the viewer can scroll down to see the rest.

✦ **Text Box**. This creates a box in which a viewer can enter a single line of text.

✦ **Text Area.** This creates a box into which a viewer can enter more than one line of text.

✦ **Submit**. This adds a button that when clicked submits the data the user supplied on the form.

✦ **Submit With Image**. Like submit, but it displays an image you choose instead of just a plain Submit button.

✦ **Reset**. This returns all the controls in the form to their default settings, and removes any data your viewer has entered.

Note
Controls on Web pages are grouped into forms. You must have one Submit or Submit with Image control within every form.

To insert controls into your Web page:

1. Place your insertion point where you want the form to begin.

2. Click the Web Tools button for the control you wish to insert. The control, when it appears, looks much like an ActiveX control in a regular Office document, except for the lines above and below indicating the beginning and end of the form (see Figure 56-5).

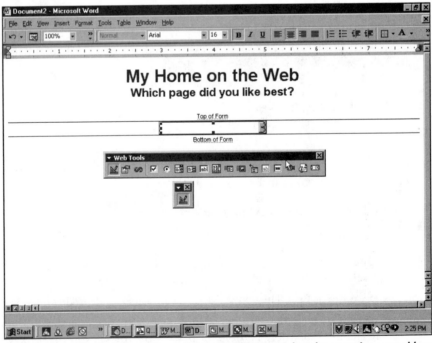

Figure 56-5: This drop-down box will let viewers respond to the question posed here.

3. Add any other controls you want to be part of the same form.

4. Add a Submit or Submit With Image control (see Figure 56-6).

5. Now set the properties of your control. Click on the control you want to set the properties for, and then click the Properties button on the Web Tools toolbar.

6. Edit each control's properties in the Properties sheet (see Figure 56-7). These vary from control to control; in this one, the names of the various pages in the Web site are entered under DisplayValues, separated by semicolons (no spaces). Under Values, enter the text (in the same order) that you want sent to the server when each option is selected. Another important property, and one that you'll see with all controls, is HTMLName; you have to give the control its own name so the information in that field will be properly identified when it's sent to the server.

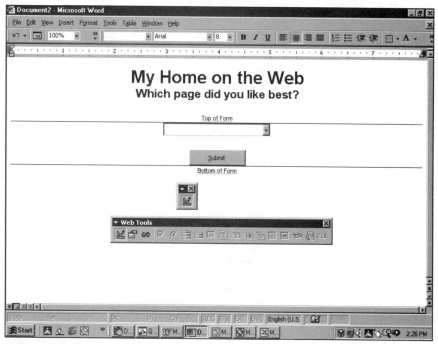

Figure 56-6: You must have a Submit or Submit with Image control somewhere in every form.

Note

Additional support files and server support are necessary for forms to work properly. Before attempting to use forms on your Web pages, check with the administrator of your network or Web-site hosting service.

For detailed information about setting properties for each of the controls in the Web Tools toolbar, consult Word Help.

Figure 56-7: Set the properties you want for each control in the Properties sheet.

7. When you've edited all the controls in the form, close Design Mode by clicking the Exit Design Mode button.

The completed drop-down box looks like the one shown in Figure 56-8.

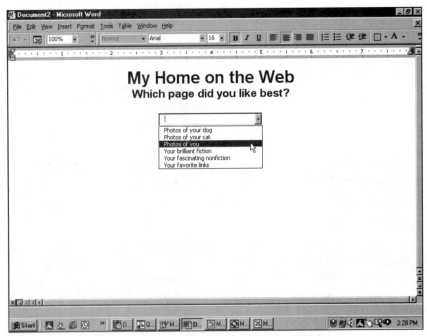

Figure 56-8: Here's what the completed Web form looks like.

Summary

In this chapter you took a brief look at ActiveX controls, and how they can add an extra level of interactivity to Web pages and other documents viewed online. Highlights included the following:

✦ To add an ActiveX control to a Word, Excel, or PowerPoint document, open the Control Toolbox by choosing View ➪ Toolbars ➪ Control Toolbox, and then click the button for the control you want to add.

✦ You can set the basic properties of each control by selecting the control and clicking Properties in the Control Toolbox.

✦ Detailed modification of ActiveX controls requires a thorough knowledge of Visual Basic; click on the control you want to modify and then click the View Code button in the Control Toolbox.

✦ When you create Web pages in Word, you can add HTML-based controls by using the Web Tools toolbar (View ➪ Toolbars ➪ Web Tools).

✦ Web tools are grouped together in forms. Enter the controls you want from the Web Tools toolbar, but remember that all forms must contain a Submit or Submit with Image button.

✦ Adjust the properties of each control by selecting the control and clicking the Properties button on the Web Tools toolbar.

✦　　✦　　✦

Cutting-Edge Office

Using the Internet from Office

In the years since the first version of Microsoft Office appeared, we've seen an explosion in the use of the Internet for communication and research worldwide, and of intranets — using the same technology on a smaller scale — for communication and research within corporations. Recognizing that fact, Microsoft has integrated each version of Office more closely with the online world. With Office 2000, the interface between your documents and the World Wide Web or your local intranet is almost seamless.

Accessing the Internet from Office Applications

Outlook and FrontPage are obviously designed to give you quick access to the Internet (or an intranet): in Outlook's case, so you can check your e-mail and exchange scheduling information; and in FrontPage's case, so you can maintain your Web site. However, Word, Excel, PowerPoint, and Access also provide instant access through the Web toolbar, which is the same in all four applications (and in Outlook as well).

Opening the Web toolbar

To open the Web toolbar:

1. Choose View ⇨ Toolbars.

2. Click Web on the list of available toolbars.

3. The toolbar appears (see Figure 57-1).

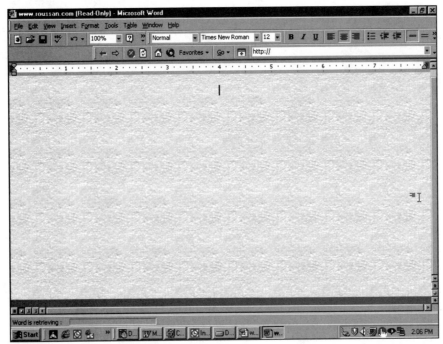

Figure 57-1: The Web toolbar makes it easy for you to access the World Wide Web.

Using the Web toolbar

To use the Web toolbar to view a Web page, just type the URL of the page you wish to visit into the address blank and press Enter. Office will automatically open your Web browser and display the indicated page.

Note You can use the Web toolbar to browse Office documents as well as Web pages. If the URL you enter is for an Office document on your own computer or local network, the application in which that document was created will open to display that document.

The Web toolbar provides several other useful buttons, which, from left to right, include the following:

✦ **Back.** This returns you to the previous document you visited, just like the Back button on your browser. If you're using your Web toolbar to browse both Office documents and Web pages, the Back button may also switch you from your browser to another Office application.

✦ **Forward.** Once you've gone backward in the list of sites and documents visited using the Back button, the Forward button should take you forward in that list again.

✦ **Stop Current Jump.** If it's taking a long time for the site or document you selected to appear, this button will be active. Click it to stop the jump to that site.

✦ **Refresh Current Page.** This reloads the latest version of the page you're viewing from the network.

✦ **Start Page.** This takes you to whatever page you currently have set to load automatically every time you open your browser.

✦ **Search the Web.** By default, this takes you to a Microsoft site that lets you search the World Wide Web.

✦ **Favorites.** This opens the list of favorite sites you have stored on your computer.

✦ **Go.** This menu includes several of the commands that already appear on the Web toolbar, including Forward, Back, Start Page, and Search the Web. You can also set a new Start Page or Search Page here by calling up the start or search page you want to use, and then choosing Go ➪ Set Start Page or Go ➪ Set Search Page. The next time you click Start Page or Search the Web, you'll go to the new sites you've selected.

✦ **Show Only Web Toolbar.** Click this to hide all other toolbars, leaving only the Web toolbar showing. Click it again to make the other toolbars reappear.

Adding Internet Objects to Your Documents

Sometimes when you're working on a document you may come across something on the World Wide Web that you'd like to add to your document just as it is. It could be a table of figures, a selection of text, or an image, to name just three possibilities. In Office 2000 it's simple to transfer items from the Internet to your document. All you have to do is drag and drop. Here's how:

1. Open Internet Explorer.

2. Open the application into which you wish to insert something from the Internet.

3. Resize the windows in which Explorer and your application appear so that you can see both of them at once. If they're both maximized, clicking the Restore button (or right-clicking on the title bar and choosing Restore from the pop-up menu) will reduce their sizes so that you can move them around to suit you. In Figure 57-2, Internet Explorer 5 and PowerPoint are arranged so that both are visible at once.

4. The next step is to highlight the item on the Web page that you want to transfer to your document. You do this just as you would in Word, by clicking and dragging your mouse pointer over the top of the material you want to highlight. In Figure 57-3, I've highlighted the image of the book cover and the accompanying text.

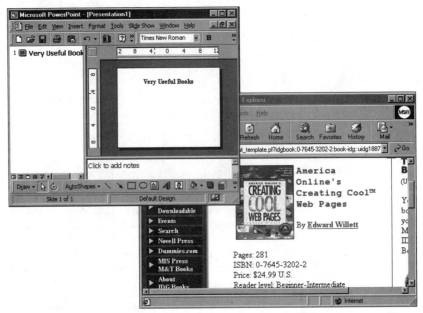

Figure 57-2: The first step to transferring items from the Internet to an Office document is to arrange your browser and Office application windows so both are visible.

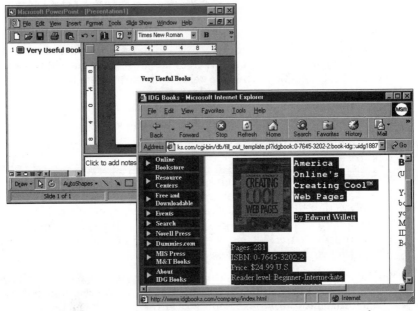

Figure 57-3: In your browser, highlight the material you want to transfer to your Office document.

5. Now place your mouse pointer anywhere inside the highlighted material, hold down the mouse button, and drag the mouse pointer to the place where you want the material to be inserted into your Office document — in this case, because it will be placed on a blank PowerPoint slide, anywhere within the boundaries of the slide. Your pointer changes to show you are dragging copied material (see Figure 57-4).

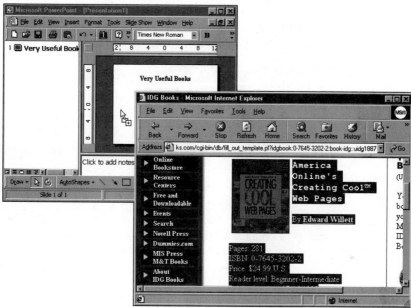

Figure 57-4: The change in your mouse pointer indicates that you are successfully transferring material from the Web page to your Office document.

6. Release your mouse button. The material from the Web page appears in your Office document. In Figure 57-5, it's a bit jumbled up; that may happen to you, too, depending on how the Web page you're taking the material from is set up and which application you're putting it into. However, once it's in your Office application, you can easily rearrange it. The important thing is that the information has all been copied.

Caution

Just because something appears on a Web page doesn't mean it's free for anyone to use. Graphics, text, sound files, etc., on the Internet are protected by copyright, just as photographs, books, and CDs are in the nonvirtual world. Before using anything from the Internet in a published document or presentation, make sure you have permission from its creator to do so. If you can't obtain that permission, or you aren't sure who owns the rights to the material in question, it's better not to use it at all — and stay on the right side of the law.

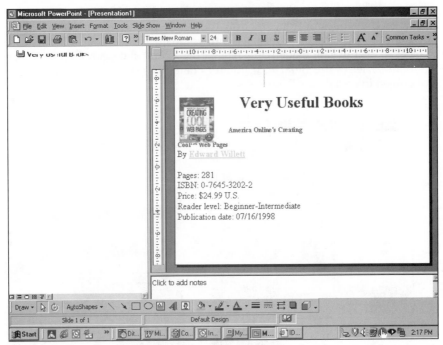

Figure 57-5: It may get a bit jumbled up in the transfer, but the material you want from the Web page is now safely ensconced in your document.

Creating Hyperlinks

In Office, you can add hyperlinks that link not only to the World Wide Web but to files on your own computer or network or even another part of the file in which the hyperlink appears. The method for adding hyperlinks to Word, Excel, and PowerPoint documents is pretty much identical, while that for adding hyperlinks to Access databases differs slightly simply because Access databases are somewhat different animals.

In Word, Excel, or PowerPoint

Follow these steps to add a hyperlink to a Word document, Excel worksheet, or PowerPoint presentation:

1. Select the text or object to which you want to apply the hyperlink.

2. Choose Insert ➪ Hyperlink, right-click and choose Hyperlink from the pop-up menu, or press Ctrl+K.

3. The Edit Hyperlink dialog box will open (see Figure 57-6).

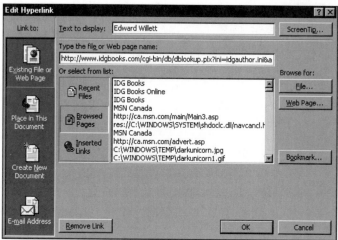

Figure 57-6: Create the hyperlink you want using this dialog box.

4. By default, the text you selected is displayed in the Text to Display box. You can change it if you want, but be aware that this will also change the text in your document.

5. If you want to create a custom screen tip (a note about the hyperlink that will pop up when people using Internet Explorer 4.0 or later place their mouse pointers on it without clicking), click Screen Tip and type the text for the tip in the small dialog box that opens; then click OK.

6. You have several options available for creating a target for your hyperlink. Down the left is a navigation bar that lets you move among these options. By default, you're looking at the options for linking to an Existing File or Web Page. You can either type in the URL in the Type the File or Web Page Name blank, or choose from lists of files you've recently opened, pages you've recently browsed, or links you've recently made use of. You can also browse for a file or Web page that's not included in any of the lists.

7. If you want to link to a place within the current document, click Place in This Document in the navigation bar. What you see next depends on which application you're using.

   • **In Word** you'll see the dialog box shown in Figure 57-7. You can choose to make the hyperlink target the top of the document, any of the headings within the document (paragraphs using one of the heading styles), or any bookmarks you may have inserted.

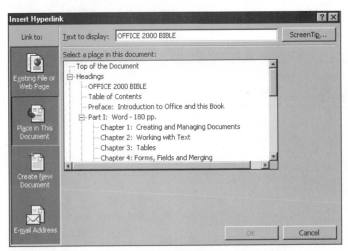

Figure 57-7: Internal links can go to the top of the document, any heading, or any bookmark within Word documents.

- **In PowerPoint** the dialog box looks a little different (see Figure 57-8). Here you can choose to link to the first slide, last slide, next slide, previous slide, or any specific slide within your presentation. The Slide Preview box shows you what the slide you've selected looks like, so you can be sure you're linking to the right one.

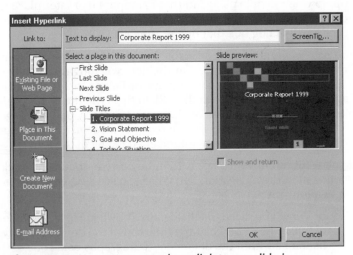

Figure 57-8: You can create a hyperlink to any slide in your PowerPoint presentation.

• **In Excel** the dialog box looks like the one shown in Figure 57-9. You can choose to reference any cell within any worksheet in the workbook, either by choosing the sheet you want and then typing in the reference number of the cell, or by linking to the cell by name, if it has one.

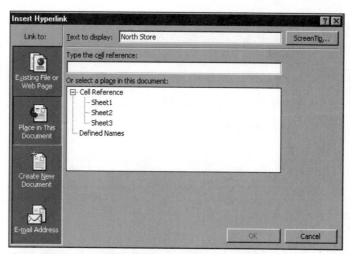

Figure 57-9: Hyperlinks within Excel go to specific cells.

8. If you want to make the target of your hyperlink a document that doesn't exist yet, click Create New Document. With the controls that appear (see Figure 57-10) you can choose a name and location for the new document, and whether you want to edit it now or later.

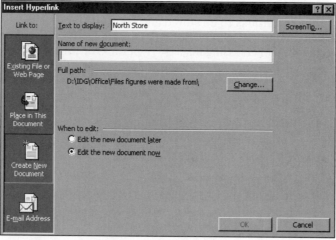

Figure 57-10: You can also choose to create a brand-new document for your hyperlink to point to.

9. Finally, you can choose to make the target of your hyperlink an e-mail address (see Figure 57-11). Type in the address you want the link to point to, or choose from the list of recently used e-mail addresses. You can also insert a subject that will automatically appear in the e-mail's header. When readers click this hyperlink, their e-mail editor will automatically open so they can send a message to the indicated recipient.

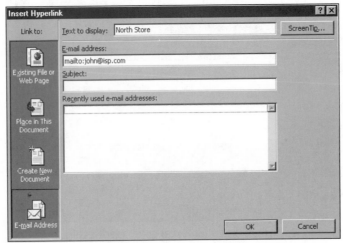

Figure 57-11: Your readers can send e-mail with the click of a button with a hyperlink to an e-mail address.

In Access

In Access, you can't simply add a hyperlink to an existing data entry. Instead, you have to make any hyperlinks a separate column of data, by opening the table in which you want the hyperlinks to be stored and choosing Insert ⇨ Hyperlink Column. Once that column exists, you can add hyperlinks to it by clicking inside any cell in the column and choosing Insert ⇨ Hyperlink, or pressing Ctrl+K.

After that the procedure is the same; the only difference is that in Access, internal hyperlinks can go to any existing database object: a table, a query, a form, etc. (see Figure 57-12).

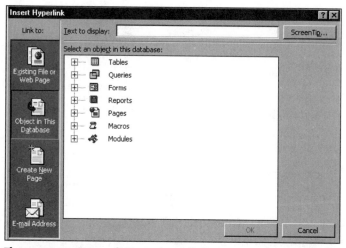

Figure 57-12: Internal Access hyperlinks can go to any database object you've created.

Using FTP

FTP stands for File Transfer Protocol: it's a method of transferring files over the Internet. Although the World Wide Web is far and away the most popular part of the Internet today, a lot of useful files are stashed all over the world on the Internet that aren't accessed through the Web at all. Many of them are stored at FTP sites instead. Office 2000 makes it easy for you to access Office documents stored at FTP sites, assuming of course that you have access to the Internet or an intranet.

Before you can access an Office document by FTP, however, you first have to add the FTP site to your list of Internet sites. To do so:

1. Choose File ⇨ Open from any Office application.

2. In the Open dialog box, pull down the Look In list (see Figure 57-13).

3. Choose Add/Modify FTP Locations. This opens the dialog box shown in Figure 57-14.

4. Enter the location of the FTP site you want to add to the list; for example, ftp.microsoft.com.

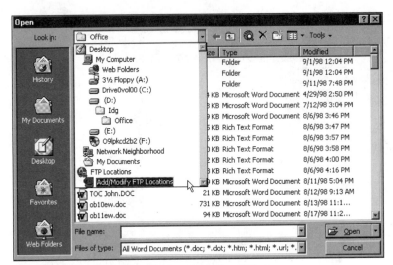

Figure 57-13: The Look in list box includes FTP sites.

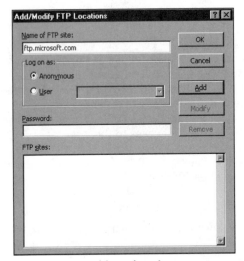

Figure 57-14: Add FTP locations to your Look In list using this dialog box.

5. If you want to log in to the site anonymously, click the Anonymous radio button; if you have an account and password at a particular site, click User and type in your user name and password.

6. Click Add to add the FTP site to the list.

7. To modify the information for an existing FTP site, highlight it in the list, and then make any changes you want to the name, user name, and password and click Modify. To remove a site from the list, highlight it and click Remove.

8. When you're done, click OK.

Now you can choose and open files from the FTP site just as if they were located on your computer, by browsing for them in the Open dialog box.

Summary

Office 2000 was designed with the increasing integration of desktop applications with the wider world of the Internet in mind. In fact, with Office 2000, the line between the two practically vanishes. Some highlights include the following:

✦ You can access the World Wide Web, or a corporate intranet, from almost any Office application by choosing View ➪ Toolbars ➪ Web to open the Web toolbar. Type in an URL to visit the indicated page.

✦ Adding an object from the Internet to an Office document is as easy as opening a Web page in your browser, highlighting what you want to move to your Office document, and dragging it into place in the Office application.

✦ Office lets you create hyperlinks to Web pages, files, e-mail addresses, and even other parts of the same document the hyperlink appears in. In most applications, simply highlight the text or object you want to attach the hyperlink to, and then press Ctrl+K.

✦ By adding FTP sites to the Look In list in your Open dialog box (pull down the list and choose Add/Modify FTP Locations) you can open Office documents stored on the Internet as easily as if they were stored on your own computer.

✦　✦　✦

International Support and Accessibility Features

♦ ♦ ♦ ♦

In This Chapter

Single worldwide
executable

Multilingual editing

Improved
accessibility features

♦ ♦ ♦ ♦

Globalization may be an overused buzzword, but that doesn't make it any less a fact. Increasingly, companies are conducting business in countries all over the world. Obviously, it helps a lot if everyone is using the same software. With Office 2000, Microsoft has come closer than ever to ensuring that you can carry out your business on any continent in any language and still enjoy all of Microsoft Office's functionality.

Single Worldwide Executable

Single Worldwide Executable is just a fancy way of saying the program code for Office 2000 is the same no matter where in the world you're running it. In other words, there won't be separate versions of the suite for different countries. That means the same product can be rolled out everywhere and still meet the needs of all users, which makes life much easier for people trying to support Office in several different languages.

With a single worldwide executable, users can enter, display, and edit information in all the languages Office supports, and it supports a lot of them, including European languages, Japanese, Chinese, Korean, Hebrew, and Arabic. (The only exceptions are the Thai, Vietnamese, and Indian languages, which still require a different executable.)

Multilingual Support

Thanks to the single worldwide executable, Office 2000 makes it easy to change the language of the user interface without affecting the operation of the various applications. It doesn't require a system administrator or an information technology specialist: It can be done by any user at any time.

Note In order to use Office 2000's multilingual support, you must have Microsoft's Language Pack installed. This can be found on the CD labeled Language Pack. Run the setup program to install it.

Changing the language

Once the Language Pack is installed, follow these steps to change the language of the user interface and enable the languages you want to use for entering and editing text:

1. Click the Windows Start button.

2. Choose Programs.

3. From the Office Tools folder, select Microsoft Office Language Setting. This opens the dialog box shown in Figure 58-1.

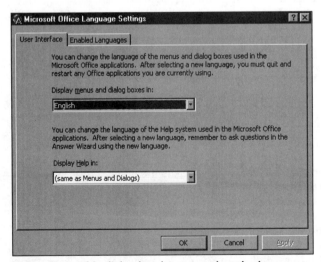

Figure 58-1: This dialog box lets you select the language in which you want to work.

4. Under the User Interface tab you'll see two list boxes: Display Menus and Dialogs In and Display Help In. Choose the languages you want to use from the lists provided (remembering, as noted earlier, that which languages you can use in your user interface depends to a certain degree on what operating

system you're running). By default, Help files are displayed in the same language as you've chosen for your user interface, but you can also change them to a different language if you wish.

5. Now click the Enabled Languages tab (see Figure 58-2). This lets you enable your Office application to work in the languages you select, and also enables any special features they may have to make working in those languages more efficient. (For example, if you are running the U.S. version of Office and you enable editing for Japanese, you'll see new commands for working with Japanese text in the Format menu in Word, PowerPoint, and Excel.) Just check the box beside each language you want to enable. When you're done, click OK.

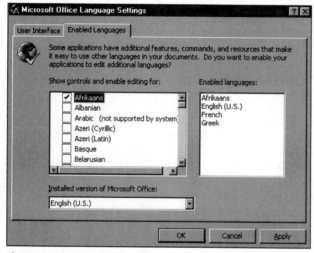

Figure 58-2: To work in different languages in Office, you first have to enable them here.

Note

If you are selecting a language that uses characters that do not appear on the standard keyboard, you'll also need to install the correct keyboard layout. You can do that by clicking Start, and then opening the Control Panel and double-clicking the Keyboard icon. If you're working in Windows 95 or Windows 98, choose the Language tab from the Keyboard Properties dialog box; if you're working in Windows NT, choose the Input Locales tab. Click Add and choose the language you want from the list provided. This dialog box also gives you several options as to which commands you want to use to switch from language to language.

6. Before the new language settings take effect, you'll have to close all Office applications and re-open them. You're given the option of doing so immediately.

7. Figure 58-3 shows Word 2000 with the user interface changed to Greek.

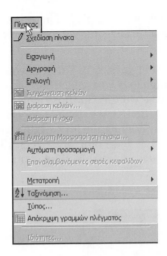

Figure 58-3: It's all Greek to Word when you change the user interface.

8. To change the language in which you enter text and edit in Word (which is the Office application most affected by changes in language, as it deals largely in text), highlight the text you want to use the new language tools for, and then choose Tools ➪ Language ➪ Set Language. Choose the language you want to use from the list (see Figure 58-4). Once it's selected, the spell-checker and other proofing tools automatically use the dictionary for that language, if it's available. If you do not want to check spelling and grammar in that language, mark the top check box of the two at the bottom of the dialog box. You can also choose to have Word automatically recognize the language you're working in and switch proofing tools accordingly, by selecting the bottom check box.

Figure 58-4: Set the language you want to work in using this dialog box.

Once you've enabled a language for use in Office applications, PowerPoint will also automatically recognize that language and use the appropriate proofing tools.

Entering language-specific characters

Things get a little more complicated when you're working in a language that doesn't use the Western European alphabet, such as Chinese, Japanese, and Korean or the Baltic, Central European, Cyrillic, Greek, and Turkish languages, and/or one that reads from right to left, such as Arabic, Hebrew, and Farsi.

For Chinese, Japanese, and Korean, you have to install software called an Input Method Editor, which is provided with Office. Input Method Editors allow you to enter Asian text in Word and Outlook.

For all other Office applications, and for the other languages mentioned, you must also be running the corresponding language version of Windows 95, Windows 98, or Windows NT.

Multilingual binary converters

The single worldwide executable means that file formats will be more easily interchangeable among users of Office who speak different languages. However, older versions of Office continue to be used, and regional versions saved files in different formats and would not allow users to save their documents in an older version in a different language. That meant, for example, that if someone using the Japanese version of Word 97 wanted to send a document to a Word 95 user in the United States, it couldn't be done, because the Japanese user couldn't save the document in the English version of Word 95.

Word 2000 has eliminated that problem. When you choose File ⇨ Save As in Word 2000, you're given the option in the Save as Type box to save in earlier file versions in European, Japanese, Korean, simplified Chinese, or traditional Chinese format.

Euro support

Excel 2000 supports the euro, the new common European currency, as one of its currency formats, allowing you to display both the euro symbol and the three letter ISO code EUR (see Figure 58-5). This is an important feature if you plan to do business with European companies or governments in the future.

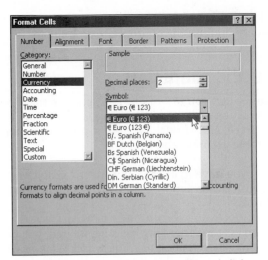

Figure 58-5: Choose Format ⇨ Cells and click the Currency category under the Number tab to call up the list box that allows you to choose the euro as the currency style for your spreadsheet.

Accessibility Features

Office has several tools that can make it easier for visually and physically impaired individuals to work with Office applications:

✦ **Zoom.** All Office applications except Outlook have, on the Standard toolbar, a list box labeled Zoom. You can choose to view documents at any percentage of full size, either by selecting one of the percentages in the list (which range from 10 percent to 500 percent) or by typing a percentage into the box. For those who find it difficult to read fine print on a computer screen, Zoom can be a major help (see Figure 58-6).

✦ **Large icons.** Another helpful feature in Office applications is the ability to enlarge icons on the toolbars. Choose Tools ⇨ Customize, click the Options tab, and then check the Large Icons check box. The change takes effect immediately (see Figure 58-7).

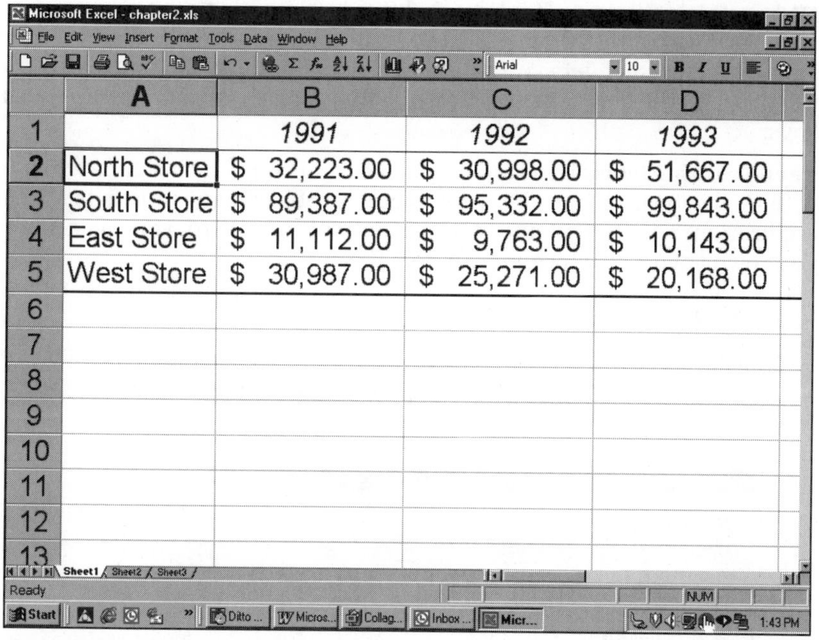

Figure 58-6: Zoom can turn any document into a large-print document for the benefit of the visually impaired.

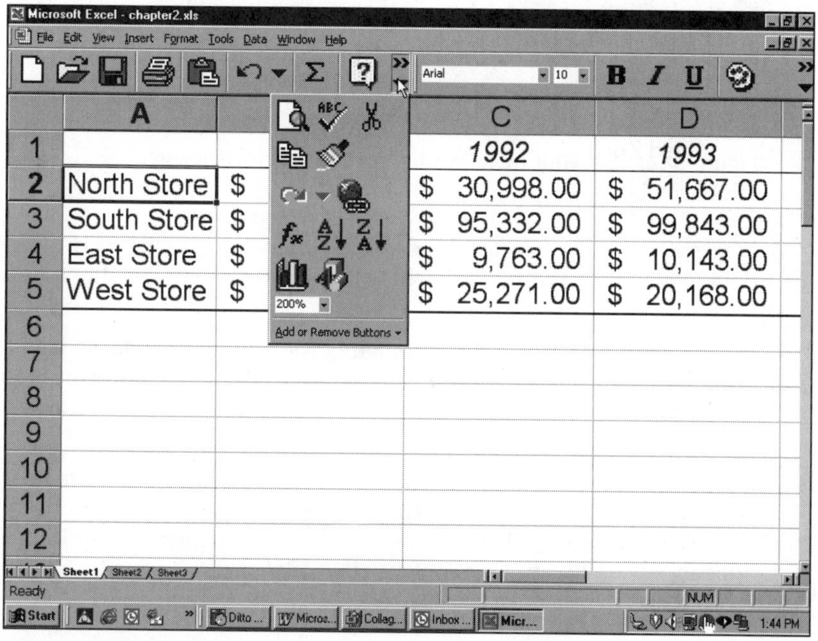

Figure 58-7: Enabling the large icons option makes it much easier to see the tools on Office's toolbars.

✦ **Microsoft IntelliMouse.** If you have difficulty operating a mouse, you might want to consider the Microsoft IntelliMouse pointing device, which Office supports and which lets you scroll and zoom more easily. For example, you can scroll to the end of the document with a single click, and without using keys.

✦ **Keyboard shortcuts.** Many Office features and commands can be activated with the keyboard alone. For a complete list of keyboard shortcuts for each application, refer to that application's Help files. In Word, you can also create your own keyboard shortcuts. To do so:

1. Choose Tools ➪ Customize.

2. Make sure the Toolbars tab is selected; then click Keyboard. This opens the Customize Keyboard dialog box shown in Figure 58-8.

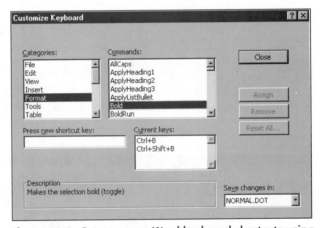

Figure 58-8: Set your own Word keyboard shortcuts using this dialog box.

3. In the Save Changes In box, click on the name of the currently open document or the template in which you want to save the shortcut key changes.

4. In the Categories box are a list of categories of commands, as well as other elements such as font, styles, AutoText, macros, and common symbols. Click on the category in which the item you want to assign a shortcut to falls.

5. In the box to the right (whose name changes to match the category you've selected), click on the specific item you want to assign the shortcut key to. Any shortcut keys currently assigned to that item appear in the Current Keys box.

6. Place your cursor in the Press New Shortcut Key box, and then press the key or key combination you want to use.

7. Click Assign.

8. You can remove an assignment by highlighting it and clicking Remove. To return all keyboard shortcuts to their original assignments, click Reset All.

9. Click Close to return to the Customize dialog box, and click Close again to return to your application.

✦ **Customize toolbars and menus.** In any application, you can also add new commands to toolbars or menus. Here's how:

1. Make sure the toolbar or menu you want to add the command to is showing.

2. Choose Tools ➪ Customize.

3. Click the Commands tab. (If you want to start a brand-new toolbar, first click the Toolbars tab and click New to create the new toolbar; then return to the Commands tab.)

4. Choose the category in which the command you want to place on the toolbar or menu falls; then choose the command you want from the list provided.

5. Click on the command you want to move to the toolbar or menu, and drag it to that toolbar or menu (see Figure 58-9). You can place it exactly where you want.

Figure 58-9: Customize your toolbars and menus by simply dragging the commands you want to place on them into place.

Summary

In this chapter you looked at Office 2000's improved multilingual support and the features it provides to make its applications more accessible to people with visual and physical disabilities. Highlights included the following:

✦ Office now has a single worldwide executable, which means that the same program code can be used in almost every country.

✦ Office offers extensive multilingual support, although you have to make a special effort to install it. Once the Language Pack, shipped on a separate CD from the regular program files, is installed, you can change the user interface language and enable various languages for entering and editing text by clicking the Start button, opening the Program files folder, looking in the Office Tools folder, and clicking Microsoft Office Language Settings. This also enables various special commands and functions that are used to work with specific languages.

✦ Once a language is enabled, most Office applications will automatically recognize which language you're working in and apply the appropriate proofing tools.

✦ Excel now offers support for the euro, the European Community's new transnational currency.

✦ Word now lets you save documents in older versions in other languages.

✦ Office offers several features to enhance its ease of use by those with visual and physical impairment. They include the Zoom command, the option to use large icons, customizable keyboard shortcuts for all commands and functions in Word, and customizable toolbars and menus in all applications. The various versions of Windows offer their own accessibility enhancements as well.

✦　　✦　　✦

Cutting-Edge Tips

Office 2000 is a major improvement over Office 97, yet they're enough alike that you could go from using one to the other without ever being aware of, or making use of, some of the most innovative features in the new version. In this chapter, we'll do our best to make sure that some of those innovations don't go unnoticed, with our list of seven cutting-edge tips to make sure you're getting the most out of Office 2000.

Using the Office Shortcut Bar

The Office Shortcut bar isn't exactly new, but it's a useful little tool that deserves mention because it sometimes goes unnoticed — many Office users probably aren't even aware that it exists.

Opening the Shortcut bar

To open the Office Shortcut bar choose Start ➪ Programs ➪ Office Tools ➪ Microsoft Office Shortcut Bar. You'll be asked if you want to configure the Shortcut bar to start automatically every time you start Windows; click Yes if you do.

When you first see the Office Shortcut bar, it's usually attached to the right side of the desktop.

To get a better look at it, we've dragged it away from the edge and made it float in Figure 59-1. You can also position it along any edge of the desktop — just drag it there and it automatically attaches.

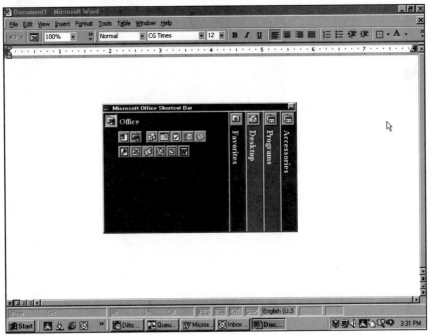

Figure 59-1: It's easier to see what's on the Shortcut bar if you float it.

What's on it

As you can see, each Office application, by default, has a shortcut on the Shortcut bar. So do two tools normally found under Start, including New Office Document and Open Office Document. In addition, several common Outlook tools have buttons here by default, including New Message, New Appointment, New Task, New Contact, New Journal Entry, and New Note.

There's more than just Office here, however. By default, there are also toolbars for Favorites (from your Internet browser), Desktop (where all the shortcuts from your desktop appear), Programs (all the folders and files you'd normally access by choosing Start ➪ Programs), and Accessories (everything you'd access by choosing Start ➪ Programs ➪ Accessories).

To activate anything on the Shortcut bar, just click its button.

Customizing the Shortcut bar

You're not limited to what's here by default; you can customize the Shortcut bar in a number of ways. To customize the Shortcut bar:

1. Right-click on it and choose Customize from the pop-up menu. This opens the Customize dialog box shown in Figure 59-2.

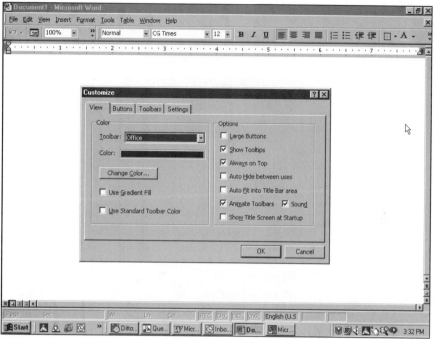

Figure 59-2: You have complete control over the appearance and contents of the Office Shortcut bar from this dialog box.

2. Customize the appearance of the bar with the controls under the View tab. Choose the toolbar you want to change the appearance of, and then choose a color by clicking Change Color. You can apply that color as a gradient fill by clicking the Use Gradient Fill check box, or you can simply use the Standard toolbar color of your current Windows color scheme by choosing that check box. Choose the additional options you want from the Options section — they're pretty self-explanatory.

3. To add or delete buttons, click the Buttons tab (see Figure 59-3). Here you can add, delete, rename, or (with the Move buttons) rearrange buttons, which can represent either files or folders.

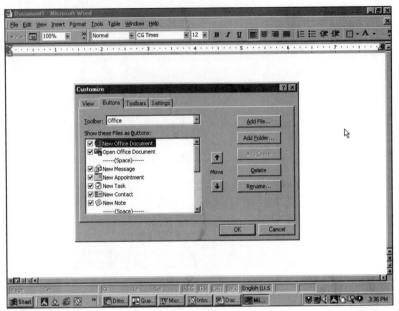

Figure 59-3: Choose and modify the buttons on the Shortcut bar from here.

4. You can make any folder on your computer into a Shortcut bar toolbar under the Toolbars tab (see Figure 59-4), or add a new toolbar by clicking Add Toolbar. You can also choose to deactivate, remove, or rename the current toolbars, or rearrange them using the Move buttons. (You can hide current toolbars by right-clicking on the Shortcut bar and unchecking the names of the toolbars you don't want displayed.)

5. Finally, under the Settings tab, you can change the default location for User and Workgroup templates.

6. When you've customized the Shortcut bar to your heart's content, click OK.

7. If you want the Shortcut bar to only show itself when you point at it, right-click on it and choose Auto Hide. (Note that this only applies when the Shortcut bar is docked, not when it's floating.)

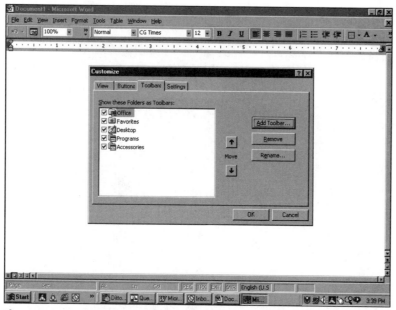

Figure 59-4: Add, delete, and rename toolbars with these controls.

Making HTML Your Default File Format

One of the most significant upgrades to Office this time around is its ability to use HTML as a native file format in addition to the regular Office formats. What's significant about this is that it means a document created in Excel, for example, and saved in HTML, can be opened in Word, PowerPoint, Internet Explorer, Netscape Navigator, or any other program that can view HTML files, with a minimal loss of formatting.

The process to make HTML the default file format varies slightly from application to application:

✦ In Word and PowerPoint, choose Tools ➪ Options, click the Save tab, and in the Save Word files as and Save PowerPoint files as list-boxes, choose Web Page.

✦ In Excel, choose Tools ➪ Options, click the Transition tab, and in the Save Excel files as list-box, choose Web Page.

Figure 59-5 shows a chart as it looks in Excel; Figure 59-6 shows the same chart viewed in Internet Explorer after it was saved in HTML format. The process of saving the chart as HTML was as fast and simple as saving in the usual Excel format.

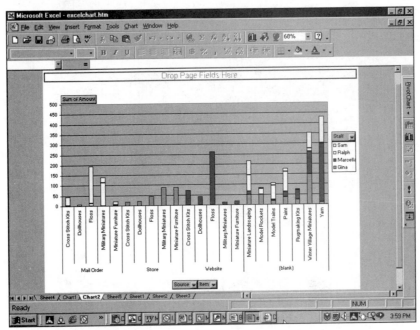

Figure 59-5: An Excel chart.

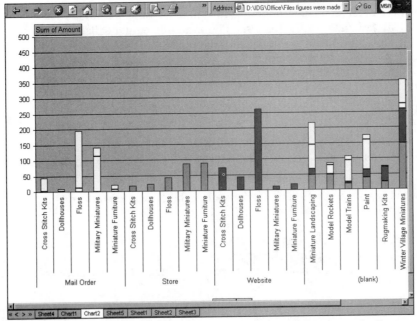

Figure 59-6: The same Excel chart after it's become a Web page, with all formatting intact.

Previewing Web Pages in Your Browser Without Saving

If you are creating Web pages in Office, you'll appreciate another advance: You can preview those pages in your browser without having to save them first, as you do now. That means you can easily and continually check the appearance of your page in your browser as you make changes to it.

To do so, just choose File ➪ Web Page Preview. Office automatically opens your default browser and displays the page you're working on in it (see Figures 59-7 and 59-8).

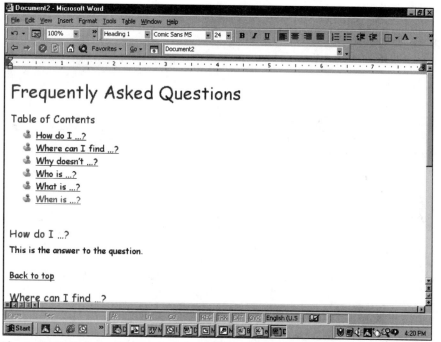

Figure 59-7: This is a Web page being created in Word (or another Office application).

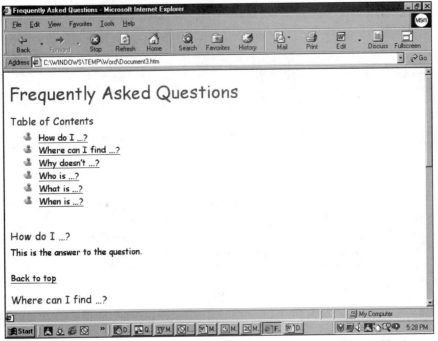

Figure 59-8: Here's a preview of that page, so you can see what it looks like in your browser.

Subscribing to Files and Folders

There's nothing worse than calling up what you think is the most recent data on a particular topic for, say, a very important report, only to find out, when you deliver your report, that all the data has changed since you accessed it.

One way to avoid this problem is by using a linked object to enter the data in your report, but this only works if the data is also stored in an Office document, or was created by some other program that supports linking. What you really need for information that doesn't fall into that category is some way of knowing when it has been changed.

Provided that the information is stored in a file published on a Web server running Office Server Extensions, Office can let you know. Just as you might subscribe to a magazine, so you can subscribe to a particular document or folder on a server running those extensions, and you'll receive e-mail on a regularly scheduled basis to tell you if the document or a document in the folder has been edited, deleted, or moved; or, in the case of a folder, if a new document has been created. Office can even let you know if a discussion remark has been added to or removed from a document.

To subscribe to a document or folder:

1. Choose Tools ➪ Online Collaboration ➪ Web Discussions.

2. Click Subscribe on the Discussions toolbar, and choose whether you want to subscribe to the currently open file (click File) or to all the files in a folder (click Folder and set the options you want or type the address of another folder). Type in the name of the file or folder you want to subscribe to.

3. In the When box, select the conditions for which you want to trigger a notification of changes being made.

4. Type your e-mail address in the Address box.

5. Choose how often you want to receive notification of changes in the Time box.

6. Click OK.

Making Good Use of the New Open Dialog Box

One thing you'll notice right away when using Office 2000 is the new Open dialog box (see Figure 59-9). It not only looks different (for one thing, it lets you view 50 percent more files with less visual clutter than the previous versions), it also offers many new features.

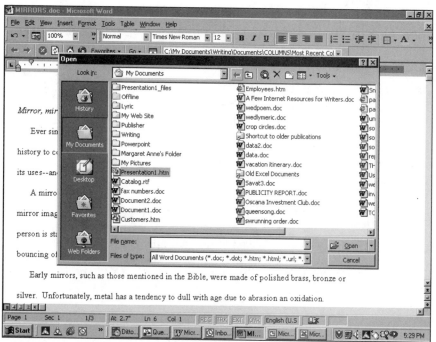

Figure 59-9: The new Open dialog box offers several improvements.

Down the left side of the box, in what's called the Places bar, are buttons that provide one-click access to the places you go most: your desktop, the My Documents folder, your folder of Favorites from your browser, Web folders (folders on a Web server you're using to save and open Office documents) and a History folder that contains links to the last 20 folders and documents on which you've worked (see Figure 59-10).

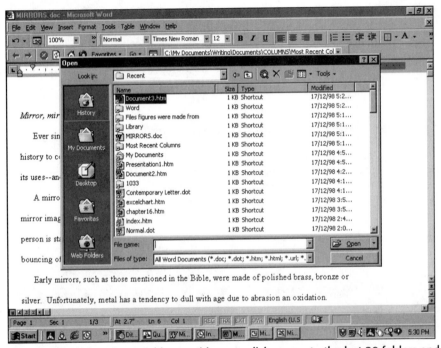

Figure 59-10: The History folder provides one-click access to the last 20 folders and documents you've opened.

Across the top are other useful tools:

✦ **Look in** lets you choose where on your computer and networked drives you want to look, including FTP locations.

✦ **Back** takes you back to the last folder you opened — and just so you can remember what that is, a screen tip appears when you point at the button, displaying the name of the previous folder.

✦ **Up One Level** takes you up one level in the folder hierarchy.

✦ **Search the Web** opens your browser so you can do just that.

✦ **Delete** deletes the currently selected file or folder (it will ask you if you're sure first).

✦ **Create New Folder** lets you do exactly that.

✦ **Views** lets you view your files and folders as a simple list of names or as a list that includes details such as file type, when modified, and size (click the down button just beside the Views button to change the view, or just click the Views button again and again to cycle through the various views). You can also view file properties (see Figure 59-11) or preview files (see Figure 59-12). Click Arrange Icons to arrange files and folders by name, type, size, or date modified.

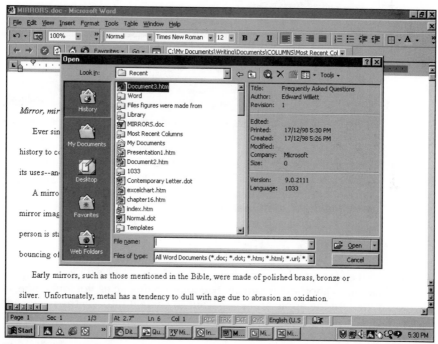

Figure 59-11: Properties view lets you see a lot of information about a file before you open it.

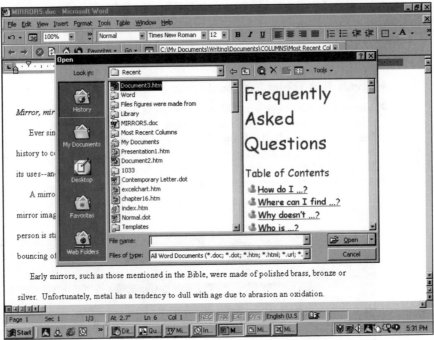

Figure 59-12: Preview view gives you a glimpse of the document itself.

✦ **Tools** opens a menu that lets you run a search for files and folders with Find; delete or rename files and folders; print files; add a file to your list of favorites; view file properties; and map a network drive (which lets you assign a drive letter to a drive on the network).

Using Collect and Paste

Have you ever found it frustrating trying to copy and paste data from one application to another? It quickly becomes confusing as you open one, copy what you want, find the application you want to paste it into, do the paste, go to the next application you need to copy something from, return to the one into which you're pasting...etc., etc., etc.

Office 2000 makes gathering information from multiple sources easier with its collect and paste capability. That means you can copy, for example, a graphic from a PowerPoint presentation, a range of figures from an Excel database, and a bit of text from a Word document and paste them all at once into a new Word document.

All of these items are copied to the Office Clipboard, which is separate from the ordinary Windows Clipboard. While the Windows Clipboard holds only one item at a time, the Office Clipboard can hold up to 12.

To use Collect and Paste:

1. Open the Clipboard toolbar by choosing View ➪ Toolbars ➪ Clipboard from any Office application (see Figure 59-13).

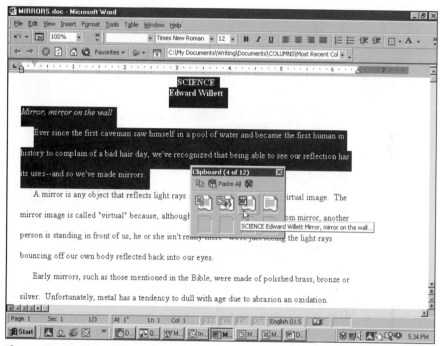

Figure 59-13: The Clipboard toolbar lets you copy and paste multiple items, with each item represented in the Clipboard by an icon.

2. Select the first item you want to copy, and click the Copy button on the toolbar.

3. Continue selecting items, in as many Office applications as you wish, until you have what you want. Each item will appear as an icon on the toolbar. If you place your mouse pointer on it, you'll even get a screen tip that can help you remember what it is.

4. When you're ready to paste an item, you can either click on an individual item to paste just it, or click Paste All to paste all the items at once — in Figure 59-14, a piece of an Excel worksheet, a couple of paragraphs of Word text, and a bit of clip art from PowerPoint have been pasted into a new Word document.

5. Rearrange the items in the document you pasted them into as necessary.

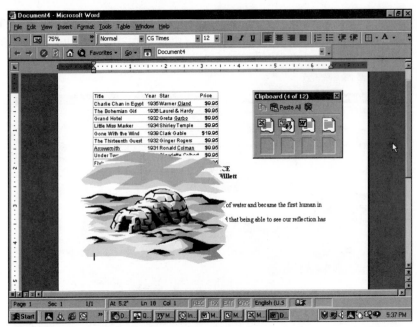

Figure 59-14: Once everything is pasted into the same document, a certain amount of rearranging is usually called for.

Using the Office Assistant

Whenever you go looking for help in Office the first time, you're probably going to find yourself requesting it from a cute cartoon character. Whether you like that sort of thing or not depends on your own personality, but even if you don't care for the character, you'll find that getting help in Office is easier than ever.

Activating the assistant

To see the Office Assistant, choose Help ➪ Show the Office Assistant and it will appear (see Figure 59-15) as an animated cat, which, when you click on it, asks you what you want to do.

Asking questions

The Assistant tries to guess what topic you might be seeking help about, based on what you've just been doing. If the links it provides aren't what you need, you can type in a keyword or two and click Search — or you can even ask a question in natural language.

For example, in Figure 59-16, I've asked the Assistant, "How do I change fonts?" and received a list of links that will, indeed, answer that question, plus others related to modifying the appearance of text.

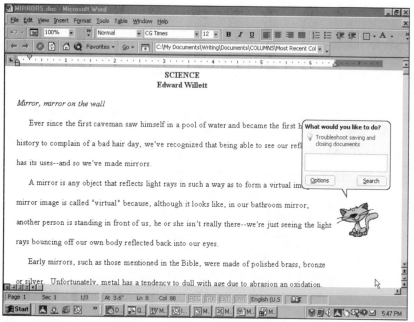

Figure 59-15: The cat in the corner isn't a virtual pet—it's your guide to the intricacies of Office 2000.

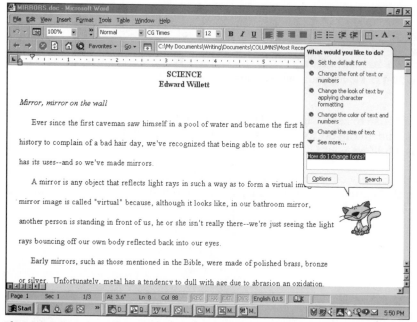

Figure 59-16: The Office 2000 Office Assistant can answer questions asked in natural language.

Modifying the assistant

You can modify the way the Assistant works by clicking Options. This opens the dialog box shown in Figure 59-17. In the top half, you can even turn off the Office Assistant entirely, if you prefer using Help in the ordinary, noncartoon-assisted way, by unchecking the Use the Office Assistant check box.

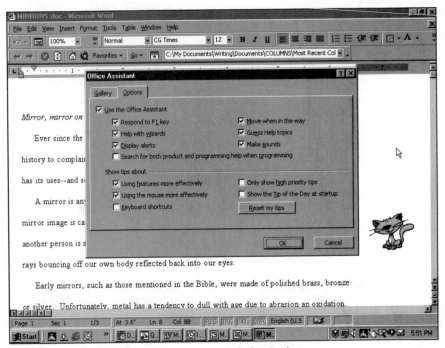

Figure 59-17: Modify your Office Assistant's behavior here.

If you choose to keep Office Assistant, you can fine-tune its behavior in the top section and, in the bottom, choose what kind of helpful tips you'd like it to relay to you as it follows your Office activities.

Click the Gallery tab to change the appearance of the Assistant; possibilities range from a claymation-looking version of an Einstein-like character to an animated Earth to a two-legged robot (see Figure 59-18).

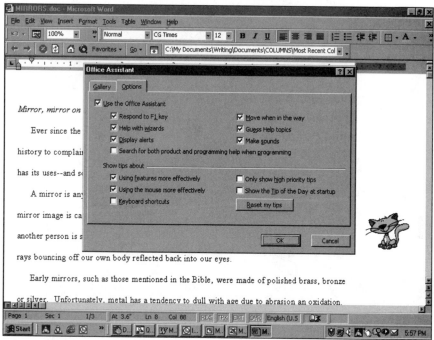

Figure 59-18: Your modified Office Assistant changes its appearance here.

Note

You can hide the assistant at any time by right-clicking on it and choosing Hide from the menu.

Getting more info on the Web

If it can't answer your question, the Assistant will offer you a link to more information on the Web. If you choose that option, you'll see a form like the one shown in Figure 59-19.

You can either send your query as is, or enter more information in the box at the bottom. Click the Send and Go to the Web button, and your query is automatically routed to the Microsoft Office Update Web site (see Figure 59-20), where it's used to conduct a search. With any luck, you'll find your answer somewhere among the articles retrieved.

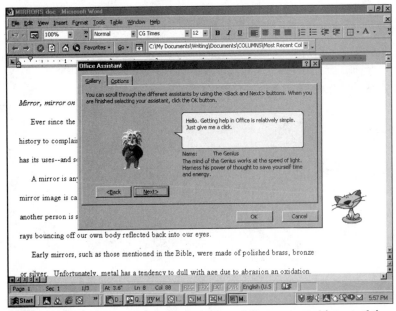

Figure 59-19: Cast a wider net for help than Office can provide out of the box by going to the Web.

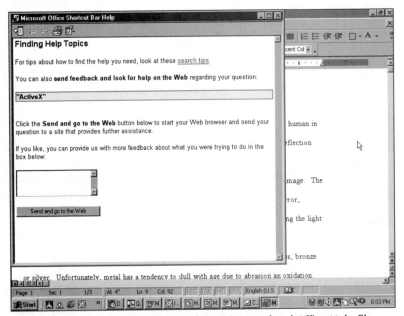

Figure 59-20: If the answer you seek isn't in your local Office Help files, maybe it's on the Microsoft Office Update Web site.

✦   ✦   ✦

What's New in Office 2000

In a word, lots. This appendix lists some of the highlights of the major Office applications.

What's New in Word

Based on extensive research and customer feedback, Microsoft came up with four goals for Word 2000:

✦ *Enable Web-centered document creation*, making it easier than ever to turn documents into Web pages, with formatting intact — which also makes it easier than ever to share documents with others, no matter what computer system or software they may be using.

✦ *Support rich e-mail creation.* In cooperation with Outlook 2000, Word 2000 can be used to create and edit all e-mail. Formatting and special elements such as tables and images are preserved when the e-mail is sent (provided recipients are using a program that permits them to view HTML e-mail).

✦ *Improve ease of use.* Word 2000 is smarter than its predecessors: it remembers your usage patterns and customizes itself to adapt to them.

✦ *Better support for international users.* Word 2000 makes it possible to work in multiple languages simultaneously.

The following tables list some of the specific improvements in each of these areas.

Table A-1
Web-Centered Document Creation:
Highlights of New and Improved Features

Feature	Description
HTML As a Native File Format	Save documents in Word, translate them into HTML, and translate them back to .doc format without losing any formatting features.
Preserve Unknown HTML Tags	If you read a Web page with Word that contains HTML code Word doesn't understand, it preserves it instead of discarding it.
Browser Compatibility	To ensure that people with earlier versions of browsers can view any document you turn into a Web page, Word 2000 lets you turn off features that aren't supported by older browsers.
Web Page Preview	You can preview Web pages you create in Word with your default browser, even before you save them.
Themes	Common Web site themes have been created and coordinated between Word (and some other Office applications) and Microsoft's popular Web-site creation software FrontPage. This makes it easier to create consistent-looking Web pages.
WYSIWYG Frames	Frames help make Web pages easier to navigate; Word 2000 lets you use them.
Table Formatting	Word 2000 supports such HTML formatting options as tables within tables and floating tables. It also provides new border formatting and AutoFormat styles appropriate to Web tables.

Table A-2
Rich E-mail Creation: Highlights of New and Improved Features

Feature	Description
Personal Stationery	You can now customize your e-mail with your own font settings, backgrounds and themes; for example, you can send a birthday-party invitation on a background of balloons.
Threading	Microsoft Office E-mail now supports in-line discussions; users can see who made what changes when in e-mail threads.
AutoSignature	Create as many signatures as you like to automatically add to the ends of e-mail messages.

Table A-3
Ease of Use: Highlights of New and Improved Features

Feature	Description
Click-n-Type	Put your cursor anywhere you want on a page, double-click, and start typing.
Print Zoom	Scale pages before printing; for example, to fit a document designed for legal-sized paper onto letter-sized paper.
Collect and Paste	Copy information from a number of sources to the Clipboard, and then select any clip to paste.
Personalized Menus	This shows up in all Office 2000 applications. Items you use most often are most prominently featured in menus.
Improved Table Tool	Now you can draw tables within tables and format and rearrange table and cell borders in many more ways. You can even draw diagonal cell borders!
24-bit Color	Word now supports 24-bit colors for text, borders, and shading.
Picture Bullets	Word 2000 makes it easy to use pictures as well as characters as bullets.
Version Compatibility	Working in an office with many different versions of Word floating around? Word 2000 lets you turn off features that aren't viewable in older versions of the program.

Table A-4
International Usage: Highlights of New and Improved Features

Feature	Description
Single Executable	All language versions (except Thai, Vietnamese, and Indian) are supported by the same version of Word, which means companies with international offices only have to install one version of the software, cutting down on support and training costs.
Microsoft Office 2000 Multi-Language Pack	This pack lets you work in the language you prefer. You can set the language of the user interface and the Help files without affecting the operation of the application, and proofing tools for various languages can be installed without changing the language of the user interface or the Help files.
Language AutoDetect	Word can automatically detect the language you're typing in, and automatically choose to use the correct spelling, grammar-checking, and other proofing tools.
Support for Asian Languages	A variety of improvements lets users work with Asian languages in Word more easily than before.

What's New in Excel

As it created Excel 2000, Microsoft took into account the changing ways that corporations are using data: in particular, the fact that more and more corporate information is being placed online for the use of employees, and that increasingly Excel is the method of choice for dealing with data of all kinds.

With those changes in mind, Microsoft came up with three goals for Excel 2000:

✦ *Enable more Web-based collaboration and information sharing.* Excel 2000 is designed to make it easier for users to share information and work with one another over the Web, and to make it possible to share data with anyone who has a Web browser.

✦ *Provide rich analysis tools for better decision making.* Excel 2000 makes it easier for employees to use their company's intranet to access important business information, and also provides tools so they can analyze and use that information more effectively.

✦ *Improve ease of use.* Excel 2000 is more intelligent than its predecessors, adapting to users' individual ways of working more readily. It's designed to let users get up and running quickly, keep working, and achieve good results with fewer resources.

The following tables list some of the specific improvements in each of these areas.

Table A-5 Web-Enabled Collaboration and Information Sharing: Highlights of New and Improved Features	
Feature	*Description*
HTML As a Companion File Format	Excel 2000 can save documents to HTML — and read HTML documents — with great accuracy. In fact, you can save documents to HTML just as easily as you can to the standard Excel file format (.xls), open them again in Excel, and still use all of Excel's features on them.
Save As Web Page	You can save an entire spreadsheet or a subset of it as a Web page, or save spreadsheet data, charts, and pivot tables as interactive Web pages.
Drag and Drop	With Excel 2000, you can drag and drop table data from your Web browser directly into an Excel spreadsheet.

Table A-6
Rich Analysis Tools: Highlights of New and Improved Features

Feature	Description
PivotTable Dynamic Views	Now you can create and manipulate the fields of a PivotTable right in your worksheet, by dragging the fields you want directly onto a PivotTable.
PivotTable AutoFormat	Save time by letting Excel do the work of formatting your data in PivotTables.
Queries	Database Queries now allow you to insert columns within a data table, to retain formatting, and to fill down formulas in adjacent columns when you refresh a query.
Enhanced Web Queries	With a new dialog box, Excel 2000 makes it easy to bring in data directly from the Web for tracking or analysis.
Refreshable Text Import	Now you can bring data from text files into Excel exactly the same way you make other database queries, retaining formatting and formulas even when the text query is refreshed.
OLAP PivotTable Views	You can now create OLAP PivotTable views against any database that supports OLE-DB for OLAP.
Large Data Stores	Excel 2000's client/server approach provides you with fast access to large server-based data stores.
Office Web Components	These components let you use Excel's analysis features while you're in a browser. The spreadsheet component lets you move worksheet models to the browser so you can analyze data and perform calculations. The charting component lets you provide basic interactive charting in a browser, and the PivotTable component enables you to pivot, filter, and summarize information within a browser.

Table A-7
Ease of Use: Highlights of New and Improved Features

Feature	Description
List AutoFill	Excel 2000 automatically extends formatting and formulas in lists, simplifying this common task.
See-Through Selection	Ordinarily, selected data appears in reverse video—white on black instead of black on white, for instance. This can sometimes hide formatting and text. See-Through Selection lightly shades selected cells so you can make changes and see the results clearly without unselecting the cells.

Continued

Table A-7 (continued)	
Feature	**Description**
New Cursors	New cursors provide you with visual cues as to what actions are possible in certain contexts.
Charting	Excel's charting capabilities now include improved formatting and the ability to create PivotChart dynamic views.
Year 2000 Dates	New date formats, custom date entry behaviors, and static date function behavior give you more options for working with dates.
Euro Currency Support	Excel 2000 now supports both the symbol and the three-letter ISO code for the new Euro currency.

What's New in PowerPoint

Until recently, people with ideas to present had to travel around the world to make their presentations to interested audiences. With PowerPoint 2000, presenters can now both collaborate with people around the world in the construction of their presentation and present to audiences equally scattered, all without leaving their office.

Microsoft developed four goals for PowerPoint 2000:

+ *Enable Web-centered information sharing.* More and more organizations are doing business in a Web-based environment. PowerPoint 2000 allows you to create and share presentations on the Web. If you wish, you can save your presentations entirely in HTML, instead of PowerPoint's .ppt format.

+ *Facilitate real-time collaboration.* PowerPoint 2000 uses Microsoft's NetShow server and NetMeeting conferencing software to enable users to collaborate over a network.

+ *Improve ease of use.* New features based on extensive user research let you get more done with less effort.

+ *Support for international users.* PowerPoint works the same, no matter what language or what country you're working in. In fact, you can use more than one language in the same presentation, and PowerPoint can still provide proofing tools.

The following tables list some of the specific improvements in each of these areas.

Table A-8
Web-Centered Information Sharing:
Highlights of New and Improved Features

Feature	Description
HTML As a Native File Format	PowerPoint 2000 can save documents to HTML — and read HTML documents — with great accuracy. You can make HTML your default file format and still take advantage of all of PowerPoint's features.
Save As Web Page	This lets you save your presentation as a Web page directly to a Web server — which means you don't have to rely on a Webmaster to post files for you on your company intranet.
Web Graphics Optimization	Microsoft Internet Explorer 5.0 will now provide better display and smaller files for HTML PowerPoint presentations.
Dual HTML Output Format	Now you can save presentations in a special dual v3-v4 mode that lets you optimize your presentations for viewing in Internet Explorer 4.0 while maintaining compatibility with Internet Explorer 3.0.
HTML Output Options	PowerPoint gives you several built-in formatting options for HTML presentations, including format, resolution, frame style, color, speaker's notes, outline, audio, and scaling of slides and graphics.
Fit to Window	Slides automatically resize to fit your display resolution and the size of your window.
Navigation Bar	HTML presentations include a navigation bar in a frame for moving around the presentation easily.
Notes Frame	Note pages are automatically created in a separate frame for easy viewing.
Design Templates	Themes have been created that are available from several Office applications, including FrontPage, to make it easier to create consistent-looking Web sites. PowerPoint 2000 includes Design Templates for these themes.
Present in Browser	PowerPoint HTML presentations provide a button that lets you view them in Internet Explorer version 4.0 or later instead of a viewer application.

Table A-9
Real-Time Collaboration:
Highlights of New and Improved Features

Feature	Description
Presentation Broadcast	This lets you deliver a presentation over an intranet, displaying the presentation slides in HTML and providing narration as streaming audio or video (as long as your audience members have Internet Explorer 4.0 or later).
Broadcast Schedule	By using Outlook's messaging and collaboration client, you can schedule online broadcasts and set up reminders; your audience members only have to click a button to join the broadcast.
Event Web Page	If you create this page, others can tune in to watch a broadcast, watch it later, or get information before the broadcast starts.
Presentations on Demand	This archives broadcasts on a Web server, so they're available for playback at any time.
Online Meeting	PowerPoint 2000 has been integrated with Microsoft NetMeeting, which lets users share Office documents for collaborative editing during online conferences.

Table A-10
Ease of Use: Highlights of New and Improved Features

Feature	Description
AutoFit Text	Text is automatically resized to fit its placeholder so it doesn't extend past the end of the slide.
Tri-Pane View	This new Normal view combines Slide, Outline, and Notes view into one, making it easier to add slides, edit text, and enter notes while creating a presentation, and to move from place to place within a presentation during editing.
Tables	Now you can create tables in PowerPoint without using Word or Excel.
Graphical Bullets	Many people like to use graphics for bullets; now PowerPoint makes it easy to do so. You can use one of the included graphical bullets or make any image you want into a bullet.

Feature	Description
AutoNumbered Bullets	Microsoft says this was one of the most frequently requested features from customers. Now you can create numbered bullets that automatically adjust their order in a logical sequence. PowerPoint recognizes what you're up to when you enter a number and automatically formats your text into a numbered list.
AutoFormat As You Type	PowerPoint also recognizes and automatically formats ordinals, fractions, em dashes, and en dashes. AutoCorrect entries are supported and smart quotes are automatically applied.
Multiple Monitor Support	If you're using Windows 98 or Windows NT 5.0, you can now drag your presentation to a secondary monitor.
Laptop Integration	This lets you disable screensavers and your laptop's low-power screen mode to avoid interruptions during presentations.
Slide-Show Usability	Now you can hide the pointer and slide-show icon automatically after a period of interactivity during a slide show. Minor movements of the mouse won't cause the pointer to reappear.
Voice Narration	The playback of narration is now synchronized with the original presentation. You can now add voice narration slide-by-slide.
Animated GIFs	Now you can add extra animation to your presentations with animated GIFs!
Additional AutoShapes	More than 50 new AutoShapes have been added, including shapes for network diagrams, Web diagrams, and office layouts.
Projector Wizard	This lets you automatically set and restore correct screen resolution for a particular projector system.

Table A-11
Support for International Users: Highlights of New and Improved Features

Feature	Description
Multilingual AutoCorrect	Now you can create an AutoCorrect list for each language you're working in.
Support for Far East Users	PowerPoint 2000 provides additional Far East date formats, improved word-breaking, and support for special Far East HTML tags.
Language Detection	PowerPoint 2000 detects what language you're working in and makes the correct proofing tools available.

What's New in Outlook

For Outlook 2000, Microsoft developed the following goals:

+ *Make it easier to use and manage.* Many people found the first version of Outlook, Outlook 97, difficult to set up and use. Microsoft hopes the changes to Outlook 2000, based on customer feedback, addresses those problems. (Many of these improvements have already appeared in Outlook 98.)

+ *Provide better support for Internet standards.* Outlook 2000 supports even more acronyms than earlier versions: SMTP/POP3, IMAP 4, LDAP, DHTML, S/MIME, NNTP. If you don't know what any of those things are, you probably don't need to worry about them. Suffice it to say that Outlook 2000 can ensure that your message gets through to just about anyone, no matter what kind of system they're using.

+ *Improve e-mail and information management.* E-mail, calendar, and contact management have all been made easier to use, and work together more closely than ever before.

+ *Enable collaboration across the Internet or with Microsoft Exchange Server.* Outlook makes it easier than ever for users to share information and collaborate in a variety of ways, both over the Internet and on internal networks.

+ *Improve remote usage functionality.* Outlook 2000 makes it easier for people to access their information even when they're away from the office where it's stored.

The following tables list some of the specific improvements in each of these areas over Outlook 97 (some of these improvements first appeared in Outlook 98):

Table A-12 **Ease of Use and Management: Highlights of New and Improved Features**	
Feature	*Description*
Outlook Today	A customizable quick overview that summarizes Mail, Calendar, and Tasks in one window.
Simplified Menus and Toolbars	The most common and useful commands are now more readily accessible in views and forms.
Improved InfoBars	InfoBars, which provide you with useful information such as the date you replied to a given e-mail, are now more colorful and easier to see.
Find Tool	Search Outlook for messages, appointments, tasks, or other information just as you'd search the Web.

Feature	Description
QuickFind Contact	Easily find and open a contact from anywhere in Outlook.
Find Exchange Server Public Folder, Send Link to Public Folder	Outlook can now search for a Microsoft Exchange Server Public Folder based on its properties, and easily send a link to it.
Organize Tool	All the e-mail organizational tools in Outlook, such as folders, views and rules, have been made easier to use.
ScreenTips	Pop-up ScreenTips are displayed when you hold your mouse pointer over column headers or truncated text.
Microsoft Internet Explorer 4.0 and 5.0 Integration	You can start Outlook from the Explorer Quick Launch Bar, send Web pages in e-mail messages, and create contacts from Internet Explorer.
Outlook Setup	Outlook Setup automatically detects the appropriate installation options. It will even automatically import existing accounts, profile information, folders and personal Address Books from earlier Outlook versions, Outlook Express, Netscape Messenger, or Eudora.
Multiple Account Management	Outlook 2000 lets you easily set up and manage multiple server connections.
Outlook Bar Shortcuts	You can easily create a shortcut in the Outlook Bar to any file, folder, or Web page.
Web Views	Clicking an Outlook Bar shortcut to a Web page displays the Web page in the right-hand Outlook pane.

Table A-13
Internet Standards Support:
Highlights of New and Improved Features

Feature	Description
Support for More Internet Standards	Outlook lets you use POP3/SMTP, IMAP4, and LDAP server connections for e-mail.
NNTP News Reader	Outlook shares a high-performance Internet news reader with Internet Explorer.
HTML and MHTML Mail	Now you can send and receive HTML-formatted mail, which can range from simple formatted text to complete Web pages.
S/MIME	Outlook 2000 lets you send and receive signed or encrypted Internet mail.
Read Receipts	Outlook tells you when the mail you sent was received and read.

Continued

Table A-13 *(continued)*

Feature	Description
vCard	You can send and receive contact information to other users using the Internet vCard format.
iCalendar	Use the iCalendar Internet Group Scheduling format to let others know when you're free or busy, and find out when they are, so you can schedule meetings. You can also send meeting requests and responses over the Internet.

Table A-14
E-mail and Information Management:
Highlights of New and Improved Features

Feature	Description
Preview Pane	View messages without opening them.
Built-in HTML Mail Editing	Edit fonts, HTML styles, hyperlinks, and more, on HTML mail right in Outlook.
Independent Editor and Send Format Choice	Use the built-in Outlook editor or Microsoft Word to edit e-mail, and choose how you'll send it: RTF, HTML, or plain-text format. You can switch among the formats at any time. If you've indicated in your Contacts list that a particular contact prefers text-only e-mail, Outlook will warn you if you send formatted mail to that contact.
Per-Message Office E-mail	Compose your e-mail using any Office application, and then send it as HTML; your recipient doesn't have to have that particular application to read it.
Automatically Spell Check in Multiple Languages	If you use Word as your e-mail editor, it can automatically detect what language you're writing in and offer appropriate proofing tools.
Multiple Signatures	You can easily set up and manage multiple signatures, again as either HTML, RTF, or plain text.
Stationery	You can use a pre-designed stationery or create your own using the fonts, hyperlinks, and background of your choice. You can use different stationery for different messages.
AutoFormat Reply	This lets you choose to automatically respond to messages in the same format as they were sent.
Send from Account	Every time you send a message, you can choose which of your POP3 or IMAP4 accounts you want to send it from.
Junk E-mail Management	Outlook can automatically recognize and dispose of unsolicited junk e-mail.

Feature	Description
Run Rules Now	You can apply a rule to any folder at any time.
Automatically Display Conversation Thread	With a single click, you can find all the messages in the same conversation thread as the current message.
AutoSave	You can automatically save unsent messages in the new Drafts folder.
Enhanced Fax Support	Symantec WinFax Starter Edition is now integrated with Outlook, making it easier to send and receive faxes within Outlook.

Table A-15
Calendar and Scheduling: Highlights of New and Improved Features

Feature	Description
Save Calendar As Web Page	You can now save a personal or team calendar as HTML.
AutoPreview and Preview Pane in Calendar	The first three lines of appointment details appear in daily and weekly calendar views, or you can use Preview Pane to view them.
ScreenTips in Calendar Views	Holding the mouse pointer in place over calendar views displays pop-up ScreenTips with complete details of appointments.
Five-Day Week View	If you wish, you can choose not to view weekend days.
Calendar Background Color	See your free and busy times more easily, thanks to the use of contrasting colors in daily and weekly views.
Enhanced Calendar Printing	Outlook can now print word-wrapped details of appointments in daily, weekly, and monthly printouts, and prints exactly one month per page.
Adding and Remove Attendees	You can now more easily change the list of attendees for a scheduled meeting.
Easily Open Other Users' Calendars	There is a most recently used list of other users' calendars.
Hide Private Appointments	You can keep private appointments private when sharing scheduling information.
NetMeeting and NetShow Integration	You can easily schedule online meetings and automatically start the NetMeeting conferencing software with an Office document to share, or schedule times to watch NetShow broadcasts and automatically start NetShow at the designated time.

Table A-16
Contacts: Highlights of New and Improved Features

Feature	Description
Fully Customizable Contacts	You can now easily add custom fields and scripts to the first page of the Contacts form.
Personal Distribution Lists	Create a personal distribution list made up of contacts from one or more Contacts folders and the Microsoft Exchange Server Global Address List.
Contact Activity Tracking	You can keep track of all e-mail, tasks, appointments, and documents linked to each contact.
Flag Contact for Follow-Up	You can now add a follow-up reminder to a contact.
Enhanced Mail Merge	You can filter your Contacts list as you wish, and then send the contacts on to Word for mail merging.
Automatic Map	Maps to a contact's address can be downloaded from Microsoft Expedia's travel-service Web site.
AutoMerge Contact Information	When you add a new contact, Outlook warns you if it looks like a duplicate and gives you the opportunity to automatically merge the new information with the old.
Multiple Contacts Folders in Address Book	You can now create and access multiple Outlook Contacts folders.
Automatically Add Message's Sender to Contacts List	Now you can automatically add the sender of an e-mail message to your Contacts list when you reply to the message.
Smart Phone Number Parsing	Outlook displays a pop-up dialog box to ensure that phone numbers are entered in the correct format.

Table A-17
Remote Usage: Highlights of New and Improved Features

Feature	Description
Enhanced Synchronization of Offline Folders and Improved Offline Address Book Synchronization	Background, scheduled, and filtered synchronization of Microsoft Exchange Server Offline Folders is now possible, and you can synchronize the Offline Exchange Server Address Book using the same commands and features.

Feature	Description
Quick Synchronization Profiles	This lets you specify collections of Microsoft Exchange Server folders to synchronize, based on speed of connection or time available.
Synchronize Message Size Limit	You can easily tell Outlook not to synchronize large messages over a slow link.
Change Connection Type	You can more easily switch between a local area network (LAN) and dial-up connection.
Background E-mail Download	You can continue to work in Outlook while mail is downloading—and the mail will download faster, too.
Scheduled Download	You can ask Outlook to periodically dial up and retrieve new e-mail.
Smart Dial-Up Options	Outlook lets you easily configure options for time- and money-saving connections to Internet e-mail providers.
AutoDetect Connection	Outlook automatically detects when a connection to an Internet service provider either becomes available or goes away.

What's New in Access

Microsoft set three main goals for Access 2000:

✦ *Make information easier to find and use.* This is the central goal of any database management program, and Access 2000 has several improvements in this area.

✦ *Enable easier sharing of information via the Web.* Enhancing Web-based collaboration is a major thrust of all of Office 2000, and Access is no exception. New features make it possible for users to share information faster and easier than ever before.

✦ *Provide rich analysis tools for managing information.* Information is power, they say; better tools for analyzing and managing it boosts that power even higher.

The following tables list some of the specific improvements in each of these areas:

Table A-18
Making Information Easy to Find and Use:
Highlights of New and Improved Features

Feature	Description
Convert Database to Prior Access Version	For the first time, you can save a database in a previous version of Access, making it easier to share it with users who haven't yet upgraded.
Database Window	The revised database window accommodates new Access 2000 objects, and has been altered to look more like the interfaces of other Office 2000 applications.
Name AutoCorrect	If you change the name of a field in a table, this feature now automatically changes that name in dependent objects such as Queries and Forms, too.
Conditional Formatting	This feature lets you use negative and positive numbers and values expressed as less than, greater than, between, or equal-to. You can also tell Access to format data entries based on functions you define.
Subdatasheets	These provide you with a picture-in-a-picture view, so you can focus on and edit related data in the same window.
Drag and Drop to Excel	Now you can export data from Access to Excel simply by dragging and dropping Access objects into Excel.
Form Enhancements	These have made it easier to make changes, such as to colors or fonts, to fields within Form view.
Print Relationships Wizard	Now you can print a visual diagram of the Relationships window, which can help you see how your database is structured.
Control Grouping	To make it easier to design forms, you can now group all controls as a single unit.
Report Snapshot	You can create a snapshot of an Access 2000 report, and then distribute it via disk, printer, Web page, or e-mail.
Compact on Close	This feature can save you disk space; Access 2000 can automatically compress a database when you close a file, to ensure it is as small as possible.
Northwind Sample Database	The Northwind Database, a fully functional sample database that's included with Access, has been updated with examples of all the latest features.

Table A-19
Sharing Information on the Web:
Highlights of New and Improved Features

Feature	Description
Data Access Pages	This lets you create data-bound HTML pages quickly and easily, which in turn makes it possible to extend database applications to the company intranet.
Grouped Data Access Pages	This lets you view and manage related information, e.g., sales by region and sales by sales manager.
Field List	This lets you add information to a Data Access Page simply by dragging and dropping field names from an easily accessible list.
Hyperlink Handling	Access 2000 makes it easier to create, edit, follow, and remove hyperlinks in databases.
Integration of Shared Components	Access takes advantage of all the new Office Web Components to give users several ways to view and analyze data.

Table A-20
Rich Analysis Tools:
Highlights of New and Improved Features

Feature	Description
Microsoft SQL Server Interoperability	Access 2000 supports OLE DB, which lets users combine the easy-to-use Access interface with the scalability of databases such as Microsoft SQL Server. You can also use Access to carry out common SQL Server administration tasks, such as replication, backup, restore, and security.
Microsoft Access Project	Access can now create a new file type (.adp) that makes it easy for you to create true client/server applications. Many of Access's wizards have been updated to support the new Access Project tasks, such as creating a new database, report, or form. New design tools also let you easily create and manage server-side objects, including tables, views, stored procedures, and database diagrams.

✦   ✦   ✦

Sources of Office Information on the Web

The following sites may provide additional useful information about using Office 2000, as well as additional macros, templates, themes, and other useful add-ons.

The Microsoft Office Home Page

Following is the official Microsoft Office Home Page, run (naturally enough) by Microsoft. Here you'll find the latest Office news, plus product information, demos, and more:

    http://www.microsoft.com/office/

Office Update

Another Office site, this one focuses on updates to the suite. This is where Office 2000 Help sends you if it can't answer your question:

    http://officeupdate.microsoft.com

Microsoft Office Tips

This free online computer reference site offers an extensive list of tips for Office users:

    http://www.computertips.com

Inside Microsoft Office

This monthly publication also has a Web site bursting with news and tips for Office users:

    http://www.zdjournals.com/o97/

CNET.com Office Suites

CNET is an excellent source for information about all aspects of computers, including Microsoft Office:

    http://cnet.com/Content/Reports/Special/OfficeSuites/

Windows Magazine

Windows Magazine's Web site is a great place to get all tips and news about anything related to Windows — including Office:

    http://www.winmag.com/

FileMine

CMPNet's FileMine and similar huge compendiums of downloadable software are great places to find templates, themes, ActiveX controls, macros, and other add-ons to increase your Office productivity:

    http://www.filemine.com/

✦   ✦   ✦

What's on the CD-ROM?

◆ ◆ ◆ ◆

In This Appendix

Freeware and
shareware

Installing programs
from the CD-ROM

◆ ◆ ◆ ◆

The *Microsoft Office 2000 Bible* CD-ROM contains interesting and useful programs, clip art, electronic documents, and more. The electronic documents include the complete text of another book in IDG Books Worldwide's Bible series, and an HTML version of the Internet directory from the Internet Bible — a compendium of nearly a thousand Web sites divided into 140 different categories, based on subject matter or general content. There's also a full electronic version of this book, in PDF format, and the Adobe Acrobat Reader, a piece of software that lets you read PDF files — a popular format for documents on the World Wide Web.

Freeware and Shareware

It's important that you understand the difference between the two types of software offered on the *Microsoft Office 2000 Bible* CD-ROM, *freeware* and *shareware*. Freeware is short for "free software." Freeware programs are made available free of charge, and can be copied and distributed as much as you wish. There's no need to register it. Adobe Acrobat Reader is freeware.

Much more common is *shareware*. Shareware is offered free for a trial period, and then the authors ask that you register it and pay a fee — generally, but not always, a smaller fee than buying a similar program in a store would cost. Some use the honor system — you can use the software indefinitely, but if you like it and find it useful, the creators would like you to register it. Some shareware continues working, but a message pops up every time you open it asking that you register. This is sometimes called *nagware*.

Some shareware ceases to function once the trial period is over, while some is disabled from the beginning so that vital functions won't work until the shareware is registered and paid for. Read the licensing agreement for all the shareware on the *Microsoft Office 2000 Bible* CD-ROM to find out which kind it is. This information is often in a labeled README file in the same folder as the program. The following table lists what's on the *Office 2000 Bible* CD, and provides a brief description.

Table C-1

Software Title	File Folder	Description	Related Web Site
MindSpring ISP Service	MindSpring	Install this software for the MindSpring ISP service. Also includes Internet Explorer.	http://www.mindspring.net
Handicalc Plus v.4.5 21-Day Evaluation Version	Abacus International	Handicalc Plus handles handicapping for small to medium sized groups of golfers. It includes all of the latest features for tracking golfers and their golf scores. Handicalc Plus also allows you to track statistics such as birdies, pars, bogeys, greens in regulation, fairways hit, and much more.	http://www.handicalc.com
ACDSee 32 v.2.3	ACD Systems	The fastest image viewer available. The 32-bit version of ACDSee is designed for use with Windows 95/98 or Windows NT.	http://www.acdsystems.com
Adarus Business Plan for Office 97 v.2.0d	Adarus Software	Develop a professional business plan quickly and easily with the help of step-by-step wizards (Sales, Expense, Asset/Loan, Business Plan). This Microsoft Excel add-in and template creates all financial reports needed for a business plan, such as cash flow, income, balance sheet, break-even, and financial ratios. A formatted business plan outline (title page, table of contents) is created in Microsoft Word, Adarus' One-Step tools (Print, Scenario, Chart) are powerful, time-saving features.	http://www.adarus.com

Software Title	File Folder	Description	Related Web Site
Adobe Acrobat Reader	Adobe Systems	The free Adobe® Acrobat® Reader allows you to view, navigate, and print PDF files across all major computing platforms.	http://www.adobe.com
ArtBeats Bundle Pack	ArtBeats Software	ArtBeats is the leader in royalty-free digital stock footage. Included here are some samples of their wares.	http://www.artbeats.com
WebVise Totality Demo	Auto FX	Auto F/X products add flair to any design, providing designers with the ability to create unique effects that would otherwise take hours and hours to do from scratch. Here are demos of several of their outstanding products.	http://www.autofx.com
The Avery Wizard Avery LabelPro 3.0 for Windows (32-bit)	Avery Dennison	With Avery LabelPro 3.0 for Windows, produce professional-looking labels and dividers in minutes from your printer. Insert your logo or other eye-catching graphics or text in your choice of color. The AutoMerge button allows quick and easy merging of your mailing list. The "Shrink-to-fit" feature automatically fits text to each label. The Avery Wizard is a software companion for Microsoft® Word that makes formatting and printing Avery products a snap.	http://www.avery.com/
Golf League Recorder v.2.5	Brown's Computerworks	Handicap and Performance tracking for League and Personal use (USGA method). Handicapping can be tailored for casual leagues that play a variety of schedules and 9-hole rounds. The math the program uses can be optionally viewed as each players' scores are entered. Personal performance graphs show trends. Includes the ability to print Handicap cards.	http://www.adsnet.com/conan.brown/index.html

Continued

Table C-1 (continued)

Software Title	File Folder	Description	Related Web Site
Drag And File Gold v.4.17 Trial Drag And View v.4.0 Trial Drag And Zip v.2.22 Trial	Canyon Software	Drag and File is a powerful file management utility; Drag and View lets you view the contents of many different types of files without opening them; and Drag and Zip zips and unzips files and even checks them for viruses!	http://www.canyonsw.com
FontLister v.3.2.6	Conquerware	FontLister is a fast Font Manager for Windows 95/98. With this program you'll never have trouble finding a font for a special task. Now you'll be able to browse all your fonts without first installing them. If you decide to install or remove a font, you only have to press one button and it's done. Furthermore, FontLister is able to print complete samples of all fonts — they don't even have to be installed.	http://www.conquerware.dk
Contact Plus Personal 97	Contact Plus Corporation	Contact's personalized map, get his stock quote — you name it! Plus, see who's closest to you by calculating the distance to your contact's locations automatically! Keep track of all those important contacts. Use Microsoft Word or Corel WordPerfect to create personalized documents.	http://www.contactplus.com
3D IMPACT! Pro	Crystal Graphics	Enhance your Web pages, presentations, and videos with 3-D animated graphics.	http://www.crystalgraphics.com/
WebSpice Sample Images WebSpice Animations Samples	DeMorgan Industries	View samples of the thousands of original & royalty-free Web images and animations created by WebSpice to reflect the growing need of businesses to create a profes-sional-looking Web site. WebSpice® is a registered trademark of DeMorgan Industries Corporation.	http://www.webspice.com

Software Title	File Folder	Description	Related Web Site
EyeWire, Inc. Images	EyeWire, Inc.	View samples of the images created by EyeWire, formerly Adobe Studios, now an independent company with over 10 years of experience delivering powerful content and tools for graphic design.	http://www.eyewire.com/
1 Cool Button Tool v.3.0	Formula Software	1 Cool Button Tool is a great new product for creating interactive Java buttons. It's perfect for rollover buttons, pop-up menus, Web-site navigation, and special effects. No Java or HTML programming required.	http://www.formulagraphics.com
3D Clock Saver EZ-Viewer Knowledge Machine Power Strip SafeKeeper Backup Grouper Video Launch Pad	Galt Technologies	A selection of useful programs from Galt Technology's vast selection of freeware and shareware.	http://www.galttech.com
Havana Street Image Sampler	Havana Images	Havana Street specializes in clip art, fonts, and stock illustrations done in a 1940s style. All images are original and created by Havana Street.	http://www.havanastreet.com
HyperCam v.1.34.00	Hyerionics	HyperCam captures the action from your Windows 95 or NT screen and saves it to AVI (Audio-Video Interleaved) movie file. Sound from your system microphone is also recorded.	http://www.hyperionics.com
Debt Analyzer 97 InfoCourier Keyboard Express 95 SmartDoc 95 SmartSum ZipExpress 95	Insight Software	A selection of programs from Insight Software Solutions, which is dedicated to developing high quality, user-friendly software products for Microsoft Windows-based operating systems.	http://www.wintools.com

Continued

Table C-1 (continued)

Software Title	File Folder	Description	Related Web Site
WS FTP Pro 5.0	Ipswitch, Inc.	WS FTP Pro is the world's most popular FTP client for Windows. Copyright, 1991-1998, Ipswitch Inc.,	http://www.ipswitch.com/
PaintShop Pro 5.01	JASC Software	Paint Shop Pro is a complete image creation and manipulation program that enhances the imaging power of business and home users with unrivaled ease of use, speed, and affordable functionality.	http://www.jasc.com
GeoClock v.8.1	Jrahlgren-GeoClock	GeoClock shows the current time (based on your computer's clock) with a high-quality map of the earth. The current sun position is displayed, and the parts of the earth in sunlight and twilight are highlighted.	http://www.clark.net/pub/bblake/geoclock
Judy's TenKey™ 4.0	Judy's Applications	Judy's TenKey is an award-winning Windows calculator that includes nearly every feature imaginable, including a scrolling tape that automatically recalculates when you edit it. You can control the appearance of your personal calculator, from choosing the types of buttons to showing negative numbers in red. More important, you can set Judy's TenKey to behave like a standard calculator, an adding machine, or a scientific calculator. A calculator is something you use ever day — why not use the best? Ziff-Davis named Judy's TenKey the 1998 Desktop Accessory of the Year.	http://www.judysapps.com
Power Utility Pak for Excel 97	Jwalk & Associates	Power Utility Pak for Excel 97 is a collection of Excel add-ins, consisting of general-purpose utilities, custom worksheet functions, enhanced shortcut menus, and even games!	http://www.j-walk.com/

Software Title	File Folder	Description	Related Web Site
Hit List Pro 21-Day Trial Version	Marketwave	Hit List Pro is the most powerful and flexible server log analysis solution for Internet and intranet sites. Pro's fast QuickList database back-end provides the ability to quickly import Web traffic data, while its reporting engine allows Web managers and marketers to quickly access the detailed data they need.	http://www.marketwave.com
Microsoft Word Viewer 97	Microsoft Corp.	Lets you view Microsoft Word 97 files.	http://www.microsoft.com
ZipMagic 98 30-Day Evaluation	Mijenix Corporation	The highest-rated zip utility just got Web and e-mail-enabled! With patent-pending technology, ZipMagic 98 actually lets you use zip files without unzipping them, so you can open, modify, launch, and save your compressed files and applications as if they were never zipped! And it now includes exclusive Internet features to easily zip up e-mail file tranfers and download and install software right from within your browser. ZipMagic 98 has helpful wizards for unzipping and zipping files, plus power features like spanning zip files over multiple disks and creating royalty-free self-extracting zip files. There is even a built-in file viewer for over 60 file formats. ZipMagic supports more compression formats than any other retail zip utility and comes with a 60-day money-back guarantee. Opens Zip, Arj, LHA/LZH, GZ, Tar, RAR, PAC, CAB, ARC, Mime/Base 64, BinHex, Uuencode, and more. Supports Windows 3.1, 95, 98, and NT. PowerDesk and ZipMagic are registered trademarks of Mijenix. FreeSpace, Mijenix, and EasyUpdate are trademarks of Mijenix Corporation. Copyright © Mijenix Corporation. All rights reserved. "The best utility we've ever seen" – PC Home	http://www.mijenix.com

Continued

Table C-1 *(continued)*

Software Title	File Folder	Description	Related Web Site
TASK FORCE Clip Art "The Free Edition"	New Vision Technologies	This sample of TaskForce Clip Art includes more than 200 full-color images and a self-extracting browser.	`http://www.nvtech.com`
WinZip 7.0 Evaluation Version	Nico Mak Computing	WinZip brings the convenience of Windows to the use of zip files and other archive and compression formats. The optional wizard interface makes unzipping easier than ever. WinZip features built-in support for popular Internet file formats, including TAR, gzip, Unix compress, UUencode, BinHex, and MIME. ARJ, LZH, and ARC files are supported via external programs. WinZip interfaces to most virus scanners.	`http://www.winzip.com`
Macro Mania	Northstar Solutions	Launch new or switch to currently running Windows programs. Send any keystroke to any Windows program — fast and easy! You can transport data between programs, schedule macros and messages, play WAV files, and much more. A friendly interface will help you quickly become a Macro Maniac.	`http://www.nstarsolutions.com`
Animation Explosion Sampler Kaboom! Sampler	Nova Dev	Animation Explosion is the ultimate library of animated Web graphics, while Kaboom! features wild and wacky sounds. Sample both of them here.	`http://www.novadevcorp.com`
CompuPic	Photodex Corporation	CompuPic Digital Content Manager helps you find, organize, and use all the photos, clip art, fonts, and video and sound files on your computer.	`http://www.photodex.com`
PhotoSpin Images	PhotoSpin	Samples of PhotoSpin's high-quality, royalty-free digital images.	`http://www.photospin.com`

Software Title	File Folder	Description	Related Web Site
PlanMagic Business	PlanMagic Corp.	PlanMagic Business is one of the finest programs available for generating business plans, from starting to running a business. It features all aspects of a professional plan (forecasts, ratios, marketing, goals, strategies, etc.), and a complete online business guide (HLP). Product key features: multiple templates to choose from, comprehensive online business guide, complete marketing concept, clear goals and strategy settings, easy-to-use in known word processors, pre-defined spreadsheets with automatic calculations, automated chart/graphs, complete financial data and automatic ratios, sales, profit and loss, and cashflow forecasting.	http://www.planmagic.com
RISS FontPak (3 files) RISS IconPack Palette Express v.1.6	RI Soft Systems	The RISS FontPak contains 10 unique, ornamental True Type fonts, while the IconPak contains more than 2,001 icons for Windows, plus the handy RISS Icon Selector. Palette Express is a must-have tool for the optimization and conversion of images and palettes.	http://www.risoftsystems.com
Retro Ad Art	Retro Ad Art© Sampler	Retro Ad Art© is a unique collection of 1,864 high-resolution, black-and-white ads cuts from the '30s, '40s, and '50s on CD-ROM. The CD comes with a large-format print book showing all the art. These authentic pieces have been carefully restored and digitized to retain the look and feel of the originals. They can be used as is or can easily be colored in any drawing or photo program. In addition to being a wonderful collection of ready-to-use art, Retro Ad Art© is a valuable historical reference and a great source of inspiration for creating your own Retro pieces that look like the real thing!	http://www.retroadart.com

Continued

Table C-1 (continued)

Software Title	File Folder	Description	Related Web Site
RFFlow v.4.00 (Trial)	RFF Electronics	Turn your ideas into charts and diagrams for documents, presentations, or the Web with RFFlow. RFFlow 4 is the first flowchart and organization chart software application for Microsoft Windows.	`http://www.rff.com`
Screen Loupe 95/NT .4.2	Software By Design	Magnify your desktop and capture screen images with Screen Loupe 95/NT.	`http://www.execpc.com/~sbd`
cgi-lib.pl v.2.17	Steve Brenner	The cgi-lib.pl library makes CGI scripting in Perl easy enough for anyone to process forms and create dynamic Web content.	`http://cgi-lib.stanford.edu/cgi-lib/`
WinFax PRO 9.0 30-day Trialware Talkworks PRO 2.0 30-day Trialware	Symantec, Inc.	WinFax Pro provides easy, reliable faxing in the office, at home, or on the road, while Talkworks Pro is perfect for those who need a complete computer-based faxing and voicemail system.	`http://www.symantec.com/winfax/`
Avi-Pro	Techno-Marketing	Hi-tech video (AVI) player for use in Windows. Record and/or play .AVI videos.	`http://www.tmi.orders.com`
Teleport Pro v. 1.29	Tennyson Maxwell	Part Swiss Army knife, part chainsaw, Teleport Pro is a fully automated, multithreaded, link-following, file-retrieving Web spider. It will retrieve all the files you want—and only the files you want—from any part of the Internet.	`http://www.tenmax.com/pro.html`

Software Title	File Folder	Description	Related Web site
Credit Card Manager 97	Turbosystems	The Credit Card Manager 97 program stores all personal credit card account-related information and helps keep track of credit card transactions on those cards. It maintains transaction information, such as charges, payments, and interest charged. When transactions are logged, they are kept in a current transaction listing for future reconciliation with the monthly account statement. After transactions are reconciled, they are retained for user-defined reporting inquiries such as account history and spending habit analyses.	http://www.turbosystems.com
MyFonts v3.2 Font Namer v.2.3	UniTech	MyFonts is a Windows font manager that lets you view and preview fonts, print font specimens, and easily install and uninstall fonts. Font Namer lets you change font names to suit yourself. Copyright© 1998; UniTech/MyTools.com (314)-770-2770	http://www.mytools.com

Installing Programs from the CD-ROM

The software that's included with the *Microsoft Office 2000 Bible* CD-ROM is simple to install. First decide which software you're interested in; then browse the CD-ROM by inserting it into your CD-ROM drive, opening the My Computer icon on your Windows desktop, and then opening the icon for the CD-ROM drive in the My Computer window.

Each folder on the CD-ROM corresponds to a program on the disk, and each holds all the files that are required to install — although exactly what you'll see depends on which program you're installing. If you see files called "license" or "readme," open them first. They'll often provide additional information about installing and using the software. If not, look for an installation file, often "setup.exe" or another ".exe" file. Double-click on it, and follow the instructions for installing the program.

If you don't find an ".exe" program, look for one with a ".zip" extension. This means the files are compressed into a special archive format. Install WinZip or one of the other zip managers included on the CD-ROM, and then use it to decompress the zip file.

To read electronic documents stored in a .PDF file, you need to install the Acrobat Reader, open it, and then use it to open the .PDF file.

✦   ✦   ✦

Index

continued

continued

E

continued

continued

continued

continued

continued

continued

continued

continued

continued

continued

continued

continued

HUNGRY MINDS, INC.
END-USER LICENSE AGREEMENT

READ THIS. You should carefully read these terms and conditions before opening the software packet(s) included with this book ("Book"). This is a license agreement ("Agreement") between you and Hungry Minds, Inc. ("HMI"). By opening the accompanying software packet(s), you acknowledge that you have read and accept the following terms and conditions. If you do not agree and do not want to be bound by such terms and conditions, promptly return the Book and the unopened software packet(s) to the place you obtained them for a full refund.

1. **License Grant.** HMI grants to you (either an individual or entity) a nonexclusive license to use one copy of the enclosed software program(s) (collectively, the "Software") solely for your own personal or business purposes on a single computer (whether a standard computer or a workstation component of a multi-user network). The Software is in use on a computer when it is loaded into temporary memory (RAM) or installed into permanent memory (hard disk, CD-ROM, or other storage device). HMI reserves all rights not expressly granted herein.

2. **Ownership.** HMI is the owner of all right, title, and interest, including copyright, in and to the compilation of the Software recorded on the disk(s) or CD-ROM ("Software Media"). Copyright to the individual programs recorded on the Software Media is owned by the author or other authorized copyright owner of each program. Ownership of the Software and all proprietary rights relating thereto remain with HMI and its licensers.

3. **Restrictions On Use and Transfer.**

    (a) You may only (i) make one copy of the Software for backup or archival purposes, or (ii) transfer the Software to a single hard disk, provided that you keep the original for backup or archival purposes. You may not (i) rent or lease the Software, (ii) copy or reproduce the Software through a LAN or other network system or through any computer subscriber system or bulletin-board system, or (iii) modify, adapt, or create derivative works based on the Software.

    (b) You may not reverse engineer, decompile, or disassemble the Software. You may transfer the Software and user documentation on a permanent basis, provided that the transferee agrees to accept the terms and conditions of this Agreement and you retain no copies. If the Software is an update or has been updated, any transfer must include the most recent update and all prior versions.

4. Restrictions on Use of Individual Programs. You must follow the individual requirements and restrictions detailed for each individual program in Appendix C, "The Office Bible CD-ROM," of this Book. These limitations are also contained in the individual license agreements recorded on the Software Media. These limitations may include a requirement that after using the program for a specified period of time, the user must pay a registration fee or discontinue use. By opening the Software packet(s), you will be agreeing to abide by the licenses and restrictions for these individual programs that are detailed in Appendix C, "The Office Bible CD-ROM," and on the Software Media. None of the material on this Software Media or listed in this Book may ever be redistributed, in original or modified form, for commercial purposes.

5. Limited Warranty.

(a) HMI warrants that the Software and Software Media are free from defects in materials and workmanship under normal use for a period of sixty (60) days from the date of purchase of this Book. If HMI receives notification within the warranty period of defects in materials or workmanship, HMI will replace the defective Software Media.

(b) **HMI AND THE AUTHOR OF THE BOOK DISCLAIM ALL OTHER WARRANTIES, EXPRESS OR IMPLIED, INCLUDING WITHOUT LIMITATION IMPLIED WARRANTIES OF MERCHANTABILITY AND FITNESS FOR A PARTICULAR PURPOSE, WITH RESPECT TO THE SOFTWARE, THE PROGRAMS, THE SOURCE CODE CONTAINED THEREIN, AND/OR THE TECHNIQUES DESCRIBED IN THIS BOOK. HMI DOES NOT WARRANT THAT THE FUNCTIONS CONTAINED IN THE SOFTWARE WILL MEET YOUR REQUIREMENTS OR THAT THE OPERATION OF THE SOFTWARE WILL BE ERROR FREE.**

(c) This limited warranty gives you specific legal rights, and you may have other rights that vary from jurisdiction to jurisdiction.

6. Remedies.

(a) HMI's entire liability and your exclusive remedy for defects in materials and workmanship shall be limited to replacement of the Software Media, which may be returned to HMI with a copy of your receipt at the following address: Software Media Fulfillment Department, Attn.: *Microsoft Office 2000 Bible,* Hungry Minds, Inc., 10475 Crosspoint Blvd., Indianapolis, IN 46256, or call 1-800-762-2974. Please allow four to six weeks for delivery. This Limited Warranty is void if failure of the Software Media has resulted from accident, abuse, or misapplication. Any replacement Software Media will be warranted for the remainder of the original warranty period or thirty (30) days, whichever is longer.

(b) In no event shall HMI or the author be liable for any damages whatsoever (including without limitation damages for loss of business profits, business interruption, loss of business information, or any other pecuniary loss) arising from the use of or inability to use the Book or the Software, even if HMI has been advised of the possibility of such damages.

(c) Because some jurisdictions do not allow the exclusion or limitation of liability for consequential or incidental damages, the above limitation or exclusion may not apply to you.

7. U.S. Government Restricted Rights. Use, duplication, or disclosure of the Software for or on behalf of the United States of America, its agencies and/or instrumentalities (the "U.S. Government") is subject to restrictions as stated in paragraph (c)(1)(ii) of the Rights in Technical Data and Computer Software clause of DFARS 252.227-7013, and in subparagraphs (a) through (d) of the Commercial Computer — Restricted Rights clause at FAR 52.227-19, and in similar clauses in the NASA FAR supplement, when applicable.

8. General. This Agreement constitutes the entire understanding of the parties and revokes and supersedes all prior agreements, oral or written, between them and may not be modified or amended except in a writing signed by both parties hereto that specifically refers to this Agreement. This Agreement shall take precedence over any other documents that may be in conflict herewith. If any one or more provisions contained in this Agreement are held by any court or tribunal to be invalid, illegal, or otherwise unenforceable, each and every other provision shall remain in full force and effect.

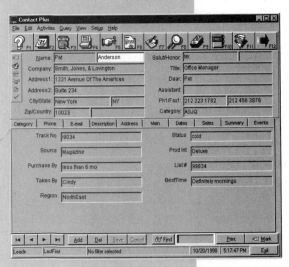

CD-ROM Installation Instructions

The *Microsoft Office 2000 Bible* CD-ROM contains all the example chapters referenced in this books along with a set of outstanding free software, demos, online catalogs, product brochures, and more.

Most of the directories or subdirectories contain installation files with a .EXE file extension. You can simply display the directories and files using your Windows Explorer and then double-click on any .EXE file to launch the install program for the file you want to copy to your hard drive. Each installation file will ask if you want a Start menu shortcut created for you.

Please read Appendix C for a complete guide to installing and using the CD-ROM.